Borland Pascal
from Square One

B O R L A N D   B A N T A M

Borland Pascal
from Square One

Jeff Duntemann

BANTAM BOOKS
NEW YORK • TORONTO • LONDON • SYDNEY • AUCKLAND

Borland Pascal from Square One
A Bantam Book / June 1993

Interior design by Nancy Sugihara.
Produced by The Coriolis Group.

ISBN 0-553-37243-2

Published simultaneously in the United States and Canada

Bantam Books are published by Bantam Books, a division of Bantam Doubleday Dell
Publishing Group, Inc. Its trademark, consisting of the words "Bantam Books" and the
portrayal of a rooster, is Registered in U.S. Patent and Trademark Office and in other
countries. Marca Registrada, Bantam Books, 1540 Broadway, New York, New York 10036.

PRINTED IN THE UNITED STATES OF AMERICA

0 9 8 7 6 5 4 3 2 1

For Carol,
who builds structures of love

Foreword

This is a great first book for learning Pascal. Jeff Duntemann's earlier book, *Complete Turbo Pascal*, probably taught Pascal to more people than all other resources combined. Jeff has a well-earned reputation as both an accomplished wordslinger and a dedicated hacker (in the nicest sense of the word). He worked for Borland as the founder of *Turbo Technix*, which has transmogrified over time into *PC TECHNIQUES*, a leading programmer's journal.

Borland Pascal from Square One, a complete revision of his earlier works, focuses on Borland Pascal, which provides a host of professional development tools, in addition to the latest Pascal compiler technology. But the book is just as relevant to Turbo Pascal programmers, due to the strong commonality of basic language elements between Turbo and Borland Pascal. As the title implies, it assumes no prerequisites. But, before your eyes glaze over at the thought of yet another boring run-through of using loops to calculate grade-point averages and the like—it's Jeff Duntemann we're talking about here—so, even if you already know a fair amount about Pascal, you're sure to find his examples amusing, entertaining, and more than slightly off-beat.

The scope of this book is intentionally limited to the "core" of the language to ensure full coverage of the fundamentals; Jeff promises to follow up with an advanced topics book in the near future that will cover objects in greater detail, along with application frameworks like Turbo Vision and ObjectWindows.

Borland has a long-term commitment to Pascal. As the technology for software development evolves, we're committed to keeping our Pascal product line right on the cutting edge. Thus, we see Borland Pascal 7.0 with Objects as the latest step in an evolutionary process—bringing you the best tools for software craftsmanship. We're sure that you'll find this book a very readable and useful source of the knowledge needed to get up to speed with Borland Pascal, and avail yourself of the tools it provides.

Philippe Kahn
CEO, Borland International

Contents

PART   TWO

The Core of the Language   113

PART   FOUR

Advanced Turbo Pascal   469

20 Dynamic Data Structures   561
Singly- and Doubly-Linked Lists on the Heap   561

21 Project Management   609
Working Smart with Make and Build   609

22 The Borland Graphics Interface (BGI)   621
Creating the Light Fantastic, Pixel by Pixel   621

ACKNOWLEDGMENTS

To Danny Thorpe at Borland, for reviewing the manuscript;

To Hugh Kenner, for ongoing feedback and assistance;

And to the whole gang at The Coriolis Group: Keith Weiskamp, Barbara Nicholson, Brad Grannis, and Robin Watkins, who took my disorderly mountain of paper and presented me with a silk purse.

Yes, Virginia, there still is magic in the world.

Introduction

COMING HOME AGAIN BY THE BACK ROADS

Yessir, this book has been around the block a few times since I began writing it in November 1983. It is now pretty close to what I had originally intended it to be, having been (in the interim) a lot of other things.

Pascal was not my first language. That honor belongs to FORTH, something I don't admit much anymore. FORTH struck a spark in my imagination, but it burned like a pile of shredded rubber tires, leaving a stink and a greasy residue behind that I'm still trying to get rid of. BASIC came next, and burned like dry pine—with fury and small explosions of insight—but there was more light than heat, and it burned out quickly. BASIC taught me a lot, but it didn't take me far enough, and left me cold halfway into the night.

Pascal, when I found it, caught and burned like seasoned ash: slow, deep, *hot*. I learned it with a measured cadence by which one fact built on all those before it. 1981 is more than 10 years gone, and the fire's still burning. I've learned a lot of other languages in the meantime, including C, which burns like sticks of dynamite: It either digs your ditch or blows you to Kingdom Come. Or both. But when something needs doing, I always come back to Pascal.

When I began writing *Pascal from Square One* in the fall of 1983, I had no particular compiler in mind. There were several, and they were all (by today's standards) agonizingly bad. The best of the bunch was the now-extinct Pascal/MT+, and I used it as the host compiler for all of my example code. The book, however, was about Pascal the *language*: how to get started using it; how to think in Pascal; how to see the language from a height, then learn its component parts one by one.

When I turned the book in at the end of summer 1984, my editor at Scott, Foresman had a radical suggestion: Rewrite the book to focus not on Pascal the language, but on Turbo Pascal the *product*. The maverick compiler from Scotts Valley was rapidly plowing all the other Pascals into the soil, and he smelled a new and ravenous audience. I took the manuscript back, and by January of 1985 I had heavily rewritten it to take into account the numerous extensions and peccadilloes of Borland's compiler, version 2.0.

The book was delayed getting into print for several months; as it happened, *Complete Turbo Pascal* was not quite the first book on the shelves focusing on Turbo Pascal. It was certainly the second, however, and it sold over 100,000 copies in the three editions that were published between 1985 and 1989. The second edition ("2E," as we publishing insiders called it) came out in 1986, and addressed Turbo Pascal V3.0. V3.0 seemed to be a stable, long-lived release, and

I busied myself writing an advanced topics book that eventually appeared in mid-1987 as *Turbo Pascal Solutions*.

Timing, timing. As luck would have it, Borland released Turbo Pascal 4.0 that fall, only a couple of months after *Turbo Pascal Solutions* hit the stands. *Solutions* was a good book, but it was an inextricably V3.0 book, and V4.0 was an absolutely clean break with the past. So *Turbo Pascal Solutions* never really had a chance to serve its audience, and I saw it on remainder piles a lot.

By that time, I had other things to do: I was working for Borland itself, hired by Philippe Kahn to create a programmer's magazine that eventually appeared in the fall of 1987 as *TURBO TECHNIX*. It was a handful, and I gladly let others write the books for Turbo Pascal 4.0. I had the insider's knowledge that V5.0 would come soon enough and change plenty, so I worked a little bit ahead; *Complete Turbo Pascal*, Third Edition, came out in early 1989.

It's tough to stay ahead in this business. Turbo Pascal 5.5 appeared in May 1989—largely as a response to Microsoft's totally unexpected QuickPascal—and brought with it the magic of object-oriented programming. While I did write the V5.5 *OOP Guide* manual (in nine sizzling days, yikes!) that Borland published with the product, I chose to pass on updating *Complete Turbo Pascal* for either V5.5 or V6.0.

It's been busy since then. I moved from Borland-land to Arizona in the beginning of 1990 to found my own programmers' magazine, *PC TECHNIQUES*. If you haven't seen it, you should—check out the coupon at the end of this book for more information.

So, here we are at version 7.0. Scott, Foresman Trade Books, publisher of all my previous titles, is history, and *Complete Turbo Pascal* is dead—but then again, *Complete Turbo Pascal* was not my title and I freely confess that I hate it. Borland's new name for its high-end compiler gave me an excellent excuse to finally come home by the back roads and use the title I have always wanted to use. *Borland Pascal from Square One* includes Turbo Pascal 7, of course. And I am no longer bound by the title to cover every last corner of the product. The documentation can do that. What I want to do is teach programming, which is an entirely different matter.

As always, I enjoy getting your letters and read every one. I may not always be able to answer, however (not if I ever expect to get another book written), and hope you won't hold my silence against me.

WHO THIS BOOK IS FOR AND WHAT IT'S ABOUT

I wrote this book for ordinary people who have the itch to try programming and (with some dedication) to get good at it over time. I didn't have Pascal experts in mind, though the experts could do worse than come back for some review now and then.

Too many people get this goofy notion that programming is a skill set apart, and that programmers are mystically anointed to somehow be able to grasp what is forever barred to the common man and woman.

Cripes!

Anyone who lives a tolerably comfortable life in this frenetic twentieth century can program. Most of us (as I'll show you shortly) engage the skills of programming to organize our daily lives. *If you want to program, you can.*

It's that simple.

WHAT THIS BOOK WILL COVER

In this book, I'm going to cover the ideas behind programming in general, and then teach programming in Pascal from the foundation of those fundamental ideas. I'll be starting from "square one"; that is, from a dead stop. Nowhere. You don't have to know a *thing* about programming to learn Pascal from this book. You should, however, be comfortable with your computer itself—how to get it up and running and how to handle the rudiments of DOS. If you have Turbo Pascal for Windows, I'll assume that you can wrestle with Windows and come out on top.

Most of the material in this book is common to all three Borland Pascal products: Turbo Pascal 7.0, Borland Pascal 7.0 with Objects, and Turbo Pascal 1.5 for Windows. I will take Pascal from the beginning through pointers, and stop. I will not go into object-oriented programming at length, nor Turbo Vision or OWL, nor assembly language through BASM or external routines. There's plenty of material there for another book, and with some luck I'll write that book, too.

For the Windows versions of Turbo Pascal, you can use the **WinCRT** unit to get the example programs running inside a simple text window. Programming for Windows proper with all the Windows folderol of dialog boxes, controls, resources, messages, and events gets hellishly complex, and it's not something easily broached without a solid grasp of all basic programming ideas up through (*especially* through) pointers.

Rather than try to cover all of Turbo Pascal or (Lord knows) Borland Pascal in one book and do justice to none of it, I'm going to take my time to help you get the basics down cold. It's tough to build a fancy house when half the bricks are missing from your foundation. This book is about foundations and getting familiar with all the skills that you will be using for the rest of your programming career, even (or especially) once you've forgotten how utterly fundamental they are.

—Jeff Duntemann
8105 East Paraiso Drive
Scottsdale, AZ 85255

April 15, 1993

PART ONE

The Idea of Pascal

This is Square One: the start of your career (formal or informal) as a Pascal programmer. It's probably not as hard as you think, nor perhaps as easy as you might have hoped. Pascal is a process, a discipline, a way of thinking—

—but most of all, it is an *idea*.

Pascal is the crystallization of one man's vision of computing. Dr. Niklaus Wirth (pronounced Veert) put forth his vision way back in 1972, drawing on earlier languages like BASIC and FORTRAN, but adding a measure of structure and organization that programming languages had never seen before. If Pascal had one purpose, it was this: to impose order on the often-chaotic process of programming, and manage the inevitable complexity that comes of solving difficult computing problems.

Wirth went on to define other languages (Modula-2 and Oberon) that continued the evolution of that original vision, but none has done as well in the world as Pascal. This book is nominally about Borland's various Pascal compilers, but behind all of Borland's compilers (and all other Pascal compilers) there remains Wirth's original idea of a language designed to manage complexity.

One job Wirth *doesn't* have is managing the complexity of the process of explaining how his language manages complexity. I guess that one falls to me. And to get started, I'm going to spend a few chapters concentrating on the idea of Pascal programming, looking at it all from a height, so that as we begin to thread the details of the language, you won't feel like you're blundering utterly in the dark.

1

For those who come into this book without any previous experience in programming, I'll lay out the fundamental ideas of programming first—ideas that lie beneath *all* programming in any language. This includes the nature of computing itself, and the mechanics of how programs are put together and perfected.

You may be surprised to discover, once you've gotten through Part I, that the skills you need to program are nothing more than the skills of thinking clearly and organizing disparate facts and actions into a coherent plan.

It sure surprised the heck out of me back when I first explored this stuff. I was looking for magic—and found a "to do" list. Ultimately, it was a relief. I'm not a magical kind of a guy. You don't have to be either.

Let me show you why.

Chapter **0**

The Box That
Follows a Plan

THE NATURE OF COMPUTING
AND HOW WE CONTROL IT

There is a rare class of human being with a gift for aphorism, which is the ability to capture the essence of a thing in only a few words. My old man was one; he could speak volumes in saying things like, "Kick ass. Just don't miss." Lacking the gene for aphorism, I write books—but I envy the ability all the same.

The patron aphorist of computing is Ted Nelson, the eccentric wizard who created the perpetually almost-there Xanadu database system, and who wrote the seminal book *Computer Lib/Dream Machines* (Tempus). It's a scary, wonderful work, and in print again after several years of oblivion. In six words, Ted Nelson defined "computer" better than anyone else probably ever will:

A computer is a box that follows a plan.

We'll come back to the box. For now, let's think about plans, where they come from, and what we do with them.

0.1 Another Scottsdale Saturday Morning

Don't be fooled. The world is virtually swimming in petroleum. What we need more of is . . . *Saturdays*.

5:30 A.M. on the start of an Arizona weekend: The neighborhood Gila woodpecker hammers on our tin chimney cap, loud enough to wake the dead, but just long enough to wake the sleeping. Mr. Byte stretches and climbs on my chest, wagging furiously as though to say, "Hey, guy, tempus is fugiting. *Shake it!*"

Over coffee and Corn Chex, I sit down with a quadrille pad and try to figure out how to cram 30 hours of doing into a 16-hour day. The toughest part comes first: simply remembering what needs to be done. I brainstorm a list, hoping it's all there:

Read EMAIL.

Pay bills.

Put money into checking account if necessary.

Go to the hardware store.

> Get Thompson's Water Seal.
>
> Get 2 4' fluorescent bulbs.
>
> Get more steel wool if we're out.
>
> Get more #120 sandpaper if we're out.
>
> See if they have high pressure hose nozzles. Check price against Alsto's catalog. Buy if cheaper.

Get birthday present for Brian. Hunter's Books?

Put together grocery list. Go to Safeway for groceries.

Sand rough spots on the deck.

Water seal the deck.

See if photo reprints are back; call first.

Replace water filter cartridge behind refrigerator.

Test pool chemicals. Add what needs adding.

Do what laundry needs doing.

Swim 50 laps.

That's a lot to ask of one day. If it's going to be done, it's going to have to be done *smart*, which is to say, in efficient order so that as little time and energy gets lost as possible. In other words, to get the most out of a day, you gotta have a *plan*.

TIME AND SPACE PRIORITIES

In lining things up for the merciless sprint through a too-short day, you have to be mindful of both time and space. Some things have to happen before other things. Some things have to happen before a certain time of the day, or within a time "window"—such as the business hours of a store you need to get to.

And on any mad dash through an area the size of the Valley of the Sun, space becomes an overwhelming consideration. You can't just go to one place, come home, then go to the next place, then come home, and go to another place, then come home again; not if each destination lies 15 or 20 miles from home. You have to think about where everything is, and visit all destinations in an order that minimizes needless travel. Hunter's Books is on the way to Home Depot, so it makes sense to visit one on the way to the other.

Furthermore, there are always hard-to-define necessities that influence how and in what order you do things. In an Arizona summer, you simply *must* do grocery shopping dead last, and perferably at a store close to home, if you expect to keep the ice cream solid and the Tater Tots frozen. Faced with 118° outside, most car air conditioners will at best keep you alive.

Finally, when pressed, most of us will admit that we rarely manage to get everything done on the day we intend to do it. Some things end up squeezed out of a too-tight day like watermelon seeds from between greasy fingers. Whether we realize it or not, we often schedule the least necessary things last, so that if we don't get to them it's no disaster. After all, tomorrow is another day.

One way or another, mostly on instinct, we put together our plan. After mulling it for a few minutes, I redrafted my plan as shown in Figure 0.1. The notes in boxes explain why I arranged some part of the plan as I did.

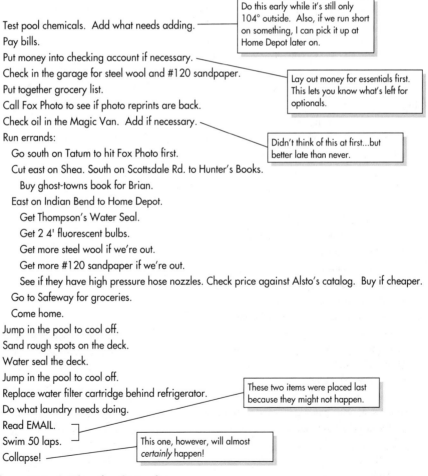

Figure 0.1 A Plan for Saturday

FROM A HEIGHT AND IN DETAIL

The plan (for it is a plan) just outlined was executed pretty much the way I wrote it. Much of the actual detail of the plan acted simply as a memory jogger. In the heat of the moment (or in the heat of an Arizona afternoon, desperate to get someplace—anyplace—air conditioned!) details are often forgotten. I knew, for example, why I wanted to go to Hunter's Books—to buy a book for my nephew's birthday. I was unlikely to forget that. But in the heat, or if the Magic Van had acted up, well, forgetfulness happens . . . .

To be safe, I wrote the plan in more detail than I might have needed.

A plan can exist, however, at various levels of detail. Had I more faith in my memory (or if I'd been stuck with a smaller piece of paper) I might have condensed some of the items above into summaries that identify them without describing them. A less detailed but no less complete form of the plan might look like the one shown in Figure 0.2.

Look carefully at the differences between this list and the previous list. Mostly I've condensed obvious, common-sense things that I was unlikely to forget. I've been to the various stores so often that I could do it asleep, so there's really little point in giving myself directions. I have an intuitive grasp of where all the stores are located, and I can plot a minimal course among them all without really thinking about it. At best, the order in which the stores are written down jogs my memory in the direction of that optimal course.

I combined items that always go together. There's not much point in testing the pool water without adjusting the chemicals. The two are really a single operation, and if I do one, I won't forget to do the other. Similarly, paying bills and adding money back into my checking account are things I always do together; to do otherwise risks disorder and insufficient funds.

Test pool and adjust chemicals.
Pay bills and replenish checking account.
Put together grocery list.
Put together a Home Depot list.
Call Fox Photo to see if photo reprints are back.
Check in the garage for steel wool and #120 sandpaper.
Check oil in the Magic Van. Add if necessary.
Run errands:
  Fox Photo
  Hunter's Books.
  Home Depot. Safeway.
Sand and water seal the deck.
Replace water filter cartridge behind refrigerator.
Do what laundry needs doing.
Read EMAIL.
Swim 50 laps.
Collapse!

Figure 0.2 Saturday's Plan from a Height

I pulled details out of the "Home Depot" item and instead added an item further up the plan, reminding me to "Make a Home Depot list." If I was already going to put together a grocery list, I figured I might as well flip it over and put a hardware store list on the other side.

There's a lesson here: Plan-making is something that gets better with practice. Every time you draft a plan, you'll probably see some way of improving it.

On the other hand, sooner or later you have to stop fooling around and execute the plan.

I'm saying all this to get you in the habit of looking at a plan as something that works at different levels. A good plan can be reduced to an "at-a-glance" form that tells you the general shape of the things you want to do today, without confusing the issue with reams of details. On the other hand, to be complete, the plan *must*, at some level, contain all necessary details. Suppose I had sprained an ankle out in the garage and had to have someone else run errands in my place? In that case, the detailed plan would have been required, down to and perhaps including directions to the various stores.

Had Carol been the one to take over errand-running for me, I might not have had to add a lot of detail to my list. When you live with a woman for 20 years, you share a lot of context and assumptions with her. But had my long-lost cousin Tony from Wisconsin been charged with dashing around Phoenix doing my day's errands, I would have had to write pages and pages to make sure he had enough information to do it right.

Or if my very distant relative Heinz from Dusseldorf were visiting—I would have had to do all that, and write the plan in German to boot.

Or, if my friend Hkrepats from Tau Ceti V (who neither knows nor cares what a swimming pool is, and might consider mustard algae a big plus) volunteered to run errands for me, I would have had to explain even the minutest detail (over and above the English language and alphabet), including what stop lights mean, how to drive a stick shift, our decimal currency (Hkrepats has 16 fingers and counts in hex) and that cats are pets, not hors d'oeuvres on the hoof.

To summarize: The shape of the plan—and the level of detail in the plan—depends on who's reading the plan and who has to follow it. Remember this. We'll come back to it a little later.

0.2 Computer Programs As Plans of Action

If you're coming into this book completely green, the conclusion may not be obvious, so here it is: *A computer program is very much a "do-it" list for a computer, written by you.* The process of creating a computer program, in fact, is very similar conceptually to the process of creating a do-it list, as we'll discover over the course of Part 1.

Ted Nelson's description of a computer as a box that follows a plan is almost literally true. You load a computer program—the plan—into the computer's memory, and the computer will follow that plan, step-by-step, with a tireless persistence and absolute adherence to the letter of the plan.

I'm not going to go into a tremendous amount of detail here as to the electrical internals of computers. If you're curious about such things, you might pick up my earlier book *Assembly Language Step By Step* (Wiley) and read its first several chapters, which take some pains to explain the CPU chip and computer memory in plain language.

THE NOTION OF AN "INSTRUCTION SET"

I had a very hard time catching on to the general concept of computing at first. Everybody who tried to explain it to me danced all around the issue of what a computer actually *was*. Yes, I knew you loaded a program into the computer and the program ran. I understood that one program could control the execution of other programs, and a host of other very high-level details. But I hungered to know what was underneath it all.

What I think was bothering me was the very important question: *How does the computer understand the steps that comprise the plan?*

The answer, like a plan, can be understood on several levels. At the highest level, you can think of it this way: The computer understands a very limited set of commands. These commands are the instructions that you write down, in order, when you sit at your desk and ponder the way to get the computer to do the things you want it to do. Taken together, the commands that the computer understands are called its *instruction set*. The instruction set is summarized in a book that describes the computer in detail. Programmers study the instruction set, and they write a program as a sequence of instructions chosen from that set.

EMILY, THE ROBOT WITH A ONE-TRACK MIND

Let's consider a very simple thought-experiment describing a gadget that has actually been built (although many years ago) at a major American university. The gadget is, in fact, a crude sort of robot. Let's call the robot Emily. (I have a reason for choosing that name. Does anyone remember what it is?)

Picture Emily as a round metal can roughly the size and shape of a low footstool or a dishpan (see Figure 0.3). Inside Emily are motors and batteries to power them, plus relays that switch the motors on and off, allowing the motors to run forward or backward, or to make right and left turns by running one motor or the other alone. On Emily's top surface are a slot into which a card can be inserted, and a button marked "GO."

Left to her own devices, Emily does nothing but sit in one place, going Whirrrrrr. However, if you take a card full of instructions and insert the card into the slot on Emily's lid and press the "GO" button, Emily zips off on her own, stopping and going and turning and reversing. She's following the instructions on the card. Eventually she reaches and obeys the last instruction on the card, and simply stops where she is, waiting for another card and another press of the "GO" button.

Figure 0.3 Emily the Robot

Figure 0.4 shows one of Emily's instruction cards. The card contains 13 rows of holes. In the figure, the black rectangles are holes punched through the card, and the empty rectangles are places where holes could be punched, but are not. Underneath the slot in Emily's lid is a mechanism for detecting holes by shining eight small beams of light at the card. Where the light goes through and strikes a photocell on the other side, there is a hole. Where the light is blocked, there is no hole.

The holes can be punched in numerous patterns. Some of the patterns "mean something" to Emily, in that they cause her machinery to react in a predictable way. When Emily's internal photocells detect the pattern that stands for "Go forward one foot" her motors come on and move her forward a distance of one foot, then stop. Similarly, when Emily detects the pattern that means "Turn right," she pivots on one motor, turning to the right. Patterns that don't correspond to some sort of action are ignored.

The card shown in the figure describes a plan for Emily. It is literally a list of things that she must do. Once the card is inserted into the slot in her lid, a press on her "GO" button sets her in motion, following the plan as surely as I followed mine by jumping into the Magic Van and heading off down Scottsdale Road to do my Saturday morning errands.

When Emily follows the plan outlined on the card, she moves in the pattern shown in Figure 0.5. It's not an especially sophisticated or useful plan—but then again, there is only room for 13 instructions on the card. With a bigger card—or more slots to put cards into—Emily could execute much longer and more complex programs.

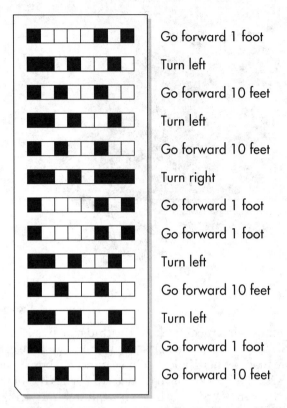

Go forward 1 foot

Turn left

Go forward 10 feet

Turn left

Go forward 10 feet

Turn right

Go forward 1 foot

Go forward 1 foot

Turn left

Go forward 10 feet

Turn left

Go forward 1 foot

Go forward 10 feet

Figure 0.4 A Program Card for Emily the Robot

EMILY'S INSTRUCTION SET

It's interesting to look at the plan-card in Figure 0.4 and dope out how many different instructions are present on the card. The answer may surprise you: *four*. It looks more complex than that, somehow. But all that Emily is doing is executing sequences of the following instructions:

Go forward 1 foot

Go forward 10 feet

Turn left

Turn right

There's no instruction to stop; when Emily runs out of instructions, she stops automatically.

Now, Emily is a little more sophisticated than this one simple card might indicate. Over and above the four instructions shown above, Emily "understands" four more:

Go backward 1 foot

Go backward 10 feet

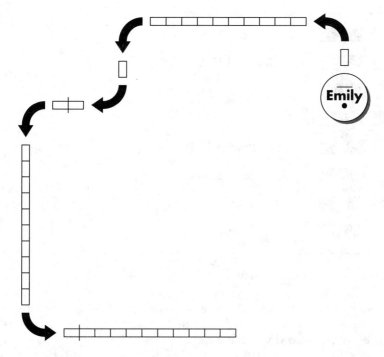

Figure 0.5 How Emily Follows Her Instructions

Rotate 180°

Sound buzzer

I've summarized Emily's full instruction set in Figure 0.6.

When you want to punch up a new card for Emily to follow, you must choose from among the eight instructions in Emily's instruction set. That's all she knows, and there's no way to make her do something that isn't part of the instruction set. However, it isn't always completely plain when something is or isn't part of the instruction set. Suppose you want Emily to move forward seven feet. There's no single instruction in Emily's instruction set called "Go forward 7 feet." However, you could put seven of the "Go forward 1 foot" instructions in a row, and Emily would go forward seven feet.

But that would take seven positions on the card, which only has 13 positions altogether. Is there a way to make Emily move forward seven feet without taking so many instructions?

Consider the full instruction set; then consider this sequence of instructions:

Go forward 10 feet

Go backward 1 foot

Go backward 1 foot

Go backward 1 foot

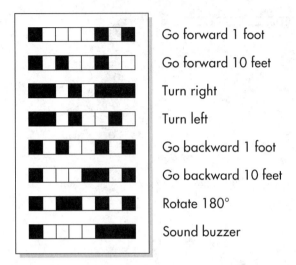

Go forward 1 foot

Go forward 10 feet

Turn right

Turn left

Go backward 1 foot

Go backward 10 feet

Rotate 180°

Sound buzzer

Figure 0.6 The Emily Instruction Set

It's the long way around, in a sense, but the end result is indeed getting Emily to a position seven feet ahead of her starting point. It takes a little longer, timewise, but it only uses up four positions on the card.

This is a lot of what the skill of programming involves: looking at the computer's instruction set and choosing sequences of instructions that get the job done. There is usually more than one way to do any job you could name—and sometimes an infinite number of ways, each with its own set of pluses and minuses. You will find, as you develop your skills as a programmer, that it's relatively easy to get a program to work—and a whole lot harder to get it to work *well*.

DIFFERENT INSTRUCTION SETS

There is something I need to make clear: An instruction set is *not* the same thing as a program. A computer's instruction set is baked into the silicon of its CPU (Central Processing Unit) chip. (There have been computers—big ones—created with alterable instruction sets, but they are not the sorts of things we are ever likely to work on.) Once the chip is designed, the instruction set is almost literally set in stone.

However, as years pass, computer designers create new CPU chips with new instruction sets. The new instruction sets are sometimes massively different from the old ones, but in many cases, a new instruction set comes about simply by adding new instructions to an existing instruction set while designing a new CPU chip.

This was done when Intel designed the 80286 CPU chip in the early '80s. The dominant PC-compatible CPU chip up to that time was Intel's 8088, used by IBM in its original PC and XT. Intel added a lot to the 8088 when it created the 80286, but the remarkable thing was that it only *added* capabilities — Intel took nothing away. The 80286's instruction set is larger than the 8088's, but it also *contains* the 8088's. That allows anything that runs on an 8088 to also run on an 80286. (This is what "upwardly-compatible" means.)

EMILY MARK II

We can return to Emily for a more concrete example. Once we've played with Emily for a few months, let's say we dismantle her and rebuild her with more complex circuitry to do different things. We add more sophisticated motor controls that allow Emily to make half-turns (45°) instead of just full 90° left and right turns. This alone allows tremendously more complex paths to be taken.

But the most intriguing addition to Emily is an electrically operated "tail" that can be raised or lowered under program control. Attached to this tail is a felt-tip reservoir brush, much like the ones sign painters use for large paper signs. One new instruction in Emily's enlarged instruction set lowers the brush so that it contacts the ground. Another instruction raises it off the ground so that it remains an inch or so in the air.

If we then put down large sheets of paper in the room where we test Emily, she can draw things on the paper by lowering the brush, moving around, then raising the brush. Emily can draw a one-foot square by executing the following set of instructions:

Lower brush

Go forward 1 foot

Turn right

Go forward 1 foot

Turn right

Go forward 1 foot

Turn right

Go forward 1 foot

Raise brush

The full Emily Mark II instruction set is shown in Figure 0.7.

The whole point I'm making here is that a computer program is a plan for action, and the individual actions must be chosen from a limited set that the computer understands. If the computer doesn't understand a particular instruction, that instruction can't be used. Sometimes you can *emulate* a missing instruction by combining existing instructions. We did this earlier by using several instructions to make Emily act as though she had a "Move forward 7 feet" instruction. Often, however, that is difficult or impossible. How, for example, might you make Emily perform a half-left turn by combining sequences of her original eight instructions? Easy. *You can't*.

Go forward 1 foot

Go forward 10 feet

Turn right

Turn left

Go backward 1 foot

Go backward 10 feet

Rotate 180°

Sound buzzer

Turn half-left

Turn half-right

Raise brush

Lower brush

Figure 0.7 The Emily Mark II Instruction Set

This is one way to understand the limitations of computers. A computer has a fundamental instruction set. This instruction set is fairly limited, and the individual instructions are very tiny in their impact. An instruction, for example, might simply add one to a location in memory. Through a great deal of cleverness, this elemental instruction set can be expanded enormously by combining a multitude of tiny, limited instructions into larger, more complex instructions. One such mechanism is the subject of this book: Turbo Pascal, as I'll come to show in the next chapter.

0.3 Changing Course Inside the Plan

If you've used a PC for any amount of time, you've probably written small batch files to execute sequences of DOS commands or utility programs. Virtually everyone has written or at least tinkered with AUTOEXEC.BAT, which sets up your machine by loading resident programs, changing video modes, checking remaining hard disk space, and things like that.

A DOS batch file is very much what we've been talking about: A "do-it" list for your computer. I have a host of them, most created to take the three or four little steps necessary to invoke some application. When I want to work with my address book file using the Paradox database, I use this little batch file:

```
D:
CD \PARADOX3\PERSONAL
VHR MDS /N
PARADOX3
```

It's not much, but it saves me having to type these four lines every time I want to update someone's phone number in my address book database. The first command moves me to the D: hard disk drive. The second command moves me into the subdirectory containing my address book database. The third line is a special utility program that resets and clears the unusual monitor and video board that I use. The fourth and last line invokes the Paradox 3.0 database program.

There's something distinctive about small batch programs like this, and about most people's "do-it" lists as well: They run straight through from top to bottom, in one path only.

DEPARTING FROM THE STRAIGHT AND NARROW

How else would it run? Well, it might contain a loop or a branch, which alters the course of the plan based on what happens while the plan is underway.

You do that sort of thing all the time in daily life, mostly without thinking. Suppose, for example, you go grocery shopping with the item "poppy-seed rolls" on your grocery list. Now when you get to Safeway, suppose it's late in the day and the poppy-seed rolls are long gone. You're faced with a decision: What to buy? If you're having hamburgers for supper, you need something to put them on. So you buy Mother Ersatz' Genuine Bread-Flavored Imitation Hamburger Buns. You didn't write it down this way and may not even think of it this way, but your "do-it" list contains this assumed entry:

If the bakery poppy-seed rolls are gone, buy Mother Ersatz' Buns.

Then again, if Mother Ersatz' products make your tummy breakdance all night after supper, you might change your whole supper strategy, leave the frozen hamburger in the freezer, and gather materials for stir-fry chicken instead:

If the bakery poppy-seed rolls are gone, then do this:
    Buy package of boneless chicken breasts.
    Buy bottle of teriyaki sauce.
    Buy fresh mushrooms.
    Buy can of water chestnuts.

Most of the time we perform such last-minute decision-making "on-the-fly," hence we rarely write such detailed decisions down in our "do-it" lists. Most of the time, Safeway *will* have the poppy-seed rolls and we operate under the assumption that they will always be there. We think of "Plan B" decisions as something that happens only when the world goes ballistic on us and acts in an unexpected fashion.

In computer programming, such decisions happen all the time, and programming would be impossible without them. In a computer program, little or nothing can be assumed. There's no "usual situation" to rely on. Everything has to be explained in full. It's rather like the situation that would occur if I sent Hkrepats the alien out shopping for me. I'd have to spell the full decision out in great detail:

If the bakery poppy-seed rolls are there, then buy one package;
  otherwise buy one package of Mother Ersatz' Buns.

This is an absolutely fundamental programming concept we call the **IF..THEN..ELSE** branch statement. It's a fork in the plan; a choice of two paths based on the state of things as they exist at that point in the plan. You can't *know* when you head out the door on your way to Safeway whether everything you want will be there—so you go in prepared to make decisions based on what you find when you get to the bakery department. In Pascal programming you'll come to use branches like this so often it will almost be done without thinking.

DOING PART OF THE PLAN MORE THAN ONCE

Changing the course of a plan doesn't necessarily mean branching off on a whole new trajectory. It can also mean going back a few steps and repeating something that may need to be done more than once.

An example of a loop to get a job done comes up often in something as simple as a recipe. When you're making a cake from scratch and the recipe book calls for four cups of flour, what do you do? You take the measuring cup, dip it into the flour canister, fill it brimful, and then dump the flour it contains into the big glass bowl.

Then you do exactly the same thing a second time . . .
  . . . and a third time . . .
  . . . and a fourth time.

The plan (here, a cake recipe) calls for flour. Measuring flour is done in one-cup increments, because you don't have a four-cup measuring cup. It's a little like the situation with Emily the Robot, when she has to move three feet forward. The instruction set doesn't allow you to measure out four cups of flour in one swoop, so you have to fake it by measuring out one cup four times.

In the larger view, you've entered a loop in the plan. You go through the component motions of measuring out a cup of flour. Then, you ratchet back just far enough in the plan to go through the same motions again. You do this as often as you must.

COUNTING PASSES THROUGH THE LOOP

You've probably been in the situation where you begin daydreaming after the second cup, and by the time you shake Julia Roberts (or perhaps Tom Cruise) out of your head, you can't remember how many times you've already run through the loop, and either go one too many or one too few. Counting helps, and since I'm a champ-een daydreamer, I'm not afraid to admit that when the count goes more than three or four, I start making tick marks on a piece of scratch paper for each, however much of whatever I throw into the bowl. This makes for much better cakes. (Or at least more predictable ones.)

You might write out (for cousin Heinz or perhaps Hkrepats the alien) this part of the plan like so:

Do this exactly four times (and count them!):
  Dip the measuring cup into the flour canister.
  Fill the cup to the line with flour.
  Dump the flour into the mixing bowl.

This is another element that you'll see very frequently in Pascal programming. It's called a **FOR..NEXT** loop, and we'll return to it later in this book.

DOING PART OF THE PLAN UNTIL IT'S FINISHED

There are other circumstances when you need to repeat a portion of a plan until . . . well, until what must be done is done. You do it as often as necessary.

It's something like the way Mary Jo Mankiewicz measures out jelly beans at Candy'N'Stuff. You ask her for a quarter-pound of the broccoli-flavored ones. She takes the big scoop, holds her nose, and plunges it deep into that rich green bin. With a scoop full of jelly beans, she stands over the scale, and repeatedly shakes a dribble of jelly beans into the scale's measuring bowl until the digital display reads a little more than .25.

Written out for Hkrepats, the plan might read this way:

Dig the scoop into the jelly beans and fill it.
Take the full scoop over to the digital scale.
Repeat the following:
  Shake a few jelly beans into the scale's measuring bowl
Until the scale's digital readout reads .25.

Exactly how many times Mary Jo has to shake the scoop over the scale depends on what kind of a shaker she is. If she's new on the job and cautious because she doesn't want to go too far, she'll just shake one or two jelly beans at a time onto the scale. Once she wises up, she'll realize that going over the requested weight doesn't matter so much, and she'll shake a little harder so that more jelly beans drop out of the scoop with each shake. This way, she'll shake a lot fewer times, and when she ends up handing you half a pound of jelly beans, that's OK—since one can't ever have enough broccoli-flavored jelly beans, now, can one?

Computers, of course, don't mind making small shakes if that's what it takes to get the final weight bang-on. This sort of loop is called a **REPEAT..UNTIL** loop, and it's also common in Pascal programming, as I'll demonstrate later on in Part 2.

THE SHAPE OF THE PLAN

The whole point I'm trying to make in this section is that a plan doesn't have to be shaped like one straight line. It can fork, once or many times. Portions of the plan can be repeated, either a set number of times, or as many times as it takes to get the job done. This is nothing new to any of us—we do this sort of thing every day in muddling through our somewhat overstuffed lives. In fact, if you've taken any effort at all to live an organized life, you'll probably make a dynamite programmer, since success in life or in programming cooks down to creating a reasonable plan and then seeing it through from start to finish.

0.4 Information and Action

Actually, we've only talked about half of what a plan (in computer terms) actually is. The other half, which some people say is by far the more important half, has been waiting in the wings for its place in this discussion.

That other half is the stuff that is acted upon when the computer acts out the plan you devise for it. When we spoke of Mary Jo Mankiewicz measuring out jelly beans, we focused on the way she ladled them out. Just as important to the process are the jelly beans themselves. And so it is, whether you characterize the plan as shopping for groceries, measuring out flour for a recipe, or building a birdhouse. The shopping, the measuring, and the building are crucial—but they mean nothing without the groceries, the flour, and all those little pieces of plywood that always split when you try to get a nail through them.

In computer terms, the stuff that a program acts on is information, by which I mean symbols that have some meaning in a human context.

CODE VS. DATA

When you create a computer program, the plan portion of the program is a series of steps, written in a programming language of some sort. In this book, that's going to mean Turbo Pascal, but there are plenty of programming languages in the world (too many by half—or maybe three quarters, I think) and they all work pretty much the same way. Taken together, these steps are called *program code*, or simply *code*. Collectively, the information acted on by the program code is called *data*. The program as a whole contains both code and data.

My friend Tom Swan (who has written some terrific books on Turbo Pascal himself) says that code is what a computer program *does*, and data is what a computer program *knows*. This is a very elegant way of characterizing the difference between program code and data, and I hesitate in using it mostly because too many people have swallowed the Hollywood notion of mysteriously intelligent computers a little too fully. A program doesn't "know" anything—it's not alive, and a consensus is beginning to form that computers can never truly be made to think in the sense that human beings think. Roger Penrose has written a truly excellent book on the subject, *The Emperor's New Mind* (Oxford), which is difficult reading in places but really nails the whole notion of "artificial intelligence" to the wall. The subject is a big one, and an important one, and I recommend the book powerfully.

But there's another reason. Thinking of code and data as "doing" and "knowing" leaves out an essential component: The gizmo that does the doing and the knowing — that is, the computer itself. I recommend that you always keep the computer in the picture, and think of the computer, code, and data as an unbreakable love triangle. No single corner is worth a damn without both of the other two. See Figure 0.8.

In summary: The program code is a series of steps. The computer takes these steps, and in doing so manipulates the program data.

Let's talk a little about the nature of data.

LET X BE . . .

A lot of people shy away from computer programming due to math anxiety. Drop an "X" in front of them and they panic. In truth, there's very little math involved in most programming, and what math there is very rarely goes beyond the high-school level. In virtually all programs you're likely to write for data processing purposes (as opposed to scientific or engineering work), you'll be doing nothing more complex than adding, subtracting, multiplying, or (maybe) dividing.

What programming *does* involve is symbolic thinking. A program is a series of steps that acts upon a group of symbols. These symbols represent some reality existing apart from the computer program itself. It's a little like explaining a point in astronomy by saying, "Let this tennis ball represent Earth, and this marble represent Moon." Using the tennis ball and the marble as symbols, you can show someone how the moon moves around the earth. Add a third

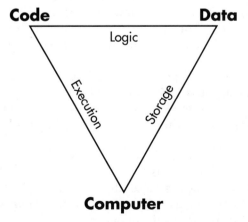

Figure 0.8 Computer, Code, and Data

symbol (a soccer ball, perhaps) to represent the Sun, and you can explain solar eclipses and the phases of the Moon. The tennis ball, marble, and soccer ball are placeholders for their real-life stone-and-hot-gas counterparts. They allow us to think about the Earth, Sun, and Moon without getting boggled by the massiveness of scale on which the solar system operates. They're *symbols*.

A BUCKET, A LABEL, AND A MASK

Using a couple of balls to represent bodies in the solar system is a good example of an interesting process called *modelling*, which is a common thing to do with computer programs; we'll come back to it at intervals throughout this book. But data is even simpler than that. A good conceptual start for thinking about data is to imagine a bucket.

Actually, imagine a group of buckets. (Your programs won't be especially useful if they only contain one item of data.) Since the buckets all look pretty much alike, you'd also better imagine that you can slap a label on each bucket and write a name on each label.

The buckets start out empty. You can, at will, put things in the buckets, or take things out again. You might place 10 marbles in a bucket labeled "Ralph," or remove five marbles from a bucket labeled "George." You can look at the buckets and compare them: Bucket Ralph now contains the same number of marbles as bucket George—but bucket Sara contains more marbles than either of them. This is pretty simple, and maps perfectly onto the programming notion of defining a *variable*—which is nothing more than a bucket for data—and giving that variable a name. The variable has a *value*, meaning only that it contains something. The subtlety comes in when you build a set of assumptions about what data in a variable *means*.

You might, for example, create a system of assumptions by which you'll indicate truth or falsehood. You make the following assumption: A bucket with one marble in it represents the logical value True, whereas an empty bucket (that is, one with no marbles in it) represents the logical value False. Note that this does *not* mean you write the word "True" on one bucket's label or "False" on another's. You're simply treating the buckets as symbols of a pair of more abstract ideas.

With the above assumptions in mind, suppose you take a bucket and write "**Mike Is At Home**" on its label. Then you call Mike on the phone. If Mike picks up the phone, you drop one marble into the labeled bucket. If Mike's phone simply rings (or if his excessively cute answering machine message greets you), you leave the labeled bucket empty.

With the bucket labeled "**Mike Is At Home**" you've stored a little bit of information. If you or someone else understands that one marble in a bucket indicates True, and an empty bucket indicates False, then the bucket labeled "**Mike Is At Home**" can tell you something useful: that it is *true* that Mike is at home. Just look in the bucket—and save yourself a phone call.

What's important here is that we've put a sort of mask on that bucket. It's not simply a bucket for holding marbles anymore. It's a way of representing a simple fact in the real world that may have nothing whatsoever to do with either marbles or buckets.

Much of the real "thinking" work of programming consists of devising these sets of assumptions that govern the use of a group of symbols. You'll be thinking things, like,

*Let's create a variable called **BeanCount**. It will represent the number of jelly beans left in the jelly bean jar. Let's also create a variable called **ScoopCapacity**, which will represent the number of jelly beans that the standard scoop contains when filled.*

In both instances, the variable itself is simply a place somewhere inside the computer where you can store a number. What's important is the mask of meaning that you place in front of that variable. The variable contains a number—and that number represents something.

This is the fundamental idea that underlies all computer data items. They're all buckets with names—for which you provide a meaning.

0.5 The Craftsman, His Pockets, His Workbench, and His Shelves

Let's turn our attention again to Ted Nelson's aphorism that *a computer is a box that follows a plan.* So far I've spoken about the plan itself—how it runs from top to bottom, perhaps branching or looping along the way. I've talked a little bit about data—the stuff that the program works on when it does its work. However, only half of the essence of computing is the plan and its data, and the other half is the nature of the box that follows the plan.

It's time to talk about the box.

DIVIDED INTO THREE PARTS

Your PC (and virtually all other kinds of computers that have ever been designed) is divided into three general areas: The *Central Processing Unit* (CPU), *storage*, and *input/output* (I/O).

The CPU is the boss of the machine. It's the part of the machine that contains the instruction set we spoke of earlier. The instruction set, if you recall, is that fundamental list of abilities that the computer has. All programs, no matter how big or how small, and regardless of how simple or how complex, are composed of some sequence of those fundamental instructions.

Storage is another term for memory, although it actually includes what we call Random Access Memory (RAM) and disk storage as well. Storage is where program code and data lives most of the time. RAM is storage that exists right next to and around the CPU, on silicon chips. The CPU can get into RAM very quickly. The disadvantage to RAM is that it's expensive, and, (worse) it goes blank when you turn off power to the computer. Disk storage, by contrast, is "farther away" from the CPU and is much slower to read from and write to. Balancing that disadvantage is the fact that disk storage is cheap and (better still) once something is written onto a disk, it stays there until you erase it or write something over it.

Input and output are similar, but differ mainly in the direction that information moves. Your keyboard is an input device, in that it sends data to the CPU when you press a key. Your screen is an output device, in that it puts up on display information sent to it by the CPU. The parallel port to which you connect your printer is another output device, and the serial port to which you connect your modem swings both ways: It both sends and receives data; thus it is both an input and an output device at once.

WHAT HAPPENS WHEN A PROGRAM RUNS

Programs are stored on disk for the long haul. When you execute a program, the CPU brings the program from disk storage into RAM. That done, the CPU begins at the top of the program in RAM and begins "fetching" instructions from the program in RAM into itself. One by one, it fetches instructions from RAM and then executes them. It's a process much like reading a step from a recipe, then performing that step. You first need to know (by reading the recipe) that you must throw four cups of flour into the bowl; then you have to go ahead and actually measure out the flour and put it into the bowl.

During a program's execution, the CPU may display information on the screen or ask for information from the keyboard. There's nothing special about input or output like this; there are instructions in the CPU's instruction set that take care of moving numbers and characters in from the keyboard or out to the screen.

What *is* more intriguing is the notion that the plan—that is, the sequence of instructions being executed by the CPU—may change based on data that you type at the keyboard. There are forks in the road (usually a multitude of them) and which road the CPU actually follows depends on what you type into data entry fields or answers to questions the CPU asks you.

You may see a question displayed on the screen something like this:

Do you want to exit the program now? (Y/N:)

If you press the "Y" key, one road at the fork will be taken, and that fork leads to the end of the program. If you press the "N" key, the other road at the fork will be taken, back into the program to do some more work.

Programs like this are said to be *interactive*, since there's a constant conversation going on between the program and you, the user. Inside the computer, the program is threading its way among a great many possible paths, choosing a path at each fork in the road depending on questions it asks you, or depending on the results of the work it is doing.

Sooner or later, the program either finishes its work or is told by you to pack up for the day; it returns control to DOS, and once again you see the good ol' C:\> prompt.

INSIDE THE BOX

That's how things appear to you, outside the box, sitting at the keyboard supervising. Understanding in detail what happens inside the box is the labor of a lifetime (or at least often seems to be) and is the subject of this entire book—and hundreds of others, including all the other books that I've ever written.

But a good place to start is with a simple metaphor. the CPU is a craftsman, trained in a set of skills that involves the manipulation of data. Just as a skilled machinist manipulates metal, and a carpenter manipulates wood, the CPU manipulates numbers, characters, and symbols. We can think of the CPU's skills as those instructions in its instruction set. The carpenter knows how to plane a board smooth—and the CPU knows how to add two numbers together to produce a sum. The carpenter knows how to nail two boards together—and the CPU knows how to compare two numbers to see if they are equal.

The CPU has a workbench in our metaphor: the computer's RAM. RAM is memory inside the computer, close to the CPU and easily accessible to the CPU. The CPU can reach anywhere it needs into RAM at any time. It can choose a place in RAM "at random—this is why we call it Random Access Memory. As the CPU stands in front of its workbench, it can reach anywhere on the workbench and grab anything there. It can move things around on the workbench. It can pick up two parts, put them together, and then place the joined parts back down on the workbench before picking up something else.

But before beginning an entirely different project, the CPU, being a good craftsman, will tidy up its workbench, put its tools away, and sweep the shavings into the trash bin, leaving a clean workbench for the next project.

Disk storage is a little different. In our metaphor, you should think of disk storage as the set of shelves in the far corner of the workshop, where the craftsman keeps tools, raw materials, and incomplete projects-in-progress. It takes a few steps to go over to the shelves, and the craftsman may have to get up on a stepstool to reach something on the highest shelves. To avoid running itself ragged (and wasting a lot of time) going back and forth to the shelves constantly, the CPU tries to take as much as it can from the shelves to its workbench, and stay to work at the workbench.

It would be like buying a birdhouse kit, opening the package, leaving the opened package on the shelves, and then traipsing over to the shelves to pull each piece out of the birdhouse kit as needed.

That's dumb. The CPU would instead take the entire kit to the workbench and assemble it there, only going back to the shelves for something too big to fit on the workbench, or to find something it hadn't anticipated needing.

One final note on our metaphor: The CPU has a number of storage locations that are actually inside itself, closer even than RAM. These are called *registers*, and they are like the pockets in a crasftman's apron. Rather than placing something back on the workbench, the craftsman can tuck a small tool or part conveniently in a pocket for quick retrieval a moment later. The CPU has a few such pockets, and can use them to tuck away a number or a character for a moment.

So there are actually three different types of storage in a computer: disk storage, RAM, and registers. Disk storage is very large (these days, hundreds of megabytes are not uncommon) and quite cheap—but the CPU has to spend considerable time and effort getting at it. RAM is much closer to the CPU, but it is a lot more expensive and rarely anything near as large. Not all computers have more than 4 or 8 megabytes of RAM these days, and worse yet, most programs that you write in Turbo Pascal will be limited to using less than a single megabyte of that. (Borland Pascal 7.0, however, can use up to 16 megabytes of memory if you have it.) Finally, registers are the closest storage to the CPU, and are in fact *inside* the CPU—but there are only a half dozen or so of them, and you can't just buy more and plug them in.

SUMMARY: TRUTH OR METAPHOR?

The electrical reality of a computer is complicated in the extreme, and getting more so all the time. I've discussed it to a much greater depth in my book *Assembly Language Step By Step* than I can possibly discuss it here; if you're curious about what RAM "really" is, that would be a good book to read.

I'm not going to that depth in *this* book because Turbo Pascal shields you from having to know as much about the computer's electrical structure and deepest, darkest corners. I'm sticking with metaphor because a computer program *is* a metaphor. A program is a symbolic metaphor for a frighteningly obscure torrent of electrical switching activity ultimately occurring in something about the size of your thumbnail.

When we declare a variable in Turbo Pascal (as I'll be explaining shortly) we're doing nothing different from saying, "Let's say that these eight transistor storage cells represent a letter of the alphabet, and we'll give it the name **DiskUnit**."

Turbo Pascal, in fact, is a tool entirely devoted to the creation and perfection of such metaphors. You could create a simple program that modeled a shopping trip taken by Hkrepats the alien to Safeway, just as I described earlier in this chapter. There was, in fact, an intriguing software product available years ago called "Karel the Robot" which was, in fact, a simulation of a robot on the computer screen. Karel could be given commands and would follow them obediently; the net effect was a very good education on the nature of computers.

This chapter has been groundwork, basically, for people who have had absolutely no experience in programming. All I've wanted to do is present some of the fundamental ideas of both computing and programming, so that we can now dive in and get on with the process of creating our program metaphors in earnest.

Chapter 1

The Nature of Software Development

UNDERSTANDING HOW PROGRAMS BECOME REALITY

As I hinted in the last chapter, a computer program is a plan, written by you, that the computer follows in order to get something done. The plan consists of a series of steps that must be taken, and some number of decisions to be made along the way when a fork in the road is encountered.

That's programming in the abstract, as simply put as possible. There are a lot of ways of actually writing a program, each way focusing on a different *programming language*. In this book, I'll be talking about only one programming language, the one called Pascal. Furthermore, I'll be focusing on only one single "dialect" of that language, the venerable Turbo Pascal, now in its tenth year and seventh major release.

This shouldn't be considered a limitation. Turbo Pascal has swept virtually all other dialects of Pascal under the rug, and has single-handedly redefined the Pascal language (as far as practical concerns go) to simply *be* Turbo Pascal. If you're going to learn Pascal programming at all, you might as well learn the dialect comprising probably 95 percent of all PC Pascal compilers ever sold.

So let's do it!

1.1 Languages and Dialects

In the "Save the Whales" episode of the *Star Trek* movie series, the crew of the Enterprise travel back in time to 1987 San Francisco. When Engineer Scottie needs to use a computer, he is shown a Macintosh (his first mistake) and immediately picks up the mouse as though it were a microphone and begins addressing the poor machine directly:

25

"Computer: We're going to design a molecular structure for transparent aluminum!"

The Mac had very little to say in response. Computers didn't understand the English language very well back in 1987, and they don't understand it much better today. So what *do* computers understand? What is their native language?

ASSEMBLY LANGUAGE

The fast answer is that computers understand something called "assembly language," in which each step in the plan is one of those fundamental machine instructions I described conceptually in Chapter 0. Machine instructions are incredibly minute in what they do; for example, a single instruction may do nothing more than fetch a byte of data from a location in RAM and store it in register AX. It takes an enormous number of such instructions to do anything useful; hundreds or thousands for small programs, and hundreds of thousands or even millions for major application programs like Word Perfect or AutoCAD.

The instructions themselves are terse, cryptic, and look more like something copied out of a mad scientist's notebook than anything you or I would call a language:

```
MOV     AX,[BX]
SUB     AX,DX
AND     AX,0FF0DH
DEC     CX
LOOPNZ  MSK13
```

Actually, the frightening truth is that even these cryptic statements are themselves "masks" for the *true* machine instructions, which are nothing more than sequences of 0's and 1's:

```
0110101000110010
0000000101110011
1110111110011011
0110110110001010
```

It is possible to program computers by writing down sequences of 0's and 1's and somehow cramming them into a computer through toggle switches, with an "up" switch for a "1" and a "down" switch for a "0." I used to do this in 1976 and thought it was great good fun, because back then it was the best that my machine and I could do.

Is it really fun?

Mmmmm . . . no. It gets old in a *big* hurry. Doing something as simple as making the PC's speaker beep requires 15 or 20 machine instructions, all laid out *precisely* the right way. Even writing assembly language in almost-words like **MOV AX,[BX]** is tiresome and done today only by the most curious and most dedicated among us. But the computer only understands machine instructions.

What to do?

HIGH-LEVEL COMPUTER LANGUAGES

The answer dates back almost to the dawn of computing. (As I said, futzing machine instructions gets old in a big, *big* hurry.) Early on, people defined what we call *high-level computer languages* to do much of that meticulous machine-instruction arranging automatically.

In a high-level language, we define words and phrases that mean something to us and perform some simple task on the computer. A good example is beeping the PC's speaker. We might decide that the word **BEEP** will be used to indicate that the computer's speaker is to be sounded. That done, we write down the sequence of machine instructions that actually causes sound to be generated on the speaker, and we associate those machine instructions with the recognizable term **BEEP**.

This sequence of instructions remains consistent and never changes. So we create a program for ourselves that, when it sees the word **BEEP**, substitutes the sequence of 20 machine instructions that actually does the speaker-beeping. We only need to remember that the word **BEEP** does the beeping. Our clever program, called a *compiler*, remembers the 20-instruction sequence that accomplishes the beep, so that we don't have to. (Perhaps our program isn't especially clever. But it remembers things *very* well.)

We go on from there and define other easily-readable words and phrases that stand for sequences of dozens or even hundreds of machine instructions. This allows us to write down easily-readable commands like the following in only a few seconds:

```
Remainder := Remainder - 1;
IF Remainder = 0 THEN
  BEGIN
    BEEP;
    Write('Warning!  Your time has run out!');
  END;
```

Once you have a feeling for the high-level language, you can look at sequences like this and know exactly what they'll do without stretching your brain too much. The reality is that it may take hundreds of machine instructions for the CPU to do the work involved in what we have written, but for *our* eyes, it's only a few short lines.

PROGRAMS THAT WRITE OTHER PROGRAMS

This clever compiler program understands a great many English-like words and phrases. We create a file, like a word processor file, containing sequences of English-like words and phrases. The compiler program reads in the source file of English-like words and phrases, and writes out an equivalent file of machine instructions. This program file of machine instructions can be loaded and executed by the CPU. But even though this program file consists of thousands or tens of thousands of machine instructions, *we never had to know even a single machine instruction to write it.* All we had to do was understand how the English-like commands of the high-level language affected the machine. The compiler takes care of the "ugly" stuff like remembering which sequence of 20 machine instructions beeps the speaker. All we have to remember is what **BEEP** does.

Much better!

Thus, a compiler program is a program that writes other programs, with some direction from us. It does its job so well that we can actually forget all about what happens with the machine instructions (most of the time, anyway) and concentrate on the logic of how the English-like words and phrases go together.

DIFFERENT LANGUAGES

A whole host of high-level languages exists for the PC. Pascal, C, C++, and BASIC are the most common, but there are hundreds of others with obscure or puckish names like COBOL, SNOBOL, SPITBOL, Forth, APL, Smalltalk, Eiffel, Actor, JOVIAL, Clarion, PL/1, Rexx, FORTRAN, IITRAN, Lisp, Scheme, AWK, and on and on and on. As different as they may seem on the surface, they all do the same thing underneath: arrange machine instructions to accomplish the work that we encode in English-like words and phrases.

Pascal, for example, uses the word **Write** to display information on the screen. BASIC, by contrast, uses the word **PRINT**. The C language uses the word **printf**. Forth uses the word **TYPE**. Others use words like **SAY**, **OUTPUT**, or **Show**. Those words were chosen by the people who designed each language for reasons they considered good ones. However, what those different words *do* is all pretty much the same.

A high-level language is defined as a set of commands, along with a set of rules as to how these commands are used alone and combined. These rules are called the *syntax* of the language, and they correspond roughly to the syntax and grammar of spoken human languages like English and French. Computer languages are not as rich as human languages, but they are *much* more precise—and needless to say, they "speak" only of things that a computer can actually accomplish.

DIALECTS OF A SINGLE LANGUAGE

Having a mob of dissimilar languages to choose from might seem confusing enough. Unfortunately, even within a single language, there are variations on a theme called *dialects*. Each person or company who creates a compiler that understands a given computer language might construct the compiler to understand things a little differently from other compilers written earlier for the same language. Thus not all Pascal compilers agree on what certain program commands mean. Nor do all BASIC compilers agree on the syntax and command set of BASIC. If you write a program in Power Basic it won't necessarily compile correctly if you hand that same program to Microsoft BASIC.

Dialects usually happen when companies who write compilers add new features and abilities to languages in order to produce a more powerful language or (at least) one perceived as different from the compilers already on the market.

Turbo Pascal is a dialect of the Pascal language. Pascal has been around for about 20 years now, and it's done some growing in the process. Pascal predates PCs; in fact, it predates all microcomputers of any design and was originally created to run on massive mainframe machines, those famous for being kept behind locked doors in air-conditioned rooms with raised floors. The man who designed Pascal, Niklaus Wirth, was trying to prove a point in computer science when he designed Pascal and really didn't finish the job. Other companies added features to Pascal over the years, and little by little the language broke into mutually exclusive dialects that were about 90 percent common. In computer languages as in horseshoes, however, "almost" just doesn't count.

For example, the original Pascal wrote information to disk files with the **Put** command. Turbo Pascal broke with this concept and used the **Write** command to write data to disk, and omitted the **Put** command completely. If you take a program written in an old version of Pascal and try to compile it using Turbo Pascal, the compiler will display an error message if it encounters a **Put** command, since it doesn't know what sequence of machine instructions **Put** is supposed to represent.

This problem of dialects is worse in most languages other than Pascal, because Turbo Pascal has dominated the Pascal world for so long that most of the earlier dialects have simply disappeared. If you ever attempt to program in different versions of BASIC, on the other hand, the dialects problem will appear in spades, and you will have a great deal of work to do making programs written for one BASIC compile correctly using another BASIC.

In general, this book will be speaking of the Turbo Pascal dialect of Pascal. Here and there, I'll be pointing out differences between Turbo Pascal and other Pascals, but as I've said before, the differences are becoming less and less important.

1.2 Getting Ready to Program

Turbo Pascal is itself a program, and needs to be installed on your hard disk before you can begin to learn how to use it. The Borland International documentation will show you how to install the product, which now consists of a great many files in several DOS subdirectories. (Many of us old-timers still recall how Turbo Pascal originally consisted of two or three files and fit very comfortably on a 360K diskette.)

PUT IT IN YOUR PATH!

Borland doesn't insist that you do this, but I will strongly suggest that you add the Turbo Pascal or Borland Pascal subdirectory to your DOS path. Borland's installer program installs Turbo Pascal in a subdirectory named TURBO on one of your hard drives; specifically the C: drive unless you tell it otherwise. (Borland Pascal is installed by the installer program in a subdirectory named BP\BIN.) If Turbo Pascal was installed in C:\TURBO, you want that path as one of the search paths displayed when you type the PATH command at the DOS command line.

If the Turbo Pascal subdirectory doesn't appear in the list of paths shown to you by the PATH command, you'll have to add it to the PATH statement in your AUTOEXEC.BAT file. Consult a DOS reference if you've never done this before. Remember that after you change your PATH statement in AUTOEXEC.BAT, you have to reboot the machine for the change to take effect.

CREATE A PATH FOR THE LISTINGS FILES

The reason I suggest putting the \TURBO subdirectory on your path is that it makes it easier to experiment with the listings files available for this book. All of the Pascal source code files presented in this book are available on diskette, either through me or through numerous on-line services, shareware vendors, and BBS systems. What works well is to go into the \TURBO subdirectory and create a new subdirectory "below" \TURBO. Then load the contents of the listings diskette into the new subdirectory. I recommend using a subdirectory name PASQ1. You can create the subdirectory this way, assuming that the \TURBO subdirectory is located on your C: drive:

```
C:
CD \TURBO
MD PASQ1
CD PASQ1
```

At this point, you'll be "in" the PASQ1 subdirectory, and can copy the listings files into the subdirectory from a diskette, or download them to the PASQ1 subdirectory using your favorite telecommunications program.

Some of the text and some of the examples I'll present in this book assume that the source code files (that is, the Pascal program files you create with the Turbo Pascal editor) will exist in the PASQ1 subdirectory beneath the TURBO subdirectory. You can store your program source code files anywhere on disk, of course, but there's little point in creating confusion by doing something deliberately different from the way things are described in the book.

1.3 The Turbo Pascal Process

Before we go ahead and run through an actual program compilation (which I suspect you're impatient to try), it might make sense to describe the process conceptually, especially if this is your first effort in programming. I'll go into the mechanics of using the Turbo Pascal Development Environment from time to time throughout the book, so this overview will be brief.

SOURCE CODE AND OBJECT CODE

Two words you may have heard before and will certainly hear in the future are *source code* and *object code*. Source code files are the "human readable" form of a program. A source code file is an ordinary DOS file that you create by typing into a text editor like the one built into Turbo Pascal. Object code files, on the other hand, contain the individual machine instructions that the CPU knows how to execute; you know, those endless runs of 0's and 1's that I described in the previous section. The whole purpose of the Turbo Pascal compiler is to take source code files that you write, and use them to generate object code files that may be executed on the computer.

Source code files for Turbo Pascal usually have a file extension of .PAS. Object code files come in two types. *Unit* files contain bits and pieces of programs that can be used again and again, but are not in themselves complete programs. I'll deal with units later on; they have a file extension of .TPU, .TPP, or .TPW. The sort of object code files that are executable program files have a file extention of .EXE (executable).

In your early explorations of Turbo Pascal, you'll be creating .PAS files and compiling them to create .EXE files. You'll then run the .EXE files and see how well they work. .EXE files may be run from the DOS prompt without any help from the Turbo Pascal product itself. However, most of the time you'll be able to test your .EXE files from inside Turbo Pascal.

THE PROGRAM DEVELOPMENT CYCLE

Creating programs in Turbo Pascal works like this: You begin by conceptualizing a design of some sort for your program. This might involve some study, some notes, and some diagrams indicating how the program is to work. With your design (that is, your notes and diagrams) close at hand, you bring up Turbo Pascal and begin writing program code based on your design into a text editor window. Every so often during this process, save your program source code file or files to disk. It's as easy as pressing the F2 function key.

Once you've completely typed the program source code file into the text editor window, you invoke the Turbo Pascal compiler. The compiler reads the source code you've typed into the text editor window and generates a .EXE file containing the appropriate object code. Once the compiler begins running, one of two things happens: The compiler either finds an error, or it doesn't. If the compiler does *not* find an error, you have what is called a *correct compilation*. This doesn't mean you have a bug-free program yet — but we'll get to *that* little matter in a moment.

Most of the time, the compiler will "complain" about something in your source code. You may have typed something incorrectly, or else misunderstood some element of Pascal and written something incomplete or nonsensical. No .EXE file will be created in this case. You'll have to stare at your code a little more, read the manuals (or this book), correct what's wrong, and try the compilation again.

Sooner or later, your program will compile correctly. At that point, you have a runnable .EXE file, and you can try running it from within Turbo Pascal.

Again, when you try running your program, one of two things happens: Either it works perfectly, or else it doesn't. And when it doesn't work perfectly, that's when we say that your program has those legendary *bugs*.

Getting rid of bugs is a lot tougher than just getting rid of compiler errors. The compiler will usually give you a good idea of where a compiler error lies and what's causing it. Bugs range from some simple, innocuous action that you didn't ask for (or one you asked for that didn't occur) all the way to locking the machine up hard and forcing you to reboot.

Turbo Pascal contains a number of built-in tools to help you flush out the inevitable bugs you'll find in your programs. Using these tools and your own good sense, you gradually find and fix the causes of whatever bugs are evident. This process can take awhile. Getting rid of disastrous and obvious bugs happens early in the cycle, because you're pretty motivated to find them and fix them. Getting rid of minor or subtler bugs that don't necessarily make your program worthless could be a long process—and may be an endless one. People say there's always one more bug, and you can devote as much time and energy as you care to rooting that last bug out.

But even when you root the "last" bug out, *there's always one more bug.* Existential, no?

THE PROCESS, SUMMARIZED

Let's run down a list of the major steps in the Turbo Pascal program development cycle:

1. You design the program on paper. This does not mean simply writing out program statements with a pencil. It usually means charts, diagrams, and notes we call *specifications*.

2. Working from your design, you type program source code into a text editor window. Save early and often!

3. Once you consider the source code complete, try to compile it.

4. Fix any compiler errors that come up, and then recompile until there are no more compiler errors.

5. Once the program compiles correctly, try running it. Take note of any bugs that appear, where a bug is anything a program does that it isn't supposed to, or something it doesn't do that it should.

6. Fix all identified bugs, and run the program some more, to see if you can identify any further bugs. This stage is called *testing*. It takes a long time.

7. When you can't find any more bugs, the program can be considered finished. This doesn't mean that the program doesn't contain any more bugs. It generally means you've simply run out of patience with bug-chasing, and will be content with what you have. Days, weeks, or months later, you

may become sufficiently irritated by one bug or another to begin the debugging process all over again, starting with Step 5.

I've summarized this process in Figure 1.1.

1.4 Let's Try It!

With all that under your belt, it's time to see the actual compilation process in action. I'd like you to type in a simple program, save it, compile it, debug it, and run it. I'm skipping the design phase for the time being, since I've found it's difficult to explain the design process to a person who isn't yet comfortable with the programming language itself. (This doesn't mean that *you* should skip the design phase later on, or dive into writing code before giving your design the attention it deserves. It's just that for the purpose of learning the software development process, you need to know a little about coding first.)

Move to the PASQ1 subdirectory. I'm showing it here beneath a subdirectory called TURBO, but if you're using Borland Pascal, PASQ1 will be under the subdirectory BP.

```
CD \TURBO\PASQ1
```

Bring up the Turbo Pascal development environment:

```
TURBO
```

What you'll see will look a great deal like the screen shown in Figure 1.2. The word NONAME00.PAS indicates that you didn't specify any file to work on when you invoked Turbo Pascal—but we'll get back to that in a moment.

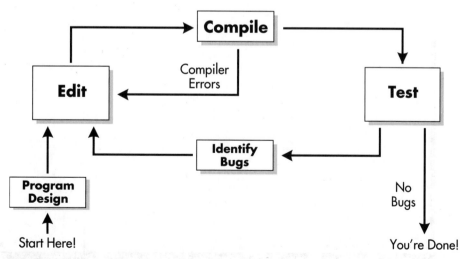

Figure 1.1 The Turbo Pascal Development Cycle

ENTERING A PROGRAM TO AN EDIT WINDOW

An edit window is already open and ready to go—it's the blue area (assuming you have a color monitor) occupying the entire screen except for the *menu bar* at the top and the *status bar* at the bottom of the screen. A white, double-line frame runs all around the window.

The test program follows. Enter it carefully, exactly as it is here:

```
PROGRAM Eat;

USES Crt

BEGIN
  ClrScr;
  GotoXY(15,11);
  Writeln('Eat at Joe''s!');
  GotoXY(15,12);
  Writeln('Ten Million Flies Can''t ALL Be Wrong!');
  Readln;
END.
```

SAVING YOUR WORK TO DISK

It's hard to overemphasize the importance of saving your work to disk frequently. What you've just typed into the open edit window exists only in RAM memory *and nowhere else.* If your machine failed for some reason right now, or if

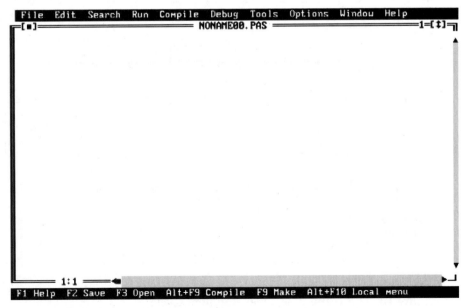

Figure 1.2 The Initial TP7 Screen

lightning hit a power pig and knocked out the electricity to your neighborhood, what you just typed would be gone for good. For a 10-line program this might not be a disaster—but if you've been furiously hammering code into the machine for a solid hour, some of what you have done might not be down on paper or even in your head. Let's get it down on disk.

At the top of your screen is the menu bar, containing words on it like **File**, **Edit**, **Search**, and so on. Through the menu bar you invoke all the various features that Turbo Pascal offers. Behind each of the words on the menu bar is a menu. You can pull down a menu either by clicking on the appropriate word with a mouse (if you have a mouse) or by pressing the Alt key with the first letter in the word. (That first letter is displayed in a different color from the rest of the word, as a memory-jogger.)

The **Files** menu, for example, can be pulled down by pressing Alt-F—or simply click on the word **Files** with your mouse. (The mouse is very useful in working with Turbo Pascal; if you don't have one, I powerfully recommend that you get one.)

There is an item on the **Files** menu called **Save as**. Move the green highlight bar down to **Save as** by pressing the arrow keys or using the mouse. Then select **Save as** by releasing the mouse or pressing Enter. You'll see a window open up in the center of the screen, as shown in Figure 1.3. This is the *Files dialog*, and you'll see it a lot as you work with Turbo Pascal. It appears when you need to name a new file or open an existing file.

Right now, we need to name a file, which is what the **Save as** menu option does for us. Your edit window has a default name already, NONAME00.PAS.

Figure 1.3 The TP7 Files Dialog

That's not much of a name, so let's give your first program its proper name, EAT.PAS. The text cursor will be in the field under the label **Save file as**. Type the filename EAT.PAS into the field. Then press Enter. The status line will (for a very short time, watch closely!) display this message:

```
Saving  C:\TURBO\PASQ1\EAT.PAS
```

At this point, your work is safe on your hard disk under its new name. Saving any further changes you make to the EAT.PAS program is even easier: You simply press the F2 function key. There's no additional fooling around with filename windows. Press F2 and the file is saved to disk.

COMPILING YOUR PROGRAM

You've now got a new program typed in and saved on disk. It's time to turn the Turbo Pascal compiler loose on it. This step will discover any errors you might have made while typing; if the program is correct, it will create an object code file that can be executed.

Compiling is done from the **Compile** menu. Pull down the **Compile** menu and select the **Compile** option. On such a small program file, Turbo Pascal does its work almost instantaneously. You'll perceive almost no delay at all. And you'll have to forgive me, but I slipped an error into the file as I printed it on page 34. And if you typed it *exactly* as shown, Turbo Pascal will be showing you an error, and your screen will look like Figure 1.4.

Figure 1.4 Screen Shot Showing Compile Error

SPOTTING AND FIXING COMPILE ERRORS

This is a compile error, and a very common one, not only for newcomers to Turbo Pascal but for the old-timers as well. Missing semicolons, like the poor, always seem to be with you. (There's a science to semicolon placement, which I'll take up in detail later on in Section 8.8.) Here, I should have placed one after the line **USES Crt**.

Notice that the compiler is giving you a hint, but also that it's not telling you exactly where the semicolon is supposed to go. The compiler is smart, but it has limitations. One of these is that it will point out an error *not* where the error actually is, but *where the compiler first noticed that there was an error*.

It's like the situation you find yourself in when you go out after supper to fill your gas tank and forget your wallet. You made a mistake when you failed to put your wallet back in your pocket when you changed pants after work. But you only notice the mistake when you've pumped a tank full of gas and reach for your credit cards. Whoops!

I make the point here because a lot of people assume that Turbo Pascal not only discovers errors but also points out where those errors are. Not true—it can only tell you where it first noticed that something was wrong. Keep that in mind as you struggle through your first few error-rich sessions in front of Turbo Pascal!

Repairing this particular error is easy. Move the text cursor back up to the end of the **USES Crt** line, and type a semicolon there. Press F2 to save the change. Then recompile.

SHORTCUT KEYS

You can recompile the same way you did the first time, by pulling down the **Compile** menu and selecting the **Compile** option. But that's more work than you need to do, especially for something that you'll be doing hundreds of times in a single session at the keyboard.

Still, pull down the **Compile** menu one more time. Notice that on the right-hand end of the **Compile** menu option is something that reads **Alt-F9**. This is called a *shortcut key*, and it's a way of selecting a Turbo Pascal feature quickly, without having to resort to the menus. Press Alt-F9 (that is, hold down the Alt key while pressing the F9 function key) and the compiler will again wake up and compile EAT.PAS. This time, the compile will go to completion without errors—assuming you really did type the program exactly as I presented it. Turbo Pascal will announce the successful compile with a *status box* in the middle of the screen. The words **Compile successful** will be flashing at the bottom of the box, as shown in Figure 1.5.

You may have already guessed, but the F2 function key—the one that saves your work—is another shortcut key. If you pull down the **Save** menu item in the **Files** menu, you'll see the "F2" shortcut indicator on the right-hand side of the **Save** item.

Figure 1.5 The Compile Status Box

The most often used features in Turbo Pascal have shortcut keys to help you work quickly once you learn your way around and don't need the menus to jog your memory anymore. You'll spot many of them in the menus as you explore, and I'll be calling most of them to your attention along the way as we continue exploring Turbo Pascal in this book.

RUNNING YOUR PROGRAM

The compile was correct, and you've got an object code file out there somewhere, waiting to be executed. You don't have to know where it is, or even what its name is. (The name is easy, though: EAT.EXE. The executable version of a Pascal program is the same as the source code name, but with .EXE as the extension rather than .PAS.) Executing your programs is also simple: Pull down the **Run** menu and select the **Run** item. Your program will be executed, and your backhanded advertising slogan will display dead-center in the screen.

The slogan will remain on the screen as long as you choose to leave it there. To end it and return to Turbo Pascal, press the Enter key.

There's a shortcut key for running your program: Ctrl-F9. You'll have it committed to memory long before you realize it.

An interesting point to be made here is that Turbo Pascal and the EAT.PAS program you've just successfully run are both programs, conceptually identical and pretty much equal in the eyes of the machine. Turbo Pascal is massively more complex; but when the time comes to execute your own programs, Turbo Pascal takes a step back and gives control of the entire computer to the program you wish to run. The programs you're writing are not "toy" programs or crippled in any way. You could write something as complex as—or even more complex than—Turbo Pascal itself. This is definitely big-time programming. Don't let anyone convince you otherwise.

When the program that you ran finishes its execution, it immediately hands the baton back to Turbo Pascal, which has stepped aside but has not gone away. Turbo Pascal returns to the screen just as it was when you ran your program, and you can continue the development cycle of write code, save, compile, and run/test.

And there's still another important shortcut key to keep in mind, when programming is done and it's time to go polish your classic Chevelle or watch *Northern Exposure*: Alt-X will cause Turbo Pascal to pack up its tent and go home.

1.5 Recapping Development Basics

As you might imagine, what you've just seen barely scratches the surface of what Turbo Pascal can do. But for the first few small programs you'll write with Turbo Pascal, that's just about all you really need to know about it.

The mechanics of elementary Turbo Pascal development come down to this:

- Enter your source code into a new, empty edit window. If such an empty window doesn't appear automatically when you invoke Turbo Pascal (and whether one does or does not depends on how Turbo Pascal is configured), you can create a new, empty edit window by selecting the **New** item in the **Files** menu.

- Save your source code under a new, meaningful name by selecting the **Save as** option in the **Files** menu. It's a good idea to save a new file before you've typed more than a screen full of source code—and save it often (by using the F2 shortcut key) after you've saved it the first time.

- Compiling the code using the **Compile** option in the **Compile** menu identifies any compile errors in your source code files. If no errors appear during a compile, your program is compilable and correct. (This *doesn't* mean it has no bugs!) You can also compile the file using the Alt-F9 shortcut key.

- Testing your new program is done by selecting the **Run** option in the **Run** menu. You can also run your program using shortcut key Ctrl-F9.

Some other points worth remembering:

- As much as you might be tempted to do otherwise, spend some time *designing* your program before you begin to write actual program code in the Turbo Pascal editor. We'll talk more about design later in this book.

- When a problem comes up during compilation, it's called an *error*. When a problem comes up during your actual testing of a program that has compiled correctly, it's called a *bug*. The compiler will give you some hints when it discovers an error. But you're pretty much on your own to identify and correct bugs.

Finally, this would be a good time to go back and take one more look at EAT.PAS. It's a series of steps bracketed between the two self-explanatory words **BEGIN** and **END**. In this simple program, the steps should be close to self-explanatory, even though you may never have looked at a single line of Pascal code before.

The only line that might have you (as a beginner) squinting hard is the last program step: **Readln**. That's the step that waits for you to press the Enter key so that the program can terminate its execution and give control of the machine back to Turbo Pascal. As with all of the fundamental elements of Turbo Pascal code, we'll return to **Readln** in more detail later in this book.

CLOSING IN ON PASCAL THE LANGUAGE

The main purpose of this chapter has been to make you comfortable with the idea of creating real, runnable programs in the Turbo Pascal fashion. EAT.PAS is a rather pointless program, but it's pretty obvious what it does and how it works. It's now time to investigate what we mean when we talk of a "structured language" and how Turbo Pascal fits the definition to several hundred decimal places.

Chapter 2

The Secret Word Is "Structure"

LOOKING AT PASCAL PROGRAM STRUCTURE FROM A HEIGHT

OK. Do you want to build a shack? Or do you want to build a cathedral? With Turbo Pascal (or with most any language, actually), *the choice is yours*. And the difference (far more than simply scale, since there can be mighty big shacks and mighty small cathedrals) is solely a matter of *structure*.

You may have heard this before. It's been said many times, and (far too often) said badly. People often lose track of the difference between small-scale knowledge and big-picture knowledge, and the corollary difference between small-scale quality and big-time mess. You can memorize perfectly the usage of every reserved word and predefined identifier in Turbo Pascal, and still not have a clue as to how to write a program with any hint of quality. Smearing individual statements around on the screen can be fun, and such smearings can actually compile and (sometimes) run, but hey, how much fingerpainting hangs in the Guggenheim Museum?

In this chapter, I'm going to explain the nature of Turbo Pascal program structure. Along the way, you'll pick up some of the fundamentals of defining and using variables, as well as some of the simpler operators and standard functions. It's tough to explain structure when you haven't yet explained the boards, bolts, and girders from which the structure is made!

2.1 Taking It Subsystem by Subsystem

In 1974, I walked out of school into the thick of a recession having a degree in English, a '68 Chevelle, and precious little else. English majors rarely get any respect (you have to be an English lieutenant colonel for that to happen, I've heard), so to keep the blood pumping and the gas tank full I got a job as a Xerox repairman.

41

And I'll never forget the horrible sinking feeling in my guts the first time I saw a Xerox copier with its panels off, merrily making copies. There were gears and drums turning, cams flipping, relays clicking, little claws grabbing a document and dragging it through a maze of harsh green fluorescent lights, crackling corotron wires, and stainless-steel paper chutes.

The instructor must have seen the expression on my face. He snorted through his bushy mustache and said, "Hey, man, *just take it subsystem by subsystem.*"

He was right, of course.

It's easy to fall into despair the first time you try to make sense of a programming language. There's five times the complexity of that gross little electromechanical copier, and each and every detail must be *exactly* right, or nothing is accomplished but the wholesale tearing of hair.

So do what I did, and take it subsystem by subsystem.

THE WAY TO WRESTLE WITH COMPLEXITY

I learned how to fix Xerox machines in record time, and spent the next several years wandering around downtown Chicago, keeping the paper pumping. But in learning how to fix Xerox machines, I learned something far more important: How to deal with complexity.

Inside almost any complicated concept (assuming that the concept makes any sense at all) there is something vitally important: *structure*. The way to understand anything complicated is to develop an eye that sees the structure in its complexity, and then to develop a set of selective blinders that allows you to focus on one element of that structure at a time.

Structure exists in layers, like an onion, and beneath one layer of structure may exist several more, each (in its turn) composed of still more layers.

Start at the very top. Examine one layer at a time. Understand the "big picture" of that one layer only, looking neither higher, to the larger principles, nor smaller, to the component details. Only when you have that layer under your belt do you delve into its component layers, and so on.

You'll find that the Pascal language is wonderfully structured, which makes it relatively easy to grasp once you have your "structure eyes."

PASCAL (LIKE GAUL) IS DIVIDED INTO THREE PARTS

Every Pascal program can be seen as having no more than three separate parts (I won't call them subsystems; parts is parts!) that can be studied separately:

- Constant and data definitions
- Procedure and function definitions
- The main block

Very tiny programs may get away without any procedures or functions (EAT.PAS had none) and totally trivial programs may not define any data. All programs, however, must have a main block, and all genuinely useful programs will have all three parts.

Let's take a look at them, one by one.

2.2 The Main Block

The little demo program EAT.PAS we compiled in the last chapter has a main block. It's *all* main block, in fact. The main block is the portion of the program delimited between the words **BEGIN** and **END**. Here's the main block from EAT.PAS:

```
BEGIN
  ClrScr;
  GotoXY(15,11);
  Writeln('Eat at Joe''s!');
  GotoXY(15,12);
  Writeln('Ten Million Flies Can''t ALL Be Wrong!');
  Readln;
END.
```

BEGIN and **END** are what we call *reserved words*. They have special meanings to the Turbo Pascal compiler and you can't use them for anything else. I'll have more to say about reserved words a little later, when we get into the detailed view of the Pascal language. They are the "framing members" of a Pascal program—the logical 2 x 4s that give a program its structure. They define its shape, and control the way execution flows within a program. In this book, reserved words will always be printed entirely in uppercase characters, as **BEGIN**, **END**, **WHILE**, **RECORD**, and so on. (Additionally, all program identifiers of *any* kind will be printed in boldface in the body text of the book.)

STATEMENTS

Between **BEGIN** and **END** are six lines, each of which is a step in the program's execution. When a program begins running, the first step in the main block executes (here, **ClrScr**), and then the second, and so on, until the last step in the main block is executed. Program execution is then finished, and the program stops running.

Each one of those steps is called a *statement*. The single word **ClrScr** is a statement, as is the more complicated line **Writeln('Eat at Joe"s!')**. Statements are separated by semicolons.

The statements in EAT.PAS are simple and easy to dope out by reading them and by watching what the program does. **ClrScr** clears the screen. **GotoXY** moves the cursor to an X,Y position on the screen. Think of your CRT screen as a Cartesian grid like the ones you worked with in high school math. The X (across) value comes first, followed by the Y (down) value. The upper left corner of the screen is the origin, 1,1. Saying **GotoXY(15,11)** moves the cursor 15 positions across, and 11 positions down. **Writeln** writes a line of text to the screen at the cursor position.

There is always a period after the **END** of the main block of a Pascal program. The period indicates that the fat lady has indeed sung, and that the program is over.

COMPOUND STATEMENTS

I'll have a lot more to say about statements later on in this book. It's important to note that, in a Pascal sense, the whole main block is itself a *compound statement*. A compound statement is some number of statements delimited by a **BEGIN** and **END** reserved word. (There are a couple of instances where a compound statement may be framed by other reserved words, like **REPEAT** and **UNTIL** rather than **BEGIN** and **END**. We'll deal with these special cases later on.)

It might help characterize the main block by considering it a collective statement that indicates the larger, single purpose that the program as a whole was designed to accomplish. Just as a sentence in the English language is a statement followed by a period, so is the main block in Pascal a compound statement followed by a period. This compound statement summarizes the program's larger purpose. By reading the main block of a Pascal program first, you should be able to garner the big picture of what the program is supposed to do.

Compound statements appear in many other parts of the Pascal language. You'll be tripping over them wherever you go. When you see one in a program, ask yourself what the unifying purpose of the compound statement is. It'll help you refine your "structure vision" and focus on just that one part of the program as a whole.

2.3 Variable Definitions

EAT.PAS has no data at all. It's a dumb billboard, and not especially interesting as a program. Real programs do significant work for us by storing and manipulating data. Another major component of any program, therefore, is a set of definitions that dictate how much data we're using in a program and how we can use it.

Since EAT.PAS lacks data, we're going to have to come up with a new program to demonstrate some data-hacking. Try this one:

```
{-----------------------------------------------------------}
{                         Aliens                            }
{                                                           }
{                    by Jeff Duntemann                      }
{                    Turbo Pascal V7.0                      }
{                    Last update 1/2/93                     }
{                                                           }
{ From: BORLAND PASCAL FROM SQUARE ONE by Jeff Duntemann    }
{-----------------------------------------------------------}
```

```
PROGRAM Aliens;

USES Crt;                    { For ClrScr, Random, and Randomize }

CONST
  MaxLength  = 9;            { The longest name we'll try to generate }
  MinLength  = 2;            { The shortest name we'll try to generate }
  LastLetter = 122;          { Lowercase 'z' in the ASCII symbol set }

TYPE
  NameString = STRING[MaxLength];   { Waste no space in our strings! }
  CharSet    = SET OF Char;         { To weed out odd symbols         }

VAR
  Printables   : SET OF Char; { Holds the set of printable letters }
  I,J          : Integer;     { General-purpose counter variables  }
  NameLength   : Integer;     { Holds the length of each name }
  NameChar     : Char;        { Holds a randomly-selected character }
  NamesWanted  : Integer;     { Holds the number of names we want   }
  CurrentName  : NameString;  { Holds the name we're working on }

BEGIN
  Randomize; { Seed the random number generator from the system clock }
  Printables := ['A'..'Z','a'..'z']; { We only want printable letters! }
  ClrScr;

  Write('How many alien names do you want? (1-10): ');
  Readln(NamesWanted);                      { Answer the question }

  FOR I := 1 TO NamesWanted DO
    BEGIN
      CurrentName := '';                          { Start with an empty name }

      REPEAT
        NameLength := Random(MaxLength); { Pick a length for this name }
      UNTIL NameLength > MinLength;

      FOR J := 1 TO NameLength DO          { Pick a letter: }
        BEGIN
          REPEAT   { We keep picking letters until one is printable: }
            NameChar := Chr(Random(LastLetter));
          UNTIL NameChar IN Printables;
          CurrentName := CurrentName + NameChar;  { Add it to the name }
        END;
      Writeln(CurrentName);          { Finally, print the completed name }
    END;
  Readln; { Pause until Enter hit; so you can admire the alien names }
END.
```

DON'T PANIC!

I mean that. You're not going to be tested on the full details of how ALIENS works at this point, so don't worry about digesting it whole. It's a full program that even does something interesting, and I'll be talking about it for a while in this chapter. So follow along as we go, and don't fret about not knowing the details of character sets or the **REPEAT..UNTIL** statement. All in good time. Remember, we're going for the big picture here. The details will crystallize out in the chapters to come.

SOLVING AN SF WRITER'S PROBLEM

The ALIENS program does a job for SF writers like myself who are too lazy to come up with imaginative names for the 17-eyed wonders who haunt the starlanes in bad space wars novels. It's a very simple program; if you have the listing entered already or have obtained the listings archive, I'd suggest that you load, compile, and run ALIENS.PAS right now.

ALIENS asks you a question: How many alien names do you want? It then waits for you to type in a number from 1 to 10 and press Enter. At that point, it will produce the exact number of names you asked for by almost literally pulling letters out of a hat and stringing them together. As each name is completed, ALIENS will display that name on the screen. This happens so quickly that all the names will seem to appear instantly.

ZEROING IN ON DATA DEFINITIONS

That's what ALIENS does. Now let's take a look at some of its machinery. We're currently focusing on the data definitions part of a Pascal program. Although there is some flexibility about where the data definition part of a program goes, most of the time you'll have to place your definitions at the very beginning of a program. The data definitions in ALIENS.PAS are shown by themselves below:

```
CONST
    MaxLength  = 9;        { The longest name we'll try to generate  }
    MinLength  = 2;        { The shortest name we'll try to generate }
    LastLetter = 122;      { Lowercase 'z' in the ASCII symbol set   }

TYPE
    NameString = STRING[MaxLength];   { Waste no space in our strings! }
    CharSet    = SET OF Char;         { To weed out odd symbols        }

VAR
    Printables  : CharSet;    { Holds the set of printable letters  }
    I,J         : Integer;    { General-purpose counter variables   }
    NameLength  : Integer;    { Holds the length of each name }
    NameChar    : Char;       { Holds a randomly-selected character }
```

```
NamesWanted : Integer;  { Holds the number of names we want   }
CurrentName : NameString; { Holds the name we're currently working on }
```

The data definition part of a Pascal program is almost literally a set of blueprints for the data that the program will be using during its execution. The Pascal compiler reads the definitions and sets up a little reference table for itself that it uses while it converts your source code file to a unit file or an executable program file. This reference table allows the Turbo Pascal compiler to tell you when something you're trying to write as part of a program is bad practice or nonsensical.

VARIABLES AS BUCKETS

Variables are defined after the **VAR** reserved word. Think of variables as buckets into which data values may be placed. In variable definitions, you declare the name of a variable followed by its *type*. The two are separated by a colon.

Variables—like buckets—come in a great many shapes and sizes. The type of a variable indicates how large the bucket is and what sorts of stuff you can safely put in it. A plastic water bucket will carry water handily—but don't try to lug molten lead in it. A colander can be thought of as a bucket suitable for carrying meatballs, but don't expect to use it to hold flour or tomato juice without making a mess.

The notion of types in Turbo Pascal exists *precisely* to keep you from making certain kinds of messes.

In ALIENS, there's a variable called **NameLength**. Its type is **Integer**, which is a signed whole number from -32,678 to 32,767. **NameLength** is thus a bucket for carrying numeric values falling in that range that don't have a decimal part. Similarly, **NameChar** is a **Char** variable, meaning it is intended to hold character values like 'A' or '*'.

TYPES AS BLUEPRINTS FOR BUCKETS

So what happens if you try to place a number like 17,234 in a **Char** variable? You can't—Turbo Pascal won't let you. The two types aren't compatible, so you'll get an error at compile time if you try to load an **Integer** value into a **Char** variable, or vise versa.

Where do types come from? Some of them are built right into Turbo Pascal and are always available. **Integer** and **Char** are two such types, and there are numerous others. On the other hand, Pascal lets you define your own types, and then create variables with those new, programmer-defined types.

ALIENS has an example. Notice the statement immediately after the **TYPE** reserved word:

```
NameString = STRING[MaxLength];  { Waste no space in our strings! }
```

This is a type definition. It defines a type called **NameString**. This type is a string type—meaning it is designed to contain data in alphanumeric strings like 'I am an American, Chicago-born' or 'THX1138'. Strings come in all sizes from 1 character to 255 characters, and you can create a string type in any of those sizes. That's what the type definition statement in ALIENS does: It creates a string type with a length given by a constant named **MaxLength**. (We'll get back to **MaxLength** and what it is shortly. For now, just assume it's a number— or look a few lines back to see how it's defined!)

NameString is a very simple type. You can create much, *much* more complex types in Turbo Pascal, as we'll explain later in this book. It's easy to see how a type is in fact a blueprint for making buckets, in that it defines what sort of data some new kind of bucket is to contain.

Then, when you actually need a bucket of this new type, you can make one in the **VAR** section:

```
CurrentName : NameString; { Holds the name we're currently working on }
```

This gives you a variable in memory that contains string data with a length given by the **MaxLength** constant.

Remember: A type is *not* a variable and holds no data. It's simply a spec that allows you to create variables with a specified size, set of attributes, and uses. Use the **TYPE** reserved word to create blueprints for buckets, then use **VAR** to create the buckets themselves.

CONSTANTS AS NAMES FOR DATA

So what, then, is **MaxLength**? It's a *constant*, which in Pascal is simply a way of giving a name to a piece of data. Long before you ever knew what programming was, you were using constants. You learned that the number 3.14159 (approximately) is called "Pi." If you took a little more math, you learned that a constant named "e" (the base of the natural logarithms) was equal to 2.71828 and change.

The actual values of constants are hard to remember unless you use them all day, every day. I had to look up the value of "e" just now, even though I know what it is and have used it many times in my life. I just haven't used it often enough to remember it.

Constants serve a similar purpose in programming: They allow you to give a descriptive name to a data value that might otherwise be hard to recall accurately. Constants have an even more important job, however: They allow you to specify a value *once*, at the top of your program, and then use that value any number of times anywhere later in the program. Later on, if you want to change that value for some reason, you change it in one place only, rather than having to hunt down dozens or hundreds of uses of the literal value in what might be a very big source code file.

MaxLength is defined in ALIENS as being 9, which is a nice maximum length for an unpronounceable name. (Hkrepats has no trouble pronouncing his name, but we both might stumble on jhuuTDplb.) We could have defined **MaxLength** as 20 and gotten much longer alien names, or as 5, and gotten much shorter ones.

Because we only use **MaxLength** once in ALIENS, it's not as obvious how useful constants are as centrally located definitions for widely used values. But there is a predefined constant in Turbo Pascal called **Pi**, which you can use anywhere you want instead of the literal value 3.14159. Later on, you can pretend to be the Tennessee Legislature and declare **Pi** equal to 3.0. None of your math will work out, but it's a great insight into the minds (if one could call them that) of politicians.

LOADING UP YOUR BUCKETS

A variable, once defined, is an empty bucket. It has no value until you give it one. (It may acquire a value by accident, as I'll explain later on. Better by far to give every variable a value early on, before it finds one on its own!)

You can give a variable a value in a number of ways, but the most straightforward way is through an *assignment statement*. An assignment statement takes a value and assigns that value to a variable. In effect, it takes the value and "loads it into" that variable, as though dropping something into a bucket.

Here's a simple assignment statement:

```
Repetitions := 141;
```

What we've done here is taken the value 141 and dropped it into the variable **Repetitions**. The two-character sequence := is called the *assignment operator*. When Turbo Pascal sees the assignment operator, it takes whatever is on the right side of the operator and drops it into whatever is on the left side.

Here's an assignment statement from ALIENS.PAS:

```
CurrentName := '';
```

What it does is drop an empty string (that is, a string containing no characters) into the variable **CurrentName**. (A string with something in it would look like this: **'Jeff'**) It may seem odd to think of dropping an empty value into a bucket, so you might consider this a way of emptying the bucket of anything else that might accidentally have fallen into it. (In Arizona, this would include dust, dead scorpions, and an occasional rattlesnake. In programming, you rarely encounter anything more lethal than a random number.)

2.4 Procedures and Functions

Compared to EAT.PAS, ALIENS.PAS is a considerably larger program. The main block in ALIENS.PAS is 26 lines long. Still manageable—but what happens when you want to write a program that does something genuinely useful? It might take hundreds of lines to write even a fairly simple utility, or easily thousands or tens of thousands of lines to write something like a custom database program to handle sales leads or invoice mail-order sales.

The secret, again, is structure. And without question, the single most powerful tool for structuring your programs is the *procedure*. (As well as those slightly special-purpose procedures called *functions*.)

The whole idea in creating a procedure is to gather together a sequence of related statements, and give them a new, descriptive name. Then later, when you need to execute that sequence of statements, you need only execute the name of the procedure, as though it were a single statement that did everything you wanted done by the group of statements hiding "inside" the procedure.

AS EASY AS BRUSHING YOUR TEETH

This sounds hairier than it is. Consider this business of brushing your teeth. You get up in the morning, and as you shake the cobwebs out of one ear or the other, you remind yourself that you can't go to work this time without brushing your teeth.

So brushing your teeth is one activity. Or is it? Watch yourself as you do it, and take note of the steps involved:

Pick up the toothpaste tube.

Twist off the cap.

Pick up your toothbrush in your other hand.

Squeeze some toothpaste (a "generous nerdle" as some forgotten toothpaste vendor so beautifully pegged it long ago) onto your toothbrush.

Sprinkle a little water on the toothbrush.

Put the toothbrush into your mouth.   Repeat:

  Work the toothbrush up and down

. . . until your mind starts to wander.

Rinse off your toothbrush.

Pick up your Flintstones cup.

Fill it with water.

Take a mouthful of water.

Swill it around.

Spit it out.

Taken as the sum of its individual steps, brushing your teeth is a real mouthful. When you actually get down and *do* it, you run faithfully through each of those steps; if you ever had to tell somebody how to do it, you could. But when you're trying to impose some order on your morning, the whole shebang shows up in your mind under the single descriptive term, "brushing your teeth."

STATEMENTS INSIDE STATEMENTS INSIDE COMPOUND STATEMENTS

Inside the term "brushing your teeth" are thus some number of other terms, in a certain order. You think of the single term "brushing you teeth" to avoid cluttering your mind with a multitude of piddly little details.

A procedure is the same thing, for the same reasons, and works much the same way. You gather together some number of Pascal statements, and then hide them behind a single identifier of your own choosing. You can execute the new identifier as though it were a single statement, masking the complexity represented by the original sequence of Pascal statements.

Suppose you have these three statements in a Pascal program:

```
DoThis;
DoThat;
DoTOther;
```

Taken together, these three statements accomplish something. Let's call that something "grimbling." We could say that the following compound statement represents what must be done in order to grimble:

```
BEGIN
  DoThis;
  DoThat;
  DoTOther;
END;
```

We can hide this compound statement behind a single statement, which we'll call **Grimble**—so that any time we need to execute those three statements together, we only have to execute this single statement:

```
Grimble;
```

Doing it is fairly easy. We mostly need to provide a name to the compound statement shown above:

```
PROCEDURE Grimble;

BEGIN
  DoThis;
  DoThat;
  DoTOther;
END;
```

What we have here are statements within a compound statement, within a procedure—which itself may be used as a kind of statement.

Structure is in many respects the placing of things within other things.

AN ADVENTURE IN STRUCTURING

To make it all click, let's do it, right now, to ALIENS.PAS. This is a slightly advanced exercise, and if you've never written a line of program code before some of it may puzzle you. Bear with me—and have faith that all of this will be explained in good time.

One of the things that ALIENS has to do is choose a length for any given alien name. It does this by "pulling" random numbers repeatedly until it pulls a random number within a specified range. This range is the range from **MinLength** to **MaxLength**, both of which are defined as constants, and in this case are equivalent to the range 2 through 9.

The code that pulls a random length within those two boundaries is this:

```
REPEAT
   NameLength := Random(MaxLength);   { Pick a length for this name }
UNTIL NameLength > MinLength;
```

Turbo Pascal contains a built-in function called **Random** that returns a random number less than the number contained in the parameter (i.e., the item in parentheses after the name **Random**) that you pass to it. That is, calling the function **Random(9)** will return a random number value between 0 and 9. This value can then be assigned to some other variable (in our case, **NameLength**) for safekeeping. (A *function*, in case you're not familiar with the term, is a procedure that returns a value, which may then be assigned to a variable.)

The three lines shown above repeatedly get a random number and test it, to make sure it's greater than **MinLength**. The **Random** function itself guarantees that the value it returns will be no larger than its parameter; that is, the constant **MaxLength** that the **Random** function holds within its parentheses.

Random numbers are useful things, and it's even more useful to be able to specify a range of values within which a random number is to be pulled. We'll find other uses for random numbers in later parts of this book. It would be nice to have a procedure of some sort that would pull a random number for us without our having to remember all the precise details of how it was done. We could call the function **Pull**, and it would be a sort of number-generating machine. We would pass it a minimum value and a maximum value, and **Pull** would return a value for us that fell within those two bounds.

CREATING A FUNCTION

So let's create the **Pull** function from the three lines in ALIENS that pull a random length for alien names:

```
FUNCTION Pull(MinValue,MaxValue : Integer) : Integer;

VAR I : Integer;

BEGIN
   REPEAT
      I := Random(MaxValue);   { Pick a length for this name }
   UNTIL I >= MinValue;
   Pull := I;
END;
```

Things have changed a little—but for a reason, as I'll explain. The central portion of **Pull** does the same thing that the three lines we lifted from ALIENS did. What we've mostly added is framework; a body for the lines to exist in.

But we've also added a strong measure of generality. The lines that pull a random name length in ALIENS can be used *only* to pull a random name length. The **Pull** function can be used to pull random numbers within a specified range for any reason. We could use it just as easily in a dice game as in an alien name generator—and that's a big, *big* advantage.

We can use **Pull** in ALIENS.PAS. Just insert the definition for **Pull** in the program file before the beginning of the main block, then replace the three lines that pull a random name length with the following single line:

```
NameLength  := Pull(MinLength,MaxLength);
```

The altered copy of ALIENS.PAS (it's on your listings diskette as ALIENS2.PAS) is shown below:

```
{----------------------------------------------------------}
{                        Aliens2                           }
{                                                          }
{                      by Jeff Duntemann                   }
{                      Turbo Pascal V7.0                   }
{                      Last update 1/2/93                  }
{                                                          }
{ From: BORLAND PASCAL FROM SQUARE ONE by Jeff Duntemann   }
{----------------------------------------------------------}

PROGRAM Aliens;

USES Crt;                   { For ClrScr, Random, and Randomize }

CONST
  MaxLength   = 9;          { The longest name we'll try to generate }
  MinLength   = 2;          { The shortest name we'll try to generate }
  LastLetter = 122;         { Lowercase 'z' in the ASCII symbol set }

TYPE
  NameString = STRING[MaxLength];   { Waste no space in our strings! }
  CharSet    = SET OF Char;         { To weed out odd symbols }

VAR
  Printables   : SET OF Char; { Holds the set of printable letters  }
  I,J          : Integer;      { General-purpose counter variables }
  NameLength   : Integer;     { Holds the length of each name }
  NameChar     : Char;        { Holds a randomly-selected character }
  NamesWanted  : Integer;     { Holds the number of names we want  }
  { Holds the name we're currently working on }
  CurrentName  : NameString;

FUNCTION Pull(MinValue,MaxValue : Integer) : Integer;
```

```
    VAR I : Integer;
BEGIN
  REPEAT
    I := Random(MaxValue);  { Pick a length for this name }
  UNTIL I >= MinValue;
  Pull := I;
END;


BEGIN
  Randomize;  { Seed the random number generator from the system clock }
  { We only want printable letters! }
  Printables := ['A'..'Z','a'..'z'];
  ClrScr;

  Write('How many alien names do you want? (1-10): ');
  Readln(NamesWanted);                  { Answer the question }

  FOR I := 1 TO NamesWanted DO
    BEGIN        CurrentName := '';          { Start with an empty name }

      NameLength := Pull(MinLength,MaxLength);

      FOR J := 1 TO NameLength DO          { Pick a letter: }
        BEGIN
          REPEAT    { We keep picking letters until one is printable: }
            NameChar := Chr(Random(LastLetter));
          UNTIL NameChar IN Printables;
          CurrentName := CurrentName + NameChar;  { Add it to the name }
        END;

        Writeln(CurrentName);      { Finally, print the completed name }
    END;
  Readln; { Pause until Enter hit; so you can admire the alien names }
END.
```

THE LEGACY OF A FUNCTION

The details of having to pull a number again and again until one appears that falls within a specified range are masked now. We only see the "front door" of the random number factory; the machinery that actually builds the random numbers is hidden away somewhere behind the door .

And that's good, because most of the time we really don't care *how* random numbers are made; we only care that they *do* get made according to our specifications.

It's true that creating the **Pull** function added a few lines to the program. Later on, we'll see how we can remove **Pull** from ALIENS2.PAS and place it in a library of functions and procedures called a *unit*. This library is available to any of your programs that need it. If 10 of your programs need a random-number puller, you can give a random number puller to all 10 of them and only have one copy of **Pull**'s 10 little lines. If you yank enough general-purpose procedures and functions out into libraries, you can actually cut the bulk of your programs considerably.

ORGANIZING PROGRAMS WITH PROCEDURES

Hiding details is the fundamental purpose of procedures and functions. The little example given here is not an especially good one, since there aren't a lot of details to be hidden in a random-number puller.

But consider a simple accounting program. A good one (even a simple one, as accounting programs go) might have 10,000 lines of code. You could write all 10,000 lines of code in one enormous main block. But how would you read and understand those 10,000 lines of code? You'd probably have to do what was done in the ancient days of programming, and literally cut a long program listing up into chunks with a scissors, and only look at the chunk you need to concentrate on at the moment.

Even *War and Peace* is divided into chapters. And procedures are often used as "chapters" in a larger program. In our accounting program example, you would have a number of accounting tasks like Payroll, Accounts Payable, Accounts Receivable, General Ledger, and so on. It's possible to make each of these accounting tasks a procedure:

```
PROCEDURE  AccountsPayable;

BEGIN
  <about  2000  lines>
END;


PROCEDURE  AccountsReceivable;

BEGIN
  <about  3000  lines>
END;


PROCEDURE  Payroll;

BEGIN
  <about  2000  lines>
END;


PROCEDURE  GeneralLedger;

BEGIN
  <about  2200  lines>
END;
```

Now at least you have a fighting chance. When you need to work on the payroll portion of your accounting program, you can print out the **Payroll** procedure and ignore the rest. All the "payroll-ness" of the accounting program is concentrated right there in one procedure, so you don't have to go searching for payroll details across the entire program. Better still, details that you *don't* have to pay attention to right now remain hidden inside their respective procedures.

With your payroll blinders on, you'll have a much easier time focusing on the payroll part of the program. The main block becomes quite small then, and is mostly a little menu manager that lets you choose which of the four big procedures you want to run.

PROCEDURES WITHIN PROCEDURES

If you're perceptive, you may have noticed something else about procedures (and functions too): They look like little programs. They *are* little programs, in fact, and procedures and functions share the same general structure with the "big" Pascal programs that contain them. This resemblance between Pascal programs and procedures and functions is reflected in a generic term that encompasses both procedures and functions: *subprograms*.

If Pascal programs are divided into three parts, then so are procedures and functions: They too have constant and data definitions, procedure and function definitions, and a main block. You may have noticed that the **Pull** function had a variable definition in it, for an integer variable named **I**. The variable **I** is what we call a *local variable*, by which we mean it is local to **Pull** and never ventures outside **Pull**'s bounds. Procedures and functions can define any number of local data items and constants, just as programs can.

But most interestingly, procedures and functions can define and contain their own local procedures and functions. Just as **Pull** was inside and thus local to ALIENS2.PAS, you could place a procedure or a function (or several of them) inside **Pull** as well. These local procedures and functions would be for **Pull**'s private use only; no procedure outside of **Pull** could make use of them.

This nesting can go on and on almost without limit: You can place procedures within procedures within procedures, like those Chinese dolls that fit one within the other. (Or, more recently, the Russian dolls that have Lenin inside Stalin inside Khrushchev inside Gorbachev inside Yeltsin.)

2.5 Program Structure Recap

This has been an overview of program structure, to get you started on your road to Pascal mastery in the right frame of mind, and with a general method for finding your way. I've touched on a great many topics without going into any of them especially deeply. In the rest of this book, I'll begin describing the Pascal language in detail.

But before getting into a hurricane of details, I wanted to lay the big picture out in front of you. Let's recap the big picture.

PASCAL PROGRAMS ARE DIVIDED INTO THREE PARTS

These three parts are data definitions, procedure and function definitions, and the main block.

Data definitions include constant definitions, type definitions, and variable definitions. Constant definitions give descriptive names to unchanging values. The value 3.14159, for example, is often made a constant with the name **Pi**. Type definitions define a particular kind of data, and act as blueprints for creating variables of that kind of data. A type definition defines how large a data type is, and what sorts of ways it can be used. A variable definition creates a little storage spot somewhere for a particular type of data. Think of type definitions as blueprints for data buckets, and variable definitions as the way the buckets themselves (the variables) are actually made.

The main block is a compound statement, which is a sequence of Pascal statements between the reserved words **BEGIN** and **END**.

Procedures and functions allow series of Pascal statements to be grouped together and "hidden" behind a single descriptive name. Calling that single name has the same effect as calling each of the individual statements within the procedure or function. Functions are procedures that return values that may be assigned to variables in assignment statements.

Procedures and functions are the primary means of masking complexity in a Pascal program. The details of a larger program task may be hidden within a procedure or function, so that your attention to that larger function will not be distracted by the details. When you need to be concerned with the details, you can examine the definition of the procedure or function to see how it operates internally.

When you need to see the details, you can. When you don't, you won't. Much of structuring a program is the artful hiding of details.

PROCEDURES AND FUNCTIONS ARE MINIATURE PROGRAMS

The essential structure of a Pascal program is echoed in the structure of procedures and functions.

Procedures and functions have data definitions and a main block; furthermore, they can contain their own local (that is, private) procedures and functions. This nesting of procedures within procedures has no explicit limits, and may continue as far as needed.

Because of their resemblances to programs, procedures and functions are often called subprograms.

PROGRAMS ARE ORGANIZED BY DIVIDING THEM INTO SUBPROGRAMS

A single monstrous program can be made conceptually manageable by dividing it into subprograms. Large subprograms can themselves be made manageable by dividing them internally into separate, smaller subprograms. By creating a program in layers in this way, you can focus your attention only on the layer you need to see, without distraction either from the big picture at a higher level, or from details at a lower level.

TAKE IT ONE SUBSYSTEM AT A TIME!

Most of all, I want you to remember the lesson of the trainer-man at Xerox: *Take it one subsystem at a time.* Being boggled gets you nowhere. Develop your structure-eyes, and learn to look selectively at a program to see the structure in it, and then work either to understand that structure (if the program was written by someone else) or to create that structure (if the program doesn't exist yet) using the structuring tools available in Turbo Pascal.

Chapter 3

The Pascal World, and Your Place in It

DISCOVERING WHAT TOOLS AND RESOURCES ARE AVAILABLE TO YOU

Turbo Pascal is more than a language. It's a whole industry, perhaps dominated by Borland but by no means limited to Borland. If you're just starting out, with nothing but a brand new compiler box in your hand, you may well be unaware of just how much stuff is out there for the use of the Turbo Pascal programmer. Let me take this short chapter to orient you a little to the Pascal world as it exists today, and what you can find to make your work easier and faster.

If you're an experienced Turbo Pascal programmer, you may already be aware of this material. Still, take a look. I see a lot of Pascal products, and you may have missed a few that are in fact listed here.

3.1 The Many Shapes of Version 7

Turbo Pascal is a tidy little industry all by itself. The product was introduced in late 1983 as a slim paperback manual with a single diskette inside of it, and only a handful of files on the diskette. The product has grown tremendously over the years, in both power and complexity. By 1993, the current top-of-the-line product from Borland comes with 10 manuals and requires 33 megabytes of hard disk storage, and does things that we couldn't have dreamed possible at the dawn of the PC era.

HOSTS AND TARGETS

Turbo Pascal was one product until 1991, when Borland introduced Turbo Pascal for Windows. The "original" Turbo Pascal then came to be called Turbo Pascal for DOS. Turbo Pascal for Windows requires that you work under Windows, and it creates programs that run only under Windows. You can't use it to program for DOS. Turbo Pascal for DOS version 6.0, by contrast, operates under DOS and for DOS; the programs it generates are not Windows programs (although they can run in a DOS window under Windows), and it does not make use of any of the Windows features like graphical UI or advanced memory management.

We say that Turbo Pascal for DOS is *hosted* under DOS, meaning that the product is intended to be operated from DOS in text mode. We also say that Turbo Pascal for DOS *targets* DOS, meaning that the programs Turbo Pascal for DOS generates are meant to run as DOS programs in text mode. (Turbo Pascal for DOS can create programs that display graphics, but not Microsoft Windows graphics.) Turbo Pascal for Windows, as you might expect, is hosted only under Windows (meaning it is a Windows application using all the Windows graphics conventions) and also targets Windows, but only Windows.

You might think this is obvious—but now, meet Version 7.

HIGH END, LOW END

The nature of the Turbo Pascal for DOS product changed drastically in the move from version 6 to 7. (Turbo Pascal for Windows remains unchanged for now, at Version 1.5.) Borland made quite a few enhancements to Turbo Pascal 6.0 and increased its version number to 7, as Turbo Pascal 7.0. However, Borland created a whole new product with a large list of new features and called it Borland Pascal 7.0.

Borland Pascal 7.0 includes Turbo Pascal 7.0 "in the box," along with a great many other things. The idea was to create a vastly more powerful new Pascal to serve the "high end" of the Pascal marketplace; primarily Pascal developers who write Pascal code for a living. Turbo Pascal 7.0 serves students, beginning programmers, and those who develop programs mostly for fun and the challenge of it. People call this the "low end," but there's nothing especially "low" about it; Turbo Pascal 7.0 has everything that Turbo Pascal 6.0 had, and more. It's low mostly by contrast to Borland Pascal, which is way off the top of the scale in terms of raw programming power.

PLATFORMS

This split came about because PC programming itself has split in two with the acceptance of Windows 3.x. You can program for DOS or Windows. The combination of an operating system like DOS with a user-interface shell like Windows is called a *platform*. DOS alone, and the DOS/Windows combination are considered two separate platforms. Generally, for any given project, you must choose one platform or another. It's hard to program for both at once, and if you try, the results will not be as good for either platform as they would if you had programmed specifically for one or for the other.

There is a third option that isn't always considered a separate platform—but it is definitely an option worth thinking about once you gain a little experience with Borland Pascal. This is *DOS protected mode*, a special operating mode for machines containing 80286 or newer CPUs. In DOS protected mode, your programs look like ordinary DOS programs on the screen . . . but they can make direct use of up to 16 megabytes of memory, and are "protected" internally from certain kinds of program errors. Some of these are errors due to your efforts as a programmer, whereas others come from interactions between different components in the system. Protected mode also helps you spot bugs during the development process, at the price of a little more complexit—but not much.

Only Borland Pascal can target DOS protected mode. Neither Turbo Pascal nor Turbo Pascal for Windows can do it. I won't have the room in this book to cover DOS protected mode, but once you get some experience you should be able to figure it out from reading Borland's documentation. It's really not that difficult at all—nothing even *close* to being as tough as programming for Windows!

Borland Pascal 7.0 is one product in a single (large) box that contains numerous programs that allow you to develop programs for either the DOS or the Windows platform. Better still, you can choose to have Borland Pascal 7.0 hosted under either DOS or Windows. By "hosted" here I mean that you can choose to have Borland Pascal operate either as a Windows application under Windows, using Windows graphics, or else as a DOS application in text mode. It's exactly the same compiler underneath the menus and the edit windows. But the face that the product turns to you, the programmer, can be either the DOS or the Windows face.

Here's an important point, however: Borland Pascal can develop DOS programs or Windows programs *regardless of which environment hosts it*. You can develop DOS programs from the Windows environment, and you can develop Windows programs from the DOS environment. How you work is entirely up to you.

3.2 Third-Party Add-On Products for Borland's Pascals

A good many companies specialize in selling "canned" code and add-on utilities for Borland's Pascal products. Some of these are sold through traditional channels, but others are distributed via "insider" means like shareware that you may not have encountered yet. There is still another body of code available for Turbo Pascal that is in the public domain, and free for the taking—if you can find it.

I'll run down some of these resources briefly, and try to steer you in their direction.

COMMERCIAL PRODUCTS

If you are aware of Borland International, you're almost certainly aware of some of the companies who create products that add value to Borland's compilers.

They're advertised in the same magazines as Borland's products are, and sold through the same specialty mail-order catalogs. If by some chance you're not aware of any of these vendors of the catalogs and magazines they're seen in, (and if not, one must wonder where you've been hiding), you should read this section carefully. Some of these products can save you an enormous amount of work and bother.

The best known of all the third-party vendors is probably TurboPower Software, a small firm operating out of Colorado. They offer a number of code libraries and utilities for the Borland Pascal and C++ compiler lines. The Turbo Professional library, in particular, is a massive collection of canned procedures and functions that can get you a third of the way through a middling programming project before you even begin working on it. If you're familiar with object-oriented programming, the firm offers a more advanced version of Turbo Professional called Object Professional, which does all of the same things, but within an object-oriented context. TurboPower's other libraries include a B-tree data-manager engine, and an asynchronous communications library.

One TurboPower strength is its technical support, particularly on the CompuServe on-line service. (See below if you've never heard of CompuServe.) TurboPower's engineers are often to be found on their forum, answering questions about their products and about programming in general. The software itself is stellar, and I highly recommend it. Furthermore, all products come with Pascal source code, which offers the additional benefit of giving you a model for excellent code design.

> TurboPower Software
> PO Box 49009
> Colorado Springs, CO 80949-9009
> (719) 260-6641

Just about as venerable is Blaise Computing of Berkeley, California. Their products include Power Tools Plus, a general-purpose code library on the order of Turbo Professional, Asynch Plus, an asynchronous communications library, and Power Screen, which allows you to paint data-entry screens interactively, and then generates code to implement those screens in Pascal. Their most unique product, however, is the Turbo Vision Development Toolkit, a combination code library and design tool for working with Borland's powerful and complex Turbo Vision object application framework.

All of the Blaise software is excellent and, like TurboPower, full Pascal source code is included with all their products.

> Blaise Computing, Inc.
> 819 Bancroft Way
> Berkeley, CA 94710
> (510) 540-5441

I don't have room to list more than these two, but any of the programmers' mail-order catalogs will list a great many more, and you will find advertisements in many programmers' magazines, including *PC TECHNIQUES*, which I publish from here in Arizona.

SHAREWARE

There is a serious problem getting commercial products out where potential buyers can hear about them and buy them. Very few computer stores offer programming products anymore, apart from the major language products themselves. Advertising products in magazines is fiercely expensive (I know; I own a magazine) and doesn't always pay for products of modest scale or very narrow interest.

Some years back, someone hit upon the notion of allowing (nay, encouraging) people to copy and distribute software among themselves, and literally trying it before laying out any money for it. That is, you copy a disk from a friend, give the software a whirl, and if you like it and intend to use it, you register your use of it by sending some amount of money (generally very little compared to the cost of commercial products) to an address specified somewhere in the product documentation. This has come to be known as *shareware* and, while the jury is still out on how well the system pays the authors of shareware software, it's certainly a clear win for the shareware *user*.

In return for your payment, many shareware vendors will send you a printed manual and notify you of new releases of the software. Some also sell more advanced or powerful versions of the shareware software as true commercial products. This makes the shareware versions "trial size" programs, serving to publicize the larger product and bring in new potential customers to the vendor. This arrangement bothers some people, but look at it as a cost-benefit equation. If the trial size is worth the modest donation, what matter that it has a more powerful (and more expensive) big brother?

A lot of programmer utilities and code libraries are available as shareware. One of the best sources for these is EMS Professional Software in Olney, Maryland, which offers a massive collection of both shareware and public domain (see below) Pascal utilities and libraries. At this writing (early 1993) the EMS Pascal library is at 21 megabytes and growing. The library costs about $80.00 and is well worth getting. (You do have to register and pay additionally for products within the library that you end up using. EMS charges mainly for their trouble of gathering and packaging the libraries, which for 21 MB of data is no small task.)

EMS Professional Software
4505 Buckhurst Court
Olney, MD 20832
(301) 924-3594

Another good commercial source of shareware code is The Programmer's Corner, described below in connection with BBS and on-line services.

I'd strongly encourage you not to wimp out and "forget" to register utilities and libraries that you use regularly. The amounts requested are modest. You, yourself, may want to release a shareware product someday, and you'd certainly want people to be honest and register what *you* create! The Golden Rule never applied more clearly than here.

THE PUBLIC DOMAIN

Finally, there is a body of programming material that has been explicitly placed in what is called the *public domain*. The public domain is the state of being without copyright protection. (You may also hear it described as "copyright-free.") Material in the public domain may be freely copied and redistributed without any payment or other consideration due the originator of the material.

Most public-domain program code is explicitly labeled as such. You have to be a little bit careful, however; the notion of "public domain software" has been muddied in recent years due to confusion with shareware (described above) and with copyrighted software that contains notices allowing "unrestricted non-commercial use" or something like that. Defining "non-commercial" is like defining "supernatural"—everybody has his own opinion, and some would deny that such a state exists.

What most people who specify "unrestricted non-commercial use" are trying to avoid is being taken for granted by big-money commercial interests who might plug their code into a major application and make millions on it. This doesn't happen often; if it does happen, you're unlikely to win a court case without blowing your life savings on it. I would recommend not worrying about it.

Two prominent sources of both shareware and public domain software are EMS (described above) and The Programmer's Corner, a national BBS mentioned in the next section.

It is a courtesy to ask the author of a piece of code if it may be used in a commercial project, even if that code is marked "public domain." If you're just another struggling loner, such permission will rarely be refused.

And remember: Grant unto others what you would have them grant unto you!

3.3 Resources On-Line and in Your Own Community

Writing program code, like writing mystery novels or almost anything else, is a pretty solitary pursuit. That is, while you're actually doing it, you're better off being alone and away from distractions and time sinks like TV, children, basketball games, political rallies, and heavy metal concerts. On the other hand, there will come times when you'll be up against the proverbial wall and in serious need of help and advice. How to find such help and advice is no small feat.

However it may feel at 3:00 A.M. when that same damned bug has you by the throat that has had you by the throat since late last week, you're probably not alone; at least not in any town with a population of more than half a dozen. The challenge is in finding other people like yourself who work in Turbo Pascal, and the organizations formed to serve computer people in general and programmers in particular. What you should look for are user groups and computer bulletin-board systems.

USER GROUPS

A user group is nothing more than a club for computer users. Most user groups meet periodically, have presentations from vendors or technical experts, and informal bull sessions after the more formal meetings. User groups exist both locally and nationally. National user groups usually focus on one particular software or hardware product and communicate largely through newsletters or on-line services. Local user groups are less product-specific as a rule and meet in person.

In the larger cities, user groups are sometimes partitioned into Special Interest Groups (SIGs) which often include groups on programming and, in some cases, specifically on Turbo Pascal programming.

It's impossible to offer general advice on finding local user groups. One of the best ways is to ask at local computer dealers, particularly those who sell more technical products than word processors and spreadsheet programs. The service department people often know where the user groups are because they often belong themselves. The smaller "clone shop" dealers are generally more in touch with local user group activities than the massive superstores like CompUSA, whose employees are less likely to care passionately about computing.

User groups often meet at public libraries. An inquiry at your local public library would be a good place to start.

Sooner or later, if you ask around enough, you'll find the local user group. Within the group is almost always an inner cadre of technical people who either comprise a programming SIG themselves or can tell you where such a SIG is, if it exists at all.

And if it doesn't, well, why not create one? That's ultimately what user groups are for: technical people offering to share their knowledge and experience with others. As you get better at Turbo Pascal, you'll become more of a source and less of a sink, and working actively within a user group is an excellent way to "pay forward" those who helped you when you were just starting out and totally green.

TURBO USER GROUP

One particular national (international, actually) user group deserves special mention: Turbo User Group (TUG), a long-time organization devoted to programmers using all of Borland's languages, but particularly Borland's Pascal. TUG's major product is *TUG Lines*, a substantial technical newsletter that remains one of the very few reliable sources of information on Turbo Pascal. TUG also offers library diskettes of Turbo Pascal source code and utilities, as well as video tapes of industry experts lecturing on programming topics.

TUG/Pro, the parent company, also sponsors Ge-TUG-ether, an annual gathering of Turbo hackers in the Pacific Northwest, in Silverdale on the west side of Puget Sound, a gorgeous ferry ride away from downtown Seattle. Numerous technical experts give seminars on the craft of programming, everything from beginner tips to expert code optimization techniques. Compared to many other industry seminar conferences, it's extremely inexpensive, and one of the most pleasant ways I know to meet other totally-committed Turbo Pascal fanatics. I generally go myself, so if you attend I may see you there!

Annual dues may seem high ($75.00, at this writing), but the *TUG Lines* newsletter is all-beef, and the code libraries contain a great deal of very good code.

TUG/Pro (Turbo User Group)
PO Box 1510
Poulsbo, WA 98370
(206) 779-9508

BULLETIN-BOARD SYSTEMS

The very first computer bulletin-board system (BBS) appeared in Chicago in the mid-1970s, and was the creation of Ward Christiansen and Randy Seuss, WB9GPM. A BBS is nothing more than a program that runs on a computer (typically a PC) and communicates with the outside world not through the keyboard and screen, but entirely through a device called a *modem* that couples to the telephone line and communicates with other computers also equipped with modems. The modem connected to the BBS computer is configured so that it can answer the phone line when it rings, and automatically connect the computer's serial port to the phone line and hence to the caller.

You communicate with a BBS by "dialing in" to the BBS phone number, and then typing to your own modem through a program often called a *terminal program* or *async program*. Your modem passes your keystrokes on to the BBS, and also accepts characters transmitted by the BBS and displays them on your screen. It sounds complicated, but it's actually fairly straightforward. I've drawn out the connection scheme in Figure 3.1.

The BBS computer is often a powerful and expensive one, and it usually has a large hard disk to hold all the messages and download files. Sometimes the operators of BBSes will request or require financial donations to help defray the cost of the equipment and the phone line.

These days, nearly all modems come with their own terminal programs, so I won't try to explain terminal programs further. Once you have the modem and terminal program installed and working correctly, you'll be able to dial into any BBS with a published phone number.

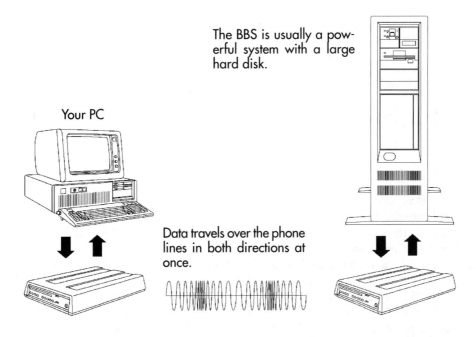

The BBS is usually a powerful system with a large hard disk.

Your PC

Data travels over the phone lines in both directions at once.

Figure 3.1 Communicating with a BBS

Most BBSes are set up so that you can be presented with a series of menus once you connect. You only need to follow the menus to enable you to do what you want to do.

And what is there to do? First and perhaps most important, BBSes contain libraries of files for you to download. Many BBSes have program source code and utility files, many of which are free for the taking.

Also, BBSes are meeting places for technical people. As the "bulletin board" portion of their name implies, BBSes allow you to post general messages for everyone to read, messages which can be, and often are, technical questions about programming. Suppose you need advice on using random access files under Turbo Pascal. You could phrase a question about what in particular is bugging you (as it were) about random files and post it on your local BBS, so that anyone else who visits the BBS could read and perhaps respond to the question.

Most BBSes additionally offer private messaging services, so that if you wanted to leave a message for Harry Hacker in particular, it would be stored on the BBS so that only Harry could read it or even know that it was there.

Not all bulletin-board systems are strictly local, and not all of them offer free access. A handful of BBSes have "gone national," usually as for-pay distributors of software and other data. You must pay for a subscription or some other type of account, and then (in almost all cases) pay for the long-distance phone call if the service is not in your immediate area. This may make such systems expensive, but you won't know until you investigate. My favorite in this group is The Programmer's Corner, which specializes in source code for all the popular programming languages, most especially including Turbo Pascal. They offer over a gigabyte (one billion bytes) of source code on-line and ready to download. Contact them for their latest rates and conditions:

The Programmer's Corner
5430 F Lynx Lane, Suite 224
Columbia, MD 21044
(301) 621-4636

PC TECHNIQUES

This is as good a place as any to mention the magazine that I founded in 1989 and still publish: *PC TECHNIQUES*. I think it's fair to say that PCT publishes more Pascal articles and source code than any other magazine now publishing, and probably will continue to do so as long as I have anything to do with it. (And since I own it, I can't exactly get fired!) We publish technical articles by all the best writers in the business, reviews of Pascal add-on products, and advertisements from virtually all the significant commercial Turbo Pascal third-party vendors.

It would be crass to say more than that. The magazine can be found at most larger newsstands and bookstores. Contact us for a sample issue or to order a subscription.

PC TECHNIQUES
7721 East Gray Road #204
Scottsdale, AZ 85260
(602) 483-0192

3.4 CompuServe

Nearly all bulletin-board systems are essentially local in nature. The one in your town is a local call, but calling Chicago or even the next town over is probably long-distance and could cost you dearly to spend any serious amount of time asking questions or downloading code libraries. There are, however, a number of worldwide bulletin-board systems that may be called through local numbers in most big American cities. You've got it both ways, this way: the benefit of a huge international base of people like yourself to talk to and ask advice of, through a local phone call. Because they're considered something larger than your average PC-based bulletin-board systems (most run on massive mainframe computers) these are usually called *on-line services* instead. Certainly the largest and the best of these is CompuServe.

CompuServe offers all of the sorts of services you can find on local BBSes: Public message-posting for questions, private messaging between individuals, and libraries of electronic goodies to download. These include source code and utilities for programmers, but go well beyond that. CompuServe contains libraries of software bug reports, electronic images ranging from Voyager photos of the outer planets to centerfold girls, stock market and investment statistics, and a great deal more. CompuServe is for more than just programmers; it serves all people with computers and modems, whether they consider themselves computer crazies or not.

To find out more about CompuServe or to inquire about getting an account, call them:

CompuServe
(800) 848-8199

GETTING IN AND FINDING YOUR WAY AROUND

To access CompuServe, you need to sign up with them and get an account. You are assigned an account number that you must type into the system when you dial in. (Most people have their communications program type it for them.) My own number is 76711,470; most numbers look a lot like that. You are also assigned a password, just as with most BBSes. *Keep that a deadly secret.* Unlike most BBSes, which are free to access, CompuServe costs real money and anyone who has both your account number and your password can use it at your expense.

CompuServe is a vast system, covering a great many topics and serving an incredible number of people. It is organized into several levels, just as the United States is organized into states, counties, and towns.

The topmost level is the forums. Forums are large divisions by topic. For example, there is a forum for railroad fans, another for ham radio operators, and a great many for the numerous facets of computer work. You move between the forums using the command GO. For example, to get to the Borland forums, you would type GO BORLAND. CompuServe would take you to the Borland forum menu and provide further directions from there. (Borland generates such intense activity on CompuServe that it has more than one forum.)

Forums require that you "join" them the first time you access them, by explicitly typing your name at a prompt. This may seem ridiculous (and it is, a little) since CompuServe already knows who you are, including your name. But there's a reason for it: Forum operators are paid a share of your connect-time charges as a reward for drawing you into CompuServe as a whole. That is, CompuServe considers the forums "bait" for its users, and is willing to share the wealth to some degree with the people and companies who operate attractive and useful forums. The more people who join a forum, the more money the forum operators make. This is why you must make an explicit choice to join a forum, and actually do a little keystroking to get in. CompuServe wants to know that you're motivated to get into a forum before it's willing to share the wealth with that forum.

Inside a forum, there are a number of sections. A section is usually a more specific subtopic of the larger topic covered by the forum as a whole. Inside sections you'll find both files to be downloaded and messages from people who have visited that section within the forum. Sometimes the messages are arranged in threads: strings of messages created when someone leaves a message, someone else answers that message, then someone else answers the answer, and so on. Sometimes threads mutate far afield from their stated subjects, and have sometimes gone on for literally hundreds of messages.

To find the files available within a section, use the command LIB <n>, where n is the section of interest. Then use the DIR command, just like in DOS, to see what's there.

WHERE THE PASCAL STUFF IS

Virtually all of the Pascal material on CompuServe is found in three places: the Borland forums, the magazine forums, and the PC vendor forums.

The Borland forums are the first place to look. Actually, all of the Pascal material is concentrated in one forum, BPASCAL. You can get to BPASCAL with the command GO BPASCAL. Be aware of Borland's "C++" forum, however, (and visit it occasionally) because you may find something there of use to programmers of any Borland language. The C++ Forum is reached with the command GO BCPP.

The PC vendor forums serve smaller companies (on a scale smaller than Borland) whose products operate in the PC environment. This goes far beyond programming tools, but there are a fair number of Pascal aftermarket vendors with sections on the PC vendor forums.

The magazine forums are operated by computer magazines as a service to those of their readers who also subscribe to CompuServe. Usually, the basic need is for a way to get code listings into reader hands without requiring that the readers either send away for listing diskettes or type listings from the magazines into their own machines, which for any serious amount of code is sheer agony.

Not many magazines publish any significant amount of Pascal code anymore. Many of the magazine forums do contain code archives from past issues, some published in the days when Turbo Pascal commanded more respect from the press. Such archives are certainly worth investigating and possibly downloading, whether or not you actually possess the magazine issue in question. Here are the worthwhile magazine forums on CompuServe:

Dr. Dobb's Journal: GO DDJ—all sections

Computer Language: GO CLM—most sections; some are devoted to smaller magazines

Windows Tech Journal: GO CLM—section 9

Windows/DOS Developer's Journal: GO CLM— section 7

PC TECHNIQUES: GO CLM—section 16

These are the only magazines still in existence that have ever published any significant amount of Pascal code. The last magazine shown, *PC TECHNIQUES*, is the one I own and publish; I read the messages posted in Section 16 of CLM almost every day.

NAVIGATOR PROGRAMS FOR COMPUSERVE

CompuServe operates on a pay-by-connect-time basis. You are billed (usually to your credit card account) a certain value per hour of time you spend connected to the system. This means it pays to know what you want to do before you dial in, and not spend a lot of time staring at the screen wondering what to do next.

There are communication programs that understand CompuServe's forum structure and command set. They have been designed to help you get into CompuServe quickly, do what you want quickly, and get out again quickly. As a class, these are called *navigator* programs, and there are several. Most of them are shareware programs as I described earlier in this chapter; when you decide to use one of them, you are required to send a registration fee to its vendor.

The oldest and best of these is called TAPCIS, and it is available for downloading from CompuServe. Its location in CompuServe's libraries has changed from time to time, so if it isn't where I say it is, don't despair — just "ask" around. Try the TAPCIS forum, section 1 first. That's where it was in early 1993.

Another, newer, navigator program is OZCIS and, while similar in intent to TAPCIS, it is quite different in operation. I haven't used OZCIS and don't have any strong opinions on it, but people I respect like it. As with TAPCIS, it may not be where I say it is when you go up on CompuServe, but try the IBMCOM forum, section 12 first.

Both TAPCIS and OZCIS are shareware programs, and either of them will save you a massive amount of money over even a few months' time. Please register them with their owners, and pay the requested fee. Furthermore, let it be some inspiration to you that both TAPCIS and OZCIS are written in Turbo Pascal!

3.5 Making Money with Turbo Pascal

Finally, a tricky question indeed, but one many new Turbo Pascal programmers ask: Is there any hope of getting jobs or otherwise making money with Turbo Pascal?

Good question. Two questions, actually, which I'll treat separately.

The first question has a pretty grim answer: There are not many traditional jobs, per se, in programming Turbo Pascal. That is, few companies will hire you as a salaried or hourly staffer simply to program in Turbo Pascal. I've heard of a few, and I've steered a few Turbo Pascal people toward some of those few jobs, but there are a lot of *very* good Turbo Pascal programmers, and the competition for such jobs is likely to be intense.

I would say you'll probably have to "luck into" such a job rather than go out hunting for one with any expectation of finding one.

This doesn't mean that nobody gets paid for programming in Turbo Pascal. The problem is that most people who program in Turbo Pascal "on the job" are programming to support their other work. I know a physician who does blood chemistry research at a major Western hospital, and he builds programs to analyze his research data in Turbo Pascal. His management takes into account the fact that he programs, but programming is not his job—blood chemistry research is. Similarly, I've heard of a lot of people in science and engineering who write Turbo Pascal software to help them get their technical work done in one way or another. Turbo Pascal is a good math language and the programming process goes quickly, especially if you use "canned" code libraries to accomplish the infrastructure of your programs (that is, the windows and menus and mouse support and other machinery that isn't directly specific to the work the program is doing).

Turbo Pascal can, in fact, make you a more productive technical person, and thus enhance your value in your technical job market—but the Turbo Pascal job market itself is very small and extremely competitive.

CONSULTING

What we call *consulting* covers a lot of ground. It can include simple advice, program design, actual programming, or some combination of all of the above. What defines "consulting" is that the consultant is not an employee of the client, and the work is generally a one-shot, closed-ended project.

A lot of such work gets done in Turbo Pascal—that's the good news. The bad news is that finding such work is difficult. What generally happens is that you become a "famous" Turbo Pascal programmer and the work finds *you*. By "famous" I only mean that you are well-known by your local computing community (often through user groups—a terrific reason to belong to and be active in your local user group) and perhaps the national community, by being a frequent contributor to CompuServe or other national on-line services in forums where Pascal people hang out. Much, if not most, consulting work is passed along on personal recommendation. Somebody knows somebody who knows somebody who knows somebody who knows you—that sort of thing. It's rare to find an ad for Pascal consulting work in the papers, or even in the trade press.

Be visible, and be known as *good*. If there's work to be had, some of it is bound to come to you sooner or later.

The problem is that it's hard to make a living on work that finds you rather than vise versa. Consulting in Turbo Pascal may best be approached as an "evenings" thing to supplement your day job. Another problem is inherent in any kind of consulting: avoiding being taken by a shrewd or unethical client who ends up getting your labor for 50 cents an hour. I can't address that problem here; it's a matter of being a tough businessman and knowing what you can and cannot accomplish in a reasonable amount of time. If you can't manage that, you're probably better off working a job for someone else rather than consulting for yourself.

CREATING YOUR OWN SHAREWARE

Writing and publishing your own products as shareware is relatively easy. Whether it pays is another matter. Some people have literally gotten rich with their shareware, but those cases are exceptional in many ways, some of them hard to define.

Shareware is basically the process of tossing your products to the four winds, accompanied by a note requesting that eventual users send you money on the honor system. (I've defined shareware in detail earlier in this chapter.) Only a few percent of those people who try or use your products will pay for them, but if the products get widely distributed, even those small percentages can add up.

I myself have never released anything as shareware, so I have no personal perspective to offer you on either success or failure. Some of my friends have made modest amounts of money on it—say, $200–$300 per month—but no one I know well has hit it really big, or even big enough to live on. The trick is to create an application that is broad in its appeal—something like a game or a word processor that *anyone* could use, rather than some arcane little routine for calculating put-option losses in the secondary market for yak hides. The catch is that an awful lot of other people have also released games and word processors as shareware, so unless your own are exceedingly good, they're not going to displace the ones that have been in the market for awhile and are being constantly recommended by strong word-of-mouth publicity.

You can definitely help your shareware products through means like sending them to magazines for reviews, but mostly you can help them by making sure that they are *everywhere*. Send them to every shareware anthology vendor you can find, give disks to user group librarians, upload them to BBSes. Beyond that, it's mostly a matter of luck. I wish I could offer better counsel, but that's the best I can do.

Still, shareware is a good place to start; and if you don't have to make a living on the proceeds, it can be fun and add a little padding to your income. There's a nice little booklet on the subject by a programmer I've met, Rob Rosenberger, who is himself a fairly successful shareware author. The booklet is *The Shareware Authors' Handbook,* and it can be purchased from Rob at his company, Barn Owl Software. It's only $7.95 postpaid, and will give you a very good idea of the process and what you can expect from it. I strongly recommend it.

The Shareware Authors' Handbook
Rob Rosenberger
Barn Owl Software
PO Box 74
O'Fallon, IL 62269
(618) 632-7345

COMMERCIAL SOFTWARE

The longest shot of all is producing a commercial product in Turbo Pascal and then marketing it yourself through traditional channels. This means doing things like advertising, and working with distributors, software stores, and mail-order catalog outlets. The problem with going the commercial route is that the actual programming is a very small part of the work involved. Selling the product comes to overwhelm all your other efforts and, if you can't sell, you won't make any money. Furthermore, you can lose a lot, in a very big hurry.

The expenses are breathtaking. Buying a full-page ad in a computer magazine can cost $10,000 per month—maybe more, for the biggest magazines. Doing any kind of mass mailing can run to $40,000 or $50,000 if you're going to get the mail piece out to enough people to do you any good. Putting a product in any kind of software store requires professionally-produced, attractive packaging. Designing the artwork for a printed product box is something like a black art, especially if you have no background in commercial graphics. Printing up such boxes costs a lot of money, and you can't just print a hundred or two at a time. You must print *thousands*—at a cost of $2.00 or $3.00 dollars each.

Projects like this require a plan, some up-front money, and probably an all-business partner who knows how to market. Don't let me discourage you if you think you have all the requisite skills. I just want you to face the prospects honestly and plainly: A great many more people lose this game than win it.

But if you've looked yourself square in the eye in the mirror and truly believe you can do it, *go for it*. If you never try, you will never win.

KIOSKWARE

Finally, I'll mention something a little new under the sun, something that I myself am in the process of trying. It's a new way to distribute software, and it could be the way of the future, especially for individual programmers without the means to do their own commercial distribution.

I call it *kioskware*, and it consists of product display racks (sometimes called kiosks) placed in mass-market retail stores that get a lot of traffic. These are the Wal-Marts, K-Marts, Targets, and so on. Each display rack may contain 50 different product titles, somewhat like a magazine or paperback book rack. The products have professional packaging, but they are not accompanied by elaborate printed manuals. Furthermore, they are priced strictly for "ah, what-the-hell" style purchases—typically $7.00 or $8.00 per package. The author's share of that isn't much. (It's usually less than a dollar per package sold. Sometimes a *lot* less.) On the other hand, if the kiosk vendor can get the kiosks into a significant number of retail outlets, you can sell a great many copies of your product, and the pennies do add up over time.

To be sold in outlets like this, the products must be non-technical in nature and very general in application. That is, you're not going to sell Turbo Pascal code libraries this way, nor special-purpose software for managing dog kennels. Games and software for handling home-related data on home computers is the preferred focus. The software must be very easy to use, but it need not compete directly with Microsoft Word for Windows. People will not expect state-of-the-art for $8.00. They will, however, expect such a product to do at least one thing well.

An example: I have recently released a small application of my own into this channel. The application is called Mortgage Vision, and it is a simple program to help people shop for mortgages and home refinancing. It doesn't do anything more than that. I *did* research its competition, however, and I made sure that it did more things better than any other similar program kicking around the industry. Remarkably, this wasn't difficult.

Is it working? I don't know yet. I should know in a few more months. In the meantime, you might get the author kit from the kiosk company I am working with:

SofSource, Inc.
Bob Falk
6285 Escondido Drive
El Paso, TX 79912
(915) 584-7670

Again, I don't expect to get rich or even make a living solely through this channel. But I do expect to make a certain amount of money, and I take considerable satisfaction in having done it using Turbo Pascal.

Chapter 4

A Place to Stand, with Access to Tools

GETTING ACQUAINTED WITH THE TURBO PASCAL IDE

"Give me a lever long enough, and a place to stand, and I will move the Earth."

Archimedes was speaking literally about the power of the lever, but behind his words there is a larger truth about work in general: To get something done, you need a place to work, with access to tools. My radio bench in the garage is set up that way: a large, flat space to lay ailing transmitters down, and a shelf above where my oscilloscope, VTVM, frequency counter, signal generator, and dip meter are within easy reach.

Much of the early success of Turbo Pascal was grounded in that simple but compelling truth. For the first time, a compiler vendor had assembled the most important tools of software development and put them together in an intuitive fashion so that the various tasks involved in creating software flowed easily and quickly from one step to the next.

Turbo Pascal versions 1 through 3 were extremely effective in this way. Turbo Pascal versions 4 and 5 were even more so—and versions 6 and 7 (about which this book was written) are nothing short of astonishing. In this section I'll give you an overview of the process of creating programs with Turbo Pascal. The emphasis here will be on the way it all fits together. In later sections, we'll look at many of the tools and the processes individually and in more detail. I won't, however, provide a complete or encyclopedic reference to the IDE—that could easily take half of this book alone. All of the information you'll need is in the Borland *User's Guide* for the Pascal product you're working on.

4.1 Using a Mouse

Before I say word one about the Turbo Pascal user interface (UI) itself, I want to point something out to those of you who may be coming to Turbo Pascal for the first time—or for the first time in a long time. The Borland Pascal products have been redesigned to work extremely effectively with the mouse. If you intend to do any significant work in Turbo Pascal and don't already have a mouse, I'd like to encourage you strongly to get one.

The mouse concept was invented at Xerox's Palo Alto Research Center in the early 1970s. Physically, a mouse is a small plastic solid about the size of a cake of hand soap, shaped to fit comfortably in the hand. A wire leads away from the front edge to some sort of interface to your computer. On top of the mouse are a number of buttons, usually two but sometimes three. (The original Xerox mice had three buttons.) On the lower surface of the mouse is some mechanism that senses the motion of the mouse over a flat surface. This is usually a rubber-coated ball, but is occasionally a tiny pair of wheels at right angles to one another. To give it good "footing," mice are usually run on a thin foam pad covered by fabric, called a *mouse pad*.

The whole idea behind the mouse is to translate continuous motion of your hand to continuous motion of a cursor on your computer screen. You're probably used to repeatedly pounding on one or another of the arrow keys to get the cursor to go where you need it to on the screen. If you have a mouse installed, the screen cursor "follows" the movement of the mouse on the mouse pad. If you move the mouse horizontally over the pad, the cursor will move horizontally across the screen, in the same direction that the mouse is moving. If you move the mouse vertically across the pad, the cursor will move a proportionate distance vertically across the screen. Even if you move the mouse in broad sweeps or weird curves, the cursor will follow the motion faithfully around the screen, as shown in Figure 4.1.

MOUSE BUTTONS

Of the buttons on the mouse's upper surface, the leftmost one gets the most action. In Turbo Pascal, in fact, the left button is the only one with a consistent

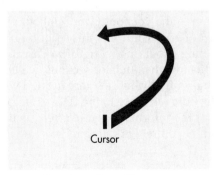

Computer Screen

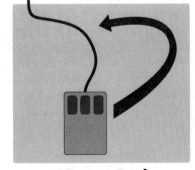

Mouse Pad

Figure 4.1 The Way a Mouse Works

function. (The left-to-right order of the mouse buttons can be reversed for the benefit of left-handed people, such that a lefty can use the right mouse button with his index finger to make selections that a righty would make with the left button. This configuration is done from the Options | Environment | Mouse menu item.)

The left button is pressed to "click" on a screen option. Some UI elements just need a quick click to make them work. In other contexts, you must depress the left button and hold it down while you move the mouse around the screen. This is called "click and drag," and is used extensively to resize and reshape windows, work the elevator button of a scroll bar, and so on.

WHY A MOUSE?

If you're not used to using a mouse, you may be wondering if you wouldn't be just as well off working completely from the keyboard. That's certainly possible; there's nothing in Borland's UI that can't be done from the keyboard, and avoiding the mouse doesn't "lock you out" of any feature of the environment.

But the UI is a complicated thing, and there are a lot of elements involved in it. You can memorize a host of shortcut keys to handle any conceivable operation—but it's probably faster and takes less hand motion to simply point and click, mouse-style. This is especially true of operations like sizing and dragging windows, where doing them with a mouse is one quick, smooth motion, whereas doing them from the keyboard involves several shortcut keys and a lot of banging on the arrow keys. In short, using a mouse makes certain things a lot easier—and you can always use some of the keyboard controls if they seem convenient to you. The mouse interface and the keyboard interface are both always active, always at the same time, side-by-side. You can mix metaphors as you like, use a little of one or a lot of the other, as your programming style evolves.

By all means give the mouse a try. You won't be disappointed.

4.2 The IDE Development Cycle

As a unit, Borland's program from which you create, test, and execute Pascal applications is called the *Interactive Development Environment* (IDE). The controls by which you manipulate your application in the IDE are collectively the user interface (UI).

Using the IDE to create programs is fairly easy, and doesn't take a great deal of study. Most of the multitude of options that the IDE supports default to reasonable values that will allow you to get started and learn enough to configure the environment to your needs. Certainly, for taking your first steps in learning Turbo Pascal, you don't have to change anything in the IDE.

From a height, the process of creating a program from within the Turbo Pascal IDE runs like this:

1. Design your program. (This is done in many ways, but it's generally done outside Borland's IDE. I use graph paper and a lead pencil. Old habits die hard.)

2. Create a new source code file or load an existing source code file into a source code window.

3. Type in new source code or change existing source code in the source code window.

4. Compile the code in the source code window.

5. If any compiler errors turn up, correct them.

6. When the program compiles without errors, run it.

7. If, when running, the program reveals any bugs, terminate program execution and return to the source code window to search for the bugs.

8. If the bugs are not found promptly "by inspection," use the Integrated Debugger to search for them.

9. When the bugs are found, correct them in the source code window and save the updated source code file to disk.

10. Recompile and retest the running program until all bugs are found.

I've illustrated this process diagramatically in Figure 4.2. Let's take a little time to discuss how this process is accomplished within Borland's IDE.

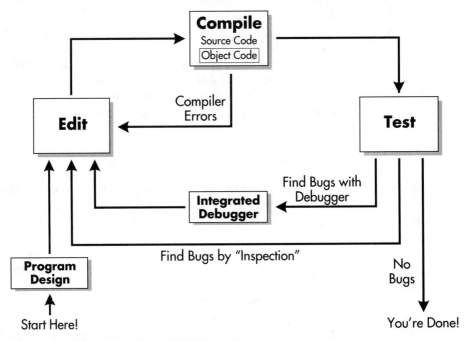

Figure 4.2 The Turbo Pascal IDE Development Process

SOFTWARE DESIGN

Designing your programs is a very personal thing. There are elaborate design-tool programs called CASE tools, but most are expensive and nearly all of them are designed for the use of teams of programmers writing monstrous multiprogram systems. You really don't need anything but pencil, paper, and some patience and concentration to design a program. It's a difficult process to describe in only a few words, but most of it cooks down to this: *Know what your program is supposed to do before you begin writing it.* This may involve drawing pictures, creating flowcharts, or just brainstorming hordes of notes on a yellow pad. However you do it, *do it.*

CREATING OR EDITING SOURCE CODE FILES

Creating a source code file is done with a *text editor*. A source code file is just a text file on disk, meaning it contains only the human-readable characters from the ASCII character set. A text editor is a program that displays a text file on the screen somehow and allows you to enter new text or change text that is already there. Think of it as elementary word processing, without all the fancy text formatting that word processing entails.

The Borland IDE has the ability to create multiple source code windows on the screen, each of which contains a fully functional text editor. You can edit more than one file at one time. (It's best to start with just one until you get your legs beneath you.) You can even edit the same file in two places at once—which may sound peculiar but can be truly useful.

When you've typed in all the text you want into the text window, you save the changes back to disk. (Actually, you should save your changes every few minutes to be safe.) Then the source code file is ready to compile.

COMPILING SOURCE CODE FILES

The fun stuff begins when you turn the Pascal compiler loose on your carefully edited source code file. The idea is to get the compiler to look at your source code file and create an executable *object-code file* of machine instructions that is, in fact, the "program" that you're creating. The compiler drinks the source code file through a straw, as it were, one character at a time, and builds your executable object-code file as it goes. It can continue building your object code file only as long as the source code file makes sense. If you write something even a little bit wrong according to the compiler's rules, the compiler will display a compile error and stop.

You then must squint at the compile error and decide what the problem is. Once you've decided (and the compiler is of limited helpfulness here), you must return to the edit window and make whatever changes are necessary to get the source code file to compile fully.

Turbo and Borland Pascal are both one-pass compilers. There is no "link step," as there is in the C and C++ languages. When the compiler is done, your program can run!

TESTING YOUR PROGRAM

Once your program has compiled successfully (and the compiler will tell you explicitly when this is the case) you must run your program and see if it does what you intended it to do. You can do this from within the IDE, through the Run menu. The IDE will automagically "step aside" and allow your program to take over the machine, and run as though the IDE were not there. You can then enter data and examine your program's responses in detail, taking notes as to things that didn't come out quite right. Perhaps the prompts are in the wrong place by a few character positions, or perhaps the colors on the screen are off a little. (You can only hope the problems will be as simple as that.) Perhaps your machine simply (as Shakespeare wrote in *Henry VI*, Part II) ". . . dies, and makes no sign." What you've got, alas, are *bugs*.

LOOKING FOR BUGS

Bugs are related to compile errors rather like diseases are related to poisons. Poisons stop you dead in your tracks—but they're fairly easy to avoid. Compile errors are like that. With some practice, you should be able to clear a program of compile errors in a few minutes—or even write programs that compile on the first try, without any compile errors.

Diseases don't usually kill you, but they can make your life miserable and can be tough to get rid of. So it is with bugs. Like the common cold, even when you locate the cause, it can be difficult to *correct* the cause. Sometimes a program bug is inherent in the program's design, and you practically have to redesign the program and rewrite it from scratch to utterly eliminate the bug.

Don't despair. Bugs are a fact of life. The question is how hard you want to work to root them out. Finding them is the first task. Borland's IDE contains a handful of superb tools for finding bugs. Fixing them, of course, is a matter of your own ingenuity.

Finding a bug is sometimes a matter of simply looking at the code that isn't working right. I call this bug-finding *by inspection*, and most of your truly blatant bugs can be found this way. When a line of text goes to the wrong location on the screen, you can probably find the bug by simply looking for the statement that writes the text to the screen and correcting the position parameters.

The downside is that with practice, you'll make fewer and fewer of such blatant bugs. This leaves the really ugly kind to find and fix, and for that you'll often need a little heavier artillery. The IDE allows you to *single-step* a program, and literally watch the contents of variables change as you step through the statements you have written. Inside the IDE, each time you press function key

F8, a highlight bar will move one statement down your program to the next program in line to be executed. You can execute *one* line of code, then sit as long as you like and think about what it's doing and what comes next.

This, my friend, is truly an education in how programs work. You set *watches* on variables, a process that places a variable's name and contents in a little window at the bottom of the screen. You then "watch" the variable as you step through the program, looking for the step that causes a peculiar or simply wrong value to appear in the variable. When the variable changes to its anomalous state, you stop, look at the code under the highlight bar, and (with a little luck) will smack yourself aside the head, saying, "Of course! How dumb of me!"

REPEAT UNTIL FINISHED

In practice, it will become a familiar cycle: Enter code into the edit window, run the compiler, and re-enter the editor to change your source code until the source code compiles without compile errors. That done, you run the compiled program and look for bugs. You'll probably find one or two bugs per search, perhaps (if you're more organized than I) ticking them off on a nice "to do" list. You'll find a few bugs, enter the editor to fix them, recompile, retest, verify that the "fixed" bugs have indeed been fixed (and that the repair work hasn't spawned even more bugs!), and then hunt for a few more.

Repeat the edit/compile/test/debug cycle a few times, and you'll have a program that begins to resemble what you set out to accomplish when you first sat down in front of the keyboard. Do this a few times, and you will learn a *lot* about programming. Do it for a few years, and you have a good chance of becoming one hell of a programmer.

4.3 The Structure of the IDE

That's the big picture of the Turbo Pascal development cycle using the IDE. Let's take a look at the overall structure of the IDE, and then we'll wrap up this chapter with a more detailed description of the IDE's major features. Later in this book we'll speak in more detail about debugging using the integrated debugger, as well as compiler configuration.

The IDE screen has three major parts that are on display all of the time. At the top of the screen is the menu bar, which summarizes the pull-down menus that are available to you. At the bottom of the screen is the *status line*, which offers hints on what the currently selected menu item means, and more occasionally, status information pertaining to the current activity being performed. In between the menu bar and the status line is the *desktop*, which is the backdrop for the windows that you open for your source code, and for the dialog boxes that you use to communicate with the IDE machinery.

Behind each of the words in the menu bar at the top of the screen is a *menu*. You can activate a menu and make it visible by clicking with the mouse on the appropriate word in the menu bar, or by using an appropriate keystroke combination called a *shortcut key*. Most shortcut keys are mnemonically related to what they activate, so that you'll have less trouble remembering them. You can activate the Window menu by clicking on the menu bar's Window word with the mouse, or you can also activate the Window menu by pressing the shortcut key Alt-W. (This means holding down the Alt key while pressing the W key briefly and releasing it.) Figure 4.3 shows the three parts of the IDE, with the Window menu dropped down and ready to select from. No source code file has been opened, so the desktop is empty.

The desktop is simply a gray pattern when you haven't loaded a source code file to work on. Nearly all of the time, however, you'll have a source code file loaded in a source code window, ready to edit, compile, or test.

A source code window is literally that: A movable porthole onto a source code file. The source code file is almost always larger than the physical screen and impossible to display all at once. You can slide this porthole up and down the length of your source code files by using the *scroll bar* that runs along the right edge of the window. Figure 4.4 shows the IDE with a source code file loaded and present in a window, ready to be edited or compiled and run.

THE SELECTED WINDOW

Notice in Figure 4.4 that the source code window has a double-line frame around it. This means that it is the *selected* or *active* window. You can have multiple windows open on the screen at once, but only *one* is the selected window. This is

Figure 4.3 Empty Desktop with Window Menu Dropped

```
   File   Edit   Search   Run   Compile   Debug   Tools   Options   Window   Help
┌─[■]═══════════════════════════ PARAMTST.PAS ═══════════════════════════1═[↕]═┐
│{------------------------------------------------------------------}         ▲
│{                          ParamTest                               }         ■
│{                                                                  }
│{ Doubly-linked list demo: Creates list of command-line parms      }
│{                                                                  }
│{                    by Jeff Duntemann                             }
│{                    Turbo Pascal V7.0                             }
│{                    Last update 1/2/93                            }
│{                                                                  }
│{  From: BORLAND PASCAL FROM SQUARE ONE  by Jeff Duntemann          }
│{------------------------------------------------------------------}
│
│
│PROGRAM ParamTest;
│
│TYPE
│   String80 = STRING[80];
│   PStringListNode = ^TStringListNode;
│   TStringListNode = RECORD
│                     Prior        : PStringListNode;
│                     StringData : String80;                                  ▼
├───── 1:1 ═════◄█████████████████████████████████████████████████████████►─┘
 F1 Help  F2 Save  F3 Open  Alt+F9 Compile  F9 Make  Alt+F10 Local menu
```

Figure 4.4 IDE with Single Source Code Window

the window with the double-line border. The selected window is the window that compiles when you select the Compile option from the Compile menu.

Sometimes you'll hear Turbo Pascal people speak of the "top" window on the screen; they don't mean "top" in the sense of the upper portion of the screen (where the menu bar is) but "top" in the sense of being on the top of a "pile" of windows on the surface of the screen. Suppose you took several small pieces of paper and "stuck" them to your CRT screen through the attraction of the static electricty produced by such screens. The pieces of paper could overlap, and in an overlapping group of paper scraps, only one scrap would be fully exposed; this would be the one on top of the little "pile" of paper scraps on your screen.

So it is with screen windows. You can have any reasonable number of windows open on the screen at once, and they can overlap quite heavily, but only one of the overlapping windows will be fully exposed and completely visible. This is the top window, the one that is considered selected. It is the window that the Turbo Pascal compiler will act upon when you select Compile from the Compile menu.

Figure 4.5 shows the IDE with several open windows overlapping on the screen. The selected window is the one with the double-line border.

MENUS AND CHOOSING MENU ITEMS

As I mentioned earlier, behind each of the several words in the menu bar is a *menu*. A menu is a vertically-arranged list of items that you can select to initiate some task or change a condition. A menu item is one of the items in the menu,

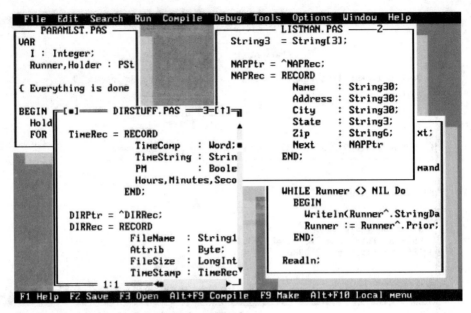

Figure 4.5 Multiple Overlapping Windows

represented by a line in that menu. There is a notation for specifying a menu item within a menu. The name of the menu comes first, and the name of the menu item follows, separated by the ASCII vertical bar character. For example, the Open item in the Files menu is tersely named Files | Open.

You can initiate an action represented by some item in a menu by *selecting* the right menu item. If you place the mouse cursor over one of the words in the menu bar and depress the left mouse button and hold it down, a menu will "drop down" from the word in the menu bar. You can then drag the highlighting bar up and down the items by simply moving the mouse up and down on its pad, while still holding the left button down. When you release the button, the menu item that was highlighted will be the item selected.

That's the "hold it down" method for menu selection with the mouse. It's the fastest way to select a menu item, and the one most Turbo experts use. There's another way that's a little more leisurely. Position the mouse cursor over one of the words in the menu bar and click once. ("Click," again, means "press and release immediately.") The menu will drop down. You can then examine the menu items at your own pace, without your mouse-button-pressing finger getting fatigued. When you decide which menu item on the dropped-down menu you wish to select, move the mouse cursor over the item and click again. The item will be selected.

ACTIVE AND "GRAYED-OUT" MENU ITEMS

As you explore the IDE's menus, you'll notice that some of the menu items are displayed in black, with one letter displayed in color. (The default color is red.)

Other menu items are displayed in gray, with no letter highlighted in red. The difference in color makes a crucial distinction: Menu items displayed in black are *active*, meaning that they can be selected and used. Menu items displayed in gray are *inactive* or *disabled*, meaning that you can click on them until the cows come home but nothing will happen. Such items, in hacker parlance, are said to be "grayed out." You cannot select a grayed-out menu item by any means. In general, if a menu item is grayed out it indicates that for the current circumstances the grayed-out menu item is meaningless.

For example, if no source code window is open, the Files I Save menu item is greyed out. If there is no open source code window, there's no source code to be saved, so selecting Files I Save would be meaningless.

MANEUVERING MENUS WITHOUT A MOUSE

As useful as the mouse is in manipulating the Borland IDE, you don't absolutely *have* to have one. The IDE can be travelled using nothing more than the PC keyboard. There are certain things (switching windows, for example) that work much more easily with the mouse, but there is nothing that absolutely *cannot* be done strictly from the keyboard. The downside is that many of the key combinations simply have to be committed to memory, and while I've done that long ago, you might find the aggravation is more than you care to endure. It's worth learning the keyboard access mechanisms if for no better reason than they're all you have if your mouse conks. (Your mouse can conk if a program you're writing mangles memory containing the mouse driver—so it isn't simply the very slight risk of your mouse failing physically or electrically.)

Here's the first thing to remember about keyboard maneuvering: *F10 gets you to the menu bar.* This is true no matter where you're starting from within the IDE. Once you're in the menu bar, reaching the rest of the system is simply a matter of steering your way left or right to the correct menu, and then down to the correct menu item within the right menu. Such maneuvering is done with the four PC arrow keys.

SHORTCUT KEYS

Getting to menu items through the keyboard is straightforward. Many of the menu items, however, can be selected without ever dropping down the menu that contains them. Take a look back at Figure 4.3. The Window menu is dropped down. Notice that on the right-hand end of the Zoom menu item is the word F5, and on the right-hand end of the Next menu item is the word F6. These are the names of function keys. The F5 function key is the *shortcut key* for the Zoom menu item. Press F5, and Window I Zoom is selected, *whether or not the Window menu is dropped down.* Zoom expands the selected window to occupy the entire desktop. Selecting Zoom again for an already-zoomed window "un-zooms" the window to the size and shape it was before it was zoomed. Press F6 and Window I Next is selected. Next makes the next window on the screen the selected window. Pressing F6 is a very quick way to switch between two opened source code windows on the screen. Table 4.1 is a quick reference of all the shortcut keys available in Turbo Pascal and Borland Pascal 7.0. Some of the keys may not quite make sense to you at this point; don't worry about it now. You'll pick them up in time.

Table 4.1 Borland and Turbo Pascal 7.0 Shortcuts

Shortcut Key	*Function*
F1	Invokes the Turbo Pascal help system
F2	Saves the file currently being edited
F3	Lets you load a new file into the editor
F4	Execute to cursor position
F5	Zooms or un-zooms the currently active window
F6	Selects the next window in the stacking order
F7	Single steps; traces into subprograms
F8	Single steps; steps over subprograms
F9	Performs a MAKE operation
F10	Returns you to the left end of the menu bar
Alt-F1	Displays the last help screen you viewed
Alt-F3	Closes the selected window (NOTE: displayed the Pick menu in V5.X!)
Alt-F5	Displays the last user (i.e., output) screen in full
Alt-F6	Switches between Watch and Output windows
Alt-F7	Go to previous error message
Alt-F8	Go to next error message
Alt-F9	Compiles the main file
Alt-F10	Brings up the local menu, if any (NOTE: Displayed the About... box in V5.X!)
Alt-B	Brings up the **B**reak/Watch menu
Alt-C	Brings up the **C**ompile menu
Alt-D	Brings up the **D**ebug menu
Alt-E	Takes you into the editor
Alt-F	Brings up the **F**iles menu
Alt-O	Brings up the **O**ptions menu
Alt-R	Brings up the **R**un menu
Alt-X	Quits the Environment and returns you to DOS
Alt-0	Displays a list of all open windows
Alt-1	Selects that window number and brings it to the top
Alt-2	Selects that window number and brings it to the top

Table 4.1 Borland and Turbo Pascal 7.0 Shortcuts (continued)

Shortcut Key	Function
Alt-3	Selects that window number and brings it to the top
Alt-4	Selects that window number and brings it to the top
Alt-5	Selects that window number and brings it to the top
Alt-6	Selects that window number and brings it to the top
Alt-7	Selects that window number and brings it to the top
Alt-8	Selects that window number and brings it to the top
Alt-9	Selects that window number and brings it to the top
Alt-Backsp	Each press undoes the next-most-recent editor change
Ctrl-F1	Shows help info for item at editor cursor
Ctrl-F2	Performs a **P**rogram reset on program under test
Ctrl-F3	Displays the **C**all Stack
Ctrl-F4	Brings up the **E**valuate dialog box
Ctrl-F5	Size or move selected window from keyboard
Ctrl-F7	Adds a watch to the watch window
Ctrl-F8	Toggles a breakpoint at the cursor line
Ctrl-F9	Runs your program
Ctrl-Del	Clear clipboard
Ctrl-Ins	Copy the highlighted text from the window to the clipboard
Shift-F1	Brings up the Turbo help index
Shift-F2	Invoke the Turbo Grep utility
Shift-F3	Invoke Turbo Assembler (BP7 only!)
Shift-F4	Invoke Turbo Debugger (BP7 only!)
Shift-F5	Invoke Turbo Profiler (BP7 only!)
Shift-F6	Select the previous window in stacking order
Shift-Del	Cut the highlighted text from the window into the clipboard
Shift-Ins	Paste text from clipboard to cursor position

Shortcut keys provide "expert access" to many elements of the IDE. (Some of the less-used menu items do not have a shortcut key, and must be accessed through the menus.) Once you've used the IDE for awhile, you'll have pressed F5 and F6 enough so that you'll remember them without any trouble. (I remember most IDE shortcut keys much better than the Magic Van's license plate number, in fact.)

One shortcut key to learn early is F2, which selects Files | Save for the selected window. You should develop a twitch in your left hand that presses F2 every five minutes or so. Turbo Pascal source code files save to disk so quickly that it won't even slow you down. Save early and often!

When learning the IDE, make it a habit to consciously try out the shortcut keys, so that you can come to remember them as soon as possible, especially for the IDE features like Zoom, Next, Save Compile, and Run that will comprise about 90 percent of all your workaday menu selections.

DIALOG BOXES AND CONTROLS

There will be times when you have to tell the IDE what to do—and just as many times when the IDE will have things to tell you as well. This give and take of information between you and the IDE happens through *dialog boxes*, which are rectangular windows that pop up as needed to accept commands from you or display information from the IDE.

Dialog boxes can be purely informational. If you select the Help menu and then click on the About... item, a dialog box will appear that gives the name and current release number of the Borland product you're using. (That is, either Borland Pascal, Turbo Pascal, Borland Pascal for Windows, or Turbo Pascal for Windows.) The dialog box has a horizontal bar toward the bottom with the word "OK" in it. When you click on the bar reading "OK" the dialog box disappears. The About... box is not much of a dialog, really, but it's a good example of how things happen between you and the IDE.

The bar that reads "OK" is a simple example of what we call a *control*. A control is a screen gadget that allows you to communicate some meaning to the IDE. It may be nothing more than a CRT pushbutton, as in the About... box, that allows you to tell the IDE to put the box away and get on with its work. A

Figure 4.6 The Open File Dialog Box

control may be a line-entry box that allows you to type words and numbers, or a list box that presents a list of items for you to pick from.

A far more complex (and far more useful) dialog box is shown in Figure 4.6. This is the Open File dialog box that allows you to specify which source code file you want to open and load into a source code window for editing.

This particular dialog box is jam-packed with controls. On the right side are four buttons, functionally equivalent to the OK button in the About... dialog box. Clicking on one of those buttons is like pushing a button on a physical control panel: It kicks off some action. Clicking on the Open button, for example, begins the process of loading the highlighted source code file into a source code window for editing. Clicking on the Cancel button closes the dialog box without taking any other action.

The bottom line of the dialog box is a read-only control: a display of the file details for the highlighted source code file. The AVERAGE.PAS file is highlighted, and down on the bottom of the box you can see how large AVERAGE.PAS is (1602 bytes) and when it was last modified.

The most interesting control is the one in the middle. It's called a *list box*, and it displays a list of things from which you can choose one item. It's like a menu, but it can contain a large number of items; more than can be displayed in the box, in fact. (Menus are limited to only the number of items that can be displayed at one time in a vertical list; something like 22.) You move the highlight bar around the file names displayed in the box by using any of the four arrow keys. You can then select the highlighted file by pressing Enter, and it will be opened and placed in a new source code window.

As with many other parts of the IDE, there's more than one way to do things with the box. You can *double-click* any of the items in the box (that is, position the mouse cursor over the item you want and click the left button twice in rapid succession) and the item you double- click on will be selected and (in this dialog box) opened and placed in a source code window.

You'll be using the Open File dialog box a lot. Experiment with it and see how all the various controls it contains interact with one another.

MANEUVERING DIALOG BOXES WITHOUT A MOUSE

As with the IDE's menu system, you don't necessarily need a mouse to use a dialog box. Everything any dialog box offers can be done from the keyboard.

The key concept here is something that doesn't really apply when you're using the mouse for everything: Every dialog box containing controls has one control at the *focus*. The focus is the destination toward which keyboard input travels. If you open a dialog box and press Enter, for example, that Enter keystroke will be sent to only one of the controls in the dialog box, the one currently at the focus.

Only controls may have the focus, and one control or another must always have the focus. You move the focus around the dialog box by pressing the Tab key. When you press Tab, the focus moves to the next control in line. Nothing else happens, though—the control to which the focus moves is not selected. You can jump the focus from one control to another all through the dialog box by repeatedly pressing the Tab key. The order in which the focus moves from control to control is called the *Tab order*. And while the tab order often broadly follows the physical left-to-right and top-to-bottom order that we might consider intuitive, *there is no guarantee that this order will prevail.*

The focus is indicated as a different color on or around the focused control. On monochrome screens, a pair of German quote marks (« and ») surrounds the focused control, because there is no distinctive color to indicate the focus.

It's worthwhile experimenting with a complex dialog box like the Open | File dialog box, just to see how the focus moves and what happens when various keystrokes are sent to the different controls as they occupy the focus.

Although it's generally spoken of in connection with dialog boxes, the notion of focus applies to the entire IDE, even when no dialog box is open. For example, when you press F10, you move the focus to the Files word on the menu bar. Unfortunately, the Tab key doesn't move the highlight along the menu bar, so the notion of Tab order breaks down some outside of dialog boxes. But in general this is a rule: Keyboard input must be directed somewhere at all times in the IDE, and that somewhere is the focus. How the focus is moved and what happens when a particular keystroke arrives at the focus may change, but there is always a focus somewhere within the IDE.

HINTS, REMINDERS, AND THE STATUS LINE

The very bottom line of the IDE is an interesting creature with several functions. It's called the *status line*, which is more than a little misleading, since most of the time what it displays is not the status of anything. Mostly what the status line does is offer you *hints* about the currently-selected menu item or control.

"Hints" is a technical term, and it means a short phrase that tells you very briefly what the selected control or menu item will do if selected. It's easy to get a feel for what the hints tell you: Pull down the IDE's various menus and watch the status line as you move from one item to another.

Hints can be extremely handy early in your IDE education, when what each of the menu items actually does is not always clear from its name alone. The Files | Save item certainly saves something, but what? Its hint reads, "Save the file in the active Edit window." This leaves almost nothing to guesswork. Over time the meaning of most of the IDE controls and menu items will become second nature and you'll probably cease noticing the hints entirely, as I generally have. But while you're still learning and uncertain of yourself, they are fine things indeed.

There will be a considerable amount of time (mostly while you're editing source code in a window) when there is no highlighted menu item, nor any highlighted control. At those times, the status line has nothing to hint about, so its function changes subtly. Look back to Figure 4.4. A single source code window is open, and no hints are needed. Instead, the status line displays several possible commands that you could select through shortcut keys. "F2 Save" reminds you that function key F2 is the shortcut key that saves the current source code window to disk. These are reminders more than hints, and again, they are most useful in the beginning when you haven't yet committed all the shortcut keys to memory.

The reminders have one additional property: If you click on them with the mouse, they execute their stated command. That is, click on "F2 Save" and your file will be saved. Click on F3, and the Files | Open command will be executed, just as though you had selected it from the menu or by pressing F3 itself. Admittedly, clicking the words "F2 Save" with the mouse may be more bother than just pressing F2. However, notice that one of the reminders reads "Alt-F9 Compile." Click on this reminder and the source code in the current source code window will be compiled. The shortcut key requires two hands (or one hand with nimble fingers): Hold down the Alt key and then press F9. If one of your hands happens already to be on the mouse, clicking the "Alt-F9" reminder may be easier than letting go of the mouse and bringing your hand to the keyboard.

The IDE often allows you a number of ways to do the same things. Learn all of them, so that you can choose the best and quickest way for the current task.

THE TURBO HELP SYSTEM

Now that you have a handle on how to "operate the controls" of the IDE, it's high time to investigate a fairly amazing resource built right into the IDE: Turbo Help. Borland has done a very good job of making their help system *context-sensitive*, meaning that different help information will be displayed depending on what you happen to be doing in the IDE when you ask for help. In many cases, just invoking help by pressing F1 will present you with a window containing a brief explanation of the part of the IDE you're currently using, or perhaps an error message that the compiler has displayed. And if the help system "guesses wrong," you always have the option of looking something up in the help index.

There are a number of ways to access the help system, and which one you use depends a lot on what sort of help you need. It can never hurt to press F1 and see what comes up. Generally, if you encounter a compile error, pressing F1 will display a short text block addressing the meaning of the error message. If you pull down a menu and move the highlight bar over one of the items in the menu, pressing F1 will bring up a help message on the highlighted menu item. Only if no windows are open and no menus are pulled down will pressing F1 bring up a generic help system "table of contents." If anything at all in the IDE is "going on," Turbo Help will try to offer its assistance!

Turbo Help will look up reserved words and predefined identifiers for you. All you need to do is place the cursor at the beginning of a reserved word or predefined (that is, defined by Borland) identifier, and then press Ctrl-F1. Turbo Help will look up the word or identifier in its index and display whatever text is available on that word or identifier. (Actually, you don't have to place the cursor slavishly at the beginning of the word or identifier to be looked up—anywhere within the word or identifier will do!)

If you try to look up an identifier that *you've* defined (or a misspelling of something Borland defined) Turbo Help will bring up the Turbo Help Index, and put the cursor on the closest item it can find to the one it looked up. Glance up and down a ways to see if you've misspelled something—and double click the correctly-spelled word or identifier to see its help text entry.

This is a specific use of some of Turbo Help's magic: Any topic listed in the Turbo Help Index is a *hot link* to the help text available for that topic. A hot link is a logical connection to a help text entry elsewhere in Turbo Help. Hot links are shown (in the default color scheme) as yellow text on the normal background. You can traverse a hot link to the text it represents by double-clicking on the yellow-colored item. The help window will clear and display the hot-linked text.

Hot links can be found here and there within the help text displayed by Turbo Help. Try double-clicking on anything in yellow text, and soon you'll get the hang of flitting around inside of the help system. Any time help is displayed, the status line will display reminders of hot keys you can use to navigate Turbo Help. A very useful one to remember if you're "threading" the hot links through Turbo Help is this: Alt-F1 "backs up"; that is, it returns you to the last help text entry you viewed. You can return all the way to your starting point by repeatedly pressing Alt-F1, so there are no "dead ends." If you can get there, you can get back.

One final help tip: If, while working with the help system, you get confused about Turbo Help's operation, press F1. You'll see "Help on Help," which explains the nuances of the help system in detail.

Pressing Esc will put the help system away and let you get back to your real work inside the IDE.

USING 43- OR 50-LINE TEXT SCREENS

Borland's IDE has the ability to work in a higher-resolution mode than the standard 25-line mode. If your CRT controller is EGA-compatible, you can display a 43-line IDE. If your CRT controller is VGA-compatible, the IDE can display as many as 50 lines of text.

The default screen configuration is 25 lines, because all PC-compatible screens can handle that. If you have an EGA or VGA and would like to use the higher-resolution text screen modes, select Options I Environment I Preferences from the menu. A large dialog box will appear. Most of what it offers are advanced configuration options that I won't be going into in this book. But in the upper left corner of the box is a pair of controls that act together to specify what text resolution your screen will use. They're labeled "Screen sizes" and there will be a small round bullet character between two parentheses to indicate which screen is currently in force. When you first bring the box up, the bullet will indicate a screen size of 25 lines. If you press the down arrow key, the bullet will move into the 43/50 line tag. (You can also click with the mouse between the empty pair of parentheses by the "43/50 lines" label to move the bullet there.) If you then click the OK button at the bottom of the box with the mouse, or tab down to the OK button and press return, the screen will instantly change to the new size.

Returning to 25-line mode is done simply by bringing up the Preferences dialog box again and moving the bullet to the "25 lines" label and clicking or tabbing to OK.

Certainly try a higher-density screen, but you have to keep in mind that the size of your monitor won't change—and the higher-density screens happen only by making the individual text characters *much* smaller. They may be too small to see comfortably on a 14" monitor. On 17" and larger monitors they work very well for me. How well they work for you depends heavily on how good your eyes are.

4.4 Creating, Saving, and Loading Source Code Files

At this point you should have a good (if perhaps rough) picture of how the IDE operates, how to get around within it, and how to engage in meaningful dialog with it. Now let's get down and spend the rest of this chapter talking about the details of using the IDE to create programs.

CREATING A BRAND NEW SOURCE CODE FILE

It starts here. When you want to create a brand new source code file, select the Files | New item. (There is no shortcut key, alas—this is one that could use a shortcut!) The IDE will create a new—and empty—source code window. At the top of the window will be the name of the window: NONAME00.PAS. If you immediately went back and selected Files | New again, you'd see a second window overlapping the first, titled NONAME01.PAS. Each time you were to select Files | New, the number at the end of the name would ratchet up by one.

To write new Pascal source code, just . . . write. Type a line, press Enter, and keep on typing. Sooner or later you'll have something resembling a program in your source code window.

SAVING SOURCE CODE IN A NEW WINDOW

But first, you had better save that new source code to disk. NONAME00.PAS to the contrary, there is no file name associated with your window. NONAME00.PAS is at best a dummy name to remind you that your program needs a name. If you go to save your file by selecting Files | Save or pressing its F2 shortcut, the Save File As dialog box appears in the center of the screen. (See Figure 4.7.) The flashing cursor will be in a line-entry control toward the top of the dialog box, marked Save File As. Enter the name of your source code file in the box and press Enter. The box will vanish, and the IDE will save your new source code in that file on disk.

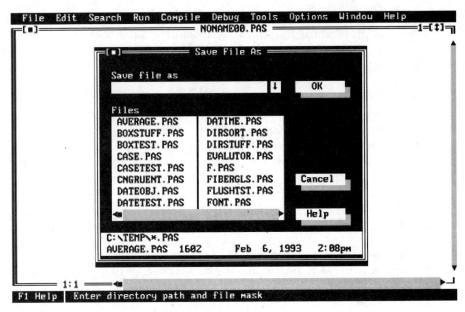

Figure 4.7 Save File As Dialog Box

There is a small and easily overlooked indicator on the bottom-left edge of every source code window that tells you if the contents of that window have been modified since the last time you saved it. It's just an asterisk, and it doesn't appear at all until you modify the contents of the window. Once you save the window's contents, the asterisk will vanish until you make some additional modifications.

LOADING SOURCE CODE THAT YOU'VE WORKED ON BEFORE

Most of the time, you'll enter the IDE to work on source code that you've worked on before. The Files | Load menu item is what you select to help you bring in an existing source code file from disk. The F3 shortcut will get select the Files | Load item without your having to go through the menus.

Files | Load brings up the Open a File dialog box, shown earlier in Figure 4.6. The list box in the center of the dialog will display the names of all of the Pascal source code files (or at least those with the file extension .PAS) existing in the working subdirectory. If the file you want to load is displayed in the list box, you can simply double-click on its name, and the IDE will load the file into a new source code window.

The file's name may not be displayed. By default, the Open a File dialog box displays files with names ending in .PAS. You can open and edit any ordinary text file in a source code window; however, the file doesn't have to contain source code, and its name doesn't have to end in .PAS. You can, for example, edit your AUTOEXEC.BAT file, or your CONFIG.SYS file in a source code window—but you'll need to be a little more clever to load it.

When you bring up the Open a File dialog box, the flashing cursor will be in the line-entry control toward the top of the box. You can simply type the name of the file—which doesn't have to be a .PAS file—into the line-entry control and press Enter. That's it—the file will be loaded into a source code window.

You may find yourself in this sort of a spot now and then: You think you remember the name of the file, but you can't quite pin it down. Was it TEST.TMP, TESTER.TMP, TESTER.SRC, or TESTEROO.TXT? Instead of entering a complete file name into the line-entry control, you can enter an *ambiguous file name*, using the same rules that apply to file names entered for the DOS DIR command. This means you can use wildcard characters like * and ? to specify what may be a group of files with similar names. To look for one of the mystery files mentioned above, you might type TEST*.* into the line-entry control, and then press Enter. If any files meeting that ambiguous file name exist in the default directory, they will be displayed in the list box. If the file you want is there, you need simply double-click on it, and the file will be loaded into a new source code window.

There's yet another possibility you may run into sooner than later: Suppose the file you want is in some subdirectory other than the default subdirectory that the Open a File dialog box displays automatically? You can cruise your hard disk's directory structure easily with the Open a File dialog, especially if you have a mouse, which makes it almost effortless. The key is to recognize directory names within the list box at the center of the dialog: *All directory names end with a backslash character.* Furthermore, directory names are displayed regardless of what other sort of file names are displayed, be they .PAS, .SRC, .TXT, or whatever. The directory names are always there.

One you should recognize from your DOS work is ..\, which is the symbol for the parent directory; that is, the directory immediately "above" your own in the DOS directory hierarchy. If you're down in C:\TP7\SOURCE, double-clicking on ..\ will take you "up" one level into C:\TP7. Once you're "up" there, you'll see the directory name SOURCE\ in the list box, indicating the directory from which you came. You can get back down there by double-clicking on SOURCE\, or you can continue by double-clicking on any other directory name, including ..\. Remember that the parent directory symbol ..\ does not exist when you're in the root directory, because the root directory has no parent directory.

4.5 Understanding Source Code Windows

Once you begin programming Pascal in earnest, you'll be spending the vast majority of your hacking hours inside an open source code window, typing text, moving text around, changing text, and (probably more than anything else) staring at text to try and figure out just what's *wrong* with it. This being the case, it would pay to spend a little time considering in detail how source code windows work and how best to use them.

MOVING AND SIZING SOURCE CODE WINDOWS

When you create a new source code window, it occupies the entire desktop. A window doesn't have to cover the entire desktop, however, and once you move into more advanced programming projects that comprise more than one source code file, you'll be having multiple source code windows on the screen at once. Screens are never as big as they should be, so some of those windows are going to overlap. You'll have to know how to move them around, and change their size.

Moving a window is easy with the mouse: You position the mouse over the top edge of the window, press the left button, and hold it down. Then you move the mouse, and the entire window will "follow" the mouse. You can even shove a goodly portion of the window right off the edge of the screen, as long as some part of the top edge of the window remains on-screen.

Sizing a window is also easy: You position the mouse cursor in the lower-right corner of the window (you'll see what I call the "elbow" character ⌋ there), press the left mouse button and hold it. Then, when you move the mouse, the size of the window will change. When the size is as you want it, just release the mouse button.

Moving or sizing a window without the mouse is a little more bother (and one superb reason to get a mouse if you don't have one!). Press the Ctrl-F5 shortcut, or select the Window|Size/Move item. The frame will change from double-line to single-line, and the status line will reflect some reminders as to what to do next. By using the four arrow keys, you can move the window in any of the four directions. By holding down the shift key while you press any of the four arrow keys, you can resize the window.

Keep in mind that while you're moving or sizing a window from the keyboard, you can't do anything else with it until you press Enter to indicate that you're done moving or sizing. Don't press Ctrl-F5, start moving or sizing the window, and get distracted. (Doorbells and phones are terrific for this, as are dogs and, for those who have them, children.) If you come back to the IDE and nothing seems to be responding to your frantic keypresses, try Enter. If you were in the middle of a size or move operation, Enter will finish things out and let you get on with your work.

But like I said, sheesh, get a mouse!

CASCADING WINDOWS VERSUS TILING THEM

Some things demonstrate a lot better than they explain. (Or at least it's better to demonstrate them *before* you explain them.) As an interesting experiment, first load a source code file into a window on an empty desktop. It will occupy the entire "gray" portion of the desktop between the menu bar and status line. Now, load a *second* file onto a desktop containing one file over the full screen. The second file will not completely cover the first. It will appear one line down and one line to the right of the first file, allowing you to see the first file's top edge and left edge. The first file's name will be clearly visible to remind you that something is indeed there, almost hidden but fully present and ready to roll when you want to go back to it.

Load a third file into a window, and look closely at what you have. (I've duplicated the display in Figure 4.8.) The three windows are arranged nicely in the fashion of three index cards in a box, offset a little so that even though only the third file is nominally visible, the names and upper edges of the first two files are still visible.

We call this technique *cascading* windows. It's a way of maximizing the exposure of the one selected window without completely hiding the other windows you had previously opened. The selected window, you recall, has a double-line border. The other two windows hiding behind it have single-line borders, indicating that they are not selected.

It's easy to move from one cascaded window to another. Just click the mouse on the top edge of the hidden window that you want to select. That window will abruptly come to the foreground; what we might consider the top of the pile of those imaginary paper scraps on the screen.

It's a little tougher to select among cascaded windows without the mouse. You must "cycle through them" by pressing the F6 shortcut key, or by selecting the Window | Next menu item. One by one the hidden windows will become selected and move to the front of the pile. Stop pressing F6 when the one you want is front-and-center. (You can press shift-F6 to "rotate" the cascaded windows in the other direction.)

There's a problem with selecting among cascaded windows. If you select the rearmost window from among the three displayed in Figure 4.8, it will come to

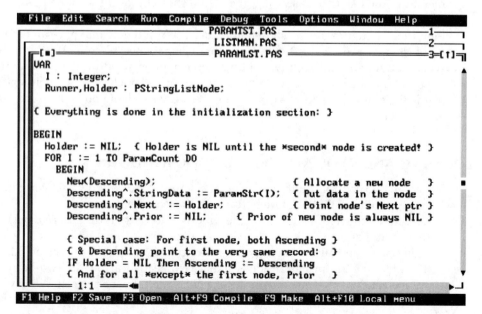

Figure 4.8 Cascaded Source Code Files

the foreground and truly cover the two other windows completely, without a trace. I've gotten confused from time to time (you will too) by forgetting that one or more windows were hiding behind the one I was working on; it was always because I had selected the rearmost of several cascaded windows, which had made it occupy the entire screen, hiding everything else that had been on-screen. The way out is to re-cascade the out-of-order windows, using the Window | Cascade menu item. They will return to their nicely "stacked" display so that all of them have at least a top edge available. Try it! Sadly, there is no shortcut key for Window | Cascade, and it's a shortcut I would dearly love to have in the IDE.

Here's a useful trick many programmers learn late or not at all: Pressing Alt-0 brings up the *window list*. The current window is listed at the top of the window list, but the last window you had on top (that is, the last one you were working in before the current window) is highlighted. You can press Enter to select the highlighted window in the window list to make it the current window. The trick is that pressing Alt-0 and Enter is a quick way to "bounce" between two windows when you have several (that is, more than just two) open at once.

Cascading is the optimal way to deal with multiple windows when you only have to see *one* window at any given time. If you actually have to look at source code within more than one open window simultaneously, it's best to use another method called *tiling*. Tiling, as its name implies, is the process of dividing the screen equally among the opened windows, much as floor space is divided equally among the linoleum tiles that cover it.

You can tile the open windows on your screen by selecting the Window | Tile menu option. (As with cascading, there's no shortcut key.) I've done this with the three windows shown cascaded in Figure 4.8, and the three windows in their tiled configuration are shown in Figure 4.9. You'll note that you can't see a whole lot in any of the three windows. In my experience, tiling is effective only when you're working with two simultaneously open windows, and no more. Beyond that, the borders of the windows take up as much room as their space inside the windows, and you don't get to see very much of your source code in any of them!

ZOOMING AND CLOSING SOURCE CODE WINDOWS

There are two controls on the top edge of a source code window that you must become familiar with: the Close button and the Zoom button.

The one on the right-hand side of the window's top edge is the *Zoom button*. It's both a control and an indicator: It tells you whether or not its window occupies the full screen, and allows you to force a window to occupy the full screen. Most of the time, the Zoom button looks like a two-headed arrow. Its two-headed arrow state indicates that your window occupies the entire text screen. When you load a file onto an empty desktop, its window will occupy the full screen, and the Zoom button's double arrow will be there at the upper-right corner.

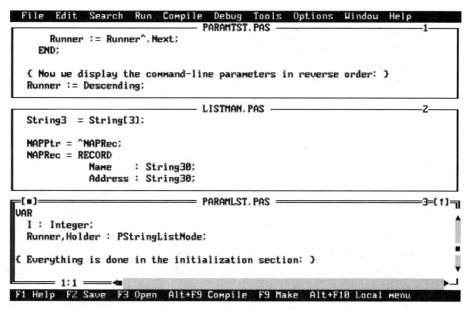

Figure 4.9 Tiled Windows

As soon as you tile or cascade multiple windows, no single window occupies the entire screen, and the Zoom button of the selected window will change to a single-headed, up-pointing arrow. Any selected window that does not, in fact, occupy the entire screen will have the single-headed arrow as its Zoom button.

The Zoom button is a way to move between the two states a window can have: occupying the entire screen ("zoomed") or occupying a portion of the screen ("un-zoomed.") If you click the mouse on the Zoom button, the window will move to its alternate state. The one exception here is that if you click the Zoom button on a new window that has always occupied the full screen, nothing will happen. The window, being new, only has one state: zoomed. Once you resize that window, or create additional windows on the screen, you'll be able to toggle between the zoomed and un-zoomed state for that or any other window on-screen.

Think of the Zoom button as alternating a window between full-screen and whatever shape/size it was before it was full-screen—including full-screen.

The button on the left-hand side of the top edge of a window is the *Close button.* As you might guess from its name, when you "push" it, the window will close and vanish. Source code windows aren't the only windows with Close buttons. Most dialog boxes have them as well. Its function is the same, wherever you see the Close button: It "puts the window away" and makes it vanish.

Here's a welcome safety feature you'll run into regularly: If you try to close a source code window that you've changed somehow but not saved, a dialog box will appear, asking you if you want to save the contents of the window before closing it. You have three choices: Save the source code in the window, *don't* save it and close the window, or cancel the close request as though nothing had happened. (See Figure 4.10.)

Why would you ever want to close a modified window without saving it? Perhaps the changes you made were a mistake. Perhaps you "tried" something by changing a few statements, and found that your experiment failed miserably and is not even worth recording. Just be careful—and don't throw away a window full of source code by accident!

4.6 Editing Text Inside a Source Code Window

The files you load into a source code window will become larger and more complex over time. Sooner than you expect, you'll begin cutting your projects up into units, each of which has one or more source code files all its own. Any significant programming project at all is going to have 10 to 20 source code files, if you've done your design correctly. Learning how to edit such quantities of source code effectively is the second most important Pascal skill there is— second only to your knowledge of the language itself.

MOVING AROUND INSIDE A WINDOW

The flashing hardware cursor is where things happen inside an edit window. If you type new text, it is placed at the hardware cursor, and if you delete text by pressing the Del key, it vanishes into the hardware cursor, with the text on the

Figure 4.10 Closing a Changed Window

right pulling over toward the cursor. Obviously, getting the cursor where you want it in a hurry is a key editing skill.

When a file is loaded into a window for editing, the cursor begins in the upper-right corner of the window. This is considered line 1, column 1. You can see the current position of the cursor displayed in the lower edge of the selected window, toward the left corner. The position is given as <line>:<column>, with the figures separated by a colon. Columns indicate the horizontal position of the cursor, lines indicate the vertical position. Both are relative to the file you're editing, and not to the source code window. That is, if you're editing line 200, it's 200 lines from the top of the file, not (obviously) from the top of the source code window you're working in!

The easiest way to move around for short distances is to use the four PC arrow keys. A press on the left or right arrow keys will move the cursor one character position to the left or right on a line. If you're already in column 1, pressing the left arrow key will *not* change the cursor position.

The PgUp and PgDn keys move the cursor one window height in the appropriate direction. A "window height" is one line less than the number of lines currently visible in the source code window you're using. For a window zoomed to the full screen, that's 20 lines. If only 10 text lines of the window were exposed, pressing PgUp or PgDn would move the cursor only nine lines.

The Home key moves the cursor to the left end of the cursor's current line; that is, to column 1. The End key moves the cursor to the last visible character (that is, to the last non-space character) in the line.

Getting to the beginning of the file or to the end of the file involves a pair of double-control character sequences. (Command sequences like this will be *very* familiar to you if you've ever spent any amount of time at all using the Wordstar word-processing product.) Moving to the top of the file is done with Ctrl-Q-R; that is, by holding down the Ctrl key and then pressing the Q and the R key in sequence. You can hold Ctrl down while pressing both keys, or you can let go after pressing the Q. Either way will execute the cursor-move command. Getting to the bottom of the file is done with Ctrl-Q-C, pressed in a similar fashion.

HOW TO USE SCROLL BARS

Source code windows in the Borland IDE have a pair of interesting gadgets attached to them: Scroll bars. A scroll bar is a way of moving the cursor's position through the entire length of the file by moving a marker up and down a vertical line that represents the full length of the file. (There are horizontal scroll bars as well; they're used less often and I'll explain them shortly.)

Look at the right-hand edge of any window containing a source code file longer than the window itself. The entire right-hand edge of the window is taken up by a gray line. This is the body of the scroll bar proper. At the top and the bottom of the scroll bar are triangles pointing up and down. Somewhere on the gray bar is a single character block with a small square or rectangle inside it.

This has various names in computing; some call it the *elevator*, and others the *thumb*. I prefer to call it the elevator, and that's the term I'll be using in this book.

The "magic" in a scroll bar is simply this: The length of the gray bar represents the length of the file. The position of the elevator on the gray bar represents the relative position of the cursor within the file. That is, if the elevator is halfway down the length of the gray bar, that means that the cursor is halfway between the top and the bottom of the file, no matter how long the file is. In a 1000-line file, the cursor would be on or near line 500; in a 200-line file, the cursor would be on or near line 100. If the elevator appears to be one third of the way down the length of the gray bar, the cursor is one third of the way down the length of the file, and so on. The scroll bar tells you at a glance about how far down the file the cursor is.

The elevator works both ways. It tells you where the cursor is, proportionately, within the edited file. It can also be used to move the cursor if you have a mouse. Place the mouse cursor block over the elevator and hold down the left mouse button. You can then drag the elevator up or down the scroll bar, and let go of the mouse button when the elevator is, proportionately, where you want the cursor to go within the file. That is, if you "drop" the elevator halfway down the scroll bar, the cursor will be moved to the halfway point in the file. If you drop the elevator to the top of the scroll bar, the cursor will be moved to the top of the file.

The triangles at the top and bottom of the scroll bar are also controls. Click on the top triangle, and the cursor will move one line toward the top of the file. Click on the bottom triangle, and the cursor will move one line toward the bottom of the file.

This is easier to try than to explain. Load a longish file into a source code window (plenty of sizable Pascal source code files come along with both Borland Pascal and Turbo Pascal) and mess around with the scroll bar. It's perhaps the one feature I can think of in the IDE that absolutely *requires* you to have a mouse to use it, and is an excellent argument for getting one.

MARKING, COPYING, AND MOVING TEXT

A fundamental editing skill is marking, copying, and moving text. The IDE makes it relatively easy. Once text is marked, you can move it from one place to another in the file, or copy it into a temporary buffer called the *clipboard*, from which you can copy it to other places in the same file, or even into other files entirely.

Marking text is easiest with the mouse. Move the mouse cursor to the start of the text you want to mark, and press the left mouse button. While holding the left button down, move the mouse cursor to the end of the text block that you wish to mark. Let go of the button. You'll see on the screen that the text has been highlighted in a distinctive color. The highlighted text is now considered marked.

You can mark text without using the mouse, though it's a lot more hammering on the keyboard. There are two ways to do it. The easy way is to hold down the shift key and move the up or down arrow key. Each line the cursor moves through while you hold down the shift key will be highlighted.

The old way is to move the cursor to the start of the text block any way you can, and press Ctrl-K-B, in the same manner as I described above for moving between the ends of the file. Ctrl-K-B indicates the beginning of the text block to be marked. Move the cursor to the end of the block to be marked, and type Ctrl-K-K. All the text between the two positions will be highlighted, indicating that it is now marked.

Once a block of text is marked, you can move it, delete it, copy it to another position in the file, or copy it into the clipboard.

Deleting it is easy. Simply press Ctrl-Del and the marked text disappears. (The older WordStar key combination Ctrl-K-Y does the same thing.)

Moving the text is also easy. Move the cursor to the position where you want the marked text to be moved, and press Ctrl-K-V. The text will vanish from its original position and reappear at the cursor position.

You can make a second copy of the marked text block (perhaps a procedure header or a boilerplate comment block) just as easily, and in much the same way: Move the cursor to where you want the duplicate text block to appear, and press Ctrl-K-C. The duplicate text will appear, and it will remain highlighted. This allows you to move the cursor yet again to a new position, and copy the highlighted text again to that new position, without having to go to the bother of marking the same block of text a second time. You can repeat the copy process as often as you like. Just move the cursor to a new position and press Ctrl-K-C.

THE NOTION OF THE CLIPBOARD

It's easy enough moving text from one place in a source code file to another. Moving text from one *window* to another (a very common operation once you begin dividing your programs up into multiple units) takes a slightly different mechanism.

The Borland IDE contains a temporary buffer area called the *clipboard*. Because the clipboard is not part of any window but is "global" to *all* windows, you can cut or copy text into the clipboard, and then "paste" this text into an entirely different source code file being edited in its own source code window.

To copy marked text into the clipboard, simply press Ctrl-Ins. The marked text will remain in the original window, since you copied it. If you want to move text from one window to another, you must "cut" the text from the first window. The Shift-Del command will remove the marked text block from the first window into the clipboard. You can then select another window, and "paste" the text from the clipboard into the second window by pressing Shift-Ins.

If you ever lose track of what's in the clipboard, you can select the Edit | Show clipboard menu item. This will open a window showing you what's in the clipboard. You can even edit the text that's in the clipboard, and your changes can be copied into other windows along with the text originally moved into the clipboard. There's one caution: For the text in the clipboard to be pasted into a file, *it must be highlighted*. Only the highlighted portions of the clipboard will paste! If you type new text into the clipboard window, be sure to highlight the entire contents of the clipboard before closing the clipboard window!

To clear the clipboard and make it totally empty, select Edit | Show clipboard, and then press Ctrl-Del.

SUMMARY OF THE EDITING COMMAND KEYS

There are a fair number of command key combinations that allow you to work without the use of the mouse. Most of them aren't on the menus anywhere, either—so remembering them is up to you. Table 4.2 summarizes the major key combinations. There are a few others I won't go into here that will be familiar to WordStar users—consult Borland's documentation for details.

4.7 Compiling Your Source Code

Compared to the complications of text editing, compiling your source code to native code is simplicity itself. This is largely due to the "I do it all—no hassles"

Table 4.2 The Keystroke Commands for Text Editing

Command	*What It Does*
Ctrl-Q-R	Move to the top (beginning) of the edit file
Ctrl-Q-C	Move to the bottom (end) of the edit file
Ctrl-Ins	Copy highlighted text into the clipboard
Shift-Del	Cut highlighted text into the clipboard
Shift-Ins	Paste text from clipboard to cursor position
Ctrl-Del	Deletes the highlighted text
Ctrl-K-B	Cursor indicates beginning of text block to be marked
Ctrl-K-K	Cursor indicates end of text block to be marked
Ctrl-K-Y	Delete the highlighted text (Identical to Ctrl-Del.)
Ctrl-K-C	Copy the highlighted text to the cursor position
Ctrl-K-V	Move the highlighted text to the cursor position
Ctrl-T	Delete the word containing the cursor
Ctrl-Y	Delete the entire line containing the cursor
Alt-BkSp	Undo last command (Goes back one change each time you press it.)
Shift-Arrow keys	Mark text

attitude of Borland's Pascal compilers. The compile and link steps are combined into one, and it happens with a speed that the C partisans can only dream about. You can do a fair amount of compiler configuration as you come to understand the programming process better, but when you're starting out, configuring the compiler simply isn't necessary. The standard compiler defaults work just about perfectly for learning projects, and you don't need to "fool with" the compiler at all until you have a fair amount of experience under your belt.

THE COMPILE DESTINATION

Borland's Pascal compilers are examples of what are called *translator* programs: They look at an input file (your source code file) and use it as a blueprint for creating an object code file. In a sense, they translate your source code into object code. How this happens is one of the blackest of black arts, and I'll only say that it does work: The compiler scans your source code file, and writes out a sequence of machine instructions. Where these machine instructions go is called the *compile destination*.

With Turbo Pascal for DOS, you have your choice of two destinations: memory or disk. (Borland Pascal and Turbo Pascal for Windows compile only to disk.) Writing object code to disk is easy to understand: The compiler creates a file with the same name as your source code file, only with a .EXE file extension. (Unit files, which also consist of object code, are compiled to files with .TPU, .TPP, or TPW extensions, as I'll explain later in this book.) It writes the machine instructions it generates to that .EXE file. Later on, you can load the .EXE file into memory and run it.

The idea behind compiling to memory as a destination is this: If you need to have your object code in memory to run it anyway, why waste time writing it out to disk? If the compiler writes your object code into memory, you can execute it right from memory without any further delay.

Compiling to disk is very fast (especially if you have a fast machine), but if you have a lot of source code to compile, and if compilation is going to produce a large .EXE file, all that disk I/O could take significant amounts of time. Compilation to memory, by comparison, is nearly instantaneous for short programs.

The IDE defaults to compiling object code to disk. You can change the compile destination by selecting the Compile | Destination item. The destination itself is displayed immediately to the right of the menu item. It will read one of two things: "Disk" or "Memory." Each time you select the Compile | Destination item, the destination is toggled to its alternate state. No other action is required of you.

If you're working in Real Mode (and if you're using Turbo Pascal, you're always working in real mode), you may find that your programs eventually take up too much room to allow them to be written out to memory. In that case you may simply have to write object code to disk. It's one of the first things you should do if you begin getting "Out of memory" errors at compile-time.

COMPILE, MAKE, OR BUILD?

The Compile menu has three options that actually do the compiling. One of them, Compile I Compile, is straightforward: It compiles the source code file in the selected window. That's the one you'll be using most often, especially as you're first learning the Pascal language. So what of the others: Compile I Make and Compile I Build? It might be a little early to explain Make and Build fully; I'll be treating them again in detail in Chapter 21. But I want to give you a sense of what they do.

Neither Make nor Build is useful until you begin cutting up your programs into multiple modules. In Turbo and Borland Pascal, a modular program consists of a single main program and one or more libraries called *units*. You compile these modules separately, and the IDE's built-in linker hooks them together into a single, runnable .EXE file. Now, when your project consists of multiple source code files, there comes the question—What gets compiled? And what gets run when you go to test your program?

It's a tricky question with a tricky answer. What gets compiled? *Everything that needs to get compiled.* And what is run when you want to test your program? Something called the *Primary File*.

THE PRIMARY FILE

The key is this: You can carve a project up into multiple source code files for editing and compilation, but when you come to run your program, it generally exists as a single piece of code. There is only *one* main program, and that main program is what is run when you choose to run your program from the IDE. You need to somehow identify the source code file that contains your main program block to the IDE. You do this by naming it as the Primary File.

You name the Primary File by selecting the Compile I Primary File item. A dialog box appears that looks a lot like the Open a File dialog box. You can either type in a new file name or click on an existing file name. Either way, the aim is to select one .PAS file from whichever ones exist as your primary file. The dialog box will allow you to enter the name of a file that doesn't exist, but the compiler will present you with an error message if you try to compile it.

Once you've identified the Primary File to the IDE, you can merrily begin writing separate modules that are to be linked into your Primary File. The mechanics of how this is done can wait until Chapter 13; look ahead if you're confident and curious. But in a nutshell, your Primary File "uses" your module (i.e., unit) files; that is, your main program can call routines written in separate source code modules. You can have just about as many of these separate source code modules as you want, and work on them in any order that you want.

What's interesting is the way the IDE pulls them all together. Any time you work on any of your separate source code modules in a multi-module program, you use the Compile I Make menu item to compile your program, which by virtue of existing in multiple modules is no longer "just" a program, but is now called a *project*. By selecting Compile | Make, you are in essence telling the IDE that you want to compile your *project*, and the IDE decides which of your project's sundry components needs compiling. It then "makes" your final .EXE file from the multiple modules as it knows best how to do.

In the process, more modules may be recompiled than the single one you happen to be working on. Why? Well, in working on your current module, you may have taken some round pegs and made them square pegs. But off in another module that you haven't worked on since last week is a set of round holes that expect to fit around your round pegs. If you've made some of those pegs square, the code won't all fit together correctly when the linker tries to glue your modules into a single .EXE file.

The IDE knows that there is a *dependency* between those two modules: One has pegs and the other has holes and the two must mesh to get their jobs done. So it compiles both modules, and when it discovers square pegs bound for round holes, it gives you a compile error, alerting you to the fact that there is still work to be done. Once you make sure all the pegs and holes match, you select Compile | Make again, and the IDE will compile everything that must be compiled according to the dependencies that it recognizes.

As I said, I'll be treating the issue of modular programming in detail in Chapter 13 and again in Chapter 21, but it won't hurt you to begin thinking about modular programming *now*. Sooner or later it will become absolutely essential.

Finally, what of Compile | Build? Unlike Make, which recompiles only those modules that the IDE knows need compiling, Build recompiles *everything*. You won't use Build much; it's a waste of time to recompile an entire multi-module project when only one or two source code files really need to be compiled. But there will come times when you suspect peculiar incompatibilities among your modules and you want to "start clean" with a total recompilation. That's mostly what Build is for. You'll know when you need it.

UNDERSTANDING COMPILE ERRORS

As a beginning student of Pascal, you'll be more concerned with compile errors than with program bugs. Just getting things to compile correctly will seem triumph enough; later on, you'll begin to see that debugging is by far the harder and more rewarding pursuit. For now, you're going to be running into compile errors by the boatload. Let's talk a little bit about how to understand them and put them right.

First of all, as soon as you attempt to compile and receive a compile error, press F1. As I've said elsewhere, F1 invokes Borland's help system, an encyclopedia of explanations about how the IDE and Pascal operate. The help system has a certain amount of understanding of what you're doing within the IDE, so when certain things like compile errors happen, it's right there waiting to offer its assistance. If you press F1 at a compile error, a dialog box will appear with a brief explanation of the error message.

Suppose, for example, that you declare a variable **I** of type **Integer**, and attempt to compile the following statement:

    I := 'A';

This will not compile, for what may not yet seem an obvious reason: That **I** and the literal constant 'A' are two incompatible types. The compile error in the red bar across the top of the screen will read: *Error 26: Type mismatch*. That's a good clue, but it isn't everything that's available. Press F1, and a window will appear looking like that shown in Figure 4.11. That gives you something a little more to chew on! That and some meditation (and perhaps some perusal of Chapter 5) should start turning on the lights. Let the IDE do as much of the work as it can. Make liberal help of Turbo Help.

4.8 Running Your Programs

Sooner or later, the compiler will present you with a clean bill of health. Then you can do what you really came here for: The chance to run a program you've written yourself. It's done via the Run I Run menu item. Select Run I Run, and the IDE will "step aside" and vanish, letting your program take control of the machine. Your program will run, and when it finishes running, will return control of the machine back to the IDE. The IDE will reappear, ready for you to edit other portions of your program and continue the edit/compile/run development cycle.

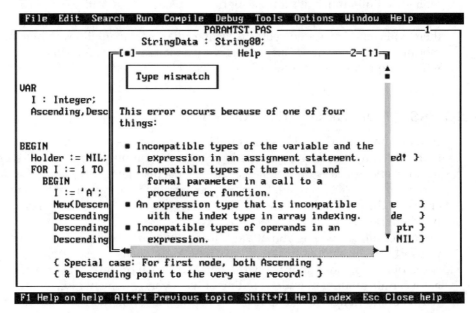

Figure 4.11 The Turbo Help Window

If your program simply runs and doesn't pause for you to press Enter before it hands the machine back to the IDE, it may run too quickly to allow you to read any information it may have written to the screen. Adding a **Readln;** right before the final **END.** statement of short programs is one easy way to pause the program and allow you to read its output. But if the output slips past you and the IDE regains control, don't panic: Your program's output is still there. To see the *output screen* (as it is called) you simply press Alt-F5 or select Window I Output.

Once the output is displayed, remember that you can only look at it; your program has *not* returned from the dead! (Don't try to type in any commands to it.) You're only seeing its effects. Press any key to return to the IDE screen.

ENDLESS LOOPS AND HUNG MACHINES

Every so often (and early in your career, lots oftener than seldomer) you'll run a program from the IDE, and the program just won't "let go." It'll appear to be running endlessly, or perhaps appear to be stuck dead in its tracks. It may be one or the other, and it's sometimes hard to tell which.

There are two different sorts of problems involved here: endless loops and program crashes. An endless loop is just that: Somehow your program is chasing around inside one of Pascal's looping statements, but cannot make the loop go to completion and end. Usually this means that the variable that governs the loop isn't being changed, or else it's being changed in a direction that won't satisfy the loop. (That is, it's being counted *up* rather than counted down.) I've pulled a slick stunt a time or two where one part of the loop counts the governing variable down, but another part a few statements later counts the same variable up again—leaving the variable "stuck" at one value and the loop endless.

A program crash is just that: Your program has written over something that the operating system needs, and has thrown your machine into some kind of anomalous state. You generally don't run into problems like this until you begin playing with pointers and machine memory, but eventually it happens to the best of us.

If your program won't complete execution and hand the machine back to the IDE, here's what you do:

1. First, press Ctrl-Break; that is, hold down the Ctrl key and press the Break key. This sometimes works and sometimes doesn't. It depends on whether you have the built-in **CheckBreak** variable set to **True** (which is its default state, and which should be maintained while you're testing and developing an application) and whether your endless loop performs some sort of screen I/O. If there is no screen I/O inside the endless loop, you won't be able to break out of the loop, regardless of the state of **CheckBreak**. See Section 8.9 for more on **CheckBreak**.

2. If Ctrl-Break doesn't work, then you aren't going to get out of your bind gracefully. The next step is to reboot out of things, by pressing Ctrl-Alt-Del. (The time-honored PC "three-finger salute.") You will lose any un-

saved changes to your edit file this way. Having done this a time or three, I now set the IDE to save the active window every time before I run the program under development.

3. Your crash may have wasted the interrupt vector table in low memory, and if that happens, even the keyboard won't be able to reboot the system. Push the hardware reset button if you have one, and power down if you don't. (Wait a full 10 seconds after the fan stops before powering up again.) Needless to say, any unsaved edit changes will be lost. Be a saver!

Finding the culprit that crashed you is always a challenge unless you did something really blatantly stupid. Initial advice: *Turn on range checking and numerical overflow checking!* Certain kinds of "mortal sins" are captured by Pascal's error-checking—if you enable error-checking. I'll be talking about these configuration options in Chapter 15.

Overall, you're unlikely to get into serious problems until you start doing more exotic things; you shouldn't try anything too terribly exotic until you have a solid grounding in Pascal and understand the issues involved in using pointers and making DOS and BIOS calls, or heaven knows, dropping down into assembly language.

As far as finding fatal bugs is concerned, look first for any statement that writes to memory. Go through a code listing with a highlighter, and highlight any suspicious statements. Then look very closely at each highlighted area. Is the statement writing to memory where it should? Is it writing *past* where you want it to, and "stepping on" anything important? See if any pointers are used before they're initialized. See if you de-referenced a NIL pointer. (Range checking will catch that one.) See if you've done any gonzo type-casting. Finally, look with suspicion on any assembly-language routines you've written yourself. That's *very* advanced Pascal, to say the least.

It sounds scary, but with experience you'll make this kind of mistake less often. And hey, if it was easy, *everybody* would be doing it—and what fun would *that* be?

PART TWO

The Core of
the Language

Having gotten a feeling for both programming and the "big picture" of Pascal itself, it's now time to focus on the details of both the Pascal language and the programming process. And therein lies a snag for me.

I'd like to be able to say, "Read this book from cover to cover and you'll learn Pascal." That's how I think books of this sort work best. The problem with teaching Pascal in a strictly linear fashion is that it's a continuous, linear narrative that weaves all of Pascal's ideas together in a single undifferentiated line. There would be no "chapter" on simple data types, because you have to introduce simple data types right alongside of reserved words, identifiers, operators, and so on. This reads well in the fashion of a novel, but it doesn't *re-read* very well. By that I mean that once you've read it, you may feel that your understanding of derived types is fuzzy, and you may want to go back and re-read a discussion of derived types. But in a strictly linear exposition of Pascal, derived types are discussed in no one place, but here, there, and in several other places. Like all the other topics, they weave in now and again in the one big story.

There's the rub: People reading about Pascal for the first time might want to see every idea introduced in its turn. People reviewing their knowledge of Pascal, by contrast, are going to want a chapter on data structures and a separate chapter on program flow control. There's no pleasing everybody, I guess. Another problem with grouping ideas into chapters by topics is that here and there you have to use concepts you haven't explained yet to explain concepts you haven't explained yet, if you know what I mean.

Once I've laid the groundwork it'll be a lot easier. But in laying the groundwork I've had to make a number of seemingly arbitrary decisions: Do I explain first what reserved words and identifiers are, and then explain what data is? Or do I explain data types first, so that I can explain how reserved words and identifiers come together to make statements?

Maybe it's a silly thing to worry about. But I'm trying hard to make this book accessible to the total newcomer to the idea of programming, and putting across the foundations of *any* idea is absolutely critical.

So I guess you'll have to cut me a little slack for the first two or three chapters in our detailed tour of Turbo Pascal. I've chosen to begin with data, because data has become more and more central to the idea of *all* programming, and not just programming in Pascal. I don't have the space to exhaustively cover object-oriented programming in this book (that's a whole separate book that I hope to write soon), but I'll get into the basics of OOP in Chapter 25. In the meantime, it might help to point out somewhat prematurely that object-oriented programming repositions data at the center of the programming universe, so you might as well get used to thinking of data in some very fundamental contexts.

It will also help if you've already read Chapter 2, which presents an overview of most of the fundamental ideas of Pascal. If you haven't, you really *really* ought to go back and read it now. The overview material will definitely help bridge the chicken-and-egg dependencies you'll find in the next several chapters.

In the interest of keeping related material close together, I've chosen to put certain facts and bits of information in these initial chapters that some people might consider "advanced Pascal." Alas, advanced is often in the eye of the beholder, and I disagree with a lot of people as to what's advanced and what isn't. I don't think it hurts to know how many bytes of memory a data type occupies. If such information doesn't seem immediately relevant, move on. All knowledge becomes valuable sooner or later.

Mostly, it will help if you just pay attention, and are willing to tuck a fuzzy fact off in the corner of your mind for a moment while I explain something else that may help bring that fuzzy fact back into focus.

Once you've got the core of the language under your belt, the problem goes away.

Really.

Chapter **5**

Simple Data Types

BECOMING FAMILIAR WITH NUMBERS, CHARACTERS, AND BOOLEANS

Data is the raw material of computing. We delight in creating the machinery that manipulates the data, but the data is what we buy or sell and ultimately live by. The machinery of programming lies empty without it. Good programs coalesce around a solid, detailed vision of what data should be, both coming into a process and leaving it.

So let's look at the idea of data, and the way that Pascal defines and manipulates it.

5.1 The Notion of Types and Type Conflicts

Data is chunks of information that your program manipulates. There are different *types* of data, depending on what the data is intended to represent. How your program handles your variables depends completely on what type you decide they are. Every variable used in a Pascal program must be declared to be of some type, with a notation like this:

```
CreditHours : Integer;
```

The variable's identifier comes first, followed by the name of the type that you choose to define that variable by. The definition shown above allows you to manipulate integer values in a variable called **CreditHours**, subject to Pascal's explicit limitations on what can be done with **Integer** types.

I didn't show it explicitly in the above definition, but variable definitions must reside in the *variable definition section* of a Pascal program. The reserved word **VAR** begins the variable definition section, and it runs until another program section (say, a procedure or a function, or the main program) begins. The variable definition section of a program (and there may be more than one in Turbo Pascal) is where you give names to variables and assign them types.

115

THE NATURE OF TYPES

At the lowest level, all data in a Pascal program (or any program, really) is stored as binary numbers somewhere in your computer's memory. The data type of a data item to some extent dictates the way those binary numbers are arranged in memory, and to a greater extent dictates how you as a human being will use that data. The type of a data item is actually a set of rules governing the storage and use of that data item. Data takes up space in memory. The type of a data item dictates how much space is needed and how the data is represented in that space. An integer, for example, always occupies two bytes of memory. The most significant bit of an integer carries the sign of the number the integer represents.

Type also governs how a data item may be used. The simplest example: What is the letter "A" plus 17? That's a meaningless question, since a letter is not the same sort of thing as a number. They're used in different ways and "mean" in different ways when we think about them. In Pascal, a letter is of type **Char** (short for "character," obviously) and 17 is type **Integer**, from the technical term for a number (either positive or negative) with no decimal part. Pascal's rules of typing prevent you from adding two incompatible types like **Char** and **Integer**. The compiler will not compile any such attempt, and would give you a type conflict error for trying.

Char and **Integer** are of different sizes in memory, so they have a sort of natural incompatibility between them. However, the size of a type has very little to do with the rules that govern it. Type **Char** and type **Byte** are both single bytes in memory, but you can add or multiply two variables of type **Byte**. Attempting to use variables of type **Char** in an arithmetic expression will generate an error.

The Pascal language incorporates *strong typing*, which means that there are strict rules concerning how individual types may be used, and especially on how variables of one type may be assigned to variables of another type. In most cases, a variable of one type may not be assigned to a variable of a different type. (The major exception is with numeric types, which have a broad compatibility with one another. We'll discuss this issue a little later.) Transferring information between variables across type boundaries is usually done with "transfer functions" that depend upon well-defined relationships between types. Transfer functions will be described in Chapter 9.

Simple types (which embrace all types described in this chapter) are "unstructured"; that is, they are data "atoms" that cannot be broken down into simpler data types.

PASCAL'S FUNDAMENTAL DATA TYPES

All compilers implementing the Pascal language share a certain number of fundamental "atomic" data types. These types express some of the most basic concepts of computing: text, numbers, and truth and falsehood. From these

fundamental types you can build data structures to model practically any data "idea" you can think of, as I'll discuss in more detail in Chapter 7.
Here are those atomic types:

- *Integers* are numbers (including negative numbers) that cannot have decimal points, like 1, -17, and 4529.

- *Characters* (indicated by predefined identifier **Char**) consist of the ASCII character codes from 0 to 127. These include all the common letters, numbers, and symbols used by all modern computers. Borland extends the definition of type **Char** to include those first 128 ASCII characters plus an additional 128 characters containing foreign language characters, mathematical symbols, and those very useful "line-draw" characters used to make boxes on the screen. Don't be confused by the fact that the ASCII character codes are numbered. **Char** is not a numeric type; just because Box #3 has a number doesn't make it a number rather than a box!

- *Boolean* types have only two possible values, **True** and **False**. They are sometimes called "flags." Pascal uses them in conditional statements like **IF/THEN/ELSE** and **REPEAT/UNTIL** to determine whether to take some action or not. Boolean types will become very important in Chapter 8, where I'll explain how you can use Boolean values and Pascal's control statements to produce structured programs.

- *Real* type variables are used to express "real numbers," numbers that may include a decimal part. 1.16, -3240, 6.338, and -74.0457 are all real numbers.

BORLAND'S SIMPLE DATA TYPES

In addition to these elementary data types understood by all Pascal compilers, Turbo Pascal adds several of its own.

- **Byte** is a numeric type that can contain values from 0 to 255. **Byte** is an example of an *unsigned* or *cardinal* numeric type, meaning that it cannot take on a negative value. (That is, it can have neither a positive nor a negative sign in front of it, as can most of the standard numeric types. **Byte** types are assumed to be positive.) Byte gets its name from the fact that it occupies one single byte in memory. (Integers occupy two bytes, and some of the more esoteric numeric types occupy as many as 10.)

- **Word** is like **Byte** in that it is unsigned and cannot hold negative values. Like **Integer** it occupies two bytes of memory. **Word** types are sometimes referred to, in fact, as "unsigned integers." They may contain values from 0 to 65,535. **Word** variables are handy at times because they can hold positive numbers twice as large as type **Integer** can.

- **LongInt** is what its name implies: a "long integer." It occupies four bytes in memory rather than two, as **Integer** types do. Its range is dazzlingly greater than **Integer**, however, and can express values from -2147483648 to

2147483647. Note that you *cannot* use commas to break up the expression of large numbers in Pascal, as we often do in ordinary day-to-day correspondence. So while spitting out a number like 214748647 seems awkward without the commas, do get used to it; it's simply the way we do things in computing.

- **ShortInt** is another numeric type related to **Integer**, in that it holds signed numeric values. Its range, however, is limited to -128 to 127, and it occupies only one byte in memory. It is, in fact, a "signed byte."

There are a number of additional numeric values defined in Borland's Pascals. These are the real number types supported by the PC's numeric coprocessors, and I'll address them in detail in Section 5.7

5.2 Simple Constants

Constants are data values that are "baked into" your source code and do not change during the execution of a program. There are two kinds of simple constants in Standard Pascal: literal and named. Turbo Pascal provides a third kind of constant that is not really a constant: typed constants; that is, constants that have a specified type and can be data structures like arrays and records. I'll discuss typed constants after I've had a chance to explain data structures, in Section 7.10.

LITERAL VERSUS NAMED CONSTANTS

A *literal constant* is a value of some sort that is stated as a value where it is used in your code. For example:

```
SphereVolume  :=  (4/3)*PI*(Radius*Radius*Radius);
```

In this line of code, "4" and "3" are literal constants, representing the values of 4 and 3.

There is another constant in that statement: The identifier **PI** was previously declared a constant in the *constant declaration part* of the program. The constant declaration part begins with the reserved word **CONST** and runs until some other part of the program begins. The constant declaration part is typically very early in a program, and is often the very first part of a program after the program name statement:

```
PROGRAM AreaCalc;

CONST
PI = 3.14159;
```

Here, **PI** is a *named constant*. We could as well have used the literal constant 3.14159 in the statement, but "**PI**" is shorter and makes the expression less cluttered and more readable. Especially where numbers are concerned, named constants almost always make a program more readable.

Another use for constants is in the setting of program parameters that need changing only very rarely. They still *might* be changed someday; if you use a named constant, changing the constant *anywhere in the program* is only a matter of changing the constant's declaration *once* in the constant declaration part of the program and then recompiling.

The alternative is to hunt through hundreds or thousands of lines of source code to find every instance of a literal constant to change it. You will almost certainly miss at least one, and the resultant bug farm may cost you dearly.

In short, don't use literal constants anywhere you will *ever* anticipate needing changes. In mathematical formulae literal constants are usually OK; but keep in mind that using a named constant in place of a literal constant allows you to control the precision of the constant everywhere in the program, from one constant definition. You may want to use pi to eight decimal places initially, but later on, to improve program performance, you may decide that five decimal places is plenty. If you define the mathematical constant pi in a Pascal named constant at the front of your program, you can change the precision instantly just by changing the definition—and not have to worry about forgetting one or two places where you had hard-coded a specific value of pi into an expression.

CONSTANTS AND THEIR TYPES

In Standard Pascal, constants may be simple types, strings, and sets only. (I'll be covering sets in detail in Chapter 7.) That group includes real numbers, integers, bytes, characters, strings, sets, and Booleans. Individual enumerated types may also be considered constants, although they are not declared the same way other constants are. (Like sets, enumerated types are derived types that I'll cover in Section 7.3.) Structured types like records, pointers, and arrays may *not* be constants in Standard Pascal. Turbo Pascal supports data structure constants, (see Section 7.10) but we must cover data structures first before we can speak of them.

Here are some sample named constants of various types:

```
CONST
    PI           = 3.14159;      { Floating point real  }
    Threshold    = -71.47;       { Negative FP real      }
    PenIOAddress = $06;          { Hexadecimal value     }
    Using8087    = True;         { Boolean               }
    DriveUnit    = 'A';          { Character             }
    Revision     = 'V2.61B';     { String                }
    Answer       = 42;           { Integer               }
    NotAnswer    = -42;          { Negative integer      }
    YesSet       = ['Y','y'];    { Set                   }
    NullString   = '';           { Null (empty) string   }
    BigNum    = 6117834 { Long integer or real }
```

I haven't said much about strings yet (and will cover them in detail in Section 7.9, and again throughout Chapter 10), but string literals are easy to understand: You enclose some sequence of ASCII characters between single-quote marks:

```
'wild (at our first) beasts uttered human words'
```

Literal string constants like this may be assigned to string variables later on in the program.

CONSTANTS VERSUS VARIABLES

How is a constant different from a variable? The obvious difference is that the value of a constant is set at compile time. You cannot assign a value to a simple constant in an assignment statement. Given the list of constants above, you could not legally code:

```
Answer := 47;
```

because **Answer** is a constant that already has a value of 42.

In Turbo Pascal, simple constants are written into the code by the compiler as immediate data. Variables are kept separate from the code portion of a program. Constants, therefore, do not take up room in your data segment. This is an advanced-topics issue, but an important one: You have only *one* data segment in Turbo Pascal, and when your program begins to get large you must use it carefully to avoid filling it completely.

The type of a constant depends, to some extent, on its context. Consider:

```
VAR
    Tiny   : Byte;      { One byte                   }
    Little : Integer;   { An integer (2 bytes)       }
    Big    : LongInt    { A long integer (4 bytes)   }
    Huge   : Real;      { A real number (6 bytes)    }

    Tiny   := Answer;
    Little := Answer;
    Big    := Answer;

    Huge   := Answer;
```

In the code snippet given a little earlier, **Answer**'s value is defined as 42. But it is perfectly legal to assign the value of **Answer** to type **Byte**, type **Integer**, type **LongInt**, or type **Real**. The code the compiler generates to do the assignment in each case is a little different. But the end result is that all three variables of three different types will each express a value of 42 in its own fashion.

Except under very special (and peculiar) circumstances, the type of a variable is fixed and unambiguous.

NOTES ON LITERAL CONSTANTS

A dollar sign ($) in front of a numeric literal means that the compiler will interpret the literal as a hexadecimal number. The numeric literal may *not* have a decimal point if it is to be considered hexadecimal.

Inside string literals, lowercase and uppercase characters are distinct. If you wish to include a single quote mark inside a string literal, you must use two single quotes together:

```
Writeln('>>You haven''t gotten it right yet...');
```

This line of code will display the following line on your CRT:

```
>>You haven't gotten it right yet...
```

5.3 Constant Expressions (Version 5.0 and Later)

With release 5.0, Turbo Pascal introduced the concept of *constant expressions* to the Pascal language. Prior to release 5.0, a named constant could be defined in only one way: by stating its name and equating it to a single literal value:

```
THR = $3F8;
```

A constant expression allows you to give a value to a named constant in terms of an expression that is evaluated at compile time. I haven't covered expressions in detail yet, but you may look ahead to Chapter 6 if you would like to understand constant expressions fully at this point; otherwise, return to this section once you've had a chance to use and understand expressions. Constant expressions are considered an advanced topic, and should be used with care, and only once you fully understand how they work.

An expression, briefly, is a combination of identifiers, values, and operators that "cooks down" to a single value. Expressions resemble portions of equations from physics, into which you plug necessary values and finally evaluate to a single value:

```
Kinetic energy = Mass * Velocity²
```

Once you know **Mass** and **Velocity**, you can plug their values into the equation and "do the math" to come up with a value for **Kinetic energy**.

It's much the same way with constant expressions. The value of a constant is given in terms of a combination of operators, values, and constants defined earlier in the program:

```
COMPORT  = 1;     { 1 = COM1:  2 = COM2: }
COMBASE  = $2F8;  { Build on this "magic number" }

{ Base I/O port is $3F8 for COM1: and $2F8 for COM2: }
PORTBASE = COMBASE OR (COMPORT SHL 8);
```

Here, **COMPORT** and **COMBASE** are simple named constants, whereas the constant **PORTBASE** is defined in terms of a constant expression. When the compiler encounters the constant expression during its compilation of the program, it "does the math" and assigns the resulting value to the named constant **PORTBASE**.

LIMITATIONS OF CONSTANT EXPRESSIONS

If you're familiar with expressions as they occur in normal Pascal statements, you may be wondering if any legal expression may be assigned to a constant. The answer is emphatically *no*; constant expressions are *much* more limited. Legal elements of a constant expression are these:

- *Literal constants.* These include numeric literals like 42 and 17.00576, the Boolean literals **True** and **False**, and quoted string and character literals.

- *Previously defined constants.* In other words, named constants defined earlier in the program, like **COMPORT** and **THRBASE** in the example above.

- *Pascal operators.* These are the arithmetic operators like addition and subtraction, the logical operators like AND and OR, and the bitwise operators like AND, OR, SHR, SHL, and so on. For a complete discussion of Turbo Pascal's operators, see Chapter 6.

- *Certain built-in functions.* A very few of Turbo Pascal's built-in functions may take part in constant expressions. These include **Ord**, **Chr**, **Odd**, **Hi**, **Lo**, **Length**, **Abs**, **Pred**, **Succ**, and **Swap**. All other functions, including those you write yourself and those built into the compiler (like **Sqr** and **Cos**) are illegal. (For those of you who can appreciate the differences, Turbo Pascal generates code for "functions" like **Abs** in-line, while other functions like **Sqrt** and **Cos** are true functions that must be called from the runtime library. **Abs** and its kin are more properly *macros* than functions, and can be evaluated in-line by the compiler during compilation.)

Although it might be obvious to veteran Pascal hackers, it's worth stating clearly that *variables cannot be part of a constant expression.* Turbo Pascal allows constants to be defined after variables are declared (as Standard Pascal does not), but not after variables are assigned values. This means that, at best, a variable would introduce an undefined quantity into a constant expression, which is far less than useful.

SOME EXAMPLES OF CONSTANT EXPRESSIONS

The best way to show what's possible with constant expressions is to put a few in front of you. The following are all legal, if not necessarily useful in every case.

```
CONST
  Platter   = 1;
  FirstSide = Odd(Platter);   { Boolean }
  FlipSide  = NOT FirstSide;  { Boolean}

  Yesses    = ['Y','y'];      { Character set }
  Noes      = ['N','n'];      { Character set }
  Answers   = Yesses + Noes;  { Union of 2 sets }

  USHoller  = 'ATTENTION!! ';     { String }
```

```
USGasMsg   = 'Fuel level is low!'; { String }
USGasWarn = USHoller + USGasMsg;  { String concatenation }
USWarnSiz = Length(USGasWarn);    { String length }

LongSide  = 17;
ShortSide = 6;
TankDepth = 8;
Volume    = LongSide * ShortSide * TankDepth;
```

WHY USE CONSTANT EXPRESSIONS?

There are two excellent reasons to use constant expressions: reconfiguration and documentation. Both relate to the use of what I call "magic numbers" in program development.

Many programs use values that may be defined once in a program and are never modified. These include mathematical constants, and I/O port numbers and bit numbers for low-level control of system hardware. These "magic numbers" aren't expected to change, but to be safe, they should always be defined as constants rather than written as dozens or hundreds of literals shotgunned throughout a program.

An excellent example of reconfiguration through constant expressions involves programming the communications port on the PC. The PC supports two serial ports, COM1: and COM2:. They are accessed through different sets of I/O ports, and the differences in the port addresses follow an unchanging relationship. By defining a single constant specifying either COM1: or COM2:, the control port addresses may be recalculated in constant expressions based on that single port number definition. This is what the following code (part of which was given earlier) does:

```
CONST
  COMPORT  = 1;       { 1 = COM1:  2 = COM2: }
  COMBASE  = $2F8; { Build on this "magic number" }

  { Base I/O port is $3F8 for COM1: and $2F8 for COM2: }
  PORTBASE = COMBASE OR (COMPORT SHL 8);

  { Transmit Holding Register is write-only at the base port: }
  THR = PORTBASE;

  { Receive Buffer Register is read-only at the base port: }
  RBR = PORTBASE;

  IER = PORTBASE + 1; { Interrupt Enable register }
  IIR = PORTBASE + 2; { Interrupt identification register }
  LCR = PORTBASE + 3; { Line control register }
  MCR = PORTBASE + 4; { Modem control register }
  LSR = PORTBASE + 5; { Line status register }
```

```
MSR = PORTBASE + 6;   { Modem status register }
SCR = PORTBASE + 7;   { Scratch register }
```

Every one of the constants defined in this code fragment has a different value depending on whether the COM1: or COM2: serial port is to be used. By changing the value of the constant **COMPORT** from 1 to 2, *all* the other constants change accordingly to the values that apply to serial port COM2:. The program does not need to be peppered with magic numbers like $2FC and $3FA. Also, your program does not need to spend time initializing all these port numbers as variables, because the compiler does all the calculation at compile time, and the resulting values are inserted as immediate data into the code generated from your source file.

The other use for constant expressions helps your programs document themselves. You may need some sort of mathematical "fudge factor" in a complicated program. You can define it as a simple named real-number constant:

```
Fudge = 8.8059;
```

No one, looking at the literal numeric value, would have any idea of its derivation. If the value is in fact the result of an established formula, it can help readability to make the formula part of a constant expression:

```
ZincOxideDensity = 5.606;
Fudge = ZincOxideDensity * (PI / 2);
```

Because the expression is evaluated at compile time, there is *no* performance penalty over using a literal constant. This will help others (or maybe even you) to keep in mind that you had to fudge things by multiplying the density of zinc oxide by pi over 2. (That is, assuming you want the world to know.)

The idea should never be far from your mind that Pascal programs are meant to be *read*. If you can't read them, you can't change them (or fix them) and then you might as well throw them away and start from scratch. Do whatever you can to make your programs readable. You (or your eventual replacement) will be glad you did.

5.4 Pascal's Ordinal Types in Detail

CHARACTERS

Type **Char** (character) is an ISO Standard Pascal type, present in all implementations of Pascal. It's considered an *ordinal type*, meaning that it has a limited number of discrete values that exist in one well-defined and ordered series. Pascal's non-numeric ordinal types include **Char** and **Boolean**. Enumerated types are also considered ordinal, but I'll treat them separately in Chapter 7.

The best way to explain ordinal types is through a close look at the most common such type: **Char**. Type **Char** includes the familiar ASCII character set:

letters, numbers, common symbols, and the "unprintable" control characters like carriage return, backspace, tab, etc. There are 128 characters in the ASCII character set. But type **Char** actually includes 256 different values, since a character is expressed as an 8-bit byte. (8 bits may encode 256 different values.) The "other" 128 characters have no names or meanings as standard as the ASCII character set. When printed to the CRT of the IBM PC, the "high" 128 characters display as foreign language characters, segments of boxes, or mathematical symbols.

How, then, to represent characters in your program? The key lies in the concept of *ordinality*. There are 256 different characters included in type **Char**. These characters exist in a specific ordered sequence numbered 0,1,2,3, and onward up to 255. The 65th character (counting from 0, remember) is always capital A. The 32nd character is always a space, and so on.

An ordinal number is a number indicating a position in an ordered series. A character's position in the sequence of type **Char** is its ordinality. The ordinality of capital A is 65. The ordinality of capital B is 66, and so on. Any character in type **Char** can be unambiguously expressed by its ordinality, using the standard "transfer function" **Chr**.

A capital A may be expressed as the character literal 'A'. It may also be expressed as **Chr(65)**. The expression **Chr(65)** may be used anywhere you would use the character literal 'A'.

Beyond the limits of the ASCII character set, the **Chr** function is the only reasonable way to express a character. The character expressed as **Chr(234)** will display on the IBM PC screen as the Greek capital letter omega (Ω) but may be displayed as something else on another computer that is not PC-compatible. It is best to express such characters using the function **Chr**.

Characters are stored in memory as single bytes, expressed as binary numbers from 0–255.

What will Pascal allow you to do with variables of type **Char**?

1. You can write them to the screen or printer using **Write** and **Writeln**:

```
Writeln('A');
Write(Chr(234));
Write(UnitChar);    { UnitChar is type Char }
```

2. You can concatenate them with string variables using the string concatenation operator (**+**) or the **Concat** built-in function: (See Section 10.2.)

```
ErrorString := Concat('Disk error on drive ',UnitChar);
DriveSpec   := UnitChar + ':' + FileName;
```

3. You can derive the ordinality or characters with the **Ord** transfer function:

```
BounceValue := 31+Ord(UnitChar);
```

Ord returns a numeric value giving the ordinality of the character parameter. **Ord** allows you to perform arithmetic operations on the ordinality of a character. I'll discuss this in more detail in connection with transfer functions in Section 9.5.

4. You can compare characters to one another with relational operators like =, >, <, >=, <=, and <>. (See Chapter 6.) This is due to the way characters are ordered in a series. What you are actually comparing is the ordinality of the two characters in their series when you use relational operators. For example, when you see:

```
'a' > 'A'
```

(which evaluates to a boolean value of **True**) the computer is actually performing a comparison of the ordinalities of 'a' and 'A':

```
97 > 65
```

Since 'a' is positioned *after* 'A' in the series of characters, its ordinality is larger, and therefore 'a' is in fact "greater than" 'A'.

5.5 Booleans

Type **Boolean** is part of ISO Standard Pascal. A Boolean variable has only two possible values, **True** and **False**. Like type **Char**, type **Boolean** is an ordinal type, which means it has a fixed number of possible values that exist in a definite order. In this order, **False** comes before **True**. By using the transfer function **Ord** you would find that:

Ord(False) returns the value 0.

Ord(True) returns the value 1.

The words **True** and **False** are predefined identifiers in Pascal. The compiler predefines them as constants of type **Boolean**. As with any predefined identifier, the compiler will allow you to define them as something other than Boolean constants, but that is a thoroughly bad idea.

A Boolean variable occupies only a single byte in memory. The actual words **True** and **False** are not physically present in a Boolean variable. When a Boolean variable contains the value **True**, it actually contains the binary number 01. When a Boolean variable contains the value **False**, it actually contains the binary number 00. If you write a Boolean variable to a disk file, the binary values 00 or 01 will be physically written to the disk. However, when you print or display a Boolean variable using **Write** or **Writeln**, the binary values are recognized by program code and the words "**TRUE**" or "**FALSE**" (in uppercase ASCII characters) will be substituted for the binary 00 and 01.

Boolean variables are used to store the results of expressions using the relational operators =, >, <, <>, >=, and <=, and the set operators +, *, -. (Operators and expressions will be discussed more fully in Chapter 6.) An expression such as "**2 < 3**" is easy enough to evaluate; logically you would say that the statement "two is less than three" is "true." If this were put as an expression in Pascal, the expression would return a Boolean value of **True**, which could be assigned to a Boolean variable and saved for later processing:

```
OK := 2 < 3;
```

This assignment statement stores a Boolean value of **True** into the Boolean variable **OK**. The value of **OK** can later be tested with an **IF..THEN..ELSE** statement, with different actions taken by the code depending on the value assigned to **OK**:

```
OK := 2 < 3;
IF OK THEN
    Writeln('>>Two comes before three, not after!')
ELSE
    Writeln('>>We are all in very serious trouble...');
```

Boolean variables are also used to alter the flow of program control in the **WHILE..DO** statement and the **REPEAT..UNTIL** statement. (See Sections 8.5 and 8.6.)

5.6 Integer Types in Detail

Turbo Pascal 4.0 and later add considerable richness to the Standard Pascal suite of numeric types. Integer types **ShortInt**, **Word**, and **LongInt**, and real types **Single**, **Double**, **Extended**, and **Comp** are all new and did not exist in version 3.0. With all that power comes a few problems, and certainly a lot more to remember.

BYTES

Numeric type **Byte** is *not* present in ISO Standard Pascal, although most microcomputer implementations of Pascal include it. Type **Byte** may be thought of as an unsigned "half-precision" integer. It may express numeric values from 0 to 255. Like **Char**, **Byte** is stored in memory as an 8-bit byte. On the lowest machine level, therefore, **Byte** and **Char** are exactly the same. They only differ in what the compiler will allow you to do with them.

Byte variables may not share an assignment statement with any type that is not an integer type. Assigning a variable of type **Byte** with a variable or constant of any of the real number types, or with **Boolean**, **Char**, or any other nonnumeric type will be flagged with this error:

```
Error 26: Type Mismatch
```

Type **Byte** may be freely included in expressions with the other numeric types described in this section. Type **Byte** may not, however, be assigned a numeric value of type **Real**, **Single**, **Double**, **Extended**, or **Comp**.

RANGE ERRORS

Variables of type **Byte** may *not* take on negative values. If you try to assign a negative constant to a variable of type **Byte**, you will get this message:

```
Error 76: Constant out of range
```

Assigning a "signed" variable (like **Integer**, **ShortInt**, or **LongInt**) to **Byte** is perfectly safe *unless the signed variable contains a negative value.*

The compiler will not detect the problem when you compile your program. Difficulties will appear at runtime; that is, when you actually run the program you have written. Two things may happen, depending on whether you have enabled range checking during the compilation of the program.

If range checking was *on*, you will see a runtime error message similar to this:

```
Runtime error 201 at 3101:0058
```

The two numbers at the end are the segment and offset address of the point in your object code at which the error occurred, and will be different depending on your machine and your program. (If this means nothing to you, that's all right; you can write fabulous programs in Turbo Pascal without ever fully understanding PC addresses. I'll cover them, however, in Chapter 24.)

If you received the error while running your program from within the Turbo Pascal Environment, you can press any key and the Environment will send you back into the Editor. At the top of the screen you will see the message:

```
Error 201: Range check error
```

and the cursor will be flashing at the point in the code where the error occurred. Of course, if you were simply executing a standalone program from DOS, the more cryptic error message will be all you'll have to go on.

If range checking was *not* on when you compiled the program, the program, in essence, will punt. It will do its best to pour a signed value into an unsigned variable; what ends up in the variable depends on the physical bit-pattern of the negative value. To put it mildly, such errors are unpredictable, and because they happen in statements that work perfectly well most of the time, they can take a *great* deal of time and headscratching to locate and fix.

This kind of error, known generically as a "range error," will also happen if you attempt to assign a value larger than 255 to type **Byte**. In general, each numeric type has a defined range, and if you enable range checking from the **Options** menu, assigning a value outside that range to a variable will generate a runtime error. This applies to the other numeric types discussed below as well as for type **Byte**.

SHORT INTEGERS

First cousin to type **Byte** is type **ShortInt**, a signed version of **Byte**. It may express values between -128 and 127. The problems of range errors exist for **ShortInt** just as they do for type **Byte**. **ShortInt** exists to provide a little bit of efficiency to programs that use a lot of small, signed values. If you use a lot of numeric variables, or (especially) large arrays of numeric variables, and can be sure the values will never wander out of the range -128..127, you can save a lot of space by using **ShortInt** variables instead of type **Integer**.

Bit 7 of a **ShortInt** is the sign bit. (See Figure 5.1.) If this bit is set to 1, the value is considered to be negative.

There is no significant speed improvement to be had by using **ShortInt** over larger numeric types, however. You might intuitively think physically small variables would be operated on more quickly than larger ones, but this is not necessarily the case. In fact, it takes the newer (that is, post-8088) Intel CPU chips *longer* to process single-byte quantities like **Byte** and **ShortInt** variables than it does to process 16-bit or even 32-bit quantities. This is because chips like the 286 fetch and process data in 16-bit chunks, and chips like the 386 and 486 fetch and process data in 32-bit chunks. The newer CPUs must "stoop and grab" more often when data exists in 8-bit chunks, and hence take longer to do repetitive operations. Use **Byte** and **ShortInt** to save space, not time!

INTEGERS

Type **Integer** is a part of ISO Standard Pascal. Integers may express a range of values from -32768 to 32767. Integers are always whole numbers. They cannot have decimal parts. In Pascal, only real number types (**Real**, **Single**, **Double**, and **Extended**) can have decimal parts.

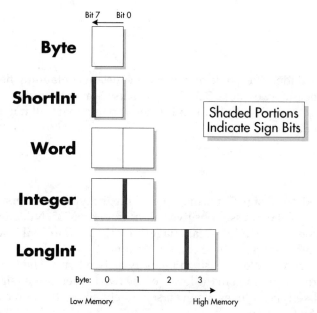

Figure 5.1 Memory Representation of Integer Types

Integers are stored in memory as two bytes. (See Figure 5.1.) The highest-order bit of the byte higher in memory is the sign bit, which indicates whether the value expressed by the integer is positive or negative. If this high bit is a binary 1, then the integer has a negative sign. If the high bit is a binary 0, the integer is positive.

HI AND LO

You separate an integer into its two bytes by using a pair of built-in functions: **Hi** and **Lo**. As you might expect, **Hi** returns the higher of the integer's two bytes in memory, and **Lo** returns the lower. For example, given the integer 17,353 (hexadecimal equivalent $43C9)

Hi(17353) will return 67 (hex $43)

Lo(17353) will return 201 (hex $C9)

Note in using **Hi** and **Lo** on integers that the sign bit is treated as just another bit in the high byte returned by **Hi**, and will not cause the value returned by either **Hi** or **Lo** to be returned as a negative quantity. For example, given the negative integer constant -21,244 (hex $AD04)

Hi(-21244) will return 173 (hex $AD)

Lo(-21244) will return 4 (hex $04)

This is definitely an advanced topic, and you'll not be doing this sort of thing a great deal.

MAXINT

There is a predefined identifier **MaxInt** which is a constant containing the maximum value an integer may express: 32767. You can use **MaxInt** in tests to ensure that you do not try to apply values to an Integer variable that will not fit, and could hence trigger a range error.

WORDS

Turbo Pascal added an unsigned partner to the **Integer** type with Version 4.0. This is type **Word**, and it expresses positive values from 0..65535. Niklaus Wirth added a similar type to his Modula-2 language, but called it **Cardinal** instead of **Word**. (Unsigned types are sometimes called "cardinal types.")

Like type **Integer**, type **Word** exists in memory as two bytes. The low-order portion of the word is contained in the lower of the two in memory, as shown in Figure 5.1. Also, like type **Integer**, you can separately access the two bytes by using the **Hi** and **Lo** functions:

```
VAR
   HiByte,LoByte : Byte;
   MyWord        : Word;

HiByte := Hi(MyWord);
LoByte := Lo(MyWord);
```

LONG INTEGERS

In Turbo Pascal 3.0, the largest number of objects you could count was only 32,767. That might seem like a lot, but on considering the computer's own ability to handle millions of bytes of RAM memory and tens or even hundreds of millions of bytes of disk storage, it suddenly looks like small change indeed. Turbo Pascal added the **LongInt** type to Version 4.0 to deal with the pressing need to count Many Things.

Type **LongInt** has the range of -2,147,483,648..2,147,483,647. This can handle any memory or disk system we're likely to be able to afford for at least another year or two. (1 gigabyte hard disks are now commonplace, if still expensive.) Note that you cannot use commas in writing long integer literal constants in compilable code.

LongInt is implemented as four bytes (see Figure 5.1) with bit 7 of the highest order byte used as the sign bit.

MAXLONGINT

Turbo Pascal 4.0 and later versions add a predefined variable of type **LongInt** named **MaxLongInt**. This is a constant with the value 2,147,483,647. It exists for the same reasons as the predefined constant **MaxInt**, and can be used in much the same ways.

5.7 Floating-Point Types in Detail

All the data types described up to this point have been ordinal types or scalar types. Ordinal types are types with a limited number of possible values, existing in a definite order. Type **Char** is an ordinal type, as is **Boolean**, and all enumerated types. (See Section 7.3 for more on enumerated types.)

If an ordinal type directly expresses a numeric value, it is called a *scalar type*. Type **Integer** is an ordinal type, since there are exactly 65,535 integer values. They are ordered and sharply defined: After 6 comes 7, after 7 comes 8, and so on, with no possible values in between. **Integer** is also a scalar type, since its values are numeric values, and not some other symbolic constants encoded internally as numeric values, as are **Boolean**'s **True** and **False**. All scalars are ordinals, but only ordinal types expressing numeric values are scalars.

Scalar types have absolute precision; that is, the value of the integer 6 is exactly six. (I have a marvelous button reading "2+2 = 5 . . . for large values of 2.")

The real world demands a way to deal with fractions. So ISO Standard Pascal supports type **Real**, which can express numbers with fractions and exponents. Numbers like this are known as *real numbers* in mathematics, and are directly expressed in type **Real**. Real numbers, especially very large ones or very small ones, do *not* have absolute precision. For example, **1.6125E10** is a real number having an exponent. You might expand the exponent and write it as 16,125,000,000. This notation implies that we know the value precisely—yet we do not. A real number offers a fixed number of *significant figures* and an exponent giving us an order of magnitude, but there is a certain amount of "fuzz" in the value. The digits after the 5 in 16,125,000,000 are zeroes because we do not know what they really are. The measurements that produced the number were not precise enough to pin down the last six digits—so they are left as zeroes to express the order of magnitude that the exponent expressed in the exponential form **1.6125E10**.

Real number types cannot be scalar types due to this lack of absolute precision.

Real numbers are "real" in that they are usually used in the scientific and engineering community to represent measurements made of things in the real world. Integers, by contrast, are largely mathematical in nature, and express abstract values usually generated by logic or calculation and not by physical measurement of some object in the real world.

Real numbers may be expressed two ways in Turbo Pascal. One way, as we have seen, is with a mantissa (1.6125) giving the significant figures, and an exponent (E10) giving the order of magnitude. This form is used for very large and very small numbers. For very small numbers, the exponent would be negative: **1.6125E-10**. You would read this number as "One point six one two five times ten to the negative tenth."

The second way to express a real number is with a decimal point: **121.402**, **3.14159**, **0.0056**, **-16.6**, and so on.

MATH COPROCESSOR TYPES

Type **Real** is represented in memory as six bytes, giving real numbers a range of 10^{-38} to 10^{38} with 11 significant figures. Type **Real** is available in all versions of Turbo Pascal, all the way back to version 1.0.

Beginning with version 4.0, a number of additional real number types become available for use. In version 4.0, these types depend on the presence of a math coprocessor; version 4.0 code making use of them will not run correctly (or possibly at all!) on machines without a math coprocessor installed.

Version 5.0 fixed this limitation, and it and all later versions of Turbo Pascal allow you to use the math coprocessor types whether you have a math coprocessor or not. They're still called "math coprocessor types" because these types are directly supported by the logic on the Intel family of math coprocessor chips. (These include the 8087, 80287, and 80387. The 486DX CPUs contain a math coprocessor right on the main CPU chip, but the 486SX does not.) Code that makes use of the math coprocessor types will run much faster on machines that have math coprocessors than on those that don't.

The math coprocessor types are **Single, Double, Extended,** and **Comp.** Whether or not the compiler will accept statements that use one of these floating-point types depends on whether the **$N** Numerics compiler directive is active. Since the default for **$N** is passive, you must either configure the compiler for numerics code generation, or else place the **{$N+}** directive at the beginning of your source file to avoid the following error:

```
Error 116: Must be in 8087 mode to compile this
```

Note that variables of one of the coprocessor-dependent types may be *defined* regardless of the state of the **$N** directive; errors occur *only* if one of the defined variables is actually *used* within a program or subprogram **BEGIN/END** block.

THE IEEE FLOATING-POINT TYPES

The coprocessor-based floating-point types (**Single, Double,** and **Extended**) are fully compatible with the IEEE floating-point specification, which is a well-established industry standard way of expressing floating-point values in memory. (**Comp** is a slightly weird special case, and I will address it separately a little later on.)

The IEEE floating-point types differ considerably in size and range:

- **Single** is a "single-precision" real number type. It is implemented in four bytes, and has a range of 10^{-38} to 10^{38}. This is the same *range* as the six-byte **Real** type, but because **Single** is implemented as only four bytes instead of six, it has less *precision* and will only yield 6 or 7 significant figures of accuracy. Calculations incorporating **Single** values will occur significantly faster than equivalent calculations using type **Real**, due both to **Single**'s smaller size and (when possible) its implementation in the silicon of the coprocessor.

- **Double** is a "double-precision" real number type. This type is identical to the 8-byte real number format used in the now-obsolete Version 3.0 Turbo-87 Pascal for the PC. *If you need to read real number values written to a physical file using Turbo-87 Pascal, read them into variables of type **Double**.* Type **Double** has a range of 10^{-307} to 10^{307}, with 16 significant figures of accuracy.

- **Extended** implements what the 8087 refers to as a "temporary real." It is expressed as 10 bytes in memory and has the astonishing range of 10^{-4932} to 10^{4932} with 19 significant figures of accuracy. This is the most accurate and widest-ranging of any numeric type understood by the math coprocessor, and there are subtle dangers involved in using it. The name "temporary" as used in Intel's math coprocessor is quite apt: Whether you use type **Extended** in your programs or not, the math coprocessor has the type available to temporarily store intermediate values that might not be fully expressible in type **Double**. If you do a lot of calculations using enormous values in variables of type **Extended**, *the math coprocessor no longer has a larger type to use to tuck away intermediate values*. In other words, if during a calculation an intermediate result appears that is larger than 10^{4932}, the math coprocessor simply doesn't have any way to express it, and a numeric overflow occurs. Your calculation will be inaccurate in range or precision or both, and a runtime error will terminate your program's execution.

INTERMEDIATE RESULTS AND SUBEXPRESSION PROMOTION

This may be further understood in terms of what happens "behind the scenes" during calculations of very involved mathematical expressions. The Turbo Pascal compiler evaluates expressions from left to right, "promoting" the type of the intermediate result to a larger numeric type as it goes. For example, consider this code snippet:

```
VAR
  RS : Single;
  RD : Double;

RS := 9.144E35; RD := 8.66543E255;
RS := ((RS*RS)*RD)/9.95E306;
```

The first portion of the expression to be evaluated is the subexpression **(RS*RS)**. Since the intermediate result generated by evaluating this subexpression has a magnitude of 10^{70}, it is well beyond the range of type **Single**, which has a maximum positive magnitude of 10^{38}. Even though both variables in the subexpression are of type **Single**, the compiler "promotes" the intermediate value to type **Double**, whose maximum positive range of 10^{308} can comfortably handle it.

Having evaluated the subexpression **(RS*RS)**, the compiler moves to the right, and multiplies that intermediate result by the value of **Double** variable **RD**, which at this point has a magnitude of 10^{255}. The new intermediate result has a magnitude of 10^{326}. This is beyond the 10^{308} expressible by type **Double**, so the compiler promotes the intermediate result to type **Extended**. Finally, the intermediate result is divided by a literal constant with a magnitude of 10^{306}. This reduces the magnitude of the intermediate result to 10^{20}, which is comfortably within the range of type **Single**.

Now, what would have happened had there not been a type **Extended** for the intermediate result to be promoted to during the evaluation of this expression? Turbo Pascal would have assigned the pseudo-value **INF** to the expression, and this pseudo-value would have carried through the evaluation and been assigned to **Single** variable **RS**, even though **RS** had enough range to accommodate the final result. And while **INF** is a defined and legal IEEE floating-point value, it is a difficult thing to respond to in ordinary arithmetical calculations.

Note that the general principles of promoting intermediate results as required applies to integer as well as floating-point expressions. The lesson in the previous example is that in expressions containing variables of type **Extended**, there is nothing larger to store intermediate results in case of an overflow to IEEE infinity. Use **Extended** with extreme care, not only in writing expressions so as to minimize the "explosion" of intermediate results, but also in keeping an eye on the values taken on by **Extended** variables at runtime.

MATH COPROCESSOR EMULATION (VERSION 5.0 AND LATER)

Turbo Pascal 4.0 requires a math coprocessor chip to make use of the IEEE floating-point real number types. This is no longer the case, starting with version 5.0. Turbo Pascal since 5.0 *emulates* the math coprocessor chip entirely in software, allowing you to run software that uses the math coprocessor types whether you have a math coprocessor in your machine or not.

Like many compromises, it's a good news/bad news situation. The good news is that having a math coprocessor allows the math coprocessor types to be used with maximum speed. The bad news is that emulating the math coprocessor makes for considerably slower real number operations. Slower, in fact, than using the old-fashioned 6-byte type **Real**.

Everything connected with floating-point operations turns on what sort of code is generated by the compiler to handle floating-point work. There are basically three kinds of floating code that can be generated. Which kind of code is generated depends on what real number types you use, and also on the state of the **$N** and **$E** compiler directives.

Software Reals. This is the code generated to support type Turbo Pascal's original type **Real**, regardless of whether you have a math coprocessor installed, and regardless of the state of the **$N** or **$E** compiler directives.

Hardware IEEE Reals. The code for hardware IEEE real number support requires the presence of a math coprocessor. Coprocessor-specific instructions are generated directly and used directly. This is the fastest and most compact floating-point support provided by Turbo Pascal. You can select it by asserting **$N+** and **$E-**, meaning that math coprocessor types are supported (**$N+**), but that math coprocessor emulation is turned off (**$E-**). Don't use it unless you *know* that your generated code will *always* be run on a machine with a math coprocessor. Executing 87-specific opcodes on a machine without an '87 will almost always send the machine into the bushes.

Emulated IEEE Reals. Emulation lets you have it both ways. For each coprocessor-specific instruction, Turbo Pascal links in an emulation routine that mimics that instruction's actions using ordinary 8086/286/386 instructions. When you run a program containing emulated IEEE real number support, the runtime library queries the machine at runtime for the presence of a math coprocessor. If no coprocessor is found, the emulation routines do the work of the coprocessor, at some cost in speed. If a math coprocessor *is* found, however, the emulation routines are "short circuited" and the coprocessor-specific instructions are used instead. Therefore, if your target machine has a math coprocessor, your math code will run nearly as fast as with pure hardware real number support. Otherwise, your math will be IEEE-compatible, but relatively slow. Emulation is selected by asserting both **$N+** and **$E+**.

SELECTING YOUR FLOATING-POINT SUPPORT

Floating-point support is controlled by the **$N** and **$E** compiler directives. The default state is **$N-** and **$E+**. **$N+** allows you to use the IEEE floating-point types, whereas **$N-** will limit you to type **Real**.

The **$E** directive was introduced with version 5.0. It stands for Emulation. **$E+** enables floating-point emulation, and **$E-** disables it. **$E** defers to **$N**, in that if **$N-** is in force, the coprocessor types may *not* be used, even if emulation is enabled with **$E+**. Also, using the **$E+** causes the floating-point emulation library to be linked into your program, increasing its size. The different combinations of **$N** and **$E** are summarized here:

- Use **$N-** and **$E-** to force the use of type **Real**. Math coprocessors are unnecessary and are ignored.

- Use **$N+** and **$E-** for pure hardware IEEE real support. This mode *requires* the math coprocessor, and gives you the fastest possible real-number calculation.

- Use **$N+** and **$E+** for emulated IEEE real support. This will allow you to use the math coprocessor types whether or not a math coprocessor is installed in the target machine. It's just as fast as compiling for pure IEEE real support when you have a math coprocessor. Otherwise, it's slower than using Borland's own **Real** type.

MANIPULATING REAL NUMBERS

Turbo Pascal includes a number of built-in mathematical and trig functions that return real number values. These are discussed at length in Section 9.3.

The arithmetic operators +, -, *, and / may all be used with all floating-point numeric types. (**Real, Single, Double,** and **Extended**.) The integer division operators **DIV** and **MOD** may *not* be used with floating-point types. (See Section 6.5 for a complete discussion of arithmetic operators.) Integers and floating-point numbers may be freely mixed within expressions; however, the result of an expression containing a floating-point number *is always a floating-point value* and must be assigned to a floating-point variable:

```
VAR
  Radius    : Integer;
  Area,PI   : Real;
```

```
PI := 3.14159;
Area := PI * Radius * Radius;
```

Here, **PI** (real) and **Radius** (integer) exist peaceably in the same expression, as long as the result of the expression is assigned to **Area**, a real number.

INTERNAL REPRESENTATION OF REAL NUMBERS

By and large, floating-point numbers should be considered "black boxes" and should not be manipulated beneath the level of Turbo Pascal. Encoding analog values in a digital fashion is complicated and subtle, and it's best to let the runtime code handle everything. Exceptions may occur when you need to pass floating-point values to an external assembly-language subprogram; if you're sharp enough to get that right, you're probably sharp enough to understand floating-point values on a bit level.

I'm not going to describe the IEEE floating-point formats in detail here. Some minimal explanation is given in the Turbo Pascal documentation. They are quite standard and thoroughly described in other publications. See *8087 Applications and Programming for the IBM and Other PCs* (Brady).

Because the six-byte **Real** format is specific to Turbo Pascal and not used elsewhere, it's worth some description.

From low memory to high: The exponent is stored in the first byte, followed by the least significant byte of the mantissa, the next most significant byte, and so on for five bytes of mantissa. 40 bits worth of mantissa will give you 11 significant figures. Beyond that point, additional precision will be lost, although the exponent will always give you the correct order of magnitude out to the limits of the range of a Turbo Pascal **Real**.

Real values actually have two signs. The most significant bit of the mantissa (bit 7 of the most significant byte of the real number) is the traditional sign bit, which indicates to which side of zero the number lies. A 1 bit indicates that the number is negative.

The other sign is the sign of the exponent, which indicates to which direction the decimal point moves when converting from scientific notation to decimal notation. The value of the exponent is offset by $80. Exponents greater than $80 indicate that the decimal point must move rightward. Exponents less than $80 indicate that the decimal point must move leftward. $80 must be subtracted from the exponent byte before the exponent can be evaluated.

Values of type **Real** in Turbo Pascal are represented internally as base two logarithms. In other words, to represent the number 4,673.450, Turbo Pascal stores the exponent to which the number two must be raised to yield 4,673.450. This makes multiplying and dividing real numbers much easier on the compiler, since numbers may be multiplied by adding their logarithms and divided by subtracting their logarithms.

The representation of type **Real** in memory is shown in Figure 5.2.

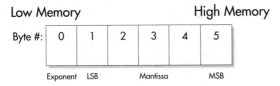

Figure 5.2 6-Byte Floating-Point Real Representation

5.8 Computational "Reals"

Turbo Pascal's suite of IEEE-compatible types contains one additional type which is functionally an integer but is often lumped in with the various IEEE real number types as a "computational real." This is type **Comp**. It has a range of -9.2×10^{18} to 9.2×10^{18}. All of the cautions that apply to using the math coprocessor types apply to using **Comp**.

While it is true that **Comp** doesn't take a decimal part as true floating-point numbers do, it acts more like a floating-point type than an integer type in several important ways. First of all, it does not work with integer disivion operators **MOD** and **DIV**. You must use the / operator to perform division on a variable of type **Comp**. Second, its default display format is the exponential format used by floating-point numbers. To display a **Comp** variable with neither exponential notation nor unused and unusable decimal places, you must format it as you would a real number. For example:

```
VAR
   BigNum : Comp;

BigNum := 17284;
Writeln(Bignum);        { Displays as 1.72840000000000E+0004 }
Writeln(BigNum:7);      { Displays as 1.7E+0004 }
Writeln(BigNum:7:2);    { Displays as 17284.00 }
Writeln(BigNum:7:0);    { Displays as 17284 }
```

Those little peculiarities aside, **Comp** can be very useful in expressing large integer quantities, particularly financial quantities that have to be penny-accurate to and beyond Gross National Product level. You must remember to express all **Comp** dollar quantities as pennies, since a **Comp** quantity may take no decimal part. Even counting pennies, **Comp** is capable of expressing dollar figures up to ten quadrillion dollars ($10,000,000,000,000,000.00) which should carry us through most reasonable financial calculations, and should even express the national debt — at least until Bill Clinton and his Democratic Congress have had a few years to "fix" the country.

Chapter 6

Pascal Atoms

RESERVED WORDS, IDENTIFIERS, OPERATORS, AND EXPRESSIONS

Pascal, by design, is a structured language.

Unlike certain "freeform" languages like APL, and older versions of BASIC and FORTRAN, it imposes a structure on its programs. Pascal will not let you string statements together haphazardly, even if every one, taken alone, is syntactically correct. There is a detailed master plan that every Pascal program must follow and the compiler is pretty stiff about enforcing the rules. A program must be coded in certain parts. Some parts must go *here,* and others must go *there.* Everything must be in a certain order. Some things cannot work together. Other things *must* work together.

Aside from some concessions to compiler designers (Pascal makes their task easier in some respects) Pascal's structure exists solely to reinforce a certain way of thinking about programming. This way of thinking represents Niklaus Wirth's emphasis on creating programs that are understandable without scores of pages of flowcharts and thousands of lines of explication. This way of thinking championed by Wirth and others is frequently called "structured programming." Although structured programming can be accomplished in any computer language (even BASIC), Pascal is one of only a few computer languages that absolutely *requires* it.

6.1 Reserved Words: The Framing Members of a Pascal Program

A structure must be made of *something.* A crystal is a structure of atoms in a particular orderly arrangement. A Pascal program is made of "atoms" that are simply English words formed from the ASCII character set. These program atoms fall into several categories. There are a very small number of words (only 51) called *reserved words,* a much larger number of words called *predefined identi-*

fiers, and then the unlimited multitude of ordinary identifiers created by you, the programmer.

Reserved words are words that have special meanings within Pascal. They cannot be used by the programmer except to stand for those particular meanings. The compiler will immediately error-flag any use of a reserved word that is not rigidly in line with that word's meaning. Examples would include **BEGIN, END, PROCEDURE, ARRAY**, and that old devil **GOTO**. Table 6.1. lists all the reserved words defined in Borland Pascal 7.0 and Turbo Pascal 7.0.

▼ *Important:*

This table has changed slightly over time and the evolution of Borland's product line; if you're using an older version of Turbo Pascal, you may find some reserved words not listed here, or some words listed here that are not reserved words in your version. It always pays to check Borland's documentation set for your version when odd things happen during compilation.

There is another class of words that are similar to reserved words, called *standard directives*. These are listed in Table 6.2. Standard directives are used in places where you cannot use your own invented identifiers, so there's no chance of conflicts with identifiers that you create. This being the case, standard directives are not "reserved"—that is, you can create your own identifiers identical to standard directives. The potential for confusion is serious, however, and unless there is a tremendously good reason to do so (I've never come across even one in my own Turbo Pascal work) treat the standard directives like reserved words and don't use them for anything else.

Table 6.1 Reserved Words in Borland/Turbo Pascal 7.0

AND	EXPORTS	MOD	SHR
ARRAY	FILE	NIL	STRING
ASM	FOR	NOT	THEN
BEGIN	FUNCTION	OBJECT	TO
CASE	GOTO	OF	TYPE
CONST	IF	OR	UNIT
CONSTRUCTOR	IMPLEMENTATION	PACKED	UNTIL
DESTRUCTOR	IN	PROCEDURE	USES
DIV	INHERITED	PROGRAM	VAR
DO	INLINE	RECORD	WHILE
DOWNTO	INTERFACE	REPEAT	WITH
ELSE	LABEL	SET	XOR
END	LIBRARY	SHL	

Historical Pascal practice has been to place reserved words in uppercase, and I'll do so throughout this book. Uppercase helps them stand out when you read your own code listings. Pascal is not case-sensitive, so you can place them in lower or mixed case if you wish. Because reserved words are the 2 x 4's of your Pascal programs and govern the very shape your programs take, I think it pays to be able to see them at a glance. The new color syntax highlighting feature introduced with version 7 will help you out a lot in that regard.

Everything that is not a reserved word or standard directive, or else a number or a symbol, is an "identifier." Some identifiers have predefined meanings to the compiler. These *predefined identifiers*, like reserved words, have a particular meaning to the compiler. However, under certain circumstances you can redefine their meanings for your own purposes. I shouldn't have to say that redefining a standard identifier is not something you should attempt until you know the Pascal language and your compiler inside and out.

Any name that *you* apply to an entity in a program is an ordinary identifier. The names of variables, of procedures and functions, and of the program itself are identifiers. An identifier you create can mean what you want it to mean (within Pascal's own rules and limits) as long as it is unique. That is, if you have a variable named **Counter**, you cannot have a procedure named **Counter**. Nor can you have another variable named **Counter**. You can give a particular identifier to only *one* entity of your program. The compiler will flag an error as soon as it spots the second usage. (There is one exception to this rule, having to do with a concept called *scope*. I'll have more to say about scope in Chapter 11.)

Combining reserved words, symbols, and identifiers gives you statements. **IF**, **THEN**, and **GOTO** are reserved words. The equal sign "=" is a symbol, in this case acting as an operator. (More on operators later in this chapter.) **GotoXY** is a predefined identifier. **Counter**, **Limit**, and **NextProg** are programmer-defined (that is, by you) identifiers.

This little snippet of code is a statement:

```
IF Counter = Limit THEN GotoXY(5,7);
```

Statements intuitively come across as "nuggets of action," much as English-language sentences are. The statement above is almost sentence-like: "If Counter equals Limit, then GotoXY at 5, 7." Combining statements in a fashion that respects Pascal's structure gives you a program. Obviously, we'll be talking about this in more detail throughout the book.

Table 6.2 Standard Directives in Borland/Turbo Pascal 7.0

ABSOLUTE	FAR	NAME	RESIDENT
ASSEMBLER	FORWARD	NEAR	VIRTUAL
EXPORT	INDEX	PRIVATE	
EXTERNAL	INTERRUPT	PUBLIC	

6.2 Identifiers

Programs are collections of things (data) and steps to be taken in storing, changing, and displaying those things (statements). The computer knows such things by their addresses in memory. The readable, English-language names of data, of programs, of functions and procedures, are for your benefit. We call such names, taken as a group, *identifiers.* They exist in the source code only. *Identifiers do not exist in the final code file.*

Identifiers are sequences of characters of any length up to 127 characters that obey these few rules:

1. Legal characters include letters, digits, and underscores. Spaces and symbols like &, !, *, or % (or any symbol not a letter or digit) are not allowed.

2. Symbols or digits (0-9) may *not* be used as the first character in an identifier. All identifiers must begin with a letter from A–Z (or lower case a–z) or an underscore.

3. Identifiers may not be identical to any reserved word.

4. Case differences are ignored. "A" is the same as "a" to the compiler.

5. Underscores are legal and significant. Note that this differs from most other Pascal compilers, in which underscores are legal but ignored. You may use underscores to "spread out" a long identifier and make it more readable: **SORT_ON_ZIP_CODE** rather than **SORTONZIPCODE**. (A better method that has become the custom in the Turbo Pascal community is to use mixed case to accomplish the same thing: **SortOnZIPCode**.)

6. *All* characters are significant in a Turbo Pascal identifier, up to 127 characters. Many other Pascals allow but ignore any character after the eighth character in an identifier.

These are all invalid identifiers that will generate errors:

Fox&Hound	Contains an invalid character, "&," that may not be in an identifier
FOO BAR	Contains a space
7Eleven	Begins with a number
Do@Noon	@ is valid only at the beginning of an identifier!
RECORD	"RECORD" is a reserved word and can't be used as an identifier

6.3 Operator Basics

As I explained earlier, a variable is a container in memory laid out by the compiler. It has a particular size and shape defined by its type. Into a variable you load an item of data which conforms to the size and shape of the variable. This data is called a "value."

You're probably familiar with this symbol, perhaps the most fundamental operator in Pascal: ":=" It is the *assignment operator*. The assignment operator is (usually) how values are placed into variables. Consider this simple assignment statement:

```
I := 17;
```

A value on the right side of the assignment operator is assigned to the variable on the left side of the assignment operator. In an assignment statement, there is always a variable on the left side of the assignment operator. On the right side may be a constant, a variable, or an expression.

An expression in Pascal is a combination of data items and operators which eventually "cooks down" to a single value. Data items are constants and variables. Operators are special symbols which perform some action involving the value or values given to it. These values are called an operator's "operands."

The simplest and most familiar examples of expressions come to us from arithmetic. This is an expression:

```
17 + 3
```

The addition operator performs an add operation on its two operands, 17 and 3. The value of the expression is 20.

An expression like "17 + 3," while valid, would not be used in a real program, where the value "20" would suffice. Considerably more useful are expressions which involve variables. For example:

```
3.14159 * Radius * Radius
```

This expression's value is recognizable as the area of the circle defined by whatever value is contained in **Radius**.

ISO Standard Pascal includes a good many different operators for building expressions, and Turbo Pascal enhances ISO Pascal with a few additional operators. They fall into a number of related groups depending on what sort of result they return: relational, arithmetic, set, and logical (also called "bitwise") operators.

6.4 Relational Operators

The relational operators are used to build Boolean expressions, that is, expressions that evaluate down to a Boolean value of **True** or **False**. Boolean expressions are the most widely used of all expressions in Pascal. All of the looping and branching statements in Pascal depend on Boolean expressions.

A relational operator causes the compiler to compare its two operands for some sort of relationship. The Boolean value that results is calculated according to a set of well-defined rules as to how data items of various sorts relate to one another.

Table 6.3 summarizes the relational operators implemented in Turbo Pascal. All return Boolean results:

Table 6.3 Relational Operators

Operator	Symbol	Operand Type	Precedence
Equality	=	scalar, set, string, pointer, record	5
Inequality	<>	scalar, set, string, pointer, record	5
Less than	<	scalar, string	5
Greater than	>	scalar, string	5
Less than or equal	<=	scalar, string	5
Greater than or equal	>=	scalar, string	5
Set membership	IN	set, set members	5
Set inclusion, left in right	<=	set	5
Set inclusion, right in left	>=	set	5
Negation	NOT	Boolean	2
Conjunction	AND	Boolean	3
Disjunction	OR	Boolean	4
Exclusive OR	XOR	Boolean	4

The set operators fall into two separate worlds; they're set operators, obviously, but they also express certain relationships between sets and set members that return Boolean values. The convention is that any operator that returns a Boolean value is relational, since Boolean values express the "truth or falsehood" of some stated relation. The three relational operators that involve sets, set membership, and the two set inclusion operators, will be discussed along with the operators that return set values, in Section 7.5. Note that the set inclusion operators share symbols with the greater than or equal to/less than or equal to operators, but the *sense* of these two types of operations are radically different.

Many of the relational operators work with scalar types. Scalar types, if you recall, are types with a limited number of ordered values. **Char, Boolean, Integer, Byte**, and enumerated types are all scalars. Real numbers, strings, structured types (records and arrays), and sets are *not* scalar types. (I defined scalar types in the last chapter.)

Some of the types mentioned briefly in this section are types I haven't yet explained in detail. Most of these will be covered in Chapter 7: sets and records, primarily. Pointers will have to wait until the last part of the book. The mentions are here not so much for you to read on your *first* linear pass through this book, but on those occasions when you return to this section for a brushup.

EQUALITY

If two values compared for equality are the same, the expression will evaluate as **True**. In general, for two values to be considered equal by Turbo Pascal's runtime code, they must be identical on a bit-by-bit basis. This is true for comparisons between like types. Most comparisons must be done between values of the same type.

The exceptions are comparisons done between numeric values expressed as different types. Turbo Pascal allows comparisons rather freely among integer types and real number types, but this sort of type-crossing must be done with great care. In particular, do not compare calculated reals (real number results of a real number arithmetic operation) for equality, either to other reals or to numeric values of other types. Rounding effects may cause real numbers to appear unequal to compiled code even though the mathematical sense of the calculation would seem to make them equal.

Integer types **Byte**, **ShortInt**, **Word**, **Integer**, and **LongInt** may be freely compared among themselves.

Two sets are considered equal if they both contain exactly the same members. (The two sets must, of course, be of the same base type to be compared at all.) Two pointers are considered equal if they both point to the same dynamic variable. Two pointers are also considered equal if they both point to **NIL**.

Two records are considered equal if they are of the same type (you cannot compare records of different types) and each field in one record is bit-by-bit identical to its corresponding field in the other record. Remember that you *cannot* compare records, even of the same type, using the greater than/less than operators >, <, >=, or <=.

Two strings are considered equal if they both have the same logical length and contain the same characters. This makes them bit-by-bit identical out as far as the logical length, which is the touchstone for all like-type equality comparisons under Turbo Pascal. Remember that this makes leading and trailing blanks significant:

```
'  Eriador' <> 'Eriador'   { True! }
'Eriador   '  <> 'Eriador'  { True! }
```

INEQUALITY

The rules for testing for inequality are exactly the same as the rules for equality. The only difference is that the Boolean state of the result is reversed:

```
17 = 17   { True }
17 <> 17  { False }
42 = 17   { False }
42 <> 16  { True }
```

In general, you can use the inequality operator anywhere you can use the equality operator.

Pointers are considered unequal when they point to different dynamic variables, or when one points to **NIL** and the other does not. The bit-by-bit rule is again applied: Even one bit's difference found during a like-type comparison means the two compared operands are unequal. The warning applied to rounding errors produced in calculated reals applies to inequality comparisons as well.

GREATER THAN/LESS THAN

The four operators greater than, less than, greater than or equal to, and less than or equal to, add a new dimension to the notion of comparison. They assume that their operands always exist in some well-defined order by which the comparison can be made.

This immediately disqualifies pointers, sets, and records. Saying one pointer is greater than another simply makes no sense, given the way pointers are defined. You could argue that since pointers are physical addresses, one pointer will always be greater or less than another nonequal pointer. This may be true, but in the spirit of the Pascal language, details about how pointers are implemented are hidden from the programmer at the purely Pascal level. (And going to the next level down and messing with pointer internals can get you into several different kinds of trouble, especially once you begin using Borland Pascal 7.0 to create applications that run in protected mode. Protected mode is *very* fussy about what you do with your pointers!)

The same applies to sets and records. Ordering them makes no logical sense, so operators involving an implied order cannot be used with them.

With scalar types, a definite order is part of the type definition. For integer types (**ShortInt**, **Byte**, **Integer**, **Word**, and **LongInt**) the order is obvious from our experience with arithmetic; integers model whole numbers between specific bounds.

The **Char** and **Byte** types are both limited to 256 possible values, and both have an order implied by the sequence of binary numbers from 0 to 255. The **Char** type is ordered by the ASCII character set, which makes the following expressions evaluate to **True**:

```
'A' < 'B'
'a' > 'A'
'@' < '['
```

The higher 128 values assignable to **Char** variables have no truly standard characters outside of the PC world, but they still exist in fixed order and are numbered from 128 to 255.

Enumerated types are limited to no more than 255 different values, and usually have fewer than 10 or 12. Their fixed order is the order the values were given in the definition of the enumerated type:

```
TYPE
  Colors = (Red,Orange,Yellow,Green,Blue,Indigo,Violet);
```

This order makes the following expressions evaluate to **True**:

```
Red < Green
Blue > Yellow
Indigo < Violet
```

The ordering of string values involves two components: The length of the string and the ASCII values of the characters present in the string. Essentially, Turbo Pascal begins by comparing the first characters in the two strings being compared. If those two characters are different, the test stops there, and the ordering of the two strings is based upon the relation of those two first characters. If the two characters are the same, the *second* characters in each string are compared. If they turn out to be the same, then the third characters in both strings are compared.

This process continues until the code finds two characters that differ, or until one string runs out of characters. In that case, the longer of the two is considered to be greater than the shorter. All of the following expressions evaluate to **True**:

```
'AAAAA' > 'AAA'
'B' > 'AAAAAAAAAAAA'
'AAAAB' > 'AAAAAAAAAA'
```

NOT, AND, OR, AND XOR

There are four operators that operate on Boolean operands: **NOT, AND, OR,** and **XOR**. These operators are sometimes set apart as a separate group called Boolean operators. In some ways, they have more in common with the arithmetic operators than with the relational operators. They do not test a relationship which already exists between two operands. Rather, they combine their operands according to the rules of Boolean algebra to produce a new value that becomes the value of the expression.

The simplest of the four is **NOT**, which takes only one Boolean operand. The operand must be placed after the **NOT** reserved word. **NOT** negates the Boolean value of its operand:

```
NOT False  { Expression is True  }
NOT True   { Expression is False }
```

Some slightly less simplistic examples:

```
NOT (6 > I){ True for I < 6 }
NOT (J = K){ True for J <> K }
```

The parentheses indicate that the expression within the parentheses is evaluated first, and only then is the resultant value acted upon by **NOT**. This expression is an instance where "order of evaluation" becomes important. I'll discuss this in detail in Section 6.7.

AND (also known as "conjunction") requires two operands, and follows this rule: *If both operands are **True**, the expression returns **True**; else the expression returns*

False. If either operand or both operands have the value **False**, the value of the expression as a whole will be **False**.

Some examples:

```
True AND True            { Expression is True }
True AND False           { Expression is False }
False AND True           { Expression is False }
False AND False          { Expression is False }

(7 > 4) AND (5 <> 3)     { Expression is True }
(16 = (4 * 4)) AND (2 <> 2)    { Expression is False }
```

All of these example expressions use constants, and thus are not realistic uses of **AND** within a program. We present them this way so the logic of the statement is obvious without having to remember what value is currently in a variable present in an expression.

OR (also known as "disjunction") requires two operands, and follows this rule: *If either (or both) operands is **True**, the expression returns **True**; only if both operands are **False** will the expression return **False**.*

Some examples, again using constants are:

```
True OR True      { Expression is True }
True OR False     { Expression is True }
False OR True     { Expression is True }
False OR False    { Expression is False }

(7 > 4) OR (5 = 3) { Expression is True }
(2 < 1) OR (6 <> 6)    { Expression is False }
```

Finally, there is **XOR**, which also requires two operands, and follows this rule: *If both operands are the same Boolean value, **XOR** returns **False**; only if the operands have unlike Boolean values will **XOR** return **True**.*

Some examples are:

```
True XOR True    { Expression is False }
True XOR False   { Expression is True }
False XOR True   { Expression is True }
False XOR False  { Expression is False }
```

GREATER THAN OR EQUAL TO/LESS THAN OR EQUAL TO

These two operators are each combinations of two operators. These combinations are so convenient and so frequently used that they were welded together to form two single operators with unique symbols: >= (read, "greater than or equal to") and <= (read, "less than or equal to").

When you wish to say:

```
X >= Y
```

you are in fact saying

```
(X > Y) OR (X = Y)
```

and when you wish to say

```
X <= Y
```

you are in fact saying

```
(X < Y) OR (X = Y)
```

The rules for applying >= and <= are exactly the same as those for < and >. They may take only scalars or strings as operands.

6.5 Arithmetic Operators

Manipulating numbers is done with arithmetic operators, which along with numeric variables, form arithmetic expressions. About the only common arithmetic operator not found in Pascal is the exponentiation operator, that is, the raising of one number to a given power. (We will, however, build a function which raises one number to the power of another in Section 9.4.) Table 6.4 summarizes the arithmetic operators implemented in Turbo Pascal.

The "operands" column lists those data types that a given operator may take as operands. The compiler is fairly free about allowing you to mix types of numeric variables within an expression. In other words, you may multiply bytes by integers, add reals to bytes, multiply integers by bytes, and so on. For example, these are all legal expressions in Turbo Pascal:

```
VAR
  I,J,K   : Integer;
  R,S,T   : Real;
  A,B,C   : Byte;
  U,V     : Single;
```

Table 6.4 Arithmetic Operators

Operator	*Symbol*	*Operand Types*	*Result Type*	*Prec.*
Addition	+	Integer, real, cardinal	same	4
Sign Inversion	-	Integer, real	same	1
Subtraction	-	Integer, real, cardinal	same	4
Multiplication	*	Integer, real, cardinal	same	3
Integer Division	DIV	Integer, cardinal	same	3
Real Division	/	Integer, real, cardinal	real	3
Modulus	MOD	Integer, cardinal	same	3

NOTES: Here, "Integer" types include **Integer**, **LongInt**, and **ShortInt**; "Cardinal" types include **Word** and **Byte**; and "Real" types include **Real**, **Single**, **Double**, **Extended**, and **Comp**.

```
W,X  : Double;
Q    : ShortInt;
L    : LongInt;

I * B        { Integer multiplied by byte }
R + J        { Integer added to real    }
L * Q        { LongInt multiplied by ShortInt }
C + (R * I) { Etc. }
J * (A / S)
```

The "result type" column in the table indicates the data type that the value of an expression incorporating that operator may take on. Pascal is ordinarily very picky about the assignment of different types to one another in assigment statements. This "strict type checking" is relaxed to some extent in simple arithmetic expressions. Numeric types may, in fact, be mixed fairly freely within expressions as long as a few rules are obeyed:

1. Any expression including a floating-point value may only be assigned to a floating-point variable.

2. Expressions containing floating-point division (/) may only be assigned to a floating-point variable *even if the operands are integer types.*

Failure to follow these rules will generate

```
Error 26: Type mismatch.
```

However, outside of the two mentioned restrictions, a numeric expression may be assigned to any numeric variable, assuming the variable has sufficient range to contain the value of the expression. For example, if an expression evaluates to 14,000, you should not assign the expression to a variable of type **Byte**, which can only contain values from 0 to 255. Program behavior in such a case is unpredictable. If range checking is on, such an assignment will generate a range error.

Addition, subtraction, and multiplication are handled the same way ordinary arithmetic is handled with pencil or calculator, and we won't need to describe them here.

THE STRANGE CASE OF COMP

Newcomers to Pascal will probably have some trouble deciding exactly what type **Comp** really is. Under Turbo Pascal 4.0, **Comp** is *only* available on machines containing a math coprocessor like the 8087 or 80287. Using release 5.0 and later, **Comp** may be used in machines without math coprocessors by taking advantage of the compiler's floating-point emulation feature. **Comp** is related to the defunct **BCD** numeric type that died with Version 3.0 Turbo BCD Pascal. While nominally an integer in function (it takes no decimal part), it acts much more like a floating-point type in most circumstances. For example:

- **Comp** may be assigned a value from an expression containing floating-point values. Any decimal parts are rounded to the closest integer.

- **Comp** *must* be used with floating-point division (the / operator) rather than integer division (the **MOD** and **DIV** operators). Trying to mix **Comp** with **MOD** and **DIV** will generate this error:

```
Error 41: Operand types do not match operator.
```

- Unless you specify a numeric format, **Comp** values will be displayed in exponential format, just as with floating-point values.

Something to keep in mind: *Comp is not a scalar type.* You cannot use the **Pred** or **Succ** functions on **Comp** variables, and **Comp** variables cannot index arrays. In a sense, **Comp** is a floating-point type that has been designed so that it has absolute whole-number precision throughout its range. This makes it suitable for numeric computations, and will probably be most valuable in financial applications, where **Comp** values may represent monetary amounts in either cents or mills. (A mill is a thousandth of a dollar, although the concept is rarely used outside the securities industry.) It is much more suitable than type **LongInt** for financial values, since **Comp** is accurate to 17 significant figures, and **LongInt** only to a measly 10 significant figures, or roughly two billion.

SIGN INVERSION

Sign inversion is a "unary" operator; that is, it takes only a single operand. What it does is reverse the sign of its operand. It will make a positive quantity negative, or a negative quantity positive. It does not affect the absolute value (distance from zero) of the operand.

Note that sign inversion cannot be used with **Byte** or **Word**. These two types are "unsigned"; that is, they are never considered negative.

DIVISION

There are three distinct division operators in Pascal. One supports floating-point division, and the other two support division for integer types. Floating-point division (/) may take operands of any numeric type, but it always produces a floating-point value, complete with decimal part. Attempting to assign a floating-point division expression to an integer type will generate error #26, *even if all numeric variables involved are integers:*

```
VAR
  I,J,K : Integer;

I := J / K;     { Won't compile!!! }
```

Division for numbers that cannot hold decimal parts is handled much the same way division is first taught to grade schoolers: When one number is divided by another, two numbers result. One is a whole number quotient; the other a whole number remainder.

In Pascal, integer division is actually two separate operations that do not depend upon one another. One operator, **DIV**, produces the quotient of its operands:

```
J := 17;
K := 3;
I := J DIV K;    { I is assigned the value 5 }
```

No remainder is generated at all by **DIV**, and the operation should not be considered incomplete. If you wish to compute the remainder, the modulus operator (**MOD**) is used:

```
I := J MOD K;    { I is assigned the value 2 }
```

Assuming the same values given above for **J** and **K**, the remainder of dividing **J** by **K** is computed as 2. The quotient is not calculated at all (or calculated internally and thrown away); only the remainder is returned.

6.6 Bitwise Operators

Turbo Pascal allows you to read and write I/O ports and other low-level data, much of which is "bit-mapped"; that is, certain bits have certain meanings apart from all other bits and must be examined, set, and interpreted individually. The way to do this is through the "bitwise" logical operators. Associated with the bitwise logical operators are the shift operators, **SHL** and **SHR**. We will speak of these shortly.

We have previously spoken of the **AND**, **OR**, **XOR**, and **NOT** operators, which work on Boolean operands and return Boolean values. The bitwise logical operators are another flavor of **NOT**, **AND**, **OR**, and **XOR**. They work with operands of all integer types (**Integer**, **Word**, **LongInt**, **ShortInt**, and **Byte**) and they apply a logical operation upon their operands, done one bit at a time.

Table 6.5 summarizes the bitwise logical operators and the shift operators.

The best way to approach all bitwise operators is to work in true binary notation, where all numbers are expressed in base two, and the only digits are 1

Table 6.5 The Bitwise Logical and Shift Operators

Operator	Symbol	Operand Types	Result Type	Precedence
Bitwise NOT	NOT	All integer types	same	2
Bitwise AND	AND	All integer types	same	3
Bitwise OR	OR	All integer types	same	4
Bitwise XOR	XOR	All integer types	same	4
Shift Right	SHR	All integer types	same	3
Shift Left	SHL	All integer types	same	3

and 0. The bitwise operators work on one binary digit at a time. The result of the various operations on 0 and 1 values is best summarized by four "truth tables":

```
NOT              AND            OR             XOR

NOT 1 = 0     0 AND 0 = 0    0 OR 0 = 0     0 XOR 0 = 0
NOT 0 = 1     0 AND 1 = 0    0 OR 1 = 1     0 XOR 1 = 1
              1 AND 0 = 0    1 OR 0 = 1     1 XOR 0 = 1
              1 AND 1 = 1    1 OR 1 = 1     1 XOR 1 = 0
```

When you apply bitwise operators to two 8-bit or two 16-bit data items, it is the same as applying the operator between each corresponding bit of the two items. For example, the following expression evaluates to **True**:

```
$80 = ($83 AND $90)    { All in hexadecimal }
```

Why? Think of the operation $83 & $90 this way:

```
Hex       Binary
$83 =1 0 0 0 0 0 1 1
          AND
$90 =1 0 0 1 0 0 0 0
           =
$80 =1 0 0 0 0 0 0 0
```

Read *down* from the top of each column in the binary number, and compare the little equation to the truth table for bitwise **AND**. If you apply bitwise **AND** to each column, you will find the bit pattern for the number $80 to be the total result.

Now, what good is this? Suppose you only wanted to examine 4 out of the 8 bits in a variable of type **Byte**. The bits are numbered 0–7 from the right. The bits you need are bits 2 through 5. The way to do it is to use bitwise **AND** and what we call a "mask":

```
VAR
     GoodBits, AllBits : Byte;

GoodBits := AllBits AND $3C;
```

To see how this works, let's again "spread it out" into a set of binary numbers:

```
AllBits =   X X X X X X X X
                   AND
$3E (mask) =0 0 1 1 1 1 0 0
                    =
GoodBits =  0 0 X X X X 0 0
```

Here, "X" means *"either* 1 or 0." Again, follow the eight little operations down from the top of each column to the bottom. The 0 bits present in four of the eight columns of the mask, $3C, force those columns to evaluate to 0 in **GoodBits**, regardless of the state of the corresponding bits in **AllBits**. Go back to the truth table if this is not clear: *If either of the two bits in a bitwise AND expression is zero, the result will be zero.*

This way, we can assume that bits 0, 1, 7, and 8 in **GoodBits** will always be zero and we can ignore them while we test the others.

SHIFT OPERATORS

We've looked at bit patterns as stored in integer types, and how we can alter those patterns by logically combining bit patterns with bitmasks. Another way to alter bit patterns in integer types is with the shift operators, **SHR** and **SHL**. **SHR** stands for SHift Right; **SHL** for SHift Left.

Both operators are best understood by looking at a bit pattern before and after the operator acts upon it. Start with the value $CB (203 decimal) and shift it two bits to the right as the **SHR** operator would do:

```
1 1 0 0 1 0 1 1 ->
 \ \ \ \ \ \
  \ \ \ \ \ \
-> 0 0 1 1 0 0 1 0
```

The result byte is $32 (50 decimal). The two 1-bits on the right end of the original $CB value are shifted off the end of the byte (into the "bit bucket," some say) and are lost. To take their place, two 0-bits are fed into the byte on the left end.

SHL works identically, but in the other direction. Let's shift $CB to the left with **SHL** and see what we get:

```
<- 1 1 0 0 1 0 1 1
    / / / / / /
   / / / / / /
   0 0 1 0 1 1 0 0 <-
```

Again, we lose two bits off the end of the original value, but this time they drop off the left end, and two 0-bits are added in on the right end. What was $CB is now $2C (44 decimal).

Syntactically, **SHL** and **SHR** are like the arithmetic operators. They act with the number of bits to be shifted to form an expression, the resulting value of which you assign to another variable:

```
Result := Operand <SHL/SHR> <number of bits to shift>;
```

Some examples are:

```
VAR
  B,C : Byte;
  I,J : Integer;

I := 17;
J := I SHL 3;  { J now contains 136 } B := $FF;
C := B SHR 4;  { C now contains $0F }
```

It would be a good exercise to work out these two examples on paper, expressing each value as a binary pattern of bits and then shifting them.

An interesting note on the shift operators is that they are extremely fast ways to multiply and divide a number by a power of 2. Shifting a number 1 bit to the left multiplies it by 2. Shifting it 2 bits to the left multiplies it by 4, and so on. In the example above, we shifted 17 by 3 bits, which multiplies it by 8. Sure enough, 17 x 8 = 136.

It works the other way as well. Shifting a number 1 bit to the right divides it by 2; shifting 2 bits to the right divides by 4, and so on. The only thing to watch is that there is no remainder on divide and nothing to notify you if you overflow on a multiply. It is a somewhat limited form of arithmetic, but in time-critical applications you'll find it is *much* faster than the more generalized multiply and divide operators.

6.7 Order of Evaluation

Mixing several operators within a single expression can lead to problems for the compiler. Eventually the expression must be evaluated down to a single value, but in what order are the various operators to be applied? Consider the ambiguity in this expression:

```
7 + 6 * 9
```

How will the compiler interpret this? Which operator is applied first? As you might expect, the authors of Turbo Pascal set down rules that dictate how expressions containing more than one operator are to be evaluated. These rules define *order of evaluation*.

To determine the order of evaluation of an expression, the compiler must consider three factors: precedence of operators, left to right evaluation, and parentheses.

PRECEDENCE

All operators in Turbo Pascal have a property called *precedence*. Precedence is a sort of evaluation prioritizing system. If two operators have different precedences, the one with higher precedence is evaluated first. There are five degrees of precedence: 1 is the highest and 5 the lowest.

When we summarized the various operators in tables, the rightmost column contained each operator's precedence. The sign inversion operator has a precedence of 1. *No other* operator has a precedence of 1. Sign inversion operations are always performed before any other operations, assuming parentheses are not present. (We'll get to that shortly.) Logical and bitwise **NOT** operators have a precedence of 2. For example:

```
VAR
   OK,FileOpen : Boolean;

IF NOT OK AND FileOpen THEN CallOperator;
```

How is the expression, "**NOT OK AND FileOpen**" evaluated? **NOT OK** is evaluated first, because NOT has a precedence of 2, whereas AND has a precedence of 3. (See Table 6.1 for the precedence of these and other relational operators.) The Boolean result is then **AND**ed with the Boolean value in **FileOpen**, to yield the final Boolean result for the expression. If that value is **True**, the procedure **CallOperator** is executed.

LEFT TO RIGHT EVALUATION

The previous example was clear-cut since **NOT** has a higher precedence than **AND**. But as you can see from the tables, many operators have the same precedence value; addition, subtraction, and set intersection are only a few of the operators with a precedence of 4, and most relational operators have a precedence of 5.

When the compiler is evaluating an expression and it confronts a choice between two operators of equal precedence, it evaluates them in order from left to right. For example:

```
VAR
   I,J,K : Integer;

J := I * 17 DIV K;
```

The * and **DIV** operators both have a precedence of 3. To evaluate the expression **I * 17 DIV K**, the compiler must first evaluate **I * 17** to an integer value, and then integer divide that value by **K**. * is to the left of **DIV**, and so it is evaluated before **DIV**.

Note that left to right evaluation happens *only* when it is not clear from precedence (or parentheses, see below) which of two operators must be evaluated first.

SETTING ORDER OF EVALUATION WITH PARENTHESES

There are situations in which the previous two rules break down. How would the compiler establish order of evaluation for this expression:

```
I > J AND K <= L
```

The idea here is to test the Boolean values of two relational expressions. The precedence of **AND** is greater than the precedence of any relational operator like > and <=. So the compiler would attempt to evaluate the subexpression **J AND K** first.

Actually, this particular expression does not even compile; Turbo Pascal will flag an error #1 as soon as it finishes compiling **J AND K** and sees another operator ahead of it.

The only way out of this one is to use parentheses. Just as in the rules of algebra, in the rules of Pascal, parentheses override *all* other order of evaluation rules. To make the offending expression pass muster, you must rework it this way:

```
(I > J) AND (K <= L)
```

Now the compiler first evaluates **(I > J)** to a Boolean value, then **(K <= L)** to another Boolean value, then submits those two Boolean values as operands to **AND. AND** happily generates a final Boolean value for the entire expression.

This is one case (and a fairly common one) in which parentheses are required to compile the expression without errors. However, there are many occasions when parentheses will make an expression more readable, even though, strictly speaking, the parentheses are not required:

```
(PI * Radius) + 7
```

Here, not only does * have a higher precedence than +, * is to the left of + as well. So in any case, the compiler would evaluate **PI * Radius** before adding 7 to the result. The parentheses make it immediately obvious what operation is to be done first, without having to think back to precedence tables and consider left to right evaluation.

I am something of a fanatic about program readability. Which of these (identical) expressions is easier to dope out?:

```
R + 2 * PI - 6
(R + (2 * PI)) - 6
```

You have to think a little about the first. You don't have to think about the second at all. I powerfully recommend using parentheses in all but the most completely simpleminded expressions to indicate to all persons (including those not especially familiar with Pascal) the order of evaluation of the operations making up the expression. Parentheses cost you *nothing* in code size or code speed. Nothing at all.

To add to your program readability, that's dirt cheap.

6.8 Statements

Put as simply as possible, a Pascal program is a series of statements. Each statement is an instruction to do something: to define data, to alter data, to execute a function or procedure, to change the direction of the program's flow of control.

There are many different kinds of statements in Pascal. We'll be looking at them all in detail in this section and Chapter 8.

Perhaps the simplest of all statements is an invocation of a procedure or function. Turbo Pascal includes several screen-control procedures for moving the cursor around, clearing the screen, and so on. Such procedures are used by naming them, and naming one constitutes a statement:

```
ClrScr;
```

This statement tells the computer to do something; in this case, to clear the screen. The computer executes the statement; the screen is cleared, and control passes to the next statement, whatever that may be.

We have been using assignment statements, type definition statements, and variable declaration statements all along. By now you should understand them thoroughly. Type definition statements must exist in the type definition part of a program, procedure, or function. They associate a type name with a description of a programmer-defined type. Enumerated types (see Section 7.3) are an excellent example:

```
TYPE
  Spectrum   = (Red,Orange,Yellow,Green,Blue,Indigo,Violet);
  LongColors = Red..Yellow;
  ColorSet   = SET OF Spectrum;
```

Each of these three definitions is a statement. The semicolons *separate* the statements rather than terminate them. This is a critical distinction that frequently escapes beginning Pascal programmers. I'll take the vexing matter of semicolons up again in Section 8.8.

Variable declaration statements are found only in the variable declaration part of a program, function, or procedure. They associate a variable name with the data type the variable is to have. The colon symbol (:) is used rather than the equal sign:

```
VAR
  I,J,K  : Integer;
  Ch     : Char;
  R      : Real;
```

Assignment statements are used in the body of the program, function, or procedure. They copy data from the identifier on the right side of the assignment operator to the variable on the left. Only a *variable* can be to the left of the assignment operator. Constants, literals, and expressions must be on the right side. Other variables, of course, can also be to the right of the assignment operator:

```
I := 17;                { '17' is a numeric Literal }
R := PI;                { PI was defined earlier as a constant }
J := (17*K) + Ord(Ch);  { An expression }
K := J;                 { The value of one variable assigned }
                        { to another }
```

We'll return in detail to the issue of statements in Chapter 8 when we confront Pascal's "flow control" machinery: loops and conditional statements.

Chapter 7

Derived Types and Data Structures

BUILDING COMPLEX DATA STRUCTURES FROM SIMPLE DATA ATOMS

All the types we've discussed up to this point have been simple types, pre-defined by Turbo Pascal and ready to use. Much of the power of Pascal lies in its ability to create structures of data out of these simple types. Derived types and data structures can make your programs both easier to write and, later on, easier to read as well.

Defining your own custom data types is easy to do. The reserved word **TYPE** begins the type definition part of your program, and that's where you lay out the plan of your data structures:

```
TYPE
   YourType = ItsDefinition;
```

In general terms, a type definition consists of the name of the type, followed by an equal sign, followed by the definition of the type. From now on, many of the types we're going to discuss must be declared and defined in the type definition part of your program. Once defined, you can declare a variable of your "custom" type in the variable declaration section of your program:

```
VAR
   ANewVariable : YourType;
```

A type *definition* does not, by itself, occupy space in your executable program file's data area, as variables do. What a type definition provides are instructions *to the compiler* telling it how to deal with variables of type **YourType** when it encounters them further down in your program source file.

With some exceptions, (strings and subranges, for example) you cannot write derived or structured types to your screen or printer with **Write** or **Writeln**. If you want to display structured types somehow, you must write procedures specifically to display some representation of the type on your CRT or printer.

159

7.1 Types As Bricks to Build With

Virtually any task can be accomplished using Pascal's fundamental data types alone. However, creating structures of data by using these fundamental data types as building blocks can help you develop a program design, and help you code the program once the design is complete. Using its basic data types, a Pascal programmer can build special-purpose types that are valid only within the program in which they are defined.

One way to build new special-purpose data types is by defining *subranges*. A subrange is a type that may have as its values only certain values in a range taken from the legal range of the fundamental data type. For example, academic grades are usually expressed as letters. Not all letters are grades, however. You might define a subrange of the basic type **Char** that can have as values only the letters from A through F. Such a type would be defined this way:

```
Grade = 'A'..'F';
```

Now, to create a variable to hold grades, you would declare a variable this way:

```
History : Grade;
```

Subranges provide a modicum of protection against certain coding mistakes. For example, if you tried to assign a grade of "W" to the variable **History**, the compiler would tell you during compilation that "W" is not a legal value of the subrange **Grade**. At runtime, the compiler would not be available for comment, but if you tried to assign a **Char** variable containing "W" to a **Grade** variable at runtime, you would generate a runtime error—if range checking were enabled.

Subranges are derived types. They're subsets of existing types—either those built into Pascal or those you define yourself. Building the other way happens when you create data structures—the most familiar of which is called a *record*. A record is a grouping of fundamental types into a larger structure that is given a name as a new type. Variables can be declared to be of this type. Those variables can be assigned, compared, and written to files just as integers or characters can.

For example, if you are writing a program that keeps track of student grades and test results, you might group together basic data types in this arrangement:

```
TYPE
   SemesterGrades = RECORD
                  StudentID    : String[9];
                  SemesterID   : String[6];
                  Math         : Grade;
                  English      : Grade;
                  Drafting     : Grade;
                  History      : Grade;
                  Spanish      : Grade;
                  Gym          : Grade;
                  SemesterGPA  : Real
                  END;
```

Now you can define a variable as having the type **SemesterGrades:**

```
VAR
   ThisSemester : SemesterGrades;
```

By a single variable name you now can control nine separate data chunks (which, when part of a record type, are called *fields*) that you would otherwise have to deal with separately. This can make certain programming tasks a *great* deal simpler. But even more important, it allows you to treat logically-connected data as a single unit to clarify your program's design and foster clear thinking about its function.

For example, when you need to write the semester's grades out to a disk file, you needn't fuss with individual subjects separately. The whole record goes out to disk at once, as though it were a single variable, without any reference to the individual fields from which the record is built. The alternative is a series of statements that write the student ID to disk, followed by the semester ID, followed by the math grade, followed by the English grade, and so on.

When you need to think of all of a student's grades taken together, you can think of them as a unit. When you need to deal with them separately, Pascal has a simple way of picking out any individual field within the record:

```
   MyMath := ThisSemester.Math;
```

You simply specify the field record name followed by the field name, separated by a period character. **ThisSemester.Math** is in a sense an expression that "cooks down" to a single value of type **Grade**.

How you think of the data now depends on how you *need* to think of the data. Pascal encourages you to structure your data in ways like this that encourage clear thinking about your problem at a high level (all grades taken together) or at a low level (each grade a separate data item.)

Much of the skill of programming in Pascal is learning how to structure your data so that details are hidden by the structure until they are needed. It's much like being able to step back and see your data as a forest without being distracted by the individual trees.

Like most tools, the structuring of data is an edge that cuts two ways. It is all too easy to create data structures of Byzantine complexity that add nothing to a program's usefulness while obscuring its ultimate purpose. If the data structure you create for your program makes the program *harder* to understand from "three steps back," you've either done it the wrong way, or done it too much.

The rule of thumb I use is this: *Don't create data structures for data structure's sake.* Unless there's a reason for it, resist. Simplicity doesn't necessarily sacrifice power or flexibility.

7.2 Subranges in Detail

The simplest derived type you can define is a subset of an ordinal type called a *subrange.* If you choose any two legal values in an ordinal type, those two values plus all values that lie between them define a subrange of that ordinal type. For example, these are subranges of type **Char**:

```
TYPE
   Uppercase  =  'A'..'Z';
   Lowercase  =  'a'..'z';
   Digits     =  '0'..'9';
```

Uppercase is the range of characters A, B, C, D, E, F, and so on to Z. **Digits** includes the numeral characters 0, 1, 2, 3, 4, on to 9. The quotes are important. They tell the compiler that the values in the subrange are of type **Char**. If you left off the quote marks from the type definition for type **Digits**:

```
Digits = 0..9;
```

you would have, instead, a subrange of type **Integer**. '7' is not the same as 7!

An expression in the form **'A'..'Z'** or **3..6** is called a *closed interval*. A closed interval is a range of ordinal values including the two stated boundary values and all values falling between them. We'll return to closed intervals later on in this chapter while discussing sets.

7.3 Enumerated Types

Newcomers to Pascal frequently find the notion of enumerated types hard to grasp. An enumerated type is an ordinal type defined by the programmer. It consists of an ordered list of values with unique names. One of the best ways to approach enumerated types is through comparison with type **Boolean**.

Type **Boolean** is, in fact, an enumerated type that is predefined by the compiler and used in special ways. Type **Boolean** is an ordered list of two values with unique names: **False**, **True**. It is *not* a pair of ASCII strings containing the English words "False" and "True." As we mentioned earlier, a Boolean value is actually a binary number with a value of either 00 or 01. We "name" the binary code 00 within type **Boolean** as **False**, and name the binary code 01 within type **Boolean** as **True**. It's a process similar in spirit to naming constants.

Consider another list of values with unique names: the colors of the spectrum. (Remember that colorful chap Roy G. Biv?) Let's create an enumerated type in which the list of values includes the colors of the spectrum, in order:

```
TYPE
   Spectrum = (Red, Orange, Yellow, Green, Blue, Indigo, Violet);
```

The values list of an enumerated type definition is always given within parentheses. The order you place the values within the parentheses defines their ordinal value, which you can test using the **Ord(X)** function. For example, **Ord(Yellow)** would return a value of 2. **Ord(Red)** would return the value 0.

You can compare values of an enumerated type with other values of that same type. It may be helpful to substitute the ordinal value of enumerated constants for the words that name them when thinking about such comparisons. The statement

Yellow > Red (think: 2 > 0) would return a Boolean value of **True**. **Green > Violet** or **Blue < Orange** would both return Boolean values of **False**.

The values of type **Spectrum** are all considered named constants. They may be assigned to variables of type **Spectrum**. For example:

```
VAR
    Color1, Color2 : Spectrum;

Color1 := Yellow;
Color2 := Indigo;
```

You cannot, however, assign anything to one of the values of type **Spectrum**. **Red := 2** or **Red := Yellow** make no sense and will not be accepted by the compiler.

Enumerated types may index arrays. (I'll be discussing arrays in detail a little later in this chapter.) For example, each color of the rainbow has a frequency (of that color of light) associated with it. These frequencies could be stored in an array, indexed by the enumerated type **Spectrum**:

```
Wavelength : ARRAY[Red..Violet] OF Real;
Frequency  : ARRAY[Red..Violet] OF Real;
Color      : Spectrum;
Lightspeed : Real;

Wavelength[Red]    := 6.2E-7;   { All in meters }
Wavelength[Orange] := 5.9E-7;
Wavelength[Yellow] := 5.6E-7;
Wavelength[Green]  := 5.4E-7;
Wavelength[Blue]   := 5.15E-7;
Wavelength[Indigo] := 4.8E-7;
Wavelength[Violet] := 4.5E-7;
```

The functions **Ord** and **Odd** work with enumerated types, as do the **Succ** and **Pred** functions. This is due to an enumerated type's having a fixed number of elements in a definite order that does not change. **Succ(Green)** will return the value **Blue**. **Pred(Yellow)** returns the value **Orange**. Be aware that **Pred(Red)** and **Succ(Violet)** are undefined. You should test for the two ends of the **Spectrum** type while using **Succ** and **Pred** to avoid assigning an undefined value to a variable.

Enumerated types may also be control variables in **FOR/NEXT** loops. (These will be discussed in detail in Chapter 8.) In continuing with the example begun above, we might calculate the frequencies of light for each of the colors of type **Spectrum** this way:

```
Lightspeed := 3.0E08      { Meters/second }
FOR Color := Red TO Violet DO
Frequency[Color] := Lightspeed / Wavelength[Color];
```

One great disadvantage to enumerated types is that they cannot be printed to the console or printer. You cannot, for example, code this up:

```
Writeln(Orange);
```

and expect to see the ASCII word "Orange" appear on the screen. Turbo Pascal will flag this as the following error:

```
Error 64: Cannot Read or Write variables of this type
```

In cases where you must print an enumerated type to the screen or printer, set up an array of strings that is indexed by the enumerated type:

```
Names : ARRAY[Red..Violet] OF STRING;

Names[Red] := 'Red';
Writeln(Names[Red]);
```

The **Writeln** statement above will print the string "Red" to the screen. You might also set up an array constant containing the names of the items in an enumerated type.

7.4 Sets

Sets are collections of elements picked from simple types. An element is either in a set, or it is not in the set. The letters "A", "Q", "W", and "Z" may be taken together as a set of characters. "Q" is in the set, and "L" is not.

Expressed in Pascal's notation:

```
VAR
    CharSet : SET OF Char;

CharSet := ['A','Q','W','Z'];
```

A pair of square brackets when used to define a set (as shown above) is called a *set constructor*.

Are sets useful? Very. For example, sets in Pascal provide an easy way to sift valid user responses from invalid ones. In answering even a simple, yes/no question, a user may in fact type two equally valid characters for yes, and two for no: Y/y and N/n. Ordinarily, you would have to test for each one individually:

```
IF (Ch='Y') OR (Ch='y') THEN DoSomething;
```

With sets, you could replace this notation with:

```
IF Ch IN ['Y','y'] THEN DoSomething;
```

The operator **IN** checks only if **Ch** is present in the set.

In Turbo Pascal, a set type may be defined for any simple type having 256 or fewer individual values. This type from which set elements are derived is called that set's *base type*. Type **Char** qualifies as a base type, as does **Byte**. The enumerated type **Spectrum** we created in the last section also qualifies, since it has only seven separate values:

```
VAR
    LowColors : SET OF Spectrum;

LowColors := [Red,Orange,Yellow];
```

Type **Integer**, however, does not qualify. There are 65,535 different values available in type **Integer**, and a set may only be defined for base types having 256 or fewer individual values. If you define an integer subrange spanning 256 or fewer values, you may define a set with that subrange type as the set's base type:

```
TYPE
   ShoeSizes  = 5..17;

VAR
   SizesInStock : SET OF ShoeSizes;
```

You may also assign a range of elements to a set, assuming the elements are of an acceptable base type:

```
VAR
   Uppercase, Lowercase,
   Whitespace, Controls : SET OF Char;

Uppercase   := ['A'..'Z'];
Lowercase   := ['a'..'z'];
Controls    := [Chr(1)..Chr(31)];
Whitespace  := [Chr(9),Chr(10),Chr(12),Chr(13),Chr(32)];
```

This is certainly easier than explicitly naming all the characters from A to Z to assign them to a set. A range of elements containing no gaps (like 'A'..'Z') is called a *closed interval*. The list of members within the set constructor can include single elements, closed intervals, and expressions that yield an element of the base type of the set. These must all be separated by commas, but they do not have to be in any sort of order:

```
GradeSet := ['A'..'F','a'..'f'];
BadChars := [Chr(1)..Chr(8),Chr(11),Chr(X+4),'Q','x'..'z'];
NullSet   := [];
```

You should take care that expressions do not yield a value that is outside the range of the set's base type. If X in **BadChars** grows to 252 or higher, the result of the expression **Chr(X+4)** will no longer be a legal character. The results of such an expression will be unpredictable, other than to say they won't do you very much good.

Sets like **Uppercase**, **Lowercase**, and **Whitespace** defined above can be very useful when manipulating characters coming in from the keyboard or some other unpredictable source. I've implemented some simple functions that make use of these character sets:

```
FUNCTION CapsLock(Ch : Char) : Char;

BEGIN
   IF Ch IN Lowercase THEN CapsLock := Chr(Ord(Ch)-32)
     ELSE CapsLock := Ch
END;
```

```
FUNCTION DownCase(Ch : Char) : Char;

BEGIN
  IF Ch IN Uppercase THEN DownCase := Chr(Ord(Ch)+32)
    ELSE DownCase := Ch
END;


FUNCTION IsWhite(Ch : Char) : Boolean;

BEGIN
  IsWhite := Ch IN WhiteSpace
END;
```

All three of these routines assume that **Uppercase**, **Lowercase**, and **Whitespace** have already been declared and filled with the proper values. Actually, the way to ensure that this is done is to do it *inside* each routine by the use of set constants, as I'll explain toward the end of this chapter.

CapsLock returns all characters passed to it in uppercase. **DownCase** returns all characters passed to it as lowercase. **IsWhite** returns a **True** value if the character passed to it is "whitespace," that is, a tab, carriage return, linefeed, or space character.

The **IN** operator we used above is not the only operator you may use with sets. There are two classes of set operators: operators that build sets from other sets, and operators that test relationships between sets and yield a Boolean result.

The set builder operators are these:

+ Union of two sets; all elements in both sets.

* Intersection of two sets; all elements that are present in both sets.

- Exclusion, ("set difference" in the Turbo Pascal Reference Manual) which yields a set of the elements in the set on the right, once all the elements in the set on the left have been removed from it. This is a tricky notion; see Chapter 7.5.

The set relational operators are these:

IN **True** if the given element is present in the set.

= **True** if both sets contain *exactly* the same elements.

<> **True** if the two given sets do not contain exactly the same elements.

<= **True** if all the elements in the set on the left are present in the set on the right.

>= **True** if all the elements in the set on the right are present in the left.

More details on these set operators, including examples, will be given in the next section.

INTERNAL REPRESENTATION OF SETS

Turbo Pascal implements set types as bitmaps. The memory required by any given set type depends on the number of elements in that set's base type. Since no set may have more than 256 elements, the largest legal set type will be 32 bytes in size (32 bytes x 8 bits = 256 possible set elements). Unlike most Pascal implementations, sets whose base types have fewer elements will be smaller.

I have to emphasize here that all sets of a given set type will *always* be the same size in memory. This figure is set at compile-time and does not change as elements are included in or excluded from a set.

The size in memory of a given set type will be:

```
(Max DIV 8) - (Min DIV 8) + 1
```

where **Max** and **Min** are the ordinal values of the largest and smallest items in the set. A set of **Char**, for example, runs from character 0 to character 255:

```
(255 DIV 8) - (0 DIV 8) + 1

31 - 0 + 1

32 bytes occupied by a set of Char
```

Now, consider a set with a smaller base type:

```
TYPE
   Printables = ' '..'^';
   SymbolSet = SET OF Printables;
```

Here, **Min** will be 32 (**Ord(' ')**) and **Max** will be 126 (**Ord('^')**):

```
(126 DIV 8) - (32 DIV 8) + 1

15 - 4 + 1

12 bytes occupied by set type SymbolSet;
```

Each possible set element has one bit in the bitmap. If a particular element is present in the set, its bit is set to binary 1; otherwise its bit remains binary 0.

The set **Uppercase** defined above is a set of **Char**. Its base type (**Char**) has 256 different elements. The set must then be represented in memory as the following sequence of 32 hex bytes:

```
00 00 00 00 00 00 00 00 FE FF FF 07 00 00 00 00
00 00 00 00 00 00 00 00 00 00 00 00 00 00 00 00

    Low memory   ->  High memory
```

This is a bitmap of the 256 possible elements in a set of **Char**. The bit that represents 'A' is bit 1 of byte 8. The bit representing 'Z' is bit 2 of byte 11. (Both bits and bytes are numbered from zero.) This might seem confusing at first since the byte order is numbered from left to right while the order of the bits within each byte is numbered from right to left. If it still seems strange, write out the sequence of bytes from 8–11 as binary patterns, but with the bits reading from left to right instead of right to left:

```
              Byte #8 of set  Uppercase

    Hex FE: 11111110       01111111
            ^       ^       ^       ^
    Bits:   7       0       0       7

    Read:Right-to-leftLeft-to-right
```

If all the bytes in the set were expressed as binary patterns reading from left to right, the set could be written as a true bitmap.

This information on the internal representation of sets will not be especially useful to you until you need to pass a set variable to a machine language subroutine. Then you will need to know exactly which binary bit corresponds to which element in the set, so that your machine language routine will be manipulating the correct elements of the set it receives from your Pascal program.

7.5 Set Operators

Set operators are used to manipulate and test values of type **SET**. To a great extent they follow the rules of set arithmetic you may have learned in grade school. Table 7.1 summarizes the set operators implemented in Turbo Pascal. All of them take set operands and return set values.

SET UNION

The union of two sets is the set that contains as members all members contained in the two sets. The symbol for the set union operator is the plus sign (+), just as for arithmetic addition. An example:

```
VAR
    SetX, SetY, SetZ : SET OF Char;

SetX := ['Y','y','M','m']; SetY := ['N','n','M','m'];
SetZ := SetX + SetY;
```

SetZ now contains '**Y**', '**y**', '**N**', '**n**', '**M**', and '**m**'. Note that although '**M**' and '**m**' exist in both sets, each appears but once in the union of the two sets. A set merely says whether or not a member is present in the set; it is meaningless to

Table 7.1 Operators that Return Set Values

Operator	*Symbol*	*Precedence*
Set union	+	4
Set difference	-	4
Set Intersection	*	4

speak of how many times a member is present in a set. By definition, each member is present only once, or not present at all.

SET DIFFERENCE

The "difference" of two sets is conceptually related to subtraction. Given two sets, **SetA** and **SetB**, the difference between them (expressed as **SetA - SetB**) is the set consisting of the elements of **SetA** that remain once all the elements of **SetB** have been removed from it. For example:

```
SetA := ['Y','y','M','m'];
SetB := ['N','n','M','m'];
SetX := SetA - SetB;
```

SetZ now contains 'Y', 'y'.

SET INTERSECTION

The intersection of two sets is the set that contains as members only those members contained in *both* sets. The symbol for set intersection is the asterisk (*), just as for arithmetic multiplication. For example:

```
SetX := ['Y','y','M','m'];
SetY := ['N','n','M','m'];
SetZ := SetX * SetY;
```

SetZ now contains 'M' and 'm', which are the only two members contained in both sets.

THE SET RELATIONAL OPERATORS

The set operators just described work with set operands to produce new set values. We have briefly mentioned the relational operators that test relationships between sets and return Boolean values depending on those relationships.

Sets, for example, can be equal to one another, if they both have the same base type and both contain the same elements. Two sets that are *not* of the same base type will generate a type mismatch error at compile time if you try to compare them:

```
VAR
   SetX : SET OF Char;
   SetQ : SET OF Color;
   OK   : Boolean;

OK := SetX = SetQ;    { Will trigger error #26! }
```

This holds true for *all* set relational operators, not just equality as demonstrated here.

The most important set relational operator is the inclusion operator **IN**. **IN** tests whether a value of a set's base type is a member of that set.

```
VAR
  Ch : Char;

Read(Ch);          { From the keyboard }
IF Ch IN ['Y','y'] THEN
  Write('Yes indeed!');
```

This example shows a clean and easy way to tell whether a user has typed the letter Y (upper- or lowercase) in response to a prompt. The **IN** operator tests whether the typed-in character is a member of the set constant ['Y','y']. (**IN** works just as well with set variables.) The alternative would be to use a more complicated Boolean expression:

```
IF (Ch = 'Y') OR (Ch = 'y') THEN
  Write('Yes indeed!');
```

The **IN** operator is also faster than using a series (especially a long series) of relational expressions linked with the **OR** operator.

The greater than (>) and less than (<) operators make no sense when applied to sets, because sets have no implied order to their values. However, there are two additional set relational operators that make use of the same symbols as used by the greater than or equal to (>=) and less than or equal to (<=) operators. These are the set inclusion operators.

Inclusion of left in right (<=) tests whether all members of the set on the left are included in the set on the right. Inclusion of right in left (>=) tests whether all members of the set on the right are included in the set on the left. The action these two operators take is identical except for the orientation of the two operands with respect to the operator symbol. Given two sets, **Set1** and **Set2**, this expression:

```
(Set1 <= Set2) = (Set2 >= Set1)
```

will always evaluate to **True**. These operators are very handy for testing and manipulating characters in a text stream. For example:

```
VAR
  Vowels,Alphabet,Samples : SET OF Char;

Vowels   :=['A','E','I','O','U'];
Alphabet :=['A'..'Z'];        { Set of all UC letters }
Samples  :=['A','D','I','Q','Z'];

IF Samples <= Vowels THEN Write('All samples are vowels.');
IF NOT(Samples <= Vowels) AND (Samples <= Alphabet) THEN
  Write('Some or all samples are uppercase letters.');
IF NOT(Alphabet >= Samples) THEN
  Write('Some samples are not uppercase letters.');
```

In addition to demonstrating the set inclusion operators, these examples also show some uses of the **AND** and **NOT** operators. Given the members assigned to **Samples** in the above example, this output will be displayed:

```
Some or all samples are uppercase letters.
```

Before going on, jot down two sets of characters that would trigger the other two messages in the above example.

7.6 Arrays

An array is a data structure consisting of a fixed number of identical elements, with the whole collection given a single identifier as its name. The program keeps track of individual elements by number. Sometimes you name the entire array to work with it as a unified whole. Most of the time you identify one of the individual elements, by number, and work with that element alone. This number identifying an array element is called an *index*. In Pascal, an index need not always be a traditional number. Enumerated types, characters, and subranges may also act as array indices, allowing a tremendous richness of expression not matched by any other computer language.

It may be helpful to think of an array as a row of identical empty boxes in memory, side by side. The program allocates space for the boxes, but it is your job as programmer to *fill* them and manipulate their contents. The elements in an array are, in fact, set side-by-side in order in memory.

An array element may be any data type except a file. Arrays may consist of data structures; that is, you may have arrays of records and arrays of arrays. An array index must be a member or a subrange of an ordinal type, or a programmer-defined enumerated type. Floating-point numbers may *not* act as array indices, nor may **LongInt** or **Comp**. Type **Integer**, **ShortInt**, **Byte**, **Word**, **Char**, and **Boolean** may all index arrays.

Here are some valid array declarations, just to give you a flavor of what is possible (if you don't understand for now what a record is, bear with us for the time being, or look ahead to Section 7.7):

```
CONST
  Districts  = 14;

TYPE
  String80   = String[80];
  Grades     = 'A'..'F';        { Subrange  }
  Percentile = 1..99;           { Ditto    }
                                { Enum. type }
  Levels     = (K,G1,G2,G3,G4,G5,G6,G7,G8,G9,G10,G11,G12);
                                { Ditto    }
  Subjects   = (English,Math,Spelling,Reading,Art,Gym);
```

```
Profile  = RECORD
              Name        : String80;
              SSID        : String80;
              IQ          : Integer;
              Standing    : Percentile;
              Finals      : ARRAY[Subjects] OF Grades
              END;

GradeDef = ARRAY[Grades] OF String80;


VAR
   K12Profile   : ARRAY[Levels] OF Profile;
   Passed       : ARRAY[Levels] OF Boolean;
   Subtotals    : ARRAY[1..24] OF Integer;
   AreaPerc     : ARRAY[1..Districts] OF Percentile;
   AreaLevels   : ARRAY[1..Districts] OF ARRAY[Levels] OF Percentile;
   RoomGrid     : ARRAY[1..3,Levels] OF Integer;
```

The declarations shown above are part of an imaginary school district records manager program written in Pascal. Note that **Passed** is an array whose index is an enumerated type. **Passed[G5]** would contain a Boolean value (**True** or **False**) indicating whether a student had passed or failed the fifth grade. Remember, "G5" is *not* a variable; it is a constant value, one value of an enumerated type.

The low limit and high limit of an array's index are called its *bounds. The bounds of an ordinary array in Pascal must be fixed at compile time.* The Pascal compiler must know when it compiles the program exactly how large all data items are going to be. You cannot **REDIM** an ordinary array as you might in BASIC, nor change its shape as you might in APL.

With this in mind, the variable **AreaPerc** deserves a closer look. At first glance, you might think it has a variable for a high bound, but actually, **Districts** is a constant with a value of 14. Writing **[1..Districts]** is no different from writing **[1..14]**, but within the context of the program it assists your understanding of what the array actually represents.

Most of the arrays shown in the above example are one-dimensional. A one-dimensional array has only one index. A two-dimensional array (like **RoomGrid**, above) has two indices. An array may have any number of dimensions, but it edges toward bad practice to define an array with more than two or (at the outside) three. Also, the more dimensions an array has, the larger it tends to be and the more memory it uses—and the more likely that parts of it are empty or full of duplicate or rarely-accessed information that does nothing for you but waste memory. There are better, less memory-wasteful ways to handle large, complicated data structures, like linked lists, as I'll demonstrate later in Chapter 20.

When Turbo Pascal allocates an array in memory, it does not zero the elements of the array, as BASIC would. In general, *Pascal does not initialize data items of any type for you*. If there was garbage in RAM where the compiler went out to set up an array, the array elements will contain the garbage when the array is allocated. If you wish to zero out or otherwise initialize the elements of an array,

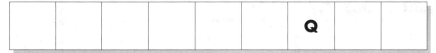

D1: ARRAY[0..8] OF CHAR;

D1[6] contains the "Q"

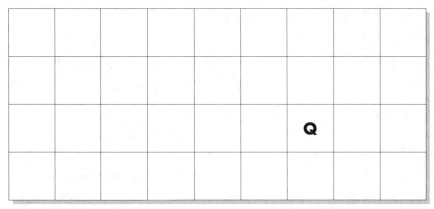

D1: ARRAY[0..8,1..4] OF CHAR;

D1[6,3] contains the "Q"

D1: ARRAY[0..7,1..4,0..3,0..2] OF CHAR;

D1[6,3,0,1] contains the "Q"

Figure 7.1 Multidimensional Arrays

you must do it yourself, in your program, before you use the array. This is not difficult, using a **FOR** loop (see Section 8.4 for more on **FOR** loops):

```
FOR I := 1 TO 24 DO Subtotals[I] := 0;
```

If portability is not a consideration, arrays (especially *large* arrays) may be initialized even more quickly with Turbo Pascal's **FillChar** statement:

```
FillChar(Subtotals,SizeOf(Subtotals),Chr(0));
```

Good examples of arrays used effectively can be found in the **ShellSort** procedure in Section 8.12 and the **QuickSort** procedure in Section 8.15.

Several special array identifiers are defined in Turbo Pascal specifically for treating all of memory as one large array. **Mem** treats memory as an array of **Byte**; **MemW** treats memory as an array of **Integer** or **Word**; and **MemL** treats memory

ARRAY[0..8] OF CHAR;

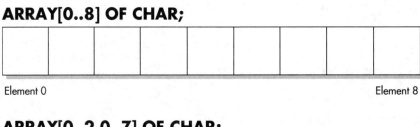

Element 0   Element 8

ARRAY[0..2,0..7] OF CHAR;

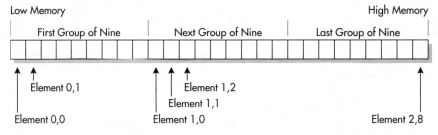

Multidimensional arrays are stored in memory with the rightmost dimensions increasing first.

Figure 7.2 Arrays in Memory

as an array of **LongInt**. The indices of these special arrays must include both an 8086 segment and an offset, separated by a colon. I won't be treating these advanced features in detail in this book, but Turbo Help can give you a good head start, and there is additional information in Borland's documentation.

INTERNAL REPRESENTATION OF ARRAYS

Arrays are contiguous sequences of the same data type. Turbo Pascal allocates array elements from low memory to high. In other words, the first byte in the first element of an array has the lowest address of any byte in the array.

For multidimensional arrays, the elements are stored with the rightmost dimension increasing first. This is best shown as a diagram. (See Figure 7.2).

7.7 Records in Detail

An array is a data structure composed of a number of identical data items all in a row and referenced by number. This sort of data structure is handy for dealing with large numbers of the same type of data; for example, values returned from an experiment of some sort. You might have a collection of 500 temperature readings and need to average them and perform analysis of variance on them. The easiest way to do that is to load them into an array and work with the temperature readings as elements of the array.

There is a data structure composed of data items that are *not* of the same type. It's called a *record*, and it gets its name from its origins as one line of data in a data file.

A record is a structure composed of several data items of different types grouped together. These data items are called the *fields* of the record.

Let's work out a short and much-simplified conceptual example. An auto-repair shop might keep a file on its spare parts inventory. For each part they keep in stock, they need to record its part number, its description, its wholesale cost, retail price, customary stock level, and current stock level. All these items are intimately linked to a single physical gadget, (a car part); so to simplify their programming the shop puts the fields together to form a record:

```
TYPE
  PartRec = RECORD
              PartNum, Class  : Integer;
              PartDescription : String;
              OurCost         : LongInt;
              ListPrice       : LongInt;
              StockLevel      : Integer;
              OnHand          : Integer;
            END

VAR
   CurrentPart, NextPart : PartRec;
   PartFile     : FILE OF PartRec;
   CurrentStock : Integer;
   MustOrder    : Boolean;
```

The entire structure becomes a new type with its own name. Data items of the record type can then be assigned, written to files, and otherwise worked with as a single entity without having to explicitly mention all the various fields within the record.

```
CurrentPart := NextPart; { Assign part record to another }
Read(PartFile,NextPart); { Read next record from file   }
```

When you need to work with the individual fields within a record, the notation consists of the record identifier followed by a period (".") followed by the field identifier:

```
CurrentStock := CurrentPart.OnHand;
IF CurrentStock < CurrentPart.StockLevel
   THEN MustOrder := True;
```

Accessing individual fields within a record this way is sometimes called "dotting."

Relational operators may *not* be used on records. To say that one record is "greater than" or "less than" another cannot be defined since there are an infinite number of possible record structures with no well-defined and unambiguous order for them to follow. In the example above we are comparing the *fields* of two records, not the records themselves. The fields are both integers and can therefore be compared by the "<" operator.

THE WITH STATEMENT

Fields within a record are accessed by dotting:

```
CurrentPart.OurCost   := 1075;  { In pennies! }
CurrentPart.ListPrice:= 4185;   { " }
CurrentPart.OnHand := 4;
```

Note the repetition of the record name before the field name. That's logically unnecessary if we know we're just going to access several fields from the same record in quick succession here. If you have to go down a list of fields within the same record and work with each field, you can avoid specifying the identifier of the record each and every time by using a special statement called the **WITH** statement.

We could simplify assigning values to several fields of the same record by writing the above snippet of code this way:

```
WITH CurrentPart DO
  BEGIN
    OurCost := 1075;
    ListPrice := 4185;
    OnHand  := 4;
  END;
```

The space between the **BEGIN** and **END** is the "scope" of the **WITH** statement. Within that scope, the record identifier need not be given to work with the fields of the record named in the **WITH** statement.

WITH statements need not have a **BEGIN/END** unless they contain more than a single statement. A **WITH** statement may include only a single statement to work with a record if that single statement contains several references to fields within a single record:

```
WITH CurrentPart DO VerifyCost(OurCost,ListPrice,Check);
```

In this example, **VerifyCost** is a procedure that takes as input two price figures and returns a value in **Check**. (Procedures are covered fully in Chapter 8.) Without the **WITH** statement, calling **VerifyCost** would have to be done this way:

```
VerifyCost(CurrentPart.OurCost,CurrentPart.ListPrice,Check);
```

The **WITH** statement makes the statement crisper and much easier to understand. By using **WITH**, we can hide the unnecessary details of what larger record we're working with during the time that we're working on a small scale with the fields of that record. There's no need to "see" the name of the embracing record every time we access a field, so the smart thing to do is put the name of the record off to one side so it doesn't get in the way. That's the spirit in which **WITH** was created.

NESTED RECORDS

A record is a group of data items taken together as a named data structure. A record is itself a data item, and so records may themselves be fields of larger records. Suppose the repair shop we've been speaking of expands its parts inventory so much that finding a part bin by memory gets to be difficult. There are 10 aisles with letters from A through J, with the bins in each aisle numbered from 1 up. To specify a location for a part requires an aisle character and a bin number. The best way to do it is by defining a new record type:

```
TYPE
  PartLocation =  RECORD
                    Aisle  : 'A'..'J';
                    Bin    : Integer
                  END;
```

Since each part has a location, **PartRec** needs a new field:

```
TYPE
  PartRec = RECORD
              PartNum, Class    : Integer;
              PartDescription   : String;
              OurCost           : LongInt;
              ListPrice         : LongInt;
              StockLevel        : Integer;
              OnHand            : Integer;
              Location          : PartLocation { A record! }
            END;
```

Location is "nested" within the larger record. To access the fields of **Location** you need *two* periods:

```
LookAisle := CurrentPart.Location.Aisle
```

If the outermost record is specified by a **WITH** statement you might have an equivalent statement like this:

```
WITH CurrentPart DO LookAisle := Location.Aisle;
```

WITH statements are fully capable of handling many levels of record nesting. You may, first of all, nest **WITH** statements one within another. The following compound statement is equivalent to the previous statement:

```
WITH CurrentPart DO
  WITH Location DO LookAisle := Aisle;
```

The **WITH** statement also allows a slightly terser form to express the same thing:

```
WITH CurrentPart, Location DO LookAisle := Aisle;
```

For this syntax you must place the record identifiers after the **WITH** reserved word, separated by commas, *in nesting order*. That is, the name of the outermost record is on the left, and the names of records nested within it are placed to its right, with the "innermost" nested record placed last.

Records are used most often as "slices" of a disk file. We will explore this use of records much more fully in the general discussion of binary file I/O in Chapter 14.

7.8 Variant Records

In the previous section we looked at Pascal's way of grouping several different data types together and calling them a record. In a *fixed* record type (which we have been discussing) the fields that make up a record are always the same data items in the same order and never change.

In a program doing real work in the real world, a record usually represents some real entity—and the real world is a varied and messy place. Pascal makes a major concession to the messiness of the real world by allowing *variant records*, the fields of which may be different data types depending on the contents of the other fields.

The notion of variant records is a subtle one. You might wish to come back to this section after reading the rest of Part 2, having paid particular attention to the discussion of **CASE OF** statements in Section 8.3. The definition of every variant record contains a **CASE OF** construct, and without a reasonable understanding of **CASE OF** you will not understand how variant records work.

BACK TO THE PARTS SHOP

Let's continue with the example of the auto repair shop's parts inventory system. In their system, each part that they keep in stock has a record in a file containing price information, stock levels, and a location in their storage room. However, in some cars there are parts that break so rarely that they are practically never needed, so it would be financially foolish to keep such parts in stock.

Still, if one breaks, the shop must have some means of ordering the part quickly. It is necessary to store (for those parts only) a vendor name and phone number for emergency ordering, and a suspected lead time on the order based on previous discussions with the vendor. If the part has to come all the way from Japan, better the customer know about it up front rather than have him haunt the repair shop for weeks while the part is in shipment.

So we can see that there are two types of parts: those kept in stock and those obtainable via emergency order only. Both types have a part number, class, description, and cost values. But there the similarity ends. We might have two separate record definitions, one for each type of part:

```
TYPE
  STPartRec = RECORD
             PartNum, Class    : Integer;
             PartDescription   : String;
             OurCost           : LongInt;
             ListPrice         : LongInt;
```

```
                StockLevel        : Integer;
                OnHand            : Integer;
                Location          : PartLocation
                END;

   EOPartRec = RECORD
                PartNum, Class    : Integer;
                PartDescription   : String;
                OurCost           : LongInt;
                ListPrice         : LongInt;
                Vendor            : String;
                OrderPhone        : String;
                OrderLead         : Integer;
                END;
```

The new part record type handles all information for emergency-order parts quite nicely. *But*—(as we will see in Section 14.3) a binary file may store only one record type, not two. Need we now keep two separate parts files, one for stocked parts and one for emergency-order only parts?

No. The two fixed record types may be combined into a single variant record type. The new record looks like this:

```
PartRec = RECORD
                PartNum, Class    : Integer;
                PartDescription   : String;
                OurCost           : LongInt;
                ListPrice         : LongInt;
                CASE Stocked      : Boolean OF
                  True :
                    (StockLevel   : Integer;
                     OnHand       : Integer;
                     Location     : PartLocation);
                  False :
                    (Vendor       : String;
                     OrderPhone   : String;
                     OrderLead    : Integer)
          END;
```

The new record type has two distinct parts. The first part, including the fields from **PartNum** to **ListPrice**, is called the *fixed part* of the record type. The rest of the record, from the reserved word **CASE** to the end, is the *variant part* of the record type. The variant part of a variant record must always be the *last* part of the record. You cannot have more fixed part fields after the variant part.

The difference between fixed part and variant part turns on the **CASE** construct. The **CASE** construct provides two or more alternative field definitions based on the value of what is called the *tag field*. The tag field of **PartRec** is the Boolean variable **Stocked**.

Stocked, being a **Boolean** variable, has only two possible values, **True** and **False**. In those **CASE**s where **Stocked** is **True** (if the record refers to a part kept in stock) the record contains the fields **StockLevel**, **OnHand**, and **Location**. In those **CASE**s where **Stocked** is **False**, (for emergency-order parts) the record instead contains the fields **Vendor**, **OrderPhone**, and **OrderLead**.

Note the use of parentheses to set off the separate variant parts of a variant record. Parentheses *must* surround the field definitions of each variant part. Do not include the tag field value constants (**True** and **False** in our example) within the parentheses.

VARIANT HASSLES

The question of what happens when you store data in a variant part, then change the value of the tag field such that another variant part comes to force. Turbo Pascal does not "wipe out" what was there before (some ancient Pascals did, however!) but simply leaves your data occupying the space it took when the earlier variant definition was in force. When the new variant definition comes into force, you can write to its fields, and that data will overwrite the memory area where your original data was placed. If you just read from the fields of the second variant without writing anything there first, Pascal will attempt to interpret the memory occupied by your first variant's fields in terms of the second variant's fields—and if that sounds ugly, well, you may not know the half of it. Sucking two bytes of a pointer into an integer variable will give you an integer, but *what* integer is almost impossible to guess.

Worse, no runtime error will be triggered if you try to do this. You'll just spawn a bug farm that could take you some time to exterminate.

Although for simplicity's sake our example record type has only two variants (because the tag field is Boolean and has only two possible values), a variant record may have up to 256 different variants, and any ordinal type may act as a tag field. This allows the (hazardous) possibility of a tag field assuming a value for which there is no defined variant. For example, if your tag field is of type **Char** and you define variants only for cases in which the tag field contains 'A', 'B', or 'C', what happens if the tag field is assigned a value of 'Z'? The behavior of the code becomes undefined, and attempts to access a field in a variant part may return unexpected garbage. *Avoid this possibility at all costs.* The best way is to make sure that *all* possible values of a tag field have a defined variant. Instead of making a tag field of type **Char**, define a subrange type instead:

```
TYPE
   TagChar = 'A'..'C';
```

and make the tag field type **TagChar** instead. Enumerated types (see section 7.3) are also extremely useful in creating data structures incorporating variant records.

It is perfectly legal for the variant parts of a variant record to be of different sizes. So how does the compiler allocate space for a variant record in memory? Every instance of a variant record type is allocated as much memory as required by the *largest* variant. If data storage space is short, you might check to see if you are wasting space by defining an enormous variant of a record and then rarely (or never!) using it. Every time you define a record of that type, the record will use all the space needed by that enormous variant even if that variant is never selected by the tag field. Rearranging your data structure to break out that enormous variant as a separate type could save you a lot of memory and disk space!

FREE UNION VARIANT RECORDS

There are actually two types of variant records defined by the Pascal language, and both of them are implemented in Turbo Pascal. The variant record we have just described is called a *discriminated union*, although the term is not used very much outside of academic circles. Discriminated union variant records always have a tag field. It is possible to define a variant record *without* a tag field. Such a data structure is called a *free union variant record*.

At first glance, a variant record without a tag field would appear to be a call to chaos. (Some experts do consider it exactly that.) Without a tag field to select one variant part from the many, how can the compiler know which variant part is currently in force?

Easy: They are *all* in force, all at once.

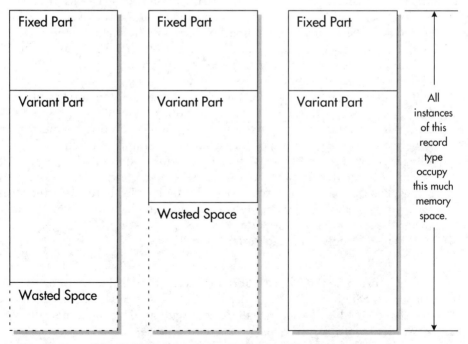

Three instances of the same variant record type, each with a different variant in force.

Figure 7.3 Variant Records

It is a peculiar concept, and one that should not be used without *complete* understanding of its implications. An example will help:

```
TYPE
   Halfer = RECORD
                 CASE Boolean OF
                    True  :  (I : Integer);
                    False :  (HiByte : Byte;
                                LoByte : Byte);
                 END;

VAR
   Porter : Halfer;
```

As you can see, there is no tag field present. There is, however (and this is the most peculiar thing about a free union) a tag field *type*, which in this case is **Boolean**. The tag field type must be present, and it must be an ordinal type with 256 or fewer values.

The tag field type is given only to specify the number of possible variant parts of the record and the values by which the variants are selected.

You'll remember that any time the tag field changes in an ordinary discriminated union variant record, the values of the fields in the previously selected variant part are essentially up for grabs as binary patterns in the underlying memory, and the fields of the initial variant part are not semantically accessible.

Here, the tag field cannot change because it does not exist. Any value assigned to any field of any variant part of a free union remains in the underlying memory, and that value will be interpreted as best can be done by all the other variant parts that share that same region of underlying memory. If this makes your head hurt, you aren't the first and you won't be the last.

To understand it, you must break a prime taboo in the Standard Pascal mindset and look closely at the actual memory locations underlying a program's data area. All variant parts of a free union are mapped onto the same region of memory. Our free union type **Halfer** has two variant parts: one has a single **Integer** field, and the other has two **Byte** fields. We know that an integer is stored as two bytes in memory. Values assigned to **Porter.HiByte** occupy the same physical byte of memory where the high-order byte of **Porter.I** exists. Values assigned to **Porter.LoByte** occupy the same physical byte of memory where the low-order byte of **Porter.I** exists.

When we assign a value to **Porter.I**:

```
Porter.I := 21217;
```

and then examine the value of **Porter.HiByte**, we will find that **Porter.HiByte** contains the high-order byte of **Porter.I**, in this case 82. In similar fashion, we can change the high-order byte of **Porter.I** without disturbing the value of the low-order byte, and vise versa.

What good is all this? Free unions can get you out of some tight spots. For example, some I/O devices are designed so that they can only move one 8-bit byte at a time to an I/O port. To send a 16-bit quantity to an I/O port you must break it down into two bytes. There are mathematical ways of deriving the values of the individual high and low order bytes of an integer, but they involve arithmetic, which takes time. (Turbo Pascal can do it with its built-in *Hi* and *Lo* functions, which, however, won't port to other implementations of Pascal.) A faster way is simply assigning your integer to a data type that can *simultaneously* be treated as both a single integer and as two 8-bit bytes. To send an integer to an 8080 I/O port using the **Halfer** free union variant record, you would do this:

```
J  := 21217;
Porter.I := J;                { Porter is type Halfer }
Port[$A0] := Porter.HIByte;  { Out to I/O port $A0   }
Port[$A0] := Porter.LOByte;  { one byte at a time... }
```

(I won't be covering the details of port I/O in this book. Check with the Borland documentation or Turbo Help if you're curious about it.) The free union variant record is actually a trick to circumvent the strong typing restrictions that Pascal places on you. It's a way of mapping one type upon another so that any type can be converted to any other type *if you know what you are doing.* Free unions are actually a concession to the vagaries of the standard-less hardware world, and should only be used to defeat problems imposed by the hardware itself.

There are terser and less "magical" ways of doing this sort of thing, mainly with type casting. (See Chapter 18.) Free unions are your best choice when portability is a consideration, however. They are often not portable in their *effects*, but are certainly more portable syntactically and symantically to other compilers than Turbo Pascal's proprietary extensions.

7.9 Strings, Fixed-Length and Variable

Manipulating words and lines of text is a fundamental function of a computer program. At minimum, a program must display messages like "Press RETURN to continue:" and "Processing completed." In Pascal, as in most computer languages, a line of characters to be taken together as a single entity is called a *string*.

STANDARD PASCAL STRINGS (FIXED LENGTH)

ISO Standard Pascal has very little power to manipulate strings. In Standard Pascal, there is nothing formally referred to as type **STRING**, as in Turbo Pascal. To hold text strings, Standard Pascal uses a *packed array of characters*, sometimes abbreviated as **PAOC**:

```
TYPE
   PAOC25 = PACKED ARRAY[1..25] OF Char;
```

This is a typical definition of a **PAOC** type. Of course, it doesn't have to be 25 characters in size; it can be as large as you like. The word **PACKED** is a hold-over from large mainframe computers; on 8- and 16-bit computers it serves no purpose. In mainframe computers with 32- and 64-bit words, the word **PACKED** instructs the compiler to store as many characters as will fit in one machine word, rather than using one machine word per character. Using **PACKED** on a mainframe could reduce the size of a string by a factor of four to eight times. Turbo Pascal always stores a **Char** value in 1 byte no matter what the word size of the computer it runs on. The word **PACKED** is still necessary, however, to define a Standard Pascal string.

What can be done with a **PAOC**-type string? Not much. A string constant can be assigned to it, if the string constant is *exactly* the same size as the definition of the **PAOC**:

```
VAR
   ErrorMsg : PAOC25;

ErrorMsg := 'Warning! Bracket missing!'; { This is OK }
ErrorMsg := 'Warning! Comma missing!';   { Illegal!  }
```

The second string constant is two characters short of 25 long, so the compiler will display

```
Error 26: Type mismatch
```

The second string constant could not be considered a **PAOC25** because it is only 23 characters long; hence the type mismatch error. Of course, you could have padded out the second constant with spaces, and the padded constant would have been acceptable.

You can compare two **PAOC**-type strings with the relational operators, read and write them from files, and print them to the screen. And that's where it ends. All other manipulations have to be done on a character-by-character basis, as though the string were just another array of any simple type.

The only reason to use **PAOC**-type strings is in situations where you are writing code that may have to be ported to a Pascal compiler that does not understand variable-length (sometimes called "dynamic") strings. Such compilers are rare, and getting rarer. As you might expect, they seem to be found mainly on enormous mainframe computers.

TURBO PASCAL VARIABLE-LENGTH STRINGS

Most modern Pascal implementors, including those who wrote Turbo Pascal, have filled this hole in the language definition by providing what are called *variable-length* strings. Like **PAOC**-type strings, variable-length strings are arrays of characters, but they are treated by the compiler in a special way. Variable-length strings have a *logical length* that varies depending on what you put into the string. Strings of different logical lengths may be assigned to one another as long as the real, physical lengths of the strings are not exceeded. The means of implementing variable-length strings in Turbo Pascal is identical to the way they have been implemented in the primordial UCSD Pascal, which has been offered by different vendors through the years, and has recently been reintroduced by a British firm.

A string type in Turbo Pascal has two lengths: a physical length and a logical length. The physical length is the amount of memory the string actually occupies. This length is set at compile time and never changes. The logical length is the number of characters currently considered to be stored in the string. This can change as you work with the string. The logical length (which from now on we will simply call the length) is a numeric value stored as part of the string itself and can be read in several ways.

A string variable is defined using the reserved word **STRING**. The default physical length for a string defined as **STRING** is 255 characters. (This differs from Turbo Pascal V3.0 and earlier, in which the **STRING** type had no default length, and derived string types of some given size had to be explicitly declared in the **TYPE** section of your programs.) You may not always need a string that physically large (for example, a telephone number fits comfortably in less than 20 characters) and you may define smaller string types to save memory by placing the physical size after the reserved word **STRING** in brackets:

```
VAR
   Message  : String[80]; { Physical size = 80 }
   Name     : String[30]; { Physical size = 30 }
   Address  : String[30]; { Physical size = 30 }
   State    : String[2];  { Physical size = 2 }
```

The legal range of physical lengths is 1 character to 255 characters.

You may also define separate string types as strings of different physical lengths. This is a much better way to deal with strings shorter than 255 characters:

```
TYPE
   String80  = String[80];
   String30  = String[30];
   Buffer    = String[255];
```

Once you have defined these types, declare all string variables that are to have a physical length of 30 characters as type **String30**. This way, all such strings will have identical types and not simply compatible types.

What is a string, physically? A string is an array of characters indexed from 0 to the physical length. Character 0 is special, however; it is the *length byte* and it holds the logical length of the string at any given time. The length byte is set by the runtime code when you perform any operation on a string that changes its logical length:

```
MyString := '';                           { MyString[0] = 0 }
MyString := 'Frodo';                      { MyString[0] = 5 }
MyString := 'Alfred E. ' + 'Newmann';     { MyString[0] = 17 }
```

The actual text contained in the string begins at **MyString[1]**. See Figure 7.4.

**VAR MYSTRING : STRING[80];
MYSTRING : = 'This is it';**

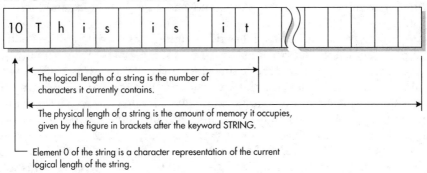

The logical length of a string is the number of characters it currently contains.

The physical length of a string is the amount of memory it occupies, given by the figure in brackets after the keyword STRING.

Element 0 of the string is a character representation of the current logical length of the string.

Figure 7.4 String Representation

Strings may be accessed as though they were in fact arrays of characters. You can reference any character in the string, including the length byte, with a normal array reference:

```
VAR
    MyString : String[15];
    CharS    : Integer;
    OUTChar  : Char;

MyString := 'Galadriel';
CharS    := ORD(MyString[0]);   { CharS now equals 9  }
OUTChar  := MyString[6];        { OUTChar now holds 'r' }
```

Even though the Turbo Pascal runtime code treats the length byte as a number, it is still an element in an array of **Char** and thus cannot be assigned directly to type **Byte** or **Integer**. To assign the length byte to a numeric variable, you must use the **ORD** transfer function, which is Pascal's orderly way of transferring a character value to a numeric value. (See Section 9.5.)

This, however, is doing it the hard way. There are a good number of predefined string-handling functions and procedures built into Turbo Pascal. The **Length** function is a good example. It returns the current logical length of a string variable:

```
    Chars := Length(MyString);   { Chars now equals 9  }
```

We will discuss **Length** and all the other built-in string handling functions and procedures in Chapter 15.

Characters and strings are compatible in some limited ways. You can assign a character value (stored either in constant form or as a **Char** variable) to a string variable. The string variable then has a logical length of one:

```
    MyString := 'A';      { Logical length = 1 }
    MyString := OUTChar;  { Ditto }
```

A string (even one having a length of zero or one) *cannot*, however, be assigned to a character variable.

You can compare a string variable to a character literal:

```
IF MyString = 'A' THEN StartProcess;
```

It is possible to assign a string to another string with a shorter physical length. This will cause neither a compile-time nor a runtime error. What it *will* do is truncate the data from the larger string to the maximum physical length of the smaller string.

C-STYLE STRING SUPPORT IN TURBO PASCAL

To support easier programming of Microsoft Windows applications in Turbo Pascal, Borland has added support for C-style null-terminated string handling. The **Strings** unit contains a large number of short procedures that manipulate C-style strings, and if you wish to use these procedures to manipulate C-style strings you must include the **Strings** unit in your **USES** statement. (More about units and **USES** in Chapter 13.)

C-style strings resemble Standard Pascal strings superficially. They are runs of characters with no explicit length byte, and their end is signalled by the use of a *null character*, the character whose ordinal value is 0. This makes it difficult to tell just how long a string is; you must scan the string to find its ending null character before you can know how long it is. The **Strings** unit has functions that perform this and a host of other services.

Using C-style strings requires that you be proficient in the use of pointers, which is a great deal to ask of beginning Pascal programmers, especially when the general payback in using C-style strings has yet to be revealed to me. I recommend not bothering with them unless you are forced to deal with Microsoft Windows API calls. Until then, C-style strings are a great deal more trouble than they are worth, and I will not be discussing them further in this book.

7.10 Typed Constants

Standard Pascal only allows simple constants: integers, characters, reals, Booleans, and strings. Turbo Pascal also provides *typed constants*, meaning constants with an explicit type that are initialized to some specific value.

Calling Turbo Pascal's typed constants "constants" is not entirely fair. Real constants are hardcoded "in-line" into the machine code produced by the compiler, with an actual physical copy of the constant dropped in everywhere it is named. The constant thus exists at no single address. Turbo Pascal's typed constants are actually static variables that are initialized at runtime to values taken from the source code. They exist at one single address, which is referenced anytime the typed constant is used.

Typed constants also violate the most fundamental proscription of constants in all languages: They may be changed during the course of a program run. Of course, you are not obligated to alter typed constants at runtime, but the compiler will not stop you if you try. In this Turbo Pascal provides less protection than in the area of simple constants. If you attempt to write to a simple constant, Turbo Pascal will display this error message:

```
Error 113: Error in statement
```

With that in mind, it might be better to think of typed constants as a means of forcing the compiler to initialize complicated data structures. Standard Pascal has *no* means of initializing variables automatically. If values are to be placed into variables, *you* must place them there somehow, either from assignment statements or by reading values in from a file. For example, you could initialize an array of 15 integers this way:

```
VAR
   Weights : ARRAY[1..15] OF Integer;

Weights[1]     := 17;
Weights[2]     := 5;
Weights[3]     := 91;
Weights[4]     := 111;
Weights[5]     := 0;
Weights[6]     := 44;
Weights[7]     := 16;
Weights[8]     := 3;
Weights[9]     := 472;
Weights[10]    := 66;
Weights[11]    := 14;
Weights[12]    := 38;
Weights[13]    := 57;
Weights[14]    := 8;
Weights[15]    := 10;
```

For 15 values this may seem manageable. But suppose you had 50 values? Or 100? At that point Turbo Pascal's typed constants become *very* attractive. This same array could be initialized as a structured constant like so:

```
CONST
   Weights : ARRAY[1..15] OF Integer =
      (17,5,91,111,0,44,16,3,472,66,14,38,57,8,10);
```

The form of a typed constant definition is this:

```
<identifier> : <type> = <values>
```

Because Turbo Pascal allows multiple **CONST** keywords within a single program, you may have a separate **CONST** declaration section for typed constants *after* the type declaration section. This allows you to declare your own custom type definitions first, and then create constants having your custom types.

ARRAY CONSTANTS

The numeric array example above is a simple, one-dimensional array constant. Its values are placed, in order, between parentheses, with commas separating the values. *You must give one value for each element of the array constant.* Turbo Pascal will not allow you to initialize some values of an array and leave the rest "blank." You must do all of them or none at all. If the number of values you give does not match the number of elements in the array, the compiler will display this error message:

```
Error 87 : ',' expected.
```

It is literally looking for another comma and more values in the list.

If you only need to initialize a few values out of a large array (and leave the others undefined), it might be more effective to go back to individual assignment statements.

You may also define *multidimensional* array constants. The trick here is to enclose each dimension in parentheses, with commas separating both the dimensions and the items. A single pair of parentheses must enclose the entire constant. The innermost nesting level represents the rightmost dimension from the array declaration. An example will help:·

```
CONST
  Grid : ARRAY[0..4,0..3] OF Boolean =
         ((4,6,2,1),
          (3,9,8,3),
          (1,7,7,5),
          (4,1,7,7),
          (3,1,3,1));
```

This is a two-dimensional array of integer constants, arranged as five rows of four columns, and might represent game pieces on a game grid. Adding a third dimension to the game (and the grid) would be done this way:

```
·CONST
  Space : ARRAY[0..7,0..4,0..3] OF Integer =

(((4,6,2,1),(3,9,8,3),(1,7,7,5),(4,1,7,7),(3,1,3,1)),
  ((1,1,1,1),(1,1,1,1),(1,1,1,1),(1,1,1,1),(1,1,1,1)),
  ((2,2,2,2),(2,2,2,2),(2,2,2,2),(2,2,2,2),(2,2,2,2)),
  ((3,3,3,3),(3,3,3,3),(3,3,3,3),(3,3,3,3),(3,3,3,3)),
  ((4,4,4,4),(4,4,4,4),(4,4,4,4),(4,4,4,4),(4,4,4,4)),
  ((5,5,5,5),(5,5,5,5),(5,5,5,5),(5,5,5,5),(5,5,5,5)),
  ((6,6,6,6),(6,6,6,6),(6,6,6,6),(6,6,6,6),(6,6,6,6)),
  ((7,7,7,7),(7,7,7,7),(7,7,7,7),(7,7,7,7),(7,7,7,7)));
```

The values given for the two-dimensional array have been retained here to see how the array has been extended by one dimension. Note that the list of values in an array constant must begin with the same number of left parentheses as the array has dimensions. Remember, also, that *every* element in the array must have a value in the array constant declaration.

Notice that this feature of Turbo Pascal allows you to intialize 160 different integer values in a relatively small space. Imagine what it would have taken to initialize this array with a separate assignment statement for each array element!

RECORD CONSTANTS

Record constants are handled a little bit differently. You must first declare a record type and then a constant containing values for each field in the record. The list of values must include the name of each field, followed by a colon, and then the value for that field. Items in the list are separated by semicolons. As an example, consider a record containing configuration values for a terminal program:

```
TYPE
   BPS         = (B110,B300,B1200,B2400,B4800,B9600);
   ParityType  = (EvenParity,OddParity,NoParity);
   TermCFG     = RECORD
                    LocalAreaCode  : String[3];
                    UseTouchtones  : Boolean;
                    DialOneFirst   : Boolean;
                    BaudRate       : BPS;
                    BitsPerChar    : Integer;
                    Parity         : ParityType
                 END;

CONST
   Config : TermCFG =
                  (LocalAreaCode  : '716';
                   UseTouchtones  : True;
                   DialOneFirst   : True;
                   BaudRate       : B1200;
                   BitsPerChar    : 7;
                   Parity         : EVEN_PARITY);
```

The structured constant declaration for **Config** must come after the type definition for **TermCFG**, otherwise the compiler would not know what a **TermCFG** was. Note that Turbo Pascal allows multiple **CONST** sections, and will allow you to place a **CONST** section *after* a **TYPE** section. This would not be allowed under Standard Pascal. Also, note that there is no **BEGIN/END** bracketing in the declaration of **Config**. The parentheses serve to set off the list of field values from the rest of your source code.

SET CONSTANTS

Declaring a set constant is not very different from assigning a set value to a set variable:

```
CONST
   Uppercase : SET OF Char = ['A'..'Z'];
```

The major difference is the notation used to represent nonprintable characters in a set of **Char**. Characters that do not have a printable symbol associated with them may ordinarily be represented in a set builder by the **Chr** transfer function:

```
MySet := [Chr(7),Chr(10),Chr(13)];
```

 Important

The **Chr** notation shown above will *not* work when declaring set constants. You have two alternatives:

1. Express the character as a control character by placing a caret symbol (^) in front of the appropriate character. The bell character, **Chr(7)**, would be expressed as **^G**.

2. Express the character as its ordinal value preceded by a pound sign (#). The bell character would be expressed as **#7**. This notation is more useful for expressing characters falling in the "high" 128 bytes of type **Char**, corresponding to the line-drawing, mathematical, and foreign language characters on the IBM PC and many compatibles.

For example, the set of whitespace characters is a useful set constant:

```
CONST
   Whitespace : SET OF Char = [#8,#10,#12,#13,' '];
```

or, alternatively:

```
CONST
   Whitespace : SET OF Char = [^H,^J,^L,^M,' '];
```

The following three routines show you how to use set constants in simple character-manipulation tools. If you do a *lot* of character manipulation and find a great deal of use for these three set constants, you might also declare them at the global program level so that any part of the program can use them. Remember that, declared as it is here locally to the individual functions, the **Whitespace** constant *cannot* be accessed from outside the function! This is a consequence of the scoping rules of procedures and functions, which I'll cover in detail in Chapter 11.

```
FUNCTION CapsLock(Ch : Char) : Char;

CONST
   Lowercase : SET OF Char = ['a'..'z'];

BEGIN
   IF Ch IN Lowercase THEN CapsLock := Chr(Ord(Ch)-32)
     ELSE CapsLock := Ch
END;
```

```
FUNCTION DownCase(Ch : Char) : Char;

CONST
  Uppercase : SET OF Char = ['A'..'Z'];

BEGIN
  IF Ch IN Uppercase THEN DownCase := Chr(Ord(Ch)+32)
    ELSE DownCase := Ch
END;


FUNCTION IsWhite(Ch : Char) : Boolean;

CONST
  Whitespace : SET OF Char = [#8,#10,#12,#13,' '];

BEGIN
  IsWhite := Ch IN WhiteSpace
END;
```

Chapter **8**

Structuring Code

MAKING EXECUTION GO WHERE YOU WANT IT TO

Controlling the flow of program logic is one of the most important facets of any programming language. Conditional statements that change the direction of the flow of control, looping statements that repeat some action a number of times, and switch statements that pick one course out of many based on a controlling value, all make useful programs possible.

Pascal, furthermore, would like you, the programmer, to direct the flow of control in a structured, rational manner so the programs you write are easy to read and easy to change when they need changing. For this reason, wild-eyed zipping around inside a program is difficult in Pascal.

The language syntax itself suggests with some force that programs begin at the top of the page and progress generally downward, exiting at the bottom when the work is done. Multiple entry and exit points and unconditional branching via **GOTO** are more trouble to set up—which is just as well, because they can be a lot more trouble to understand and debug when they don't go quite where you want them to, when you want them to.

And making things go where you want them to is the fundamental purpose of this admittedly large chapter.

8.1 BEGIN, END, and Compound Statements

We have already looked at several simple types of statements like assignment statements and data definition statements. In Pascal you frequently need to group a number of statements together and treat them as though they were a single statement. The means to do this is the pair of reserved words **BEGIN** and **END**. A group of statements between a **BEGIN** and **END** pair becomes a *compound statement*. The bodies of procedures and functions, and of programs themselves, are compound statements:

193

```
PROGRAM Rooter;

VAR
  R,S : Real;

BEGIN
  Writeln('>>Square root calculator<<');
  Writeln;
  Write('>>Enter the number: ');
  Readln(R);
  S := Sqrt(R);
  Writeln(' The square root of ',R:7:7,' is ',S:7:7,'.')
END.
```

The statements bracketed by **BEGIN** and **END** in the above example are all simple statements, but that need not be the case. Compound statements may also be parts of larger compound statements:

```
PROGRAM BetterRooter;

VAR
  R,S : Real;

BEGIN
  Writeln('>>Better square root calculator<<');
  Writeln;
  R:=1;
  WHILE R<>0 DO
    BEGIN
      Writeln('>>Enter the number (0 to exit): ');
      Readln(R);
      IF R<>0 THEN
      BEGIN
        S := Sqrt(R);
        Writeln(' The square root of ',R:7:7,' is ',S:7:7,'.');
        Writeln
      END
    END;
  Writeln('>>Square root calculator signing off...')
END.
```

This program contains one compound statement nested inside another, and both nested within a third compound statement that is the body of the program itself.

This is a good place to point out the "prettyprinting" convention that is virtually always used when writing Pascal code. The rule on prettyprinting turns on compound statements: *Each compound statement is indented two spaces to the right of the rest of the statement in which it is nested.*

It's also crucial to remember that *prettyprinting is ignored by the compiler.* It is strictly a typographical convention to help you sort out nested compound statements by "eyeballing" rather than counting **BEGIN**s and **END**s. You could as well (as some do) indent by three or more spaces instead of two. You could also (as some do) not indent at all. The compiler doesn't care. But the readability of your program will suffer if you don't use prettyprinting.

There is one other thing about compound statements that might seem obvious to some but very unobvious to others: *Compound statements can be used anywhere a simple statement can.* Anything between a **BEGIN/END** pair is treated syntactically by the compiler just as a single simple statement would be.

Compound statements may also be bounded by the reserved words **REPEAT** and **UNTIL**, as I'll show a little later in this chapter.

8.2 IF/THEN/ELSE

A *conditional statement* is one that directs program flow in one of two directions based on a Boolean value. In Pascal the conditional statement is the **IF/THEN/ELSE** statement. The **ELSE** clause is optional, but every **IF** reserved word *must* have a **THEN** associated with it. In its simplest form, such a statement is constructed this way:

```
IF <Boolean expression> THEN <statement>
```

The way this statement works is almost self-explanatory from the logic of the English language: If the Boolean expression evaluates to **True**, then **<statement>** is executed. If the Boolean expression evaluates to **False**, control "falls through" to the next statement in the program.

Adding an **ELSE** clause makes the statement look like this:

```
IF <Boolean expression> THEN <statement1>
   ELSE <statement2>
```

Here, if the expression evaluates to **True,** then **<statement 1>** is executed. If the expression evaluates to **False,** then **<statement 2>** is executed. If an **ELSE** clause exists, you can be sure that one or the other of the two statements will be executed.

Either or both of the statements associated with **IF/THEN/ELSE** may be compound statements. Remember that a compound statement may be used anywhere a simple statement may. For example:

```
IF I < 0 THEN
   BEGIN
     Negative := True;   { Set negative flag   }
     I := Abs(I)        { Take abs. value of I  }
   END            { Never semicolon here! }
ELSE Negative := False;  { Clear negative flag   }
```

An important point to remember: There is *no* semicolon after the **BEGIN/END** compound statement. The entire code fragment above is considered a single IF statement. A crucial corollary: There is *never* a semicolon immediately before the **ELSE** reserved word in an **IF/THEN/ELSE** statement. Adding one will give you a "freestanding **ELSE**," which is meaningless in Pascal and will trigger a syntax error. The only place you'll ever find a semicolon immediately before an **ELSE** word is inside a **CASE** statement, as I'll explain a little later in connection with **CASE** statements.

NESTED IF STATEMENTS

Since an **IF** statement is itself a perfectly valid statement, it may be one or both of the statements contained in an **IF/THEN/ELSE** statement. **IF**s may be nested as deeply as you like—but remember that if someone reading your code must dive too deeply after the bottommost **IF**, he may lose track of things and drown before coming up again. If the sole purpose of multiply nested **IF**s is to choose one alternative of many, it is far better to use the **CASE** statement, which will be covered in Section 8.3. Structurally, such a construction looks like this:

```
IF <Boolean expression1> THEN
 IF <Boolean expression2> THEN
  IF <Boolean expression3> THEN
   IF <Boolean expression4> THEN
    IF <Boolean expression5> THEN
     <statement>;
```

The bottom line here is that all Boolean expressions must evaluate to **True** before **<statement>** is executed.

Such a downward escalator of **IF**s is often hard to follow. Sharp readers may already be objecting that this same result could be done with **AND** operators:

```
IF <Boolean1> AND <Boolean2> AND <Boolean3>
   AND <Boolean4> AND <Boolean5> THEN
   <statement>;
```

This is entirely equivalent to the earlier nested **IF** with one sneaky catch: Here, *all* the Boolean expressions are evaluated before a decision is reached on whether or not to execute **<statement>**. With the nested **IF**, the compiler will stop testing as soon as it encounters a Boolean expression that turns up **False**. In other words, in a nested **IF**, if **<Boolean3>** is found to be **False**, the compiler never even evaluates **<Boolean4>** or **<Boolean5>**.

Nitpicking? No! There are times when, in fact, the reason for **<Boolean3>** might be to make sure **<Boolean4>** is not tested in certain cases. Divide by zero is one of those cases. Consider this:

```
IF AllOK THEN
 IF R > PI THEN
  IF S <> 1 THEN
   IF (R / ((S*S)-1) < PI) THEN
    CalculateRightAscension;
```

Here, a value of **S** = 1 will cause a divide-by-zero error if the code attempts to evaluate the next expression. So the code *must* stop testing if **S > 1** turns up **False** or risk crashing the program with a runtime divide-by-zero error.

With nested **IF**s you can determine the sequential order in which a series of tests is done. A string of **AND** operators between Boolean expressions may evaluate those expressions in any order dictated by the code generator's optimization logic. If one of your tests carries the hazard of a runtime error, use nested **IF**s.

NESTED ELSE/IFS

The previous discussion of nested **IF**s did not include any **ELSE** clauses. Nesting **IF**'s does not preclude **ELSE**s, though the use and meaning of the statement changes radically. Our previous example executed a series of tests to determine whether or not a single statement was to be executed. By using nested **ELSE/IF**s you can determine which of many statements is to be executed:

```
IF <Boolean1> THEN <statement1>
  ELSE
   IF <Boolean2> THEN <statement2>
    ELSE
     IF <Boolean3> THEN <statement3>
      ELSE
       IF <Boolean4> then <statement4>
        ELSE <statement5>;
```

The code will descend the escalator, and as soon as it finds a Boolean with a value of **True**, it will execute the statement associated with that Boolean. The tests are performed in order; even if **<Boolean4>** is **True**, it will not be executed (or **<Boolean4>** even evaluated) if **<Boolean2>** is found to be **True** first.

The final **ELSE** clause is not necessary; it provides a "none of the above" choice, in case none of the preceding Boolean expressions turned out to be true. You could simply omit it and control would fall through to the next statement without executing any of the statements contained in the larger **IF** statement.

As with nested **IF**s described above, nested **ELSE/IF**s allow you to set the order of the tests performed, so that if one of them carries the danger of a runtime error, you can defuse the danger with an earlier test for the dangerous values.

The **CASE** statement is a shorthand form of nested **ELSE/IF**s in which all of the Boolean expressions are of this form: **<value> = <value>** and the type of all **<value>**s is identical. We'll look at the **CASE** statement in detail in Section 8.3.

SHORT-CIRCUIT BOOLEAN EVALUATION

Apart from nesting **IF** statements, there is another, considerably less portable means of dictating the order in which the compiler evaluates Boolean expressions. It involves a compiler optimization technique introduced with Turbo Pascal 4.0 called *short-circuit Boolean evaluation*.

A few paragraphs back we looked at a nested **IF** construction that avoided the possibility of a divide-by-zero error by testing for a divide-by-zero condition before performing the actual divide operation. Consider that nested **IF** expressed as a single Boolean expression:

```
IF AllOK  AND
   (R > PI) AND
   (S <> 1) AND
   (R / ((S*S)-1) < PI)     { Could trigger divide-by-zero! }
THEN CalculateRightAscension;
```

Without short-circuit Boolean Evaluation (which is the default), the compiler will evaluate all four of the Boolean subexpressions before combining them into a single Boolean value as the result of the entire, larger expression. As we mentioned earlier, if **S** ever takes on a value of 1, the fourth subexpression will trigger a divide-by-zero error, since when **S** equals 1, **R** is divided by **((S*S)-1)** which equals zero.

When short-circuit Boolean evaluation is in force, the compiler is forced to evaluate Boolean expressions from left to right, and it will stop evaluation as soon as it is sure that testing further will not change the ultimate value of the expression.

How can it be sure that further testing won't change things? Think about the meaning of the **AND** operator. If any number of Boolean subexpressions are **AND**ed together, *a single FALSE value will force the whole expression to FALSE*. So once that first **FALSE** turns up in evaluating an expression from left to right, the whole expression will be **FALSE** no matter what else waits to be evaluated further to the right.

This technique is called "short circuit" because it quits when possible before evaluating an entire expression. The primary reason for it is that it can make your programs run more quickly if there are many Boolean expressions to be evaluated. Any time you can perform the same job by executing less code, the job will go more quickly.

However, the side benefit of allowing you to arrange your Boolean expressions so that "dangerous" subexpressions are to the right of "sentinel" subexpressions that guard against the dangerous condition is perhaps more generally useful. Returning to the example above: If short-circuit Boolean evaluation is enabled, the compiler will evaluate the subexpression **(S <> 1)**. If **S** is equal to 1, evaluation stops there, and the dangerous expression **(R / ((S*S)-1) < PI)** will never be evaluated, eliminating the possibility of a divide-by-zero runtime error bringing the program to a halt.

Short-circuit evaluation doesn't only apply to the **AND** operator. A string of expressions **OR**ed together will be evaluated *only* until the first **TRUE** value is encountered. More complicated expressions are simply ground through until the compiler is certain that nothing further can change the ultimate Boolean value. Then it will stop.

Using short-circuit Boolean evaluation is made easier by the fact that the compiler assumes it by default. What is called "complete" Boolean expression evaluation must be explicitly chosen if you want to use it. (Turbo Pascal 3.0 and earlier versions *always* used complete expression evaluation, which is in keeping with the Standard Pascal definition.) Forcing complete Boolean expression evaluation is done from the Options I Compiler menu item in the IDE, or through the **/B+** switch when using the command-line version of the compiler.

You can also force complete Boolean expression evaluation by inserting a **{$B+}** compiler command in your source code. By bracketing a region of code between a **{$B+}** command and a **{$B-}** command, you can force complete evaluation *only* between the two commands, and use short-circuit evaluation throughout the rest of your program.

Why would you ever want to use complete Boolean expression evaluation? Just as you sometimes need to ensure that a certain subexpression will *never* be evaluated (as we saw above), you must sometimes ensure that *every* subexpression is *always* evaluated.

Almost all such cases involve Pascal functions that return Boolean values after doing some sort of necessary work that must be completed regardless of which value the function returns. (For those of you reading this book serially who may not yet understand Pascal functions and how they return values, look ahead to Section 8.10.)

```
IF AllocateBigBuffer(BigBuffPtr) AND
  AllocateLittleBuffer(LittleBuffPtr)
   THEN LoadBothBuffers ELSE
    BEGIN
     IF BuffPtr1 <> NIL THEN LoadBuffer1
      ELSE IF BuffPtr2 <> NIL THEN LoadBuffer2
      ELSE UseDiskSwap := True
    END;
```

This example comes from a program that needs a lot of memory for buffers. It attempts to allocate both its large and its small buffers if possible. If only the large buffer can be allocated without leaving enough RAM for the small buffer, so be it. Or, if the large buffer cannot be allocated but the small buffer can, the small buffer will be allocated and used. Finally, if the program can't find enough memory to allocate either RAM-based buffer, it will use a disk-swapping system to make disk space serve as (slower) memory space for buffer operations. **BuffPtr1** and **BuffPtr2** are pointers that are initialized to point to their buffers when those buffers are allocated. If there isn't enough memory to allocate a buffer, its pointer is returned with a value of **NIL** to indicate that its buffer could not be created.

Whether or not both buffers can be created in memory, *both* pointers must be initialized to some value, either a legitimate pointer value to an allocated buffer, or else **NIL**. Later on in the program, the logic will need to test those pointers to see if a given buffer exists. Having either pointer in an uninitialized state could be disastrous. If we allowed short-circuit Boolean expression evaluation here, function **AllocateLittleBuffer** would never be executed if **AllocateBigBuffer** failed to find enough memory to allocate the large buffer. **LittleBuffPtr** would be left in an uninitialized state, and later on, the program could malfunction if it tried to test the uninitialized **LittleBuffPtr**.

In this situation, the entire Boolean expression

```
IF AllocateBigBuffer(BigBuffPtr) AND
   AllocateLittleBuffer(LittleBuffPtr)
```

must be evaluated, regardless of the outcome of executing function **AllocateBigBuffer**. The only way to guarantee this is to force complete Boolean expression evaluation, either by issuing a command to the IDE or to the command-line compiler, or by bracketing this area of code between **{$B+}** and **{$B-}** commands.

As the somewhat specialized and arcane nature of this example suggests, short-circuit Boolean evaluation will be your method of choice in the vast majority of instances.

8.3 CASE

Choosing between one of several alternative control paths is critical to computer programming. We've seen how **IF/THEN/ELSE** in its simplest form can choose between two alternatives based on the value of a Boolean expression. By nesting **IF/THEN/ELSE** statements one within another, we can choose among many different control paths, as we saw in the previous section.

The problem of readability appears when we nest **IF** statements more than two or three deep. Nested **IF/THEN/ELSE** gets awkward and non-intuitive in a great hurry when more than three levels exist. Consider the problem of flashing a message on a CRT screen based on some input code number. A problem reporting system on a CRT-equippped computerized car might include a statement sequence like this:

```
Beep;
Writeln('*****WARNING*****');
IF ProblemCode = 1 THEN
  Writeln('[001] Fuel supply has fallen below 10%')
ELSE IF ProblemCode = 2 THEN
  Writeln('[002] Oil pressure has fallen below min spec')
ELSE IF ProblemCode = 3 THEN
  Writeln('[003] Engine temperature is too high')
ELSE IF ProblemCode = 4 THEN
  Writeln('[004] Battery voltage has fallen below min spec')
ELSE IF ProblemCode = 5 THEN
  Writeln('[005] Brake fluid level has fallen below min spec')
ELSE IF ProblemCode = 6 THEN
  Writeln('[006] Transmission fluid level has fallen below min spec')
ELSE IF ProblemCode = 7 THEN
  Writeln('[007] Radiator water level has fallen below min spec')
ELSE
  Writeln('[***] Logic failure in problem reporting system')
```

This will work well enough, but it takes some picking through to follow it clear to the bottom. This sort of selection of one statement from many based on a single selection value is what the **CASE** statement was created for. Rewriting the above statement with **CASE** gives us this:

```
Beep;
Writeln('*****WARNING*****');
CASE ProblemCode OF
   1 : Writeln('[001] Fuel supply has fallen below 10%');
   2 : Writeln('[002] Oil pressure has fallen below min spec');
   3 : Writeln('[003] Engine temperature is too high');
   4 : Writeln('[004] Battery voltage has fallen below min spec');
   5 : Writeln('[005] Brake fluid level has fallen below min spec');
   6 : Writeln('[006] Transmission fluid level is below min spec');
   7 : Writeln('[007] Radiator water level has fallen below min spec')
ELSE
   Writeln('[***] Logic failure in problem reporting system')
END; { CASE }
```

Here, **ProblemCode** is called the *case selector*. The case selector may be an expression or simply a variable. It holds the value upon which the choice among statements will be made. The numbers in a line beneath the word **CASE** are called *case labels*. Each case label is followed by a colon, and then a statement. The statement may be simple (as are all in the example) or compound.

When the **CASE** statement is executed, the case selector is evaluated and its value is compared, one by one, against each of the case labels. If a case label is found that is equal to the value of the case selector, the statement associated with that case label is executed. Once the statement chosen for execution has completed executing, the work of the **CASE** statement is done and control passes on to the rest of the program. Only one (or none, see below) of the several statements is executed for each pass through the **CASE** statement.

If no case label matches the value of the case selector, the statement following the **ELSE** keyword is executed. **ELSE** is optional, by the way; if no **ELSE** keyword is found, control falls through to the next statement in the program.

The general form of a **CASE** statement is this:

```
CASE <case selector> OF
   <constant list 1> : <statement 1>;
   <constant list 2> : <statement 2>;
   <constant list 3> : <statement 3>;
                ....
   <constant list n> : <statement n>
   ELSE <statement>
END;
```

There may be as many case labels as you like, up to 256. You may be puzzling over the fact that what we pointed out as case labels are called *constant lists* in the general form. In our first example, each case label was only a single numeric constant. A case label may also be a list of constants separated by commas.

Remember that the case label is the *list* of constants associated with a statement; each statement can only have *one* case label. And do not forget that a case label may *never* be a variable!

For another example, let's look into part of the code for a mail-in questionnaire analysis system. The responses are to be grouped together by geographical regions of the country. **State** is an enumerated type including all the two-letter state name abbreviations, in alphabetical order. This particular code fragment tallies the number of responses from each geographical region:

```
TYPE
   {II = Indiana; OG = Oregon to avoid reserved word conflict}
   State = (AK,AL,AR,AZ,CA,CO,CT,DE,DC,FL,GA,HI,ID,IL,II,
            IA,KS,KY,LA,MA,MD,ME,MI,MN,MO,MS,MT,NE,NV,NH,
            NJ,NM,NY,NC,ND,OH,OK,OG,PA,RI,SC,SD,TN,TX,UT,
            VA,VT,WA,WI,WV,WY)

VAR
   FromState : State;

CASE FromState OF
CT,MA,ME,NH,
RI,VT             : CountNewEngland := CountNewEngland + 1;
DC,DE,MD,NJ,
NY,PA             : CountMidAtlantic := CountMidAtlantic + 1;
FL,GA,NC,SC       : CountSoutheast := CountSoutheast + 1;
IA,IL,II,MI,
MN,OH,WI,WV       : CountMidwest := CountMidwest + 1;
AL,AR,KY,LA,
MO,MS,TN,VA       : CountSouth := CountSouth + 1;
KS,ND,NE,SD,
WY                : CountPlains := CountPlains + 1;
AK,CA,CO,HI,
ID,MT,OG,UT,
WA,               : CountWest := CountWest + 1;
AZ,NM,NV,OK,
TX                : CountSouthwest := CountSouthwest + 1;
END; { CASE }
```

Here you can see that a case label can indeed be a list of constants. Also note that there is no **ELSE** clause here because every one of the possible values of type **State** is present in one of the case labels.

CASE CAUTIONS

The most important thing to remember about case labels is that they must be constants or lists of constants. A particular value may appear only once in a **CASE** statement. In other words, the value **IL** (from the last example) could not appear in both the **CountMidwest** and the **CountSouth** case labels. The reason for this should be obvious; if a value is associated with more than one statement, the **CASE** logic will not know which statement to execute for that case label value.

You should be careful when using a case selector of type **Integer**. Case selectors may only have an ordinality between 0 and 255. An integer case selector may have a value much larger than 255, and when it does, the results of executing the **CASE** statement are undefined. If you work a lot with numeric codes (and intend to use **CASE** structures to interpret those codes) it is a *very* good idea to define those codes as subranges of **Integer**:

```
TYPE
   Keypress = 0..255;
   Problem  = 0..32;
   Priority = 0..7;
```

Any of these named subrange types may act as case selectors.

ISO STANDARD PASCAL LACKS ELSE IN CASE

I should point out an important variance between Turbo Pascal and ISO Standard Pascal here.

One of the puzzling lapses of logic in ISO Standard Pascal is the lack of an **ELSE** clause in its definition of **CASE**. In Standard Pascal, a case selector value for which no case label exists is supposed to cause a runtime error. The programmer is supposed to ensure, with range testing, that each value submitted to a **CASE** statement is in fact legal for that **CASE** statement. No good explanation for why this should be necessary has ever crossed my desk.

So it is not surprising that every single commercial implementation of Pascal that I have ever tested includes an **ELSE** clause in its definition, to cover that "none of the above" possibility. Turbo Pascal uses the reserved word **ELSE** for this purpose. A number of Pascal compilers (such as Apple Pascal, UCSD Pascal, and now-extinct Turbo Pascal for the Macintosh) use the keyword **OTHERWISE** instead of **ELSE**, but the meaning and function are exactly the same.

8.4 FOR Loops

There are many occasions when you must perform the same operation or operations on a whole range of values. The most-used example would be the generation of a square roots table for all the numbers from 1 to 100. Pascal provides a tidy way to loop through the same code for each value, dropping through to the next statement in the program when all the loops have been performed. It's called the **FOR** statement, and it is one of three ways to perform program loops in Pascal.

Printing the table of square roots becomes easy:

```
FOR I := 1 TO 100 DO
   BEGIN
```

```
        J := Sqrt(I);
        Writeln('The square root of ',I,' is ',J)
      END;
```

There are better ways to lay out a square roots table, but this gets the feeling of a **FOR** loop across very well. **I** and **J** are integers. The compound statement between the **BEGIN/END** pair is executed 100 times. The first time through, **I** has the value 1. Each time the compound statement is executed, the value of **I** is increased by 1. Finally, after the compound statement has been executed with the value of **I** as 100, the **FOR** statement has done its job and control passes on to the next statement in the program.

The preceding example is only a particular case of a **FOR** statement. The general form of a **FOR** statement is this:

```
      FOR <control variable> :=
         <start value> TO <end value> DO <statement>
```

<start value> and **<end value>** may be expressions. **<control variable>** is any ordinal type, including enumerated types. When a **FOR** statement is executed, the following things happen: If **<start value>** and **<end value>** are expressions, they are evaluated and tucked away for reference. Then the control variable is assigned **<start value>**. Next, **<statement>** is executed. After **<statement>** is executed, the *successor value* to the value already in the control variable is placed in the control variable. The control variable is now tested. If it exceeds **<end value>**, execution of the **FOR** statement ceases. Otherwise, **<statement>** is executed. If **<start value>** is greater than **<end value>**, **<statement>** is never executed to begin with.

The loop repeats until the control variable is incremented past **<end value>**.

Note that the general definition of a **FOR** statement does not speak of "adding one to" the control variable. The control variable is incremented by assigning the successor value of the current value to the control variable. "Adding" is not really done at all, not even with integers. To obtain the successor value, the statement evaluates the expression

```
      Succ(<control variable>)
```

The function **Succ** is discussed in Section 9.6. If you recall our enumerated type **Spectrum**:

```
      TYPE
         Spectrum = (Red, Orange, Yellow, Green, Blue,
                         Indigo, Violet);
```

the successor value to **Orange** is **Yellow**. The successor value to **Green** is **Blue**, and so on.

A variable of type **Spectrum** makes a perfectly good control variable in a **FOR** loop:

```
      LightSpeed := 3.0E06;
      FOR Color := Red TO Violet DO
         Frequency[Color] := Wavelength[Color] / LightSpeed;
```

So do characters:

```
FOR Ch := 'a' to 'z' DO
  IF Ch IN CharSet DO Writeln('CharSet contains ',Ch);
```

If **<start value>** and **<end value>** are the same, the loop is executed once. If **<start value>** is *higher* than **<end value>**, the loop is not executed at all. That is, **<statement>** is not executed, and control immediately falls through to the next statement in the program.

CONTROL VARIABLE CAUTIONS

A control variable must be an ordinal type or a subrange of an ordinal type. Real numbers cannot be used as control variables. There is no distinct successor value to a number like 3.141592, after all. For similar reasons you cannot use sets or structured types of any kind.

Also, an error message will appear if the control variable is a formal parameter passed by reference (see Section 8.12), that is, a **VAR** parameter in the function or procedure's parameter line. You *cannot* do this:

```
PROCEDURE Runnerup(Hi,Lo   : Integer;
                    VAR Limit : Integer);

VAR
   Foo : Integer;

BEGIN
   <statements>;
   FOR Limit := Lo TO Hi DO <statement>;
   Foo:=Limit;
   <statements>
END;
```

Turbo Pascal will respond here with

```
Error 97: Invalid FOR control variable
```

Standard Pascal requires that control variables be local and nonformal. Turbo Pascal is somewhat more lenient, and allows control variables to be nonlocal (this is, not declared in the current block; see Chapter 11 for more on this) and also allows formal parameters to be control variables as long as they are passed by value; that is, if the procedure is given its own copy of the parameter to play with.

As in many of Pascal's rules and restrictions, this one was designed to keep you out of certain kinds of trouble. Understanding what kind of trouble requires a little further poking at the notion of control variables in **FOR** loops: To make faulty procedure **Runnerup** shown above work, some sort of local control variable would have to be declared in the data declaration section of the procedure, like this:

```
PROCEDURE Runnerup(Hi,Lo   : Integer;
                    VAR Limit : Integer);
```

```
VAR
  Foo,I : Integer;

BEGIN
  <statements>;
  FOR I := Lo TO Hi DO <statement>;
  Foo := I;
  <statements>
END;
```

Now the **FOR** loop will compile correctly. But there is still something wrong with this procedure. What it's trying to do is make use of the control variable immediately after the loop has executed by assigning its value to **Foo**. This is also illegal. *Immediately after a FOR statement, the value of the control variable becomes undefined.* This is not a problem, since the end value is accessible in **Hi**. To make use of the final value of the control variable, assign **Hi** to **Foo** instead of **I**. The end result will be the same:

```
PROCEDURE Runnerup(Hi,Lo    : Integer;
                   VAR Limit : Integer);

VAR
  Foo,I : Integer;

BEGIN
  <statements>;
  FOR I := Lo TO Hi DO <statement>;
  Foo := Hi;
  <statements>
END;
```

There is a good reason for the control variable becoming undefined after its loop has run its course. After each pass through **<statement>** the successor value to the current value in the control variable is computed. In the process, that successor value *may in fact become undefined* if the ordinal type being used runs out of values. Going back to our type **Spectrum**, what is the successor value to **Violet**? There is none; **Succ(Violet)** is undefined. Consider:

```
FOR Color := Red TO Violet DO <statement>;
```

After the loop runs through its seven iterations, **Color** would hold an undefined value. If you were allowed to "pick up" the control variable's value after the run of a **FOR** loop, you might in fact be picking up an undefined, nonsense value and have no way of knowing it were so. So the Standard Pascal definition declares that control variables are *always* undefined after a **FOR** loop to remove the temptation to "save" the final value of a control variable for later use.

In the 7.0 version of Borland's Pascal compilers a **Break** statement has been added. **Break** interrupts execution of a **FOR, WHILE, or REPEAT** loop before the loop has run through all the iterations called for. With **Break** now an option, you cannot always be sure that the **<end value>** will match the control variable's value at the end of the loop, so you must use a separate variable if you want to keep track of the value in the control variable.

Within the **FOR** loop (that is, within **<statement>**) the control variable must be treated as a "read-only" value. You *can* change the value of the control variable within the **FOR** loop, but you should do so with extreme hesitation. The **REPEAT/UNTIL** and **WHILE/DO** statements are designed to support this kind of "moving target" loop, which will execute as often as required to make a control variable equal to some final value. **FOR** loops, by contrast, were designed to execute a fixed number of times, and while executing, the value of the control variable should be solely under the control of the **FOR** loop itself.

Now (finally!) you may understand why Turbo forbids using **VAR** parameters as control variables. Pascal reserves the right to force a control variable into an undefined state after its loop is done. Using a **VAR** parameer as a control variable might "reach up" out of the procedure and force the **VAR** parameter into some unexpected and possibly undefined state. Allowing a procedure to "undefine" a parameter passed to it is asking for trouble, since it may not be obvious to the calling logic that its parameter may come back undefined.

Preserve sanity in your programs. Keep your **FOR** loop control variables local.

FOR WITH DOWNTO

The **FOR** statement as we've seen it so far always increments its control variable "upward"; that is, it uses the successor value of the control variable for the next pass through **<statement>**. It is sometimes useful to go the other way: to begin with a "high" value and count down to a lower value. In this case, the *predecessor* value of the value in the control variable becomes the new control variable value for the next pass through **<statement>**. This predecessor value is calculated with the predefined function **Pred(<control variable>)**; see Section 9.6. Otherwise, its operation is identical to that of **FOR** with **TO**:

```
FOR I := 17 DOWNTO 7 DO <statement>;

FOR Color := Indigo DOWNTO Orange DO <statement>;

FOR Ch := 'Z' DOWNTO 'X' DO <statement>;
```

When using **DOWNTO**, keep in mind that if **<start value>** is *lower* than **<end value>**, **<statement>** will not be executed at all. This is the reverse of the case for **FOR/TO** loops.

THERE'S NO STEP IN TURBO PASCAL!

One thing to keep in mind when learning to use **FOR** loops: The loop can only "step through" — one value at a time — the range the control variable must take. Some languages like BASIC allow a **STEP** parameter to specify that the loop is to "count by five" or some other value. Turbo Pascal does not allow you to do this. If you want the loop to count up or down by some value other than one, you need to either skip the "in-between" values while counting (the **MOD** operator can be handy for this) or else take the gutsy road and jigger the value of the control variable on each pass. This can be done, but be careful!

8.5 WHILE/DO Loops

As we have seen, a **FOR** loop executes a specific number of times, no more, no less, unless you use the **Break** or **Continue** procedures, as I'll describe in Section 8.7. The control variable should not be altered during the loop. There are many cases in which a loop must run until some condition occurs that stops it. The control variable *must* be altered during the loop, or the loop will just run forever. Pascal offers two ways to build such loops: **WHILE/DO** and **REPEAT/UNTIL**.

The general form of a **WHILE/DO** loop is this:

```
WHILE <Boolean expression> DO <statement>
```

The **<Boolean expression>** can be an expression that evaluates to a Boolean value, such as I > 17, or it can simply be a Boolean variable. As with **FOR** loops, **<statement>** can be any statement including a compound statement framed between **BEGIN** and **END**.

WHILE/DO loops work like this: The code first evaluates **<Boolean expression>**. If the value of the expression is **True**, then **<statement>** is executed. If the value is **False**, **<statement>** is not executed even once, and control falls through to the next statement in the program. (Don't forget that the **WHILE/DO** loop as a whole is considered a statement.)

Assuming **<Boolean expression>** came out **True** the first time, then after executing **<statement>** the code goes back and evaluates **<Boolean expression>** again. If it is still true, **<statement>** is executed again. If it evaluates to **False**, the **WHILE/DO** loop ends and control passes on to the next statement in the program.

In short, as long as **<Boolean expression>** is **True**, **<statement>** will be executed repeatedly. Only when the expression comes up **False** will the loop end. For example:

```
VAR
  pH : Real;

FillTank;      { Fill tank with raw water  }
Take(pH);      { Take initial PH reading   }
WHILE pH < 7.2 DO
  BEGIN
    AddAlkali;   { Drop 1 soda pellet in tank }
    AgitateTank; { Stir }
    Take(pH);    { Read the PH sensor        }
  END;
```

This snippet of code is a part of a control system for some sort of chemical processing apparatus. All it must do is fill a tank with water, ensuring that the pH of the water is at least 7.2. If the water from the water supply comes in as too acidic (water quality varies widely in some parts of the country), its pH must be brought up to 7.2 before the water is considered useable.

First the tank is filled. Then the initial pH reading is taken. The water may in fact be useable from the start, in which case the loop is never executed. But if the water comes up acidic, the loop is executed. A small quantity of an alkali is added, the tank is stirred for a while, and then the pH is taken again. If the pH has risen to 7.2, the loop terminates. If the pH remains too low, the loop is executed again, more alkali is added, and the pH is tested once more. This will continue until the pH test returns a value in the variable pH that is higher than 7.2.

It is crucial to note that an initial pH test was performed. If the variable **pH** were not used before, its value is undefined, and testing it for **True** or **False** will not reflect any real-world meaning. *Make sure the Boolean expression is defined before the WHILE/DO loop is executed!* Every variable in the expression must be initialized somehow before the expression can be "trusted."

The most important property of a **WHILE/DO** loop is that its Boolean expression is tested *before* **<statement>** is executed. A corollary to this is that there are cases when **<statement>** will never be executed at all. Keep this in mind while we discuss **REPEAT/UNTIL** below.

8.6 REPEAT/UNTIL Loops

REPEAT/UNTIL loops are very similar to **WHILE/DO** loops. As with **WHILE/DO**, **REPEAT/UNTIL** executes a statement until a Boolean expression becomes **True**. The general form is this:

```
REPEAT <statement> UNTIL <Boolean expression>;
```

It works this way. First, **<statement>** is executed. Then **<Boolean expression>** is evaluated. If it comes up **True**, the loop terminates, and control passes on to the next statement in the program. If **<Boolean expression>** evaluates to **False**, **<statement>** is executed again. This continues until **<Boolean expression>** becomes **True**.

The important fact to notice here is that *<statement> is always executed at least once.* So unlike **WHILE/DO**, you needn't initialize all variables in **<Boolean expression>** before the loop begins. It's quite all right to assign all values as part of executing the loop.

For an example, let's return to the chemical process controller and consider a snippet of code to handle a simple titration. Titration means adding small, carefully measured amounts of one chemical to another while watching for some chemical reaction to go to completion. Usually, when the reaction is complete, the mixture will begin changing color, or will become electrically conductive, or give some other measurable signal.

In Pascal, it might be handled this way:

```
VAR
   Drops   : Integer;
   Complete : Boolean;

Drops := 0;
REPEAT
   AddADrop;              { Opens valve for 1 drop  }
   Drops := Drops + 1;    { Increment counter       }
   Signal(Complete)       { Read the reaction sensor }
UNTIL Complete;
```

Note that the drops counter is initialized before the loop begins. A drop is added to the test vessel, and the drop counter is incremented by one. Then the reaction sensor is read. If it senses that the reaction has gone to completion, the Boolean variable **Complete** is set to **True**.

Since it takes at least one drop to complete the reaction (without any drops of the chemical, the reaction can't even begin), this series of events must be done at least once. If the first drop completes the reaction, the loop is performed only once. Most likely, the loop will have to execute many times before the chemical reaction completes and **Complete** becomes **True**. When this happens, **Drops** will contain the number of drops required to complete the reaction. The value of **Drops** might then be displayed on an LED readout or other output device attached to the chemical apparatus.

One interesting thing about **REPEAT/UNTIL** is that the two keywords do double duty if **<statement>** is compound. Instead of bracketing the component statements between **BEGIN** and **END**, **REPEAT** and **UNTIL** perform the bracketing function themselves. In all Pascal, only **BEGIN/END** and **REPEAT/UNTIL** may frame a compound statement.

WHILE/DO OR REPEAT/UNTIL?

These two types of loops are very similar, and it is sensible to ask why both are necessary. Actually, **WHILE/DO** can accomplish anything **REPEAT/UNTIL** can, with a little extra effort and occasional rearranging of the order of the statements contained in the loop. The titration code could be written this way:

```
Drops := 0;
Complete := False;
WHILE NOT Complete DO
 BEGIN
  AddADrop;
  Drops := Drops +1;
  Signal(Complete)
 END
```

This method requires that **Complete** be set to **False** initially to ensure that it will be defined when the loop first tests it. If **Complete** were left undefined and it happened to contain garbage data that could be interpreted as **True**, (if bit 0 is binary 1, for example) the loop might never be executed, and the code would report that the titration had been accomplished with zero drops of reagent—which is chemically impossible.

Using **REPEAT/UNTIL** would prevent that sort of error in logic. Quite simply: *Use REPEAT/UNTIL in those cases where the loop **must** be executed at least once.* Whenever you write code with loops, always consider what might happen if the loop were never excuted at all—and if anything unsavory might come of it, make sure the loop is coded as **REPEAT/UNTIL** rather than **WHILE/DO**.

8.7 Labels, GOTO, Break, and Continue

The bane of ancient unstructured languages like BASIC, FORTRAN, and CO-BOL is freeform **GOTO** branching all over the program body without any sort of plan or structure. Such programs are very nearly impossible to read. The problem with such programs, however, is not the **GOTO**s themselves but bad use of them. **GOTO**s fill a certain need in Pascal, but they have a seductive power and are eminently easy to understand:

```
GOTO 150;
```

and *wham!* you're at label 150. This straightforwardness leads inexperienced programmers (especially those first schooled in BASIC, and today, most everybody is first schooled in BASIC) to use them to get out of any programming spot that they do not fully understand how to deal with in a structured manner.

I will not caution you, as some people do, never to use a **GOTO** no matter what. What I *will* tell you to do is never use a **GOTO** when something else will get the job done as well or better.

LABELS

In order to use **GOTO**, **GOTO** must have somewhere to go, and in Pascal that somewhere must be marked by something called a *label*. Labels, like most everything else in Pascal, must be predeclared before they are used. Declaring labels is done in the label declaration section of a program, immediately following the reserved word **LABEL**:

```
LABEL
  100,150,200,250,300;
```

This example **LABEL** definition statement conforms to ISO Standard Pascal. The labels themselves must be numeric for Standard Pascal, in the range 0-9999. A label may mark only one point in a program.

Turbo Pascal extends the label syntax and allows labels to be ordinary identifiers just like those you use for constants and variables. You can mix numeric and identifier labels in the same label definition statement:

```
LABEL
    100,ShutDown,PowerGlitch,200,300,HardwareFailure;
```

When you mark a statement with a label, you must put a colon after the label. Look to the code a few paragraphs down for an example.

Numeric and identifier labels are used identically in **GOTO** statements:

```
GOTO ShutDown;
GOTO 200;
```

The effect is the same in either case: Execution continues at the statement in the program marked by the label.

GOTO LIMITATIONS IN TURBO PASCAL

Use of **GOTO**s with Turbo Pascal carries a few limitations. You may **GOTO** a label *within* the current block. This means that you may *not* **GOTO** a label inside another procedure or function, or from within a procedure or function out into the main program code.

You should not **GOTO** a label within a structured statement. In other words, given this **WHILE/DO** statement:

```
WHILE NOT Finished DO
  BEGIN
    Read(MyFile,ALine);
    IF EOF(MyFile) THEN GOTO 300;
    IF ALine = 'Do not write this...' THEN GOTO 250;
    Write(YourFile,ALine);
    LineCounter := LineCounter + 1;
    250:
  END
300: Close(MyFile);
```

you could not, from some other part of the block, **GOTO** label 250. However, assuming that this snippet of code is not part of some larger structured statement, you could in fact **GOTO** label 300 from some other part of the current block. Whether or not that would perform any useful function is a good question.

This example is *very* bad practice, but we include it here only to indicate that you cannot branch into the middle of a **WHILE/DO** statement from somewhere outside the statement. Label 250 is accessible only from somewhere between the **BEGIN** and **END** pair.

In general, **GOTO**s are used to get *out* of somewhere, not to get *in*. Standard Pascal and versions of Turbo Pascal prior to 7.0 lack two general looping functions that Turbo Pascal now has: **Break** and **Continue**. **Break** leaves the middle of a loop and sends control to the first statement after the loop. **Continue** stops executing the loop and begins the loop at the top, with the next value of the control variable.

Without **Break** and **Continue**, GOTO often provides the only reasonably clean way to get out from inside complicated loops in which a lot is going on and more than one condition value affects exiting from the loop. Logically speaking, you can always get out of a loop safely by using the facilities provided by the loop (exiting at the top with **WHILE/DO** and at the bottom with **REPEAT/UNTIL**), but there are cases when to do so involves tortuous combinations of **IF/THEN/ELSE** that might in fact be harder to read than simply jumping out with **GOTO**. But for clarity's sake, always **GOTO** the statement *immediately* following the loop you're exiting. (This is what the **Break** statement does.)

Break and **Continue** were finally added to Version 7.0 of Turbo and Borland Pascal, as I'll describe below in more detail. That being the case, the possible situations requiring **GOTO** have dwindled down to practically nothing.

What remains is the very rare need to get somewhere else *now*, especially when the code you need to get to is code to handle some impending failure or emergency situation that requires immediate attention to accomplish an orderly shutdown of the equipment, or something of similar seriousness. This would tend to come up in embedded-system type software that has direct control over some rather complicated hardware. In 12 years of working with Pascal I have never had to do this. I suspect that if you ever do, you will know it.

BREAK AND CONTINUE

With version 7, Borland's Pascal compilers provide the **Break** and **Continue** procedures I spoke of above. Both procedures may *only* be used in connection with looping statements **FOR**, **WHILE/DO**, and **REPEAT/UNTIL**.

Break amounts to a **GOTO** to the statement that immediately follows the loop statement. Consider:

```
Total := 0;
TotalAveraged := 0;
FOR I := 1 TO DataTally DO
   BEGIN
      IF (Total+DataPoints[I]) >= MaxLongInt THEN Break;
      Total := Total + DataPoints[I];
      Inc(TotalAveraged);
   END;
WriteDataToFile;
```

Here, a **FOR** loop is totaling data values stored in an array, for averaging. A statement has been added to prevent the total from overflowing a long integer variable. If the total plus the next data value is greater than **MaxLongInt** (a built-in constant containing the largest legal **LongInt** value), the **Break** procedure is executed. **Break** takes execution to the first statement after the end of the **FOR** loop's compound statement; in this example, to the **WriteDataFile** procedure call. It's an "early exit" from the **FOR** loop, and that's about all to be said for it.

One caution: Don't count on the value of the **FOR** loop's control variable being available and meaningful once you leave the loop via **Break**. In my example, I'm keeping a separate count of the number of items successfully tallied, in the variable **TotalAveraged**. That's always a good idea—even if it seems to complicate the logic.

Continue is a little subtler. It's a "restart" procedure that allows you to "short circuit" the remaining logic in a loop, and start again at the *first* statement *inside* the loop. If the loop is a **FOR** loop, the control variable is bumped to its next value before the loop is restarted. If the loop is a **WHILE/DO** or **REPEAT/UNTIL** loop, the loop is restarted at the top, but no variables are affected in any way.

The following example isn't the best possible coding practice, but it's simple and shows what the **Continue** statement actually does. The example reads a line from a text file and tests to see if there's anything in the line. That is, it tests to see if the length of the line read from the file is 0. If the line contains data and has a nonzero length, the **AddLineToList** procedure adds the line to a linked list.

```
WHILE NOT EOF(InFile) DO
BEGIN
   Readln(InFile,InLine);
   IF Length(InLine) <=0 THEN Continue ELSE
     AddLineToList(InLine);
END;
```

On the other hand, if the length of the line read from the text file is zero, there's really no more work to be done with that line anyway—so restart the loop from the top, which reads the next line from the file.

The real situations where **Continue** is likely to be useful are complex loops that do a lot of things and test a lot of different conditions—and such loops make poor examples because their complexity confuses what they're really trying to demonstrate.

There can be multiple **Break** or **Continue** calls inside the same loop. Be careful, however, that you don't find yourself using the two procedures carelessly, as an excuse not to think through a loop's logic. **Break** and **Continue** are used more often than **GOTO**—but not so often that you'll have them in every loop you write.

8.8 Semicolons and Where They Go

Nothing makes newcomers to Pascal cry out in frustration quite so consistently as the question of semicolons and where they go. There are places where semicolons *must* go, places where it seems not to matter whether they go or not, and places where they cannot go without triggering an error. Worse, it seems at first to have no sensible method to it.

Of course, like everything else in Pascal, placing semicolons *does* have a method to it. Why the confusion? Two reasons:

1. Pascal is a "freeform" language that does not take line structure of the source file into account. Unfortunately, most new Pascal programmers graduate into Pascal from BASIC, which is about as line-oriented a language as ever existed.

2. Semicolons in Pascal are statement *separators*, not statement *terminators*. The difference is crucial, and made worse by the fact that the C language and PL/1 use semicolons as statement terminators.

Clarifying these two issues should make semicolon placement Pascal-style second nature.

FREEFORM VS. LINE-STRUCTURED SOURCE CODE

Pascal source code is "freeform"; that is, the boundaries of individual lines and the positioning of keywords and variables on those lines matter not at all. The prettyprinting customary to Pascal source code baffled me in my earliest learning days until I realized that the compiler completely ignored it. The compiler, in fact, sucks the program up from the disk as though through a drinking straw, in one long line. The following two program listings are utterly identical as far as Turbo Pascal is concerned:

```
PROGRAM Squares;

VAR
   I,J : Integer;

BEGIN
   Writeln('Number    Its square');
   FOR I := 1 TO 10 DO
     BEGIN
       J := I * I;
        Writeln(' ',I:2,'        ',J:3)
     END;
   Writeln;
   Writeln('Processing completed!')
END.

PROGRAM Squares;VAR I,J : Integer;BEGIN Writeln
('Number    It''s square');FOR I:=1 TO 10 DO
BEGIN J:=I*I;Writeln(' ',I:2,'        ',J:3)
END;Writeln;Writeln('Processing completed!') END.
```

Although the second listing appears to exist in four lines, this is only for the convenience of the printed page; the intent was to express the program as one continuous line without any line breaks at all.

The second listing above is the compiler's eye view of your program source code. You must remember that although you see your program listing "from a height" as it were, the compiler scans it one character at a time, beginning with the 'P' in 'PROGRAM' and reading through to the "." after END. All unnecessary "whitespace" characters (spaces, tabs, carriage returns, linefeeds) have been removed as the compiler would remove them. Whitespace serves only to delineate the beginnings and endings of reserved words and identifiers, and as far as the compiler is concerned, one whitespace character of any kind is as good as one of any other kind. Once the compiler "grabs" a word or identifier, literal or operator, it tosses out any following whitespace until it finds a non-whitespace character indicating that a program element is beginning again.

SEMICOLONS AS STATEMENT SEPARATORS

Note the compound statement executed as part of the FOR loop:

```
BEGIN J:=I*I;Writeln(' ',I:2,'      ',J:3) END
```

There are two statements here, framed between **BEGIN** and **END**. Smart as the compiler may seem to you, it has no way to know where statements start and end unless you tell it. If the ';' between **I** and **Writeln** were not there, the compiler would not know for sure if the statement that it sees (so far!) as **J:=I*I** ends there or must somehow continue on with **Writeln**.

Note that there is no semicolon after the second statement. There doesn't have to be; the compiler has scanned a **BEGIN** word and knows that an **END** should be coming up eventually. The **END** word tells the compiler unambiguously that the previous statement is over and done with. *BEGIN and END are not statements.* They are reserved words, acting as delimiters, and only serve to tell the compiler that the group of statements between them is a compound statement.

I find it useful to think of a long line of statements as a line of boxcars on a rail siding. Separating each car from the next is a pair of linked couplers. Anywhere two couplers connect is where, (if boxcars were program statements) you would need a semicolon. You don't need one at the front of the first car, nor at the end of the last car because the last car doesn't need to be separated from anything; behind it is just empty air.

THE NULL STATEMENT

Why, then, is it legal to have a semicolon after the last statement in a compound statement? This is perfectly all right (and adds to the confusion):

```
BEGIN
  ClrScr;
  J := J + 5;
  IF J > 100 THEN PageEject;
  DoPage;          { ; not needed here }
END
```

The answer, of course, is that there *is* a statement after statement **DoPage**; and that statement is the null statement. This might be clearer with the example rewritten this way:

```
BEGIN
  ClrScr;
  J := J + 5;
  IF J > 100 THEN PageEject;
  DoPage;
                { Null statement here! }
END
```

There is a semicolon between **DoPage** and the null statement, but none between the null statement and the **END** word.

The null statement is a theoretical abstraction; it does no work and generates no code, not even a **NOP** (No-Op) instruction. (Don't try to use it to pad timing loops!) It serves very little purpose other than to make certain conditional statements a little more intuitive and readable. For example:

```
IF TapeIsMounted THEN { NULL } ELSE RequestMount;
```

I find this more readable than the alternative:

```
IF NOT TapeIsMounted THEN RequestMount;
```

but I suspect it is a matter of taste. Note the convention of inserting the comment {**NULL**} wherever you use a null statement. It's like the bandages around the Invisible Man; they make the guy easier to see and thus keep him out of trouble.

Another use of the null statement is in **CASE** statements in which nothing need be done for a selector value:

```
CASE Color OF
   Red     : { NULL };          { No filter needed }
   Orange  : InsertFilter(1);   { Density 1      }
   Yellow  : InsertFilter(5);   { Density 5      }
   Green   : InsertFilter(11);  { Density 11     }
   ELSE InsertFilter(99)        { Opaque (99)    }
END; { CASE }
```

In some sort of optical apparatus there is a mechanism for rotating a filter in front of an optical path. The density of the filter depends on the color of light being used. No filter is needed for red, and for blue, indigo, or violet the test will not function and an opaque barrier is moved into the optical path instead of a filter. A null statement is used for the **Red** case label.

SEMICOLONS WITH IF/THEN/ELSE STATEMENTS

More errors are made placing semicolons within **IF/THEN/ELSE** statements than any other kind, I suspect. This sort of thing is fairly common and oh so easy to do when you're a beginner:

```
IF TankIsEmpty THEN FillTank(Reagent,FlowRate);
   ELSE Titrate(SensorNum,Temp,Drops);
```

The temptation to put a semicolon at the end of a line is strong. Furthermore, in most dialects of BASIC you *must* put a colon between an **IF** clause and its associated **ELSE** clause.

But semicolons are statement *separators*, and the example above is *one single statement*. There is nothing to separate. Remember this rule with regard to placing semicolons in **IF/THEN/ELSE** statements: *Never place a semicolon immediately before an ELSE word in an IF statement!* With that in mind you will avoid 90 percent of all semicolon placement errors.

To make things slightly more confusing, it *is* legal (and sometimes necessary) to place a semicolon before an **ELSE** word in a **CASE** statement. If a future release of Turbo Pascal allows the use of the **OTHERWISE** word as an alias for **ELSE** within a **CASE** statement, it will become possible to say, simply, *never place a semicolon immediately before ELSE*. In the meantime, keep the null statement in mind and semicolon placement won't seem quite so arbitrary.

8.9 Halt and Exit

These two statements are *not* part of Standard Pascal, and in many respects are not good practice—like **GOTO**, they are easily abused and can make your programs difficult to read and debug. But like any good tools, they have some legitimate uses.

HALT

Turbo Pascal provides a means of stopping a program in its tracks from anywhere within the program. **Halt** will terminate any running program and throw you back into Turbo Pascal's IDE or (if you're not working from the IDE) out into your operating system.

Halt is a creature of limited usefulness. If you have the foresight to envision a condition in which a complicated program gets so confused that it cannot continue to function meaningfully, it may be best to call a **Halt** with an appropriate error message. One example I might cite involves a situation in which a large application consisting of multiple overlay files discovers that one or more of its overlay files cannot be read or may be missing from disk. This is the sort of anomalous situation from which there is no truly graceful exit—it may be better to print an informative error message and return to the operating system.

In PC DOS or MS DOS versions of Turbo Pascal V3.0 and later, the **Halt** statement may take an optional parameter:

```
Halt(ErrorCode : Integer);
```

When **Halt** returns control to DOS, it sets DOS **ERRORLEVEL** to the numeric value in the optional **ErrorCode** parameter. Note that **ERROR LEVEL** is a *byte* value; your integer will be truncated to the range 0-255 by **Halt**.

ERRORLEVEL is a pseudo-variable that can be tested by the **IF** batch command in order to perform conditional processing in a DOS batch file. After a program is run from a batch file, some value is set into **ERRORLEVEL**, typically zero. A program can set **ERRORLEVEL** if it wishes, and then the batch file can "branch" at that point depending on the value set into **ERRORLEVEL** by the program.

Aside from its name, there is nothing hard-coded into **ERRORLEVEL** connected with DOS errors. I use **Halt** with a parameter as a means of building small utilities to extend the usefulness of DOS's batch facility, typically by writing a short program to test some machine condition for which no test exists in ordinary batch commands.

For example, the following program tests whether a monochrome or graphics display is installed in the system, using the **Query Adapter Type** function described later on in Section 12.4:

```
PROGRAM IsMono;

USES Dos; { For Registers type }

TYPE
   AdapterType = (None,MDA,CGA,EGAMono,EGAColor,VGAMono,
                  VGAColor,MCGAMono,MCGAColor);

{$I QUERYDSP.SRC }

BEGIN
  IF QueryAdapterType IN [MDA,EGAMono,VGAMono,MCGAMono]
    THEN Halt(5)
  ELSE Halt(0);
END.
```

If a monochrome screen is present, the program returns a code of 5 to DOS **ERRORLEVEL**; otherwise it returns a 0.

A batch file can test **ERRORLEVEL** to see which display is installed in the machine:

```
ECHO off
ISMONO
IF ERRORLEVEL 5 GOTO mono
ECHO on
REM  It is a graphics screen.
GOTO exit
:mono
ECHO on
REM  It is a monochrome screen.
ECHO on
:exit
```

Your batch file could use this information to install a different set of CRT drivers for an application program, depending on the type of display adapter installed on the machine.

If you do use **Halt** in anything but the simplest programs like the one above, *highlight its presence with glow-in-the-dark comments!* Generally, Pascal programs begin at the top and end at the bottom. Ducking out in the middle via **Halt** or **Exit** (see below) is nonstandard procedure and can complicate the reading and debugging of your programs.

EXIT

Release 3.0 and later of Turbo Pascal offers the **Exit** statement. **Exit** jumps out of the current block into the next highest block. In other words, if you execute an **Exit** within a function or procedure, execution of that function or procedure will cease, and control returns to the statement immediately following the invocation of the function or procedure. If **Exit** is encountered in the main program, Turbo Pascal will end the program and return to the IDE (if you were working from within the IDE) or into DOS, if your program is a standalone .EXE file.

Use **Exit** with care. One of the strengths of the Pascal structure is the assurance that a block of code begins at the top and ends at the bottom. Sprinkling a block with **Exit**s makes code much harder to read and debug.

INTERRUPTING A PROGRAM WITH CTRL-BREAK

Invariably, you're going to grow impatient with some program's plodding along, and you're going to want to cut the run short. An easy exit inherited from BASIC is simply to press CTRL-Break. If the conditions are correct, your program will terminate, and control will return to DOS if you were running a standalone .EXE file, or to the Turbo Pascal IDE if you were running from within the IDE.

What are the correct conditions? A program may be "broken" any time it writes to the CRT *if* a system Boolean variable called **CheckBreak** in the **Crt** unit is set to **True**. To modify **CheckBreak** you must USE the **Crt** unit, as **CheckBreak** exists within **Crt**.

If **CheckBreak** is set to **True** (its default state) you'll have a way out of infinite loops, so long as somewhere within the infinite loop the program writes something to the screen. You pay a heavy price in performance, however, because the Turbo Pascal runtime code must check frequently to see if a CTRL-Break has been typed.

CheckBreak defaults to **True**, so you can simply leave it alone and have the protection of being able to break out of your program's execution. It makes sense to leave **CheckBreak** as **True** during development and debugging, when endless loops tend to happen. Once the program has been solidly debugged, you can set **CheckBreak** to **False** and pick up the additional speed.

A note to Turbo Pascal 3.0 users: **CheckBreak** serves the same function as the undocumented system variable **CBreak** in Turbo Pascal 3.0.

8.10 Structuring with Procedures and Functions

Some people think looping statements like **WHILE/DO** and **REPEAT/UNTIL** (and the corresponding lack of need for **GOTO**s) are the touchstone of structured programming. Not so—at the bottom of it, *structured programming is the artful hiding of details.* The human mind's ability to grasp complexity breaks down quickly unless some structure or pattern can be found in the complexity. I recall (with some embarrassment) writing a 1300 line FORTRAN program in high school, and by the time I wrote the last of it (this being done over a six-week period), I no longer remembered how the first part worked. The entire program was a mass of unstructured, undifferentiated detail.

How does one hide details in computer programs? By identifying sequences of code that do discrete tasks, and setting each sequence off somewhere, replacing it by a single word describing (or at least hinting at) the task it does. Such code sequences are properly called "subprograms."

In Pascal, there are two types of subprograms: procedures and functions. Both are sequences of Pascal statements set off from the main body of program code. Both are invoked, and their statements executed, simply by naming them. The only difference between functions and procedures is this: The identifier naming a function has a type and takes on a value when it is executed. The name of a procedure has no type and takes on no value.

Two simple examples: The procedure **ClrScr**, when executed, clears the CRT screen:

```
ClrScr;
```

ClrScr will be discussed along with the other CRT control procedures in Section 12.1. It is a complete statement in itself. Although **ClrScr** has no parameters, a procedure may have any number of parameters if it needs them.

A function, by contrast, is *not* a complete statement. It is more like an expression, which returns a value that must be used somehow:

```
VAR
   Space,Radius : Real;

Radius := 4.66;
Space := Area(Radius);
```

Note that prior to version 7 you could *not* simply have put the invocation of **Area** on a line by itself:

```
Area(Radius);
```

This would generate an error at compile-time:

```
Error 122: Invalid variable reference
```

(In the next subsection I'll explain how this can be done using the version 7 compilers.) **Area** calculates the area for the value **Radius**, which is passed to it as a parameter. After it calculates the area for the value passed to it in **Radius**, the area value is taken on by the identifier **Area**, as though **Area** were a variable.

Functions in Turbo Pascal may return values of any ordinal type (**Integer**, **Char**, **Byte**, **Real**, **Boolean**), any enumerated type, a subrange of an ordinal or enumerated type, or any pointer type. Unlike virtually all other Pascal compilers, functions in Turbo Pascal may return values of type **STRING** or types derived from **STRING**.

Using the **Area** function hides the details of calculating areas. There aren't many details involved in calculating areas, but for other calculations (matrix inversion comes to mind) a function can hide 30 or 40 lines of complicated code. Or more. So when you're reading the program and come to a function invocation, you can think, "Ah, here's where we invert the matrix" without being concerned about *how* the matrix is actually inverted. At that level in reading the program, the *how* is not important, so those details are best kept out of sight.

The **ClrScr** function illustrates another facet of detail-hiding. The **ClrScr** function clears the CRT screen. How this is done varies widely from computer to computer. The IBM PC requires a software interrupt to clear the screen, whereas the Victor 9000 and certain other less-than-compatible PC compatibles only require that a control character be sent to the system console driver. If you're writing a program that is to run on many different computers, it is best to hide machine-specific details in functions and procedures and put those functions and procedures in a machine-specific library that can be included into your main program code for each specific machine. This way, a single source file can be compiled to run on many different computers without changes, simply by including a different machine-specific library for each different computer.

"THROWING AWAY" FUNCTION RESULTS

Starting with Turbo Pascal 6.0, it has been possible to configure the compiler to allow you to "throw away" the value returned by a function, and thus invoke the function as though it were a procedure, without having to use the function within an expression or on the right side of an assignment statement.

This doesn't make sense for most functions that you write, since in most cases, the return value is the whole purpose for writing the function to begin with. However, as your functions grow more complex, you might, on occasion, wish to invoke a function merely to make its "side effects" happen—that is, the things it does that don't involve the return value.

This happens most often when programmers create a function that does something significant like file access, and returns a code as its function return value that indicates whether or not the action was a success. In most cases, you'll want to check the function result to see how things went. There may, however, be an occasion where you simply want to do the deed regardless of the status value. So instead of coding it this way:

```
FileActionStatus := CloseTheFile;
```

you could simply code it this way:

```
CloseTheFile;
```

Turbo Pascal 6.0 won't ordinarily allow functions to be invoked this way. To do it, you must place a **{$X+}** command somewhere in your source code file before you make the function invocation. You can also set the same directive from the Options | Compiler dialog box, by checking the Extended Syntax check box.

With Turbo and Borland Pascal 7.0, the default state was changed to $X+, so you don't have to configure the compiler or do anything to your source code files to execute functions as standalone statements.

One important caution: You can't treat any function defined in the **System** unit as a statement, regardless of the state of the $X switch. **System** unit functions are functions now and always, and their return values must always be dealt with.

THE STRUCTURE OF FUNCTIONS AND PROCEDURES

Procedures and functions are, in effect, miniature programs. They can have label declarations, constant declarations, type declarations, variable declarations, and procedure and function declarations as well as the expected code statements. Consider these two entities:

```
PROGRAM HiThere;          PROCEDURE HiThere;

BEGIN                     BEGIN
  Writeln('Hi there!')      Writeln('Hi there!')
END.                      END;
```

The only *essential* differences between a program and a procedure are the keyword **PROGRAM** and the punctuation after the final **END**.

Functions are a little different. A function has a type and takes on a value that it returns to the program logic that invokes it:

```
FUNCTION Area(R : Real) : Real;

CONST
  PI = 3.14159;

BEGIN
  Area := PI * R * R;
END;
```

The type of function **Area** is **Real**. As you can see from the function's single line of code, an expression computing area for the given radius R is evaluated, and the value is assigned to the function's name. Aside from these two distinctions, functions are identical to procedures and are also miniature programs.

8.11 Formal and Actual Parameters

Passing data to procedures and functions can be done two ways: by using global variables that any procedure or function can read from or write to, and through each procedure or function's parameter list. The first method (sometimes called "common," from an old FORTRAN scheme) is a thoroughly bad idea, to be avoided as much as possible. It is good practice to hand a procedure everything it needs through its parameter list.

The following program contains a procedure to draw boxes on the CRT screen with characters, as opposed to true pixel graphics:

```
{-------------------------------------------------------------------}
{                              BoxTest                              }
{                                                                   }
{    Character box-draw demo program; demos concept of procedures   }
{                                                                   }
{                         by Jeff Duntemann                         }
{                         Turbo Pascal V7.0                         }
{                         Last update 1/23/93                       }
{                                                                   }
{       From: BORLAND PASCAL FROM SQUARE ONE   by Jeff Duntemann    }
{-------------------------------------------------------------------}

PROGRAM BoxTest;

USES Crt;

TYPE
  LineRec = RECORD
              ULCorner,
              URCorner,
              LLCorner,
              LRCorner,
              HBar,
              VBar,
              LineCross,
              TDown,
              TUp,
              TRight,
              TLeft : String[4]
            END;

  String80 = String[80];

CONST
  PCLineChars : LineRec =
    (ULCorner : #201;
```

```
                URCorner : #187;
                LLCorner : #200;
                LRCorner : #188;
                HBar    : #205;
                VBar    : #186;
                LineCross: #206;
                TDown   : #203;
                TUp     : #202;
                TRight  : #185;
                TLeft   : #204);


VAR
   X,Y            : Integer;
   Width,Height : Integer;


PROCEDURE MakeBox(X,Y,Width,Height : Integer;
                     LineChars    : LineRec);

VAR
   I,J : Integer;

BEGIN
   IF X < 0 THEN X := (80-Width) DIV 2;   { Negative X centers box }
   WITH LineChars DO
      BEGIN                                { Draw top line }
      GotoXY(X,Y); Write(ULCorner);
      FOR I := 3 TO Width DO Write(HBar);
      Write(URCorner);
                                             { Draw bottom line }
      GotoXY(X,(Y+Height)-1); Write(LLCorner);
      FOR I := 3 TO Width DO Write(HBar);
      Write(LRCorner);
                         { Draw sides }
    FOR I := 1 TO Height-2 DO
      BEGIN
         GotoXY(X,Y+I); Write(VBar);
         GotoXY((X+Width)-1,Y+I); Write(VBar)
      END
    END
END;


BEGIN
   Randomize;           { Seed the pseudorandom number generator }
   ClrScr;              { Clear the entire screen }
```

```
    WHILE NOT KeyPressed DO   { Draw boxes until a key is pressed }
      BEGIN
        X := Random(72);      { Get a Random X/Y for UL Corner of box }
        Y := Random(21);
        REPEAT Width := Random(80-72) UNTIL Width > 1;
        { Get Random Height & }
        REPEAT Height := Random(25-Y) UNTIL Height > 1;
        { Width to fit on CRT }
         MakeBox(X,Y,Width,Height,PCLineChars);         { and draw it! }
        Delay(25);
      END
  END.
```

The **PCLineChars** typed constant is an excellent example of the use of record constants, as I described them in the last chapter. But what I wanted this little program to demonstrate is the use of a procedure to hide some program details.

Procedure **MakeBox** has a parameter list with five parameters in it. In the parameter list of the procedure's declaration they are named: **X**, **Y**, **Width**, **Height**, and **LineChars**. Notice that the types of these parameters are given in the procedure declaration. **X**, **Y**, **Width**, and **Height** are all identical types, so they may be given as a list separated by commas. You could also have defined each of the four separately, like this:

```
PROCEDURE MakeBox(X     : Integer;
              Y         : Integer;
              Width     : Integer;
              Height    : Integer;
              LineChars : LineRec);
```

The parameters defined in a procedure's declaration are called "formal parameters" and must always be given a type, separated from the formal parameter by a colon. In the example, **X**, **Y**, **Width**, **Height**, and **LineChars** are all formal parameters.

When a procedure is invoked, values are passed to the procedure through its parameters. The parameter types are not given:

```
MakeBox(25,BoxNum+2,30,3,PCLineChars);
```

Furthermore, in this example, the values may be values stored in variables, or values expressed as constants or expressions. The parameters that are present in the parameter list of a particular invocation of a procedure are called *actual parameters*. (All parameters passed to **MakeBox** are passed *by value*. If they were passed *by reference*, the actual parameters would have to be variables of identical type to the formal parameters. This will be fully explained in the next section.)

Identifiers used as formal parameters are local to their procedure or function. As such, their names may be identical to identifiers defined in other procedures or functions, or in the main program, without any conflict. (You'll find more on this particular subject in Chapter 11.) The **X** and **Y** formal parameters in **MakeBox** have no relation at all to an **X** or **Y** identifier used elsewhere in the program. Of course, the flipside of this is also true: If you are using an X or **Y** variable global to the entire program they will *not* be accessible from within **MakeBox**. If you try to access a global **X** or **Y** variable from within **MakeBox**, you will access the formal parameters **X** and **Y** instead.

Also remember that formal **VAR** parameters may not act as control variables in **FOR** loops. Local variables (such as **I** in **MakeBox**) should be declared for this purpose. Non-**VAR** formal parameters may be used freely as control variables in **FOR** loops.

8.12 Passing Parameters by Value or by Reference

When a function or a procedure is invoked, the actual parameters are "meshed" with the formal parameters, and then the function or procedure does its work. The meshing of actual parameters with formal parameters is done two ways: by value and by reference.

PASSING PARAMETERS BY VALUE

A parameter passed by value is just that: A value is copied from the actual parameter into the formal parameter. The movement of the value to the procedure is a one-way street. Nothing can come back out again and be used by the calling program. This applies whether the actual parameter is a constant, an expression, or a variable.

There are powerful advantages to one-way data movement *into* a procedure. The procedure can fold, spindle, and mutilate the parameter any way it needs to, and not fear any side effects outside of the procedure. The copy of the actual parameter it gets is a truly private copy, strictly local to the procedure itself.

If a variable is passed to a procedure by value the type of the variable must be compatible with the type of the formal parameter.

PASSING PARAMETERS BY REFERENCE

There are many occasions when the whole point of passing a parameter to a function or procedure is to have it modified and returned for further use. To have a procedure or function modify a parameter and return it, the parameter must be passed by reference.

Unlike parameters passed by value, a parameter passed by reference (often called a **VAR** parameter) cannot be a literal, a constant, or an expression. The values of constants and literals by definition cannot be changed, and the notion of changing the value of an expression and stuffing it back into the expression makes no logical sense.

To be passed by reference, an actual parameter must be a variable of the *identical* type as the formal parameter. Compatible types will not do; the types must evaluate down to the same type definition statement.

The one exception to this rule in Turbo Pascal involves string types. Strings, if you recall from Section 7.9, may be defined in any physical length from 1 to 255, with the default length being 255 unless you specify some other length. Under strict type checking a **VAR** string parameter passed to a procedure must be of the identical type declared in the procedure's header:

```
VAR
    String1 : String80;
    String2 : String30;

PROCEDURE Grimble(VAR WorkString : String255);
```

In this example, strict type checking would prohibit passing either **String1** or **String2** as a parameter to procedure **Grimble**.

However, strict type checking may be relaxed with the **$V** compiler command to allow strings of any physical length to be passed as **VAR** parameters regardless of the formal **VAR** parameter's physical length. To relax strict type checking include the {**$V-**} command in your code. Note that the default for type checking is strict, and you must explicitly use the **$V-** command to relax type checking if desired.

The draconian nature of strict type checking for **VAR** parameters makes a little more sense when you realize that the variable itself is not copied into the formal parameter (as with parameters passed by value). What is passed is actually a pointer to the variable itself. Data is not being moved from one variable to another. Data is being read from one variable and written back into the same variable. To protect other data items that may exist to either side of the variable passed by reference, the compiler insists on a *perfect* match between formal and actual parameters.

Using **$V-** is still possible for compatibility with existing Turbo Pascal code, but it's always been a little hazardous, and version 7.0 has provided a new feature, *open string parameters*, that does the same thing a lot more safely. Open string parameters will be discussed a little later in this chapter.

The procedure **MakeBox** had several parameters, all passed by value. For an example of a parameter passed by reference, consider the Shell sort procedure below:

```
{->>>>ShellSort<<<<------------------------------------------------}
{ Filename : SHELSORT.SRC — Last Modified 1/24/93               }
{                                                              }
{ This is your textbook Shell sort on an array of key records,  }
{ defined as the type shown below:                             }
{                                                              }
{       KeyRec = RECORD                                        }
{                    Ref    : Integer;                         }
{                    KeyData : String30                        }
{                END;                                          }
{                                                              }
{       From: BORLAND PASCAL FROM SQUARE ONE  by Jeff Duntemann }
{--------------------------------------------------------------}
```

```
PROCEDURE ShellSort(VAR SortBuf : KeyArray; Recs : Integer);

VAR
  I,J,K,L : Integer;
  Spread : Integer;


PROCEDURE KeySwap(VAR RR,SS : KeyRec);

VAR
  T : KeyRec;

BEGIN
  T := RR;
  RR := SS;
  SS := T
END;


BEGIN
  Spread := Recs DIV 2;    { First Spread is half record count }
  WHILE Spread > 0 DO      { Do until Spread goes to zero:     }
    BEGIN
    FOR I := Spread + 1 TO Recs DO
      BEGIN
      J := I - Spread;
      WHILE J > 0 DO
        BEGIN          { Test & swap across the array }
          L := J + Spread;
          IF SortBuf[J].KeyData <= SortBuf[L].KeyData THEN J := 0 ELSE
             KeySwap(SortBuf[J],SortBuf[L]);
          J := J - Spread
        END
      END;
    Spread := Spread DIV 2  { Halve Spread for next pass }
  END
END;
```

This procedure sorts an array of sort keys. A sort key is a record type that consists of a piece of data and a pointer to a file entry from which the data came. The fastest and safest way to sort a file is not to sort the file at all, but to build an array of sort keys from information in the file and sort the array of sort keys instead.

The array can then be written out to a file. Since the data in the array is in sorted (usually alphabetical) order, it can be searched using a fast binary search function. Once a match to a desired string is found (in the **Key** field of a **KeyRec** record) the **RecNum** field contains the physical record number of the record in the file where the rest of the information is stored.

Look at the parameter line for **ShellSort**:

```
PROCEDURE ShellSort(VAR SortBuf : KeyArray; Recs : Integer);
```

The first parameter, **SortBuf**, is passed by reference. The second parameter, **Recs**, is passed by value. The difference is that **SortBuf** is preceded by the keyword **VAR**. **VAR** indicates that the parameter following it is passed by reference.

The reason for passing **SortBuf** by reference should be obvious: We want to rearrange the sort keys in **SortBuf** and put them in a certain order. **ShellSort** does this rearranging. We will need to get **SortBuf** "back" when the rearranging is done. Had we passed **SortBuf** to **ShellSort** by value, **ShellSort** would have received its own private copy of **SortBuf**, would have sorted the copy, and then would have had no way to return the sorted copy to the rest of the program.

Recs contains a count of the number of sort keys loaded into the array **SortBuf**. While knowing the value stored in **Recs** is essential to sorting **SortBuf** correctly, it need not be changed, and thus **Recs** can be passed by value. Only the *value* of **Recs** is needed.

Summing up: An actual parameter passed by value is copied into the formal parameter. The copy is local to the procedure or function and changes made to the copy do not "leak out" into the rest of the program.

Passing a parameter to a procedure by reference actually gives the procedure a pointer to the physical variable being passed. Changes made to the parameter within the procedure are actually made to the physical variable outside the procedure.

To pass a parameter by reference, precede the parameter by the keyword **VAR**. When passed by reference, actual parameters must be variables of *identical type* to the formal parameter.

8.13 Open Array and String Parameters

One of the hassles of working with arrays is that Pascal will not allow you to pass an array to a procedure in a formal array parameter that does not match the actual array parameter in every respect, including element type, upper bound, and lower bound. This makes it difficult to create a general-purpose array-sorting procedure, for example, since you must define in the array formal parameter exactly how many elements will be in the array passed into the procedure.

Turbo Pascal 7.0 adds *open array parameters* to address this problem. Students of other Pascal compilers will recognize this feature as what Niklaus Wirth calls *conformant arrays*.

In the header of your procedure or function, a formal array parameter is declared with the *type* of the elements in the array, but without any declared bounds. We might declare a new version of the **ShellSort** procedure presented a little earlier this way:

```
PROCEDURE ShellSort(VAR SortBuf : ARRAY of KeyRec; Recs : Integer);
```

The new **SortBuf** parameter is an open array parameter. We are told that it is an array of **KeyRec**, but not how large an array **SortBuf** is. Turbo Pascal is flexible enough to be able to handle the meshing of the formal array parameter **SortBuf** with an actual array of **KeyRec** at runtime. Either of the array variables below can be passed to the new **ShellSort** procedure in the **SortBuf** open array parameter:

```
VAR
   BigBuffer : ARRAY[0..500] OF KeyRec;
   LilBuffer : ARRAY[0..100] OF KeyRec;
```

No other changes need to be made to **ShellSort** to allow it to work perfectly well with any size array of **KeyRec** passed to it, assuming that the **Recs** value accurately reflects the number of significant elements in the array passed. If **Recs** is larger than the upper bound of the array passed in the open array parameter, a range error will be triggered.

Now, inside of the new **ShellSort**, how does the procedure know what it's dealing with? To manipulate the arrays passed to it, the procedure must know what any array's upper and lower bounds are. The answer lies in two pre-defined functions: **High** and **Low.** (Make sure before using open array parameters that you have not defined your own identifiers **High** and **Low.**) Inside of a procedure having an open array parameter, **High(<open array>)** returns a value indicating the zero-adjusted high bound of the actual parameter, and **Low(<open array>)** returns 0. The zero-adjusted high bound is equal to the high bound minus the low bound; in essence, the low bound is dropped to zero and the high bound is dropped by an equal value.

The consequences are important: *High and Low work intuitively only with 0-based arrays.* That is, that regardless of the defined value of the lower bound of an array passed in an open array parameter, **Low** will always return it as 0 inside the procedure! If you define an array as

```
MyArray = ARRAY[10..200] OF Integer;
```

and then pass **MyArray** to a procedure in the **MyOpenArray** parameter, you will find that **Low(MyOpenArray)** returns 0—and that **High(MyOpenArray)** returns 190. If you're going to get into the habit of using open arrays, define your arrays as zero based:

```
MyArray = ARRAY[0..190] OF Integer;
```

This will minimize confusion.

The **Recs** parameter of the **ShellSort** procedure exists to allow a partially-filled array of records to be sorted—**Recs** simply tells **ShellSort** how many elements of the **SortBuf** array really contain data. We can build some safety into **ShellSort** by using **High** to check whether **Recs** accidentally contains a higher number than the upper bound of the **SortBuf** array. In that case, we can set **Recs** equal to the high bound of **SortBuf**, so that **ShellSort** will find itself passed an array that might be partly full, or full—but not over-full. It only takes one simple statement, the first in the revised **ShellSort**:

```
PROCEDURE ShellSort(VAR SortBuf : ARRAY OF KeyRec; Recs : Integer);
VAR
  I,J,K,L : Integer;
  Spread : Integer;

PROCEDURE KeySwap(VAR RR,SS : KeyRec);
VAR
  T : KeyRec;
BEGIN
  T := RR;
  RR := SS;
  SS := T
END;

BEGIN
  { First we make sure Recs isn't higher than the upper bound: }
  IF Recs > High(SortBuf) THEN Recs := High(SortBuf);
  Spread := Recs DIV 2;    { First Spread is half record count }
  WHILE Spread > 0 DO      { Do until Spread goes to zero:    }
    BEGIN
      FOR I := Spread + 1 TO Recs DO
        BEGIN
          J := I - Spread;
          WHILE J > 0 DO
            BEGIN        { Test & swap across the array }
              L := J + Spread;
              IF SortBuf[J].KeyData <= SortBuf[L].KeyData THEN J :=
                0 ELSE KeySwap(SortBuf[J],SortBuf[L]);
              J := J - Spread
            END
        END;
      Spread := Spread DIV 2  { Halve Spread for next pass }
    END
END;
```

There are some restrictions on open array parameters. You cannot assign to an open array parameter in its entirety; that is, you cannot treat the array as a whole in any way. You can only work with an open array parameter on an element-by-element basis. Open array parameters passed by value (that is, without the **VAR** reserved word) are allocated on the stack, and can crash your machine if they take more stack than you've allocated for stack use.

High and **Low** are actually usable on any scalar type to return the highest and lowest values legal within that type. This can be especially valuable for use with subranges or enumerated types.

OPEN STRING PARAMETERS

Open string parameters use the same machinery as open array parameters to allow you to pass strings of different sizes through a formal parameter without a specified string size. A string, after all, is simply an array of **Char** that receives special treatment from the runtime library in a few limited ways.

You declare an open string parameter using the predefined identifier **OpenString**. Here's a simple procedure that forces the case of its open string parameter to upper. You can pass a string value of any legal length (that is, up to 255 characters) in **Target** without running afoul of strong type checking:

```
PROCEDURE UCString(VAR Target : OpenString);

VAR
  I : Integer;

BEGIN
  FOR I := 1 TO Length(Target) DO
    Target[I] := UpCase(Target[I]);
END;
```

Inside the procedure, the standard **Length** string function works the way it does on any sort of string. **High(Target)** would return the defined length of the actual parameter passed in **Target. Low(Target)** always returns 0, since strings are always zero-based arrays.

Somewhat oddly (to my view), the identifier **OpenString** will not act this way when it is used to declare a value parameter (that is, without **VAR**). As a value parameter, **OpenString** yields a string parameter that is always of type **STRING**; that is, the maximum string length of 255, and the **High** function will always return 255. *You should only use OpenString as a VAR parameter!*

OPEN STRINGS WITH $P+

With version 7.0, Borland introduced a new compiler command, $P+, as an alternate way to declare open string parameters. If you place the {$P+} command toward the top of your source code file (or else check the check box for Open parameters in the Options|Compiler dialog box), **VAR** parameters declared using the **STRING** reserved word act as open string parameters, and not simply as strings with a maximum length of 255. However, value parameters of type **STRING** remain type **STRING** and do *not* become open array parameters. As with **OpenString**, the **VAR** has to be there!

This was done to provide backward compatibility to older Turbo Pascal code that used **STRING** as a way of safely passing strings of any size to a procedure or function. If you're writing new code, the advised method is to use the **OpenString** predefined type instead.

8.14 Recursion

Recursion is one of those peculiar concepts that seems to defy understanding totally, and depends completely on mystery for its operation, until eventually some small spark of understanding happens, and then, *wham*! It becomes simple or even obvious. A great many people have trouble understanding recursion at first glance, so if you do too, don't think less of yourself for it. For the beginner recursion is simple. But it is *not* obvious.

Recursion is what we call it when a function or procedure invokes itself. It seems somehow intuitive to beginners that having a procedure call itself is either impossible or else an invitation to disaster. Both of these fears are unfounded, of course. Let's look at them both.

Recursion is indeed possible. In fact, having a procedure call itself is no different from a coding perspective than having a procedure call any other procedure. What happens when a procedure calls another procedure? Only this: First, the called procedure is "instantiated"; that is, its formal parameters and local variables are allocated on the system stack. Next, the return address (the location in the code from which the procedure was called and to which it must return control) is "pushed" onto the system stack. Finally, control is passed to the called procedure's code.

When the called procedure is finished executing, it retrieves the return address from the system stack and then clears its variables and formal parameters off the stack by a process we call "popping." Then it returns control to the code that called it by branching to the return address.

None of this changes when a procedure calls itself. Upon a recursive call to itself, new copies of the procedure's formal parameters and local variables are instantiated on the stack. Then control is passed to the start of the procedure again.

The problem shows up when execution reaches the point in the procedure where it calls itself. A third instance of the procedure is allocated on the stack, and the procedure begins running again. A fourth instance, and a fifth . . . and after a few hundred recursive calls the stack has grown so large that it collides with something important in memory, and the system crashes. If you had this kind of procedure, such a thing would happen very quickly:

```
PROCEDURE Fatal;

BEGIN
  Fatal
END;
```

Such a situation is an unlimited feedback loop. It is this possibility that makes newcomers feel uneasy about recursion.

Obviously, the important part of recursion is knowing when to stop.

A recursive procedure must test some condition before it calls itself, to see if it still needs to call itself to complete its work. This condition could be a comparison of a counter against a predetermined number of recursive calls, or some

Boolean condition that becomes true (or false) when the time is right to stop recursing and go home.

When controlled in this way, recursion becomes a very powerful and elegant way to solve certain programming problems.

Let's go through a simpleminded example of a controlled recursive procedure. Read through this code *very* carefully:

```
PROGRAM PushPop;

CONST
  Levels = 5;

VAR
  Depth : Integer;

PROCEDURE Dive(VAR Depth : Integer);

BEGIN
  Writeln('Push!');
  Writeln('Our depth is now: ',Depth);
  Depth := Depth +1;
  IF Depth <= Levels THEN Dive(Depth);
  Writeln('Pop!')
END;


BEGIN
  Depth := 1;
  Dive(Depth);
END.
```

The program itself is nothing more than setting a counter to one and calling the recursive procedure **Dive**. Note constant **Levels**. **Dive** prints the word "Push!" when it begins executing, and the word "Pop!" when it ceases executing. In between, it prints the value of the variable **Depth** and then increments it.

If, at this point, the value of **Depth** is less than the constant **Levels**, **Dive** calls itself. Each call to **Dive** increments **Depth** by one, until at last **Depth** is greater than **Levels**. Then recursion stops.

Running program **PushPop** produces this output. Can you tell yourself exactly why?

```
Push!
Our depth is now 1
Push!
Our depth is now 2
Push!
Our depth is now 3
Push!
Our depth is now 4
Push!
Our depth is now 5
```

```
Pop!
Pop!
Pop!
Pop!
Pop!
```

Follow the execution of **PushPop** through, with a pencil to touch each keyword, if necessary, until the output makes sense to you.

8.15 Appplications of Recursion

Certain programming problems simply cry out for recursive solutions. Perhaps the simplest and best-known is the matter of calculating factorials. A factorial is the product of a digit and all the digits less than it, down to one:

```
5! = 5 * 4 * 3 * 2 * 1
```

A little scrutiny here will show that 5! is the same as 5 * 4!, and 4! is the same as 4 * 3!, and so on. In the general case, N! = N * (N-1)! Whether you see it immediately or not, we have already expressed the factorial algorithm recursively by defining it in terms of a factorial. This will become a little clearer when we express it in Pascal:

```
FUNCTION Factorial(N : LongInt) : LongInt;

BEGIN
   IF N > 1 THEN Factorial := N * Factorial(N-1)
     ELSE Factorial := 1
END;
```

And that is it. We express it as a conditional statement because there must always be something to tell the code when to stop recursing. Without the N > 1 test the function would merrily decrement N down past zero and recurse away until the system crashed.

The way to understand this function is to work it out for N=1, then N=2, N=3, and so on. For N=1, the N > 1 test returns **FALSE**, so is assigned the value 1. No recursion involved. 1! = 1. For N=2, a recursive call to **Factorial** is made: **Factorial** is assigned the value **2 * Factorial(1)**. As we saw above, **Factorial(1) = 1**. So 2! = 2 * 1, or 2. For N=3, two recursive calls are made: **Factorial** is assigned the value **3 * Factorial(2)**. **Factorial(2)** is computed (as we just saw) by evaluating (recursively) **2 * Factorial(1)**. And **Factorial(1)** is simply = 1. Catching on? One interesting thing to do is add (temporarily) a **Writeln** statement to **Factorial** that displays the value of **N** at the beginning of each invocation.

A sidenote on the power of factorials: Calculating anything over 7! will overflow a 2–byte integer. This is why the **Factorial** function returns a **LongInt** parameter. Here's something for you to figure out: How high a value can you pass in **N** without overflowing a long integer?

A RECURSIVE QUICKSORT PROCEDURE

A considerably more useful application of recursion lies in the "quicksort" method of sorting arrays, invented by C.A.R. Hoare. Quicksort procedures can be written in a number of different ways, but the simplest way is by using recursion.

This will not be an easy procedure to understand if you are a beginner. If you can't make sense of it right now, come back to it after you have had a chance to use Pascal for awhile.

The quicksort procedure below does the same job that the procedure **ShellSort** did in the last section. **QuickSort** is passed an array of **KeyRec** and a count of the number of records to be sorted in the array. It rearranges the records until they are in ascending sort order in the array:

```
{->>>>QuickSort<<<<-------------------------------------------}
{                                                             }
{ Filename : QUIKSORT.SRC - Last Modified 1/24/93             }
{                                                             }
{ This is your textbook recursive quicksort on an array of key }
{ records, which are defined as the type shown below:         }
{                                                             }
{   KeyRec = RECORD                                           }
{       Ref    : Integer;                                     }
{       KeyData : String30                                    }
{     END;                                                    }
{                                                             }
{   From: BORLAND PASCAL FROM SQUARE ONE by Jeff Duntemann    }
{-------------------------------------------------------------}

PROCEDURE QuickSort(VAR SortBuf : KeyARRAY;
                        Recs  : Integer);


PROCEDURE KeySwap(VAR RR,SS : KeyRec);

VAR
  T : KeyRec;

BEGIN
  T  := RR;
  RR := SS;
  SS := T
END;


PROCEDURE DoSort(Low, High : Integer);
```

```
VAR
  I,J   : Integer;
  Pivot : KeyRec;

BEGIN
  { Can't sort if Low is greater than or equal to High... }
  IF Low < High THEN
    BEGIN
      I := Low;
      J := High;
      Pivot := SortBuf[J];
      REPEAT
        WHILE (I < J) AND (SortBuf[I].KeyData <= Pivot.KeyData) DO I
          := I + 1;
        WHILE (J > I) AND (SortBuf[J].KeyData >= Pivot.KeyData) DO J
          := J - 1;
        IF I < J THEN KeySwap(SortBuf[I],SortBuf[J]);
      UNTIL I >= J;
      KeySwap(SortBuf[I],SortBuf[High]);
      IF (I - Low < High - I) THEN
        BEGIN
          DoSort(Low,I-1);   { Recursive calls to DoSort! }
          DoSort(I+1,High)
        END
      ELSE
        BEGIN
          DoSort(I+1,High);  { Recursive calls to DoSort! }
          DoSort(Low,I-1)
        END
    END
END;



BEGIN
  DoSort(1,Recs);
END; { QuickSort }
```

QuickSort's *modus operandi* is summarized in Figure 8.1. One of the elements is chosen arbitrarily (here it is the last element in the array) to be the "pivot value." The idea is to divide the array into two partitions so that all elements on one side of the partition are greater than the pivot value, and all elements on the other side of the partition are less than the pivot value.

This is done by scanning the array from both ends toward the middle by counters **I** and **J**. **I** scans from the low end upward; **J** from the high end downward. The **I** counter samples each element, and stops when it finds an element whose value is *higher* than the pivot value. Then the scan begins from the top end down, with the **J** counter looking for a value that is *less* than the pivot value.

When it finds one, the two found elements are swapped, thus putting them on the proper side of the pivot value.

When **I** and **J** collide in the middle somewhere (*not* necessarily in the center!), the array has been partitioned into two groups of elements: one that is larger than the pivot value, and one that is smaller than the pivot value. These two groups are not necessarily equal in size. In fact, they usually will not be. The only thing that is certain is that all the elements in one group are less than the value of the pivot element, and all of the elements of the other group are greater than the pivot element. The two *groups* are sorted with respect to one another: All elements of the low group are less than all elements of the high group.

Enter recursion: This same process is now applied to each of the two groups by calling **DoSort** recursively for each group. A new pivot value is chosen for each group, and each group is partitioned around its pivot value, just as the entire array was originally. When this is done, there are four groups. A little thought will show you that low-valued elements of the array are being driven toward the low end of the array, and high-valued elements are being driven toward the high end of the array. Within each group there is no guarantee that the elements are in sorted order. What you must understand is that the *groups themselves* are in sort order. In other words, *all* the elements of one group are greater than all the elements of the group below it.

Pressing on: Each of the four groups is partitioned again by more recursive calls to **DoSort**. The groups are smaller. Each group taken as one is sorted with respect to all other groups. With each recursive call, the groups have fewer and fewer members. In time, each group will contain only one element. Since groups are always in sort order, if each group is a single element, then all elements of the array are in sorted order, and **QuickSort**'s job is finished.

How does **QuickSort** know when to stop recursing? The first conditional test in **DoSort** does it: If **Low** is greater than or equal to **High**, the sort is finished. Why? Because **Low** and **High** are the bounds of the group being partitioned. If

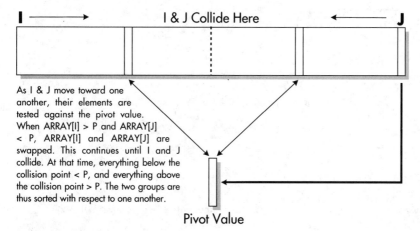

Figure 8.1 A QuickSort Scan

Low = **High**, the group has only one member. When the groups have only one member, the array is in sort order and work is done.

If this makes your head spin, you are in good company. Follow it through a few times until it makes sense. Once you can follow **QuickSort**'s internal logic, you will have a *very* good grasp of the uses of recursion.

This particular Quicksort algorithm works best when the original order of the elements in the array is random or nearly so. It works least well when the original order is close to fully sorted. For an array of random elements, it is one of the fastest of all sorting methods. For sorting arrays that are close to being in order, the **ShellSort** procedure given earlier will be consistently faster.

The following program puts the two sort procedures to the test. It will also give you a flavor for using keyed files. (I'll be talking about files a little later, in Chapter 14.) It generates a file of random keys, and allows you to display the random keys to verify how random they are. (Thoroughly.) Finally, it will sort the file by either of the two methods. Once the file has been sorted, you can display the keys once more to be sure that they have in fact been sorted.

SORTTEST.PAS uses a lot of concepts I haven't introduced in the book yet, and calls routines that I haven't described so far. It is, however, a very straight-forward program, and it would be an interesting exercise to see just how much of it you can understand based on what you've learned so far.

```
{----------------------------------------------------------------}
{                          SortTest                              }
{                                                                }
{              Data sort demonstration program                   }
{                                                                }
{                      by Jeff Duntemann                         }
{                      Turbo Pascal V7.0                         }
{                      Last update 1/23/93                       }
{                                                                }
{    From: BORLAND PASCAL FROM SQUARE ONE by Jeff Duntemann      }
{----------------------------------------------------------------}

PROGRAM SortTest;

USES CRT,DOS,  { Standard Borland units }
     BoxStuff; { Unit for drawing boxes; see Chapter 13 }

CONST
   Highlite   = True; { These first 4 constants are used by WriteAt }
   CR         = True;
   NoHighlite = False;
   NoCR       = False;
   Shell      = True; { Which sort procedure will we be using? }
   Quick      = False;
```

```
TYPE
 String255  = STRING[255];
 String80   = STRING[80];
 String30   = STRING[30];

 KeyRec     = RECORD
                 Ref   : Integer;
                 KeyData : String30
              END;

 KeyArray   = ARRAY[0..500] OF KeyRec;
 KeyFile    = FILE OF KeyRec;

VAR
 IVal      : Integer;  { Holds integer value for user's response }
 WorkArray : KeyArray;
 Randoms   : KeyFile;  { Files should generally be declared global }


{$I BEEP.SRC}        { Described in Section 16.13 }
{$I UHUH.SRC}        { Described in Section 16.13 }
{$I PULL.SRC }       { Described in Section 16.12 }
{$I CLREGION.SRC}    { Described in Section 18.1 }
{$I YES.SRC }        { Described in Section 18.3 }
{$I WRITEAT.SRC}     { Described in Section 18.3 }
{$I GETSTRIN.SRC}    { Described in Section 15.2 }
{$I SHELSORT.SRC}    { Described in Section 14.2 }
{$I QUIKSORT.SRC}    { Described in Section 14.4 }


PROCEDURE GenerateRandomKeyFile(KeyQuantity : Integer);

VAR WorkKey : KeyRec;
    I,J    : Word;

BEGIN
  Assign(Randoms,'RANDOMS.KEY');
  Rewrite(Randoms);
  FOR I := 1 TO KeyQuantity DO
    BEGIN
       FillChar(WorkKey,SizeOf(WorkKey),0);
      FOR J := 1 TO SizeOf(WorkKey.KeyData)-1 DO
        WorkKey.KeyData[J] := Chr(Pull(65,90));
       WorkKey.KeyData[0] := Chr(30);
       Write(Randoms,WorkKey);
    END;
```

```
      Close(Randoms)
  END;


PROCEDURE DisplayKeys;

VAR WorkKey : KeyRec;

BEGIN
   Assign(Randoms,'RANDOMS.KEY');
   Reset(Randoms);
   Window(25,13,70,22);
   GotoXY(1,1);
   WHILE NOT EOF(Randoms) DO
     BEGIN
        Read(Randoms,WorkKey);
        IF NOT EOF(Randoms) THEN Writeln(WorkKey.KeyData)
     END;
   Close(Randoms);
   Writeln;
   Writeln('    >>Press (CR)<<');
   Readln;
   ClrScr;
   Window(1,1,80,25)
END;


PROCEDURE DoSort(Shell : Boolean);

VAR I,Counter : Word;

BEGIN
   Assign(Randoms,'RANDOMS.KEY');
   Reset(Randoms);
   Counter := 1;
   WriteAt(20,15,NoHighlite,NoCR,'Loading...');
   WHILE NOT EOF(Randoms) DO
     BEGIN
        Read(Randoms,WorkArray[Counter]);
        Counter := Succ(Counter)
     END;
   Close(Randoms);
   Write('...sorting...');
   IF Shell THEN ShellSort(WorkArray,Counter-1)
     ELSE QuickSort(WorkArray,Counter-1);
   Write('...writing...');
```

```
    Rewrite(Randoms);
    FOR I := 1 TO Counter-1 DO Write(Randoms,WorkArray[I]);
    Close(Randoms);
    Writeln('...done!');
    WriteAt(-1,21,NoHighlite,NoCR,'>>Press (CR)<<');
    Readln;
    ClearRegion(2,15,77,22)
  END;


BEGIN
  ClrScr;
  MakeBox(1,1,80,24,PCLineChars);
  WriteAt(18,3,HighLite,NoCR,'THE BORLAND PASCAL FROM SQUARE ONE SORT
    DEMO');
  REPEAT
    WriteAt(25,5,NoHighlite,NoCR,'[1] Generate file of random keys');
    WriteAt(25,6,NoHighlite,NoCR,'[2] Display file of random keys');
    WriteAt(25,7,NoHighlite,NoCR,'[3] Sort file via Shell sort');
    WriteAt(25,8,NoHighlite,NoCR,'[4] Sort file via Quicksort');
    WriteAt(18,10,NoHighlite,NoCR,'Enter 1-4, or 0 to quit, and press
     Enter: ');
    IVal := 0;
    Readln(IVal);
    CASE IVal OF
      0 :;                    { Null statement here }
      1 : GenerateRandomKeyFile(500); { 500 is as high as you can
      go...}
      2 : DisplayKeys;
      3 : DoSort(Shell);
      4 : DoSort(Quick);
      ELSE IVal := 0;
    END; {CASE}
  UNTIL (IVal = 0);
END.
```

8.16 Forward Declarations

In almost all cases, you must declare a type in the type declaration section of your program before you can declare a variable of that type. There's one well-known exception to this rule that I'll be discussing toward the end of this book when we take up the difficult issue of pointers: You can use an identifier in a pointer definition before that identifier is defined. In other words, this pair of type definitions is completely legal:

```
TYPE
  RecPtr = ^DynaRec;
```

```
DynaRec = RECORD
             DataPart : String;
             Next     : RecPtr
          END;
```

Ignore for now what **^DynaRec** means if you haven't been exposed to pointer notation before. What's significant here is that Turbo Pascal "takes our word" that we will, in fact, define **DynaRec** before the type definition section ends, and thus allows the definition of **RecPtr** *before* the definition of **DynaRec**—even though **DynaRec** is an integral part of the definition of **RecPtr**. This use of an undefined identifier is called a "forward reference."

The context of defining pointer types is the *only* context in which Pascal will accept a forward reference without any special persuasion. In certain circumstances, however, Pascal can be persuaded to accept a procedure or function identifier before that procedure or function has been defined. In a sense, we must promise the compiler that we will, in fact, define the identifier. Or, if you prefer, we have to declare that we will declare such an identifier somewhere down the source code trail.

This promise is called a "forward declaration." It is accomplished with a Pascal standard directive, **FORWARD**, and it is done this way:

```
PROCEDURE NotThereYet(Foo,Bar : Integer); FORWARD;
```

What we have here is the procedure header all by itself, without any procedure body or local declarations of constants, types, or variables. People who understand Turbo Pascal units (see Chapter 13) will think that this resembles the declarations in the interface section of a unit, and they are right.

Later on in the program, sometime before the **BEGIN** that marks the start of the main program block, procedure **NotThereYet** must be declared in its entirety. If it isn't, Turbo Pascal will give us this error:

```
Error 59: Undefined forward (NOTHEREYET)
```

The eventual declaration of the procedure is perfectly ordinary. No special syntax indicates that the procedure had earlier been declared as **FORWARD**.

You do have the option of *not* re-declaring the forward-declared procedure's parameter list. In other words, you could in fact define an (empty) procedure **NotThereYet** without parameters:

```
PROCEDURE NotThereYet;

BEGIN
END;
```

This shorthand, also, will be familiar to people who understand Turbo Pascal's units. I consider it bad practice, however. The compiler allows you to re-declare the parameters, and re-declaring parameters contributes to the clarity of the program to have the parameter list in both places: the forward declaration, (where they are essential) and the full definition.

At last we come to the question: What good is all of this? The answer is: not much. The only situation that genuinely requires forward declaration is circular (also called mutual) recursion. Consider these two procedure definitions:

```
PROCEDURE Egg;

BEGIN
    .

    .
    Chicken;

    .

END;

PROCEDURE  Chicken;

BEGIN
    .

    .
    Egg;

    .

    .
END;
```

Which comes first? You can't declare **Chicken** without calling **Egg**, and you can't declare **Egg** without calling **Chicken**. Pascal will call foul on the whole thing unless you forward-declare one or the other. Adding the forward declaration makes everything copacetic:

```
PROCEDURE Chicken; FORWARD;

PROCEDURE Egg;

BEGIN
    .    { Other program logic keeps this from }
    .    { being an infinite loop. }
    Chicken;   { Without the FORWARD, we get an error here. }
    .

    .

END;

PROCEDURE  Chicken;

BEGIN
    .

    .
    Egg;

    .

    .
END;
```

That is what circular recursion *is*, but what it's good for has thus far escaped me. If any reader has come across a use more compelling than the mathematical oddity **Catch22** in the old *Turbo Pascal 3.0 Reference Manual*, I would like to hear about it. My hunch is that any program that appears to require circular recursion can probably be rewritten a different way without it.

I look upon the reserved word **FORWARD** much as I do the spokeshave sitting in the bottom drawer of my tool cabinet. I have never yet used it, but by God, if I ever need to shave some spokes, I know just where it is.

Chapter 9

Standard Functions

BUILT-IN SOFTWARE GADGETS TO HELP YOU GET THINGS DONE

The ISO Standard Pascal definition includes a number of "standard functions" that are built into the language and need not be declared and coded into your program. These functions fall into two basic groups: mathematical functions, which provide fundamental operations such as square and square root, absolute value, natural logarithms, and trig functions; and transfer functions, which define relationships between otherwise incompatible data types like **Integer** and **Char**.

Many books refer to the parameter passed to a standard function as its "argument." This borrows jargon from the world of mathematics and may be confusing, since some people end up wondering what the difference is between an argument and a parameter. There is no difference other than the term. To lessen the confusion, I will use the term "parameter," which we have been using with respect to functions all along.

All of the standard functions described in this section may accept expressions as parameters, as long as those expressions evaluate to a value of the correct type. In other words, you may say **Sqrt(Sqr(X)+Sqr(Y))** as well as **Sqrt(16)**. Just make sure you don't try to extract the square root of a **Boolean** value, or of an enumerated type, and so on.

Turbo Pascal implements all the standard functions from ISO Pascal, and quite a few of its own. In this section we'll discuss them in detail.

9.1 Round and Trunc

Round and **Trunc** are fence sitters. They are both mathematical functions, in the sense that they provide a mathematical service, and they are also transfer functions, in that they provide a bridge between the partly incompatible types **Real** and **Integer**.

We have already seen, in Chapter 5, that any integer value may be assigned to a variable of type **Real**. But the reverse is *not* true, since a **Real** value may have a decimal part, and there is no way to express a decimal part in type **Integer**. **Round** and **Trunc** give us our choice of two ways to "transfer" a **Real** value into an **Integer** value. **Round** and **Trunc** both accept parameters of type **Real** and return values that may be assigned to either type **Integer** or **Real**.

ROUND

In mathematics, "rounding" a number means moving its value to the nearest integer. This is the job done by **Round**. **Round(X)** returns an integer value that is the integer closest to **X**. The direction in which a real number with a fractional part is rounded is usually given as "up" or "down." This can be confusing when you start dealing with negative real numbers. I prefer to visualize a number line and speak of "toward zero" or "away from zero."

For **X** *greater than* 0: Rounds *away from zero* (up) for fractional parts greater than or equal to .5. Rounds *toward zero* (down) for fractional parts less than .5.

For **X** *less than* 0: Rounds *away from zero* (down) for fractional parts greater than or equal to .5. Rounds *toward zero* (up) for fractional parts less than .5.

Some examples are:

```
Round(4.449)    { Returns 4 }
Round(-6.12)    { Returns -6 }
Round(0.6)      { Returns 1 }
Round(-3.5)     { Returns -4 }
Round(17.5)     { Returns 18 }
```

Because the way rounding works with **Round** is symmetric with respect to zero, **Round(-X)** is equal to **-Round(X)**.

Note that using **Round(X)** for **X > MaxInt** will return a value that cannot be assigned to an integer without generating a runtime error:

```
Error 201: Range check error
```

This will occur if range checking is enabled; if range checking is *not* enabled, your program will continue executing, but the value actually assigned to the integer will be unpredictable, but predictably meaningless.

TRUNC

Truncating a real number simply means removing its fractional part and dealing with what's left. **Trunc(X)** returns the closest integer value *toward* zero—and if you ponder that for a moment, you'll see that it is equivalent to removing the fractional part and calling the whole number part an integer. Examples:

```
Trunc(17.667)     { Returns 17 }
Trunc(-3.14)      { Returns -3 }
Trunc(6.5)        { Returns 6 }
Trunc(-229.00884) { Returns -229 }
```

Turbo Pascal 4.0 removed a restriction imposed by V3.0 that prevented you from using **Round** and **Trunc** from rounding or truncating large real numbers, even if you intended to assign the resulting value to type **Real**. Turbo Pascal 3.0 actually worked with intermediate integer values internally, and would trigger a range error if **Round** or **Trunc** were passed a parameter greater than **MaxInt**. No longer. Assuming the type to which you assign the value returned by **Round** or **Trunc** has the range to contain the value, there will be no problems. When returning values to real numbers, **Trunc** is now the equivalent of the Turbo Pascal functions **Int**.

9.2 Sqr and Sqrt

Nothing complicated here. **Sqr(X)** squares **X**. It is completely equivalent to **X * X**, and Pascal includes it because squaring is done so frequently in mathematics, and also because (as we will discuss later) there is no exponentiation operator in Pascal and hence no clean notation for **X** raised to a power of two.

Sqr may operate on both integers and reals. If you square an integer with **Sqr**, the returned value is an integer. If you square a real with **Sqr**, the returned value is real.

Sqrt(X) may also operate on either an integer or real **X**, but the value returned is *always* type **Real**.

A few examples are:

```
CONST
  PI = 3.14159;

VAR
  I : Integer;
  R : Real;

I := 64;
R := 6.077;

Sqrt(16)    { Returns 4.0; a real number! }
Sqrt(PI)    { Returns 1.77245 }
Sqrt(I)     { Returns 64; real number }
Sqr(2.4)    { Returns 4.8; again, real }
Sqr(7)      { Returns 49; integer or real }
Sqr(I)      { Returns 4096; integer }
Sqr(R)      { Returns 36.92993; real }
```

The following procedure calculates the length of the hypotenuse of a right triangle, given the other two sides:

```
FUNCTION Hypotenuse(Side1,Side2 : Real ) : Real;

BEGIN
  Hypotenuse := Sqrt(Sqr(Side1) + Sqr(Side2))
END;
```

The algorithm, of course, is the Pythagorean Theorem.

9.3 Trigonometric Functions

There are three trigonometric functions among the standard functions of Pascal: **Sin**, **Cos**, and **ArcTan**. Where are **Tan**, **ArcSin**, and all the others? Well, given **Sin**, **Cos**, and **ArcTan**, all other trigonometric functions are easily derived. Insisting that they be built into the compiler would make the compiler more complex and prone to errors. It would also make the Pascal language more cluttered than it has to be.

Sin(X), **Cos(X)**, and **ArcTan(X)** all return real results. **X** may, however, be an integer or a real number. Note well that *X represents radians, not degrees.* A radian equals 57.29578 degrees. Radians, however, are usually thought of in terms of pi (3.14159) and fractions of pi. 360 degrees = 2pi radians; 180 degrees = pi radians, and so on. Pascal's trigonometric functions behave as you would expect them to behave from textbook discussions of trigonometry.

DERIVING OTHER TRIG FUNCTIONS

With **Sin**, **Cos**, and **Arctan**, one can build functions returning all other trigonometric relationships. For example:

```
FUNCTION Tan(X : Real) : Real;

BEGIN
  Tan := Sin(X) / Cos(X)
END;

FUNCTION Cot(X : Real) : Real;

BEGIN
  Cot := Cos(X) / Sin(X)
END;

FUNCTION Sec(X : Real) : Real;

BEGIN
  Sec := 1 / Cos(X)
END;

FUNCTION Csc(X : Real) : Real;

BEGIN
  Csc := 1 / Sin(X)
END;
```

Note that even though the **X** parameter passed to these functions is declared as type **Real**, Turbo Pascal will allow you to pass an integer literal or variable in **X** without error, and will treat the value as a real number without a fractional part during the calculations.

9.4 Absolute Value, Natural Logs, and Exponents

ABSOLUTE VALUE

Absolute value in mathematics is the distance of a number from zero. In practical terms, this means stripping the negative sign from a negative number and leaving a positive number alone. The Pascal function **Abs(X)** returns the absolute value of **X**. **X** may be type **Real** or **Integer**. The type of the returned value is the same as the type of **X**. For example:

```
Abs(-61)      { Returns 61; type Integer }
Abs(484)      { Returns 484; also Integer }
Abs(3.87)     { Returns 3.87; type Real }
Abs(-61.558)  { Returns 61.558; also Real }
```

The **Abs** function is actually a shorthand form of the following statement:

```
IF X < 0 THEN X := - X;
```

NATURAL LOGARITHMS

There are two Pascal standard functions that deal with natural logarithms. Natural logarithms are mathematical functions that turn on a remarkable irrational number named e, which, to six decimal places, is 2.718282. Explaining where e comes from, or explaining natural logarithms in detail, is somewhat outside the charter of this book. Do read up on them (in any senior high math text) if the concept is strange to you.

Exp(X) returns the exponential function for **X**. **X** may be a real number or an integer, but the returned value is always real. The exponential function raises e to the **X** power. Therefore, when you evaluate **Exp(X)**, what you are actually evaluating is e^X.

Ln(X) returns the natural logarithm (logarithm to the base e) of **X**. **X** may be type **Integer** or **Real**, and the returned value, again, is always type **Real**. The sense of the **Ln(X)** function is the reverse of **Exp(X)**: Evaluating **Ln(X)** yields the exponent to which e must be raised to give **X**.

Natural logarithms are the most arcane of Pascal's mathematical standard functions. They are most used in mathematics that many of us would consider "heavy." However, there is one use for which natural logarithms fill an enormous hole in Pascal's definition: exponentiation. Unlike most languages, Pascal contains no general function for raising X to the Yth power. (In FORTRAN the exponentiation operator is the double asterisk: X**Y raises **X** to the Yth power.) **Exp** and **Ln** allow us to create a function that raises one number to a given power:

```
FUNCTION Power(Mantissa, Exponent : Real) : Real;

BEGIN
```

```
    Power := Exp(Ln(Mantissa)*Exponent)
END;
```

This almost certainly looks like magic unless you really understand how natural logarithms work. Two cautions: The result returned is type **Real**, not **Integer**. Also, do not pass a zero or negative value to **Mantissa**. Runtime error 4: Ln argument error will result. Reason: **Ln(X)** for a negative **X** is undefined!

9.5 Ord and Chr

The functions **Ord** and **Chr** are true transfer functions, providing you with a well-documented, "legal" pathway between the otherwise incompatible types **Integer** and **Char**. **Ord** actually provides the pathway between integers and *any* ordinal type—hence the name.

ORD

As its name suggests, **Ord(X)** deals with ordinal types. Ordinal types are those types that can be "enumerated"; that is, types with a fixed number of values in a well-defined order.

Ord(X) returns the ordinal position (an integer) of the value X in its ordinal type. The sixty-sixth character in the ASCII character set is the capital letter 'A'. **Ord('A')** returns 65. The third color in our old friend type **Spectrum** is **Yellow**. **Ord(Yellow)** returns 2—remember (for both examples) that we start counting at 0!

CHR

Chr goes in the opposite direction from **Ord**: **Chr(X)** returns a character value corresponding to the **X**th character in the ASCII character set. (**X** is an integer.) **Chr(65)** returns the capital 'A'. **Chr(66)** returns capital letter 'B', and so on. The most important use of **Chr(X)** is generating character values that are not expressed by any symbol that you can place between single quote marks. How do you put a line feed in quotes? Or worse yet, a bell character? You don't—you express them with **Chr**:

```
Chr(13)    { Returns ASCII carriage return (CR) }
Chr(7)     { Returns ASCII bell (BEL) }
Chr(127)   { Returns ASCII delete (DEL) }
Chr(8)     { Returns ASCII backspace (BS) }
```

Chr allows you to return a character based on an integer expression. The procedure **CapsLock**, for example, uses **Ord** and **Chr** to translate a character into an integer, manipulate the integer, and then translate the integer back into a character:

```
PROCEDURE CapsLock(VAR Target : String);
```

```
VAR Lowercase : SET OF Char;
    I       : Integer;

BEGIN
    Lowercase := ['a'..'z'];
    FOR I := 1 TO Length(Target) DO
        IF Target[I] IN Lowercase THEN
            Target[I] := Chr(Ord(Target[I]) - 32)
END;
```

(Turbo Pascal has a built-in procedure, **UpCase**, which will accomplish the same thing as the expression

```
Chr(Ord(Target[I]) - 32)
```

but the procedure **CapsLock** as given above will compile under any Pascal with a UCSD-style string type.)

Don't try to pass **Chr** an integer value higher than 255. The results will be undefined, probably garbage.

9.6 Pred and Succ

We discussed these two standard functions informally in Section 8.4, in connection with **FOR** loops. Now it's time for a closer look.

One of the properties of an ordinal type is that its values exist in a fixed and well-defined order. In other words, for type **Integer**, 3 comes after 2, not before. For type **Char**, 'Q' follows 'P' which follows 'O', and so on. The order is always the same.

This order is called the *collating sequence* or *collating order* of an ordinal type. Given a value of an ordinal type, **Ord** tells you which position that value occupies in its collating sequence. Given a value of an ordinal type, **Pred** and **Succ** return the next value before that value or after that value, respectively.

```
Pred('Z')      { Returns 'Y' }
Succ('w')      { Returns 'x' }
Pred(43)       { Returns 42 }
Succ(19210)    { Returns 19211 }
Pred(Orange)   { Returns Red }
Succ(Green)    { Returns Blue }
Pred(Red)      { Undefined! }
```

This last example bears a closer look. The predecessor value of **Red** is undefined. Recall the definition of our enumerated type **Spectrum**:

```
Spectrum = (Red,Orange,Yellow,Green,Blue,Indigo,Violet);
```

Red is the very first value in the type. There is nothing before it, so **Pred(Red)** makes no sense in the context of type **Spectrum**. Similarly, **Succ(Violet)** makes no sense, since there is no value in **Spectrum** after **Violet**.

Pred(<value>) of the first value of an ordinal type is undefined. **Succ(<value>)** of the last value of an ordinal type is undefined.

Pred and **Succ** provide a means of "stepping through" an ordinal type to do some repetitive manipulation on a range of the values in that ordinal type. For example, in printing out the names on a telephone/address list, we might want to put a little header before the list of names beginning with 'A', and then before the list of names beginning with 'B', and so on. Assuming that the names are stored in sorted order in an array, we might work it this way:

```
VAR
   Names     : ARRAY[1..200] OF String[35];
   NameCount : Integer;

PROCEDURE Header(Ch : Char);

BEGIN
   Write(LST,Chr(13),Chr(10));
   Writeln(LST,'[',Ch,']---------------')
END;

PROCEDURE PrintBook(NameCount : Integer);

VAR I   : Integer;
    Ch  : Char;
    AName : String[35];

BEGIN
   Ch := 'A';
   Header(Ch);
   FOR I := 1 TO NameCount DO
     BEGIN
       AName := Names[I];
       IF AName[1] <> CH THEN
         REPEAT
           CH := Succ(CH);
           Header(Ch)
         UNTIL AName[1] = CH;
       Writeln(LST,AName)
     END
   END;
```

Assume that the array **Names** has been filled somehow with names, and that the number of names has been placed in **NameCount**. The names must be in sorted order, last name first. When **PrintBook** is invoked, the list of names in **Names** is printed on the system printer, with a header for each letter of the alphabet:

```
[A]---------------
Albert*Eddie
Aldiss*Brian
Anselm*Jo
Anthony*Piers
```

```
[B]--------------
Brooks*Bobbie
Bentley*Mike

[C]--------------
Chan*Charlie
Charles*Ray
Cabell*James  Branch

[D]--------------

[E]--------------

[F]--------------
Farmer*Philip  Jose
Foglio*Phil
Flor*Donna
```

and so on. Letters for which no names exist in the list will still have a printed header on the list. The printed listing, if cut into memo-book sized sheets, would make the core of a "little black book" for names and addresses.

Look at the listing of **PrintBook**. **Ch** is given an initial value of A. As the names are printed, the first letter of each name is compared to the letter stored in **Ch**. If they don't match, the loop

```
REPEAT
   Ch := Succ(Ch);
   Header(Ch)
UNTIL AName[1] = Ch;
```

is executed. The letter in **Ch** is "stepped" along the alphabet until it "catches up" to the first letter in **AName**. For each step along the alphabet, a header is printed.

We might have written **Ch := Chr(Ord(Ch)+1)** instead of **Ch := Succ(Ch)**. **Succ** provides a much crisper notation. And because **Chr** does not work with enumerated types, **Succ** is the only way to step along the values of a programmer-defined enumerated type like **Spectrum**.

9.7 Odd

The last of the standard functions from ISO Pascal is a transfer function: **Odd(X)**. **X** is an integer value. If **X** is an odd value **Odd(X)** returns the Boolean value **True**. If **X** is an even value, **Odd(X)** returns **False**.

Odd is thus a way of expressing an integer value as a Boolean. Any even number can express the value **False**, and any odd number can express the value **True**. (Although it doesn't fit the classic definition of "even" as "dividable by 2," 0 is considered an even number by virtue of lying between two odd numbers, 1 and -1.)

Up to this point, all the functions described have been present in ISO Standard Pascal. Turbo Pascal provides a number of other built-in functions that ISO Standard Pascal does not.

9.8 Frac and Int

With these two functions you can "take apart" a real number into its whole number part and its fractional part.

Frac(R) returns the fractional part of real number **R**. In other words, **Frac(24.44789)** would return 0.44789.

Int(R) returns the whole number part of real number **R**. In other words, **Int(241.003)** would return 241.0.

Both **Frac** and **Int** return values of type **Real**. You cannot directly assign the return values from either of these functions to an integer type. For returning the whole number part of a real number to an integer type, use **Trunc** instead.

9.9 Hi, Lo, and Swap

Type **Integer**, if you recall, is represented in memory as two bytes. There are times when it is necessary to obtain the value of each of the 2 bytes apart from its brother. Functions **Hi** and **Lo** allow you to do this:

Hi(I) returns the value of the high-order byte of **I**. Technically, what happens is that the value of **I** is shifted 8 bits to the right, so that the high-order byte becomes the low-order byte. The high-order byte is filled with zero bits. For example:

Hi(256) returns 1. Why? Can you picture it happening?

Hi(17341) returns 67.

Hi(-10366) returns 215. How does the negative sign figure in?

Lo(I) returns the low order byte of **I**. All that happens here is that the high 8 bits of **I** are forced to zero. For example:

Lo(256) returns 0.

Lo(17341) returns 189.

Lo(-10366) returns 130. Can **Lo** ever return a negative number?

Swap(I) *exchanges* the 2 bytes of integer **I**. The high-order byte becomes the low-order byte, and the low-order byte becomes the high-order byte. For example:

Swap(17341) returns -17085. Where does the negative sign come from?

Swap($66FF) returns $FF66. Hexadecimal notation makes things a good deal clearer!

Hi, **Lo**, and **Swap** find good use when you must move values into and out of CPU registers. Many 8086 registers are 2 bytes wide and must be filled all at once; yet many operating system calls require that the two halves of a CPU register be filled with unrelated bytes of data. Furthermore, after a DOS call the 2 bytes of a register may contain necessary but unrelated data, and must be separated.

Suppose, for example, that you need to pass $01 to register AH and $06 to register AL. AH and AL are two halves of 8086 register AX, and AX must be passed to the operating system as a unit. Turbo Pascal treats AX as an integer, part of an important data structure called **Registers** (see Section 19.3). How to load two separate numbers into one integer? Try this:

```
VAR
    AX,JMask,QBit : Integer;

JMask := $06;      { The high bytes of both these }
QBit  := $01;      { variables are zero! }
AX    := QBit;     { QBit goes into the low byte of AX; }
AX    := Swap(AX); { then Swap flips low byte for high; }
AX    := AX + JMask; { so that adding JMask to AX puts it }
                   { into AX's low byte. }
```

Hi and **Lo** come into play when the operating system returns a value to your program in register **AX**. You want to extract **JMask** and **QBit** from **AX** again, like so:

```
JMask := Lo(AX);   { JMask comes back in AX's low byte; }
QBit  := Hi(AX);   { and QBit in AX's high byte }
```

The need for **Hi**, **Lo**, and **Swap** will become more apparent after you understand what is involved in making DOS calls and software interrupts. We'll go into this more in Chapter 19.

9.10 Pi

Turbo Pascal also includes a standard function **Pi** that returns the value of pi to as many significant figures as the variable to which it returns the value may express. The value returned is a real number type and so may not be assigned to any integer type, but (as with any real number type) may be assigned to the IEEE math coprocessor types **Single**, **Double**, **Extended**, and **Comp**.

You should keep in mind that differences in precision in the type receiving a value from **Pi** will affect the exact decimal values returned, although for all but the most exacting requirements these differences can be ignored.

To illustrate, the following code displays the actual values returned by function **Pi** to the various real number types:

```
VAR
    RS : Single;
    RR : Real;
    RD : Double;
    RE : Extended;
    RC : Comp;

RS := Pi; RR := Pi; RD := Pi; RE := Pi; RC := Pi;
Writeln('Type Single:    ',RS:4:25);
Writeln('Type Real:      ',RR:4:25);
```

```
Writeln('Type Double:   ',RD:4:25);
Writeln('Type Extended: ',RE:4:25);
Writeln('Type Comp:     ',RC:4:25);
```

And here is the screen output you'll see:

```
Type Single:    3.141592741012573240
Type Real:      3.141592653588304530
Type Double:    3.141592653589793120
Type Extended:  3.141592653589793240
Type Comp:      3.000000000000000000
```

Note that type **Comp** can accept a value from **Pi** without triggering an error but will *not* store the fractional part!

9.11 Inc and Dec

Turbo Pascal 4.0 added two new standard procedures to its already considerable toolkit: **Inc** and **Dec**. They both operate only on ordinal types. Their function is simple: **Inc** increments an ordinal value, and **Dec** decrements an ordinal value. Functionally, they are equivalent to **Pred** and **Succ** *except* that **Pred** and **Succ** are functions rather than procedures.

In other words, **Inc** and **Dec** may stand alone as statements:

```
VAR
  I : Integer;
  Ch : Char;

I := 17;
Ch := 'A';
Inc(I);   { I now contains 16 }
Dec(Ch);  { Ch now contains '@' }
```

Pred and **Succ**, by contrast, need to be placed on the right side of an assignment statement, either alone or inside of an expression:

```
I := 17;
Ch := 'A';
I := Succ(I);   { I now contains 17 }
Ch := Pred(Ch); { Ch now contains '@' }
```

Why use **Inc** and **Dec** if the standard and much more portable **Pred** and **Succ** are available? Only one reason: speed. To understand this you need to consider what the compiler has to do when it generates native 8086 code from a Turbo Pascal statement. An assignment statement like

```
I := Succ(I);
```

is treated as any assignment statement: First the compiler generates code to evaluate the expression on the right side of the assignment statement, and then it moves that intermediate value to replace the current value of the variable on the left side of the assignment statement. Moving things from one location in memory to another takes a fair amount of time compared to the time it takes simply to increment or decrement a variable that fits neatly in either one or two 8086 registers.

A statement like

```
Inc(I);
```

on the other hand, generates code that goes directly to the location of variable **I** and increments it. Nothing unnecessary is done, and the code generated is faster than the code generated for **Succ**. It may not seem a *lot* faster, and it won't be noticeable until you need to increment something thousands of times in succession within a tight loop. Then, all those microscopic fragments of wasted time add up to significant program delays.

Like so many other things in life, it's a tradeoff. You, the program developer, will have to decide whether the gain in speed is worth the loss in portability, or vise versa.

9.12 Random Number Functions

Built into Turbo Pascal are two functions that return pseudorandom numbers, **Random** and **Random(I)**. **Random** returns a real number, and **Random(I)** returns an integer.

Random returns a pseudorandom number of type **Real** that is greater than or equal to zero and less than one. This statement:

```
FOR I := 1 TO 5 DO Writeln(Random);
```

might display:

```
7.0172090270E-01
7.3332131305E-01
8.0977424840E-01
6.7220290820E-01
9.2550002318E-01
```

The E-01 exponent makes all these numbers fall in the range 0.0 - 0.9999999999. All random numbers returned by the function **Random** fall within this range; but, of course, if you need random real numbers in another range, you need only shift the decimal point the required number of places to the right.

Random(I) returns random integers. The parameter is an integer that sets an upper bound for the random numbers returned by the function. **Random(I)** will return a number greater than or equal to zero and less than **I**. **I** may be any integer up to **MaxInt**. **I** may be negative; however, making **I** *any* negative value has the same effect as passing **MaxInt** to **Random(I)**. There is no way to make **Random(I)** return negative random numbers.

There is frequently a need for a random number in a particular range, say between 15 and 50 or between 100 and 500. The procedure **Pull** meets this need by extracting random integers until one falls in the range specified by **Low** and **High**.

```
{<<<< Pull >>>>}
{ From: BORLAND PASCAL FROM SQUARE ONE   }
{ by Jeff Duntemann -- Last mod 1/25/93 }

FUNCTION Pull(Low,High : Integer) : Integer;

VAR
  I : Integer;

BEGIN
  REPEAT              { Keep requesting random integers until }
    I := Random(High + 1); { one falls between Low and High }
  UNTIL I >= Low;
  Pull := I
END;
```

RANDOMIZE

The **Randomize** procedure exists because Turbo Pascal's random numbers, like all random numbers generated in software, are not random at all but only "pseudorandom," which means that a series of such numbers approximates randomness. The *series* of such numbers may well repeat itself each time the program is run, unless the random number generator is "reseeded" with a new seed value. This is the job of **Randomize**.

Randomize should be called at least once in every program, and to make your pseudorandom numbers more nearly random, might be called each time you want a new random number or series of random numbers.

Randomize did not work correctly in Turbo Pascal releases 1 and 2. In release 3.0 and later, **Randomize** appears to work correctly.

A DICE GAME

The following program shows one use of random numbers in a game situation. **Rollem** simulates the roll of one or more dice—up to as many as will fit across the screen. Procedure **Roll** may be placed in your function/procedure library and used in any game program that must roll dice in a visual manner. It will display a number of text-mode dice at location **X,Y** on the screen, where **X,Y** are the coordinates of the upper-left corner of the first die. The **NumberOfDice** parameter tells **Roll** how many dice to roll; there is built-in protection against attempting to display more dice than space to the right of **X** will allow.

Rollem is also a good exercise in **REPEAT/UNTIL** loops. The **MakeBox** procedure was described in Section 8.11.

```
{-----------------------------------------------------------------}
{                    Rollem                                       }
```

```
{                                                              }
{  A dice game to demonstrate random numbers and box draws     }
{                                                              }
{                  by Jeff Duntemann                           }
{                  Turbo Pascal V7.0                           }
{                  Last update 1/25/93                         }
{                                                              }
{ From: BORLAND PASCAL FROM SQUARE ONE by Jeff Duntemann   }
{-------------------------------------------------------------}

PROGRAM Rollem;

USES Crt,BoxStuff;

CONST
  DiceFaces : ARRAY[0..5,0..2] OF STRING[5] =
              (('   ',' o ','   '), { 1 }
               ('o  ','   ','  o'), { 2 }
               ('  o',' o ','o  '), { 3 }
               ('o  o','   ','o  o'), { 4 }
               ('o  o',' o ','o  o'), { 5 }
               ('o o o','     ','o o o')); { 6 }

TYPE
  String80 = String[80];

VAR
  I,X,Y      : Integer;
  Width,Height : Integer;
  Quit     : Boolean;
  Dice,Toss  : Integer;
  DiceX    : Integer;
  Ch       : Char;
  Banner     : String80;


PROCEDURE Roll(X,Y        : Integer;
               NumberOfDice : Integer;
               VAR Toss   : Integer);

VAR I,J,Throw,XOffset : Integer;

BEGIN
  IF (NumberOfDice * 9)+X >= 80 THEN { Too many dice horizontally }
    NumberOfDice := (80-X) DIV 9; { will scramble the CRT display! }
  FOR I := 1 TO NumberOfDice DO
    BEGIN
```

```
      XOffset := (I-1)*9;        { Nine space offset for each die }
      MakeBox(X+XOffset,Y,7,5,PCLineChars); { Draw a die }
      Throw := Random(6);            { "Toss" it }
      FOR J := 0 TO 2 DO             { and fill it with dots }
        BEGIN
          GotoXY(X+1+XOffset,Y+1+J);
          Write(DiceFaces[Throw,J])
        END
    END
END;


BEGIN
  Randomize;          { Seed the pseudorandom number generator }
  ClrScr;             { Clear the entire screen }
  Quit := False;      { Initialize the quit flag }
  Banner := 'GONNA Roll THE BONES!';
  MakeBox(-1,1,Length(Banner)+4,3,PCLineChars); { Draw Banner box }
  { Put Banner in it }
  GotoXY((80-Length(Banner)) DIV 2,2); Write(Banner);
  REPEAT
    REPEAT
      FOR I := 6 TO 18 DO    { Clear the game portion of screen }
        BEGIN
          GotoXY(1,I);
          ClrEol
        END;
    GotoXY(1,6);
    Write('>>How many dice will we Roll this game? (1-5, or 0 to
          exit): ');
    Readln(Dice);
    IF Dice = 0 THEN Quit := True ELSE { Zero dice sets Quit flag}
      { Show error for dice out of range }
      IF (Dice < 1) OR (Dice > 5) THEN
        BEGIN
          GotoXY(0,23);
          Write('>>The legal range is 1-5 Dice!')
        END
    UNTIL (Dice >= 0) AND (Dice <= 5);
    GotoXY(0,23); ClrEol; { Get rid of any leftover error messages }
    IF NOT Quit THEN       { Play the game! }
      BEGIN
        DiceX := (80-(9*Dice)) DIV 2; { Calculate centered X for dice }
        REPEAT
          GotoXY(1,16); ClrEol;
          Roll(DiceX,9,Dice,Toss);               { Roll & draw dice }
          GotoXY(1,16); Write('>>Roll again? (Y/N): ');
          Readln(Ch);
```

```
        UNTIL NOT (Ch IN ['Y','y']);
        GotoXY(1,18); Write('>>Play another game? (Y/N): ');
        Readln(Ch);
        IF NOT (Ch IN ['Y','y']) THEN Quit := True
      END
   UNTIL Quit   { Quit flag set ends the game }
 END.
```

9.13 Sound Routines

Turbo Pascal contains two procedures that control sound production from the PC's speaker. These two procedures, **Sound** and **NoSound**, plus the built-in procedure **Delay** enable you to generate specified frequencies for specified periods of time.

Sound(Frequency) "turns on" a sound with a frequency given as Hertz (cycles per second) in **Frequency**. **Sound** says nothing about how *long* the sound will be generated; it will remain "on" until turned off by **NoSound**.

NoSound turns the speaker off again.

As a simplest-case example, to generate a 1 Khz (kilohertz) tone for one second, these three statements would be required:

```
Sound(1000);      { Initiate sound at 1000 Hertz }
Delay(1000);      { Delay for 1000 milliseconds }
NoSound;          { Turn sound off again }
```

Breaking away from the proverbial beep as a signal from your programs is easy enough, once you convince yourself that creative noise is not exclusively for video games. One simple signal I use is an audio "uh-uh" to signal that something is not right, especially character input from the keyboard:

```
{<<<< UhUh >>>>}

{ From: BORLAND PASCAL FROM SQUARE ONE }
{   by Jeff Duntemann -- Last mod 1/25/93 }

PROCEDURE UhUh;

VAR
  I : Integer;

BEGIN
  FOR I := 1 TO 2 DO
    BEGIN
      Sound(50);
      Delay(100);
      NoSound;
      Delay(50)
```

```
    END
  END;
```

Type this one in and try it—you'll get the idea.

Another interesting and very simple application of Turbo Pascal's sound support is shown below. It's a beeper with a difference—one that sounds like those fancy telephones you hear in lawyers' offices.

```
{<<<< Beep >>>>}

{   From: BORLAND PASCAL FROM SQUARE ONE   }
{   by Jeff Duntemann -- Last mod 1/25/93 }

PROCEDURE Beep;

VAR
  I : Integer;

BEGIN
  FOR I := 1 TO 3 DO
  BEGIN
    Sound(800);
    Delay(50);
    Sound(500);
    Delay(50)
  END;
  NoSound;
END;
```

Earlier versions of Turbo Pascal had the problem that **Sound** and **Delay** were clock-speed dependent. In other words, on faster machines, a given tone generated by **Sound** would be higher than on a slower machine, and the time delay generated with **Delay** would vary depending on a machine's clock speed as well. With Turbo Pascal 3.0 and later, these problems have been corrected, and both routines are now acceptably clock-speed independent.

A MORSE CODE GENERATOR

Another example of both **Sound** and **Delay** in use lies in the generation of Morse code characters. Procedure **SendMorse** accepts strings containing plain ASCII text, and will use the computer speaker to transmit the code audibly. Two additional parameters specify the code speed in words per minute (WPM) and the frequency of the speaker tone used, in Hertz.

The amateur radio practice of blending two separate Morse characters together for certain purposes (such as SK, meaning "end of contact") is handled by prefixing the pair to be "blended" with an asterisk ('*'), a character for which there is no common Morse equivalent. The blended SK would then be passed to **SendMorse** as "*SK".

Local procedure **Morse** accepts strings containing information already encoded as "dits" and "dahs," where the ASCII period character ('.') represents a dit and the ASCII dash ('-') represents a dah. **Morse** was set out apart from the body of **SendMorse** so that it could be rewritten to output the code through some other port than the audible speaker—perhaps a serial port used to control a transceiver, or a bit in the parallel port that drives a keying relay. **SendMorse** uses the ARRL's (American Radio Relay League's) published definition for WPM as

```
WPM = 1.2 * B
```

where B is the baud rate of the transmission; essentially the rate at which the smallest units of information are passed. This unit is the length of the audible portion of a 'dit', though it must be remembered that the dit properly includes the dit-length silence following it. The baud rate is thus *twice* the rate of an uninterrupted series of dits. The length of each dit can be derived from the above formula as

```
           1.2
DitLength = ----
           WPM
```

which, when multiplied by 1000, becomes an integer that can be passed to the **Delay** procedure as the integer number of milliseconds by which to delay.

The **Delay** procedure is tolerably clock-speed independent, and **SendMorse** will transmit code within a few percent of the passed code speed figure regardless of the speed of the host computer. I have tested this on a 4.77 Mhz PC and a 33 Mhz 80486 AT compatible, and the speeds are close enough to count on for code practice leading to the FCC amateur exams.

```
{->>>>SendMorse<<<<---------------------------------------------}
{                                                               }
{ Filename : SENDMORS.SRC -- Last Modified 1/26/93              }
{                                                               }
{ This procedure converts plain text to audible Morse Code at}
{ a specified code speed and tone frequency. The times are   }
{ fairly accurate and have been tested on a 4.77 Mhz PC and a}
{ 16 Mhz 80386 machine without significant difference in     }
{ code speed. (Turbo's V3.0 DELAY procedure is finally clock}
{ speed independent.) The useful range of the procedure is   }
{ from 10-35 WPM, with best "feel" at 15-25 WPM.             }
{                                                               }
{ Text is passed to SendMorse as quoted strings of plain      }
{ text. If two characters are to be sent as one without an   }
{ intermediate delay, an asterisk ('*') must precede the two}
{ characters. This replaces the overbar used in most amateur}
{ literature.                                                   }
{                                                               }
{ From: BORLAND PASCAL FROM SQUARE ONE by Jeff Duntemann      }
{---------------------------------------------------------------}
```

```
PROCEDURE SendMorse(PlainText : String;
                    ToneFrequency : Integer;
                    CodeSpeed    : Integer);

VAR
  I         : Integer;
  ToneLength  : Integer;
  DitLength  : Integer;
  CodeChar   : String;
  BlendNextTwo : Boolean;


{ Code is passed to local procedure Morse as literal dots and }
{ dashes: '-.-.' = 'C', and so on. SendMorse converts from   }
{ text to the dot/dash code representation. }

PROCEDURE Morse(CodeChar : String);

VAR
  I : Integer;

BEGIN
  FOR I := 1 TO Length(CodeChar) DO
    BEGIN
      IF CodeChar[1] IN ['.','-'] THEN
        BEGIN
          IF CodeChar[I] = '.' THEN ToneLength := DitLength
            ELSE ToneLength := DitLength * 3;
          Sound(ToneFrequency);
          Delay(ToneLength);
          NoSound;
          Delay(DitLength)
        END
    END
END;

BEGIN
  BlendNextTwo := False;
  { Code speed calculation is derived from formulae published in }
  { the 1986 ARRL Handbook, Section 9-8.  I recommend running   }
  { this procedure at 10 WPM or greater; 15-20 WPM is its most  }
  { effective range. Timer resolution interferes above 35 WPM. }
  DitLength := Round((1.2 / CodeSpeed) * 1000.0);
  FOR I := 1 TO Length(PlainText) DO IF PlainText[I] = '*' THEN
    BlendNextTwo := TRUE ELSE
    BEGIN
      PlainText[I] := UpCase(PlainText[I]);
```

```
    CASE PlainText[I] OF
     'A' : CodeChar := '.-';
     'B' : CodeChar := '-...';
     'C' : CodeChar := '-.-.';
     'D' : CodeChar := '-..';
     'E' : CodeChar := '.';
     'F' : CodeChar := '..-.';
     'G' : CodeChar := '-.';
     'H' : CodeChar := '....';
     'I' : CodeChar := '..';
     'J' : CodeChar := '.-';
     'K' : CodeChar := '-.-';
     'L' : CodeChar := '.-..';
     'M' : CodeChar := '-';
     'N' : CodeChar := '-.';
     'O' : CodeChar := '-';
     'P' : CodeChar := '.-.';
     'Q' : CodeChar := '-.-';
     'R' : CodeChar := '.-.';
     'S' : CodeChar := '...';
     'T' : CodeChar := '-';
     'U' : CodeChar := '..-';
     'V' : CodeChar := '...-';
     'W' : CodeChar := '.-';
     'X' : CodeChar := '-..-';
     'Y' : CodeChar := '-.-';
     'Z' : CodeChar := '-..';
     '1' : CodeChar := '.--';
     '2' : CodeChar := '..-';
     '3' : CodeChar := '...-';
     '4' : CodeChar := '....-';
     '5' : CodeChar := '.....';
     '6' : CodeChar := '-....';
     '7' : CodeChar := '-...';
     '8' : CodeChar := '-..';
     '9' : CodeChar := '--.';
     '0' : CodeChar := '--';
     '?' : CodeChar := '..-..';
     '.' : CodeChar := '.-.-.-';
     ',' : CodeChar := '-..-';
     '/' : CodeChar := '-..-.';
     '$' : CodeChar := '...-..-';
     '-' : CodeChar := '-....-';
    ELSE CodeChar := ''
    END; {CASE}
    Morse(CodeChar);
    IF NOT BlendNextTwo THEN Delay(DitLength * 2);
```

```
        BlendNextTwo := FALSE
    END;
END;
```

SendMorse works best at code speeds between 15 and 25 WPM, and gets dicey below 10 or above 35. For practice at lower speeds it would make sense to modify the code to insert additional "dead time" between characters and keep the character elements themselves at 10 WPM or faster.

The short program **MorseTest** demonstrates the use of **SendMorse**.

```
PROGRAM MorseTest;

USES Crt;

TYPE
    String80 = String[80];

    {$I SENDMORS.SRC}

BEGIN
    ClrScr;
    SendMorse('CQCQCQ DE KG7JF *SK',850,15);
END.
```

Chapter 10

Strings and How to Use Them

TURBO PASCAL'S "TEXT CONTAINERS" AND TEXT OPERATORS

ISO Standard Pascal lacks a "clean" way to deal with text. There is no **STRING** type in ISO Pascal; to work with strings in ISO Pascal you must confine your text to arrays of characters, keep your own logical length counters, and write all the procedures for manipulating strings yourself.

Given the pervasiveness of text in the work that computers do, it is not surprising that most implementors of Pascal have extended the language by providing a **STRING** data type and some built-in procedures and functions to manipulate strings.

10.1 Defining String Types

Turbo Pascal is no exception. We looked briefly at the **STRING** data type in Section 7.9. A **STRING** variable is actually an array of characters with a counter attached to keep tabs on how many characters have been loaded into the array. The Turbo Pascal type **STRING** has a physical length of 255 characters.

You can define physically shorter string types by using the word **STRING** followed by the maximum physical length of the string (up to 255) in brackets. For example, a string type capable of holding 80 characters of information would be defined this way:

```
TYPE
   String80 = STRING[80];
```

The type **String80** is actually an array 81 physical bytes long. Byte 0 is the length counter. It can hold a number from 0 to 80. Bytes 1 through 80 hold the actual text characters that make up the string. It may be helpful to think of this string type as a record type:

```
TYPE
   String80 = RECORD
                 Counter : Char;
                 ARRAY[1..80] OF Char
              END;
```

This is just a comparison, however—type **STRING** is treated specially by the compiler in a number of ways, and you cannot define a record type named **STRING** and expect it to get the same special treatment. In fact, the word **STRING** is a reserved word that cannot be redefined by you the programmer. (That's why I print **STRING** here in caps, as I do all reserved words.)

When you assign a string literal to a string variable, the length counter is automatically updated to reflect the number of characters assigned:

```
VAR
   MyText : STRING;

MyText := '';
MyText := 'Let the wookie win.';
```

Before this text assignment, **MyText** had been assigned the null string ('') and its length counter was 0. After the assignment, the length counter was automatically updated to 19.

Turbo Pascal provides a number of powerful string procedures and functions for manipulating text stored in strings. In the next section we'll look at each in detail.

10.2 Built-In String Procedures and Functions

LENGTH

The length counter of a string variable is accessible in two ways. One way is simply to examine element 0 of the string:

```
Count := Ord(MyText[0]);
```

This will put the length counter of string **MyText** into the integer variable **Count**. The length counter of string variables, just like the data in the string itself, is type **Char**, which needs the transfer function **Ord** to be assigned to an integer.

A considerably better way to do the same thing is to use the function **Length**. It is a built-in function predefined this way:

```
FUNCTION Length(Target : STRING) : Integer;
```

Length returns the value of the length counter, which indicates the logical length of string **Target**:

```
Count := Length(MyText);
```

This is functionally equivalent to accessing the length byte directly and is somewhat easier to read. **Length** is a function that returns an integer value, and obviates the use of transfer function **Ord**.

The length of the null string ('') is 0.

The following procedure, **CapsLock,** accepts a string parameter and returns it with all lowercase letters changed to their corresponding uppercase letters. Note the use of the **Length** function:

```
PROCEDURE CapsLock(VAR MyString : OpenString);

VAR
  I : Integer;

BEGIN
  FOR I := 1 TO Length(MyString) DO
    MyString[I] := UpCase(MyString[I]);
END;
```

CapsLock makes use of a convenient Turbo Pascal built-in function, **UpCase.** **UpCase** accepts a character value as a parameter and returns the uppercase equivalent of that character, if the parameter is lowercase. If the parameter is not a lowercase character, it is returned unchanged.

Keep in mind that to compile **CapsLock**, you must be using Turbo Pascal 7.0, which supports open string parameter types through the predefined type **OpenString**. In earlier versions of the compiler, to pass strings physically shorter than 255 characters to **CapsLock** (or any subprogram with a string **VAR** parameter) you need to relax strict type checking with the {$V-} compiler command.

CONCAT

Concatenation is the process of taking two or more strings and combining them into a single string. Turbo Pascal gives you two separate ways to perform this operation.

The easiest way to concatenate two or more strings is to use Turbo Pascal's string concatenation operator (**+**). Many BASIC interpreters also use the plus symbol to concatenate strings. Simply place the string variables in order, separated by the string concatenation operator:

```
BigString := String1 + String2 + String3 + String4;
```

STRING variable **BigString** should, of course, be large enough to hold all the variables you intend to concatenate into it. If the total length of all the source strings is greater than the physical length of the destination string, all data that will not fit into the destination string is truncated off the end and ignored.

The built-in function **Concat** performs the same function as the string concatenation operator. It is included in Turbo Pascal because several older Pascal compilers (notably UCSD Pascal and Pascal/MT+) used a **Concat** function and did not have a string concatenation operator. Borland included a number of features in early versions of its compilers to allow easy porting of code written for competitive compilers that no longer exist today.

Concat is a function returning a value of type **STRING.** It accepts any number of string variables and string literals as parameters, separated by commas.

The following example shows how both string concatenation methods work:

```
VAR
    Subject,Predicate,Sentence : String[80];

Subject := 'Kevin the hacker';
Predicate := 'crashed the system';
Sentence := Subject + Predicate;
Sentence :=
    Concat(Sentence,', but brought it up again.');
Writeln(Sentence);
```

Here, two string variables and a string literal are concatenated into a single string variable. The CRT output of the **Writeln** statement would be the single string "built" from the smaller strings via concatenation:

```
Kevin the hacker crashed the system, but brought it up again.
```

DELETE

Removing one or more characters from a string is the job done by the built-in **Delete** procedure, predefined this way:

```
PROCEDURE Delete(Target : STRING; Pos,Num : Integer);
```

Delete removes **Num** characters from the string **Target** beginning at the character number passed in **Pos**. The length counter of **Target** is updated to reflect the deleted characters.

```
VAR
    Magic : STRING;

Magic := 'Watch me make an elephant disappear...';
Delete(Magic,15,11);
Writeln(Magic);
```

Before the **Delete** operation, the string **Magic** has a length of 38 characters. When run, this example will display:

```
Watch me make disappear...
```

The new length of **Magic** is set to 27.

One use of **Delete** is to remove "leading whitespace" from a string variable. *Whitespace* is a set of characters that includes space, tab, carriage return, and linefeed. Whitespace is used to format text files for readability by human beings. However, when that text file is read by computer, the whitespace must be removed, as it tells the computer nothing.

The following procedure strips leading whitespace from a string variable:

```
PROCEDURE StripWhite(VAR Target : OpenString);

CONST
    Whitespace : SET OF Char = [#8,#10,#12,#13,' '];
```

```
BEGIN
  WHILE (Length(Target) > 0) AND (Target[1] IN Whitespace) DO
    Delete(Target,1,1)
END;
```

Whitespace is a set constant (see Section 7.10) containing the whitespace characters. Set constants are a feature unique to Turbo Pascal—keep that in mind if you intend to export your code to another Pascal compiler. Also, remember that open string parameters require version 7.0 of the compiler.

Delete(Target,1,1) deletes one character from the beginning of string **Target**. The second character is then moved up to take its place. If it, too, is a whitespace character it is also deleted, and so on until a nonwhitespace character becomes the first character in **Target**, or until **Target** is emptied of characters completely.

POS

Locating a substring within a larger string is handled by the built-in function **Pos. Pos** is predefined this way:

```
FUNCTION Pos(Pattern : <string or char>; Source : STRING) : Integer;
```

Pos returns an integer that is the location of the first occurence of **Pattern** in **Source. Pattern** may be a string variable, a **Char** variable, or a string or character literal.

For example:

```
VAR
  ChX,ChY   : Char;
  Little,Big : STRING;

Big := 'I am an American, Chicago-born. Chicago, that somber city.'
Little := 'Chicago';
ChX := 'g';
ChY := 'G';

Writeln('The position of ',Little,' in "Big" is ',Pos(Little,Big));
Writeln('The position of ',ChX,' in "Big" is ',Pos(ChX,Big));
Writeln('The position of ',ChY,' in "Big" is ',Pos(ChY,Big));
Writeln('The position of somber in "Big" is ',Pos('somber',Big));
Writeln('The position of r in "Big" is ',Pos('r',Big));
```

When executed, this example code will display the following:

```
The position of Chicago in "Big" is 19
The position of g in "Big" is 24
The position of G in "Big" is 0
The position of somber in "Big" is 48
The position of r in "Big" is 12
```

Pos *does* distinguish between upper- and lowercase letters. Note that if **Pos** cannot locate **Pattern** in **Source**, it returns a value of 0.

COPY

Extracting a substring from within a string is accomplished with the **Copy** built-in function. **Copy** is predefined this way:

```
FUNCTION Copy(Source : STRING; Pos,Num : Integer) : STRING;
```

Copy returns a string that contains **Size** characters from **Source**, beginning at character #**Index** within **Source**:

```
VAR
   Roland,Tower : STRING;

Roland := 'Childe Roland to the Dark Tower came!';
Tower := Copy(Roland,22,10);
Writeln(Tower);
```

When run, this example will print:

```
Dark Tower
```

In this example, **Index** and **Size** are passed to **Copy** as constants. They can also be passed as integer variables or expressions. The following function accepts a string containing a file name, and returns a string value containing the file extension. (The extension is the part of a file name from the period to the end; in "TURBO.COM" the extension is ".COM".)

```
FUNCTION GetExt(FileName : STRING) : STRING;

VAR
   DotPos : Integer;

BEGIN
   DotPos := Pos('.',FileName);
   IF DotPos = 0 THEN GetExt := '' ELSE
      GetExt := Copy(FileName,DotPos,(Length(FileName)-DotPos)+1);
END;
```

GetExt first tests to see if there is, in fact, a period in **FileName** at all. (File extensions are optional.) If there is no period, there is no extension, and **GetExt** is assigned the null string. If a period is there, **Copy** is used to assign to **GetExt** all characters from the period to the end of the string.

Since the length of a file extension may be 2, 3, or 4 characters, the expression **(Length(FileName)-DotPos)+1** is needed to calculate just how long the extension is in each particular case.

If **Index** plus **Size** is greater than the logical length of **Source**, **Copy** truncates the returned string value to whatever characters lie between **Index** and the end of the string. Note that unlike most Pascal compilers, Turbo Pascal allows you to write functions that return string values.

INSERT

A string can be added to the end of another string by using the **Concat** function. Copying a string into the middle of another string (and not simply tacking it on at the end) is done with the **Insert** procedure.

Insert is predefined this way:

```
PROCEDURE Insert(Source     : STRING;
                 VAR Target : STRING;
                 Pos        : Integer);
```

When invoked, **Insert** copies **Source** into **Target** starting at position **Pos** within **Target**. All characters in **Target** starting at position **Pos** are moved forward to make room for the inserted string, and **Target**'s length counter is updated to reflect the addition of the inserted characters.

```
VAR
   Sentence,Ozzie : STRING;

Sentence := 'I am King of Kings.';
Ozzie := 'Ozymandias, ';
Insert(Ozzie,Sentence,6);
Writeln(Sentence);
```

The output from this example would be:

```
I am Ozymandias, King of Kings.
```

If inserting text into **Target** gives **Target** more characters than it can physically contain, **Target** is truncated to its maximum physical length:

```
VAR
   Fickle,GOP : STRING[18];

Fickle := 'I am a Democrat.';
GOP := 'Republican.';
Insert(GOP,Fickle,8);
Writeln(Fickle);
```

This prints:

```
I am a Republican.
```

Note in this example that the word "Democrat" was not overwritten; it was appropriately pushed off the end of string **Fickle** into nothingness. After the insert, **Fickle** should have contained

```
I am a Republican.Democrat.
```

however, **Fickle**, defined as **STRING[18]**, is only 18 physical characters long. "I am a Republican." fills it completely. "Democrat." was lost to truncation.

STR

It is important to remember (and easy enough to forget) that a number and its string equivalent are *not* interchangeable. In other words, the integer 37 and its string representation, the two ASCII characters '3' and '7' *look* the same on your screen but are completely incompatible in all ways but that.

Unlike most other Pascals, Turbo provides a pair of procedures for translating numeric values into their string equivalents, and vise versa.

Translating a numeric value to its string equivalent is done with the procedure **Str**. **Str** is predefined this way:

```
PROCEDURE Str(<formatted numeric value>; VAR ST : STRING);
```

The formatted numeric value can be either an integer or a real number. It is given as a *write parameter*. (See Section 14.3 for a complete discussion of write parameters as they apply to all simple data types, numeric and non-numeric.) Briefly, a write parameter is an expression that gives a value and a format to express it in. The write parameter **I:7** (assuming **I** was previously declared an integer) right-justifies the value of I in a field 7 characters wide. **R:9:3** (assuming **R** was declared **Real** previously) right-justifies the value of **R** in a field 9 characters wide with three figures to the right of the decimal place.

The use of **Str** is best shown by a few examples:

```
CONST
  Bar = '|';

VAR
  R  : Real;
  I  : Integer;
  TX : STRING[30];

R := 45612.338;
I := 21244;

Str(I:8,TX);
Writeln(Bar,TX,Bar);     { Displays: |   21244| }

Str(I:3,TX);
Writeln(Bar,TX,Bar);     { Displays: |21244| }

Str(R,TX);
Writeln(Bar,TX,Bar);     { Displays: | 4.5612338000E+04| }

Str(R:13:4,TX);
Writeln(Bar,TX,Bar);     { Displays: |   45612.3380| }
```

Note from the third example that if you do not specify any format for a real number, the default format will be scientific notation in a field 18 characters wide.

VAL

Going in the other direction, from string representation to numeric value, is accomplished by the **Val** procedure. **Val** is predeclared this way:

```
PROCEDURE Val(ST : STRING; VAR <numeric variable>;
VAR Code : Integer);
```

Val's task is somewhat more complicated than **Str**'s. For every numeric value there is a string representation that may be constructed from it. The reverse is not true; there are many string constructions that *cannot* be evaluated as numbers. So **Val** must have a means of returning an error code to signal an input string that cannot be evaluated as a number. This is the purpose of the **Code** parameter.

If the string is evaluated without any problem, **Code**'s value is 0 and the numeric equivalent of the string is returned in the numeric variable. If Turbo Pascal finds that it cannot evaluate the string to a number, **Code** returns the character position of the first character that does not jive with the evaluation scheme. The numeric variable in that case is undefined:

```
PROGRAM Evaluator;

VAR
   SST    : STRING;
   R      : Real;
   Result : Integer;

BEGIN
   REPEAT
      Write('>>Enter a number in string form: ');
      Readln(SST);
      IF Length(SST) > 0 THEN
         BEGIN
            Val(SST,R,Result);
         IF Result <> 0 THEN
            Writeln
               ('>>Cannot evaluate that string. Check character #',Result)
         ELSE
            Writeln
               ('>>The numeric equivalent of that string is ',R:18:10)
      END
   UNTIL Length(SST) = 0
END.
```

This little program will allow you to experiment with **Val** and see what it will accept and what it will reject. One regrettable shortcoming of **Val** is that *it considers commas an error*. A string like '5,462,445.3' will generate an error on character #2.

In the next section we'll be using **Val** in slightly more sophisticated sur-
roundings to build a generalized data entry routine. In the meantime, Table 10.1
contains a summary of all of Turbo Pascal's built-in string-handling routines.

10.3 A String Input Procedure

Pascal provides only one built-in way to enter a string from the system console.
Readln will accept character input from the keyboard, waiting for characters to
be typed until Enter is pressed. While **Readln** is waiting for input, you can
backspace over mistyped characters. This is a fairly typical example of entering
a string from the console using **Readln**:

```
VAR
   Buff10 : STRING[10];

Write('Type up to 10 letters: ');
Readln(Buff10);
```

Here, once you've typed 10 letters, **Readln** will allow you to type as many more
as you like. However, it will only return as many characters as the string has
room for. If you have set up a complicated data entry form on your CRT, nothing will stop the operator from typing beyond the right boundary of any field
and disrupting other fields to the right of the one being filled.

What you need is a slightly more disciplined string input routine. Ideally,
such a routine should show you before you begin typing how large the string
can be, accept characters up to that maximum limit, and then ignore further
characters until previous characters are deleted with backspace, or until Enter
or Esc is pressed.

Table 10.1 Built-in String-handling Routines

```
FUNCTION Concat(Source1,Source2...SourceN : STRING) : STRING
FUNCTION Copy(Source : STRING; Index,Size : Integer) : STRING
PROCEDURE Delete(Target : STRING; Index,Size : Integer)
PROCEDURE Insert(Source     : STRING;
                 VAR Target : STRING;
                 Index      : Integer)
FUNCTION Length(Source : STRING) : Integer
FUNCTION Pos(Pattern : STRING or Char;
             Source  : STRING) : Integer
PROCEDURE Str(Num : <write parameter>, VAR StrEquiv : STRING)
PROCEDURE Val(Source     : STRING;
              VAR NumEquiv : <Integer or Real>;
              VAR Code     : Integer)
```

The following string input routine does all this and more. First, read it over and try to understand how it works:

```
{->>>>GetString<<<<-------------------------------------------}
{                                                             }
{ Filename : GETSTRIN.SRC - Last Modified 1/26/93             }
{                                                             }
{ This is a generalized string-input procedure. It shows a    }
{ field between vertical bar characters at X,Y, with any       }
{ string value passed initially in XString left-justified in   }
{ the field. The current state of XString when the user        }
{ presses Return is returned in XString. The user can press     }
{ ESC and leave the passed value of XString undisturbed, even   }
{ if XString was altered prior to his pressing ESC.            }
{                                                             }
{ NOTE THAT THIS ROUTINE USES OPEN STRING PARAMETERS AND WILL  }
{ NOT COMPILE UNDER EARLIER VERSIONS OF TURBO PASCAL!         }
{                                                             }
{   From: BORLAND PASCAL FROM SQUARE ONE by Jeff Duntemann    }
{-------------------------------------------------------------}

PROCEDURE GetString(  X,Y      : Integer;
              VAR XString      : OpenString;
                  MaxLen       : Integer;
                  Capslock     : Boolean;
                  Numeric      : Boolean;
                  GetReal      : Boolean;
              VAR RValue       : Real;
              VAR IValue       : Integer;
              VAR Error        : Integer;
              VAR Escape       : Boolean);

VAR I,J       : Integer;
    Ch        : Char;
    Cursor    : Char;
    Dot       : Char;
    BLength   : Byte;
    ClearIt   : String80;
    Worker    : String80;
    Printables : SET OF Char;
    Lowercase  : SET OF Char;
    Numerics   : SET OF Char;
    CR         : Boolean;


BEGIN
  Printables := [' '..'}'];          { Init sets }
```

```
Lowercase := ['a'..'z'];
IF GetReal THEN Numerics := ['-','.','0'..'9','E','e']
  ELSE Numerics := ['-','0'..'9'];
Cursor := '_'; Dot := '.';
CR := False; Escape := False;
FillChar(ClearIt,SizeOf(ClearIt),'.'); { Fill the clear string }
ClearIt[0] := Chr(MaxLen);              { Set clear string to MaxLen }

                      { Convert numbers to string if required: }
IF Numeric THEN        { Convert zero values to null string: }
  IF (GetReal AND (RValue = 0.0)) OR
    (NOT GetReal AND (IValue = 0)) THEN XString := ''
  ELSE            { Convert nonzero values to string equiv: }
    IF GetReal THEN Str(RValue:MaxLen,XString)
      ELSE Str(IValue:MaxLen,XString);

                    { Truncate string value to MaxLen }
IF Length(XString) > MaxLen THEN XString[0] := Chr(MaxLen);
GotoXY(X,Y); Write('|',ClearIt,'|');  { Draw the field }
GotoXY(X+1,Y); Write(XString);
IF Length(XString)<MaxLen THEN
  BEGIN
    GotoXY(X + Length(XString) + 1,Y);
    Write(Cursor)              { Draw the Cursor }
  END;
Worker := XString;   { Fill work string with input string   }

REPEAT          { Until ESC or (CR) entered }
                { Wait here for keypress:  }
  WHILE NOT KeyPressed DO BEGIN {NULL} END;
  Ch := ReadKey;

  IF Ch IN Printables THEN        { If Ch is printable... }
    IF Length(Worker) >= MaxLen THEN UhUh ELSE
      IF Numeric AND (NOT (Ch IN Numerics)) THEN UhUh ELSE
        BEGIN
            IF Ch IN Lowercase THEN IF Capslock THEN Ch :=
            Chr(Ord(Ch)-32);
            Worker := CONCAT(Worker,Ch);
            GotoXY(X+1,Y); Write(Worker);
            IF Length(Worker) < MaxLen THEN Write(Cursor)
        END
ELSE  { If Ch is NOT printable... }
  CASE Ord(Ch) OF
    8,127 : IF Length(Worker) <= 0 THEN UhUh ELSE
              BEGIN
                  Delete(Worker,Length(Worker),1);
```

```
                    GotoXY(X+1,Y); Write(Worker,Cursor);
                    IF Length(Worker) < MaxLen-1 THEN Write(Dot);
                 END;

     13 : CR := True;       { Carriage return }

     24 : BEGIN             { CTRL-X : Blank the field }
             GotoXY(X+1,Y); Write(ClearIt);
             Worker := '';   { Blank out work string }
          END;

     27 : Escape := True;   { ESC }
     ELSE UhUh              { CASE ELSE }
   END; { CASE }

 UNTIL CR OR Escape;         { Get keypresses until (CR) or }
                { ESC pressed }
 GotoXY(X + 1,Y); Write(ClearIt);
 GotoXY(X + 1,Y); Write(Worker);
 IF CR THEN                { Don't update XString if ESC hit }
   BEGIN
     XString := Worker;
     IF Numeric THEN        { Convert string to Numeric values }
       CASE GetReal OF
          True : Val(Worker,RValue,Error);
          False : Val(Worker,IValue,Error)
       END { CASE }
     ELSE
       BEGIN
         RValue := 0.0;
         IValue := 0
       END
   END

END; { GETString }
```

This routine makes use of the **GotoXY** procedure to locate the cursor on your CRT screen. Turbo Pascal's CRT control procedures are described in Section 12.1. Remember that to use **GotoXY** you must place the **Crt** unit in your **USES** statement.

GetString begins by drawing a field on the screen. The field consists of two vertical bar characters (ASCII character 124) with periods between them. The number of periods is the maximum length of the string you wish to enter, passed to **GetString** in **MaxLen**:

```
|......................|
```

This example would be drawn for a **MaxLen** value of 25. The left vertical bar character is located at X,Y on the screen.

GetString can accept a string value to edit in the parameter **XString**. If **XString** has anything in it, those characters are displayed left-justified in the field:

```
|I am a man of letters....|
```

GetString then positions an underscore character for a nonflashing cursor immediately after the displayed characters, or at the left margin if no characters were displayed:

```
|I am a man of letters_...|
```

At this point **GetString** begins to accept typed characters. No **Read** or **Readln** statements are used in this procedure at all. A DOS call is performed in a tight loop to test for a keypress. If a key was pressed, the **MSDOS** function (see Section 19.5) returns the character pressed; if no key was pressed, it returns character 0.

Once a keypress is accepted, **GetString** decides if it is printable or not. Control characters (ASCII 1-31) are never printable. If the **Numerics** parameter is **True**, only digits, decimal points, the letter 'E', and minus signs will be accepted as printable. Then, after the string has been completed by the pressing of Enter, **Val** evaluates the string and places the value in **Value**.

If the **CapsLock** parameter is **True**, lowercase letters will be forced to uppercase as they are entered.

Only a few control characters are obeyed. Enter will end string entry and replace the previous contents of **XString** with the entered string. Esc will end string entry but leave **XString** the same as it was on entry. CTRL-X (CANcel) clears the entire string to zero length and erases it from the displayed field. BS and DEL destructively backspace over one character.

Any character that is not printable and not a recognized control character causes the **UhUh** procedure (see Section 9.13) to be invoked, signalling to the user that a keypress was ignored. Trying to backspace past the left margin of the field will trigger an error signal, as will trying to enter more characters than the field will hold.

USING GETSTRING FOR SCREEN DATA ENTRY

GetString is the most complex piece of Pascal code we've examined so far. If you intend to write a lot of programs that interact extensively with the user, you might also find it one of the most useful tools in your software toolbox. It makes the programming of interactive data-entry screens neat and easy.

For many years all computer interaction was done on the "glass teletype" model: Computer and user took turns typing their halves of a dialog on the bottom line of a terminal, with the screen scrolling up one line after each one's turn. Much tidier is the notion of a *data entry screen*. The computer "paints" one or more fields on a cleared screen, and then the user fills in the fields in some well-defined order. The computer uses some reserved portion of the screen (usually the top or bottom lines) to send messages to the user.

The following program is a simple example of a data entry screen, using the **GetString** procedure to provide several fields for the user to fill in. Nothing is done with the information after it is accepted, but in a functional program of this type the data is typically stored in a file.

GetString is another good example of hiding detail in a Pascal program. If you're programming a data entry screen, what's important is what data fields are being entered and what is done with them afterward. The excruciating details of accepting a string character-by-character and converting it (if necessary) into a numeric value are not necessary to understanding the logic of the data entry screen. So the details are shoved off into a black box named **GetString** where they will not interfere with the clarity of the code that handles the data itself.

```
{-------------------------------------------------------------}
{                          Screen                             }
{                                                             }
{            Full-screen input demo program                   }
{                                                             }
{                   by Jeff Duntemann                         }
{                   Turbo Pascal V7.0                         }
{                   Last update 1/26/93                       }
{                                                             }
{  From: BORLAND PASCAL FROM SQUARE ONE by Jeff Duntemann     }
{-------------------------------------------------------------}

PROGRAM Screen;

USES DOS,Crt,BoxStuff;

CONST
   Capslock     = True;
   NoCapslock   = False;
   Numeric      = True;
   NonNumeric   = False;

TYPE
   String80 = STRING[80];
   String30 = STRING[30];
   String6  = STRING[6];
   String4  = STRING[4];
   String3  = STRING[3];

   NAPRec  = RECORD
                Name    : String30;
                Address : String30;
                City    : String30;
                State   : String3;
                Zip   : String6
```

```
                    END;

        AdapterType = (None,MDA,CGA,EGAMono,EGAColor,VGAMono,
                VGAColor,MCGAMono,MCGAColor);



    VAR
        CH              : Char;
        CurrentRecord   : NAPRec;
        Edit            : Boolean;
        Quit            : Boolean;
        Escape          : Boolean;
        WIDTH,HEIGHT    : Integer;
        I,J             : Integer;
        R               : Real;



    {$I UHUH.SRC }          { Described in Section 16.11 }
    {$I QUERYDSP.SRC }
    {$I FONTSIZE.SRC }
    {$I CURSOFF.SRC }       { Described in Section 17.2 }
    {$I CURSON.SRC }        { Described in Section 17.2 }
    {$I YES.SRC }           { Described in Section 17.2 }
    {$I GETSTRIN.SRC }      { Described in Section 15.2 }



    PROCEDURE GetScreen(VAR ScreenData : NAPRec;
                            Edit       : Boolean;
                        VAR Escape     : Boolean);

    BEGIN
      MakeBox(1,1,79,20,PCLineChars);    { Draw the screen box }
      IF NOT Edit THEN WITH ScreenData DO { If not editing, clear record }
        BEGIN
          Name := ''; Address := ''; City := ''; State := ''; Zip := ''
        END;
      GotoXY(23,2);
      Writeln('<< Name / Address Entry Screen >>');
      GotoXY(29,4);
      Writeln('Press ESC to exit...');
      WITH ScreenData DO
        BEGIN            { First draw field frames: }
          GotoXY(5,7);
            Write('>>Customer Name:    |..............................|');
          GotoXY(5,9);
            Write('>>Customer Address: |..............................|');
          GotoXY(5,11);
            Write('>>Customer City:    |..............................|');
```

```
      GotoXY(5,13);
       Write('>>Customer State:    |...|');
      GotoXY(5,15);
       Write('>>Customer Zip:      |......| ');
       IF Edit THEN WITH ScreenData DO { If editing, show current
       values }
         BEGIN
           GotoXY(26,7); Write(Name);
           GotoXY(26,9); Write(Address);
           GotoXY(26,11); Write(City);
           GotoXY(26,13); Write(State);
           GotoXY(26,15); Write(Zip)
         END;                  { Now input/Edit field data: }
       GetString(25,7,Name,30,NoCapslock,NonNumeric,False,R,I,J,Escape);
       IF NOT Escape THEN
        GetString(25,9,Address,30,NoCapslock,NonNumeric,False,R,I,J,Escape);
       IF NOT Escape THEN
        GetString(25,11,City,30,NoCapslock,NonNumeric,False,R,I,J,Escape);
       IF NOT Escape THEN
        GetString(25,13,State,3,Capslock,NonNumeric,False,R,I,J,Escape);
       IF NOT Escape THEN
           GetString(25,15,Zip,6,Capslock,NonNumeric,False,R,I,J,Escape);
     END
END;


BEGIN    { SCREEN MAIN }
  Edit := False;
  CursorOff;
  REPEAT
    ClrScr;
    GetScreen(CurrentRecord,Edit,Escape); { Input/Edit a data screen }
    IF Escape THEN Quit := True ELSE      { Quit if ESC pressed }
      BEGIN                    { Otherwise summarize data }
        Quit := False;             { and ask for approval }
        GotoXY(1,22);
        Write('>>Summary: ');
        WITH CurrentRecord DO
          BEGIN
            Write(Name,'/',Address,'/',Zip);
            GotoXY(1,23); Write('>>OK? (Y/N): ');
            IF YES THEN Edit := False ELSE Edit := True
          END
      END
  UNTIL Quit;
  ClrScr;
  CursorOn
END.
```

10.4 More Examples of String Manipulation

Perhaps the first ambitious program most beginning programmers attempt is a name/address/phone number manager. Sooner or later, in designing such a program, the problem comes up: how to sort the list on the name field, when names are stored first name first and sorted last name first?

Storing the first name in a separate field is no answer—suppose you want to store The First National Bank of East Rochester? What is its first name?

The best solution I have found is to store the name last name first, with an asterisk (*) separating the last and first names. For example, Jeff Duntemann would be stored as Duntemann*Jeff. Clive Staples Lewis would be stored as Lewis*Clive Staples. Names maintained in this order are easily sorted by last name. All we need is a routine to turn the inside-out name rightside-in again.

The following routine does just that—and uses **Pos**, **Copy**, **Delete**, and **Concat**, all in four lines!

```
{<<<< RvrsName >>>>}
{ From: BORLAND PASCAL FROM SQUARE ONE }
{ by Jeff Duntemann - Last mod 1/25/93 }

PROCEDURE RvrsName(VAR Name : OpenString);

VAR
  TName : String;

BEGIN
  IF Pos('*',Name) <> 0 THEN
    BEGIN
      TName := Copy(Name,1,(Pos('*',Name)-1));
      Delete(Name,1,Pos('*',Name));
      Name := Concat(Name,' ',TName)
    END
END;
```

The theory is simple: If there is no asterisk in the name, it's something like "Granny Maria's Pizza Palace" and needs no reversal. Hence the first test. If an asterisk is found, the last name up to (but not including) the asterisk is copied from **Name** into **TName**, a temporary string. Then the last name is deleted from **Name**, up to *and* including the asterisk. What remains in **Name** is thus the first name. Finally, concatenate **TName** (containing the last name) to **Name** with a space to separate them. The name is now in its proper, first-name-first form.

Obviously, if you try to store and sort on a name of some sort that rightfully contains an asterisk, the name is going to be mangled by **RvrsName**.

A CASE ADJUSTER FUNCTION FOR STRINGS

Turbo Pascal provides a built-in character function called **UpCase**, predeclared this way:

```
FUNCTION UpCase(Ch : Char) : Char;
```

UpCase accepts a character **Ch** and returns its uppercase equivalent as the function return value. If **Ch** is already uppercase, or a character with no uppercase equivalent (numerals, symbols, and so on), the character is returned unchanged.

UpCase is a character function, but it suggests that a string function could be built that accepts an arbitrary string value and returns that value converted to uppercase. And although no "down-case" function exists in Turbo Pascal, an equivalent is not hard to put together. A two-way case adjuster function looks like this:

```
{<<<< ForceCase >>>>}
{ From: BORLAND PASCAL FROM SQUARE ONE }
{ by Jeff Duntemann — Last mod 1/25/93 }

FUNCTION ForceCase(Up : BOOLEAN; Target : STRING) : STRING;

CONST
   Uppercase : SET OF Char = ['A'..'Z'];
   Lowercase : SET OF Char = ['a'..'z'];

VAR
   I : INTEGER;

BEGIN
   IF Up THEN FOR I := 1 TO Length(Target) DO
     IF Target[I] IN Lowercase THEN
       Target[I] := UpCase(Target[I])
     ELSE { NULL }
   ELSE FOR I := 1 TO Length(Target) DO
     IF Target[I] IN Uppercase THEN
     Target[I] := Chr(Ord(Target[I])+32);
   ForceCase := Target
END;
```

In Turbo Pascal, functions may return string values the same as any other values. However, the string type must either be the default type **STRING** or have been declared before the declaration of your string function. In other words, if you wish your function to return a string with a physical length of 80, you must have declared a string type with that physical length:

```
TYPE
   String80 = STRING[80];
```

You *cannot* use the bracketed string-length notation on a string function return value. That is, you could not have declared **ForceCase** this way:

```
FUNCTION ForceCase(Up    : Boolean;
                   Target : String80) : String[80];
                                      {^Invalid! }
```

ForceCase will convert all uppercase characters in a string to lowercase, or all lowercase characters in a string to uppercase, depending on the Boolean value of parameter **Up**. If **Up** is true, lowercase is forced to uppercase. Otherwise, uppercase is forced to lowercase. The string **Target** is scanned from character 1 to its last character, and any necessary conversion of character case is done character-by-character. The "down-case" function is done by taking advantage of the ordering of the ASCII character set, in that lowercase characters have an ASCII value 32 higher than their uppercase counterparts. Add 32 to the ordinal value of an uppercase character, and you have the ordinal value of its lowercase equivalent.

Also note that although the parameter string **Target** is modified during the scan, the modifications are not made to the actual parameter itself, since **Target** was passed by value, not by reference. **ForceCase** received its own private copy of **Target,** which it could safely change without altering the "real" **Target**. See Section 8.12 for more on the passing of parameters by value or by reference.

ACCESSING COMMAND-LINE STRINGS

Most operating systems allow some sort of program access to the command-line tail; that is, the optional text that may be typed after the program name when invoking a program from the operating system command prompt:

```
A>CASE DOWN B:FOOFILE.TXT
```

In this example, the characters typed after the program name "CASE" constitute the command-line tail:

```
DOWN B:FOOFILE.TXT
```

Turbo Pascal provides a very convenient method of getting access to the command-line tail. Two predefined functions are connected with the command-line tail: **ParamCount** and **ParamStr**. They are predeclared this way:

```
FUNCTION ParamCount : Integer;
FUNCTION ParamStr(ParameterNumber : Integer) : STRING;
```

The function **ParamCount** returns the number of parameters typed after the command on the operating system command line. Parameters must have been separated by spaces or tab characters to be considered separate parameters. Commas, slashes, and other symbols on will *not* delimit separate parameters!

ParamStr returns a string value that is one of the parameters. The number of the parameter is specified by **ParameterNumber**, starting from 1. If you typed several parameters on the command line, for example,

```
ParamStr(2)
```

will return the second parameter.

Keep this in mind: You *must* read the command-line tail before opening your first disk file! The same area used to store the tail is also used in buffering disk accesses in some cases. The best way to do this is to keep an array of strings large enough to hold the maximum number of parameters your program needs, and read the parameters into the array as soon as your program begins running. This is easy enough to do:

```
VAR
   I : Integer;
   ParmArray : ARRAY[1..8] OF STRING[80];

FOR I := 1 TO ParamCount DO
   ParmArray[I] := ParamStr(I);
```

Now you have the parameters safely in **ParmArray** and can examine and use them at your leisure. For examples of **ParamCount** and **ParamStr** in use, see the **Caser** program in Section 14.7.

PART THREE

Journeyman Turbo Pascal

In Part I, I presented the elementary components of a Pascal program: basic data types, control structures, standard functions, and strings. Without those, you're nowhere—but even with those, you've barely gotten out of the gate.

Creating useful programs demands a second level of understanding: not only of the basic pieces, but of how they should be put together, and how to fix the problems that come of putting them together incorrectly. Those are the sorts of things we have to take up now.

Not to mention pointers.

It's time to start applying your structure eyes to the language itself. With a firm grounding in the basic components, you now need to see how higher-level concepts like locality and scope contribute to the structure of programs that you write. You need to get a handle on modularity; that is, how to divide a big program into separate files that can be perfected and maintained separately.

The Pascal language has been the focus so far, but the language doesn't exist in a vacuum. You now need to study the ways Turbo Pascal interacts with the machine itself, through the CRT, printer, and disk systems. This is when programs "get real" and start doing useful work for you. By the time you've worked your way through Part III, you'll be a tolerably experienced Pascal programmer, ready to attack the dragons lurking in the more advanced corners of the language.

Say no more. Let's go.

Chapter **11**

Locality and Scope

HIDING WHAT NEEDS HIDING, AND REVEALING WHAT NEEDS REVEALING

At the heart of structured programming is that old saw about the artful hiding of details. You want to be able to focus in on the level of detail where you're currently working, and not be excessively concerned with either the details down lower, or the larger view from above. On a purely structural level, the best way of hiding details is to divide a program into *subprograms* (that is, procedures and functions) and by grouping data into data structures like arrays and records. When you need to think of the task that a subprogram does, you simply think of it as a little black box that does one or two well-defined things. You don't worry about what's inside the box—*unless* you're actually going to tinker with what's inside the box. That's when you open the box and take a look.

This sounds simple enough on the surface, but there are some subtle issues surrounding it that I found *most* confusing when I was first picking up the language, back in the late 1970s. There's not a lot to discuss (which is why this chapter is so short), but what's there is extremely important, especially if you expect to become a truly world-class programmer.

11.1 The Innards of a Subprogram

Functions and procedures aren't called *subprograms* for nothing. Their structure is almost identical to that of your Pascal main program: They have a name, they have definitions, and they have a body consisting of a compound statement bounded by reserved words **BEGIN** and **END**. They can even have their own subprograms, nested inside them like Chinese boxes.

Here's a subprogram we've seen before (I removed the comment header to save space):

```
PROCEDURE ShellSort(VAR SortBuf : KeyArray; Recs : Integer);

VAR
```

```
    I,J,K,L : Integer;
    Spread  : Integer;

PROCEDURE KeySwap(VAR RR,SS : KeyRec);

VAR
   T : KeyRec;

BEGIN
   T := RR;
   RR := SS;
   SS := T
END;


BEGIN
   Spread := Recs DIV 2;        { First Spread is half record count  }
   WHILE Spread > 0 DO          { Do until Spread goes to zero:       }
     BEGIN
       FOR I := Spread + 1 TO Recs DO
         BEGIN
           J := I - Spread;
           WHILE J > 0 DO
             BEGIN                   { Test & swap across the array }
               L := J + Spread;
               IF SortBuf[J].KeyData <= SortBuf[L].KeyData THEN J := 0
                 ELSE KeySwap(SortBuf[J],SortBuf[L]);
               J := J - Spread
             END
         END;
       Spread := Spread DIV 2     { Halve Spread for next pass }
     END
END;
```

The **ShellSort** procedure defines five of its own variables, and has a subprogram of its own, **KeySwap**. The **KeySwap** procedure, moreover, defines its own variable, **T**.

The **KeySwap** procedure is only called from one place inside **ShellSort**. Its whole job is to hide the details of swapping two keys so that those details don't get in the way while you're reading **ShellSort**. At the time the swap happens, *how* the swap happens is unimportant. You simply need to know that the two parameters are exchanged.

The *ShellSort* procedure itself exists to hide the details of sorting an array of keys. When you're writing a data manager program that keeps a data file and a sorted key file, you don't necessarily want to be bothered with the details of how the sort happens. That's why you only need to see this much of *ShellSort* when you actually want to use it to perform a sort:

```
ShellSort(MySortBuf,KeyCount);
```

All you need to know at this point is that you're going to sort the key array **MySortBuf**, which contains **KeyCount** key records. The details of how the sort happens are irrelevant. Later on, if you want to mess with the sort routine a little bit, you can go to the source code file that contains **ShellSort** and poke at it. But when you're simply building a sort call into a program you're writing, the call itself is sufficient.

11.2 Global versus Local

When one subprogram is defined inside another, we say that the inner subprogram is *local* to the outer one. The same term applies to variables and other definitions that exist inside a subprogram. The variables **I,J,K,L**, and **Spread** are local to **ShellSort**. Variable **T** is local to **KeySwap**.

A different term is applied to definitions that you place in the main program itself. These are called *global* definitions. The difference between local and global follows the sense of the terms themselves: Global definitions are "known" (we say, *visible*) throughout the entire program and everything within it. Local definitions are visible *only* from within their containing entity.

The term visible is a technical one here, and it amounts to an ability to make a reference to an identifier. If you can reference an identifier from some place in a program, the identifier is visible from that place in the program.

The local variable **T** defined by **KeySwap** is an excellent example. **KeySwap** uses **T** as a temporary bucket to put a key record in during the swap process. Inside **KeySwap**, T is obviously visible, because **KeySwap**'s internal logic uses it.

Now, how about from within **ShellSort**? Could a statement in **ShellSort**'s body reference **T**? No! **T** is local to the **KeySwap** procedure, and is only visible from within **KeySwap**. If you tried to read from or write to T from **ShellSort**'s body, the compiler would issue Error 3: Unknown identifier. And that's the truth: From within **ShellSort**'s procedure body, variable **T** really is unknown. It's local to **KeySwap**, and unknown anywhere outside **KeySwap**'s procedure body. The same would be true from the main program block; you could not reference **T** at all.

SCOPE

This "visibility" property of a Pascal identifier is called its *scope*. The scope of an identifier is that area of the program from which the identifier can be referenced. As we saw in the last section, the scope of **T** is limited to the **KeySwap** procedure alone. The scope of the **KeySwap** procedure is limited to **ShellSort**. The main program cannot directly call **KeySwap**. (Nor could some other procedure, like **QuickSort**, call **KeySwap**.) Only **ShellSort** can call **KeySwap**.

In general (and more technical) terms, the scope of an identifier is limited to the block in which it is defined, and to all blocks defined within that block.

What this means is that scope extends "down" the nesting hierarchy, but not "up." That is, the scope of variable **Spread** in **ShellSort** extends down into **KeySwap**, but the scope of **T** in **KeySwap** does not extend up into **ShellSort**. If it needed to, **KeySwap** could read the current value in **Spread**, but nothing in **ShellSort** could read the current value of **T**.

11.3 Identifier Conflicts and Scope

There's an interesting consequence of Pascal's scoping rules: You can have more than one identifier in a given program with exactly the same name, and nobody will complain. (You might complain, if you don't understand the rules—which is the purpose of this chapter!)

Let's take a look at a short and highly contrived Pascal program to try to get a more precise handle on this:

```
PROGRAM Hollow;

VAR
   Z     : Integer;
   Ch, Q : Char;
   Gonk  : String[80];

PROCEDURE LITTLE1;

VAR
   Z : Integer;

BEGIN
END;

PROCEDURE LITTLE2;

VAR
   Z : Integer;
   Q : Char;

BEGIN
END;


BEGIN     { Main for Hollow }
   Little1;
   Writeln('>>We are the hollow programs.');
   Little2;
   Writeln('>>We are the stuffed programs.')
END.
```

Program **Hollow** is nothing more than the merest skeleton of a program, constructed to illustrate the concept of identifier scope. If you're sharp and have looked closely at **Hollow**, you may be objecting to the fact that there are three instances of a variable named *"Z"*—and I already told you that Pascal does not tolerate duplicate identifiers. Well, due to Pascal's scoping rules, the three **Z**s are *not* duplicates at all.

Up near the top of the source file, in program **Hollow**'s own variable list, is a variable named **Z**. In **Little1** is a variable named **Z**, but *this* **Z** is local to **Little1**. **Little2** also has a **Z** that is local to **Little2**. Each **Z** is "known" only in its own neighborhood, and the extent of that neighborhood is its scope. The scope of **Little1**'s **Z** is *only* within **Little1**. Likewise, **Little2**'s **Z** is known only within **Little2**. You *cannot* access the value of **Little2**'s **Z** (or, for that matter, *any* variable declared within **Little2**) from within **Little1**. Furthermore, while you're in the main program, you cannot access either of the two **Z**s that are local to **Little1** and **Little2**. They might as well not exist until you enter one of the two procedures in which those local **Z**s are declared.

This gets a little slipperier when you consider the **Z** belonging to program **Hollow** itself. That **Z**'s neighborhood encompasses the entire program, which includes both **Little1** and **Little2**. So while we're within **Little1** or **Little2**, which **Z** is the real **Z**? Plainly, we need a rule here, and the rule is called "precedence." *When the scopes of two identical identifiers overlap, the most local identifier takes precedence.* In other words, while you're within **Little1**, **Little1**'s own local **Z** is the only **Z** you can "see." The **Z** belonging to **Hollow** is hidden from you while you're within the scope of a more local **Z**. **Hollow**'s **Z** doesn't go away and doesn't change; you simply can't look at it or change it while **Little1**'s **Z** takes precedence.

THE MIKE SMITH METAPHOR

Or think of it this way: There are way too many Mike Smiths in the world. A large national liquor company based in New York City has a vice president named Mike Smith. The company also has two regional salesmen named Mike Smith, one in Chicago and one in Geneseo, New York. When you're at corporate headquarters in New York and mention Mike Smith, everyone assumes you mean the Vice President of Whisky Keg Procurement. However, if you're in Chicago and mention Mike Smith to a liquor-store owner, he thinks you mean the skinny chap who sells him Rasputin Vodka. He's never heard of the VP or the salesman in Geneseo. Furthermore, if you're in Geneseo and mention Mike Smith, the restaurant owners think of the fellow with the red beard who distributes Old Tank Car wines. They don't know (and could not care less about) the VP of Whisky Keg Procurement or the vodka salesman in Chicago.

Look back at **Hollow** for a moment and consider the variable **Q**. **Hollow** has a **Q**. **Little2** also has one. **Little1** does not. Within **Little2**, **Little2**'s **Q** is king, and **Hollow**'s **Q** is hidden away. However, **Little1** can read and change **Hollow**'s **Q**. There is no precedence conflict here because there is no **Q** in **Little1**. Since the scope of **Hollow**'s **Q** is the entire program, any function or procedure within **Hollow** can access **Hollow**'s **Q** as long as there is no conflict of precedence. We say that **Hollow**'s **Q** is global to the entire program. In the absence of precedence conflicts, **Hollow**'s **Q** is "known" throughout **Hollow**.

Hollow has a variable named **Gonk** that can be accessed from either **Little1** or **Little2** because it is the only **Gonk** anywhere within **Hollow**. With **Gonk**, the question of precedence does not arise at all.

Unless you can't possibly avoid it, don't make your procedures and functions read or change global variables (like **Ch** or **Gonk**) *unless* those variables are passed to the procedure or function through the parameter line. This prevents data "sneak paths" among your main program and procedures and functions. Such sneak paths are easy to forget when you modify a program, and may bollix up legitimate changes to the program in (apparently) inexplicable ways.

To sum up: An identifier is local to the block (procedure, function, module, or program) in which it is defined. This block is the *scope* of that identifier.

You cannot access a local identifier unless you are *within* that block, or *contain* that block.

Where a duplicate identifier conflict of scope exists, the *more local of the two* is the identifier that you can access.

WHY?

This can be a lot of abstract logic and rules to swallow without some firm peg in the real world to hang it on. I don't know about you, but understanding the physical reality of a program helps me understand its more abstract logic. So if you're feeling ambitious, I'll spend a few words explaining why Pascal does things this way.

Identifiers defined within a subprogram are not visible from outside that subprogram because until that subprogram is called, *its identifiers do not physically exist*. We who see the whole program and all of its subprograms laid out on the screen or on sheets of paper, all at once, sometimes forget the time-sequential nature of a Pascal program.

Global variables are allocated in an area of memory called the data segment. They are brought into existence when the program is loaded into memory, and remain in existence until the program hands control back to the operating system, or to the IDE. (The IDE can sometimes play games with a program such that the program and the IDE can bounce back and forth during the debugging process, and the IDE can "see" variables within the program. This is a separate issue, and involves some magic you won't be using in ordinary Pascal programming.) Local variables, by contrast, do not exist until the very moment that their subprograms are called.

When a subprogram is called, it receives a little slice of an area of memory called the *stack*. Inside that little slice of the stack are allocated its local variables. Now, the stack is strictly temporary, reusable storage; when a subprogram finishes executing and returns control to its caller, the region of the stack that it had is freed up for some other subprogram to use. *A subprogram's local variables exist on the stack only during the time that the subprogram is executing.* When the subprogram returns, its variables go poof and are no longer anywhere to be seen.

We say that subprograms have a limited *lifetime*—the time that they are executing and own their little slice of the stack containing their local variables. Before and after that lifetime, a subprogram's local variables do not exist.

So scoping rules are not simply the compiler being authoritarian. It can't allow you to reference something that no longer exists. *Rules are for reasons!* Don't gripe about the rules. Strive to know the reasons.

Chapter **12**

Controlling Your CRT

DISPLAYING INFORMATION IN TEXT MODE

Such a simple thing as controlling the placement of information on a CRT screen has been a thorn in the side of computer programmers as long as there have been computers. Each manufacturer of computers and terminals has considered his own set of screen control codes the best set possible, and the result has (predictably) been chaos. Most vendors of computer languages have simply given up, and left CRT control as an exercise for the programmer.

Turbo Pascal is one of the few native-code Pascal compilers for microcomputers that attempts to define its own CRT interface standard. Its screen control procedures are not part of ISO Standard Pascal, but *someone* must set a standard if we are to have both portable Pascal code and full-screen Pascal applications. Other Pascal vendors have begun to implement Turbo Pascal's screen control procedures in their own compilers, and my feeling is that the standard has firmly taken root.

I make a fuss about CRT control because it is *important*. The manner in which a program interfaces to its user is in my way of thinking the most crucial attribute of that program. The days of the Mystical Order of the Computer Priesthood are over. A computer program that is hard to use will be left unused. In designing the concept of a computer program, lay out the face that the program presents to the user *first*. Your primary allegiance as a programmer is to the needs of your user.

12.1 The CRT Unit's Text-Oriented Functions and Procedures

Starting with version 4.0, Turbo Pascal accomplishes its text-mode CRT control through a number of functions, procedures, and predefined variables contained in a unit called **CRT**. These routines are a superset of the text support routines contained in version 3.0 of the compiler. The extended graphics procedures from Turbo Pascal 3.0 are now present in a unit called **Graph3**. These are part of Turbo Pascal since version 4.0 *only* for compatibility purposes; for new development I recommend starting fresh with the much-superior Borland Graphics Interface (BGI) contained in the unit **Graph**. The BGI is described in Chapter 22.

301

USING THE CRT UNIT

Like any unit, **CRT** is used by specifying it in your program's **USES** statement:

```
PROGRAM JiveTalk;
  USES CRT,DOS,CommStuf;
```

You can do minimal screen output without using **CRT**, but the only screen routines actually available outside of **CRT** are **Read** and **Readln** for screen input, plus **Write** and **Writeln** for screen output. These routines are defined in the **System** unit and are always available. However, they only perform "glass teletype" screen output. You have no control over where the text appears on the screen. It appears at the beginning of the first clear line, and moves down the screen until the screen is full. At that point, the screen scrolls upward one line, much like a piece of paper in an old teletype printer.

DOS VIDEO VERSUS BIOS VIDEO VERSUS DIRECT VIDEO

This is not necessarily a bad thing in all applications. Using **Readln** and **Writeln** without **CRT** uses DOS for screen input and output. DOS is slow, but it allows you to *redirect* screen input from text files and output to text files. For example, a file search routine like **Locate** (described in Section 19.9) doesn't need to position the cursor or clear the screen. By eschewing **CRT**, **Locate** allows you to redirect its output to a text file, essentially taking a "snapshot" of the information it gathers. This redirection is done with the ">" operator on the DOS command line:

```
C:\>LOCATE *.BAK > BAKLIST.TXT
```

Running **Locate** in this way displays nothing at all to the screen, but instead writes a file named BAKLIST.TXT containing its information:

```
 4919   09/20/92   9:23a   \HACKS\POORBACK.BAK
10875   10/24/92   9:34p   \HACKS\VECTORS.BAK
 2454   10/24/92   8:53p   \HACKS\HEXTEST.BAK
29256   08/08/92   9:12p   \LOCATE2.BAK
```

Less useful is *input* redirection, which takes a text file of strings and "feeds" them one by one to the **Readln** statements within your program:

```
C:\>GENSWEEP < SWEEPCMD.TXT
```

Here, a program called **GenSweep** takes its commands from a text file called SWEEPCMD.TXT. **GenSweep** then works automatically, rather than requesting input from you through the screen. This feature is handy for creating utility programs that must be used either interactively from the command line or else automatically from within batch files.

The final advantage to using "glass teletype" I/O through DOS is that your programs will work correctly on any machine that can run DOS. Even ancient machines like the Victor 9000, which are *not* screen-compatible with the PC, will run programs like **Locate** that do not use the **CRT** unit. This limits your options to a certain kind of command-line oriented utility, but you should be aware of the option if you ever feel like building replacements for the utility programs that come with DOS.

When you use the **CRT** unit, you have two additional choices: BIOS screen I/O and *direct* screen I/O. The default is direct screen I/O, which is both the fastest method and the most specific to the PC video architecture.

THE DIRECTVIDEO VARIABLE

Your choice is specified through a predefined Boolean variable called **DirectVideo**. When **DirectVideo** is **True**, screen output is sent directly to the video buffer, without any BIOS involvement. When **DirectVideo** is **False**, all screen I/O is performed through BIOS calls. (Essentially, through software interrupt $10.) The default value is **True**.

DirectVideo is set to **True** in the initialization section of the **CRT** unit, and after any call to the **TextMode** procedure. If you wish to use the BIOS to perform screen I/O, you must set **DirectVideo** to **False** *before* sending anything to the screen, and after *every* invocation of **TextMode**.

Is there any compelling reason to work through the BIOS? Not really. Any computer that is BIOS-compatible for text video is almost certainly video-buffer compatible as well. If you have trouble with screen output, try using BIOS output by setting **DirectVideo** to false. By and large, BIOS calls are extremely wasteful of CPU time, and you are much better off using direct video I/O.

DEALING WITH CGA VIDEO "SNOW"

On IBM's original CGA (Color Graphics Adapter) and many other early CGA-compatible video boards, writing directly to screen memory generates a scattering of random "snow" across the screen during the instant it takes to write a character directly into memory. Newer video boards like the EGA and VGA and nearly all recent CGA lookalikes use dual-ported memory and avoid snow. If you use Turbo Pascal's direct video I/O and notice snow on your screen during screen updates, you can suppress the snow with a predefined Boolean variable named **CheckSnow**.

CheckSnow defaults to **False**. When set to **True**, it forces the Turbo Pascal runtime code to write characters to the screen buffer *only* during horizontal retrace periods. In this way, the snow can only happen when the monitor's electron gun is turned off, and the snow will not be visible. *However*, this interval is rather small, and forcing all video to be displayed during horizontal retrace will slow your screen displays down enormously. If at all possible, buy a newer video board that is immune to snow, and leave **CheckSnow** set to **False**.

SCREENS VERSUS WINDOWS

As I'll explain below, Turbo Pascal's CRT display routines operate relative to the current screen window. Ordinarily, Turbo Pascal considers the current window to be the entire physical screen. There are times, however, when it would be very convenient to treat separate areas of the screen as though each were a separate screen. Writing an application that does two or more separate things comes to mind, as in a split-screen editor or a communications program that monitors both COM1: and COM2: at the same time.

The **Window** procedure exists for this purpose. It is predeclared this way:

```
PROCEDURE Window(X1,Y1,X2,Y2 : Integer);
```

Parameters **X1** and **Y1** define the column and row of the upper left corner of the window to be defined, and **X2** and **Y2** define the lower right corner. Once a window is defined with **Window**, it remains in force until another window is defined, or until you execute the **TextMode** statement.

On the PC, all screen commands operate with respect to the current window, which is either the full-screen default or the last window set via **Window**. In other words, if you define a window this way:

```
Window(10,10,70,20);
ClrScr;
```

only the screen in the rectangular region defined by the given coordinates will be cleared. Surrounding areas of the screen will not be affected.

Similarly, using **GotoXY** within a window *always* uses the upper left corner of the window as the coordinate origin. In other words, with the window mentioned above set at 10,10 and 70,20, performing a **GotoXY(1,1);** will position the cursor at what appears to be screen location 10,10. However, because the window was set, Turbo Pascal treats 10,10 as though it were the upper left corner of the entire screen. Physical screen position 10,10 becomes the logical screen position 1,1.

Window makes it possible to selectively clear rectangular areas of the PC screen very quickly—more quickly, in fact, than you can follow by eye, and certainly more quickly than writing lines full of spaces. Using this procedure you can clear any rectangular area of the screen:

```
{<<<< ClearRegion >>>>}
{    From: BORLAND PASCAL FROM SQUARE ONE   }
{    by Jeff Duntemann - Last mod 1/30/93   }

PROCEDURE ClearRegion(X1,Y1,X2,Y2 : Integer);

BEGIN
  Window(X1,Y1,X2,Y2);
  ClrScr;
  Window(1,1,80,25)
END;
```

The coordinates of the current window are available in a pair of predefined variables contained in the **Crt** unit, **WindMin** and **WindMax**, both of type **Word**. **WindMin** contains the upper-left X,Y coordinates, with X in the low-order byte, and Y in the high-order byte. Similarly, **WindMax** contains the lower-right X,Y coordinates of the current window, with X in the low-order byte and Y in the high-order byte. To separate them out, you need to use the built-in functions **Lo** and **Hi**. (See Section 5.6.) The other thing to remember in using **WindMin** and **WindMax** is that they contain the current window coordinates *relative to zero*. In other words, if you have set the current window to 10,10 - 50,18, **WindMin** will contain 9,9 and *not* 10,10. **WindMax** will contain 49,17 rather than 50,18.

WindMin and **WindMax** are actually a peek at the storage area where the Turbo Pascal runtime keeps its own low-level information on the window, and the runtime thinks of window coordinates as relative to zero. Remember to add one to the individual coordinates (and *not* to the entire word variable **WindMin** or **WindMax**!) before you use them.

SCREEN-CONTROL ROUTINES DEFINED IN CRT

The rest of this section describes the routines that actually send characters to the screen. There are other routines in **CRT** that have nothing to do with screen output. These include **Delay**, **Sound**, and **NoSound**. They really belong among Turbo Pascal's standard functions, and I describe them in Section 9.13.

All of the routines described below operate *within the current window*. The default window is the full screen, but if you define a smaller window to be the current window, the action of these routines will be limited to within that actual window.

CLRSCR

This command blanks the current window and returns the cursor to the upper left-hand corner. If the current window is the entire screen (the default) the entire screen will be blanked. Turbo Pascal considers the coordinates of the upper left corner of the screen to be 1,1, *not* 0,0 as many other programming environments (such as dBase II) do.

The **TextMode** procedure also clears the screen, but it clears the entire physical screen, and not simply the current window.

GOTOXY(X,Y)

This command moves the cursor to position **X,Y** in the current window where **X** is the column (counting across from the left) and **Y** is the row (counting down from the top.) **X** and **Y** may be type **Integer**, **Byte**, **Word**, **LongInt**, or **ShortInt** but not any real number type. The upper left corner is position 1,1.

CLREOL

The "EOL" in this command means "End Of Line." **ClrEOL** will clear the line containing the cursor from the cursor to the end of the line. The cursor itself does not move. Keep in mind that the line will only be cleared within the current window.

DELLINE

The cursor line is deleted, and lines are moved upward to fill in. An empty line is inserted at the bottom of the current window.

INSLINE

An empty line is inserted at the cursor line. The line that previously contained the cursor is moved down beneath the inserted line, and all lines further down move down one line. The bottom screen line will be pushed off the bottom of the screen and lost.

LOWVIDEO

LowVideo clears the high-intensity bit in the video attribute byte used in displaying text sent to the screen. (This byte is available to you as the predefined variable **TextAttr**.) In essence, this maps colors 8-15 onto colors 0-7. The end result is that characters sent to the screen after **LowVideo** is executed will show up as the lower-intensity version of the currently selected color. On a monochrome screen, this means the characters will be dimmer than characters normally appear.

NORMVIDEO

What **LowVideo** does, **NormVideo** undoes. Text sent to the screen after **NormVideo** is executed will be displayed using the video attribute that was in force before **LowVideo** was invoked.

12.2 Text Modes, Colors, and Attributes

In the past few years, the PC has established what must be the closest thing to a CRT display standard that now exists in the microcomputer industry. Unlike previous versions, Turbo Pascal 4.0 and later are highly specific to the PC family of machines, especially in terms of CRT handling.

In this section we'll discuss text modes, text colors, and monochrome text attributes.

TEXT MODES

There are several different variations in text mode for the IBM display adapter standard. The **TextMode** command will select among the variations. Unlike version 3.0, Turbo Pascal 4.0 and later will not allow you to call **TextMode** without a parameter to select the current or last text mode selected. In V4.0 and later, the predefined constant **Last** must be used. The other predefined constants that may be used as parameters to **TextMode** are given in the examples below:

```
TextMode(Last);      { Selects current or last mode used }
TextMode(C40);       { Selects 40-column with color enabled }
TextMode(C80);       { Selects 80-column with color enabled }
TextMode(BW40);      { Selects 40-column with color disabled }
TextMode(BW80);      { Selects 80-column with color disabled }
TextMode(Mono);      { Selects 80-column on mono adapter }
```

On the monochrome display adapter, there is, of course, no color available. Neither is there really a 40-column mode as we know it on the color card; if you select the C40 or BW40 parameters, text will be displayed on the left half of the screen only, with characters their normal size and width. IBM's monochrome card cannot display the double-width characters used by the color card in 40-column mode. There is no point, then, in using the **BW40** or **BW80** parameters with **TextMode** when you have the monochrome card installed in your computer. Use **Mono** instead.

No matter which display adapter you are using or what variation of text mode you select, **TextMode** *always* clears the screen. **TextMode** also resets the current window to the entire physical screen.

TEXT COLORS AND MONOCHROME ATTRIBUTES

If you're using one of the video boards that supports color (CGA, EGA, or VGA) you have complete control over both the foreground and background colors for each individual character position on the screen. Furthermore, if you wish, you can make a character of any color blink. Two built-in procedures give you control of text colors: **TextColor** and **TextBackground**.

These same two procedures also work if you have the monochrome display adapter installed, but what they do is a great deal different. The monochrome display does not display colors, but it allows you to set attributes on a character-by-character basis. These attributes include underline, dim, and blink. Setting an attribute is done the same way you would set a text-mode color on a color board.

Setting character color or attribute is done by passing a parameter to **TextColor**. The parameter is an integer having a value from 0-31:

```
TextColor(4);        { Selects yellow on color card }
```

The meaning of the parameter for color or monochrome is summarized in Table 12.1.

Table 12.1 Color and Monochrome Attribute Values

		Mode of Operation	
Value	*Constants*	*Color*	*Monochrome*
0	Black	Black	Off
1	Blue	Blue	Dim underline
2	Green	Green	Off
3	Cyan	Cyan	Dim
4	Red	Red	Dim
5	Magenta	Magenta	Dim
6	Brown	Brown	Dim
7	LightGrey	Light grey	Dim
8	DarkGrey	Dark grey	Off
9	LightBlue	Light blue	Normal Underline
10	LightGreen	Light green	Off
11	LightCyan	Light cyan	Normal
12	LightRed	Light red	Normal
13	LightMagenta	Light magenta	Normal
14	Yellow	Yellow	Normal
15	White	White	Normal
16		Black	Off
17		Blue blink	Dim blink underline
18		Green blink	Off
19		Cyan blink	Dim blink
20		Red blink	Dim blink
21		Magenta blink	Dim blink
22		Brown blink	Dim blink
23		Light grey blink	Dim blink
24		Dark grey blink	Off
25		Light blue blink	Normal blink underline
26		Light green blink	Off
27		Light cyan blink	Normal blink
28		Light red blink	Normal blink
29		Light magenta blink	Normal blink
30		Yellow blink	Normal blink
31		White blink	Normal blink

The "constants" column in the table lists the 16 integer constants predefined by Turbo Pascal for the values 0–15. By using these constants you can make your code a little more self-explanatory:

```
TextColor(LightGreen);
```

There is one additional predefined integer constant, **Blink**. **Blink**'s value is 128. If you add **Blink** to a color constant, you will get that color character that blinks:

```
TextColor(Red + Blink);
```

Again, this is only to make your code clearer; you could just as easily have plugged the numeric literal 132 into the parameter and the result would have been the same.

The difference between the normal colors and the "light" colors is the intensity signal in the color graphics adapter's RGB outputs. Light red is actually red with the intensity signal on, and so on. Some low-cost color monitors do not make use of the intensity signal, and on those monitors your light colors will be identical to their corresponding normal colors.

On monochrome video boards the color values select various combinations of the dim, underline, and blink attributes. To display underlined text, you would invoke **TextColor** with a value that selects the underline attribute, display the text, and then invoke **TextColor** again with the attribute value previously in force. Although there are no predefined constants for the various attributes, nothing would prevent you from defining constants of your own for that purpose:

```
CONST
   Blink        = 27;
   Dim          = 3;
   Normal       = 11;
   Underline    = 9;
   DimBlink     = 19;
   DimUnderline = 1;


TextColor(Underline);        { Select normal underline text }
Writeln('Be sure to back up your data!');
TextColor(Normal);           { Select normal text display }
```

The background color of a character is the color taken on by the rest of the little rectangular cell that contains the character itself. For the background color you have your choice of the seven normal colors 1–8 and of course, color 0, black:

```
TextBackground(Blue);
```

As we show here, the predefined color constants may be used for **TextBackground** as for **TextColor**.

On the monochrome adapter, the background color translates to a black background (colors 0 and 2) or a white background (colors 1,3,4,5,6,7). To display in inverse video, for example, you must display text in color black on a white background:

```
TextColor(Black);
TextBackground(1);
Writeln('Use inverse video for emphasis.');
TextColor(Normal);
TextBackground(Black);
```

People converting text applications from Turbo Pascal 3.0 or earlier should bear in mind that the **GraphBackground** procedure is no longer supported, starting with Turbo Pascal 4.0. An undocumented use of **GraphBackground** was in setting the text border color. You must eliminate all references to **GraphBackground** or your program will not compile. On the EGA and VGA, the text border is so narrow it is not much worth bothering with.

SAVING THE CURSOR POSITION

Turbo Pascal includes two functions that return the current X and Y positions of the cursor:

```
FUNCTION WhereX : Byte;
FUNCTION WhereY : Byte;
```

WhereX returns the X coordinate of the cursor. **WhereY** returns the Y coordinate. Both return byte values.

What are **WhereX** and **WhereY** good for? One application lies in the saving of entire text screens. "Painting" a screen with **GotoXY** and **Write** statements takes a certain amount of time. If your application needs to switch frequently among a number of different screens, you'll find yourself spending a noticeable amount of time watching the screens regenerate themselves.

It is possible to save a screen after it is drawn by using Turbo Pascal's built-in **Move** routine to move a copy of the entire 4K text-mode video buffer to another location in free RAM. Then you can bring in another screen in a fraction of a second (assuming it had been saved to RAM as well after being painted to the screen or loaded from a screen file). The problem with this is that the cursor position is *not* saved in the video refresh buffer, but elsewhere in system RAM. If you need to save a cursor position along with a screen, you must save it yourself. **WhereX** and **WhereY** allow you to assign the current cursor position to a pair of integer variables. When bringing in a previously-saved screen, you can then restore the cursor position from those two variables with **GotoXY**.

12.3 Useful Screen Control Tactics

In this section I'll give you some tips on creating effective text displays from Turbo Pascal.

The **LowVideo** procedure provides a way to highlight (or lowlight, if you prefer) text as a way of setting it off from normal text. The problem is that making text dimmer than the bulk of the text on the screen is a backhanded way of calling attention to it. A better method to accent text is to execute **LowVideo** *immediately* at the start of your program so that half brightness is used for the bulk of the text displayed from your program. Then, when you want to highlight something, drop into normal video for a line or two and your text will stand out nicely:

```
NormVideo;
Writeln('Please call your service rep immediately!');
LowVideo;
```

You'll find after awhile that you'll be using familiar sequences of statements to do many display chores. For instance, to place a message at a particular place on the screen takes at least two statements:

```
IF ERROR THEN
  BEGIN
    GotoXY(10,24);
    Writeln('>>That file is missing or damaged!')
  END;
```

Highlighting your message with a video attribute (half-brightness or inverse video) adds two more statements to the compound statement:

```
IF ERROR THEN
  BEGIN
    LowVideo;
    GotoXY(10,24);
    Writeln('>>That file is missing or damaged!');
    NormVideo
  END;
```

If you want to center a message you will have to determine its length, subtract its length from 80 (the width of your typical screen) and divide the difference by two. All of this fooling around may be done inside a single text display procedure:

```
{<<<< WriteAt >>>>}
{ From: BORLAND PASCAL 7 FROM SQUARE ONE   }
{   by Jeff Duntemann - Last mod 1/25/93   }

PROCEDURE WriteAt(X,Y : Integer;
                  Highlite : Boolean;
                  UseCR    : Boolean;
                  TheText  : String);

BEGIN
  IF Y < 0 THEN Y := 12;
  IF X < 0 THEN X := (80-Length(TheText)) DIV 2;
```

```
      GotoXY(X,Y);
      IF Highlite THEN LowVideo;
      IF UseCR THEN Writeln(TheText) ELSE Write(TheText);
      NormVideo
   END;
```

WriteAt will automatically center a line of text on your screen from side to side and from top to bottom, either or both as required. If you pass **WriteAt** a negative **X** parameter, your text line will be centered from side to side. If you pass it a negative **Y** value, the text line will be placed on line 12, which is centered on a 25-line screen.

In the constant declaration part of your program you should define a few Boolean constants for the use of **WriteAt**:

```
CONST
   Highlite : True;
   Normal   : False;
   CR       : True;
   NoCR     : False;
```

Rather than plugging the nondescript literals **True** and **False** into **WriteAt**'s parameter line, you can use the descriptive constants given above and make the intent of the parameters clear at a glance:

```
IF Error THEN WriteAt(-1,24,Highlite,NoCR,'<<DISK ERROR!>>');
```

This particular invocation of **WriteAt** will place a highlighted error message centered on line 24 of the screen. Since sending a carriage return to the screen after line 24 will scroll the screen up, the **UseCR** parameter is passed a **False** value by Boolean constant **NoCR**.

WriteAt's purpose is actually to hide the details involved in centering a text line on the screen, highlighting it, and placing it at a particular X,Y position. These details add to the bulk of your code and may serve to obscure the real job of the program. When displaying an error message the important thing to understand is why an error message must be displayed at that point, not how one highlights and centers a text line on the screen.

This is also a good place to point out that it is perfectly legal to break up a procedure call into several separate lines. This can make for a less cluttered, easier-to-read source code. Pascal, which does not ordinarily respect the line structure of text files, does not care:

```
WriteAt(HPos + 6, YPos + Offset + 2,
        Highlite, NoCR,
        'This is a raid.  I repeat, this is a raid!');
```

The only thing you *can't* break out into more than one line is a text literal. You could not, in the line above, have written:

```
WriteAt(HPos + 6, YPos + Offset + 2,
        Highlite, NoCR,
        'This is a raid.
           I repeat, this is a raid!');
```

Turbo Pascal would stop with Error 8: String constant exceeds line. To pass **WriteAt** a string literal longer than will fit on a single line, you must concatenate two shorter string literals:

```
WriteAt(HPos + 6, YPos + Offset + 2,
        Highlite, NoCR,
        'This is a raid.  I said, son, this is a raid.' +
        ' Listen up in there!  Did you hear me?  THIS IS A RAID!');
```

Unless the screen were wider than 80 characters (unlikely), the above message would likely "wrap" around to the next line down when displayed on the screen.

A FUNCTION FOR YES/NO QUESTIONS

Perhaps the most common questions to occur during dialogs between a computer program and a user are simple yes/no questions. Coding such a question up involves something close to this:

```
Write('>>Do you want to add another record? (Y/N): ');
Read(Ch);
IF NOT (Ch IN ['Y','y']) THEN
   Quit := True ELSE Quit := False;
```

These lines of code (with a different prompt, of course) would have to be repeated for every yes/no question in the program. Everything except the prompt can be bundled into a single function called **Yes**:

```
{<<<< Yes >>>>}
{ From: BORLAND PASCAL 7 FROM SQUARE ONE   }
{    by Jeff Duntemann - Last mod 1/25/93 }

FUNCTION Yes : Boolean;

VAR
  Ch : Char;

BEGIN
  Read(Ch);
  IF Ch IN ['Y','y'] THEN Yes := True ELSE Yes := False
END;
```

Now you can do this instead:

```
Write('>>Do you want to add another record? (Y/N): ');
IF Yes THEN Quit := True ELSE Quit := False;
```

The details of getting a character from the keyboard and seeing what it is are hidden by function **Yes**. The dialog-nature of the interchange remains the important and visible characteristic of this piece of code. It is a cleaner, more readable way of handling yes/no interchanges in your programs.

A DATA-ENTRY ROUTINE FOR BOOLEAN VARIABLES

Lots of different types of data come in pairs. Human beings are male or female, alive or dead. Telephones are TouchTone or pulse dial. Cars are US or foreign made. Such data can be conveniently expressed as Boolean values:

```
VAR
    TouchDial,Male,Deceased,USMade : Boolean;
```

Displaying and entering Boolean values within a data-entry screen involves a certain amount of rigamarole. For example, one way of displaying the current value of a Boolean variable and entering a new value might be this:

```
REPEAT
  Quit := False;
  GotoXY(1,5); Write('>>TouchTone or Pulse dialing? ');
  IF TouchDial THEN Write('TouchTone')
    ELSE Write('Pulse dial');
  Write(' Change? (Y/N): ');
  IF Yes THEN TouchDial := NOT TouchDial ELSE Quit
UNTIL Quit
```

Yes is the yes/no question function described earlier in this section. A cleaner and more self-explanatory method of getting a Boolean value from the keyboard is the following procedure:

```
{->>>>FlipField<<<<---------------------------------------------}
{                                                               }
{ Filename : FLIPFLD.SRC - Last Modified 4/8/93                 }
{                                                               }
{ This routine facilitates entry of "toggle" fields--fields     }
{ that have one of only two different values: Male/Female,      }
{ Citizen/Non-citizen, etc.  You specify an X,Y position for   }
{ the field, a string for each of the True and False case, and }
{ an initial Boolean value that specifies which of the two     }
{ alternatives will be initially displayed.  Pressing ESC      }
{ during entry changes nothing and sets the ESC parm to True.  }
{ Whichever state is displayed at the point the user presses   }
{ Return is the Boolean value returned in VAR parm State.      }
{                                                               }
{   From: BORLAND PASCAL FROM SQUARE ONE  by Jeff Duntemann     }
{---------------------------------------------------------------}


PROCEDURE FlipField(X,Y        : Integer;
                    VAR State  : Boolean;
                    TrueString : OpenString;
                    FalseString : OpenString;
                    VAR Escape : Boolean);
```

```
VAR Blanker    : String80;
    KeyStroke  : 0..255;
    WorkState  : Boolean;
    Ch         : Char;
    IsExtChar  : Boolean;
    ScanCode,ShiftBits : Byte;


PROCEDURE ShowState(NowState : Boolean);

BEGIN
  GotoXY(X,Y); Write(Blanker);    { Erase the old label }
  IF NowState THEN
    BEGIN
      GotoXY(X,Y);
      Write(TrueString)    { Write TrueString for NowState = True }
    END
  ELSE
    BEGIN
      GotoXY(X,Y);
      Write(FalseString);  { Write FalseString for NowState = False }
    END
END;



BEGIN
  Escape := False; Ch := Chr(0);
  LowVideo;                                        { Use highlighting }
  FillChar(Blanker,SizeOf(Blanker),' ');      { Set up Blanker String }
  WorkState:=State;                             { Temporary Boolean }
  IF Length(TrueString)>Length(FalseString) THEN    { Adjust Blanker }
    Blanker[0] := Chr(Length(TrueString)) ELSE {  String for lengths }
    Blanker[0] := Chr(Length(FalseString));    {  of meaning labels }
  ShowState(WorkState);                         { Display initial label }
  REPEAT
   {GetKey from Ch. 19 }
     WHILE NOT GetKey(Ch,IsExtChar,ScanCode,ShiftBits)
       DO BEGIN {NULL} END; { Loop & do nothing between keystrokes }
     KeyStroke := Ord(Ch);
     IF KeyStroke = 27 THEN Escape := True ELSE
       IF KeyStroke<>13 THEN WorkState := NOT WorkState;
     ShowState(WorkState);
  UNTIL (KeyStroke=13) OR Escape;       { ...until CR or ESC is pressed }
  IF NOT Escape THEN State:=WorkState;          { Update State if CR }
  NormVideo;
  ShowState(State);           { Redisplay State in non-highlighted text }
END;
```

When you use a Boolean variable in a program, it probably has a distinct and important meaning connected with each of its two states, **True** and **False**. **FlipField** displays the meaning of variable **State** and allows you to flip between its two states by pressing any key that is neither the escape key nor Enter.

FlipField is passed two text labels in its parameter line: **TrueString** describes the meaning of **State** when **State** is **True**. **FalseString** describes the meaning of **State** when **State** is **False**. For example, if **State** were a Boolean variable called **PatientSex**, **TrueString** might hold the string "Male" and **FalseString** might hold the string "Female." When **FlipField** begins running, it displays at **X,Y** the label corresponding to the current state of **State** as passed in the parameter line.

FlipField then waits on the keyboard for keypresses. If an Esc is entered, **FlipField** returns without making any change to **State**. If Enter is entered, **FlipField** updates **State** to reflect the currently selected meaning and returns. If any other key is pressed, **FlipField** flips to the other meaning for **State** and updates the screen display at **X,Y** to match. Going back to our example, by pressing a key (space bar works well) repeatedly, **FlipField** will rapidly display "Male" and "Female" at the same location until either Esc or Enter is pressed.

All the user must do to pick one of two states for a Boolean value is press Enter when the meaning he wants is displayed on the screen. All possible keypresses are accounted for and he doesn't have to type a string at the keyboard with the possibility of misspellings.

FlipField requires **GetKey**, a function that performs non-echo keyboard I/O through a BIOS call. See Section 19.4. The short program below demonstrates **FlipField**.

```
PROGRAM FlipTest;

USES Crt,DOS;

TYPE
  String80 = STRING[80];
  String30 = STRING[30];

VAR
  Sex,Quit : Boolean;
  Male,Female : String30;

{$I GETKEY.SRC }
{$I FLIPFLD.SRC }

BEGIN
  ClrScr;
  Sex := False; Male := 'Male'; Female := 'Female';
  GotoXY(1,10);
  Writeln('Press space bar until desired sex is displayed;');
  Write('then press Enter to select the displayed sex: ');
  FlipField(47,11,Sex,Male,Female,Quit);
```

```
    Writeln;
    Write('The chosen sex is: ');
    IF Sex THEN Writeln(Male) ELSE Writeln(Female);
    Readln;
END.
```

12.4 Determining Which Display Adapter Is Installed

Not counting the shunned and mediocre Professional Graphics Controller and the display board from the defunct PCjr, IBM has released only four distinct display adapters, the CGA, MDA, EGA, and VGA, as of July 1988. (Yet another adapter, the MCGA, exists, but it is a subset variant of the VGA and is nearly identical to the VGA in text modes. Besides, to my knowledge the MCGA has only existed as a set of chips on IBM PS/2 motherboards and has never been cloned by third-party vendors.) A host of third-party display adapters is available, but in general they all try to "look like" one of these IBM boards to software. This mimicry is driven by a need to fall under one of four different DIP switch settings on the PC system board, or one of four possible adapter values in AT-compatible SETUP programs.

Switches 5 and 6 of IBM PC switch block 1 must be set to reflect the kind of display adapter installed in the system. These switch settings are summarized in Figure 12.1. Switches 5 and 6 are what the PC looks at when it wishes to determine what sort of display it has. It does *not* go out and somehow examine the board to see what is actually present on the bus. This seems to be a risky system on the surface, since there is no promise that a third-party board pretending to be an MDA is actually similar enough to an MDA not to cause trouble. In fact, this risk has perhaps driven third-party display board manufac-

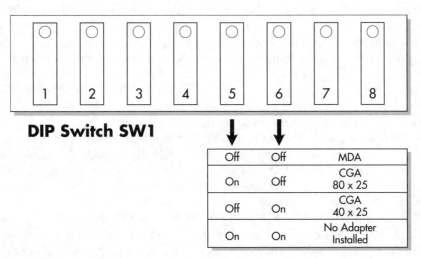

Figure 12.1 Display DIP Switch Settings

turers to be a little more careful of how compatible their products actually are with the IBM standard.

On the SETUP screen of AT-compatible PCs (which is virtually all machines still being sold today) you generally have a choice of four options: Color 40, Color 80, Monochrome, and EGA/VGA. Sometimes AT SETUP programs imitate the older PC's DIP switches, and list "No adapter installed" instead of EGA/VGA.

It is important to remember that the setting marked "No display adapter installed" means, more properly, a statement from the PC ROM BIOS stating "I don't know what adapter is installed--*yet*." It is a way of allowing ROM BIOS to hedge its bets and defer a decision to a better authority.

What authority? Unlike the older CGA and MDA cards, the EGA and VGA contain a ROM BIOS extension in a ROM chip right on the display board. This ROM contains software that is better able to assess the machine environment and decide how to handle video. The EGA or VGA BIOS code takes control during the *ROM scan* period after the motherboard-based ROM BIOS completes its power-on self-test (POST) and initializes the BIOS data areas. The EGA or VGA BIOS then alters the BIOS data areas as it sees fit.

We know where in memory the BIOS data areas are located, but IBM does not promise not to move them in future releases or future additions to the PC family. Therefore, the safe bet (and speed matters little here since it needs to be done only once) is to access this information through the BIOS. PC ROM BIOS function $11 returns 16 bits' worth of information on what equipment the PC thinks it has installed. This information comes from the BIOS data areas, *not* directly from the DIP switches or CMOS storage as some people believe. The DIP switches or CMOS storage are read *only* at POST time.

This is an important distinction, because the EGA and VGA BIOS overwrite the DIP switch/CMOS information when they perform tests and initialization on the EGA or VGA board during ROM scan. Recall that the EGA and VGA installation instructions direct the user to set DIP switches 5 and 6 to indicate *no* display adapter installed. The EGA and VGA determine through their own means whether a color or monochrome monitor is attached to the system; if a color monitor is attached, the EGA/VGA BIOS sets the BIOS data area as though the DIP switches had been set to reflect a CGA. Likewise, if the EGA or VGA detects a monochrome monitor attached to the system, it sets the BIOS data areas as though the DIP switches had indicated an MDA.

So *don't* make the mistake of assuming that you will get a 0 code back from BIOS function $11 if the installed video display adapter is an EGA or VGA. If an EGA or VGA is installed, BIOS will tell you there is a CGA installed if a color monitor is attached to the system, or BIOS will say an MDA is installed if a monochrome display is attached.

Obviously, BIOS function $11 alone will *not* tell you whether an EGA or VGA is actually installed or not. Remarkably, there is no really straightforward way of detecting the presence of an EGA or a VGA in a system. The method I use has proven reliable for IBM's own EGA and VGA plus a large number of clone boards, and I suspect it will work reliably on any EGA or VGA with a responsi-bly-written ROM BIOS on the board.

The generalized display-board detection method works this way: In a sense, we are detecting BIOS upgrades rather than boards. The VGA BIOS routine for VIDEO contains a new function call, $1A, that returns a code number identify-ing the nature of the installed display adapters and monitors. You might won-der why the VGA BIOS would bother returning a code for older cards — since if the VGA BIOS is present, the adapter must be a VGA, right?

Wrong. In a sense, the VGA BIOS is the new standard for *all* display card BIOSes in the PS/2 world, and there would be nothing to stop IBM from creat-ing a low-cost monochrome display adapter with a BIOS containing the new VIDEO function calls.

So we start by trying to invoke VIDEO function call $1A. If the function call is present, it will return the function call number (here, $1A) in register AL. (This is a general standard for behavior in the PS/2 BIOS — if a function call exists and is called, it will return its function number in AL.) If call $1A happens, we accept its sayso for the current display card type. While all display adapter types are covered, in reality you'll only see the VGA or the MCGA (standard with the PS/2 models 25 and 30).

If we determine (from testing AL against $1A) that no PS/2 BIOS exists in the machine, the next step is to test for an EGA BIOS. Like the PS/2, the EGA ROM BIOS adds a few extensions to the interrupt $10 VIDEO service included in the PC/XT/AT motherboard ROM BIOS. One extension is service AH=$12, Alter-nate Function. Service $12 currently includes two subfunctions. We are inter-ested in subfunction BL=$10, Return EGA Information. This subfunction will poll the installed EGA and return 1) the mode in effect, either color or mono-chrome; 2) the amount of EGA memory installed; 3) the bits from the EGA feature connector; and 4) the settings of the DIP switch on the spine of the EGA.

Consider what might happen if you made this subfunction call on a machine that did *not* contain an EGA. In such machines, VIDEO service AH=$12 is not defined. VIDEO handles such cases in a chivalrous manner and ignores them, restoring all registers and returning to the caller without changing anything.

In a sense, if we ask for EGA information in a machine with an EGA, we get back EGA information in register BX. If we ask for EGA information in a machine *without* an EGA, we get back *exactly* what we passed to VIDEO in BX, which (thank fate!) is *not* valid EGA information. So the method consists of performing a Return EGA Information call to VIDEO and seeing if BX changes in the process. If BX changes, we have an EGA. If BX stays the same, no EGA is installed.

Finally, if we find neither a VGA nor an EGA, we poll Interrupt $11 and see what it tells us. At that point the choice is essentially between a CGA and an MDA.

This series of tests allows us to build a function that returns a value indicat-ing which card is installed in the machine. Ideally, a function should return a distinct value for each kind of display card. While returning a plain numeric value (0, 1, 2, etc.) would be adequate, Pascal allows us to define an enumerated type that will make programs much more self-explanatory:

```
TYPE
    AdapterType = (MDA,CGA,EGAMono,EGAColor,VGAMono,
                   VGAColor,MCGAMono,MCGAColor);
```

The EGA, VGA, and MCGA appear in two incarnations since they can be configured to look (in text mode, at least) nearly identical to either the CGA or the MDA, including the starting address for the video buffer. The two EGA/VGA/MCGA incarnations are sufficiently different (especially since they cannot be switched from one to another under software control) to consider them, from a software perspective, as two different kinds of display adapter.

QueryAdapterType returns a value of type **AdapterType**, which means that you must define **AdapterType** in any program that uses **QueryAdapterType**, or else build the type and and the function into a unit.

```
{->>>>QueryAdapterType<<<<-------------------------------------}
{                                                              }
{ Filename : QUERYDSP.SRC - Last Modified 1/30/93              }
{                                                              }
{ This routine determines the currently installed primary     }
{ display adapter and returns it in the form of a value from   }
{ the enumerated type AdapterType.                            }
{                                                              }
{ AdapterType must be predefined:                              }
{                                                              }
{ AdapterType = (None,MDA,CGA,EGAMono,EGAColor,VGAMono,       }
{                VGAColor,MCGAMono,MCGAColor);                 }
{                                                              }
{   From: BORLAND PASCAL FROM SQUARE ONE  by Jeff Duntemann   }
{-------------------------------------------------------------}

FUNCTION QueryAdapterType : AdapterType;

VAR
  Regs : Registers;
  Code : Byte;

BEGIN
  Regs.AH := $1A;   { Attempt to call VGA Identify Adapter Function }
  Regs.AL := $00;   { Must clear AL to 0 ... }
  Intr($10,Regs);
  IF Regs.AL = $1A THEN  { ...so that if $1A comes back in AL...  }
    BEGIN                 { ...we know a PS/2 video BIOS is out there }
      CASE Regs.BL OF     { Code comes back in BL }
        $00 : QueryAdapterType := None;
        $01 : QueryAdapterType := MDA;
        $02 : QueryAdapterType := CGA;
        $04 : QueryAdapterType := EGAColor;
```

```
        $05 : QueryAdapterType := EGAMono;
        $07 : QueryAdapterType := VGAMono;
        $08 : QueryAdapterType := VGAColor;
        $0A,$0C : QueryAdapterType := MCGAColor;
        $0B : QueryAdapterType := MCGAMono;
        ELSE QueryAdapterType := CGA
      END { CASE }
    END
  ELSE
  { Next we have to check for the presence of an EGA BIOS: }
    BEGIN
      Regs.AH := $12;        { Select Alternate Function service }
      Regs.BX := $10;        { BL=$10 means return EGA information }
      Intr($10,Regs);        { Call BIOS VIDEO }
      IF Regs.BX <> $10 THEN { BX unchanged means EGA is NOT there...}
        BEGIN
          Regs.AH := $12;    { Once we know Alt Function exists... }
          Regs.BL := $10;    { ...we call it again to see if it's... }
          Intr($10,Regs);    { ...EGA color or EGA monochrome. }
          IF (Regs.BH = 0) THEN QueryAdapterType := EGAColor
             ELSE QueryAdapterType := EGAMono
        END
      ELSE  { Now we know we have an EGA or MDA: }
        BEGIN
          Intr($11,Regs);    { Equipment determination service }
          Code := (Regs.AL AND $30) SHR 4;
          CASE Code of
            1 : QueryAdapterType := CGA;
            2 : QueryAdapterType := CGA;
            3 : QueryAdapterType := MDA
            ELSE QueryAdapterType := CGA
          END { Case }
        END
    END;
END;
```

CHARACTER CELL SIZE AND CURSOR MANIPULATION

Before the introduction of the EGA, dealing comprehensively with text video was a much simpler thing. The CGA used an 8 x 8 character cell; the MDA used a 8 x 14 character cell. (For the sake of you purists: Yes, it is a 9 x 14 character cell, but the ninth pixel row doesn't really exist!) The EGA has *both* sizes of fonts in its ROM, as we mentioned above, for both monochrome and color modes. The VGA complicates matters still further by having both the 8 and 14 pixel fonts, plus an 8 x 16 pixel font as well. The MCGA, just to be perverse, has the 8 x 16 pixel font but *not* the 8 x 8 or 8 x 14 fonts.

Knowing what font the EGA or VGA happen to be using at any given time is important mostly because turning the cursor on and off correctly depends on it. It's *easy* to turn the cursor off; a simple call to VIDEO service 1 with bit 5 of CX high will do it:

```
{<<<< CursorOff >>>>}
{  From: BORLAND PASCAL FROM SQUARE ONE   }
{    by Jeff Duntemann - Last mod 1/30/93 }
{ From section 12.4-HIGHLY specific to the PC }


PROCEDURE CursorOff;

VAR
  Regs : Registers;

BEGIN
  WITH Regs DO
    BEGIN
      AX := $0100;
      CX := $2000;    { Set CH bit 5 hi to suppress cursor }
    END;
  INTR(16,Regs);
END;
```

Turning the cursor back *on* again is another story. The PC's text cursor is defined as a range of scan lines within the character cell, with the top scan line 0, and the bottom scan line either 15, 13, or 7, depending on the font in use at the time. Although any range of scan lines, including the entire character cell, can be set to flash at the cursor, the default text cursor consists of the bottom two scan lines in the character cell. Turning the cursor on again requires passing to VIDEO the starting scan line and ending scan line of our desired cursor. There is no way to "turn the cursor on as it was before we turned it off." VIDEO doesn't "remember" the old cursor settings. They get thrown away when you turn the cursor off. We need to know how many scan lines are in the current character cell before we can turn the default cursor back on correctly.

The function **DeterminePoints** returns the number of scan lines in the font currently in use. (Calling it "**Points**" hearkens back to "point sizes" of printed fonts, although the number of pixels in a font does not map in any way to the standard unit of type size measure called a "point," which is about 1/72 of an inch.) For the CGA, the value will always be equal to 8; for the MDA, equal to 14. For the EGA and VGA it could be either, or for the VGA it could also be 16; an additional query must be made to figure out the point size for the more advanced adapters. Again, a call to BIOS VIDEO accomplishes this, through the EGA BIOS extension service $11, Character Generator Functions. Subfunction $30, Return Information, provides the number of bytes per character (and hence the number of scan lines, since all characters in IBM text displays are 8 bits or one byte wide) in register CX.

```
{->>>>DeterminePoints<<<<-----------------------------------------}
{                                                                 }
{ Filename : FONTSIZE.SRC - Last Modified 1/26/93                 }
{                                                                 }
{ This routine determines the character cell height for the       }
{ font currently in use.  For the MDA and CGA this is hard-       }
{ wired; for the EGA, VGA, and MCGA the value must be obtained    }
{ by querying the ROM BIOS.                                       }
{                                                                 }
{   From: BORLAND PASCAL FROM SQUARE ONE  by Jeff Duntemann       }
{-----------------------------------------------------------------}


FUNCTION DeterminePoints : Integer;

VAR
  Regs : Registers;

BEGIN
  CASE QueryAdapterType OF
    CGA        : DeterminePoints := 8;
    MDA        : DeterminePoints := 14;
    EGAMono,         { These adapters may be using any of   }
    EGAColor,        { several different font cell heights,  }
    VGAMono,         { so we need to query the BIOS to find  }
    VGAColor,        { out which is currently in use. }
    MCGAMono,
    MCGAColor : BEGIN
                  WITH Regs DO
                    BEGIN
                      AH := $11;  { EGA/VGA Information Call }
                      AL := $30;
                      BH := 0;
                    END;
                  Intr($10,Regs);
                  DeterminePoints := Regs.CX
                END
    END  { CASE }
END;
```

The main use of **DeterminePoints** is in turning the cursor back on after it has been suppressed. The following procedure turns the cursor on, assuming the default text cursor of the two bottommost scan lines of the character cell. All font sizes are covered by specifying the cursor starting scan line as **Points-2** and the ending scan line as **Points-1**. The bottom scan line is not given by **Points** alone because **Points** gives the *number* of scan lines in the cell, and VIDEO requires the ordinal value of a line, counting from zero. For example, for the MDA font, there are 14 lines in the character cell, and the lines are numbered from 0–13.

```
{<<<< CursorOn >>>>}
{   From: BORLAND PASCAL FROM SQUARE ONE  }
{    by Jeff Duntemann - Last mod 1/30/93 }
{ From section 12.4-HIGHLY specific to the PC }

PROCEDURE CursorOn;

VAR
  Points : Byte;
  Regs   : Registers;

BEGIN
  Points := DeterminePoints;
  Mem[$40:$87] := Mem[$40:$87] OR $01;
  WITH Regs DO
    BEGIN AX := $0100; CH := Points-2; CL := 0; END;
  INTR(16,Regs);
END;
```

FONT SIZE AND SCREEN SIZE

We've become so used to 25-line screens that we often forget that the EGA and VGA have the ability to display other, larger screen sizes. The EGA can display a 43-line screen, and the VGA can display a 43- or a 50-line screen. If you've never seen one of these large format screens, try it from the IDE: Select Options | Environment | Preferences and check the "43/50 lines" checkbox under "Screen sizes." (This option will be disabled unless you have either a VGA or EGA installed in your system.) The screen will be changed to the larger size, whichever is appropriate for your display adapter.

It's all done with fonts. As we've seen, the size in pixels of an IBM display adapter font may be 8, 14, or 16. The default font on an EGA is 14 pixels high. The default font on the VGA and MCGA is 16 pixels high. However, the EGA and VGA can both use an 8-pixel font, and when they do, they display 43 or 50 lines, respectively.

There is no separate "mode" for 43- or 50-line screens. You set the screen size by simply changing the fonts. This is done through yet another EGA/VGA/MCGA BIOS call.

The program FONT.PAS not only demonstrates how to select fonts on the EGA/VGA/MCGA, but provides several useful services as well. It identifies the installed display adapter. (On monochrome systems, which adapter is installed is not always obvious at a glance.) It identifies the current font size, and passes that value to DOS ERRORLEVEL, so that batch files can take action based on the current font size (and hence screen) size. Finally, it allows you to enter a font size on the command line and change to that font size.

As with all good utility programs, the bulk of **Font**'s logic is user error-trapping. **Font** determines the installed display adapter, and it does not allow a font change BIOS call to be attempted on an adapter that does not support a given font size. For example, trying to load the 16-pixel font on an EGA is not allowed.

The only "magic" in **Font** involves the suppression of BIOS cursor emulation. IBM's original EGA BIOS could not emulate the earlier cursors due to a rather blatant bug in the BIOS logic. For this reason, IBM did not push 43-line mode on the EGA. To take control of the cursor style you have to remove the BIOS's own grip on the cursor, and this is done by setting a bit in a location in low memory:

```
MEM[$40:$87] := MEM[$40:$87] OR $01;
```

The only caution here is that some inexpensive third-party EGA clone adapters have even buggier BIOSes that may react peculiarly to this kind of treatment. If your EGA goes berserk when you run **Font** for an 8-pixel font, you will not be able to use 43-line mode, which depends on the 8-pixel font. Get a better adapter; I have found both Paradise and Video 7 to be accurate copies of IBM's original EGA, right down to IBM's BIOS bugs.

Greater love than that, no clone hath.

```
{------------------------------------------------------------------}
{                             FONT                                 }
{                                                                  }
{      Display adapter text font query and change utility          }
{                                                                  }
{                             by Jeff Duntemann                    }
{                             Turbo Pascal V7.0                     }
{                             Last update 1/30/93                   }
{                                                                  }
{    From: BORLAND PASCAL FROM SQUARE ONE    by Jeff Duntemann      }
{------------------------------------------------------------------}

PROGRAM Font;

USES Crt,DOS;

TYPE
   AdapterType = (None,MDA,CGA,EGAMono,EGAColor,VGAMono,
                   VGAColor,MCGAMono,MCGAColor);
   FontSizes   = SET OF Byte;

CONST
   AdapterStrings : ARRAY[AdapterType] OF String =
                   ('None','MDA','CGA','EGAMono','EGAColor',
                    'VGAMono','VGAColor','MCGAMono','MCGAColor');
```

```
VAR
  InstalledAdapter : AdapterType;
  LegalSizes       : FontSizes;
  AdapterSizes     : FontSizes;
  ErrorPos         : Integer;
  ErrorSize        : String;
  NewFont          : Byte;
  FontCode         : Byte;
  OldAdapters      : SET OF AdapterType;
  Regs             : Registers;


{$I QUERYDSP.SRC} { Contains function QueryAdapterType; see Section 12.4 }
{$I FONTSIZE.SRC} { Contains function DeterminePoints; see Section 12.4 }


PROCEDURE ShowFontSizeError(BadSize : String);

BEGIN
  Writeln(BadSize,' is not a valid font size.');
  Writeln('Legal values are 8, 14, and 16,');
  Writeln('*if* your display adapter supports them.')
END;


BEGIN   { MAIN }
  LegalSizes := [8,14,16];   { IBM adapters only use these three sizes }
  OldAdapters := [CGA,MDA]; { The CGA and MDA cannot change fonts }

  IF ParamCount < 1 THEN
    BEGIN
      InstalledAdapter := QueryAdapterType;
      Writeln('>>FONT<<  V2.0 by Jeff Duntemann');
      Writeln('     From the book, BORLAND PASCAL FROM SQUARE ONE');
      Writeln;
      Writeln('The installed adapter is: ',
              AdapterStrings[InstalledAdapter]);
      Writeln('The current font size is: ',DeterminePoints);
      Writeln;
      Writeln
      ('To change the current font size, invoke FONT.EXE with the
        desired');
      Writeln
      ('font size as the only parameter, which must be one of 8, 14,
        or 16:');
      Writeln; Writeln('   C>FONT 14'); WRITELN;
      Writeln('Remember that the font size of the CGA and MDA cannot
              change.');
      Writeln
```

```
('The EGA supports 8 and 14, while the VGA supports 8, 14, or 16.');
        Writeln('The MCGA supports the 16 pixel font size *only*.');
        Writeln
('FONT.EXE passes the current font size in ERRORLEVEL for use in batch
files.');
        Halt(DeterminePoints)  { Make point size available in ERRORLEVEL }
        { THIS IS AN EXIT POINT FROM FONT.PAS!!! }
    END
  ELSE
    BEGIN
      Val(ParamStr(1),NewFont,ErrorPos);
      IF ErrorPos <> 0 THEN ShowFontSizeError(ParamStr(2))
      ELSE
        IF NOT (NewFont IN LegalSizes) THEN
          BEGIN
            Str(NewFont,ErrorSize);
            ShowFontSizeError(ErrorSize)
          END
        ELSE       { At this point entered font size is OK... }
          BEGIN    { ...but we must be sure the adapter supports it: }
            InstalledAdapter := QueryAdapterType;
            CASE InstalledAdapter OF
              CGA                  : AdapterSizes := [8];
              MDA                  : AdapterSizes := [14];
              EGAMono,EGAColor     : AdapterSizes := [8,14];
              VGAMono,VGAColor     : AdapterSizes := [8,14,16];
              MCGAMono,MCGAColor   : AdapterSizes := [16];
            END; { CASE }
            IF NOT (NewFont IN AdapterSizes) THEN
              BEGIN
                Writeln('That font size does not exist');
                Writeln('on your display adapter.')
              END
            ELSE       { Finally, do the font switch }
              BEGIN
                ClrScr;
                IF NOT (InstalledAdapter IN OldAdapters) THEN
                  BEGIN
                    CASE NewFont OF
                      8  : FontCode := $12;
                      14 : FontCode := $11;
                      16 : FontCode := $10;
                    END; { CASE }
                    Regs.AH := $11;  { EGA/VGA character generator
                                             services }
                    Regs.AL := FontCode;  { Plug in the code for this
                                             size... }
                    Regs.BX := 0;
```

```
                Intr($10,Regs);  { ...and make the BIOS call. }
                { Suppress BIOS cursor emulation: }
                MEM[$40:$87] := MEM[$40:$87] OR $01;
                { Now reset the cursor to the appropriate lines: }
                Regs.AX := $100;
                Regs.BX := 0;
                Regs.CL := 0;
                Regs.CH := NewFont - 2;  { i.e., 6, 12, or 14 }
                Intr($10,Regs);  { Make the BIOS call. }
                HALT(DeterminePoints);
           END
         END
       END
     END
 END.
```

Chapter 13

Separate Compilation and Overlays

HOW TO BREAK UP LARGE PROGRAMS INTO MANAGEABLE MODULES

Why compile the whole shebang when you only need to compile the piece you're working on?

We've been asking this question for years. Pascal naturally separates a program into logical chunks (or it does when you don't fight the spirit of the language); good program design calls for relatively independent modules which may be compiled separately, and then linked together in one quick, final step before testing the completed program.

This is called *separate compilation*. Separate compilation has never been part of the Pascal language definition, but time has shown that it's very hard to manage large projects without it. Turbo Pascal 3.0 and earlier versions did not allow any kind of separate compilation. Turbo Pascal 4.0 and later adopt the *units* paradigm for separate compilation pioneered by UCSD Pascal years ago. This chapter covers the mechanisms by which separate compilation happens in Turbo Pascal.

13.1 The Packing List Metaphor

Let's say the UPS man rolls up to your door one day and drops a cardboard box in your lap. You know where it came from (in my case, probably Hosfelt Electronics, which sells a great many strange and wonderful things) but your memory of what the order contains has gotten a little fuzzy.

So you rip open the little plastic slap-on window and pull out the goldenrod sheet of paper marked "packing list." Right in a row is a summary of what's in the box: 2 spur gears, 96 tooth, brass. One pillow block ball bearing, 1/4". One alarm clock, Navy Surplus. (Original cost $900.) One tank prism.

Without actually ripping open the box, you know what's in it. If, for example, the packing list read something like, "25 polyethelene shower curtains, mauve," I would suspect the UPS man had dropped the wrong box in my lap.

Units are a little like a sealed box with a packing list. Each unit has two primary parts:

1. an *interface* part; and

2. an *implementation* part.

The interface part is a lot like a packing list. It is an orderly description of what is in the unit, *without* the actual code details of the functions and procedures within the unit. The interface part includes constant, type, and variable definitions, along with the parameter line portions of the functions and procedures within the unit.

This last item may seem a little strange. Consider the following line of code:

```
PROCEDURE FogCheck(InString : String; VAR FogFactor : Integer);
```

This isn't all of the procedure, obviously—but like it or not, it's all you really need to see of **FogCheck** to be able to make use of the procedure in your own programs. You need to know the relationship between the input parameter **InString** and the output parameter **FogFactor**, of course, but that's a documentation issue. Knowing *what* procedure **FogCheck** does is an entirely separate matter from knowing *how* it does it. If you know that the foggier the input string is, the higher a value will come back in **FogFactor**, well, that's sufficient.

Where is the rest of **FogCheck**? In the *implementation* part of the unit. In other words, inside the sealed box. The box contains the substance of the order, the actual goods. The packing list contains a description. That is the critical difference between interface and implementation.

At this point the packing list metaphor begins to break down, because in order to do anything with my brass gears and tank prism I have to rip open the box and take the goods out. A separately-compiled unit may remain a sealed box in that you cannot read the details of what lies inside, but the interface part of the unit allows your own programs to hook into and use the contents of the box.

USING UNITS

Turbo Pascal since 4.0 comes with several precompiled units full of routines for use in your own programs. This works to your advantage in many ways, not the least of which is that the procedures and functions within those readymade units are already compiled, and do not need to be compiled again every time you compile your own programs, as was the case with Turbo Pascal 3.0. (Turbo Pascal 3.0 only supported "libraries" of routines as *include files,* which needed to be compiled every time the main program was compiled.) Without having to recompile the units you use, compilation in general goes much more quickly.

How do you use these ready-made units? Just like that—you **USE** them:

```
PROGRAM Caveat;

USES Crt;

BEGIN
  ClrScr;                        { In unit Crt }
  GoToXY(12,10);      { ditto }
  Writeln('Better to light one single candle...'); { NOT in Crt!}
  Writeln('...than to trip on a rake while changing the fuse.');
END.
```

Here, the program **Caveat** contains a new type of Pascal statement: The **USES** statement. (**USES** is a reserved word.)

Caveat uses a unit called **Crt** that is included with Turbo Pascal. **Crt** contains (as you might imagine) routines that deal with screen handling. These include many routines familiar from Turbo Pascal 3.0 that used to be "built-in" to the compiler itself. **ClrScr** and **GotoXY** are the most common examples. Such routines were never really part of the Pascal language; but because Turbo Pascal 3.0 did not have any way to perform separate compilation, they had to be built into the compiler to be easily used. There is nothing "magical" or peculiar about either **ClrScr** or **GotoXY**. They are both ordinary procedures that you could have written yourself.

The same isn't quite true about those other stalwarts, **Read**, **Readln**, **Write**, and **Writeln**. These are *not* procedures in the strictest Pascal sense. If you're sharp you'll know why without being reminded: They can take a variable number of parameters of many different types in any order at all, which is a gross violation of Pascal's rules and regulations regarding procedures. This being the case, they *must* be built into the compiler, because the compiler has to generate different object code to perform each separate call to **Read** or **Write** depending on the number and types of the parameters used. I consider them Pascal statements, the same way **REPEAT/UNTIL** and **WHILE/DO** are statements.

So while most people think of **Writeln** as a CRT-oriented procedure (forgetting, perhaps, its use in writing to text files), it does not "live" in the same unit with all the other CRT-oriented functions and procedures supplied with Turbo Pascal.

The **USES** statement can take any number of unit names, separated by commas. The order you place them in the **USES** statement is not important.

WHERE UNITS MUST BE PLACED ON YOUR DISK

Units physically exist in one of two places: either as separate files with their own names, or as parts of the Turbo Pascal **System** unit. Unit files may have one of three different extensions, depending on what sort of Turbo Pascal programming you're doing: .TPU for Turbo Pascal for DOS; .TPP for Borland Pascal protected mode units, or .TPW for units compiled for use under Microsoft Windows. The **System** unit resides in a file that *always* has a .TPL extension. The name of the unit, however, depends on what sort of programming you're doing.

System for DOS lives in the file TURBO.TPL; **System** for protected mode resides in TPP.TPL, and **System** for Windows resides in TPW.TPL.

You may have any number of files on you working disk containing units, but with Borland Pascal there can only be three .TPL (Turbo Pascal Library) files, as described above. (Turbo Pascal will only have TURBO.TPL, and Turbo Pascal for Windows will only have TPW.TPL.)

For DOS work, TURBO.TPL is read into memory whenever you load and run the Turbo Pascal compiler or environment. It thus takes up a certain amount of memory that cannot be used for other things, like data and heap space for programs run under the Turbo Pascal Environment. If you know that you will not be using some of the standard units resident in TURBO.TPL, you can remove them with a standard utility called TPUMOVER.EXE. This will make TURBO.TPL smaller and allow the memory to be used for other things. The use of TPUMOVER is explained in Chapter 1 of the *Tools and Utilities Guide* shipped with the product.

Units that are not part of TURBO.TPL must be kept somewhere the compiler can find them. Unfortunately, you can't place a drive specifier or a path specifier in the **USES** statement. In other words, these are not legal **USES** statements:

```
USES Crt,DOS,C:RingBuf;        { Won't compile! }
USES Crt,D:\JIVETALK\RINGBUF;  { Won't compile! }
```

The best explanation as to why, is that unit names are *not* file names, but Pascal identifiers.

Here are the conditions under which the compiler can find your unit files:

- If they're in the current directory. In other words, your current directory is C:\JIVETALK, and the compiler is in C:\TURBO. Because C:\TURBO is in your DOS path, you can invoke the compiler from C:\JIVETALK. If the units you wish to use are in C:\JIVETALK, the compiler will find them.

- If you have set up a path to your units in the Options | Directories dialog box in the IDE. There is a specifier string for unit directories in that menu that you can fill with one or more paths to directories containing units:

```
C:\TURBO;C:\JIVETALK;C:\IKONYX
```

This is how the prompt would appear on your screen if you had these directories correctly specified to contain units. Notice that the three paths are separated *only* by semicolons—if you leave a space after the semicolon, any following paths will *not* be recognized! When a unit name is called out in **USES** statement, the compiler will search each path until it finds a unit of the correct name. The danger here is having units of the identical name but with different contents in several places on your disk. The *first* one the compiler finds will be the one it uses. If that isn't the one you want, you had better be more specific, as shown in the next item.

REFERENCING IDENTICAL IDENTIFIERS IN DIFFERENT UNITS

It is perfectly legal to have identical identifiers within two units and use both units from the same program. In other words, you could have a unit called **CustomCRT** that contained a procedure called **ClrScr**, which is the same name as the familiar screenclearing routine found in standard unit **Crt**:

```
USES DOS,Crt,CustomCrt;
```

A program could use both units as shown above and no error message would be generated.

But—which **ClrScr** would be actually incorporated into the program?

With no more information than the procedure name to go on, Turbo Pascal will link the *last* procedure named **ClrScr** that it finds in scanning the units named in the **USES** statement. In the example above, it would scan **CustomCrt** after scanning **Crt**, and thus it would link the custom-written **ClrScr** routine into the program.

You could exchange the unit names **Crt** and **CustomCrt** in the **USES** statement, and the compiler would then link the standard **ClrScr** routine into your program:

```
USES DOS,CustomCrt,Crt;
```

However, if you arrange the **USES** statement like this, nothing in **CustomCrt** can use any of the many useful routines in **Crt**. This may not be an issue, but it does limit your options.

There is a better way. You can specify the name of the unit that contains an identifier *when you use the identifier*. The notation should be familiar to you from working with Pascal record types, and works in a very similar fashion:

```
PROGRAM WeirdTextStuff;

USES DOS,Crt,CustomCrt;

BEGIN
  Crt.ClrScr;          { Clears the visible PC text screen }
  ClrScr;              { Clears the other text screens too }

  .  .  .

END.
```

This is often called *dotting*. In the same way that you can have two different record types with identical field names, you can have two or more units containing identical identifiers, and there will be no conflict. You simply choose the one you want by prefixing it with the unit name and a period character at each invocation. The default identifier in cases where no unit name precedes the reference is the first one found in scanning the units in the **USES** statement.

Note that the resemblance to record references ends there. There is no **WITH** statement feature regarding unit names.

13.2 Unit Syntax

In its simplest form, a unit source code file is very much like a Pascal program source code file without a program body. (A unit may have an optional "program body" called the *initialization section*, as I'll explain a little later on.) Typically, units contain procedures and functions, and often other declarations like constants, types, and variables.

A minimal unit with nothing inside it looks like this:

```
UNIT Skeleton;
INTERFACE
IMPLEMENTATION
END.
```

There are several immediate departures from the expected here. The reserved words **INTERFACE** and **IMPLEMENTATION** are *not* statements, and therefore are not followed by semicolons. Like the reserved words **BEGIN** and **END**, they serve to set off groups of statements that belong together.

Also, there is an **END** but no **BEGIN**. Most units do not have a program body. The **BEGIN** is optional, and may be used if the standalone **END** makes you uncomfortable. The **BEGIN** is required if you intend to add an initialization section to the unit.

Fleshing out our unit a little bit will bring out the differences between the interface and implementation parts:

```
UNIT Skeleton;

INTERFACE

USES DOS, Crt;

TYPE
  MyType = ItsDefinition;

VAR
   MyVar : MyType;

PROCEDURE MyProc(MyParm : MyType);

FUNCTION MyFunc(I,Y : Integer) : Char;

IMPLEMENTATION

VAR
   PrivateVar : MyType;

PROCEDURE MyProc(MyParm : MyType);

VAR Q,X : Integer;
```

```
BEGIN
END;

FUNCTION MyFunc(I,Y : Integer) : Char;

BEGIN
END;


END.
```

Note here that the **INTERFACE** keyword must come *before* the **USES** statement, if any. Nothing but comments and compiler directives may come between the unit name and the **INTERFACE** reserved word.

One type and a variable of that type are defined in the interface section. Both of these definitions are "visible" to any program or unit that uses **Skeleton**. A function and a procedure are also defined in the interface part of **Skeleton**, and like **MyType** and **MyVar**, are visible to any unit or program that uses **Skeleton**.

Now look down to the implementation section, where the bodies of the function and procedure are given. Notice that a variable name **PrivateVar** is defined in the implementation section. As its name implies, **PrivateVar** is known *only* within the implementation section of the unit. No other program or unit can reference the identifier **PrivateVar** or in any other way know that it exists.

PrivateVar can, however, be accessed by any of the procedures or functions defined within the unit. So, in a sense, the *effects* of **PrivateVar** can be "felt" by outside programs or units that use the subprograms that have access to **PrivateVar**, but the variable itself remains invisible to anything outside the unit in which it is defined.

Why is this important? Like so many of Pascal's structural limitations, it is done to minimize the possibility of "sneak paths" occurring between routines when those paths are not desired. Such sneak paths make possible bugs of a truly insidious nature.

A USEFUL UNIT EXAMPLE

A very simple example involves the **MakeBox** procedure I presented in Section 8.11. I've gathered together the **LineRec** and **PCLineChars** definitions, along with the **MakeBox** procedure itself, and created a short unit to "box it all up" and make it all available simply by placing the name **BoxStuff** in your **USES** statement. By now this should all be pretty easily digestible. Read it carefully to make sure you understand all the details.

```
{--------------------------------------------------------------}
{                        BoxStuff                              }
{                                                              }
{ Unit to demonstrate separate compilation - draws text boxes  }
{                                                              }
```

```
{                           by Jeff Duntemann                      }
{                         Turbo Pascal V7.0                        }
{                        Last update 1/23/93                       }
{                                                                  }
{    From: BORLAND PASCAL FROM SQUARE ONE   by Jeff Duntemann      }
{------------------------------------------------------------------}

UNIT BoxStuff;

INTERFACE

USES Crt;       { For GotoXY }

TYPE
  LineRec = RECORD
                ULCorner,
                URCorner,
                LLCorner,
                LRCorner,
                HBar,
                VBar,
                LineCross,
                TDown,
                TUp,
                TRight,
                TLeft : String[4]
              END;


{ PCLineChars: }
{ Contains box-drawing strings for MakeBox.}
{ Any program or unit that USES BoxStuff    }
{ can access the PCLineChars constant just }
{ as though it had been defined within the }
{ USEing program or unit.                   }

CONST
  PCLineChars : LineRec =
    (ULCorner : #201;
     URCorner : #187;
     LLCorner : #200;
     LRCorner : #188;
     HBar     : #205;
     VBar     : #186;
     LineCross: #206;
     TDown    : #203;
     TUp      : #202;
```

```
      TRight    : #185;
      TLeft     : #204);



{<<<< MakeBox >>>>}
{ This is all that the "outside world" really needs to see of the }
{ MakeBox procedure.  *How* it happens is irrelevant to using it. }

PROCEDURE MakeBox(X,Y,Width,Height : Integer;
                  LineChars        : LineRec);

IMPLEMENTATION

{ <<<<MakeBox>>>> }
{ Note here that the parameter line does not have to be repeated. }
{ (We gave the full parameter list definition in the INTERFACE.)  }
{ But since it does no harm, you might as well re-state the       }
{ parameter list.  That makes it easier to read the full source   }
{ for MakeBox. }

PROCEDURE MakeBox(X,Y,Width,Height : Integer;
                  LineChars        : LineRec);

VAR
  I,J : Integer;

BEGIN
  IF X < 0 THEN X := (80-Width) DIV 2;    { Negative X centers box }
  WITH LineChars DO
    BEGIN                                 { Draw top line }
      GotoXY(X,Y); Write(ULCorner);
      FOR I := 3 TO Width DO Write(HBar);
      Write(URCorner);
                                          { Draw bottom line }
      GotoXY(X,(Y+Height)-1); Write(LLCorner);
      FOR I := 3 TO Width DO Write(HBar);
      Write(LRCorner);
                                          { Draw sides }
      FOR I := 1 TO Height-2 DO
        BEGIN
          GotoXY(X,Y+I); Write(VBar);
          GotoXY((X+Width)-1,Y+I); Write(VBar)
        END
    END
END;

END.
```

13.3 The Initialization Section of a Unit

Structurally, units are very much like Pascal programs without program bodies. The important parts are the definitions of constants, types, variables, and subprograms. A unit may in fact have a "program body," that is, statements between the optional **BEGIN** reserved word and the required **END.** reserved word and period. Any statements in the body of a unit make up that unit's *initialization section*, and they are run *before* the main program body runs.

In a program that uses several units, the initialization section (if there is one) for each one of those units will execute before the main program body begins executing. The order in which the unit initialization sections run is the same order that the units are named in the **USES** statement. For example:

```
USES  Crt,Mouse,MenuStuff;
```

When the program that contains this statement is run, the initialization section for **Crt** executes first, followed by the initialization section for **Mouse**. There is no initialization section for the unit **MenuStuff**, so as soon as the initialization section of **Mouse** finishes executing, the main program body begins executing.

Of what advantage is an initialization section? There are many, although most of them are relatively advanced concepts that you may not need to use until you have come up to speed in Pascal programming in general.

Most simply, an initialization section can initialize global variables declared in the unit to some desired initial value. This relieves the program itself of the responsibility, and avoids the possibility that the programmer will forget to add initialization code to the beginning of his program that uses the unit. Also, in situations where a vendor sells a unit as a separate product, the initialization section guarantees that any globals that need to be initialized *will* be initialized so that the unit (which may not be fully understood by the programmer who uses it) will work correctly without depending on the programmer.

THE INITIALIZATION SECTION AS WATCHDOG

Another, somewhat more advanced use of the initialization section of a unit is to act as a watchdog to be sure certain conditions are just right before proceeding to execute the program as a whole. If something isn't right, the initialization section can call a halt to the whole program right then and there.

A fairly simple example of this notion concerns the installable device driver used with virtually all mouse pointing devices sold today. Programs that intend to use the mouse need to have the mouse installed in the computer or no pointer will appear and the elaborate pull-down menus often used in conjunction with a mouse will be worthless.

A program that depends on having a mouse installed should always check to see if the mouse driver is in fact loaded and available. This is not difficult, and it is an ideal task for the initialization section of a unit providing high-level language interface to the mouse driver.

The standard Microsoft mouse driver is called by way of an 8086 software interrupt. The Microsoft mouse driver loads in memory and then arranges for the pointer (more commonly called a "vector") at position 51 in the interrupt vector table to point to it. Programs that wish to use the mouse need only call interrupt 51 and pass it information in the 8086 machine registers.

Now, the question arises: How do we tell if the mouse driver has been installed somewhere in system memory? The answer is to look at interrupt vector 51 in the table. If the vector is **NIL** (that is, if all 32 bits are set to zero), then the driver is not installed. Or, if there is an address in the vector, but that address points to a certain 86-family machine instruction called an **IRET** (Interrupt RETurn), then the mouse driver has not been installed. Any vector at position 51 in the table that is neither **NIL** nor pointing to an **IRET** can be assumed to be pointing to a loaded mouse driver.

There are two negative possibilities here because not all computers set up the interrupt vector table the same way when you power-up your machine. Some fill the vector table with zeroes, some place a pointer to an **IRET** in all unused vector positions. It depends on the manufacturer of the BIOS. IBM's PC BIOS places a pointer to an **IRET** in vector 51, but many of the Far East BIOSes I have tried simply zero-fill the table before setting up the essential vectors.

There is a procedure in Turbo Pascal's standard unit **DOS** that fetches any given interrupt vector from the vector table. By fetching the interrupt 51 vector through the **GetIntVec** procedure, and then testing the pointer returned for a **NIL** value or an **IRET** byte at its target address, the unit's initialization section can decide whether or not the mouse driver is installed. If the driver is not there, the initialization section code halts the program with an error message before the main program block ever gets control.

The MOUSE.PAS unit shown below provides a number of functions for using the mouse from your Turbo Pascal programs. **Mouser** is the only procedure in the unit that actually calls interrupt 51. All the other procedures and functions are higher-level "wrappers" that handle register manipulation invisibly, allowing you to use the common mouse functions without being concerned about mouse function numbers, register values, and so on. **Mouser** is available if you need it for whatever reason to make mouse calls directly.

Notice the initialization section for MOUSE.PAS. It's a good example of both general reasons for having initialization sections: to make sure conditions are right before allowing application execution to continue, and (assuming conditions are right) to set a few things up ahead of the main application.

The **Mouse** unit checks to see if a mouse driver is in fact installed. If no mouse is there, it aborts the entire application to DOS. (You can easily remove this logic if you want to adapt MOUSE.PAS for use in mouse-optional applications.) **Mouse** also queries the mouse to see how many buttons are present on the installed mouse. The Microsoft Mouse has two buttons, but the Xerox mice I learned on back in the late 1970s had three, as does the Logitech Mouse I use to this day. It can be handy to know what hardware one has to work with, and **Mouse** helps out a little in that regard. The exported variable **ButtonCount** contains the number of buttons on the installed mouse even before the application using **Mouse** gets control.

Through considerable testing I've discovered that much of what **Mouse** tells you depends on the installed mouse driver more than on the actual physical mouse device. Microsoft's mouse driver only reports two buttons, regardless of how many buttons your mouse may have. My Logitech Mouse will work with the Microsoft driver, but in the process it "becomes" a Microsoft Mouse and the third button isn't accessible.

We'll be making use of the **Mouse** unit later on in the book.

```
{--------------------------------------------------------------}
{               TURBO PASCAL MOUSE INTERFACE UNIT              }
{                                                              }
{                     by Jeff Duntemann                        }
{                     Turbo Pascal V7.0                        }
{                     Last Updated 1/31/93                     }
{                                                              }
{   From: BORLAND PASCAL FROM SQUARE ONE   by Jeff Duntemann   }
{--------------------------------------------------------------}


UNIT Mouse;

INTERFACE

USES DOS;


VAR
   ButtonCount : Integer;         { Number of buttons on mouse }
   M1,M2,M3,M4 : Word;            { For low-level mouse calls  }

FUNCTION IsLogitechMouse : Boolean;             { Looks at driver }

PROCEDURE ResetMouse;          { Standard Mouse function call 0 }

PROCEDURE PointerOn;                                     { 1 }

PROCEDURE PointerOff;                                    { 2 }

PROCEDURE PollMouse(VAR X,Y : Word;
                    VAR Left,Center,Right : Boolean);    { 3 }

PROCEDURE PointerToXY(X,Y : Word);                       { 4 }

PROCEDURE SetColumnRange(High,Low : Word);               { 7 }

PROCEDURE SetRowRange(High,Low : Word);                  { 8 }
```

```
PROCEDURE Mouser(VAR M1,M2,M3,M4 : Word);




IMPLEMENTATION


FUNCTION NumberOfMouseButtons : Integer;

BEGIN
  M1 := 0;  { Must reset mouse to count buttons! }
  Mouser(M1,M2,M3,M4);
  NumberOfMouseButtons := M2
END;




FUNCTION MouseIsInstalled : Boolean;

TYPE
  BytePtr = ^Byte;

VAR
  TestVector : BytePtr;

BEGIN
  GetIntVec(51,Pointer(TestVector));
  { $CF is the binary opcode for the IRET instruction; }
  { in many BIOSes, the startup code puts IRETs into   }
  { most unused vectors. }
  IF (TestVector = NIL) OR (TestVector^ = $CF) THEN
    MouseIsInstalled := False
  ELSE
    MouseIsInstalled := True
END;


{---------------------------------------------------------------}
{       PROCEDURES ABOVE THIS BAR ARE PRIVATE TO THIS UNIT      }
{---------------------------------------------------------------}


PROCEDURE Mouser(VAR M1,M2,M3,M4 : Word);

VAR
  Regs : Registers;

BEGIN
```

```
      WITH Regs DO
        BEGIN
          AX := M1; BX := M2; CX := M3; DX := M4
        END;
      Intr(51,Regs);
      WITH Regs DO
        BEGIN
          M1 := AX; M2 := BX; M3 := CX; M4 := DX
        END
    END;



    FUNCTION IsLogitechMouse : Boolean;

    TYPE
      Signature = ARRAY[0..13] OF Char;
      SigPtr = ^Signature;

    CONST LogitechSig : Signature = 'LOGITECH MOUSE';

    VAR
      TestVector : SigPtr;
      L          : LongInt;

    BEGIN
      GetIntVec(51,Pointer(TestVector));
      LongInt(TestVector) := LongInt(TestVector) + 16;
      IF TestVector^ = LogitechSig THEN
        IsLogitechMouse := True
      ELSE
        IsLogitechMouse := False
    END;



    PROCEDURE  ResetMouse;

    BEGIN
      M1 := 0;
      Mouser(M1,M2,M3,M4);
    END;



    PROCEDURE  PointerOn;

    BEGIN
      M1 := 1;
```

```
    Mouser(M1,M2,M3,M4)
END;



PROCEDURE  PointerOff;

BEGIN
  M1 := 2;
   Mouser(M1,M2,M3,M4)
END;



PROCEDURE  PollMouse(VAR X,Y : Word; VAR Left,Center,Right : Boolean);

BEGIN
  M1 := 3;              { Perform mouse function call 3 }
   Mouser(M1,M2,M3,M4);
   X := M3; Y := M4;    { Return mouse pointer X,Y position }
   IF (M2 AND $01) = $01 THEN Left := True ELSE Left := False;
   IF (M2 AND $02) = $02 THEN Right := True ELSE Right := False;
   IF (M2 AND $04) = $04 THEN Center := True ELSE Center := False;
END;



PROCEDURE  PointerToXY(X,Y : Word);

BEGIN
  M1 := 4;
  M3 := X; M4 := Y;
   Mouser(M1,M2,M3,M4)
END;



PROCEDURE  SetColumnRange(High,Low : Word);

BEGIN
  M1 := 7;
  M3 := Low;
  M4 := High;
   Mouser(M1,M2,M3,M4)
END;



PROCEDURE  SetRowRange(High,Low : Word);

BEGIN
  M1 := 8;
```

```
    M3 := Low;
    M4 := High;
    Mouser(M1,M2,M3,M4)
  END;


  {------------------------------------------------------------------}
  {                   INITIALIZATION SECTION                         }
  {                                                                  }
  {  Function MouseIsInstalled goes out and checks the interrupt }
  {  51 vector-if it is either NIL (zeroed) or points to an          }
  {  IRET, the mouse is assumed NOT to be installed.  Note that      }
  {  a vector table full of garbage may be taken to mean the         }
  {  mouse driver is there.  Use the VECTORS utility to check        }
  {  the state of your vector table after cold boot.  Some Asian }
  {  schlock BIOSes (BII?) may not initialize the table properly }
  {  and cause false readings on testing for an installed driver.}
  {------------------------------------------------------------------}


BEGIN
  IF NOT MouseIsInstalled THEN
    BEGIN
      Writeln
      ('>>>ERROR:  Mouse driver not detected.  Aborting to DOS.');
      HALT(1)
    END;
  ButtonCount := NumberOfMouseButtons
END.   {Mouse}
```

13.4 Unit Exit Procedures

Pascal programs that use units don't necessarily begin their execution at the top of the main program block. If any of the units it uses have initialization sections, the program actually begins with the initialization section of the first unit named in the **USES** statement.

The flipside is also true: A program that uses units doesn't necessarily end after the final **END.** of the main program block. An alter-ego of the initialization section is available under Turbo Pascal that executes *after* the main program block finishes running: the *exit procedure*.

EXIT PROCEDURES FROM A HEIGHT

Exit procedures are trickier to understand than initialization sections, because they involve pointers to procedures. You might wish to come back to this section after digesting some of the pointer and address material explained in Chapter 24.

Exit procedures exist primarily to undo what an initialization section may do: set the machine up in some application-specific fashion. If the initialization section sets up one or more interrupt vectors to point to interrupt service routines contained within the application, something had better restore those vectors to what they were before the application began running.

Exit procedures may also be used simply to "clean house" and ensure that whatever needs doing before returning control to DOS gets done. This might include closing all files, erasing unneeded temporary files, or purging sensitive data from RAM-based buffers.

An exit procedure is an ordinary procedure without parameters. It may not be a function, or an **INLINE**, or an interrupt procedure. There is no reserved word or other qualifier in Turbo Pascal that brands it as an exit procedure. What makes it an exit procedure is the way it is called, and that one thing only.

THE EXIT PROCEDURE CHAIN

Every unit may have an exit procedure, as may the main program. Exit procedures are called after the main program finishes executing, by completing its tasks normally, or by encountering a **Halt** statement, or by falling prey to a runtime error. When a program ceases execution for any of those three reasons, any existing exit procedures are executed in the following order: First, the main program's exit procedure runs, then the unit exit procedures run in *reverse* order of the units as they were declared in the **USES** statement. In other words, given this **USES** statement:

```
USES  Unit1,Unit2,Unit3;
```

the main program's exit procedure will run first, followed by Unit3's, then Unit2's, and finally Unit1's.

The manner in which exit procedures are called is interesting and more than a little tricky. The Turbo Pascal runtime library maintains a generic pointer called **ExitProc**. Ordinarily this pointer is set to **NIL** (**NIL** is a reserved word representing a pointer value indicating a pointer that points to nothing; see Chapter 17); however, a unit or the main program can set **ExitProc** to point to a procedure designated as an exit procedure. Then, when the runtime library takes control back from the main program and prepares to return to DOS, it tests **ExitProc** and transfers control to the address **ExitProc** contains if **ExitProc** is not equal to **NIL**.

This works simply and well if there is only one exit procedure in a given program. However, with a little attention to details, the main program and every unit can have an exit procedure, and all may make use of the same exit procedure pointer, **ExitProc**.

This process is a rough one to digest without some visual aid. Figure 13.1 can be read two ways: Read from the bottom to the top, it shows the sequence in which an exit procedure chain is built. Read from the top to the bottom, it shows the sequence in which exit procedures in a chain are called, and the chain dismantled in the process.

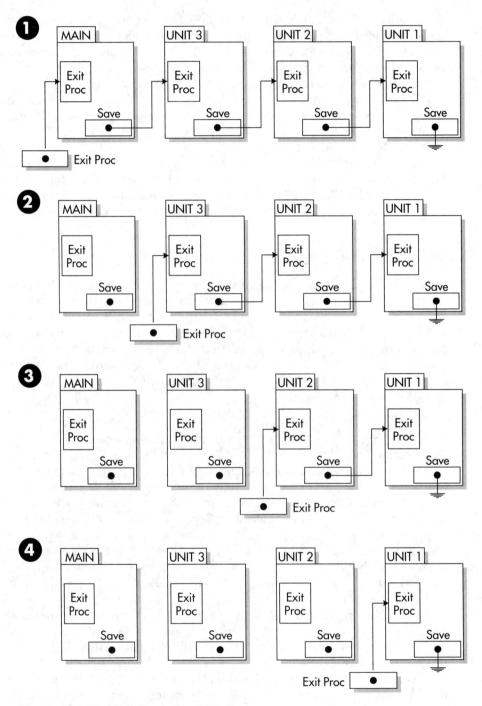

Figure 13.1 The Exit Procedure Chain

Figure 13.1 shows the main program and three units it uses, as would happen in a program with the following **USES** statement:

```
PROGRAM Main;
USES Unit1, Unit2, Unit3;
```

Each unit and the main program have a procedure defined that is to serve as an exit procedure. Also, the main program and each unit has a generic pointer defined which for this example we'll call **Save**.

```
VAR Save : Pointer;
```

Save is local to each unit and can therefore have the same name as both the main program's **Save** and the **Save**s belonging to the other units. As we mentioned above, the predefined generic pointer **ExitProc** is ordinarily set to **NIL** by the Turbo Pascal runtime code.

Creating an exit procedure chain is begun in the initialization section of the first unit that executes prior to **Main**, which in our example is **Unit1**. **Unit1** saves the *current* value of **ExitProc** in its **Save** pointer:

```
Save := ExitProc;
```

Since the initial value of **ExitProc** is **NIL**, **Save** now contains the value **NIL**. **Unit1** next assigns the address of its exit procedure to the pointer **ExitProc**:

```
ExitProc := @Unit1ExitProcedure;
```

This is the situation as shown in row 4 of Figure 13.1. The @ operator means "address of" and it returns the machine address of its operand, which in this case is the procedure **Unit1ExitProcedure**.

Now, the truly clever thing about the process is that the *next* unit performs *exactly* the same two tasks in its initialization section: It assigns the current value of **ExitProc** to its own **Save** pointer, and then assigns the value of its exit procedure to **ExitProc**. This is the situation shown in row 3 of Figure 13.1. Because **ExitProc** had been pointing to **Unit1**'s exit procedure, **Unit2**'s **Save** pointer points now to **Unit1**'s exit procedure, and **ExitProc** now points to **Unit2**'s exit procedure.

For the next step, **Unit3** does exactly the same thing: It places the current value of **ExitProc** into its own **Save** pointer, and assigns the address of its own exit procedure to **ExitProc**. We then have the situation shown in row 2 of Figure 13.1. Finally, in the first few lines of the main program, **Main** continues the process and does what the units did: It puts the current value of **ExitProc** into its **Save** pointer, and puts the address of its own exit procedure into **ExitProc**. The chain is then complete, as shown in the top row of Figure 13.1.

It is crucial that you understand one thing: There is *nothing* about the order of execution built into the units that form the chain of exit procedures. You could change the order of the **USES** statement to

```
USES Unit2, Unit1, Unit3;
```

and the process would happen the same way, save that **Unit2** would be the first unit in the chain, followed by **Unit1** and finally **Unit3**. Furthermore, none of the units know how many other units are in the chain, or even if there *are* any other units in the chain.

When **Main** ceases running, whether by ending normally, through a **Halt** statement, or through a runtime error, the entire chain of exit procedures is executed. The order of execution is the reverse of the order in which the units constructed the chain. The process can be followed by reading Figure 13.1 from the top row down. It is a little more subtle than the process of building the chain.

The Turbo Pascal runtime library begins the process by testing **ExitProc** to see if it holds a value of **NIL**. If not, it transfers control to the address contained in **ExitProc** via a **CALL** instruction. In our example, the first exit procedure to execute will be the one belonging to **Main**. This is the situation in the top row of Figure 13.1.

Just before calling the address contained in **ExitProc**, the runtime library moves the address into registers and sets **ExitProc** to **NIL**. This is important in ensuring that the chain is executed in sequence, as we'll see in a moment. Because the exit procedure took control via a **CALL** instruction and not a **JMP** instruction, *control returns to the runtime library when the exit procedure finishes executing*. The runtime library then tests the value of **ExitProc** against **NIL** again— and calls the address in **ExitProc** if **ExitProc** is not equal to **NIL**.

If this sounds like an infinite loop, you're right. It is. However, the exit procedure has one task to perform before it returns control to the runtime library, and that is to assign the value of its **Save** pointer to **ExitProc**:

```
ExitProc := Save;
```

Save, if you recall (or can see from Figure 13.1), contains the address of the *next* exit procedure in the chain. So when the first exit procedure returns control to the runtime library, **ExitProc** contains the address of the next exit procedure in the chain. The runtime library tests **ExitProc** against **NIL** again, and calls the second exit procedure in the chain. This is the situation in row 2 of Figure 13.1.

Just before returning control to the runtime library, the exit procedure for **Unit3** assigns its own **Save** pointer to **ExitProc**, bringing us to the situation shown in row 3 of Figure 13.1. Once again, the runtime library calls the address in **ExitProc** and the execution of the chain continues.

Now, suppose for a moment that the first exit procedure had *not* set **ExitProc** to **NIL** before returning to the runtime library. In that case, **ExitProc** would still contain the address of the first exit procedure. The runtime library might then call the same exit procedure over and over again in an infinite loop. However, there is a safety mechanism built into the runtime library: Before calling an exit procedure, the runtime library sets **ExitProc** to **NIL**. That way, if the exit procedure fails to set **ExitProc** to the address of the next exit procedure in the chain, **ExitProc** will contain **NIL** on return to the runtime library, and the runtime library will stop executing the chain.

All things come to an end. Consider what happens when the last exit procedure, that belonging to **Unit1**, terminates. It assigns the value of its **Save** pointer to **ExitProc**. But because it was the first exit procedure in the chain, the value it stored in its **Save** pointer was the default value placed in **ExitProc** by the runtime library: **NIL**. Therefore, when control returns to the runtime library, **ExitProc** will contain **NIL**, and the runtime library will consider the chain finished. The runtime library will then complete its own housecleaning and return to DOS.

This business of exit procedure chains is complicated, but it *is* reliable, and provides a level of safety unknown in earlier versions of Turbo Pascal and in most other language compilers.

I have written four simple source code files that perform the sequence of events we have been describing in the last few pages. They do nothing more than create an exit procedure chain and then execute it, finally returning to DOS. Follow the code through until it all makes sense to you.

```
UNIT Unit1;

INTERFACE

IMPLEMENTATION

VAR Save : Pointer;

{$F+} PROCEDURE Unit1ExitProcedure; {$F-}

BEGIN
  Writeln('Unit #1 - Exit procedure...');
  ExitProc := Save
END;

BEGIN
  Save := ExitProc;
  ExitProc := @Unit1ExitProcedure;
  Writeln('Unit #1 - Initialization procedure...');
END.

UNIT Unit2;

INTERFACE

IMPLEMENTATION

VAR Save : Pointer;

{$F+} PROCEDURE Unit2ExitProcedure; {$F-}

BEGIN
  Writeln('Unit #2 - Exit procedure...');
  ExitProc := Save
END;
```

```
BEGIN
  Save := ExitProc;
  ExitProc := @Unit2ExitProcedure;
  Writeln('Unit #2 - Initialization procedure...');
END.

UNIT Unit3;

INTERFACE

IMPLEMENTATION

VAR Save : Pointer;

{$F+} PROCEDURE Unit3ExitProcedure; {$F-}

BEGIN
  Writeln('Unit #3 - Exit procedure...');
  ExitProc := Save
END;

BEGIN
  Save := ExitProc;
  ExitProc := @Unit3ExitProcedure;
  Writeln('Unit #3 - Initialization procedure...');
END.

{-------------------------------------------------------------}
{                          Main                               }
{                                                             }
{      Exit procedure chaining demonstration program          }
{                                                             }
{                   by Jeff Duntemann                         }
{                   Turbo Pascal V7.0                         }
{                   Last update 1/31/93                       }
{                                                             }
{   From: BORLAND PASCAL FROM SQUARE ONE   by Jeff Duntemann  }
{-------------------------------------------------------------}

PROGRAM Main;

USES Unit1,Unit2,Unit3; { In UNIT1.PAS, UNIT2.PAS, & UNIT3.PAS }

BEGIN
  Writeln('Main program execution begins here.');
  Writeln('Main program execution ends here.');
END.
```

Once you understand how they work, compile and link them together into an executable file and run them. If what you see when they run seems natural to you, then you have digested all there is to know about Turbo Pascal's exit procedures.

13.5 Units As Overlays

Turbo Pascal 1.0 did not have overlays. Turbo Pascal 2.0 and 3.0 had overlays. Turbo Pascal 4.0 did not. Overlays came back with release 5.0, and seem to be here to stay. With overlays, your program can get a great deal larger than the DOS 640K memory limit, as long as your disk system is large enough to hold the program's component parts.

OVERLAYS FROM A HEIGHT

The idea behind overlays is just that: You cut a program into parts, and arrange it so that several of the parts share the same place in memory. When the main program begins running, an initial overlay is loaded into a slot in memory. When the second overlay is required, it is loaded into memory into the same slot as the first overlay, "overlaying" the first overlay. Later on, when a third, fourth, or fifth overlay is required, it is simply loaded on top of whatever overlay had previously occupied the overlay area in memory. In this way, you can have megabytes of code that all run handily in 256K RAM or even less—you simply need to carve those megabytes of code up into a sufficient number of overlays.

Turbo Pascal 5.0's overlay system is based on units. Any number of units may be specified as overlays, which means that each will occupy the same region of memory when loaded. The overlaid units, in a sense, take turns at executing in memory and, on loading, each unit overwrites the unit existing in memory before it.

All units specified as overlays are linked to a *single* separate file, with the same name as the main program but with an extension of .OVR. In other words, MYPROG.PAS, if it contains overlaid units, will compile to MYPROG.EXE and MYPROG.OVR. *All* overlaid units are contained in MYPROG.OVR.

Unlike Turbo Pascal's earlier overlay system, there is only one overlay area in memory. This is called the *overlay buffer*, and it is actually allocated on the heap before the main program takes control, in effect bumping the heap up by the size of the overlay buffer. So there is no need to be concerned about multiple overlay areas. You simply specify that a unit is to be overlaid, and the compiler takes care of the rest.

The overlay buffer is initially made as large as it must be to contain the largest overlaid unit. The overlay buffer can be made larger if desired, as I'll explain later. Smaller overlaid units simply use as much space as they must in the overlay buffer. Any unused space is wasted—which is a good reason to make your overlaid units all of a similar size. One whopper overlay and a lot of little ones will waste most of the overlay buffer during any time the big unit is not in memory.

If the runtime library detects expanded (EMS) memory in the system at runtime, it will allow the .OVR file to be loaded into EMS RAM. From that point on, all accesses will be made from EMS RAM to the overlay buffer at RAM speed, without any further access to the disk-based copy of the .OVR file. Because expanded RAM is only slightly slower than DOS RAM, the end result of using EMS RAM is to defeat the DOS 640K barrier. By using EMS, your programs can be completely memory-based and as large as they need to be, up to the practical limits of the runtime library.

Turbo Pascal's overlay system is laid out in Figure 13.2.

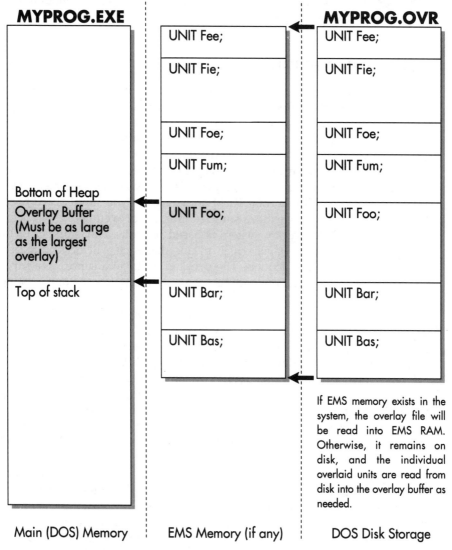

Figure 13.2 Overlay Files and Buffers

SETTING UP AN OVERLAID APPLICATION

Turbo Pascal provides an overlay manager that handles access to overlays, in a unit called **Overlay**. If you intend to use overlays, you must include **Overlay** in your **USES** statement, before *all* of the overlaid units. As a safety precaution, you might get in the habit of specifying **Overlay** first any time you specify it at all.

A unit is specified as overlaid through compiler directive **$O**. This directive has two forms: a toggle form and a parameter form. The toggle form consists of the **$O** directive followed by either a plus or a minus symbol. The parameter form consists of the **$O** directive followed by its parameter, which in this case is the name of a unit to be overlaid. Both forms of the **$O** directive appear within comment delimiters in the usual fashion for compiler directives.

The two forms of the **$O** directive go in two different places, but actually in the service of the same purpose: to define a unit as an overlay. The toggle form goes in the unit source code file itself, to "turn on" overlay support code generation *within that unit*. The parameter form is placed in the main program, to tell the compiler which units are to be treated as overlays. You are given two chances to specify overlays because you may want the option of making a unit an overlay in one program or not an overlay in another, as required. By placing the **$O+** directive in the unit source file, you *enable* its use as an overlay, but you don't *require* its use as an overlay. It can still be linked normally if desired.

The parameter form of the toggle, by contrast, tells the main program that the named unit is to be treated as an overlay. Such **$O** directives must be placed *after* the **USES** statement:

```
PROGRAM JiveTalk;

{$F+}

USES  Overlay,DOS,CRT,CircBuff,XMODEM,Kermit,Packet1K,Parser;

{$O XMODEM}
{$O Kermit}
{$O Packet1K}
```

This example overlays some but not all of its units. **Overlay** is first in the **USES** statement. There is no necessary order in placing the **$O** directives.

A common error is to place the **$O** parameter directives in the main program with the names of units that do *not* have a **$O+** directive in them. Without **$O+** in the unit source code file, *that unit cannot be overlaid*, and the compiler and linker will tell you so.

There was definitely a method in choosing which units in program **JiveTalk** were to be made overlays. The three overlaid units contain code for three file transfer protocols. Since the program services only a single communications session at a time, only one of the three protocols will be active at any one time. Furthermore, once a file transfer has been initiated, it will carry through without requiring the use of any protocol other than the one currently operating.

On the other hand, while the **DOS** unit could be overlaid, to do so would be insane, since nearly every other unit in the program calls the **DOS** unit. If another overlay is called **DOS**, the two would be waltzing in and out of memory by turns in a process we call "thrashing," which would be slow indeed.

This means don't put "toolkit" units out as overlays. Instead, design major subsystems as giant overlaid units, and arrange it so that none of the subsystems call elements of other subsystems. For example, in an accounting application put the accounts payable module out as an overlaid unit, the accounts receivable module out as another unit, payroll as a third unit, and so on; but keep screen control and menuing routines out of the overlay scheme. In short, overlay the *highest* level routines, and leave low-level and utility routines in memory, to be available to all and sundry. Keep in mind that Payroll *never* calls Accounts Receivable, but both probably call any number of routines in your general-purpose screen or file toolkit.

One additional point to note in the example declarations above is the presence of a **$F+** compiler directive immediately after the **PROGRAM** statement. One of the requirements of a program containing overlays is that all calls must be far calls. Place a **$F+** directive at the start of any program using overlays, as well as one **$F+** at the start of each unit. Failing to do so may cause a subprogram call to walk off the edge of the Earth, taking your program session with it.

OVERLAY MANAGEMENT

The overlay manager needs to be initialized at runtime before any of the routines in the overlay file are called. The **Overlay** unit provides a procedure to accomplish this:

```
PROCEDURE OverInit(OverlayFileName : String);
```

The name of the DOS file containing the overlays is passed in **OverlayFileName**. This name can be a full pathname, including drive unit specifier and subdirectory path. If no drive unit is specified, the overlay manager searches the current drive, and if no path is specified, the overlay manager searches the current directory. If the file is not found in the current directory, the overlay manager will then search the directory containing the .EXE file (providing you're using DOS 3.X) and then will search directories listed in the DOS PATH environment variable.

If an error occurs during overlay manager initialization, an error is reported in the predefined variable **OvrResult**. All of the routines in unit **Overlay** report errors in **OvrResult**. Each of the possible values is represented by a predefined constant in **Overlay**. A table of the constants, their values, and their meanings is given in Table 13.1.

OvrResult should be tested immediately after calling **OvrInit**. If an error is returned by **OvrInit**, it will typically be **OvrNotFound**, meaning the overlay manager cannot locate the specified overlay file. The generic **OverError** code may also be returned, indicating an error not covered by any of the other codes. If anything other than **OvrOK** is returned in **OvrResult** after a call to **OvrInit**, the overlay manager will not be installed; and if you attempt to call a routine in an overlaid unit, runtime error 208 will occur, halting your program.

Table 13.1 Overlay Initialization Error Codes

Code	Constant	Meaning
0	OvrOK	A-OK; no problems encountered
-1	OvrError	"None of the above" error code
-2	OvrNotFound	Specified overlay file not found
-3	OvrNoMemory	Not enough heap for overlay buffer
-4	OvrIOError	I/O error loading overlay file
-5	OvrNoEMSDriver	EMS driver not installed
-6	OvrNoEMSMemory	Not enough EMS memory for overlay file

Something to note about **OvrResult**: Unlike **IOResult**, which it resembles functionally, **OvrResult** is not set to zero immediately after being read, but instead remains unchanged until the next call to a routine in the **Overlay** unit. You needn't copy **OvrResult** into a variable for safekeeping if you don't want to, unless for some reason you need to keep the error status of one call to an overlay manager routine during or after a call to another.

USING EMS MEMORY FOR THE OVERLAY FILE

Turbo Pascal's overlay manager has the ability to detect the presence of EMS memory at runtime. If EMS memory is detected, the overlay manager can use it; if not, no harm is done, and the overlay file can remain on disk. However, in order for this detection to work, you need to explicitly call an overlay manager routine:

```
PROCEDURE OvrInitEMS;
```

Note that there are no parameters, and that it is *not* a function. Also keep in mind that **OvrInitEMS** in no way *replaces* **OvrInit**. Once you have successfully initialized the overlay manager, you should call **OvrInitEMS** to see if any EMS is available. If enough EMS memory is available to hold the overlay file, the overlay file will be loaded into EMS memory. It's as simple as that, and totally automatic. This is a chunk of an overlaid application I wrote once, and it shows how these things should go together:

```
OverlayName := 'JIVETALK.OVR';
OvrInit(OverlayName);
IF OvrResult <> OvrOK THEN
CASE OvrResult OF
  OvrNotFound :  { Overlay file not found on disk }
    BEGIN
      Writeln('Overlay file ',OverlayName,' not found.');
      Writeln('Please reinstall JiveTalk and run again.');
```

```
          Halt(OvrResult)
       END;
    OvrIOError :    { I/O error loading overlay file }
       BEGIN
          Writeln('I/O error reading overlay file ',OverlayName,'.');
          Writeln('The file may be corrupted.  Please re-install');
          Writeln('JiveTalk from the master disk.');
          Halt(OvrResult)
       END;
    OvrNoMemory :   { Not enough heap to allocate overlay buffer }
       BEGIN
          Writeln('There is not enough memory in your computer');
          Writeln('to run Jivetalk.  You need at least 384K RAM.');
          Writeln('Without additional memory, Jivetalk cannot run.');
          Halt(OvrResult)
       END;
    ELSE              { Miscellaneous overlay system error }
       BEGIN
          Writeln('Jivetalk overlay system error.  Please reboot');
          Writeln('your system and run again.  If error persists,);
          Writeln('re-install JiveTalk from the master disk.');
          Halt(OvrResult)
       END;
  END; { CASE }


  OvrInitEMS;       { Detect and use EMS RAM if available }
  IF OvrResult <> OvrOK THEN
     IF OvrIOError THEN
       BEGIN
          Writeln('I/O error reading overlay file ',OverlayName,'.');
          Writeln('The file may be corrupted.  Please re-install');
          Writeln('JiveTalk from the master disk.');
          Halt(OvrResult)
       END;
```

This code fragment from a communications program illustrates an unavoidable truth about commercial-quality applications: Most of their bulk is devoted to detecting and dealing gracefully with either system or user errors. The days when a commercial application can simply roll over on its back and die are long past. Your users deserve better. Try to be ready for all errors, and at the very least exit to DOS with some sort of "last words."

Note that no special action is taken on an **OvrResult** value indicating that there is no EMS driver installed or no EMS memory in the system. These are normal situations—many or most people do not have EMS memory in their system.

SETTING THE OVERLAY BUFFER SIZE

When **OvrINIT** runs, it allocates a buffer on the heap large enough to contain the largest overlaid unit. (See Figure 13.2.) If you can afford to give the overlay manager more heap memory than that, it will speed overall system performance by allowing the overlay manager to keep more than one unit in memory at a time. An algorithm that keeps an eye on which overlays are called most frequently allows the overlay manager to decide which overlays to maintain in memory and which to leave on disk. You, however, must tell the overlay manager how large it may make the overlay buffer, using another procedure from the **Overlay** unit:

```
PROCEDURE OvrSetBuf(BufferSize : LongInt);
```

Here, **BufferSize** specifies the total desired size of the overlay buffer, in bytes. This amount of memory is allocated on the heap. Two conditions are necessary for a call to **OvrSetBuf** to succeed: 1) The heap must be *empty*. If *any* dynamic variables have been allocated on the heap before you call **OvrSetBuf**, the call will fail and the **OvrError** error code will be returned in **OvrResult**. 2) There must be enough memory on the heap to satisfy the request. If there is insufficient heap memory available, an **OvrNoMemory** error is returned in **OvrResult**.

Keep in mind that by the time you call **OvrSetBuf**, it is assumed that you have already called **OvrInit**, and that **OvrInit** has been able to successfully allocate enough memory on the heap to contain the largest single overlaid unit. Therefore, if a call to **OvrSetBuf** fails, your program can continue operating; it will simply have to be content with an overlay buffer as large as—but no larger than—the largest overlay.

QUERYING THE OVERLAY BUFFER SIZE

A companion routine to **OvrSetBuf** allows you to query the current size of the overlay buffer:

```
FUNCTION OvrGetBuf : LongInt;
```

Quite simply, the size of the overlay buffer in bytes is returned by **OvrGetBuf**. **OvrGetBuf** and **OvrSetBuf** allow your programs to do some smart memory allocation by looping through a series of attempts—perhaps starting by asking for enough heap space to hold the entire overlay file—until a memory allocation value small enough to succeed is found.

OVERLAY CAUTIONS

There are a number of things to keep in mind when designing a program that is to be divided into overlays:

- *Do not attempt to overlay the **Overlay** unit.* The compiler will allow it, but the resulting program will not run.

- *Do not overlay any unit that contains an interrupt handler.* An interrupt handler must be in memory at all times, because when interrupts are triggered, there is no mechanism to intercept control long enough for the overlay manager to load an overlay containing the handler into memory. Again, the compiler will not forbid you to put interrupt handlers into overlays, but if an interrupt is triggered while that overlay is not in memory, your program will crash *hard*.

- *Avoid designing initialization sections into overlaid units.* There is no real danger in doing this, but you must remember that on program startup, every unit initialization section is run. If you have 17 overlays, each with an initialization section, each of the 17 will be loaded into memory just long enough for its initialization section to run. This means a period of constant disk access at the start of your program that will only make the program look bad to impatient users.

Chapter 14

Printer and Disk File I/O

DEVICES FOR DATA PRINTOUT, STORAGE, AND RETRIEVAL

A computer program is a universe unto itself. Within its bounds data structures are created, changed, and deleted. Calculations are performed and the results used in still more calculations. Lots goes on in a computer program's universe in the cause of getting a job done.

But it's out here in *our* universe where the job comes from and the finished work is needed. Somehow some of the critters living in a computer program have to cross the threshold between the program universe and the real universe. The pathways between the computer program and the outside world are collectively called "input/output" or, more tersely, "I/O." In Pascal, all I/O is handled under the umbrella category of files.

THE NOTION OF A FILE

To most people, the word "file" conjures images of filing cabinets and various other places to store things away for future perusal and reuse. However, another connotation of the word "file" strikes closer to the heart of the Pascal file: a long row of people or objects in a straight line, often in the process of moving from one place to another in an orderly fashion. Soldiers file from the parade ground to the mess hall, and so on.

A Pascal file is a stream of data, either coming or going. Not all "files" are data stored on disk or tape. Your keyboard is a file: a stream of characters triggered by your fingers and sent inward to the waiting program. Your CRT screen is a file: a flat field painted with visible symbols by a stream of characters sent from the program inside the computer. Your printer is a file: a device that accepts a stream of characters from the program and places them somehow onto a piece of paper.

The last example contains an important word: "device." Your keyboard is a device, as is your CRT screen, as is your printer, as is your modem. All are files that have one endpoint in the computer program and another endpoint in a physical gadget that absorbs or emits data. (Sometimes a file may do both.) This kind of file we call a "device file."

The other kind of file is the more familiar kind: a collection of data recorded as little magnetic disturbances on a clean piece of magnetic plastic. These are "disk files." Files in Turbo Pascal are of one type or another, either device files or disk files.

14.1 Logical and Physical Files

ISO Standard Pascal does not make a distinction between device and disk files. In ISO Pascal, a file is a file—a stream of data either coming or going. One end of the line is inside the Pascal program, and Pascal simply doesn't care what sort of thing is on the other end of the line.

Turbo Pascal has to modify this notion a little—for random files, as an example—but the "everything Out There is a file" bias remains. By not getting involved in the downdeep details of how a character is printed or sent to the screen, Pascal the language (that is, its workaday syntax) can present a uniform front to many different operating systems. This makes for less work in translating a Pascal program from one operating system environment to another.

This separation between *what* a file does and *how* it does it is sharply drawn in Pascal, between the concepts of "logical" and "physical" files.

A logical file is a Pascal abstraction, beginning with the declaration of a file variable in the variable declaration part of a program:

```
StatData : FILE OF Integer;
```

This tells us that **StatData** is a file and contains integers, nothing more. It says nothing about whether or not the file exists on a disk, which disk, or how much data exists in the file.

That information falls under the realm of physical files. A physical file is an actual device (for device files) or an actual collection of data on some sort of storage medium. A physical disk file has a file name, a size, a record length, an access mode, (read only, read/write, hidden, system, etc.), perhaps a timestamp for last access and an interleave factor, and other things as well. It is *not* an abstraction, and by not being an abstraction a physical file must pay attention to all those gritty little details that make storing and retrieving data on disk possible.

All these little details are very much hardware and operating system dependent. If Pascal had to take care of such details, it would be nearly an entirely separate language for each computer/operating system combo it ran on, as is very nearly the case these days with BASIC. (And it has always been the case with FORTH.)

So Pascal provides logical files, and the operating system provides physical files. When a logical file becomes associated with (or "assigned to" as is often said) a physical file, a path exists between the program's inner universe and the outside world. That file is then said to be "open."

14.2 Declaring, Assigning, and Opening Files

Declaring a file gives the file a name and a data type:

```
FileVariableName : FILE OF <type>;
```

<type> may be any valid data type except a file type. (A file of files makes no logical sense and is illegal.) <Type> can be a standard type like **Integer** or **Boolean**, or it can be a type that you have defined, like records, sets, enumerated types, or arrays. A file can be a file of only one type, however; you cannot declare a file of **Integer** and then write records or sets to it.

Declaring a file also creates a file buffer in your data area. This file buffer is a variable of the type the file is declared to be. It is a "window" into the file; the actual open end of the data pipe between the program and the outside world.

Unlike ISO Standard Pascal and most other commercial implementations of Pascal, Turbo Pascal does *not* allow direct access to the file window via **Get**, **Put**, or the caret notation:

```
VAR
   NumFile : FILE OF Integer;

NumFile^ := I;    { Illegal in Turbo Pascal; OK in Standard Pascal }
Put(NumFile);
```

This was the source of some conflict early on, but now that Turbo Pascal defines the standard for commercial Pascal, no one is complaining much. The **Get/Put** notation was awkward and hard to understand to begin with, and I feel that accessing all files through **Read** and **Write** is a much better choice.

CONNECTING LOGICAL TO PHYSICAL WITH ASSIGN

Before you can open a file, there must first be a connection between a logical file that is declared in the program, and a physical file that exists outside the program. Creating this connection is the job of the built-in procedure **Assign**.

Assign takes two parameters: a file variable that has been declared in the program, and a string variable or literal that names a physical file:

```
PROCEDURE Assign(AFile : <filetype>; FileName : String);
```

Assign creates the File Information Block (usually called a FIB) which each file must have to be used by the program. Once associated with a physical file, a logical file may be opened for write access or read access. This is done with **Reset** and **Rewrite**.

OPENING FILES WITH RESET AND REWRITE

The **Assign** procedure is *not* part of ISO Standard Pascal. Most commercial Pascal compilers use it as the means of connecting logical to physical files.

However, **Assign** does only half the job of opening a file; its job is limited to linking a logical file with a physical file. Getting a logical file ready to be written to or read from involves two built-in procedures: **Reset** and **Rewrite**. These procedures *are* part of ISO Standard Pascal.

An open file has in its FIB what we call a *file pointer*. This is not a pointer variable as we know it, but rather a logical marker indicating which element in the file will be read or written to next.

Reset opens a file for reading. Some device files allow both read access and write access at the same time; these files are opened with **Reset** also. When a file is to be opened for random file I/O using **Seek** (see Section 14.9), **Reset**, again, is used.

Reset does not disturb the previous contents of a disk file. The file pointer is positioned at the first data item in the file. If the file is empty when **Reset** is executed, the **EOF** function returns **True** for that file.

Some examples are:

```
Assign(MyFile,'A:ADDRESS.TXT');
Reset(MyFile);

Assign(ConsoleInput,'CON');
Reset(ConsoleInput);
```

Reset can also be used on a file that is already open. For an open disk file, this will reposition the file pointer to the first record in the file. Performing a **Reset** on an open device file does nothing. If the device file is one of Turbo Pascal's predefined logical devices, **Reset** will generate an error.

Rewrite opens files that are *only* to be written to, and not read from while they are currently open. When **Rewrite** is executed on a disk file, all previous contents of the disk file are overwritten and lost. Note that you may use either **Reset** or **Rewrite** on device files; the action on the device file is identical for both.

```
Assign(MyFile,'B:GRADES.DAT');    { Old grades are lost! }
Rewrite(MyFile);

Assign(BitBucket,'NUL');          { Anything written to BitBucket }
Rewrite(BitBucket);               { will quietly vanish away...    }
```

DEVICE FILES AND DOS DEVICE NAMES

All files have names. You're certainly familiar with the list of file names that comes up when you use the DOS DIR facility. DIR displays a directory of disk file names on a given disk drive. Device files have names as well, if not such easily displayable ones.

Each operating system has its own means of getting information to and from devices. Most operating systems have a set of standard devices that are supported by function calls to the operating system BIOS (Basic Input/Output System). Turbo Pascal recognizes names for all standard DOS devices. These names are used by the Turbo Pascal file handling machinery just as names for disk files are used. Table 14.1 summarizes the DOS device names usable from Turbo Pascal.

Be careful with devices COM1 and COM2. The fact that they are input/output devices implies that they could be used to write a "dumb terminal" program to read characters from the keyboard and send them to the modem, and read characters from the modem and send them to the screen. Unfortunately, there is no way to test COM1 or COM2 to see if a character is ready to be read before you actually go in and read one. And if a character is *not* ready, the **Read** statement will wait until one is ready, effectively "hanging the system" until something comes in on the modem line. In practice, you need to go to the BIOS or to the hardware to do effective input from COM1 or COM2, because you need to test for the *presence* of a character before you try to *read* a character.

These device names are *not* files and cannot be used as file identifiers. To use them you must assign them to a Pascal file variable, and then either **Reset** or **Rewrite** them as appropriate.

INPUT AND OUTPUT

All Pascal programs are capable of accepting input from the keyboard and writing output to the screen. Two standard device files are always open for this purpose: **Input** and **Output**.

In some Pascals you must explicitly name **Input** and **Output** when using them with **Read**, **Write**, **Readln**, and **Writeln**:

```
Writeln(Output,'Files do it sequentially...');
```

Table 14.1 Supported DOS Device Names

Name	*Device Definition*
CON	Buffered system console. Echoes input characters CR as CR/LF; BS as BS/SP/BS. As OUTPUT, echoes CR as CR/LF; LF alone is ignored. HT (horiz. tab) is expanded to every 8 columns. CAN (CRL-X) erases input line and returns cursor to its starting column.
LPT1 LPT2 LPT3	These are output-only devices generally attached to PC parallel ports. PRN is a synonym for LPT1. The **Printer** unit assigns LPT1 to a text file variable named **LST**.
COM1 COM2	These refer to the PC's standard serial ports. There is no status call; if you read one of these devices when no character is ready it will wait for a character, effectively hanging the system.
NUL	"Bit bucket" device. Absorbs all output without effect. Generates EOF immediately on any read.

In Turbo Pascal, **Input** and **Output** are the default files for use with **Read, Write, Readln**, and **Writeln**. If you omit the name of a file in one of those statements, the compiler assumes **Input** for **Read** and **Readln**, and **Output** for **Write** and **Writeln**. You need only write:

```
Writeln('Files do it sequentially...');
```

and Turbo Pascal will know to send the text line to your CRT screen.

Similarly, to accept input from the **Input** logical file, which is always connected to your keyboard and always open, you need only write:

```
Readln(AString);
```

and the program will wait while you type text at the keyboard, going on only when it detects that Enter was pressed, or when you have filled the string variable out to its maximum physical length. The text you typed will be immediately available in the variable **AString**. There is no need to include the identifier **Input** in the **Readln** statement, although you may if you wish—nothing will change.

Input and **Output** are considered text files, which means that only printable ASCII characters and a few control characters may be read from them or written to them. *However,* **Read, Readln, Write**, and **Writeln** do contain limited abilities to convert binary data types like **Integer** to printable representations. So it is in fact legal to **Write** an integer to **Output** because **Write** converts the integer to printable ASCII characters before **Output** ever sees it. For a fuller discussion see Section 14.7 under "Using **Read** and **Write** with text files."

Under Turbo Pascal 4.0 and later, **Input** and **Output** are assigned to DOS standard input and DOS standard output, respectively. This means that characters written to **Output** may be redirected to a DOS file by use of the DOS redirection feature. Also, characters read from **Input** may be redirected to come from a DOS disk file instead of from the console keyboard.

An important thing to remember about **Input** and **Output** is that when you use the **CRT** unit (see Chapter 12) *they are no longer assigned to DOS standard input and standard output*, but are assigned directly to Turbo Pascal's low-level screen and keyboard support. This means that DOS redirection will *not* work once you **USE** the **CRT** unit.

BINARY FILES VERSUS TEXT FILES

All disk files can eventually be seen as collections of bytes grouped somehow on a diskette or hard disk. Pascal makes a distinction between files that can contain absolutely any binary pattern in a stored byte, and those files that are allowed to contain only printable characters and certain (very few) control characters. Files that may contain any byte pattern at all are called *binary* or *non-text* files. Files that are limited to printable characters are called *text files*.

Text files are allowed to contain printable ASCII characters plus *whitespace* characters. Whitespace characters include carriage return ($0D), linefeed ($0A), formfeed ($0C), horizontal tab ($09), and backspace ($08). Although not technically a whitespace character, the bell character ($07) is also permitted in text files.

Text files may be "typed" (via the DOS TYPE command) directly from disk to the screen without sending the display controller into suicide fits.

An important consequence of allowing only printable characters is that text files created under PC DOS may contain an end-of-file (EOF) marker character. Binary files may *not* contain an EOF marker because binary files are allowed to have any 8-bit character pattern as valid data. Therefore, the operating system (and thus Turbo Pascal) could not tell an EOF marker character from just more legal binary data.

Text files under the DOS operating system have traditionally used CTRL-Z (hex 1A) as the EOF marker. This is a holdover from DOS's origins in CP/M-80, which did *not* keep track of the size of files down to the byte, as DOS does. CP/M-80 only knew how many 128-byte blocks were in a file; to mark the true end of data within the last data block, an application had to place a CTRL-Z character after the last true byte of data.

Turbo Pascal writes a CTRL-Z after the last data byte in a text file. Furthermore, when reading a text file, it reports EOF at *either* the true EOF reported by DOS *or* at the first CTRL-Z character found in the file. This could be important if you allow a CTRL-Z character to be written somewhere in the middle of a text file, perhaps by way of the **Write** procedure as used for binary data like records, sets, integers, etc. If you later read that file as text through **Read** or **Readln**, you will be able to read *only* up to the CTRL-Z, at which point EOF will become true.

Text files in Turbo Pascal are declared this way:

```
VAR
   MyFile   : FILE OF Text;    { Both forms are legal }
   YourFile : Text;
```

Any file that is not declared to be a **FILE OF Text** or simply **Text** is considered a binary file. The difference between the two becomes critical when you need to detect where data ends in the file. We will examine this problem in detail in connection with the **EOF** function in Section 14.4.

14.3 Reading from and Writing to Files

ISO Standard Pascal has a pair of file procedures called **Get** and **Put**. These work with a data structure called the *file window*, which is a "slice" of the file to be read or written to. When you **Get** from a file, the next item in the file is placed in the file window, from which it may be accessed at leisure. Similarly, when you wish to write an item to a file, you place it in the file window and then **Put** the file window out to the disk.

Turbo Pascal does *not* implement **Get** and **Put**, nor does it make the file window directly available to the programmer. If you are porting Pascal code from another compiler, all **Gets**, **Puts**, and file window references will have to be edited to use **Read** and **Write** instead.

USING READ AND WRITE WITH NON-TEXT FILES

I won't say much more about **Get** and **Put**. They do nothing that can't be done with **Read** and **Write**. That, and their awkwardness, and the need to keep the size of the compiler down are the reasons Turbo Pascal does not implement **Get**, **Put**, and the file window concept of file I/O.

The following discussion deals with *typed* files, that is, binary files that are not files of **Text**. Text files are a special case and will be covered in the next section.

Once a file has been opened with **Reset**, data may be read from the file with the **Read** procedure. **Read** takes at least two parameters: a file variable and one or more variables with the same type as the file:

```
VAR
   StatRec,Rec1,Rec2,Rec3   : NameRec;
   MyFile : FILE OF NameRec;

Assign(MyFile,'B:NAMES.DAT');
Reset(MyFile);

Read(MyFile,StatRec);
Read(MyFile,Rec1,Rec2,Rec3);
```

Here, **NameRec** is a record type defined earlier in the program. In this example, the **Read** statement reads the *first* record from **MyFile** into the record variable **StatRec**. There is no mention of the file window variable, although the file window is involved beneath the surface in the code that handles the **Read** function. The second **Read** statement reads the next three elements of **MyFile** into **Rec1**, **Rec2**, and **Rec3**, all at one time. This is a convenient shorthand; there is no difference in doing this than in executing three distinct **Read** statements.

Write works just the same way, with the same parameters; the only difference is the direction the data is flowing:

```
Assign(MyFile,'B:NAMES.DAT');
Rewrite(MyFile);

Write(MyFile,StatRec);
Write(MyFile,Rec1,Rec2,Rec3);
```

Read and **Write** work *sequentially*; each time **Read** or **Write** is used, the file pointer is bumped to the next element down the file. The process never works backwards; you cannot begin at the end of the file and work your way back. (Again, for that sort of thing you need random file I/O—see Section 14.9.)

USING READ AND WRITE WITH TEXT FILES

A text file is a stream of printable characters between the program and a device file or disk file. The **Read** and **Write** statements are used to transfer a data item (or list of data items) to or from the text file character stream. The data items do not have to be of the same type. We've been doing things like this informally all through this book:

```
VAR
   Unit  : Char:
   Count : Integer;

Write('The number of files on disk ',Unit,' is ',Count);
```

What is happening here is that a list of four data items is being sent to device file **Output**. Two are string literals, one is a character, and one is an integer.

Text files, as we saw in the previous section, may contain only printable ASCII characters and certain control characters. Integer variables are not ASCII characters; rather, they are 2-byte binary numbers that are not necessarily printable to the screen.

Yet when you write

```
VAR
   I : Integer;

I := 42;
Write(I);
```

the two ASCII characters "4" and "2" appear on your screen. They are an ASCII representation of a 2-byte binary integer that could as well have been written in base 2 as 00000000 00101010. **Read** and **Write** contain the machinery for converting between numeric variables (which are stored in binary form) and printable ASCII numerals.

Write also has the ability to take Boolean values (which are actually binary numbers 0 or 1) and convert them to the words "TRUE" and "FALSE" before passing them to a text file. **Read**, however, does *not* convert the ASCII strings "TRUE" or "FALSE" to Boolean values!

Read and **Write** when used with text files can accept data types **Integer, Char, Byte, Word, LongInt, ShortInt** and subranges of those types; type **String** and derived string types; plus type **Real, Single, Double, Extended**, and **Comp. Write** will also accept Boolean values; remember that **Read** will not. Enumerated types, pointers, sets, arrays, and record types will generate errors during compilation. Attempting to **Read** a Boolean value from a text file will trigger this error:

```
Error 64: Cannot Read or Write variables of this type
```

Although **Read** will accept a string variable, it's better practice to use **Readln** for reading strings. (See below on **Readln**.) The problem is that strings on a text file character stream carry no information about how long they are. If you **Read** from a text file stream into a string variable, the string variable will accept characters from the file until it is physically filled. If the file ends before the string is completely filled, the system may hang or fill the remainder of the string with garbage.

READLN AND WRITELN

Pascal includes a pair of I/O statements that work only on text files: **Readln** and **Writeln**. They introduce a whole new concept: dividing a Pascal text file into "lines."

Ordinary text on a printed page is a series of lines. A Pascal text file is a one-dimensional stream of characters; it has none of the two-dimensional quality of a printed page. To model text as we see it in the real world, Pascal defines an end-of-line character (EOL) that is inserted into the character stream of a text file after each line of printable characters. The definition of the EOL character may vary from system to system. For most microcomputers EOL is not one character but two: the sequence carriage return/linefeed ($0D/$0A). This is a holdover from teletype's heyday when it took one control character to return the typehead to the left margin, and yet another to index the paper up one line.

The **Writeln** procedure is exactly like **Write**, save that it follows the last item sent to the text file character stream with the EOL character. For our discussion EOL will always be the pair CR/LF.

```
PROGRAM WriteInt;

VAR
  IntText : Text;
  I,J     : Integer;

BEGIN
  Assign(IntText,'B:INTEGERS.DAT');
  Rewrite(IntText);
  FOR I := 1 TO 25 DO Writeln(IntText,I);
  Close(IntText);
END.
```

This program writes the ASCII equivalent of the numbers from 1–25 to a text file. Each numeral is followed by a CR/LF pair. A hexdump of file INTEGERS.DAT will allow you to inspect the file character stream:

```
0000   31 0D 0A 32 0D 0A 33 0D    0A 34 0D 0A 35 0D 0A 36
0010   0D 0A 37 0D 0A 38 0D 0A    39 0D 0A 31 30 0D 0A 31
0020   31 0D 0A 31 32 0D 0A 31    33 0D 0A 31 34 0D 0A 31
0030   35 0D 0A 31 36 0D 0A 31    37 0D 0A 31 38 0D 0A 31
0040   39 0D 0A 32 30 0D 0A 32    31 0D 0A 32 32 0D 0A 32
0050   33 0D 0A 32 34 0D 0A 32    35 0D 0A 1A 1A 1A 1A 1A
0060   1A 1A 1A 1A 1A 1A 1A 1A    1A 1A 1A 1A 1A 1A 1A 1A
0070   1A 1A 1A 1A 1A 1A 1A 1A    1A 1A 1A 1A 1A 1A 1A 1A
```

If you know your ASCII well (or have a table handy) you can see the structure of the character stream in this file: ASCII numerals separated by 0D/0A pairs. Turbo Pascal fills out the 128-byte block after the end of data with CTRL-Z characters. In text files, the first CTRL-Z signals end-of-file; more on that shortly.

In a sense, **Writeln** writes only strings (minus length bytes) to its files. If you hand it a variable that is not a string, **Writeln** will (if the conversion is possible) convert it to a string before writing it to its file.

Readln reads one line from a text file. A line, again, is a series of characters up to the next EOL marker. If **Readln** is reading into a string variable, the number of characters read becomes the logical length of the string. So unlike **Read** and **Write**, **Readln** and **Writeln** can in fact maintain information on string length in a file, since all strings written by **Writeln** are bounded by EOL markers.

FORMATTING WITH WRITE PARAMETERS

Write and **Writeln** allow certain formatting options when writing data to text files, including the screen (**Output**) and system printer. These options as given to the **Write** and **Writeln** statements are called *write parameters*.

The simplest write parameter applies to any variable that may be written to a text file, and specifies the width of the field in which the variable is written.

```
<any Writeable variable> : <field width>
```

When written, data (if any) in the variable will be right justified within a field of spaces <field width> wide. For example:

```
CONST
  Bar = '|';

VAR
  I    : Integer;
  R    : Real;
  CH   : Char;
  OK   : Boolean;
  Txt  : String;

I  := 727;
CH := 'Z';
R  := 2577543.67;
OK := False;
Txt := 'Grimble';

Writeln(Bar,I:5,Bar);
Writeln(Bar,CH:2,Bar);
Writeln(Bar,R:12,Bar);
Writeln(Bar,OK:7,Bar);
Writeln(Bar,TXT:10,Bar);
```

```
Writeln(Bar,-R,Bar);
Writeln(Bar,R,Bar);
```

When run, this code snippet produces this output:

```
|   727|
| Z|
|  2.577544E+06|
|   FALSE|
|    Grimble|
|-2.57754E+06|
|  2.57754E+06|
```

Note that the real numbers are always expressed in exponential (also called "scientific") notation, that is, as powers of 10, even though originally expressed with a decimal point and no exponent. To express a real number *without* the exponent, you must include a second write parameter for the width of the decimal part of the field:

```
<real value> : <field width> : <decimal width>
```

The value <decimal width> indicates how many decimal places are to be displayed. For example:

```
R := 7.775;
S := 0.123456789;
T := 7765;

Writeln(Bar,R:10:3,Bar);
Writeln(Bar,R:10:1,Bar);
Writeln(Bar,R:5:2,Bar);
Writeln(Bar,S:6:6,Bar);
Writeln(Bar,S:12:6,Bar);
Writeln(Bar,S:12:12,Bar);
Writeln(Bar,S:5,Bar);
Writeln(Bar,T:5:2,Bar);
Writeln(Bar,T:5,Bar);
Writeln(Bar,T:6:6,Bar);
```

This code produces the following output:

```
|     7.775|
|       7.8|
| 7.77|
|0.123457|
|    0.123457|
|  1.2345678E-01|
| 1.E-01|
|7765.00|
```

```
|  8.E+03|
|  7.7650003E+03|
```

A reminder here: You cannot begin a fractional real number (such as .123456789, above) with a decimal point. You *must* begin the number with a 0 as shown, or suffer this error during compilation:

```
Error 42: Error in expression
```

WRITING TO THE SYSTEM PRINTER

Your printer is a physical device that may be accessed as a text file. You have the option of assigning one of the DOS device names LPT1, LPT2, LPT3, COM1, or COM2 to a text file of your choosing and **Reset**ing that text file, or using the standard unit **Printer**. **Printer** assigns DOS device name LPT1 to a text file named **LST**, and opens **LST** before the main program begins execution. Thus **LST** will be immediately available to your code without any action from you other than to **USE** the **Printer** unit. Either way you set up a printer text file; writing any text to that text file will print the text on your printer:

```
PROGRAM PrinTest;

USES Printer;

VAR
  PrintDevice : Text;

BEGIN
  Assign(PrintDevice,'LPT1');        { Open a printer file }
  Rewrite(PrintDevice);

  Writeln(PrintDevice,'This text will now appear on the printer.');
  Writeln(LST,'This will too, and it''s easier!');
END.
```

Using **Writeln** to the printer will end each line with a carriage return/linefeed pair that will bring the printhead to the left margin of the next line. Using **Write** will leave the printhead where it is after printing the text:

```
Write(LST,'Active drive units now include: ');
FOR Drive := 'A' to 'P' DO
  IF CheckDrive(Drive) THEN Write(LST,Drive,' ');
Writeln(LST,' ');
```

This will print:

```
Active drive units now include: A B D M N
```

Even if you open a printer file yourself (rather than use the **Printer** unit's file **LST**), you need not close the file.

14.4 IOResult and EOF

IORESULT

Working with creatures like disk files that lie outside the borders of the program itself is risky business. You can build machinery into your program to make sure that the program never attempts to divide by zero, or never attempts to index past the bounds of an array. But how do you make sure that (when you want to open a disk file) the file is on the disk and the disk is in the proper disk drive?

The program does not have absolute control over disk files in the way it has absolute control over numbers, arrays, and other variables. The only way to be sure a file is on the disk is to go out and try to read it. If the file isn't out there, there must be some way to recover gracefully.

The runtime code that Turbo Pascal adds to every program it compiles guards against runtime errors such as an attempt to open (for reading) a file that does not exist. Such an attempt will generate an I/O error 01: File does not exist. Your program will terminate and, if you are running from within the IDE, Turbo Pascal will begin searching for the location of the **Reset** statement that tried to open the file.

Obviously, if there is a legal possibility of a file not existing on the disk, you cannot allow your program simply to crash. Better to determine that an error has happened *without* crashing, so that the program could do something about it, like create a new file or look somewhere else for the old one. Turbo Pascal provides the **IOResult** function to let the program know how successful it has been in striking a path to the outside world. It is predeclared by Turbo Pascal this way:

```
FUNCTION IOResult : Integer
```

After each I/O statement is executed, a value is given to the **IOResult** function. This value can then be tested to determine whether the I/O statement completed successfully. A 0 value indicates that the I/O operation went normally; anything else constitutes an error code.

However, the runtime code's error traps will still crash your program when an error is encountered, whether or not you use **IOResult**. To keep the program running in spite of the error, you must disable the error trap with the compiler directive **$I**. This is done by surrounding the I/O statement with an **{$I-}** directive (turn traps off) and an **{$I+}** directive (turn traps on again).

For example:

```
Assign(MyFile,'B:BOWLING.DAT');
{$I-} Reset(MyFile); {$I+} { Suspend error traps during Reset }
IF IOResult <> 0 THEN
  BEGIN
    Beep;
```

```
    Writeln('>>The bowling scores file cannot be opened.');
    Writeln('  Make sure the scores disk is in the B: drive');
    Writeln('  and press (CR) again:')
  END;
```

This code snippet checks **IOResult** immediately after executing a **Reset** to open a file for read. If **IOResult** returns a nonzero value, the program displays a message to the operator.

IOResult is cleared to zero and refilled with a new value at the beginning of *all* I/O primitives. This includes **Readln** and **Writeln** when used (as we have been using them all along) to talk to the keyboard and the screen via device files **Input** and **Output**. This means you *cannot* directly write the value returned by **IOResult** to the screen or to a file!

```
{$I-} Reset(MyFile); {$I+}
Writeln('The result of that Reset is ',IOResult);  { No! }
```

No matter what happens when **Reset(MyFile)** is executed, the above snippet will *always* display:

```
The result of that Reset is 0
```

Given that restriction, it is probably good practice to assign the value of **IOResult** to an integer variable immediately after an I/O statement and work with the integer variable rather than the function itself.

Another example of **IOResult** in use lies in the **Averager** program in the next section. **Averager** opens and reads a binary file of integers until the end of the file and then averages the integers it has read. If it cannot open the file of integers, it recovers and issues an error message with the help of **IOResult**.

EOF

Knowing where a disk file ends is critical. A built-in function called **EOF** (End Of File) provides this service to your programs. **EOF** is predeclared this way:

```
FUNCTION EOF(FileVar : <any file type>) : Boolean
```

FileVar can be any legal file type. The EOF function returns **True** as soon as the last item in the file has been read. At that point the file pointer points just past the end of data in the file, and *no further reads should be attempted*. A runtime error will occur if you try to read beyond the end of a file. This applies to both text files and binary files.

Turbo Pascal's runtime code determines **EOF** by using information stored by DOS for each disk file. For text files it keeps a count of characters read from the file and compares that to the size of the file at each read; when bytes read equals or exceeds the number of bytes DOS says are in the file, **EOF** returns **True**. For binary files, Turbo Pascal knows the size of each record read (since every file is a **FILE OF <something>**, where **<something>** is a declared data type with a fixed size) and compares a similar count of records read against the DOS file size figure.

Text file EOF is also triggered by the presence of a CTRL-Z character ($1A) in the file. For CP/M-80, this was the *only* way to determine true EOF, since CP/M only kept count of the number of 128-byte blocks in a file, not the actual number of bytes. The CTRL-Z was the only way to tell where within the last block of data the last significant character actually fell.

DOS knows exactly how many bytes are in every file at all times, so with DOS text files, Turbo Pascal reports EOF either when DOS indicated the last character had been read, or when a CTRL-Z was encountered in the text stream from the file.

The following program assumes a binary file of integers named INTEGERS.BIN. (I provide such a file on the listings diskette for this book, or you can generate your own.) It reads all the integers in the file, testing **EOF** at each read. As it reads each integer it keeps a running total and a running count, and then produces an average value for all the integers in the file. Note the use of the **$I** compiler directive when opening the file:

```
{----------------------------------------------------------------}
{                          Averager                              }
{                                                                }
{            Binary file I/O demonstration program               }
{                                                                }
{                       by Jeff Duntemann                        }
{                       Turbo Pascal V7.0                        }
{                       Last update 1/31/93                      }
{                                                                }
{   From: BORLAND PASCAL FROM SQUARE ONE   by Jeff Duntemann    }
{----------------------------------------------------------------}

PROGRAM Averager;

VAR
   IntFile        : FILE OF Integer;
   I,J,Count      : Integer;
   Average,Total  : Real;

BEGIN
   Assign(IntFile,'INTEGERS.BIN');
   {$I-} Reset(IntFile); {$I+}
   I := IOResult;
   IF I <> 0 THEN
     BEGIN
       Writeln('>>File INTEGERS.BIN is missing or damaged.');
       Writeln('  Please investigate and run the program again.')
     END
   ELSE
     BEGIN
```

```
         Count := 0; Total := 0.0;
         WHILE NOT EOF(IntFile) DO
           BEGIN
             Read(IntFile,J);
             IF NOT EOF(IntFile) THEN
               BEGIN
                 Count := Count + 1;
                 Total := Total + J
               END;
           END;
         Close(IntFile);
         AVERAGE := Total / Count;
         Writeln;
         Writeln('>>There are ',Count,' integers in INTEGERS.BIN.');
         Writeln('  Their average value is ',Average:10:6,'.');
       END
     END.
```

14.5 FileSize and FilePos

Turbo Pascal supplies two built-in functions for determining the size of a binary disk file and the position of the file pointer within a disk file. Note that **FileSize** and **FilePos** may *not* be used with text files!

FileSize is predeclared this way:

```
FUNCTION FileSize(FileVar : <binary filetype>) : LongInt
```

The function **FileSize** returns a long integer count of the number of items stored in the file. **FileVar** is an open binary file. (*Not* a text file.) An empty file will return a zero value.

Function **FilePos** is predeclared this way:

```
FUNCTION FilePos(FileVar : <binary filetype>) : LongInt
```

A binary file's file pointer is a counter that indicates the next item to be read from the file. The **FilePos** function returns the current value of a file's file pointer. **FileVar** is an open binary file. (*Not* a text file.) The first item in a file is item number 0. When a file is first opened, its file pointer is set to 0. Each **Read** operation will increment the file pointer by one. The **Seek** procedure (see Section 14.9) will put the file pointer to a particular value to enable random access to a binary file.

14.6 Miscellaneous File Routines

The last group of Turbo Pascal file routines we'll discuss are all extensions to the ISO Standard Pascal definition. Most Pascals have routines like these, but sadly, their invocation syntax and parameters vary widely. Any time you use file I/O, you can be almost certain that your programs will be nonportable. (There is no way even to close a file in ISO Pascal!) This is yet another reason why I have not stressed adherence to the ISO Standard in this book. If file I/O cannot be made portable, you might as well hang it up.

FLUSH

Every file has a buffer in memory, and when you write to a file, the data you've written actually goes to the buffer rather than directly to the physical disk file. Periodically, based on decisions it makes on its own, the Turbo Pascal runtime code will flush the buffer to disk, actually transferring the data to the physical disk file. You can force such a flush to disk with the **Flush** procedure. It is predeclared this way:

```
PROCEDURE  Flush(<filevar>);
```

<filevar> is any file variable opened for output. **Flush** has no effect on a file opened for input. **IOResult** will return a 0 value if the file was flushed success-fully. *Do not use Flush on a closed file!*

CLOSE

Closing a file that you have opened ensures that all data written to the file is physically transferred from the file buffer to disk. In Turbo Pascal the **Close** procedure does this job:

```
PROCEDURE  Close(<filevar>);
```

As with **Flush**, **<filevar>** is any opened file. It is all right to close a file that has been closed already.

Closing files that had not been changed while open used to be optional. With Turbo Pascal 3.0 and later, this is not the case. You *must* close all opened disk files to keep the operating system happy. Turbo Pascal 3.0 and later use DOS file handles, of which there are only 16 available. File handles, once allocated by opening a file, will not be freed for further use until the file is closed. If you neglect to close a few temporary files, you may soon run out of file handles.

And of course, if you exit a program before closing a file that has been written to, the runtime code makes no guarantee that all records written to the file buffer will actually make it out to the physical disk file. As with most file-related routines, **IOResult** will be set to 0 if the file was closed successfully. Otherwise, **IOResult** will contain a nonzero DOS error code.

ERASE

Deleting a disk file from within a program is done with the **Erase** procedure:

```
PROCEDURE Erase(<filevar>);
```

<filevar> is any file variable that has been assigned to a physical file. In other words, if you try to **Erase** a file variable to which no physical file has yet been assigned, the runtime code has no way of knowing which file you want to delete:

```
VAR
   NumFile : FILE OF Integer;

Assign(NumFile,'VALUES.BIN');
Erase(NumFile);
```

Do not attempt to **Erase** an open file. Close it first, or the results could be unpredictable. **IOResult** will return a 0 if the file was successfully deleted.

RENAME

Turbo Pascal gives you the ability to change the name of a disk file from within a program with the **Rename** procedure:

```
PROCEDURE Rename(<filevar>; NewName : String80);
```

<filevar> is any file that has been assigned to a physical file with **Assign**. As with **Erase**, trying to rename a file without connecting it with a physical file is meaningless.

Use **Rename** with some caution. It is possible to rename a file to a name that another disk file already uses. No error will result, but you will have two files with the same name, and getting the *right* one when you need one of the two files will be a problem indeed.

As with **Erase**, renaming an open file is a no-no. **IOResult** will return a 0 if the file was successfully renamed.

APPEND

Append provides a way to quickly move the file pointer to the end of a text file without having to explicitly read the file and throw away the characters read up to EOF.

Append is used instead of **Rewrite**:

```
PROCEDURE Append(<filevar>);
```

<filevar> must first be assigned to some physical file before **Append** can be used. The contents of the file are not destroyed, as they are with **Rewrite**. The file is opened for output, however, at EOF. Adding text to the file with **Write** or **Writeln** will position the new text at and following EOF.

IOResult will return a 0 if the operation was successful. Keep in mind that **Append** may be used *only* with text files. Attempting to use **Append** with a non-text file type will trigger

```
Error 63: Invalid file type
```

TRUNCATE

Truncate is conceptually similar to **Append**. Both prepare a file for the adding of additional data via **Write** or (for text files) **Writeln**. Unlike **Append**, **Truncate** may be used with any type of file: text, binary, or untyped. **Truncate** is predeclared this way:

```
PROCEDURE Truncate(<filevar>);
```

When executed, **Truncate** chops a file off at the current position of the file pointer. In other words, if you have read part way down a file and execute **Truncate**, the remainder of the file will be thrown away. The file is then ready for output, even if you opened the file with **Reset**.

Standard Pascal does not allow writing to a file that contains data. When a file is opened for output in Standard Pascal, all previous contents of the file are destroyed. This defies the logic of the real world, in which files are built by an ongoing process of reading, writing, updating, and deleting. **Append** and **Truncate** make real-world use of data files a great deal more convenient than in Standard Pascal.

14.7 Using Text Files

Given its variable-length string type, its built-in string functions and procedures, and Standard Pascal's **Readln** and **Writeln** procedures, Turbo Pascal is a natural choice for working with text files. In this section we'll show you a real-life example of a useful program for manipulating text files.

FILTER PROGRAMS

There is a whole class of programs that read a file in chunks, perform some manipulation on the chunks, and then write the transformed chunks back out to another file. This type of program is called a "filter" program because it filters a file through some sort of processing step. The data changes according to a set of rules as it passes through the processing part of the program.

A good example would be a program to force all lowercase characters in a file to uppercase. Turbo Pascal is not sensitive to character case but some programs and language processors (particularly COBOL and APL) do not interpret lowercase characters correctly. To pass a text file between Pascal and COBOL, all lowercase characters in the file must be set to uppercase.

A filter program to accomplish this task would work this way:

```
Open the input file for read and create a new output file.
While not end-of-file keep doing this:
   Read a line from the input text file.
   Force all lowercase characters in the line to uppercase.
   Write the line out to the output text file.
Close both files.
```

This basic structure is the same for all text file filter programs, except for the processing that is actually done line-by-line. You could just as easily force all uppercase characters in the line to lowercase, count the words in the line, remove all BEL characters (CTRL-G) from the line, expand HT (tab; CTRL-I) characters to 8 space characters, and so on.

You could in fact combine two or more processes into one filter program; say, force lowercase to uppercase and count characters.

A TWO-WAY CASE FILTER PROGRAM

The program shown below can perform two distinct functions: It can force all lowercase characters in a text file to uppercase, or all uppercase characters to lowercase. (Not both at the same time, however.) Which of the two actions is taken depends on a parameter entered on the command line:

```
CASE UP B:COBOL.SRC          Forces lower to upper

CASE DOWN B:PASTEXT.SRC       Forces upper to lower
```

Note that the name of the program source *file* is "CASE.PAS," while the name of the *program* (from the program statement) is "**Caser.**" The reason is that **CASE** is a reserved word and may not be used as a programmer-defined identifier within a program. However, you may name a program source code *file* anything you like, and in this case (so to speak) **CASE** is the best name for the actual runnable program file on disk.

CASE.PAS incorporates a good many of the file routines we've been discussing in this chapter, and understanding how it works will help you understand how those routines interact within a program.

```
{ --------------------------------------------------------------- }
{                            Case                                 }
{                                                                 }
{ An upper/lower case conversion filter program for text files }
{                                                                 }
{                       by Jeff Duntemann                         }
{                       Turbo Pascal V7.0                         }
{                       Last update 1/31/93                       }
{                                                                 }
{    From: BORLAND PASCAL FROM SQUARE ONE   by Jeff Duntemann    }
{ --------------------------------------------------------------- }


PROGRAM Caser;   { "Caser" because "CASE" is a reserved word... }

CONST
  Upper = True;
  Lower = False;
```

```
TYPE
  String40   = String[40];
  String80   = String[80];
  String255  = String[255];

VAR
  I,J,K      : Integer;
  Quit       : Boolean;
  Ch         : Char;
  WorkFile   : Text;
  TempFile   : Text;
  NewCase    : Boolean;
  WorkLine   : String80;
  WorkName   : String80;
  TempName   : String80;
  CaseTag    : String80;



{$I FRCECASE.SRC }     { Described in Section 10.4 }



{>>>>MakeTemp<<<<}

PROCEDURE MakeTemp(FileName : String80; VAR TempName : String80);

VAR
  Point : Integer;

BEGIN
  Point := Pos('.',FileName);
  IF Point > 0 THEN Delete(FileName,Point,(Length(FileName)-Point)+1);
  TempName := Concat(FileName,'.$$$')
END;



{ CASER MAIN }

BEGIN
  Quit := False;
  IF ParamCount < 2 THEN    { Missing parms error }
    BEGIN
      Writeln('>>CASE<<  V2.00  By Jeff Duntemann');
      Writeln('          From the book, BORLAND PASCAL FROM SQUARE ONE');
      Writeln('          Bantam Books, 1993');
      Writeln;
      Writeln
      ('This program forces all characters of a text file to either ');
```

```
        Writeln
        ('upper or lower case, as requested.  Characters already in ');
        Writeln('the requested case are not disturbed.');
        Writeln;
        Writeln('CALLING SYNTAX:');
        Writeln;
        Writeln('CASE UP|DOWN <filespec>');
        Writeln;
        Writeln('For example, to force all lowercase characters of file');
        Writeln('FOO.COB to uppercase, invoke CASE this way:');
        Writeln;
        Writeln('CASE UP FOO.COB');
        Writeln;
      END
  ELSE
    BEGIN
      WorkName := ParamStr(2);
      Assign(WorkFile,WorkName);  { Attempt to open the file }
      {$I-} Reset(WorkFile); {$I+}
      IF IOResult <>0 THEN
        BEGIN
          Writeln('<<Error!>> File ',WorkName,' does not exist.');
          Writeln
          ('          Invoke CASE again with an existing FileName.');
        END
      ELSE
        BEGIN                       { See if UP/DOWN parm was entered }
          CaseTag := ParamStr(1);
          CaseTag := ForceCase(Upper,CaseTag);
          IF CaseTag = 'UP' THEN NewCase := Upper ELSE
            IF CaseTag = 'DOWN' THEN NewCase := Lower ELSE
              Quit := True;
          IF Quit THEN
            BEGIN
              Writeln
              ('<<Error!>> The case parameter must be "UP" or "DOWN."');
              Writeln
              ('        Invoke CASE again using either "UP" or "DOWN".');
            END
          ELSE
            BEGIN
              Write('Forcing case ');
              IF NewCase THEN Write('up ') ELSE Write('down ');
              MakeTemp(WorkName,TempName);
              { Generate temporary FileName }
              Assign(TempFile,TempName);    { Open temporary file }
              Rewrite(TempFile);
```

```
                  WHILE NOT EOF(WorkFile) DO
                    BEGIN
                      Readln(WorkFile,WorkLine);
                      Write('.');                   { Dot shows it's working }
                      WorkLine := ForceCase(NewCase,WorkLine);
                      Writeln(TempFile,WorkLine)
                    END;
                  Close(TempFile);        { Close the temporary file }
                  Close(WorkFile);        { Close original source file... }
                  Erase(WorkFile);           { ...and delete it. }
                  Rename(TempFile,WorkName);
                  { Temporary file becomes source }
                END
            END
        END
    END.
```

Most of **Caser** is actually setup: making sure files exist; making sure valid commands were entered at the command line, and so on. The real meat of the program is simplicity itself:

```
WHILE NOT EOF(WorkFile) DO
  BEGIN
    Readln(WorkFile,WorkLine);
    Write('.');                   { Dot shows it's working }
    WorkLine := ForceCase(NewCase,WorkLine);
    Writeln(TempFile,WorkLine);
  END;
```

This loop executes repeatedly as long as there are lines to be read in **WorkFile**. A line is read, **ForceCase** adjusts the case of the characters in the line, and then the line is written to **TempFile**. When **Readln** reads the last line in the text file, the **EOF** function will immediately return **True**. The text file is "filtered" through **ForceCase** into a temporary file. When the original file has been read completely, it is erased with **Erase** and the temporary file is renamed to become the original file.

If you're nervous about deleting your original text file (and that is not a totally unhealthy feeling) you could close it with **Close** instead of **Erase** and then give **TempFile** a new file extension instead of .$$$. (I have used ".ZZZ" in the past.) If you're careless about backing up important files, this is a very good idea.

14.8 Using Binary Files

A text file is distinctive in being the *only* type of Pascal file that may contain records of varying lengths. Pascal treats text files specially in other ways, by limiting the range of characters that may legally reside in the file, and by the EOF character that accurately flags where written data ends. Binary files, by contrast, are given none of this special treatment.

A binary file is a file containing some number of data items of a given type:

```
TYPE
  KeyFile = FILE OF KeyRec;
  CfgFile = FILE OF CfgRec;
  IntFile = FILE OF Integer;
```

Only one data type may be stored in a binary file. You could not, for example, write one variable of type **KeyRec** and another variable of type **CfgRec** to the same logical file.

Each instance of a data item in a binary file is called a "record," whether the data item is actually a Pascal record type or not. One integer stored in an **IntFile** as defined above could be considered a record of the **IntFile**.

One common use of binary files puts only one record in the file: the "configuration file." Consider a complicated program that performs file maintenance and telecommunications. The program is used at a great many sites owned by a large corporation. The names of the files it works with change from site to site, as do the telephone numbers it must call to link with the host mainframe computer.

Rather than "hard-code" things like telephone numbers into the Pascal source file, it makes more sense to store them out to a configuration file. The easiest way is to define a record type containing fields for all the site-specific information:

```
TYPE
  CfgRec  = RECORD
              SiteName    : String;
              SiteCode    : Integer;
              AuthOp      : String;
              HostCode    : Integer;
              PhoneNum    : String;
              P1FileName  : String;
              P2FileName  : String;
              AXFileName  : String
            END;

  CfgFile = FILE OF CfgRec;

VAR
  SiteFile : CfgFile;
  CfgData  : CfgRec;
```

All the data items that change from site to site are present in one single record. When loaded with the correct site values for a particular site, the record can be easily written to disk:

```
Assign(SiteFile,'B:SITEDATA.CFG');
Rewrite(SiteFile);
Write(SiteFile,CfgData);
Close(SiteFile);
```

Here, once **SiteFile** is opened, the single **CfgRec** is written to disk with the **Write** statement.

14.9 Using Random-Access Files

All file access methods we have discussed so far have been *sequential*. That is, when you open a file you may access the first record, and then the second, and then the third, and so on until you run out of records. All records in the file are accessible, but only at the cost of always starting at the beginning and scanning past all records up to the one you really need.

In contrast, *random access* of a file means the ability to open a file and simply—*zap!*—read record #241, without having to read anything else first. Then, without any further scanning, simply—*zap*—write data to record #73. Turbo Pascal gives you this ability through the **Seek** procedure.

Random access is possible with all binary files. Text files may *not* be accessed randomly; for random access to work, all records in a file must be the same length. Binary files that were written sequentially with **Write** may be read or rewritten randomly by using **Seek**. Binary files written randomly by using **Seek** may be read sequentially with **Read**.

Seek is not part of ISO Standard Pascal, although several other Pascals including UCSD Pascal implement it much the same way. **Seek** is predeclared this way:

```
PROCEDURE Seek(FileVar : <binary filetype>; RecNum : LongInt);
```

Seek manipulates the file pointer of opened binary file **FileVar**. **Seek** may *not* be used with text files! It sets the file pointer of **FileVar** to **RecNum**. The next **Read** done on **FileVar** will read the **RecNum**'th record from the file:

```
VAR
   Keys : KeyFile;
   AKey : KeyRec;

Assign(Keys,'NAMES.KEY');
Reset(Keys);

Seek(Keys,17);
Read(Keys,AKey)
```

In this example, record 17 of the file **NAMES.KEY** is read from disk and assigned to the variable **AKey**.

You should be careful not to **Seek** past the end of the file. I/O error #91: Seek beyond end-of-file will result. Testing **FileSize** before **Seek**ing is always a good idea.

Turbo Pascal 3.0 and earlier did not have type **LongInt** and used integer variables to specify record positions for small files. A separate procedure requiring a parameter of type **Real**, **LongSeek**, was used for files with more than 32K records. **LongSeek** is still available in the **Turbo3** compatibility unit, but you should convert any code using it to the cleaner and faster **Seek** using long integers.

A BINARY SEARCH PROCEDURE

Finding a particular record in a file is perhaps the central problem of all business-related computer science. If you know the record number there is no problem;

you either go directly to the record with **Seek** or scan sequentially through the file with **Read**, counting records up to the desired number. But in most cases you want to locate a record *based on what's in the record*.

A sequential search is simple enough: You start reading at the beginning of the file, and test each record to see if it's the one you want. If it's a big file, or if your search criteria are complicated enough, such a search can take minutes or even hours on hard-disk based systems. Since such a search ties up the computer completely while the search is underway, it can become a costly way to work.

There are many ways to approach the searching of files, but no method is as easy to understand and use as that of *binary search*.

Binary searches depend upon the file being sorted on the data you wish to search for. In other words, if you want to find a person's name in a file, the records in the file (each containing someone's name) must be in alphabetical order by the name field.

We presented a couple of very fast sorting methods in earlier sections. The Shell sort and quicksort can both be modified to sort any type of data structure that can exist in an array. Sorting a file involves loading its records from disk into an array, sorting the array, and writing the sorted records back out to the file on disk. The file can then be binary searched.

Briefly, binary searching involves dividing a file in half repeatedly, making sure that the desired record is somewhere in the half that is retained at each division. In time the halves divide down to nothing, and if the record is not found at that point it does not exist in the file.

In detail: The binary search procedure is passed a file to search (called a key file for reasons we'll explain shortly); the number of records in the file; and a data item (in our example, a string) containing the data we're searching for.

Starting out, a variable **Low** contains the record number of the first record in the file (1) and a variable **High** contains the record number of the last record in the file. **High** and **Low** are always the bounds of the region we will be searching. At the outset, they encompass the entire file.

The search begins: The procedure calculates a record number halfway between **High** and **Low** and stores that in **Mid**. The record at **Mid** is read and tested. If the data part of the record at **Mid** matches our "key," the search is over. It probably won't happen quite so quickly.

Because the file is sorted, we can state this: If our key is *greater* than the data at **Mid**, we must now search the half of the file *above* **Mid**. If our key is *less* than the data at **Mid**, we must search the half of the file *below* **Mid**.

The procedure thus sets up a new **High** and **Low** for the half of the file in which our desired record must exist. The process begins again, now with only half of the file. A new **Mid** is calculated, and the record at the new **Mid** is read and tested. If **Mid** isn't the record we want, we have our choice of two new, smaller sections of the file to search. And so we continue, setting up **High** and **Low** as the bounds of a still smaller section of the file.

This continues until one of two things happens: 1) We find that the record we read at **Mid** is the record we want, or 2) **Mid** collides with either **High** or **Low**. If that happens, the search is over without finding what we want. Our key does not exist in the file.

(Of course, if the file is not fully sorted, our desired record may in fact exist in the file and yet the binary search may not find it. The file must be completely and correctly sorted or all bets are off!)

The actual Pascal code for such a binary search function follows. **KeySearch** requires the following type definitions prior to its own definition:

```
TYPE
   KeyRec = RECORD
               Ref     : Integer;
               KeyData : String30;
            END;

   KeyFile = FILE OF KeyRec;
```

The **KeySearch** routine itself is shown below:

```
{->>>>KeySearch<<<<------------------------------------------------}
{                                                                  }
{ Filename : KSEARCH.SRC - Last Modified 2/2/93                    }
{                                                                  }
{ This routine searches file Keys for key records containing       }
{ the key string contained in parameter MatchIt.  The method      }
{ is your classic binary search, and the key record type is        }
{ defined as the type shown below:                                 }
{                                                                  }
{      KeyRec = RECORD                                             }
{                  Ref     : Integer;                             }
{                  KeyData : String30;                            }
{               END;                                              }
{                                                                  }
{ The function returns True if a matching record is found,         }
{ else False.                                                     }
{                                                                  }
{   From: BORLAND PASCAL FROM SQUARE ONE  by Jeff Duntemann       }
{-----------------------------------------------------------------}


FUNCTION KeySearch(VAR Keys      : KeyFile;
                   VAR KeyRef    : Integer;
                       MatchIt   : String80) : Boolean;

VAR High,Low,Mid : Integer;
    SearchRec    : KeyRec;
    Found        : Boolean;
    Collided     : Boolean;
    RecCount     : Integer;
```

```
BEGIN
  KeyRef := 0;                       { Initialize variables     }
  RecCount := FileSize(Keys);
  High := RecCount;
  Low := 0;
  KeySearch := False; Found := False; Collided := False;
  Mid := (Low + High) DIV 2;   { Calc first midpoint      }

  IF RecCount > 0 THEN            { Don't search if file empty}
    REPEAT
      Seek(Keys,Mid);            { Read midpoint record      }
      Read(Keys,SearchRec);
      { Collision between Mid & Low or Mid & High?   }
      IF (Low = Mid) OR (High = Mid) THEN Collided := True;
      IF MatchIt = SearchRec.KeyData THEN  { Found it! }
        BEGIN
          Found := True;             { Set found flag...    }
          KeySearch := True;         { ...function value... }
          KeyRef := SearchRec.Ref  { ...and file key      }
        END
      ELSE                { No luck...divide & try again   }
        BEGIN
          IF MatchIt > SearchRec.KeyData THEN Low := Mid
            ELSE High := Mid;        { Halve the field  }
          Mid := (Low + High) DIV 2;    { Recalc midpoint }
          KeyRef := Mid { Save Mid in parm }
        END
    UNTIL Collided OR Found
END;
```

KEYED FILES

KeySearch has some machinery in it that goes beyond simply searching a file for a matching data string. **KeySearch** returns an integer parameter **KeyRef**, which it takes from the **KeyRec** record it locates. The **Ref** field of the **KeyRec** type allows us to build a *keyed* file system.

It is both difficult and hazardous to sort a large data file composed of large ("wide") records. It's difficult because the entire file (or big chunks of it for a sort/merge system) must be in memory at one time; hazardous because sorting involves rewriting the entire file after every sort. Rewriting an entire file greatly increases vulnerability to disk errors that can corrupt data in the file, or even (worst case) make the file unreadable.

Furthermore, sorting a file involves swapping many large records around, even if the part of the record that is sorted (called the *key field*) is a very small part of the entire record. A lot of that swapping time is simply wasted.

It would be better, faster, and safer to extract and sort only that part of the record that needs to be sorted. This is what a key file is for. The **KeyData** field is the data that is sorted. The **Ref** field is the record number of the record in the main data file from which the **KeyData** field was extracted. If we binary search a key file for a given string, **Ref** will give us the record number where we can find the rest of the data associated with that string. In other words, if we binary search a key file containing only names, **Ref** will allow us to read the record containing the address, phone number, and other information associated with the name we found. See Fig. 14.1.

The following simple program assumes the existence of a data file and key file sorted on the data file's **Name** field. (Two such files are provided on the listings diskette for this book.) The program waits for a name to be entered, then searches the key file for the name. If the name is present in the key file, the program reads the data record for the rest of the data associated with that name, and displays it.

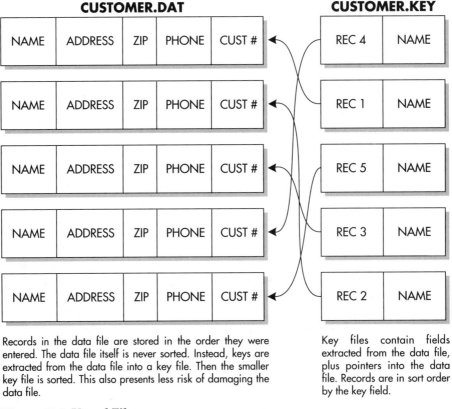

Records in the data file are stored in the order they were entered. The data file itself is never sorted. Instead, keys are extracted from the data file into a key file. Then the smaller key file is sorted. This also presents less risk of damaging the data file.

Key files contain fields extracted from the data file, plus pointers into the data file. Records are in sort order by the key field.

Figure 14.1 Keyed Files

```
{-------------------------------------------------------------------}
{                          ShowName                                 }
{                                                                   }
{           Keyed file binary search demo program                   }
{                                                                   }
{                       by Jeff Duntemann                           }
{                       Turbo Pascal V7.0                           }
{                       Last update 2/2/93                          }
{                                                                   }
{   From: BORLAND PASCAL FROM SQUARE ONE  by Jeff Duntemann         }
{-------------------------------------------------------------------}


{ Unlike most programs in this book, this program requires two }
{ external files to operate: FRIENDS.NAP and FRIENDS.KEY. The }
{ two files will be included on the source listings diskette.  }
{ FRIENDS.NAP is a file of NAPRec containing some number of    }
{ name/address/phone records.  FRIENDS.KEY is a sorted key     }
{ file containing keys extracted from FRIENDS.NAP.  You can    }
{ write a utility to extract keys from a .NAP file and sort    }
{ them using either the SHELLSORT or QUIKSORT procedures given }
{ in Chapter 7. }


PROGRAM ShowName;

TYPE
  String3    = STRING[3];
  String6    = STRING[6];
  String30   = STRING[30];
  String40   = STRING[40];
  String80   = STRING[80];
  String255  = STRING[255];

  NAPRec = RECORD
              Name    : String30;
              Address : String30;
              City    : String30;
              State   : String3;
              Zip     : String6
           END;

  NAPFile = FILE OF NAPRec;

  KeyRec  = RECORD
              REF : Integer;
```

```
                  KeyData : String30
               END;

   KeyFile = FILE OF KeyRec;


VAR I,J,K     : Integer;
    RecNum    : Integer;
    Parm      : String80;
  . WorkRec   : NAPRec;
    TempKey   : KeyRec;
    WorkFile  : NAPFile;
    WorkKey   : KeyFile;



{$I KSEARCH.SRC}    { Contains KeySearch }


{ SHOWNAME MAIN }

BEGIN
  IF ParamCount < 1 THEN            { Missing parms error }
    BEGIN
      Writeln
      ('<<Error!>> You must enter a name on the command line:');
      Writeln('          A>SHOWNAME Duntemann*Jeff ');
      Writeln
      ('          Or else enter "*" to show all keys in key file.')
    END
  ELSE
    BEGIN
      Parm := ParamStr(1);
      Assign(WorkFile,'FRIENDS.NAP');  { Open the names data file }
      Reset(WorkFile);
      Assign(WorkKey,'FRIENDS.KEY');   { Open the names key file }
      Reset(WorkKey);
      IF Parm = '*' THEN
        WHILE NOT EOF(WorkKey) DO
          BEGIN
            Read(WorkKey,TempKey);
            Writeln(TempKey.KeyData);
          END
      ELSE
       IF KeySearch(WorkKey,RecNum,Parm) THEN  { If key is found...}
         BEGIN                      { We have record # into data file }
            Seek(WorkFile,RecNum);  { Seek to record # in data file }
            Read(WorkFile,WorkRec); { Read data record from data file }
```

```
            WITH WorkRec DO            { and display the name/address data }
               BEGIN
                 Writeln('>>NAME    : ',Name);
                 Writeln('  ADDRESS : ',Address);
                 Writeln('  CITY    : ',City);
                 Writeln('  STATE   : ',Zip);
               END
          END
        ELSE
           Writeln('>>Sorry, ',Parm,' not found.');
        Close(WorkFile);
        Close(WorkKey);
      END
   END.
```

Records are added to the data file at the end of the file, and are never rewritten unless the data must be changed somehow.

Another important advantage of a keyed file system is that your main data file can effectively be sorted on two or more of its fields at the same time. You can just as easily have a key file keyed on the **Address** or **Zipcode** field. There is the disk space overhead required for the additional key files, but that is nothing like the space it would take to hold the same data file duplicated in its entirety once for each field!

14.10 Using MS-DOS Structured Directories

Version 2.0 and later of MS-DOS supports *structured directories;* that is, directories that may contain not only files but also subsidiary directories called *subdirectories.* These subdirectories are functionally identical to the root directory on a disk, and may contain files or subdirectories of their own.

Versions 1 and 2 of Turbo Pascal did not contain support for structured directories. Versions 3.0 and later support DOS structured directories. This section describes that support.

GETDIR

This procedure allows Turbo Pascal programs to determine what the current directory is on any drisk drive on the system. It is predeclared this way:

```
PROCEDURE GetDir(Drive : Byte; VAR CurrentDirectory : String);
```

The input to **GetDir** is **Drive**, a **Byte** parameter containing a value that specifies which disk drive is to be queried. The correspondence between values passed in **Drive** and physical drive specifiers runs like this:

```
0 = The logged drive
1 = A:
```

```
2 = B:
3 = C:
```

and so on.

GetDir's output is **CurrentDirectory**, a string that returns the path of the current directory on the specified disk drive.

The following program will display the current directories for the logged drive and drives A through D:

```
{-----------------------------------------------------------------}
{                           ShowDir                               }
{                                                                 }
{             "GetDir" demonstration program                      }
{                                                                 }
{                    by Jeff Duntemann                            }
{                    Turbo Pascal V7.0                            }
{                    Last update 2/2/93                           }
{                                                                 }
{   From: BORLAND PASCAL FROM SQUARE ONE   by Jeff Duntemann      }
{-----------------------------------------------------------------}


PROGRAM ShowDir;

VAR
  I     : Byte;
  Error : Integer;
  CurrentDirectory : String;

BEGIN
  FOR I := 0 TO 4 DO
    BEGIN
      GetDir(I,CurrentDirectory);
      IF I = 0 THEN Write('Logged drive: ')
        ELSE Write('Drive        ',Chr(64+I),': ');
      Writeln(CurrentDirectory)
    END
END.
```

On some machines there must be a diskette in any diskette drives when **ShowDir** is run, or DOS will generate its familiar "Abort, Retry, or Ignore?" error. You can press I for Ignore to continue program execution. On my own machine this is not the case, but I've seen machines where the diskettes must be present to avoid the DOS message.

One unfortunate weakness of **GetDir** is that it does not return any error condition for checking on a disk drive that doesn't exist; for example, if you have a drive A: and drive C:, but no drive B:, **IOResult** returns 0 in all cases.

Determining what disk drives actually exist from within Turbo Pascal is not trivial, and I have not worked out a totally reliable way of doing so in all cases.

MKDIR

Creating a new subdirectory is the job of **MkDir**, predeclared this way:

```
PROCEDURE MkDir(NewDirectory : String);
```

When invoked, **MkDir** will create a new subdirectory with the path specified in **NewDirectory**.

When you use **MkDir**, *always* disable runtime error checking around it, as you should always do with **Reset** (see Section 14.4) followed by an invocation of the **IOResult** function. Trying to create a subdirectory that already exists, or a subdirectory on a volume that has been marked Read Only, or with an invalid path, will trigger a runtime error and terminate your program unless runtime error-checking has been disabled. **IOResult** will return 1 for all ordinary errors, and 0 if the operation completed successfully.

RMDIR

Deleting a subdirectory is accomplished with **RmDir**:

```
PROCEDURE RmDir(TargetDirectory : String);
```

The path of the subdirectory to be removed is passed to **RmDir** in **TargetDirectory**. As with **MkDir**, runtime error-checking should be disabled around the **RmDir** statement, as runtime errors can occur if the subdirectory does not already exist or if it still contains undeleted files. Again, the returned error code from **IOResult** will be 1. 0 indicates that the subdirectory was successfully removed.

You cannot delete the root directory, the current directory (often indicated by a single period in a pathname: "."), or the parent directory (often indicated in a pathname with two periods: ".."). If you try to delete what looks like an empty directory and still get an error, there may be files in the directory marked as "hidden" or "system" files, and therefore not displayed from the DOS DIR command. Inspect the subdirectory with a directory utility like **The Norton Utilities**, **Window DOS**, or one of the many good public-domain directory utilities available from your user group. If there are files of any kind in a directory, you cannot delete it!

CHDIR

The current directory of a disk drive can be simply thought of as the directory named in the DOS prompt with the (essential, as far as I'm concerned) PROMPT

PG command in force. In other words, if you're working on drive C: and the command prompt says

```
C:\TURBO\HACKS\GRAPHICS>
```

the current directory for drive C: is \TURBO\HACKS\GRAPHICS. The current directory is where DOS looks for programs and files when no pathname to a specific directory is given.

Even though you may execute a program from a particular directory (say, \TURBO), your program can change the current directory to something entirely different. When it finishes executing, the current directory will remain changed; nothing in Turbo Pascal's runtime code will automatically change it back. If you want to change the current directory back to what it was originally, you must first save the current directory path in a string variable by invoking **GetDir** (see above) and then changing back to the original directory by executing another **ChDir** just before your program terminates.

ChDir is predeclared this way:

```
PROCEDURE ChDir(TargetDirectory : String);
```

Just as with the other procedures that operate with subdirectories, **ChDir** can trigger runtime errors if the specified directory does not exist, of if the given path in **TargetDirectory** is somehow invalid. Turn runtime error-checking off around **ChDir** and sample the error condition with **IOResult** after each invocation.

Chapter 15

Using and Configuring the Compiler

GENERATE CODE THE BEST WAY FOR THE JOB YOU NEED TO DO

In a sense, everything in Turbo Pascal exists to support the compiler. The compiler is very much the heart of the product and the process of creating native code programs in Pascal. In this chapter we'll look closely at the compiler, its commands, and the options it recognizes that govern the way it generates code.

15.1 Compiling and Running Code

Turbo Pascal compiles the source code file in the active window to pure native code that runs without the assistance of an intermediate code interpreter in the manner of UCSD Pascal or BASICA. For most program development you can compile a source code file in a window (which already exists in RAM) directly to native code in RAM, a process that happens with such speed as to astonish any programmer who has previously worked only with disk-to-disk filter-type compilers.

Once your program has compiled to RAM it can be run from the Interactive Development Environment (IDE) by selecting the Run | Run menu item. When you run your program, the IDE "steps aside" while the program executes, and when the program terminates, the IDE reappears. It is thus possible to develop programs *without any disk access at all*. This kind of no-disk-access development is both dizzyingly fast and somewhat dangerous. A frantic session of edit/compile/run, edit/compile/run, can load your RAM memory with irreplaceable code existing nowhere else—perhaps not on paper, in your notes, or (at three ayem, after ten hours at the tube) even in your head. Working with Turbo Pascal is undeniably intoxicating, and the tendency to work without ever saving to disk is strong.

Avoid that temptation.

One power glitch, one blown fuse, one little brother tripping over your machine's power cord and yanking it out of the wall will send all your hard work into the mystical bit bucket in the sky. Be wise. Save your program source work file to disk after each modification. It's as easy as pressing F2. And back up your hard disk after every session! (Borland Pascal compiles *only* to disk— but that doesn't excuse you from backing up your hard disk files!)

THE RUN ITEM

At the top of the Run menu is the Run item. (The version 4.0 **Run** word on the menu bar had no menu behind it.) If you select Run I Run, two things will happen without further assistance from you:

1. If your program has changed since the last time it was compiled, it will be recompiled. A *compile status box* will appear in the middle of your screen, providing a running tally of lines compiled. It goes fast. On a 50 Mhz 486 machine like mine, it often happens too quickly to follow.

2. The compiled program will run. The screen will clear, and your program will be given full control. Once it runs its course, the IDE will reappear, ready for your next program modification.

SPECIFYING COMMAND-LINE PARAMETERS

When you run a newly-compiled program from within the IDE, there is no obvious way to simulate the command-line parameters that you would normally pass to the program from the DOS command line. The Run I Parameters item allows you to set up a set of parameters for testing purposes while you are working within the IDE.

Selecting Run I Parameters brings up a dialog box entitled Program Parameters. You may enter up to 128 characters of command-line text (which is all that DOS allows) and press Enter. The next time you select Run I Parameters, the text that you entered will be displayed in the dialog box. You may append to it or edit it as you desire. The parameter text is saved along with the configuration file (whatever name you give it) so that you can have a set of "standard" command-line parameters for each project you're working on, assuming you keep each different project in a different subdirectory. The IDE will load a configuration file when it runs, and if you keep a file called TURBO.TP in each project subdirectory, that configuration file (which contains your command-line parameters) will be loaded when you change to that subdirectory from DOS and run the IDE. Note that you must *not* include the name of the program being run as part of the parameter text!

The other items in the Run menu are all connected with debugging, and will be addressed in Chapter 16.

15.2 The Compile Menu

No matter where you are within the IDE, pressing Alt-C will bring up the Compile menu. The top item in the compile menu is Compile, and by selecting Compile | Compile, your program will be compiled and made ready to run.

THE COMPILE ITEM

Assuming that the Pascal source code in the active window has no errors, compilation is a remarkably simple thing. When selected, the Compile item begins compilation on the source code in the active window.

While compilation is underway, the compiler displays a compile status box in the middle of the screen. The running tally of lines compiled is there to give you some flavor for how far along it is (and, not coincidentally, how fast it is going). If the compilation completes without any errors, the compiler will leave the compile status box on the screen, with its summary of the lines compiled and the amount of available memory. To continue, press any key.

WHOOPS!

No matter how good a programmer you will become, you will write programs with errors. Turbo Pascal is quite helpful in spotting errors in your programs. When the compiler discovers an error in your source code, it will stop the compilation and print a message similar to this in a highlighted line (in red if you have a color screen):

```
Error 85: ";" expected.
```

Beneath the error message line, the editor will be displaying your source code file with the cursor at the location where it noticed the error. *This is not necessarily where the problem exists*, but rather is always where the compiler first suspects that something is wrong.

For example, if you leave out a **BEGIN** in the middle of the program, the compiler will not necessarily notice that a **BEGIN** is missing until further down in the file, when something else doesn't add up. It may be that it finds, at the bottom of the program, that it has one too many **END**s. There are a fair number of other ways that a missing **BEGIN** will make itself known to the compiler; which one eventually tips the compiler off will depend on how your program is laid out.

The point of all this is that while the compiler will give you a good hint when it passes the baton to the editor and places the cursor where it noticed a problem with your program, you may in fact have to do some further hunting to find the real cause of the problem.

THE COMPILE DESTINATION

Immediately beneath the Compile I Compile item are the Make and Build items, which I won't discuss in this chapter. They are part of Turbo Pascal's project management feature, and I'll take them up in Chapter 21.

Next on the menu is Destination, which is a toggle that directs the output of the compiler to either memory or a disk file. The default state is Memory. This makes for very fast compiles, and when your program is fairly small, there's very little need to create a separate disk file for the executable code.

Problems will appear when your program starts to get ambitious. The Turbo Pascal IDE takes a fair amount of space in memory, since the executable file is 120K-130K depending on the release, with an additional 64K of memory allocated to the editor work file alone. Version 5.0 and later will place the editor buffer in EMS memory if the IDE detects it in your system. Once your program starts to push thirty or forty thousand lines of code (and this may happen sooner than you think, if you use a lot of units) you may have to abandon in-memory compiles.

Changing the Destination item to Disk writes an .EXE file to the current directory *unless* a directory has been specified for executable files in the EXE and TPU Directories line of the Options I Directories dialog box. (See Section 15.7.) You can toggle Destination between its two states simply by selecting it. Select it when it reads Memory and it will change to Disk. Select it once more, and it will change back to Memory.

FINDING RUNTIME ERRORS

Turbo Pascal 3.0 had an extremely convenient system for finding the location in the source code of a runtime error, given the reported address of the error. The compiler simply recompiled the source code until it reached the offset in the object code that matched the address of the runtime error.

This system only works with the .COM code files produced by versions of Turbo Pascal prior to 4.0. Things are far more complex now; with multiple code segments and .EXE files, the compiler needs additional information to relate the location of a runtime error in the object code to a line in the source code file.

You can insert this information into your program object code file by using the Debug information item in the Options I Compiler dialog box. The Debug information item is either checked or not checked; make sure that it is checked when you compile. When the item is checked, the compiler generates additional information about the line structure of your source code and inserts it into the .EXE file or memory image. Generating the debug information adds a little to the size of your file, and code speed will be reduced slightly. This is why you should compile with Debug information *off* (not checked) once you've shaken the bugs out of a program.

Once you have checked the Debug information item to generate the necessary information and inserted it into your file, there are two methods of locating runtime errors.

The first is when you are running your program from within the IDE. If a runtime error occurs, you will be bounced back into the IDE without a normal exit from your program. The editor will load the source code (if available) for the code module in which the error occurred. In other words, if your program uses a number of units, and the runtime error occurs within one of the units, the source code for that unit will be loaded into the editor, and the cursor will be positioned as close to the runtime error location as Turbo Pascal can pin it. If the error occurred in the main program module, the main program source code will be loaded instead.

If the compiler cannot find the source code for the code module that is at fault, a dialog box will appear, entitled **Cannot find run-time error file:**. The name of the source code file it wants to load will appear within the box. You then have the option of editing the file name or path within the dialog box to reflect the current location or name of the source code file. Once you press Return, the editor will attempt to load the file again.

This first method makes use of all the features of the Turbo Pascal IDE, and is nearly automatic. All you have to do is make sure that the Debug information item is turned on, and that the source code files of all code modules you are developing are available to the IDE if it needs them.

The second method is necessary when you run your program from DOS and trigger a runtime error. An error message will appear, similar to this:

```
Runtime error 200 at 0028:02BF.
```

You need to manually write down the code and the address, because the IDE is not in memory to note it for you.

With that information written down, bring up the IDE and load the source code for your main program, regardless of where the runtime error occurred. To find the error, the IDE must begin with the main program.

Select the Search | Find error item. A dialog box will appear, entitled **Error Address**. Type in the full address you copied from the runtime error message on the screen, and press Return. The IDE will take it from there, load the appropriate source code file as described above, and put the cursor as close to the error as it can. Keep in mind that when using this second method, the IDE cannot tell you what kind of runtime error occurred. You have to look the error code up yourself.

Don't forget that for either method of locating runtime errors, you must have Debug information turned on before the last compile. If you were running an application that was compiled *without* Debug information checked when a runtime error happened, you'll have to recompile the program and run it again to the point where the runtime error happened. Taking note of a runtime error address produced by a program compiled without Debug information checked won't help you.

15.3 The Active Window and the Primary File

The next item on the Compile menu is the Primary file item. This item affects which source code file is compiled when you request a compile operation. Ordinarily, the file in the active edit window (the edit file) is what you compile when you want to compile something. For simple programs that exist in only one piece, this will always be the case.

However, once you start cutting a program source code file up into several separate units, the picture gets more complicated. You may be editing and testing a unit file, but you can't simply compile and run a unit all by itself. The unit must be linked to the main program file, and then run along with the main program.

What happens is that you are editing a unit file, but you need to compile, link, and run the entire program. You can, of course, compile the unit to disk as a .TPU file, then load and compile the main program and run that as a way of testing the unit file you're working on.

It doesn't have to be that difficult. The IDE recognizes what is called the *primary file*. The primary file is the source code file that is compiled and linked when either the Make or Build items in the Compile menu are selected. By setting the primary file to the main program file, you can edit the unit file in the active window, and then press F9 (the shortcut key to the Make item) to re-Make the whole program, starting with the main program specifed in the primary file name.

Understanding that last sentence requires that you know what it means to *make* or *build* a program. This is part of Turbo Pascal's project management feature, which I'll be describing in detail in Chapter 21. I'll define the words only briefly here; you might look ahead to Chapter 21 for the details if you're still puzzled.

When you *make* a program file, you recompile the main program and any units that were modifed *since the last time the main program was compiled*. If none of the units were modifed, only the main program is recompiled. The units' .TPU files are *linked* with the main program, but the unit source code is not *recompiled*.

On the other hand, when you *build* a program, you recompile *everything*, including all units the main program uses, regardless of what was modified when.

In reality, make and build are a little more complicated than that. Again, refer to Chapter 21 for more information. For now, simply understand that in order for the idea of the primary file to mean anything at all, you must use Make or Build. Simply selecting Compile | Compile will *always* compile the file in the active edit window, regardless of what the primary file is.

DISPLAYING COMPILE INFORMATION

The last item on the Compile menu, Information, brings up an information box containing a summary of the various aspects of the last compile that was successfully completed. An example of a Compile | Information box is given in Figure 15.1.

Figure 15.1 The Compile Information Box

The box summarizes the source file size, code size, stack size, heap minimum and maximum size, and remaining system memory. It also indicates whether your compiled code resides in memory or on disk, as specified by the Destination item in the Compile menu.

If your program exits through a **Halt** statement with an exit code as **Halt**'s optional parameter, that code will be reported at the bottom of the information box, along with information on any runtime error that was detected during the last time the program was run.

15.4 Compiler Directives

There are two ways to control the nature of the code produced by the Turbo Pascal compiler. One is through the Options|Compiler dialog box, shown in Figure 15.2. The other way is through commands that you place directly into your source code as you edit it. These are called *compiler directives*. Most of them can be set through the Options|Compiler dialog box, but as I'll explain a little later, I think it's a better idea to set them individually in your source code files, as needed.

There are actually three very different types of compiler directives:

- **Switch directives** turn some condition on or off, by naming the condition and then using the "+" symbol to turn the condition on, and the "-" symbol to turn the condition off.

- **Parameter directives** provide parameters to the compiler, such as file names or values for memory allocation.

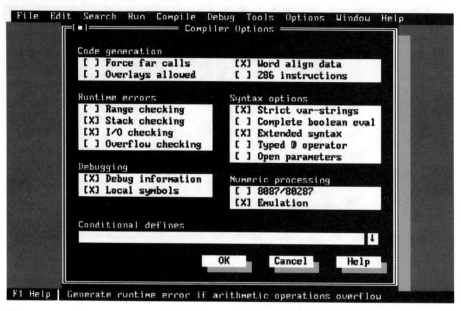

Figure 15.2 The Options | Compiler Dialog Box

- **Condition directives** provide for the compilation of different portions of a single source file depending on parameters defined by you the programmer. This is an advanced technique, and I will not be covering condition directives in this section.

COMPILER COMMANDS OR IDE OPTIONS?

In virtually every case, you can set up the same compiler commands either through the IDE Options | Compiler dialog box, or through compiler directives in the source code. There are several good reasons to use compiler directives rather than the Options | Compiler dialog box. Most of the compiler directives have the advantage of being changeable during the course of program compilation. The most common example is the turning on and off of runtime error-trapping. There are times when you will want the compiler to trap serious computational errors, and other times when you will prefer to be notified of them (via **IOResult**, for example) and take action on your own. The **$I+/-** compiler directive lets you turn off error-trapping for a statement or two and then turn it back on again.

Then there is the more practical issue of having to load in a new configuration file every time you change source code, if you choose to depend on the menus to configure compilation. It makes much more sense to set up a series of default conditions that make sense for the work you generally do, and then use compiler directives in your source code to set things up specifically for the project you are working on in the form of that particular source code file. Loading the source code loads its options for you automatically (because the options are compiler directives that are part of the source code), and saves that extra step.

COMPILER DIRECTIVE SYNTAX

Syntactically, compiler directives are special-purpose comments. If the first character in a comment is a dollar sign ($) that comment will be interpreted by the compiler as a compiler directive. *There can be no space or other characters between the left comment delimiter (either "(*" or "{") and the dollar sign.*

Several compiler directives may be included in a single comment as a list separated by commas. In this case only the first directive need be preceded by a dollar sign. Here are some valid example compiler directives:

```
{$I-}
{$I A:MOUSELIB.SRC}
{$C-,R-}
(*$B- *)
(*$U-,V-,C-*)
```

As with all comments, you must close the compiler directive comment with the same delimiter it starts with. In other words, compiler directives like **{$I-*}** or **(*$B+}** are invalid and dangerous, since one kind of comment delimiter cannot close a comment begun by the other.

Keep in mind that switch directives (those directives followed in the discussions below by "+/-") are toggles which are either on "+" or off "-". You must pick only one in practice; in other words, a directive like "**$I+/-**" is not valid in your source code, but is used here as a typographical device only to indicate that the **$I** switch directive has two states specified by plus and minus symbols.

Now let's go through Pascal's supported compiler options in detail, one by one. Keep in mind that some of these directives address issues that we haven't covered in detail in this book yet, and a few others that I won't be covering in detail at all. In every case, I'll try to present a brief description of what's going on, but if you don't fully understand some of the more advanced compiler directives, you do have the option of simply not using them!

$A+/- : WORD ALIGNMENT; DEFAULT +

The 86-family of processors can access data more quickly if that data is *word-aligned*; that is, if the start of data occurs at an even-numbered address. Even-numbered addresses represent what are called *word boundaries,* and beginning a data item on a word boundary makes that data word-aligned.

It may be that a data item would fall on an odd-numbered address because it follows another data item containing an odd number of bytes. In that case, if word alignment is in force, the compiler will add a single-byte "pad" to force the new data item to begin on a word boundary.

Word alignment makes for faster programs, at the cost of some (but not a great deal) of wasted space in your single data segment. The default is word alignment; if you begin to run out of data segment space, the first thing you should do is disable word alignment so that the compiler will pack data in the data segment nose-to-tail and make the best use of space, at the cost of some (but not much) code performance. If you'd like to know a little more about PC memory addressing, make sure you read Chapter 24.

The **$A+/-** compiler directive controls word alignment. **$A+** (the default) specifies word alignment, while **$A-** disables word alignment, so that data may fall on either an even or an odd address. This is sometimes called byte alignment, because data may be aligned on any byte address.

This directive is equivalent to the Word align data item on the Options | Compiler dialog box.

$B+/- : BOOLEAN EVALUATION; DEFAULT -

There are two different ways that the compiler can generate code to support Boolean expression evaluation: complete and short-circuit. Complete evaluation evaluates every part of an expression that strings several expressions together with **AND** and **OR** operators, even when some early part of the expression determines the outcome of the entire expression early on. Short-circuit evaluation stops evaluation of the expression as soon as the outcome of the expression is determined. This concept is discussed in detail in Section 8.2.

{**$B+**} forces the compiler to generate code that performs complete Boolean expression evaluation. {**$B-**} forces the compiler to generate code that performs short-circuit Boolean evaluation.

This directive is equivalent to the Complete Boolean eval item on the Options | Compiler dialog box.

$C <ATTRIBUTE ATTRIBUTE...>: SPECIFY CODE SEGMENT ATTRIBUTE

This is one of those truly advanced compiler directives that I won't be discussing in detail in this book. It applies only in protected mode and for Windows programming, and specifies how certain generated code segments are to be treated. Valid attribute constants for V7.0 are **MOVEABLE, FIXED, DEMANDLOAD, PRELOAD, DISCARDABLE**, and **PERMANENT**.

Until you begin working in Windows or in protected mode with Borland Pascal 7.0, this directive won't be of much use to you.

$D+/- : GENERATE DEBUG INFORMATION; DEFAULT -

In order to locate the position of a runtime error in your source code, the compiler needs more information than simply the address at which the error occurred. (This process was discussed earlier in this chapter.) When directed to with the {$D+} directive, the compiler creates a table of line number addresses for each procedure in the program. This table allows the IDE to use an address provided by you to "zero in" on a specific line number in your source code.

When compiling a unit, the debug information is recorded in the unit's .TPU file. When compiling a program into memory, this informaton is retained in memory. When compiling a program to disk, the information is written out to a separate .TPM file, *if* the generation of .TPM files is enabled with the {$D+} directive.

If the generation of debug information is disabled by the {$D-} directive (the default condition) the IDE will be unable to pinpoint the location of a runtime error for you.

The matter of debug information will be taken up again in Chapter 16, when we talk about the debugging process in detail.

$E+/- : FLOATING-POINT EMULATION; DEFAULT +

Version 5.0 and later has the ability of emulating the '87 family of math coprocessors if one is not present in the system. This allows you to make use of the IEEE floating-point types **Single**, **Double**, **Extended**, and **Comp**, even if you don't have an '87 installed. Turbo Pascal 4.0 users need to have the actual chip in their systems to use these types.

The default is to have emulation enabled ({$E+}). If you turn emulation off, you will need to have an '87 to use the IEEE floating-point types, but your code will be somewhat more compact and only slightly faster. The $E directive works closely in concert with the $N directive, which governs whether or not the IEEE floating-point types may be used at all. If $N- is in force, the state of the $E directive really doesn't matter, and the only real number type available to you will be the built-in type **Real**.

$F+/- : FORCE FAR CALLS; DEFAULT -

The code that calls procedures or functions can be generated two ways: If the call must venture outside the current 64K code segment, the call is a *far* call; otherwise, the call is limited to the current 64K code segment and is considered a *near* call. The main program and all its subprograms are contained within a single code segment, so the subprograms are accessed using near calls. The subprograms defined within a unit, however, must be called as far calls because they can be called from the main program's code segment or any of the other unit code segments.

In most cases, the compiler decides whether to generate a subprogram using near or far calls. This happens most often when you call a subprogram residing in a unit. Such a call is always a far call, and the compiler knows this well enough to do it automatically; you don't have to explicitly specify far calls.

However, there are certain situations in which a subprogram within the main program's segment must be compiled for far calls. The main program's exit procedure is the most common example, because it is joined into a chain with all unit exit procedures that spans several code segments. (See the discussion of exit procedures in Section 13.4.)

All subprograms compiled after a {$F+} directive are compiled for far calls. It's not enough simply to turn far calls on, however, since typically only one or two subprograms within a program need to be compiled for far calls. The correct way to use $F is to bracket a far procedure or function with {$F+} and {$F-}:

```
{$F+}

PROCEDURE MyFarProc;

BEGIN
  ...
END;

{$F-}
```

This way, only the single procedure becomes a far procedure, which is as you want it. Far procedures and functions take up more room and require more time to execute because of the extra burden of pushing both a segment address and an offset address on the stack, rather than just an offset address.

For this reason, it is not a good idea to enable far calls through the equivalent Force far calls item on the Options | Compiler dialog box. Using the dialog box control makes *all* calls in a program far calls, indiscriminately. Use a razor, not a club.

Overlays since V5.0 require that far calls be used *throughout* a call chain that ends with a procedure within an overlay. In other words, if procedure **A** calls procedure **B**, procedure **B** calls procedure **C**, procedure **C** calls procedure **D**, and **D** is within an overlay, then **A**, **B**, **C**, and **D** must *all* be compiled as far. The safest way to anticipate all combinations is to simply use far calls for everything in an overlaid application. For overlays, use the club—the razor might kill you.

$G+/-: ENABLE 286 CODE GENERATION; DEFAULT - FOR REAL MODE, + FOR PROTECTED MODE AND WINDOWS

Intel's newer CPUs added powerful machine instructions that earlier CPU types didn't have. Using these newer instructions can make your code faster and more compact—at the cost of its not being able to run on older processors like the 8088 and 8086.

By default in real mode programming, 286 code generation is disabled. You can enable it for real mode by placing the $G+ directive at the front of your source code file. If you're working in Windows or in DOS protected mode, 286 code generation defaults on, because Windows and DOS protected mode require at least a 286 CPU to function.

There are additional, rather arcane Windows-related issues connected with $G that I won't be covering here. If you're curious, consult Borland's *Programmer's Reference*, Chapter 2.

$I+/- : I/O ERROR-TRAPPING; DEFAULT +

This toggle determines whether I/O errors are trapped or simply reported. With {$I+} in force (the default) the Turbo Pascal runtime code traps I/O errors with an error message and then brings the program to a halt. With {$I-} in force, trapping is turned off. Errors will still be *reported* by the **IOResult** function (see Section 14.4) but it will be up to you to test **IOResult** for errors and take appropriate action when errors are reported.

As mentioned above in connection with the $F directive, don't just turn trapping off and leave it off. I/O trapping is there for a reason, and it can be very helpful in tracing a problem when an I/O error occurs. It's good practice to turn trapping off only around the single statement that would generate a predictable, trappable I/O error; for example, **Reset** or **Rewrite**:

```
Assign(MyFile,'FOO.TXT');
{$I-} Reset(MyFile); {$I+}
IF IOResult <> 0 THEN CallFileErrorProc;
```

Trapping should be left on at all other times to capture the unexpected. It's usually better to crash than to continue operating with garbage data.

As with **$F**, you can turn off I/O trapping through the **I/O** checking item on the Options I Compiler dialog box, but again, *using the menus with this directive is a bad idea*. Turn off error-trapping only when you must, leaving as little of your code as possible exposed to unreported I/O errors.

$I <FILENAME> : INCLUDE FILE

In my opinion it was a bad idea to have two different forms of the **$I** directive for two different functions—so take special note that **$I <filename>** has *nothing* to do with **$I+/-** as described above, especially since the two of them are among the most-used of all Pascal's compiler directives.

$I <filename>** is a parameter directive that allows you to "include" a file during compilation. This is a way to cut your source code up into chunks. When the compiler encounters the **$I <filename> directive, it opens the disk file **<filename>** and begins compiling it. The file **<filename>** is not actually read into memory as a whole; the compiler simply reads it line by line, compiles the line to machine code, then throws the line away and reads the next line.

Note that starting with Turbo Pascal 4.0, include files *may* include any other files, up to eight nested levels deep. One notable restriction on **$I <filename>** is that it may not appear between any **BEGIN..END** block. (Turbo Pascal 3.0 and earlier versions allowed include files to be included anywhere within a source file.)

Using include files was once the only way to divide a large Turbo Pascal program up into manageable chunks. Many programmers created libraries of procedures and functions that were include files, and then used **$I <filename>** to "link" these libraries into their main programs. This system will still work, but I strongly encourage you to place your libraries of utility functions into separately-compiled units. Not only does this save the time spent compiling trusty, proven routines each time you compile the main program, but it also takes your utility libraries out of your main program's code segment. Once your program begins to require more than 64K of code, this will be your only way out. Use units—not include files—for subprogram libraries!

$K+/-: ENABLE SMART CALLBACKS FOR WINDOWS CODE; DEFAULT +

This is an *extremely* arcane compiler feature relating to Windows programming only, and even then only for those who know their way around. I won't be covering it in this book.

$L+/- : ENABLE LOCAL SYMBOL GENERATION; DEFAULT +

To use the IDE's Integrated Debugger with programs that contain subprograms (for example, 98 percent of all sensible programs) you must explicitly enable the generation of a table of local symbols, that is, symbols belonging to the subprogram rather than the main program. Disabling local symbol generation releases a little memory but has no other real consequence. The default is to generate local symbols and there is little reason to disable it.

Note: Version 4.0 used $L for a totally different reason. If you're still using V4.0, check with your documentation before using $L!

In general, when you use **$D+** to generate local symbol information, you should use **$L+** to enable local symbol generation. Once you're through debugging a program, you can change both directives to their "off" state and make your programs a little leaner and a little faster.

$L <FILENAME> : LINK OBJECT FILE

This parameter directive specifies the name of an external machine-code file to the Turbo Pascal linker. The linker then loads the file into memory and links it into the generated code when the external routine is called.

For example, if you have an external file called GAMEBORD.OBJ and wish to link it into your program, you would use this syntax:

```
{$L GAMER.OBJ}
PROCEDURE Stick(Sticknumber : Integer; VAR X,Y : Integer);
            EXTERNAL;
```

This assumes that a file named GAMER.OBJ resides in the current directory. You could specify a file in a different directory by including directory path information in the **$L** directive. Alternatively, you can store a directory name in the Include directories item on the Directories submenu of the Options menu. The Turbo Pascal compiler will search there for an external file if no path is given within the **$L** directive, and the file is not found in the default directory.

$L assumes a .OBJ extension. Specifying GAMER is equivalent to specifying GAMER.OBJ. If you wish to link an external file with some other extension, you must specify the extension explicitly.

Keep in mind that if you specify a file name in a **$L** directive and then fail to make use of the file through an **EXTERNAL** declaration later in the program, Turbo Pascal will generate this error

```
Error 51: Invalid PUBLIC definition (GAMER)
```

after it reaches the end of the file.

$M <STACKSIZE>, <HEAPMIN>, <HEAPMAX> : MEMORY ALLOCATION;   DEFAULT {$M 16384,0,655360}

You have the power to alter the allocation of memory to your program. Specifically, you can specify how much memory is to be used for the stack segment, and how much is to be made available to the heap for storage of dynamic variables. The way you specify allocation values is through the **$M** parameter directive. The **$M** directive can be used *only* within program files. If you place one in a unit source file, no error will be generated, but the directive will be ignored and will have no effect. When used in a program compiled for real mode, **$M** takes three numeric parameters: stack allocation, minimum heap allocation, and maximum heap allocation. The three values are placed within the comment delimiters, separated by a space from the **$M** directive name, and separated from one another by commas. For example, in the following directive

```
{$M 65520,0,32768}
```

the stack allocation is 65,520 bytes; the minimum heap allocation is 0 bytes, and the maximum heap allocation is 32,768 bytes.

Stack allocation is the amount of memory in your program's stack segment. Turbo Pascal uses the stack heavily, for keeping temporary values, and especially for the passing of values to and from subprograms. Therefore, you must have some minimum amount of memory available for stack use, or your programs will not run at all. The minimum amount of stack that you can allocate to a Turbo Pascal program is 1024 bytes. If you try to allocate less than that, you will receive an error:

```
Error 17: Invalid compiler directive
```

The maximum amount of memory allocatable to the stack is 65,520 bytes, *not* 65,536 bytes (what we often call "64K"). The default stack allocation (that is, the allocation granted automatically unless you override it with a **$M** directive) is

16,384 bytes. This is a good working value, and should be left alone unless you really need to change it.

More stack is often required when your program makes heavy use of recursion (see Section 8.14). Every time a recursive procedure calls itself, it allocates a new "stack frame" on the stack with new instantiations of all parameters and local variables. Make a few hundred recursive calls, and this adds up—which you must keep in mind if you intend to build recursion into your programs. If you run out of stack space, you will generate runtime error 202, *if* stack overflow checking is enabled. (See the **$S+/-** directive, below.) If stack checking is not enabled, your program will crash mutely, leaving you scratching your head and reaching for the power switch.

Minimum heap allocation is the minimum amount of memory that your program must be able to allocate to the heap, or it will refuse to run. This is a "guarantee" that your program, once it runs, will have a certain amount of RAM available for essential buffers and variables on the heap. The default value is 0; that is, your program can run by default without any memory for the heap at all. If you make *any* use of the heap, decide how much memory your program needs to get its work done, and make this the minimum heap allocation value.

Maximum heap allocation is the amount of memory that your program should reserve for the heap, if the memory is available. The default value is 655,360 bytes, which (if you know your PC architecture) is the entire usable RAM area for PC DOS applications.

The default values for minimum and maximum heap allocation means that, by default, your PC will *promise* you *no* heap memory, but will *take* all the memory it can find, right up to the end of DOS memory.

If you intend to make use of **Exec** in the **DOS** unit to spawn child processes, you *must* cut back on the maximum heap allocation by the amount of memory required by your child process.

You can set memory allocation through the **Memory sizes** item on the **Compiler** submenu of the **Options** menu, but again, I don't think that's a very good idea. Use the defaults when you can, and override them when you must on a program-by-program basis, by using the **$M** directive.

If you're working in protected mode with Borland Pascal 7.0, you cannot set minimum and maximum heap sizes. Heap allocation in protected mode is handled in other ways. In protected mode, you can only place one value after the $M directive, and that value will be the stack size value. The default stack size in protected mode, as in real mode, is 16384.

For Windows programming, you can set a total heap size, but not separate maximum and minimum values. Both the default stack size and heap size for Windows is 8192.

$N+/- : NUMERIC PROCESSING; DEFAULT -

There are two broad categories of real numbers available within Turbo Pascal. One is the "software-only" real numbers, of the predefined type **Real**, which occupy 6 bytes. The other is the "8087-style" IEEE real number types: **Single**, **Double**, **Extended**, and **Comp**.

In Turbo Pascal 4.0, the 8087 real number types *required* a math coprocessor like the 8087, 80287, or 80387 to compile and run. The Turbo Pascal 4.0 compiler could detect the presence or absence of a math coprocessor on your system, and if it failed to find a math coprocessor it would not even let you use the 8087 types.

Floating-point support starting with Turbo Pascal 5.0, on the other hand, resembles that of Turbo C and C++ in that the math coprocessor is used if available, and *emulated* if not. You needn't be concerned whether someone running your compiled program has a math coprocessor or not, except that emulating a coprocessor is considerably slower than using a real one. Since version 5.0, emulation may be turned on and off through the {**$E+/-**} directive, as explained earlier in this section.

The **$N** switch allows or forbids the use of the 8087 types. The default condition is {**$N-**}, meaning that you cannot use the 8087 types. Inserting a {**$N+**} directive into your program allows you to compile a program using the 8087 types. Keep in mind that under version 4.0, if you don't have an 8087 (or one of the more advanced Intel math coprocessors) installed, *the compiler will not let you use the 8087 types, whether {$N+} is in force or not!* Another point to be noted is that the compiler will call you down when you attempt to use an IEEE real type, *not* when you *define* a variable of that type. You can define all the variables you want, but as soon as they begin taking part in statements, you'll get a compiler error reading

```
Error 116: Must be in 8087 mode to compile this.
```

The **$N** directive is equivalent to the **N**umeric processing item on the Options | Compiler dialog box. The 8087/80287 check box in the dialog box is equivalent to {**$N+**}, while the Emulation check box is equivalent to {**$N-**}.

$O+/- : ENABLE UNIT OVERLAY COMPILATION; DEFAULT -

For a unit to be compiled as an overlay under Turbo Pascal, the unit must contain a {**$O+**} directive enabling overlay compilation of the unit. When enabled, the directive allows the unit containing it to be compiled to the .OVR overlay file rather than the main program's .EXE file. Note that including a {**$O+**} directive in a unit does not *force* a unit to be overlaid; it merely *allows* the unit to be overlaid. To be overlaid, a unit must contain the {**$O+**} directive, *and* the main program must name the unit in a **$O <unit name>** directive as described below.

Note that Turbo Pascal 4.0 did not have overlay support at all, while versions 3.0 and earlier handled it in a totally different way.

$O <UNIT NAME> : SPECIFY OVERLAY UNIT NAME

Every unit to be used as an overlay must be named as an overlay in the main program source file, within a {**$O**} directive. Each unit must have its own separate directive, existing *after* the **USES** statement but before anything else:

```
PROGRAM JiveTalk;

{$F+}

USES  Overlay,DOS,CRT,CircBuff,XMODEM,Kermit,Packet1K,Parser;

{$O XMODEM}
{$O Kermit}
{$O Packet1K}
```

Note that each overlaid unit must (as you might expect) be named in the **USES** statement. Also, each unit to be overlaid must contain a {$O+} directive, as explained above.

$P+/-: DEFINE VAR STRING PARAMETERS AS OPEN STRINGS; DEFAULT -

Back in Section 8.13, I explained open string parameters, a feature new to version 7.0 that allows you to pass a string of any length in a **VAR** string parameter. There are two ways to use open strings. Perhaps the easiest is the one I emphasized in Section 8.13: Use the **OpenString** predefined identifier as the type of a **VAR** string parameter.

The other way is to assert the **$P+** state of the **$P** directive. Any code falling between **$P+** and **$P-** directives will be generated such that **VAR** string parameters are open string parameters. If you place a **$P+** directive at the start of your program source code file, **VAR** string parameters throughout the entire program will be generated as open strings.

The **$P** directive is equivalent to the Open parameters item in the Syntax block of the Options | Compiler dialog box. The Open parameters item also allows or forbids the use of open array parameters (conformant arrays) in a program.

$Q+/-: OVERFLOW CHECKING; DEFAULT -

Overflow checking is similar to range checking (see below). The runtime code can check several common numeric operations to ensure that the results returned by those operations fall within the range of legal values for the operation. If **$Q+** is asserted and the result falls outside a legal range, a runtime error halts your program.

The operations watched by the runtime code when **$Q+** is asserted are: +, -, *, **Abs**, **Sqr**, **Succ**, and **Pred**. **Inc** and **Dec**, while similar functionally to **Succ** and **Pred**, are not checked, regardless of the state of **$Q**.

If an overflow happens with **$Q** in its "off" (minus) state, your program will not halt on an overflow, but the variable into which an out-of-range value is supposed to go will receive an undefined "garbage" value instead. If you act on such a value assuming it to be valid, you could have further problems as well.

Your programs will run a little faster with **$Q-** asserted, so once you've gotten your overflow errors out of your system, turn overflow checking off.

$Q is equivalent to the Overflow checking check box in the Options | Compiler dialog box.

$R+/-: INDEX RANGE ERROR CHECK; DEFAULT -

Ordinarily, if you attempt to index an array or string outside of its legal bounds, no runtime error occurs. If indexing outside the bounds of an array or string trashes adjacent data items, the resulting bugs will be peculiar and rough to define. You have the option of turning on runtime index range error-trapping, so that when an index range error happens, the Turbo Pascal runtime code will trap a runtime error and halt your program. The **$R** directive turns this error-trapping for index range errors on and off. **{$R+}** turns index range error-trapping on. **{$R-}** (the default) turns trapping off.

Like all of Pascal's safeguards, range checking costs your program a little in terms of execution speed, and makes the generated code a little larger. For ease of debugging you might turn index range trapping on while you're developing a program. Once you have thoroughly debugged your program, you might wish to recompile it with trapping turned off. Your program will then run a little faster.

This directive is equivalent to the Range checking item on the Options | Compiler dialog box.

$R <RESOURCE FILENAME>: SPECIFY NAME OF RESOURCE FILE

In Windows and protected mode programming, you can incorporate a *resource file* into your .EXE or .DLL file written with Borland Pascal 7.0. A resource file typically contains icons, bitmaps, or string lists used to internationalize an application. Resource files can exist as separate .RES files, but to reduce "file clutter" you can have the compiler combine a .RES file with the executable file it is generating. That's what the parameter form of **$R** does; keep in mind that resource files have *nothing* to do with range checking.

Resource files are an advanced topic and I won't be dealing with them further in this book.

$S+/-: STACK OVERFLOW CHECKING; DEFAULT +

Ordinarily, the Turbo Pascal runtime code checks to see if space is available on the stack for local variables and value parameters before each call to a function or procedure. If space is not available, a runtime error will occur and execution will cease.

With **{$S+}** (the default) in force, the compiler will generate code to make this check. With **{$S-}** in effect, that code will not be generated, and the runtime library will simply assume that space is always available on the stack. This will usually be true. However, in recursive applications where heavy use of the stack is expected, it may be a good idea to use **{$S+}**.

With {$S-} in force, a stack collision will almost always crash your system hard, requiring a reboot or even a power-down.

This directive is equivalent to the **S**tack checking item on the Options | **C**ompiler dialog box. It also directly replaces the {**$K+/-**} directive from version 3.0 and earlier. There are further **$S** issues connected with Windows and protected mode programming, but I won't be covering them here.

$T+/- : TYPE-CHECKED POINTERS RETURNED BY @; DEFAULT -

This directive has had a long and checkered history. It was not present in versions 1–3; was present and governed map file (.TPM) generation in V4.0, was not present in V5.0, 5.5, or 6.0, and returned with an entirely new meaning in V7.0. Currently, **$T** dictates whether or not type checking will be performed on pointers returned by the address-of operator, @.

Previous to V7.0, and when **$T-** is in force, the pointer returned by the @ operator is a true untyped pointer, and is assignment-compatible with all other pointer types. In V7.0, when **$T+** is asserted, pointers returned by @ are assignment-compatible only with pointers to the type of variable @ was applied to.

This explains better with examples.

```
TYPE
   PCharSet : ^CharSet;
   CharSet : SET OF Char;

VAR
   Foo : Integer
   Bar : PCharSet

Bar := @Foo; { Type conflict if $T+ asserted! }
```

This code snippet will *not* compile with **$T+** asserted. **Bar** is defined as a typed pointer, because it is a pointer to a **SET** of Char. **Foo** is an integer. @**Foo** returns a true untyped pointer when **$T-** is in force, but once you assert **$T+**, what @**Foo** returns is a pointer to an integer, which is not assignment-compatible with a pointer to a **SET** of characters, but only with other pointers to integers.

$T+/- corresponds to the Typed @ operator check box in the Options | Compiler dialog box.

$V+/- : STRING VAR-PARAMETER LENGTH CHECKING; DEFAULT +

All string types have a specific physical length. The default length of type **STRING** without a length qualifier is 255 bytes. (See Section 10.1). String types of shorter lengths are defined as **String[20]**, **String[80]** and so on, with the length given in brackets after the identifier **STRING**. When you pass a string type to a function or procedure by reference (as a **VAR** parameter, in other words), the physical length of the formal parameter and the physical length of the actual parameter are ordinarily required to be exactly the same. Attempting to plug a larger or smaller actual parameter into the formal parameter will generate a compile-time error.

The **$V** directive allows you to turn this restriction off and on. **{$V+}** (the default) enforces this physical length matching restriction. **{$V-}** allows you to pass actual parameters of any length to a given formal parameter.

The consequences of passing an actual parameter *larger* than its formal parameter can be overwriting of adjacent data, very much like array index range errors.

This directive is equivalent to the **VAR** string checking item on the **Compiler** submenu of the **Options** menu. The "strict" state from the menu is equivalent to **{$V+}**, and the "relaxed" state is equivalent to **{$V-}**.

Note that the $V directive is obsolete with V7.0. Open string parameters make it unnecessary ever to assert **$V-**. Using the predefined **OpenString** type or **$P+/-** (see above) allows you to get the same results in a "safe" fashion that will always be defined by the runtime code. Use **$V** *only* to compile old pre-7.0 code that you need and haven't converted to open string parameters yet.

$Y+/-: ENABLE SYMBOL REFERENCE INFORMATION; DEFAULT +

The **$Y** directive is new with Borland Pascal 7.0 *only* (it is not supported by Turbo Pascal 7.0), and is related to the debug information directive **$D** and local symbols directive **$L**. With directive **$Y+** asserted (the default) Borland Pascal generates information about the units, objects, and global variables and procedures used in your program. After compiling, you can open a browser that allows you to scan browsable symbols in a browser window. The browser can display the value held by constants, and the names of any defined subprograms, variables, or objects.

Note well that unless **$D+** and **$L+** are both asserted, **$Y** will have no effect, and your symbols will not be browsable. In general, you assert **$D+**, **$L+**, and **$Y+** as a group, and then assert their "minus" versions once debugging of a program is complete.

15.5 The Options | Linker Dialog Box

The Options | Linker dialog box specifies various options for the Turbo Pascal smart linker. (See Figure 15.3.) Ordinarily (especially as a beginner in Pascal) you won't need to be configuring the linker. This is an advanced topic, and you probably won't need to alter any of the linker configuration items until you begin doing very subtle or very ambitious projects.

The Linker submenu has only two items:

- *Map file* specifies the level of detail written into Turbo Pascal map (.MAP) files. .MAP files are human-readable summaries of program address and line number information, generated during compilation. By default, map file generation is disabled. The **Map** file item allows you to turn on map file generation and specify how much information the map file is to contain.

Selecting **Map** file brings up a menu of four choices:

Off means that map files are completely disabled.

Segments specifies that *only* segment name, address, and length information are to be included in the map file.

Publics specifies that the map file is to include the segment information mentioned above, plus all public symbol names in the program (including symbols **USE**d in resident units) and the address of the program's entry point.

Detailed specifies that the map file is to contain all the information mentioned above, plus an additional table providing a 32-bit code address for each line number of source code that was available to the compiler during compilation. As you might imagine, this portion of the .MAP file can be enormous, so unless you need the information you'd best select some lesser degree of detail.

* *Link buffer* specifies whether the Turbo Pascal link buffer is to be kept on disk or in memory. When the link buffer is in memory, link operations proceed more quickly; on the other hand, the link buffer occupies memory that might also be given to the program under development. When the link buffer is kept on disk, link operations go more slowly because disk I/O is a great deal slower than memory access. The choice is yours: The default condition is to leave the link buffer in memory, and this will work well for

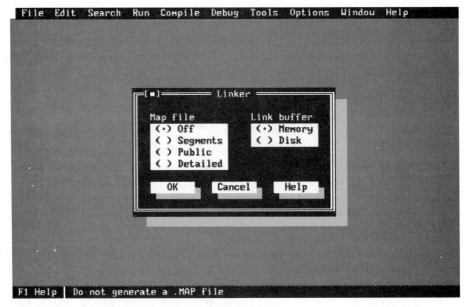

Figure 15.3 The Options | Linker Dialog Box

all but the very largest programs. Once your program grows to the point that you are having a hard time compiling it within the IDE, the first thing you should do is change the Link buffer item to **Disk**.

15.6 The Options | Environment Submenu

Most of the Options menu items lead directly to dialog boxes. Options | Environment is a *submenu*; that is, a menu within a menu, and it leads, ultimately, to five different dialog boxes full of configurable options. (See Figure 15.4.) As you might imagine, the suite of Options | Environment dialog boxes exists to help you set up the Turbo Pascal IDE to suit your own preferences and needs. For that reason, there are no equivalent source code directives or command-line compiler directives. The things you're configuring with the Options | Environment submenu dialog boxes apply *only* to the IDE.

In writing this book, I'm *not* trying to create a replacement for the Borland manuals; what I'm trying to do is help you understand the most important facets of Borland and Turbo Pascal. There are quite a number of options available for fiddling-with behind the Options | Environment submenu, and I could use half the book in describing them all. What I'll describe here are only the ones I consider most significant. If you want to investigate any of the others, try pressing F1 for on-line Help. Borland has done a truly amazing job with their help system, and between Help and a little experimentation, you will be able to understand any of the IDE's numerous configurable options.

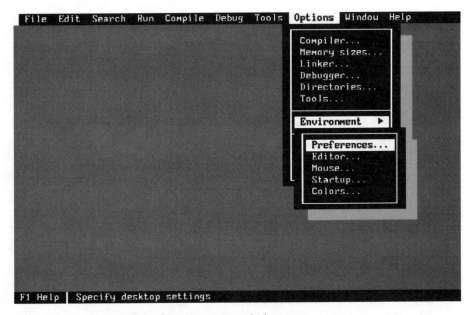

Figure 15.4 The Options | Environment Submenu

BACKING UP SOURCE FILES

Turbo Pascal 3.0 and its predecessors always created a backup file with the .BAK extension every time you saved your source code file out to disk. With Turbo Pascal 4.0 and later, you have the option to turn this feature off. The Options l Environment l Editor l Create backup files item exists to let you make that choice. It's part of the dialog box used to set options for the editor embodied in Turbo Pascal's edit windows. See Figure 15.5.

Create backup files is a check box, and can be set to either On or Off. The default is On, (checked) which means that a backup file will be created each time you save the editor file out to disk. The file as it existed before the edit began becomes the .BAK file, and the new file as written to disk takes on the old file's name.

ENABLING OR DISABLING SYNTAX HIGHLIGHTING

Version 7 originated syntax highlighting, by which different elements of your programs are shown in different colors while displayed for editing in an edit window. People seem to either love or hate this feature, and many do not realize that you can turn it off if you want to. (I heard of one chap who laboriously set all the syntax highlighting colors to yellow before realizing that syntax highlighting can be disabled with a single option!)

There is a checkbox in the Options l Environment l Editor dialog box called Syntax highlight. (See Figure 15.5.) If it's checked (the default) the IDE will

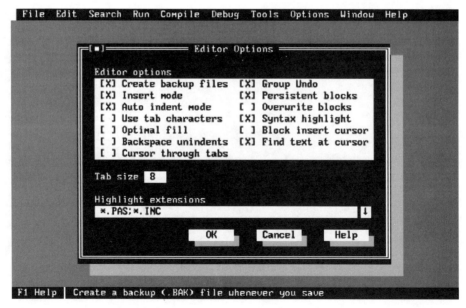

Figure 15.5 The Options l Environment l Editor Dialog Box

display program elements in different colors. Uncheck it (by clicking it with the mouse) and when you close the dialog box your source code windows will revert to single-color operation.

CHANGING THE SIZE OF EDIT WINDOW HARD TABS

Turbo Pascal's edit windows support either Borland's original *smart tabs,* whose spacing varies depending on the contents of the file, or more traditional *hard tabs,* which are the traditional tab stop every *n* characters, where *n* defaults to 8. That is, with hard tabs, every time you press the Tab key, the cursor moves eight characters to the right on the current line. The number of characters between tab stops may be set to any value from 2 to 16 by using the Tab size field inside the Options | Environment | Editor dialog box. (See Figure 15.5.)

Tab size is an editable line that appears displaying the current tab size value (usually 8). You can type in any value between 2 and 16, which will become the new tab size for hard tabs.

FILE EXTENSIONS TO HIGHLIGHT

Not everyone likes version 7's new syntax highlighting feature in the edit windows, but I'd say most people would prefer not to have to fight with it when editing files that are *not* Pascal source code. Opening an edit window into an ordinary ASCII data file is easy enough, and it's pointless having a data file peppered with colored words that just happen to be reserved words or comments.

You can define which file extensions are treated as Pascal source with the Highlight extensions field in the Options | Environment | Editor dialog box. The field displays a list of file extensions that the IDE performs syntax highlighting on. (See Figure 15.5.) This list defaults to *.PAS and *.INC. You may have other file extensions for Pascal source; I used .SRC a lot. Or you may want to use .INC for nonsource data files. To add an extension to the last, simply add a semicolon and *.<extension> to the list. Don't put a space between the semicolon and the "*" character!

AUTOMATIC SAVING BEFORE RUNNING A PROGRAM OR "SHELLING OUT"

For those who can't always remember to save early and often, Turbo Pascal provides a safety feature in the form of automatic edit file saving before leaving the editor to do dangerous things.

By "dangerous things" I mean running the compiled program or "shelling out" to DOS using the **DOS** shell item on the Files menu. In both of these cases, the Turbo Pascal IDE loses all control over what happens to the machine, and you, the programmer, regain the opportunity to lock the system up by running a faulty program or doing hazardous things from the DOS command line.

The Editor files check box in the Auto save block in the Options | Environment | Preferences dialog box enables or disables this feature. (See Figure 15.6.) The default condition is Off (not checked), which means you have sole responsibility for saving your source code files out to disk. You toggle the check box (as with all check boxes) by clicking on it with the mouse. With an X in the check box, the IDE will save your edit file before running the compiled program or before shelling out to DOS.

AUTOMATIC SAVING OF DESKTOP AND CONFIGURATION FILES

If you don't explicitly save options configured through the Options | Save item, you lose them when you leave Turbo Pascal. The Environment check box in the Auto-save block of Options | Environment | Preferences allows you to have the IDE save your options to disk automatically when you exit. (See Figure 15.6.) The default condition of this item is off (not checked), meaning that the options are *not* saved. Turning it on will save all options to a disk file whenever you exit Turbo Pascal to DOS.

The default name of this disk file is TURBO.TP, but you may name it anything you like when you save it to disk.

You auto-save the configuration of windows opened on the IDE desktop as an entirely separate matter from saving the IDE's configuration options. By this I mean that you can exit the IDE, and even turn the machine off, and when you

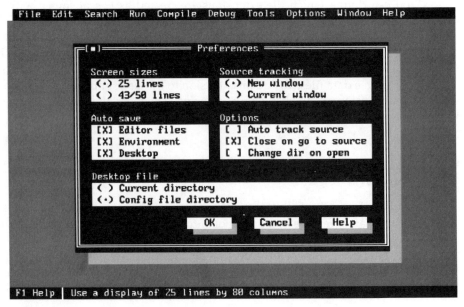

Figure 15.6 The Options | Environment | Preferences Dialog Box

come back the next day and execute the IDE, your various source code windows will be opened to the same source code files, and in the same sizes and arrangement that they took when you exited the system. This is called "saving the desktop" and you enable automatic saving of the desktop when you check the Desktop check box in the Options | Environment | Preferences dialog box. The default is *not* checked, and nothing will be saved unless you specify that you want the desktop saved by checking the Desktop check box.

CHANGING THE SCREEN SIZE

Most early PC-compatible display adapters only display 25 lines of 80 characters. IBM's EGA, introduced in 1984, can display as many as 43 lines at once, while the IBM VGA and its compatibles, introduced in 1987, can display as many as 50 lines.

The Turbo Pascal IDE defaults to a 25-line screen. However, using the Screen sizes block in the Options | Environment | Preferences dialog box you can change the number of lines on your screen to a larger number *if your installed display adapter supports it*. Turbo Pascal can detect the presence of an EGA or VGA display, and will allow you to set the larger screen sizes only for those adapters that support the larger sizes.

The Screen sizes block has two items on it: **25** lines for the standard display on any adapter; and **43/50** lines for the EGA and VGA. (See Figure 15.6.) If you have an older CGA or MDA display, only the 25-line item will be accessible. The other one will be visible, but will be displayed in a fainter shade to indicate that it is "grayed out" and therefore dormant. Under 7.0 you can have a 43-line display with an EGA adapter and a 50-line display with a VGA, but the VGA will no longer (as it did under version 4.0) allow you a 43-line screen.

When you choose a screen size, the screen changes instantly to that size, and will remain at that size until you change it again or leave the IDE. To keep a screen size across sessions, you must save out your options to a disk file using the Save item on the Options menu, as explained below.

15.7 The Directories Dialog Box

In a system like DOS that supports subdirectories, knowing where things are is critical. Turbo Pascal offers you considerable flexibility as to where you store the compiler file, your unit files, include files, and so on. Managing this flexibility is the job of the Options | Directories dialog box. See Figure 15.7.

This dialog box allows you to specify pathnames of four different directories for the use of the IDE. Some earlier versions of Turbo Pascal allowed entry of a fifth subdirectory, specifying where the Turbo Pascal product itself resided on your hard disk. This is no longer necessary, as the product searches the DOS path for any of its component data files. *You should always place the Turbo Pascal product directory in your DOS path!* Without putting the product subdirectory on

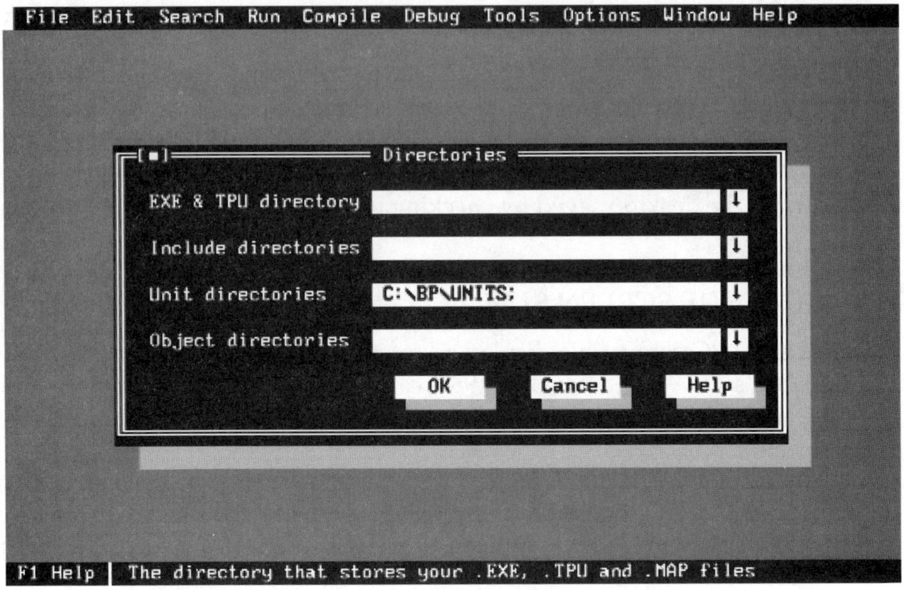

Figure 15.7 The Options I Directories Dialog Box

your DOS path, you won't be able to work from any project subdirectories
separate from the Turbo Pascal subdirectory.

SPECIFYING THE DIRECTORIES FOR COMPILED .EXE FILES

Ordinarily (and I think wisely) the .EXE files generated by the compiler are
written into the current directory. You can change that directory to another
directory if you choose by the EXE and TPU directory field. You simply type the
full path (including the disk specifier like C:, D: etc.) of the subdirectory you
want. Don't add a final backslash! Note that, unlike the other directory options
defined below, you can enter only *one* directory for executable files, since it is a
"write to" rather than a "read from" option.

I rarely use this option, as I generally move the current directory to my
project subdirectory, and then execute Turbo Pascal from there. Without any
entry in the EXE and TPU field, all generated object code files are written to the
current directory.

SPECIFYING THE DIRECTORIES FOR INCLUDE FILES

The compiler will always search the current directory for an include file specified by the **$I** compiler directive. You have the option of specifying additional

directories to be searched for include files that are not found in the current directory. This may be done through the Include directories item.

You simply type into the edit line all the names of all directories you want the compiler to search for include files. You have 128 characters in which to specify all directories, which isn't all that much if you plan to specify lots of directories or only a few that are nested *way* down deep inside the DOS directory tree. Here's an example of only two real-world search paths that, taken together, devour 46 bytes of the 128 allowed:

```
C:\TURBO\SOURCE\COMM;C:\TURBO\SOURCE\LASERJET;
```

I've begun limiting my search paths to two levels, and am using short directory names where possible. Note that multiple directories as shown here are separated by a semicolon *only. Do not leave any spaces between one directory and the next.* If you do, the space will cause the compiler to ignore any subsequent directory information.

For example, if you type the following two directory paths into the dialog box, only the first will be recognized by the compiler:

```
C:\TURBO4;  C:\JIVETALK
```

SPECIFYING THE DIRECTORIES FOR UNIT FILES

Just as with include files, the compiler will always search the current directory for any .TPU files named in a **USES** statement. You may wish to keep generally-useful units in a specific place or places, however, rather than copy them all into every project directory you have. (In fact, doing otherwise is ridiculously wasteful of your disk space.)

Note that you don't have to specify a directory in order to use units that have been moved into TURBO.TPL system library file. (This file is named TPP.TPL for units linked into protected mode programs.) This library typically includes **DOS**, **Crt**, **Printer**, and the special **System** unit, but not the BGI unit **Graph**.

But for other units (and this includes **Graph**) there ought to be a specified location. When the compiler installs itself on your hard disk, it generally places an entry in the Unit directories field for the units that Borland provides. By and large, you won't have to tell your code where to find Borland's units. You may, however, have a standard unit depository for your own code, apart from your development directories. This path leading to this depository needs to be entered into the Unit directories field so that all of your projects, regardless of where they exist on your hard disk, can access your own home-grown utility units.

The **Unit** directories item allows you to enter one or more directories separated by semicolons into its edit line, to a maximum length of 128 characters. *Do not separate the directories by space, or anything but a single semicolon.* You will see no error if you do, but any directories named after the space will be ignored and will not be searched for units named in your **USES** statements.

SPECIFYING THE DIRECTORIES FOR .OBJ FILES

Turbo Pascal links object code generated by 8086 assemblers into its own code by the use of the **$L** directive and the **EXTERNAL** standard directive. When the compiler encounters a **$L** directive, it first searches the current directory for the .OBJ file named in the directive. If the named .OBJ file doesn't exist in the current directory, the compiler will search any directory paths you have specified using the Object directories field in the Options I Directories dialog box.

As with the other directories fields described above, you can specify as many directories as you like, to a total length of 128 characters. Separate directory paths with a single semicolon, and, as I have emphasized above, *do not put any space or other characters between the named directories*. You will get no error message, but nothing after the first space or invalid character the IDE encounters will be scanned while searching!

15.8 Loading and Saving Configuration Files

Once you have spent some time and thought configuring the IDE optimally for a given project, it makes sense to save that hard-won configuration to disk for reuse later on. The Options I Save and Options I Save as items allows you to do this.

The default name of the configuration file is TURBO.TP, and Turbo Pascal will open and load a configuration file named TURBO.TP from the current directory each time you load Turbo Pascal—if it finds a file named TURBO.TP in the current directory. So you should save any "global" configuration (that is, common to all your projects) options in a file named TURBO.TP, and store that TURBO.TP in the Turbo Pascal "home" directory. (That is, where all the compiler executables are kept.) If you have an EGA display you might, for example, keep a common screen size of 43 lines at all times. This kind of information should be kept in your "global" TURBO.TP.

Other configuration data, like a set of command-line parameters, directory paths, linker setup, and so on, are specific to a given project and should be kept in a project-specific configuration file. The best way to do this (in my opinion) is to confine each major project to its own subdirectory, and within that subdirectory store a "local" TURBO.TP containing project-specific configuration information. When you begin a new project, copy the "global" TURBO.TP from the home directory into your new project directory. This gets you started on all your "standard" configuration options. Then, as your project evolves, keep saving the project-specific information to that same copy of TURBO.TP stored in the project subdirectory. That TURBO.TP will be loaded automatically every time you invoke the IDE from within the project subdirectory.

OPENING A NONDEFAULT CONFIGURATION FILE

If the IDE can find a TURBO.TP in your project subdirectory (assuming it is the current subdirectory), it will open that TURBO.TP. If there's no TURBO.TP in your project subdirectory, the IDE will open a copy of TURBO.TP from the IDE home directory (typically \TURBO or \BP\BIN). You also have the option of manually opening a configuration file with any name at all, though it's wise for the sake of quelling confusion to use the .TP extension for all configuration files.

Opening a nondefault configuration file is done with the Options I Open dialog box. (See Figure 15.8.) At the top of the dialog box is an edit line containing the name of the current configuration file. It will probably be a copy of TURBO.TP in the current directory, if the current directory is a project directory. If not, it will show the path of the IDE's home directory. All you need to do to open an entirely different configuration file is type the name of the file into the edit line. You don't even have to "erase" the line that's already there—you simply type the name or path and name, and on the first keystroke the existing line will disappear. When you press Enter, that configuration file will be loaded and replace the one currently controlling the IDE.

SAVING A NEW CONFIGURATION FILE

The IDE will not automatically create a configuration file for you. Once such a file is created, it can be told to faithfully save each time you leave the IDE, but that first step taken has to be yours.

Once you have configured the IDE the way you want it, select Options I Save as. This will bring up a dialog box very similar to the one for loading a configuration file. Again, you simply need to type a file name, or a path and a file name, into the edit line at the top of the dialog box. As soon as you press enter, the current IDE configuration will be stored to disk in the specified file.

Figure 15.8 The Open Options Dialog Box

You must do this at least once to create a TURBO.TP for each project subdirectory. The configuration will go into the current directory if you don't specify any path information. In other words, you simply type TURBO.TP, and a file of that name will go out to disk in the current subdirectory with all your configuration data inside it.

SAVING THE CONFIGURATION TO THE DEFAULT CONFIGURATION FILE

I set my copy of the IDE up to save the configuration automatically every time I leave the IDE. This way, nothing is ever lost to my own forgetfulness. However, you can handle it manually if you like. Once there is a defined configuration file somewhere (either in your project subdirectory or in the IDE's home directory) you can save the configuration to disk with a single mouse click, simply by selecting Options I Save. The configuration will immediately go to whichever configuration file you're using.

For safety's sake, however, automatic saving (through the Options I Environment I Preferences I Auto save item) is definitely the way to go.

Chapter 16

Seeing What's Wrong, and Putting Things Right

DEBUGGING WITH THE INTEGRATED DEBUGGER

The single most important thing Turbo Pascal 5.0 brought to the Pascal developer was the IDE's integrated high-level debugger. Debugging is something that all Pascal programmers have to do, but until now, there have been few tools available to help them do it. Most of us continue to resort to sticking **Writeln** statements here and there in the code to display the value of a maverick variable as the program code unfolds and does its work. This is definitely the hard way to do it. Let me show you the easy way, and you'll never go back.

16.1 The Debugging Lexicon

The debugging process brings to Turbo Pascal a whole new suite of terms and concepts. People with experience in C or assembly language will be familiar with most of these terms, but people coming from BASIC or who have never stepped beyond Pascal may find the new lexicon confusing in the extreme. Before getting into the details of how to use Turbo Pascal's built-in debugging features, it will help to define some terms and describe the debugging process itself from a height.

LOW-LEVEL VERSUS HIGH-LEVEL DEBUGGING

"Debugging" is nothing more than seeing what your program code and variables are doing as the program runs. If you can watch a bug happen, you can fix it. The problem is that a program, when running, is very much a black box. All you see are its output: words or graphics written to the screen or printer. The program's innards cannot be examined unless you take deliberate steps to examine them.

427

So a debugger's job is simply to let you look inside a program while it runs. This looking can take place from two different perspectives:

From Pascal's perspective. A Pascal program consists of Pascal statements and Pascal variables. The vast majority of program bugs can be detected simply by watching the sequence in which statements execute along with the values as they change within program variables. Debugging that limits itself to the examination of language statements and variables is called *high-level debugging.*

From the machine's perspective. A computer program of any stripe is a series of machine-code instructions that act on locations in memory. The CPU chip executes the machine instructions, which act upon internal memory bins called *registers* as well as external memory bins that we call *system memory.* A portion of system memory set aside for short-term storage is called the *stack.* Each statement in a Turbo Pascal program is equivalent to some number of machine-code instructions, and each Turbo Pascal variable is some number of bytes of memory somewhere in the system memory map. *Low-level debugging* involves examining the CPU registers, the stack, the individual machine-code instructions, and the individual bytes that make up system memory as the program runs.

In a sense, high-level debugging is looking down on your program from above, while low-level debugging is looking *up* at your program from beneath. It's the same program in either case, but from above it appears as a sequence of Pascal statements, and from beneath as a sequence of machine instructions.

As you might imagine, low-level debugging is somewhat more difficult but *much* more potent. Borland Pascal 7.0 (but not Turbo Pascal 7.0) is shipped with a low-level debugger called Turbo Debugger that works very well with Turbo Pascal. I don't have the space here to describe low-level debugging, which merits a book all to itself. The rest of this chapter will limit itself to the high-level debugging features built into Turbo Pascal.

BREAKPOINTS

People who cut their teeth on interpreted BASIC probably did a lot of debugging by "control-breaking" out of program execution, and then using the **RESUME** statement to continue execution after examining or changing some variables. Something like this is possible in Turbo Pascal (though much more powerful and tidy) using the concept of *breakpoints.* A breakpoint is a flag raised at some program statement, indicating that the program is to halt temporarily at that statement. "Halting" here is not the same as "terminating." It's more like pausing in neutral with the motor running. All the values stored in the program's variables are still intact. When the program halts, the IDE takes control, putting all its resources at your disposal. You can examine and change variables and do other things before putting the program back in gear and letting it go on its way once more.

STEPPING VERSUS TRACING

Turbo Pascal also allows you to follow the step-by-step execution of a program by placing a highlight bar over the line of source code that is currently being executed. You can then execute program statements one at a time by pressing a function key. Each time you press the function key, the highlight bar moves to the next Pascal statement in sequence. This single-stepping process is sometimes called *code animation*, especially in mainframe environments.

You have two ways to execute any statement. *Stepping* through the statement treats the statement as a single indivisible step, and executes it. If the statement is a subprogram call, the subprogram is executed normally, that is, without treating *its* statements as steps to be executed individually while you watch. Essentially, the subprogram is executed as one "lump" and you do not get to see the flow of individual instructions *within* the subprogram.

Tracing a statement, on the other hand, enters subprograms and allows you to single-step a subprogram's statements as well, with a pause between each while you decide what to do next.

While debugging a program, you can step over a subroutine call or trace into it as you desire, simply by choosing the proper function key.

WATCHES

A *watch* is a window into the guts of a program variable, showing you the variable's value and how it changes during program execution. Each time you execute a single program statement, the value in the watch window for a given variable will be updated, if the executed statement changes that variable. If you have a watch open on a counter variable, you can watch its value grow as the program increments the counter variable. If that counter variable doesn't seem to be counting, you can see what's happening to it and find out what's going wrong.

Perhaps one statement increments the counter normally, but another statement later on unexpectedly *decrements* the variable. With a watch on the variable, you'll be able to see the variable first increment up to the next higher value, then decrement down to its original value. Furthermore, you'll be able to tell exactly which statement is erroneously decrementing the counter, because when the counter decrements, the highlight bar will be resting on the statement that's doing the decrementing.

EVALUATION

It may not be necessary to continuously monitor the value that changes within a variable, as happens with a watch. You can at any point *evaluate* a variable or an expression by bringing up an evaluation window. The evaluation window will allow you to enter the name of a variable. It will immediately display the current contents of that variable. Furthermore, you have the opportunity of *chang-*

ing the contents of that variable as a means of testing the effects of the change on program operation from that point on. You can't change the value of a variable from a watch window.

In general, watches are used while stepping or tracing, and evaluation is used when you run and halt a program by means of breakpoints.

DISPLAY SWAPPING

A problem arises when you try to watch a program's innards: Where do you watch them? The program under test is, presumably, using the screen to communicate with its user. Using the screen to examine statement execution and variable contents will disrupt the screen's normal output.

Turbo Pascal does something called *display swapping* that effectively shares a single physical screen between the IDE, where debugging takes place, and the program's output screen. Each time the program writes to its screen, the IDE saves the updated display out to a buffer, so that the display can be restored when you want to see it, or when the program updates it again. The IDE and the program being tested bounce back and forth, each using the screen when it must. It sounds a little crazy, but it works remarkably well.

16.2 Watching a Simple Program Run

With all of those terms defined and fresh in your mind, it makes sense to load up a simple program and trace through its execution, just to get an initial feel for the high-level debugger. A good sample program is ROOTER2.PAS, which was first presented in Section 8.1. It's a very simpleminded program that requests an integer value from the keyboard and then displays the square root of that value. It repeats this action until you enter a value of zero, which signals the code that it's time to halt and return to DOS.

```
PROGRAM BetterRooter;

VAR
  R,S : Real;

BEGIN
  Writeln('>>Better square root calculator<<');
  Writeln;
  R:=1;
  WHILE R<>0 DO
    BEGIN
      Write('>>Enter the number (0 to exit): ');
      Readln(R);
      IF R<>0 THEN
      BEGIN
        S := Sqrt(R);
```

```
        Writeln('  The square root of ',R:7:7,' is ',S:7:7,'.');
        Writeln
     END
   END;
  Writeln('>>Square root calculator signing off...')
END.
```

Load **BetterRooter** into the editor as you would if you were simply intending to compile and run it. Before trying to debug the program, compile and run it (if you haven't before) just so that you know what to expect from it. That done, let's trace through it one statement at a time.

Bring down the Run menu—remember that Alt-R is the easiest way to do it if you don't have a mouse. Begin the trace by selecting the Step over item on the Run menu. (F8 is a shortcut for Step over, by the way, and is also the way you continue stepping once stepping has begun.) The Run menu will disappear and a highlight bar will appear over the **BEGIN** word at the start of the main program block. Unless you're using units with initialization sections, stepping and tracing *always* begin at the start of the main program block. Constant, type, and variable definition statements do not take part in the actual step-through of the program.

A single step is taken by pressing the F8 function key once. *When you press F8, the highlighted statement is executed.* I put that sentence in italics because you *must* keep that straight: The highlight is placed on a line *before* the line is executed, and the line is *not* executed *until* you press F8 (or F7, if you are tracing rather than stepping).

Something that may seem a little odd will happen when you execute most statements during a step-through. The IDE will vanish for a moment, and the output screen (essentially the screen you left behind when you loaded Turbo Pascal from DOS) will appear very briefly. Just as briefly, the output screen will vanish again, and the IDE will return, with the highlight bar on the next statement in sequence.

What gives? This is Turbo Pascal's display swapping machinery in action. Because many statements have the power to write to the display, the IDE, before it executes a statement, will "bring in" the output screen from its buffer and put it into display memory. This is *not* done so that you can see it (so don't complain that it comes and goes too quickly!), but rather to allow the executed statement to write to the display. As soon as the executed statement has done its thing, the IDE saves the output screen back to its buffer and reappears on your display.

On an 8088-based PC, the swapping happens slowly enough for you to glimpse what's happening on the output screen. On AT-type machines (and especially fast 386- or 486-based machines) display swapping will happen so quickly that the screen simply flashes, and that's all you'll see of the output screen. Remember, the output screen is just "passing through" for the program's benefit, and you are not expected to be able to see it.

If you want to see the output screen, all you need to do is press Alt-F5. The output screen will appear instantly. Pressing Alt-F5 again (or any other key, actually) will bring back the IDE.

You may also notice that display swapping does not happen on *all* statements. The Turbo Pascal IDE does its best to avoid swapping the display unless necessary, so on some statements that cannot possibly write to the screen (a simple assignment statement, for example) the statement will execute without the IDE swapping the display. This is called "smart" display swapping, and is the default mechanism. Later on we'll explain how display swapping may be disabled altogether, or done on every single statement.

So, step away! Every time you press F8, the highlight bar will move down by one line. There is a loop in **BetterRooter**, and you can watch execution go around the loop again and again, calculating the square root for a different number each time.

You'll notice that when you execute the **Readln** statement, the output screen comes in and stays in. While **Readln** waits for your input, the output screen will remain in view. As soon as you enter some value and press Enter, the IDE will return.

Step through to the end of **BetterRooter** by entering a 0 at the **Readln** statement. When you step off the end of the program, the highlight bar will disappear.

16.3 Tracing a Program with Subprograms

BetterRooter is an extremely simple program. It has only one loop and no procedures or functions. Far more of the power of the high-level debugger comes into play when you trace a program that has subprograms.

Let's move ahead by debugging a fairly simple program presented in Section 9.13, **MorseTest**. This program demonstrates Turbo Pascal's sound routines by translating text strings into Morse code.

```
PROGRAM MorseTest;

USES Crt;

TYPE
  String80  = String[80];

{$I SENDMORS.SRC}

BEGIN
  ClrScr;
  SendMorse('CQCQCQ DE KI6RA *SK',850,15);
END.
```

The main program of **MorseTest** contains only two statements. The first clears the screen, and the second actually sounds the Morse code equivalent of the string parameter through the speaker. Load the program and step through it as we did with **BetterRooter**, using F8 to execute each of the two statements in turn. When the first statement executes, the output screen will clear. When the second statement executes, you will hear Morse code from the system speaker.

After executing the call to **SendMorse**, the step-through is finished and the highlight bar will disappear.

You've probably already decided that this won't help you much if you have a problem *inside* the **SendMorse** procedure. Fortunately, there is a way to step through subprograms as well as main program blocks: Trace into (the shortcut is F7).

Begin another step-through for **MorseTest**, but this time, press F7 rather than F8 to execute each statement. The **ClrScr** statement will execute just as before. However, when you execute the call to **SendMorse** by pressing F7, the **MorseTest** program vanishes from the screen and the source code for the **SendMorse** procedure appears in its place, with the highlight bar over the opening **BEGIN** of the **SendMorse** procedure body.

THE DIFFERENCE BETWEEN TRACE INTO AND STEP OVER

This is a good place to ponder the difference between Step over (F8) and Trace into (F7). Step over executes the highlighted statement *as a single entity*. In other words, a procedure call is executed as a procedure call without any attempt to step through the procedure's statements as well. Trace into, by contrast, follows subprogram calls down into the subprogram source code, and will single-step all program statements (including subprogram statements) as it encounters them.

You are not obliged to use one or the other during a step-through of a program. Each time you see that the highlight bar is over a subprogram call, you can decide which way to go: to step over the subprogram call (executing it without single-stepping it) or to descend into the subprogram and single-step its statements as well.

So give it a try. When the **SendMorse** procedure call is highlighted, press F7 rather than F8. The source code for **SendMorse** will be loaded into the editor, and you can begin single-stepping the procedure.

The bulk of procedure **SendMorse** is one enormous **CASE..OF** statement. You might expect that the **CASE..OF** statement would be executed in one blow (since only one of its case labels can be found equal to the case selector), but Turbo Pascal bends its rules a little bit and acts as though each individual test within the **CASE..OF** statement were itself a separate statement.

So once you enter the **CASE..OF** statement, each press of F7 moves one case label down into the **CASE..OF** statement until the case selector matches the case label. Only then does the highlight bar skip to the end of the **CASE..OF** statement and highlight the next statement in sequence.

The statement that immediately follows the **CASE..OF** statement is another procedure call, to a local procedure named **Morse**. When the call to **Morse** is highlighted, you can again take your choice: to step through procedure **Morse** or simply to execute it. If you choose to execute it, you will hear a generated Morse code character sound off on the speaker. Choosing to step through **Morse**, however, will demonstrate something important: Single-stepping will disrupt the operation of programs (like **MorseTest**) that depend on system timing.

Try it and see. Procedure **Morse** uses Turbo Pascal's sound-generating procedures and the **Delay** procedure to create audible Morse code characters. The **Sound** procedure turns on the tone through the speaker. The **Delay** procedure is supposed to dictate how long the tone is to remain on. Once you execute the **Sound** procedure, however, the tone will remain on while the IDE waits for you to press F7 again. Stepping through **Morse** will create some sound, but it won't necessarily sound like Morse code. Keep this effect in mind: Single-stepping a program isn't always possible without seriously altering the program's intended output. Fortunately, your ability to execute a procedure call without single-stepping the procedure allows you to avoid stepping through those parts of the program that won't take single-stepping gracefully.

STATEMENTS VERSUS SOURCE CODE LINES

Up until now I haven't drawn any distinction between a program statement and a line of source code, but the distinction must be made. The Turbo Pascal integrated debugger is a *line-oriented* debugger. It executes one *line* of source code with each single step rather than one *statement*.

I have on occasion combined several statements onto one source code line, particularly assignment statements that assign initial values to a whole clutch of program variables. Cramming many statements onto one line is generally bad practice from a readability standpoint, and now, with integrated debugging, you have even more reason to avoid overdense lines of code. One statement per line is the most readable format you can write, and also the most amenable to sanity in debugging with Turbo Pascal.

TRACING INTO UNITS

The **MorseTest** program in the single-stepping example above brings in an include file containing its single subprogram in source code form. The include file has to be present for the program as a whole to compile, so the compiler can assume with confidence that the include file can be loaded in for single-stepping.

But what about subprograms existing in units? The compiler will try to trace a subprogram in a unit by searching for the source code for that unit. If the source code for the unit is found, it will be loaded into an edit window and tracing will continue. If the source code is *not* found, no error is generated, but the subprogram will be executed without tracing through it, exactly as it would be if **Step** over were executed rather than **Trace** into. Note that units residing in SYSTEM.TPU are *never* traced, whether or not their source code is available to the compiler. But since these contain Borland's commonest utility routines, you have some confidence that bugs, if present, will be in your code rather than Borland's.

16.4 Examining Variables through Evaluation and Watches

Single-stepping allows you to see the order in which statements are executed, which can often be a great help in deciding what is wrong with a balky program. Statements are only half of what a program is about, though—looking "inside" a variable is just as important as single-stepping statements, and Turbo Pascal provides plenty of power in this area as well.

USING THE EVALUATION WINDOW

While the IDE is paused, waiting for you to execute the next statement via F7 or F8, you have the ability to examine any program variable in or above the current scope. This is done by bringing up a window especially for that purpose. The window can be invoked from the Debug menu, by selecting Debug|Evaluate/modify. (Ctrl-F4 is the shortcut for Evaluate/modify.) The evaluation window is divided into three fields, as shown in Figure 16.1. Each field of the evaluation window has a name, indicating its function.

The top field of the evaluation window is the Expression field. It accepts the identifier or expression that you wish to evaluate. The middle field is the Result field, which displays the result of the IDE evaluating what you enter into the top field. The bottom field is the New value field, into which you can enter a new value for a modifiable identifier currently shown in the Expression field.

When you bring up the evaluation window, perhaps at a breakpoint during a debug session, the word containing the editor cursor will be in the Expression

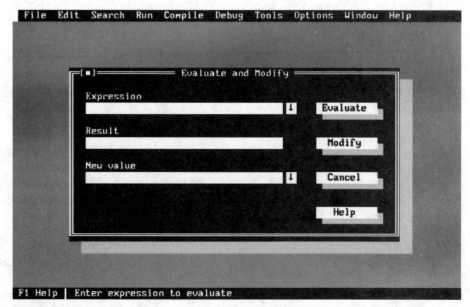

Figure 16.1 The Evaluation Window (EVAL.CAP)

field. This is done blindly by the IDE, and certainly does not guarantee that the identifier is an evaluatable item. The cursor may be within the reserved word **BEGIN**, for example, or the name of a subprogram, neither of which make any sense in the context of the Expression field. If the word at the cursor is *not* what you want to evaluate, you can move the cursor around the screen, and place it at the start of any evaluatable identifier. Then, when you bring up the evaluation window, the identifier that starts under the cursor will be in the Expression field. You need only press Enter to evaluate it.

A further extension to this slick trick is that you can copy in additional text from the edit window to the Expression field by pressing the right arrow key. When you want to evaluate an entire expression, this will be a valuable feature, because the Expression field will initially only copy in the single word containing the cursor, and not an entire expression. Its ability to "guess" what you want is strictly limited.

Of course, you also have the option of typing in the name of an identifier to evaluate. If you wish to evaluate an expression that does exist anywhere on the screen, typing it in will be your only option.

The most obvious use for the evaluation window is in inspecting and modifying program variables. Any time your program is paused, either at a breakpoint or between single steps, you can enter the name of an identifier in the Expression field and its value will be displayed in the Result field. This allows you to peek at your program variables whenever you want.

One of the most desirable features of the evaluation window is its ability to display the values of data items that have no easily-printable form. A set, for example, will be displayed as the values present in the set between the set builder brackets. For example, a set of characters containing the upper- and lowercase 'Y' characters plus the BEL character (ASCII character 7) would be displayed as:

```
[#7,'Y','y']
```

If the displayed value is wider than the 50-odd characters that can be seen in a field at one time, the field may be scrolled rightward and leftward as desired, using the arrow keys.

EVALUATING EXPRESSIONS

The evaluation window will also evaluate expressions, within certain limits. The expression must be a true expression, in that it must "cook down" to some single value. In addition to program variables it can involve numeric, character, and Boolean literals; constants; any arithmetic or logical operator; and certain built-in functions. The list of valid functions is not long, and it is not obvious which built-in functions are valid and which are not. The list of functions that I have found to be valid include: **@**, **Abs**, **Addr**, **Chr**, **CSeg**, **DSeg**, **Hi**, **Length**, **Lo**, **Odd**, **Ofs**, **Ord**, **Pred**, **Ptr**, **Seg**, **SizeOf**, **TypeOf**, **SPtr**, **SSeg**, **Succ**, and **Swap**.

Even this short length of functions allows you to do some very useful things, like locating program identifiers (including subprograms) by address in memory; checking the length of strings; and watching the stack pointer register. Unfortunately, all of the functions that act on real numbers are excluded from expressions. This includes **Pi**, the trig functions, and the integer/real transfer functions.

The evaluation window can also act as a primitive programmer's calculator, in allowing you to determine the result of masking operations, shifting quantities, and so on, simply by typing the expressions to be evaluated; for example,

```
$F4 SHR 3
133 OR 51
MyMask AND $CB
```

The window will convert hexadecimal values to decimal; all you need to do is type a hex value like $D3 into the Expression field, and its decimal equivalent will appear in the Result field. Sadly, you can't force it to work the other way, and convert decimal to hex.

The evaluation window will reject an Expression field entry that cannot be evaluated with an error message in the Result field, typically, "Error in expression." Also, it will not allow you to modify a nonvariable in the New value field.

DISPLAY FORMATS AND FORMAT DIRECTIVES

Turbo Pascal provides considerable flexibility in how you display the data contained in the variables you evaluate. The default display format for each type of data is the one that makes the most sense, but there are *format directives* that you can use when evaluating data that will display data in a slightly different way. These format directives are characters that are appended to the data item in question with a comma, as in:

```
BelChar,C
```

The format directives are summarized in Table 16.1.

Characters are displayed in one of two ways: "Printable" characters are shown in their standard ASCII form, in single quotes, as in 'B'. "Control" characters 0–31 are displayed as their numeric equivalents with a preceding pound sign, as in #7 for the ASCII BEL character 7. You can override this format using the **c** format directive, which forces the use of IBM standard symbols for control character display. Characters in the high-order character set are displayed in quotes using the standard IBM symbols, as in '⊤' for character 209.

Sets are displayed as you would build them, within set builder brackets, with the elements of the set separated by commas. If the compiler identifies a closed interval within the set, the items in the closed interval will be displayed as a closed interval rather than as individual elements. Given our enumerated type **Spectrum** from Section 7.3, a **SET OF Spectrum** might be displayed as shown below:

```
[RED..YELLOW,INDIGO]
```

Table 16.1 Format Directives

Directive	Function
C	Displays "control characters" 0–31 as their respective IBM-standard character-set symbols rather than the default of a pound sign followed by the character's numeric equivalent; i.e., character 1 will be shown as a "smiley face" rather than as "#1." Works *only* on characters or elements of strings.
D	Dumps the preceding data item (which may be of any type) as a series of hexadecimal values.
Fn	**n** specifies the number of visible digits for display of any floating-point types.
nM	Displays **n** bytes of memory in hex dump format starting at the address defined by the given expression. If you don't provide an n value, the size of the memory region to be displayed is assumed to be the size of the variable in the expression.
P	Overrides the default pointer format **PTR($<seg>,$<ofs>)** to a simple (and shorter) display of **<seg>,<ofs>** with both in hex. May be used with any address type or expression that cooks down to an address, such as **Addr**, and **@**. Legal but unnecessary for **CSeg**, **DSeg**, **Seg**, and **Ofs**.
R	Applies the record field label to the value of each field in the display of records, as in **LASTNAME : 'Duntemann'** rather than merely **'Duntemann'**.
S	Modifies a memory dump specified by nM such that ASCII 0–31 will be displayed as #XX rather than in hex.
X,$,H	Any of these three directives forces integer types to display as hexadecimal rather than the default of decimal. Legal but ignored for other simple types; i.e., you cannot force control characters to be displayed in hex with **X**; use **d** instead.

Note that even though we originally defined the constants of type **Spectrum** in mixed case, they will always be shown in uppercase when displayed in the Expression field, because the compiler forces all program identifiers to uppercase before it processes them. This is true for the constants comprising an enumerated type in all circumstances, not simply in set display.

Booleans are displayed as one of the two uppercase constants **TRUE** or **FALSE**.

Pointers are displayed using the syntax of the built-in **Ptr** function:

```
Ptr($6180,$30)
```

You can use a terser display format by appending the **P** format directive to a pointer identifier, as in **MyPtr,P**. This form simply displays the hexadecimal formats of the segment and offset values, separated by commas:

```
6180,30
```

Note that you can dereference pointers in the Expression field by using the familiar pointer notation **MyPtr^**, which will display whatever data **MyPtr** points to, rather than the address **MyPtr** contains. Dereferencing can also be done to generic (untyped) pointers, but *only* if you include the format specifier **D**. This will display a hex dump of the 86 bytes following the address to which the untyped pointer points. (86 since each byte requires three characters to dump, and 3 x 86 fills the 255 character limit of the Result field.)

Records default to a list of field values separated by commas and enclosed within parentheses:

```
(NIL,'Sprightly',42,Ptr($A134,$131))
```

You can also display the field names in front of each value by appending the **r** format directive to the end of the record identifier:

```
(Next:NIL,KeyName:'Sprightly',KeyVal:42,Prev:PTR($A134,$131))
```

Records that contain nested records will be displayed with the inner records enclosed in parentheses.

Arrays are displayed, like records, enclosed by parentheses with commas separating individual values. Most arrays are too long to display entirely within the Expression field, and the compiler will show only the part of the array that will fill 255 characters. (For an integer array, this is only 86 elements—not very much!) Displaying some portion of the array that does not fall within the first equivalent 255 characters requires a little more finesse. You need to specify the starting element to display, followed after a comma by the number of elements to be displayed. For example, to show 10 elements of an array starting at element 1,677, you would enter this into the Expression field:

```
MyArray[1677],10
```

If you intend to use a format directive in addition to the repeat count value, the format directive must come *after* the repeat count.

File variables are displayed with the status of the logical file followed by the name of the physical file (if any) connected with the logical file. The status is given as one of the four uppercase words **OPEN**, **CLOSED**, **READ**, or **WRITE**. A file currently being read would be displayed as

```
(READ,'STARDATA.BIN')
```

A logical file that is not connected with any physical file is displayed simply as **(CLOSED)**.

Looking more closely at a file variable's innards can be done by casting the file variable onto a record of type **FileRec**. (Type casting in the Expression field will be explained more fully a little later in this section.) The **FileRec** type is defined in the **DOS** unit, and if you intend to perform such a type cast, your program must **USE** the **DOS** unit *even if you make no other use of anything from the DOS unit*. The cast is entered this way:

```
FileRec(StarFile),R
```

This essentially converts **StarFile** to a record, and will be displayed as any other record would be displayed. The **R** format directive helps comprehension of the display a little bit by preceding each of the **FileRec** field values with the field's name. This will allow you to monitor the file handle, the file mode, the record size, and other file internals.

MODIFYING PROGRAM VARIABLES IN THE NEW VALUE FIELD

The third field in the evaluation window is the New value field. It will allow you to alter the values of program variables during a program pause, and then continue execution of the program to see what happens when the modified variable takes on its new value. This allows you to play some interesting "what if?" games with malfunctioning programs, by letting you enter what you think is the correct value of a wayward variable to see how the program responds.

With a variable or typed constant in the Expression field, you can enter any assignment-compatible value into the New value field, and that value will be stored in the variable or typed constant. This value may be an expression, as long as the expression cooks down to a value assignment compatible with the identifier in the Expression field. The New value field performs some range checking and assignment-compatibility checking on the entered new value, and will display an error message if the new value is out of range or cannot be assigned to the identifier in the Expression field.

You can enter new values only for simple types and strings; in other words, you cannot enter a complete array or record, even a short one that could be entered within the limits of the field. You *can* enter a new value for any simple type or string element of an array or field of a record.

You cannot enter new values at all for sets or files.

Keep in mind that by modifying the values of pointers into system memory, or absolute variables defined over some essential part of system memory, that you can crash your system without any protection from the Turbo Pascal IDE. Be careful.

LOCAL SYMBOLS

There is a very basic conceptual difference between global variables and variables belonging to subprograms. Global variables exist in a program's data segment and exist throughout the time the program has control of the machine. Identifiers connected with subprograms are local, and are allocated on the stack *only* during the period that the subprogram has control. When the subprogram terminates and returns control to its caller, the subprogram is *de-instantiated*, and all of its parameters and local variables *are removed from the stack*.

This is why you cannot examine a local variable unless you are currently tracing into the subprogram that "owns" that local variable. If you are outside the subprogram, the subprogram's local variables are no longer on the stack and do not, in fact, exist at all. That's why the Result field in the Evaluate/modify window will tell you "unknown identifier" when you try to evaluate a local variable belonging to a subprogram that you're not currently tracing. It's not so much that the identifier is unknown as that it just doesn't exist at the moment.

Ordinarily, when you compile a program with the intent to debug it, all local symbols are compiled into the IDE's symbol tables. Thus, when you trace into a subprogram, you can evaluate a variable or put it into the watch window (see below on watches.) However, to save IDE memory when you are not intending to debug a program, you can turn off this access to local symbols. The means is the $L- compiler directive, or the Local symbols item in the **Debug** menu.

THE CALL STACK

Another very handy inspection tool offered by Turbo Pascal is the *call stack*, which is a window that will show you how deeply you are nested in subprogram execution, along with (most usefully!) the parameters with which the current instantiation of each nested subprogram was called. A screen display showing the call stack from within the **Morse** procedure of the **MorseTest** program is shown in Figure 16.2. Note that the call stack builds from the bottom up; the most recently entered subprogram will be on top.

Keep in mind that while as many as 128 levels are tracked by the call stack, only nine levels will be displayed at a time. To inspect more than nine, use the arrow keys to move the displayed stack up and down within its window, or else maximize the window temporarily. If the window appears in front of code you want to examine (perhaps in conjunction with examining the call stack itself), simply move the window to one side or another by "grabbing" the top line of the window with the mouse and moving the mouse. This applies to any IDE window, of course—but it's amazing how often I forgot, early on, that I could position the various IDE windows anywhere I wanted them.

Another interesting thing to do is inspect the call stack at various points during the execution of a recursive function, like the **Factorial** function and **QuickSort** procedure from Section 8.15. The names of the subprograms on the call stack will be the same, but the parameter *values* will be different for each call. The best way to do this is to set a breakpoint (see the next section on breakpoints) at the beginning of the main block of the recursive subprogram, so that you can inspect the call stack during the breakpoint pause each time the recursive routine takes control.

Another useful call stack feature allows you to double-click on any function call listed in the call stack, and the IDE will immediately take you to the source code implementing that function call. Very slick!

One thing to keep in mind: The call stack will *not* display the names of nested subprograms if you have disabled access to local symbols by using the $L- compiler directive or the Local symbols item on the **Debug** menu. Subprograms are, after all, local entities from the global perspective of the main program. Without access to local symbols, you can't see the subprograms themselves any more than subprogram parameters or variables.

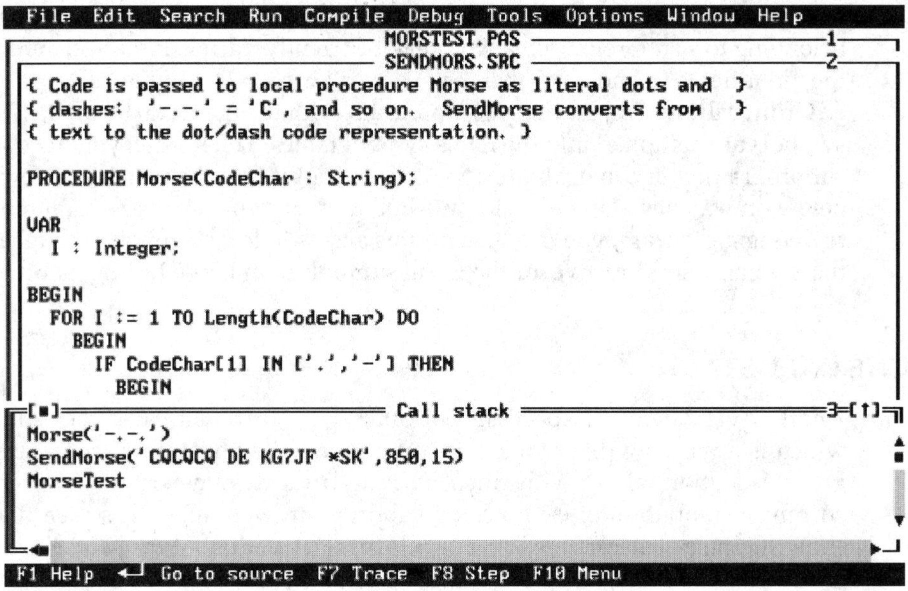

```
 File  Edit  Search  Run  Compile  Debug  Tools  Options  Window  Help
┌──────────────────────── MORSTEST.PAS ─────────────────────────1───┐
│──────────────────────── SENDMORS.SRC ─────────────────────────2─  │
│ { Code is passed to local procedure Morse as literal dots and  }  │
│ { dashes:  '-.-.' = 'C', and so on.  SendMorse converts from   }  │
│ { text to the dot/dash code representation. }                     │
│                                                                   │
│ PROCEDURE Morse(CodeChar : String);                               │
│                                                                   │
│ VAR                                                               │
│   I : Integer;                                                    │
│                                                                   │
│ BEGIN                                                             │
│   FOR I := 1 TO Length(CodeChar) DO                               │
│     BEGIN                                                         │
│       IF CodeChar[1] IN ['.','-'] THEN                            │
│         BEGIN                                                     │
┌─[■]═══════════════════════ Call stack ════════════════════════3─[↑]┐
│ Morse('-.-.')                                                     │
│ SendMorse('CQCQCQ DE KG7JF *SK',850,15)                          ▲│
│ MorseTest                                                        ▓│
│                                                                  ▼│
└─◄─────────────────────────────────────────────────────────────►─┘
 F1 Help  ◄┘ Go to source  F7 Trace  F8 Step  F10 Menu
```

Figure 16.2 The Call Stack

WATCHES

Turbo Pascal offers another window into the private lives of program variables: Watches. A *watch* is, in essence, a continuous evaluation window into a single variable, updated after each step taken when stepping through a program. Without having to take any ongoing action, you can observe the continuous changes in a variable's value as you step your way through the program.

Watches exist in a window of their own called the *watch window*. A watch consists of the name of a variable or of an expression that is evaluated and updated after each step taken while stepping a program. Any symbol or expression that may be evaluated in the evaluation window (as described above) may also be a legal watch. The display format and format directives are identical.

Adding a watch to the watch window is done through the Debug|Add Watch menu item. Alternatively, you can use the Ctrl-F7 shortcut key to add a watch. Regardless of which way you choose to add a watch, a dialog box entitled Add Watch will appear. The window will already contain the identifier (if any) currently under the cursor in the edit window. Generally, the cursor follows the highlight bar, but you can move the cursor independently of the highlight bar with the arrow keys to select an identifier for the Add Watch window.

You can also type the name of the identifier into the Add Watch window. If you wish to add a format directive to the identifier in the Add Watch window, you will have to type that out explicitly, just as you would in working with the evaluation window, described earlier. Pressing Enter will add a watch on that identifier to the watch window.

Once a watch is in the watch window, it will be updated each time you take a program step. Of course, if the value of the watch item doesn't change through the action of a step, it won't change after that step. The IDE evaluates every watch in the watch window after each program step taken, and updates each watch any time its value changes.

You can edit or delete existing watches by switching from the Edit window to the Watch window, either by clicking anywhere on the watch window with the mouse or by pressing F6 repeatedly to cycle active windows until the watch window becomes active. When the watch window is active, a highlight bar will highlight the current watch. This watch can be edited by pressing Enter, which brings up the Add Watch dialog box again. The highlighted watch can be deleted by pressing the Delete key. You can also add a new watch to the watch window while it's active, by pressing Ins.

Although watches are tailor-made for watching program variables while single-stepping a program, they operate identically when you run a program with breakpoints. At any breakpoint pause, the IDE will update watches in the watch window before turning control back to you.

16.5 Using Breakpoints

Single-stepping through a program from start to finish (as we've done in the simple examples above) can be enlightening, but it isn't practical for larger projects. (The potential tedium of single-stepping through a 10,000-iteration loop should be obvious.) What makes a lot more sense is to execute a malfunctioning program normally until execution gets close to the suspected site of the trouble, and *then* begin single-stepping until the source of the problem is found. For this, another type of tool is needed: breakpoints.

A *breakpoint* is a stop sign inserted into your code by the compiler at your request. When your code is executing and encounters a breakpoint, it will pause and the IDE will take over the screen. The source code will appear in an edit window, with the highlight bar over the source code line containing the breakpoint.

At this point, you can do whatever you need to do; all the resources of the IDE are at your service. You can examine or modify variables using the evaluation window. You can single-step your way further into the program. You can hot-key the output screen into view (using Alt-F5) to see what the program has accomplished up to that point. Or you can continue full-speed execution of the program until it terminates, or until it encounters another (or re-encounters the same) breakpoint.

SETTING AND CLEARING BREAKPOINTS

Breakpoints are *line-oriented*. In other words, a breakpoint can only be set at the start of a program line, not at some individual statement within a multi-statement line. This is yet another reason to confine yourself to one program statement per line.

There are two ways to set breakpoints in your code, and they are not the same. The simple way is by using a shortcut key: Ctrl-F8 is the "toggle breakpoints" shortcut key. When you press Ctrl-F8, the line containing the cursor becomes highlighted, and the IDE marks it as an *unconditional breakpoint*. When code execution encounters an unconditional breakpoint, it simply stops, no questions asked. Clearing (removing) an unconditional breakpoint is done the same way: Place the cursor on a line that already contains a breakpoint, and then press Ctrl-F8 to toggle the breakpoint off again. When a line contains a breakpoint of any kind, it is set to a different color or highlight level, depending on what sort of screen your copy of Turbo Pascal has been installed for. You can always tell at a glance when looking at your edit window where the breakpoints are.

The other method for setting breakpoints is more versatile, and more interesting. When you select the Debug | Add breakpoint item, the Add breakpoint dialog box appears. See Figure 16.3. You can set an unconditional breakpoint through the Add breakpoint dialog box if you want. (Pressing Ctrl-F8 is a lot easier.) But you can also set a *conditional breakpoint*, which means a breakpoint that pauses execution only if some testable condition is met at the time execution reaches the breakpoint.

SETTING CONDITIONAL BREAKPOINTS

Every time a step is taken while single-stepping a program, the IDE evaluates each watch and redisplays the contents of the watched variables. A conditional breakpoint is handled similarly: Every time execution reaches a conditional

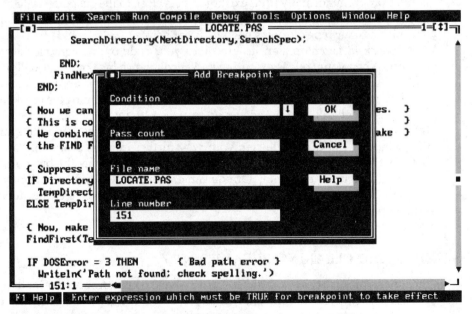

Figure 16.3 The Add Breakpoint Dialog Box

breakpoint, the IDE performs a predefined test attached to that breakpoint. If the test succeeds, execution is paused, allowing you to use the machinery of the IDE to examine the state of your program. If the test fails, execution keeps right on going through the breakpoint.

Why is this useful? Suppose you have a 1000-step loop in your program, and the program crashes with a range error somewhere on the 700th iteration of the loop or thereabouts. Stepping through a loop 700-odd times would try the patience of a stone. Better yet—set your breakpoint to pause execution *only* after execution has passed the breakpoint 700 times. If you crash before you get there, ratchet back on the number of times execution is to pass the breakpoint. (We call this the *pass count.*) If execution reaches the 700th pass unscathed, you can single-step a few more times through the loop, or perhaps try again with a pass count of 725, to get as close as possible to the crash point without quite reaching it. From that vantage point, you can watch some likely variables to see which one is growing out of range.

Or, if a loop isn't the problem, you can set a *Boolean condition* on the breakpoint. This is some sort of expression that evaluates to a Boolean value. Each time execution passes the breakpoint, the IDE quickly evaluates the Boolean expression connected with that breakpoint. Perhaps you set the expression **BlockReceived = True**. If the **BlockReceived** variable is equal to **True**, execution will pause. If **BlockReceived** is equal to **False**, execution will keep on going. Unless something somewhere in the program eventually sets **BlockReceived** to **True**, that particular breakpoint may never in fact pause execution.

But hey, that tells you something right there.

In a sense, a breakpoint on a Boolean condition is a watch that the IDE watches so that you don't have to. The machinery that generates Turbo Pascal code can easily tell when a variable changes from False to True, so why go crosseyed staring at the screen until the variable does something?

Setting a Boolean condition on a breakpoint is done in the top field of the Add breakpoint dialog box shown in Figure 16.3. Type any legal Boolean expression.

*Note: The IDE will not parse the expression **until the breakpoint expression is evaluated at runtime.** Nothing is checked when you enter the expression, so be extra careful how you spell variable names.*

You can enter more than one expression for a single line. This has the effect of an **OR** operation on the several conditions: All the expressions are evaluated when execution hits that line, and if any one of the expressions comes up **True**, execution pauses at the breakpoint.

You can enter a breakpoint with a pass count simply by typing the pass count into the Pass field in the Add breakpoint dialog box. You can have a breakpoint with both a pass count and a conditional expression; however, the Boolean conditional expression will not be evaluated until execution has passed it by the number in the pass count.

ODD NOTES ON BREAKPOINTS

Here's an interesting problem with breakpoints: The IDE does not remove a breakpoint from its list of breakpoints even when you "put away" a source code file by deleting its window. Before you start another project, you have to manually clear all the previous project's breakpoints from the breakpoint list. This is done through the Debug | Breakpoints item. Select Clear all and all breakpoints in the list will be cleared. If you don't clear breakpoints "left over" from a previous project, the IDE will give you an error message for every "orphan" breakpoint that it encounters.

Another potential problem lies in the way the IDE keeps breakpoints between sessions. You can load a file into the IDE, and if it had a breakpoint when you saved it and deleted its window, that breakpoint will still be there when you open it. That's because the IDE keeps a list of breakpoints between sessions, and each breakpoint on the list is associated with a source code file name and a line number. *Nothing in the source code file itself tells the IDE that a breakpoint exists at any given line.* There is no "hidden marker" in your source code file. If you edit a source code file *outside* of the IDE (say, with another source code editor of some kind) and change the number of lines or the order of the lines in the file, the breakpoints will be in the wrong places when you reload that file into the IDE. If you're going to use IDE breakpoints and keep them between sessions, don't edit your files anywhere but inside the IDE!

You can remove any breakpoint by placing the cursor within the breakpoint line (which is typically highlighted in red) and pressing Ctrl-F8. This is true whether you entered the breakpoint by pressing F8 originally, or through the Add breakpoint dialog box.

USING BREAKPOINTS TO EXAMINE PROGRAM OPERATION

There's no better way to get a good feel for how breakpoints are used than just to use them. Let's give it a try, and in the process I'll demonstrate the various things that can be done using the many facilities that Turbo Pascal's integrated debugger can offer.

An interesting program to observe is the **Locate** program described in Section 19.9. Load LOCATE.PAS into the Edit screen, and take a moment to read and become familiar with the general logic of the program, if you haven't already. (Only one note of warning: **Locate** is a relatively advanced program, incorporating a number of DOS calls, recursion, and some pretty involved understanding of the DOS file system. If you're a thoroughly green Turbo Pascal programmer, it might make sense to come back to this section once you've had a chance to bone up on other Turbo Pascal topics and have had some experience in programming larger programs.)

Locate is a "whereis" program. It searches your entire hard-disk directory for files that match a given file spec. In other words, if you know you have a little utility program somewhere on your 40MB hard disk called GRIMBLE.EXE, (or was it GRIMBLE.COM?) you can find it by typing

```
LOCATE GRIMBLE.*
```

Any time **Locate** encounters a file matching the **GRIMBLE.*** filespec anywhere on your hard disk, it will print out the full pathname, size, and time/date stamp of the file to your screen.

The main program of **Locate** is only a frame for a large procedure called **SearchDirectory**. Although **Locate** searches the entire DOS directory tree on each invocation, it only searches one subdirectory at a time, by invoking **SearchDirectory** to search each subdirectory. If, in the course of searching a subdirectory, **SearchDirectory** encounters a child directory, it calls itself recursively to search that child directory.

Before running **Locate**, enter a command-line parameter by selecting the **Parameters** field of the **Options** menu. A good one is *.BAK, since almost everyone has some .BAK backup files somewhere on their hard disk system.

ADDING SOME BREAKPOINTS

Now you're ready to add breakpoints to **Locate**. Before you can do that, however, you need to decide just what you're looking for. In a real debugging situation, an errant program would be doing something odd, or failing to do something that you consider correct. The place to go in the source code has to be your best guess as to the location of the trouble. You may be (or will probably be) wrong on your first guess, but you have to start somewhere. Debugging is not an exact science, but a process of successive refinement of hunches.

Perhaps **Locate** isn't locating all the files it should be locating. The place to go, pretty obviously, is the point at which **Locate** decides that it has found a file to match the search file specification. Once you're there, you can inspect certain variables to see just what's going on.

Locate tests the **DOSError** flag every time it executes **FindFirst** or **FindNext**. If the value is 0, then a file has been found. A good spot for a breakpoint would be immediately after the **FindFirst** invocation that looks for files (an earlier **FindFirst**/**FindNext** cycle searches separately for subdirectories) in the **BEGIN..END** block executed when **DOSError** is equal to 0:

```
{ Now, make the FIND FIRST call: }
  FindFirst(TempDirectory,0,CurrentDTA);

IF DOSError = 3 THEN        { Bad path error }
  Writeln('Path not found; check spelling.')

{ If we found something in the current directory matching the filespec, }
{ format it nicely into a single string and display it: }
ELSE IF (DOSError = 2) OR (DOSError = 18) THEN
  { Null; Directory is empty }
```

```
  ELSE
    BEGIN
      DTAtoDIR(CurrentDIR);        { Convert first find to DIR format.. }
      DisplayData(Directory,CurrentDIR);         { Show it pretty-like }

      IF DOSError <> 18 THEN { More files are out there... }
        REPEAT
          FindNext(CurrentDTA);
          IF DOSError <> 18 THEN  { More entries exist }
            BEGIN
              DTAtoDIR(CurrentDIR);
              { Convert further finds to DIR format }
              DisplayData(Directory,CurrentDIR)    { and display 'em }
            END
        UNTIL (DOSError = 18) OR (DOSError = 2)  { Ain't no more! }
    END
```

The breakpoint position is marked through shading. You mark a breakpoint by moving the cursor to the desired line and pressing Ctrl-F8, which is a shortcut to the **T**oggle breakpoint item on the **Break**/watch menu. Note that there are *two* shaded lines on the code fragment above. Remember, **FindFirst** and **FindNext** operate together. If you want to break on every file found by **Locate**, you must set a breakpoint after each. Breaking after **FindFirst** will happen only on the *first* file located in each subdirectory. Mark both breakpoints shown.

ADDING SOME WATCHES

Next, you need to decide what to examine when you pause for breakpoints. When a file is found by **Locate**, file information is retained in a record called **CurrentDTA**, of type **SearchRec**. How about a watch on **CurrentDTA**? That wouldn't be hard to set up, but for purely practical reasons you would not want to display the whole record, as the first 21 bytes are private to DOS and not especially meaningful. Better would be to set two separate watches on the **Attr** field and the **Name** field, so you can check each file's attribute byte. Adding a watch to the watch window is done by pressing Ctrl-F7, which is a shortcut to the **A**dd watch item on the **Break**/watch menu. Add those two watches to the watch window.

EXECUTING TO A BREAKPOINT

Now we're ready to do a little breakpoint dancing. Run the program by pressing Ctrl-F9, which is a shortcut to the **R**un item on the **R**un menu. (Choosing from the menus gets tedious in a hurry during a debugging cycle. Learn your shortcuts and use them!)

What happened? One of two things: Either **Locate** found a file with a .BAK extension, or it didn't. If it didn't (and you are a tidy person indeed!) the highlight bar will not appear at the breakpoint, or be visible anywhere on the screen at all. You'll see the following in the watch window:

```
CurrentDTA.Name: Unknown identifier
CurrentDTA.Attr: Unknown identifier
```

This doesn't mean anything is wrong; it merely means that because no file was ever found, no meaningful values were ever placed in **CurrentDTA**.

More likely, a file will have been found, and the highlight bar will be displayed over the **FindFirst** breakpoint. Down in the watch window, you'll see information on the found file:

```
CurrentDTA.Name: AFILE.BAK
CurrentDTA.Attr: 32
```

The 32 indicates that the file has been changed since it was last copied by an archiving utility. Most of your files will carry an attribute byte value of 32. Files that have *not* been changed since they were last archived (assuming they are neither hidden files nor system files) will have an attribute byte of 0.

RUNNING FROM BREAKPOINT TO BREAKPOINT

So, onward. We could single-step through the program from this point, but that would be tedious and unnecessary. Pressing Ctrl-F9 (the **R**un shortcut) will set the program running again, picking up with the statement at the first breakpoint. **Locate** will run until it encounters the second breakpoint, and will display another file name and attribute byte in the watch window. By pressing Ctrl-F9 repeatedly, you can continue executing **Locate** and pause each time a file is found, until no more files are located.

RESETTING THE PROGRAM BEING DEBUGGED

Now let's put **Locate** through another debug run with a different search specification. Select the Parameters item from the Options menu and enter C:*.COM as the parameter. (I want you to specify your boot drive here, as well as *.COM. If you boot from A: instead, use A:*.COM, etc.) We're changing the command-line parameters, but we're probably somewhere in the middle of a program run. **Locate** is paused, but it's still in the middle of executing, with the *.BAK specification in force. To start again from the top with a new search specification, we must reset the program.

This is done using the Program reset item on the Run menu. Selecting Program reset "wipes the slate," clearing all variables so that the program will begin executing without any assumptions left over from a previous debug run.

Once the program is reset, run it again with Ctrl-F9. **Locate** will show you all the .COM files on your boot drive—or will it? Sharp DOS hackers will notice that the two famous lurkers of the PC-DOS file system, IBMBIO.COM and IBMDOS.COM, which are always the first two files in any PC-DOS boot directory, will not be displayed. (In systems containing MS-DOS the two files will be IO.SYS and MSDOS.SYS instead. If you're running this scenario on an MS-DOS system, change the Run I Parameters item to C:*.SYS.) This may be a bug or it may be a feature; which it is depends on what you want **Locate** to do. If you want **Locate** to examine *all* files for the search spec (say, everything matching *.COM), then it's definitely a bug. Let's see how it could be fixed.

IBMBIO.COM and IBMDOS.COM (and IO.SYS and MSDOS.SYS) differ from almost all other files in that they have attribute bits 0, 1, and 2 set. These are the Read-only, Hidden, and System bits, respectively. (See Figure 19.4 in Chapter 19.) To match these bits, **FindFirst** and **FindNext** must be asked for them. Notice in the code fragment from **Locate** shown earlier, the invocation of **FindFirst**:

```
FindFirst(TempDirectory,0,CurrentDTA);
```

The 0 parameter is the attribute byte we wish to search for. DOS is funny about attribute bits; an attribute byte of 0 will locate files having an attribute byte value of 0 *or* 32; i.e., all "normal" files. Setting the attribute byte to 8, to locate the DOS volume label, will find *only* files whose attribute byte is 8. Setting the Read-only, Hidden, and System bits in the attribute byte will find files with those bits and other files as well; *not* setting them will locate only normal files.

So change the middle parameter to 7, which sets Read-only, Hidden, and System. Press Ctrl-F9 to begin **Locate** executing. Notice that whenever you change the source code of the program being debugged, Turbo Pascal will recompile the program before running it. If other .COM files exist in subdirectories on your boot volume, they will probably be displayed, but ultimately, you will see the watch window display IBMBIO.COM and IBMDOS.COM. With an attribute byte of 7, **Locate** really will locate *all* files, with the sole exception of volume label files, which are not really files in the truest sense of the word.

CHANGING BREAKPOINTS

Finding most bugs won't be quite as easy as *that*. You may discover that your path of inquiry is a dead end, and that stopping at your chosen breakpoints won't help. You can change breakpoints easily, in one of two ways: You can toggle an individual breakpoint off the same way you toggled it on, by placing the cursor on the breakpoint line and pressing Ctrl-F8. If you feel that *all* your breakpoints are completely useless, you can clear them all at once by selecting the Clear all button in the Debug I Breakpoints dialog box.

Let's do that, and clear both the breakpoints we've been using thus far. For a new breakpoint, we might decide to watch the point at which procedure **SearchDirectory**—the heart of **Locate**—calls itself recursively. That point is clearly marked in the source code, at the line shown below:

```
{ Here's where we call "ourselves." }
SearchDirectory(NextDirectory,  SearchSpec);
```

Set a breakpoint on the **SearchDirectory** line by pressing Ctrl-F8. Also, add a watch to the watch window for the identifier **NextDirectory**. (Hint: The shortcut is Ctrl-F7.) Remember that we still have the original two watches, on **CurrentDTA.Name** and **CurrentDTA.Attr**. (We only cleared the breakpoints, not the watches!)

Set the command-line parameter back to our original *.BAK. Reset the program (this may be done by selecting Run | Program reset or its shortcut, Ctrl-F2) and run it. (Ctrl-F9.) What happens obviously depends on how complex the structure of your hard disk is, but if you have lots of nested subdirectories you're in for an interesting ride.

Remember how **Locate** works: It searches the root directory for subdirectories. If it finds a subdirectory, it calls itself recursively to search the subdirectory. If the subdirectory has a subdirectory, yet another recursive call descends into that subdirectory to search it, and so on. (See the detailed discussion of **Locate** in Section 19.9.) **Locate** descends into the directory tree until it finds a subdirectory that has no subdirectories. Then it searches that subdirectory for files that match the search specification. That done, it "climbs" back up through the subdirectory tree, searching for more subdirectories, and not searching for files in any given subdirectory until it runs out of subdirectories in that subdirectory.

Each time you press **Run** (Ctrl-F9) **Locate** will execute until it encounters a new subdirectory. Then it will pause, just before it makes a recursive call to itself to search the new subdirectory. Notice the watch window. Once you're a few levels deep, you'll see something like this:

```
NextDirectory:   '\WINDOWS\ACTOR\CLASSES'
CurrentDTA.Name:  'CLASSES'
CurrentDTA.Attr:  16
```

The breakpoint pauses execution just *before* the recursive call is made. When the call is made, **NextDirectory** will contain the path for the search spec passed to **FindFirst**. Note also the attribute value of 16, which indicates a set Subdirectory bit. The directory entry with the name 'CLASSES' is thus a subdirectory, and not an ordinary file or a volume label. Attribute bits are important—it's nice to be able to see them at every step as the program executes.

TRACING INTO A RECURSIVE CALL

Something interesting can happen at this point. Suppose you trace into the recursive call by pressing **Trace into** (F7). Abruptly, the values in the watch window will change to something like this:

```
NextDirectory:   #21'0098GHf'#0'hggJ9'#7#11'H99'#0#0#0'*7^^'#0
CurrentDTA.Name:  'GGHy'#7
CurrentDTA.Attr:  19
```

What gives? All of a sudden, the variables we've been watching have inexplicably turned to garbage. Well, maybe not ... think for a moment: By tracing into

SearchDirectory, we kick off a brand new instantiation of the subprogram on the stack, including all new instantiations of **SearchDirectory**'s local variables. Both **NextDirectory** and **CurrentDTA** are local variables. What you're seeing in the watch window are local variables allocated on the stack but not yet filled with anything, and what the watch window displays is the random trash in memory underlying the newly allocated local variables.

No, the **NextDirectory** value we were watching as a local variable in the previous instantiation of **SearchDirectory** was passed to the new instantiation as a parameter. To verify this, we can bring up the evaluation window, and take a peek at the parameters to this latest instantiation of **SearchDirectory**. Select Debug|Evaluate/modify (Ctrl-F4). Enter the name of **SearchDirectory**'s first formal parameter, **Directory**. Voila! There's the path value again, in the Result field of the evaluation window:

```
'WINDOWS\ACTOR\CLASSES'
```

Type the second parameter, **SearchSpec**, into the Expression field, and there's our faithful, unchanging search specification originally entered as a command-line parameter:

```
'*.BAK'
```

If you continue to single-step through the new instantiation of **SearchDirectory**, you will eventually see the local copies of **NextDirectory** and **CurrentDTA** take on new values—if, of course, any additional child subdirectories are found.

LOOKING AT THE CALL STACK

How many levels deep are you into the recursive traversal of the directory tree? In our particular example, you can count the number of subdirectories in the path that was just passed to the latest instantiation of **SearchDirectory**. In most cases, however, you won't have such a nice, convenient roadmap telling you where you are in terms of subprogram nesting. Turbo Pascal has such a roadmap, and you can call it up by selecting the Debug|Call stack item, or pressing its shortcut, Ctrl-F3. What you'll see is the "call stack," and it will be displayed in a window. The actual data in the window will look something like this:

```
SEARCHDIRECTORY('\WINDOWS\ACTOR\CLASSES','*.BAK');
SEARCHDIRECTORY('\WINDOWS\ACTOR','*.BAK')
SEARCHDIRECTORY('\WINDOWS','*.BAK')
SEARCHDIRECTORY('\','*.BAK')
LOCATE
```

(Obviously, this depends on what's in your hard disk!) The call stack tells us that we're executing a program called **LOCATE**, and that we're four levels deep in recursive calls to **SEARCHDIRECTORY**. Furthermore, it shows us the actual parameters passed to each instantiation of **SearchDirectory**.

The call stack can be extremely handy for debugging complex programs that contain many levels of subprogram nesting. Such programs sometimes crash for what seems like no identifiable reason, when a previous (and similar) run of the program operated correctly. What actually happens may have less to do with code bugs than with something else: stack space.

MONITORING AVAILABLE STACK SPACE

A program begins its life with a fixed amount of stack space, either the default 16,384 bytes, or some other amount set with the $M compiler directive. (See Section 15.4.) When you run out of stack space, you crash with a runtime error. It's that simple.

Programs using recursive algorithms are particularly prone to stack crashes. Each recursive call needs stack space for allocation of parameters and local variables. If you recurse down too many levels, your program will use up its stack allocation and crash. If you write a program that uses recursion, you should keep an eye on your stack space. Here's how, using our current example.

Add a watch to the watch window. (Ctrl-F7.) This time, the watch will not be a variable or parameter, but the built-in function **Sptr**. **Sptr** returns the stack pointer value at any given time. Because the stack pointer starts at the high end of the stack and works its way downward, the value returned by **Sptr** is an accurate indicator of the amount of stack space you have left.

Reset the program and run it again. At the first breakpoint, the watch window will contain a line something like this:

```
Sptr: 14476
```

Keep on recursing. The next time **SearchDirectory** calls itself, the value returned by **Sptr** will have changed to 12826. Taking the difference of the two figures will show you that each instantiation of **SearchDirectory** takes *1,650 bytes!* If you start out with 16,384 bytes of stack, you have at best nine levels of recursion available before you crash.

I, too, was surprised at the 1,650 byte figure for each instantiation of **SearchDirectory**. But consider: **SearchDirectory** contains two parameters of type **STRING**, and two local variables of type **STRING**. Each instance of type **STRING** is 256 bytes in size—we're up to 1,024 bytes already, just in string storage. Add to that the size of a **SearchRec** (43 bytes), a **DIRRec** (295 bytes), and a **Registers** record (20 bytes), and you're up to 1,382 bytes. Then there's the additional overhead of return addresses, pointers to temporary string values, and local storage private to the compiler ... suddenly, 1,650 bytes per call doesn't seem so outlandish.

Quick tip: To determine how large a given variable or data type is, just bring up the evaluation window (Ctrl-F4) and enter an expression like

```
SizeOf(DIRRec)
```

*into the Expression field. The size of **SizeOf**'s operand will appear in the Result field. Let the computer do what computers do best!*

If you start having mysterious stack crashes, put **Sptr** into your watch window and keep an eye on it. If you're like most Pascal programmers, you're not used to figuring out the sizes of variables, nor imagining that stack space is anything but infinite. Like natural resources, stack space is limited. You have to keep an eye on it.

Locate is a good program to trace. It does a lot of interesting things, and yet it's simple enough to understand without many hours of study. I'd recommend spending some time with it, setting breakpoints here and there, and using the watch window and the evaluation window to examine its variables at different points of execution. As an exercise, add to **Locate** the ability to locate a subdirectory as well as a file or files. It's not as simple as you might think at first thought—nor as difficult as it might seem after a minute mulling it over.

An entire book could (and probably should) be written on the art of debugging Turbo Pascal programs. I've done little more than scratch the surface here in the hope of getting you interested. Be aware of what the compiler offers. Turbo Pascal's integrated debugger can tell you lots of useful things you never knew how to determine before—and in doing so can keep you out of many different flavors of trouble.

16.6 The Run and Debug Menus: A Summary

Turbo Pascal's menu structure has changed over time. The **Run, Debug,** and **Break/watch** menus were introduced in V5.0 and were *not* present in V4.0. The **Break/watch** menu disappeared in V6.0, with its items migrating into the Debug menu.

In this section I'll provide a quick reference to the two menus that govern program execution and debugging. I've described most of the items on the menus during the debugging walk-throughs in the previous section, but it may be handy to have them all in one place for review and quick reference.

THE RUN MENU

Turbo Pascal 4.0 had a Run item on the main menu bar—but there was no menu behind it. When you selected Run, the program ran, and that was that. With V5.0 and later, the Run item, like all other items on the menu bar, has a menu behind it.

The top item on the **Run** menu is *Run*. Select it, and your program runs. The shortcut is Ctrl-F9. If any breakpoints have been set in your program, execution will pause at the first breakpoint encountered, as long as any pass count or Boolean conditions associated with that breakpoint are met.

Beneath Run is *Step over* (shortcut: F8) which single-steps to the next line of source code. If the next line is a subprogram, the trace will skip over the subprogram call. The subprogram call will be *made* and the subprogram executed normally; however, you simply won't see it occur line by line.

Trace into (shortcut: F7), like Step over, single-steps to the next line of source code. If the next line is a subprogram, the trace will move into that subprogram. This will happen *only* if the source code for the subprogram is available to the IDE. Also, you cannot trace into a unit compiled with the {$D-} or {$L-} compiler directives in force, even if the source code is available. These two directives (see Section 15.4) turn off the generation of essential debugging information needed by the IDE to step through the code and examine local symbols.

Also, tracing with **Trace into** will not enter interrupt procedures, exit procedures, or **INLINE** macros. Tracing will, however, trace into assembly language statements created with the **ASM** standard directive. (I won't be covering ASM statements in this book.) Tracing into external machine code subprograms will occur if the subprograms were assembled with debug information enabled. Tracing code within an exit procedure may be done by setting a breakpoint at the start of the exit procedure and then beginning to step once normal execution pauses for the breakpoint.

Trace into and Step over exist to give you a choice. By intelligently choosing one or the other while single-stepping a program, you can examine the subprograms you *need* to examine and not be bothered tracing the ones that you know already work correctly.

The *Go to cursor* item (shortcut: F4) is a portable breakpoint. Quite simply, selecting **Go** to cursor will execute the program code until execution encounters the statement on the current cursor line. This can be handy if you're stepping through a program and wish to skip ahead by a screen or two. Moving the cursor quickly downward by using the PgDn key and then pressing F4 will execute the code between the current position of the highlight bar and the new position of the cursor.

The IDE will refuse to begin execution if you place the cursor over a part of the program that does not represent executable code, such as constant, type, or variable declarations.

There is one "gotcha" to keep in mind, however: If you move the cursor to a line in the program that isn't in the direct path of execution, execution will keep on going until the program terminates or encounters a breakpoint. For example, if your cursor lands within a **BEGIN..END** block controlled by the **ELSE** clause of an **IF** statement, and the **ELSE** clause is not selected, execution will breeze right by the **BEGIN..END** block containing the cursor.

A corollary of this that should be obvious is that you can't move the cursor *up* in the source file and somehow expect execution to go backward toward the cursor. If you move the cursor up the source file and press F4, execution will move forward relentlessly until it encounters the end of the program or a breakpoint. Of course, if execution loops *back* to the line containing the cursor, execution will pause, but there is nothing "magical" about **Go** to cursor that alters the essential control path specified by your program.

Next on the menu is *Program reset*. Its function echoes its name: It reinitializes the current program and gets everything ready for another run through it, "from the top." If you're stepping through the program and things seem hopelessly muddled, selecting **P**rogram reset is a good way to begin again. The highlight bar that indicates which statement executes next will disappear, and all the values currently displayed in the watch window will go "out of scope" and become undefined.

Finally, you have *Parameters*, which allows you to specify up to 128 characters' worth of command-line parameters that will be addressed by **ParamCount** and **ParamStr**, just as though you had typed them after the name of the program while executing it from the command-line prompt.

THE DEBUG MENU

The **D**ebug menu was introduced with Turbo Pascal 5.0. It contains most of the selectable items that involve debugging, except for those directly connected with program execution, such as Step Over and Trace Into, which exist in the Run menu. It became a considerably more important menu with the introduction of V6.0, when the Debug and Break/watch menus were combined to save space on the menu bar. Many of the items that were individual menu line items in V5.5 and earlier became buttons in the Breakpoints and Watch dialog boxes with V6.0 and later.

The first item on the menu is *Breakpoints*. It brings up a dialog box that displays all currently active breakpoints, and allows you to clear them or edit them individually. There is a Clear all button in the Breakpoints dialog box that clears all breakpoints from the breakpoint list maintained in the dialog box.

The *Call stack* item was described in detail in Section 16.4, and demonstrated during the trace of **Locate** in Section 16.5. The **C**all stack displays the current nesting level of program execution. In other words, it shows the names of all subprograms into which execution has progressed, including the actual parameters passed to each instantiation of the subprogram. During debugging, the IDE keeps track of up to 128 nested subprograms and their parameters, of which it can display up to nine in the call stack window. (The others may be seen by scrolling the window with the arrow keys or by resizing the window to make it a little larger.)

The call stack cannot be examined unless a program has been compiled and execution begun.

Beneath Call stack is *Register* which, when selected, brings up a small window that displays the state of the CPU registers while you single-step. I can't explain the use of this window in detail, but I will point out that when any register changes value from one step to the next, the IDE highlights the value in white. If you know anything at all about the 86-family of CPUs, you'll find it interesting to display this window while debugging. It gives you a taste of what you can watch using the "big time" Turbo Debugger product shipped with Borland Pascal 7.0.

The *Watch* item brings up a dialog box listing all currently defined watches. Buttons along the lower edge of the dialog box allow you to edit and clear watches individually.

The *Output* item opens a window to which "glass teletype"-type program output may be sent. The Output window is useful for testing command-line utilities, but it's not very handy for testing any program that displays to the full screen using **GotoXY**. Open the Output window and then single-step through the BOXTEST.PAS program I presented in Chapter 8 — you'll see what I mean. If you need to look at the output from your programs while debugging, use the User screen item or its shortcut Alt-F5 instead.

The *User screen* item "flips" to the current state of the full output screen to which all Turbo Pascal programs send their output. You'll probably use this one a lot — but through its shortcut, Alt-F5, more than through the User screen item.

Evaluate/modify (shortcut: Ctrl-F4) brings up the evaluation window, which is described in detail in Section 16.4. Through the evaluation window you can examine the contents of program constants and variables, either alone or as part of simple expressions. Furthermore, you can modify the contents of typed constants and program variables, so that execution can continue with the new values in place.

Next on the Debug menu is *Add watch*. Selecting **Add** watch through the menu or its shortcut, Ctrl-F7, brings up a dialog box that allows you to view the list of current watches, and enter the name of a program or typed constant, or of an expression to be added to the watch window. You can clear watches from this window as well.

Finally, there is *Add breakpoint* (no shortcut), which similarly allows you to add a new breakpoint to the list of active breakpoints. Remember that you can toggle a simple, unconditional breakpoint on and off for a given source code line by placing the cursor in that line and pressing Ctrl-F8.

Chapter 17

Pointer Basics

CREATING AND DESTROYING VARIABLES AS YOU NEED THEM

If you were born mortal, I'll expect you to admit it: When you first found yourself face-to-face with Pascal pointers, you bumped your nose on a wall 10 miles high. I certainly did, and my nose still carries the bruises. I hit it, and hit it *hard*.

This is the reason that I didn't cover pointers earlier in this book. Pointers are definitely the demilitarized zone between beginning Pascal and advanced Pascal. You can write perfectly good Pascal programs without pointers. But sooner or later it dawns on you that it's impossible to write *great* Pascal programs without them.

So pointers are inevitable, and approached the right way, not all that tough to deal with either. So c'mon—follow along and get them down cold. Then you, too, can learn to stop worrying and love the heap...

...and save your nose in the process.

INSIGHT OUT

A very large part of the problem with understanding pointers is the way they're taught. University profs insist that their students place pointers off in the abstract somewhere, vehemently refusing to answer the very pertinent question, "But what *is* a pointer?" It isn't enough to say, "A pointer is a data item that points to something else." That means *nothing*. And while it's true that it's far less important to understand what a pointer *is* than what it *does*, knowing the underlying implementation of pointers goes a long way toward cementing understanding of how pointers work.

The profs mean well, of course, but inside their minds, programming tends to be a branch of mathematics or logic, where it's fine to put concepts in the abstract and divorce them from anything connected to the real world. Most of us have trouble with concepts that we can't hang on something made out of steel and plastic, or at least attribute to a specific location inside a specific (and visible) chip.

459

It's just the way we tend to learn: We count apples before we ponder the mystery of prime numbers. Concrete before abstract. Makes sense, no?

So in this chapter I'm going to turn the process on its ear. I'm going to explain some of the ugly stuff behind the pointer abstraction *first*, and not start building linked castles in the abstract air until well along in the discussion.

If any profs in the audience care to send bricks, that's fine. I've got a barbecue pit in the works.

17.1 The Forbidden Truth

The mystery ends here: *A pointer is a variable containing the memory address of something else.*

Everything you define in a Pascal program has a definite location in memory. Each location is numbered (although in something less than a straightforward fashion) and the number of a location is what we call the *machine address* of that location.

So just as you can define a variable that contains a character, a string, or an integer, you can define a variable whose entire job is to contain machine addresses. Such variables are called *pointer variables*.

When we say that a variable "points to" something, we only mean that the variable in question contains the address of that something in question. If you've got the address of a Pascal variable, you've got considerable power over that variable. Pascal contains machinery that allows you to manipulate data through a pointer to that data, machinery that I'll be describing in detail throughout this chapter and also in Chapters 20, 23, and 24.

REFERENTS, DEREFERENCING, AND NIL

The Wall of Pointers is made higher by the use of some pretty forbidding jargon that is rarely defined in the textbooks. Let me take a moment to pin that jargon down.

Most of the time, pointer variables point to other variables. The variable pointed to by a pointer is that pointer's *referent*. A pointer may be connected to its referent in a number of ways, but all those ways involve determining the address of the referent and placing that address into the pointer. The easiest to understand is the @ ("address of") operator, to which I'll return later. It's a good illustration of how a pointer may be associated with another variable:

```
MyPtr := @MyVar;
```

Here, the @ operator takes the address of the variable **MyVar** and places the address in the pointer **MyPtr**. **MyVar** thus becomes the referent of **MyPtr**. (There is another way of specifying the "address of" operator: **Addr**. It's exactly the same thing to write **Addr(MyVar)** as to write **@MyVar**. Your choice.)

A pointer's referent may be read from or written to through the pointer. This is done by way of the ^ ("dereference") operator. Placing the ^ operator *after* the name of a pointer indicates that you are now working on the pointer's *referent* rather than on the pointer itself:

```
Writeln(MyPtr^);
```

Here, what we're writing to the screen is *not* the pointer variable **MyPtr**, but **MyPtr**'s referent, **MyVar**. Using a pointer to access the pointer's referent is called *dereferencing* the pointer, and it's done through the **^** operator. I don't much care for the terms "dereference" or "dereferencing" because for the beginner they sometimes carry a certain sense of turning the pointer away from its referent, which of course isn't true. Still, they're standard terminology and we might as well get them right.

A pointer either points to something, or it points to nothing. A pointer that has explicitly been pointed to nothing is called a *NIL pointer*. You point a pointer to nothing by assigning it a predefined Pascal value called **NIL**:

```
MyPtr := NIL;
```

NIL, by the way, is a Pascal reserved word, and cannot be used for any other purpose. People sometimes say "null pointer" when they mean "**NIL** pointer." This sort of confusion in the jargon doesn't make things any easier.

17.2 The Why of It All: Static versus Dynamic Variables

People who spend any amount of time pondering the simple truth about pointers stated above soon come up with a pretty good question: If you can manipulate a variable directly, what's the use of manipulating a variable through a pointer?

Ahhh, to the very heart of the matter...

Until now in your programming career, you've probably made the assumption that all data items used in a Pascal program are known to the compiler when it compiles the program. That is, in order to use three integer variables **I**, **J**, and **K**, those three variables must be declared in the program source code:

```
VAR
    I,J,K : Integer;
```

The compiler uses this line to create three integer variables that remain available as long as the program is running. The three variables are each given their proper place in the program's data segment and there they remain. The program (assuming it has only these three variables) cannot decide on the basis of its work that it needs another variable, and create it. What it got at compile time is what it has, period.

Variables of this sort are called *static variables*. Static variables are those variables defined in the **VAR** section of programs and subprograms. Pascal allows another kind of variable, which a program can in fact create as it needs them. These are called *dynamic variables*.

Dynamic variables are identical in form and in function to static variables. In other words, a static integer variable *does* the very same things as a dynamic integer variable. The same integer value can be stored in either. What is different about them is how they are created and (as I showed briefly above) how they are accessed.

OUT IN THE GREAT ELSEWHERE

Almost by definition, the static data segment of a program is set at compile time and can never be rearranged while the program is running. Dynamic variables, if they can be created and destroyed during a program's run, must exist somewhere else. This "somewhere else" is a region of memory set aside by the compiler specifically to hold dynamic variables. It is called *heapspace* or *the heap*.

The word *heap* was coined in contrast to the word *stack*, which is a memory-management method in which items are stored in strict order and must be stored and retrieved in that order, like plates placed in a stack: The top one must come off first, then the next-to-top, and so on. In a heap of plates, (rather like the heap left in our kitchen cabinets after the Great California Quake of '89) the plates are in no special order. If you want a plate, you can reach in and grab any of them you like in any order.

So it is with dynamic variables placed in heapspace. If you need a new dynamic variable, you create it. (I'll explain how shortly.) Once a dynamic variable is created, you can store a value in it or read a value back at any time. Assuming you have enough room on the heap, dynamic variables you create later on have no effect on ones created earlier. You can get at them in any order, at any time.

Furthermore, once you're done using one or more of your dynamic variables, you can destroy them, and release the memory they occupy for use by new and different dynamic variables. (I'll explain how dynamic variables are destroyed a little later.) This use and reuse of memory can happen any number of times during a program's run.

THE MISSING LINK

So what's this got to do with pointers? *Everything.* Pointers are the link between dynamic variables and the rest of your program. The major purpose of pointer variables is to act as the bridge between a program's static data segment and the heap. It may not be immediately obvious, but keep this in mind: *Dynamic variables have no names!* How could they? Dynamic variables don't exist at compile time, when the Turbo Pascal compiler runs through your source code, building lists of things you've defined and given names to.

A pointer variable *can* have a name, and is in one sense a way of naming a dynamic variable; the only way, in fact, of "getting at" a dynamic variable in any way.

The other, somewhat scarier use of pointers is to build links between multiple-record structures created at runtime on the heap. You can use pointers to construct massive, complex structures on the heap, with the pointers acting as the "glue" that links the nameless component records into a single unified whole.

These things have a number of names, but I'll be describing two different kind of heap-based structures called *linked lists* in Chapter 20.

17.3 Defining Pointer Types

Pointer types are defined in the **TYPE** section of a program, just as derived types and structured types are. A pointer may be defined as a pointer to a standard type like **Integer** or **Char**, or to some programmer-defined type that you've defined yourself:

```
TYPE
   YourPtrType = ^Integer;
   HisPtrType  = ^Char;

   AType       = String[20];
   MyPtrType   = ^AType;
```

Most of the time, a pointer type is defined as a pointer to some other type. The notation **^AType** is read, "pointer to **AType**." The data type associated with a pointer is called the pointer's *base type*. A pointer's base type may be any type except a file type. There is also a special kind of pointer called an *untyped* or *generic* pointer that does *not* have any base type associated with it. Untyped pointers are definitely advanced-level magic, and I'll return to them toward the end of this book, in Chapter 24.

CHICKENS AND EGGS

One peculiarity of defining pointer types is that a pointer may be defined as pointing to a type that has itself not been defined yet. Consider the problem of defining a pointer variable that points to a record type containing (as a field) a pointer like itself, which points to a record of that type:

```
TYPE
   PDynaRec  = ^TDynaRec;
   TDynaRec  = RECORD
                  DataPart : String;
                  Next     : PDynaRec
               END;
```

This is not some weird sort of pathological case; in fact, this is the core structure of even the simplest linked lists, as I'll demonstrate in Chapter 20. By the way, prefixing pointer type names with "P" and other type names with "T" is a common convention in Turbo Pascal programming, and one that I heartily recommend when you begin working with pointers, dynamic data structures, and objects.

Ordinarily, you cannot use an identifier until the compiler already knows what it is. But there is a "chicken and egg" conflict here: If we define **PDynaRec** first, the compiler doesn't know what **TDynaRec** means. If we define **TDynaRec** first, the compiler doesn't know what **PDynaRec** means. So by convention, Pascal allows us to define a pointer to a type that will later be defined. Of course, if you never get around to defining **DynaRec**, an error will be generated and the compilation will fail, with this message:

```
Error 19: Undefined type in pointer definition (TDynaRec)
```

Note that **TDynaRec** must be defined somewhere within the *same* **TYPE** section as **^TDynaRec**. Turbo Pascal allows multiple **TYPE** sections within a single program, but a pointer type and its base type must both be defined within the same section.

17.4 Creating Dynamic Variables with New

If you want a pointer variable as a static variable in your program, you declare it in the VAR section of the program just as you would any other static variable of any type:

```
VAR
    MyPtr : TMyPtrType;
```

When a pointer variable declared this way is allocated by the compiler, the pointer's value is undefined, as with any static variable. You can't even say that it points to nothing—when a pointer must point to nothing, it must be given a special value called **NIL**, as mentioned earlier. An undefined pointer is simply undefined and should not be used until it has been given something (or nothing, via **NIL**) to point to. *Using undefined pointers is one of the classic hair-puller bugs of our time!* (Be warned—but I'll come back to this subject later on.)

Dynamic variables are created by a predefined Pascal procedure called **New**:

```
VAR
    APtr : PDynaRec;

New(APtr);    { Create a new dynamic TDynaRec }
```

The type **PDynaRec** (as we saw above) was previously defined as a pointer to type **TDynaRec**. Because **APtr** is of type **PDynaRec**, the program (*not* the compiler; this is done at runtime!) knows to create a variable of type **TDynaRec** off in heapspace. It then sets up **APtr** to point to the new dynamic variable of type **TDynaRec**. **APtr**, which was previously undefined, now indeed points to something: a brand new **TDynaRec**.

Figure 17.1 shows a generalized diagram of this way of using **New**. Note in the diagram that **TDynaRec** is not the *name* of the new dynamic variable, but its *type*.

Accessing a dynamic variable is done through its pointer. Going back to the text example, if we wish to assign some value to the **DataPart** field of the new **TDynaRec**, we must use this notation:

```
APtr^.DataPart := 'Be dynamic!';
```

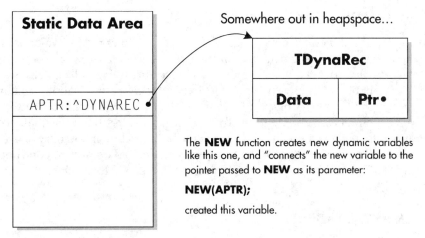

The **NEW** function creates new dynamic variables like this one, and "connects" the new variable to the pointer passed to **NEW** as its parameter:

NEW(APTR);

created this variable.

Figure 17.1 A Pointer

Assigning a dynamic variable (or a field of a dynamic record) to a static variable is done just as easily:

```
AString := APtr^.DataPart;
```

Accessing a dynamic variable through its pointer in this way (both reading from and writing to) is an example of dereferencing the pointer. In fact, *any* use of the ^ operator in connection with a pointer is dereferencing the pointer.

There is no "clean" way to pronounce **APtr^** other than "that which pointer **APtr** points to" or (better) "**APtr**'s referent." The notation "**APtr^**" is the closest the new dynamic variable will ever come to having an actual name.

17.5 Operations on Pointers

A pointer is either undefined, or it points to a dynamic variable, or it points to nothing. Making a pointer point to nothing is done by assigning it a special predefined pointer value called **NIL**:

```
APtr := NIL;
```

It can now be said that **APtr** points to nothing. It's a truly excellent idea to assign **NIL** to all pointers soon after a program begins running. Using a pointer with a value of **NIL** is *loads* safer than using a pointer that is undefined.

Pointers may be compared for equality. When two pointers are said to be equal, it means that they both point to the identical dynamic variable, or that they both have a value of **NIL**. Both pointers must be of the same type to be compared at all.

POINTER COMPARISON TRAPS

More important, neither pointer should have been "tweaked" in value by low-level means (what we sometimes call *pointer arithmetic*) prior to the comparison. The segmented nature of the PC memory architecture (which I'll explain in some detail in Chapter 24) allows two pointers to point to the same location in memory, even though their binary bit-patterns are not identical. If the binary bit-patterns of a pair of pointers are not identical, Turbo Pascal considers them unequal, even if both pointers do in fact point to the same physical location in memory.

Comparing two undefined pointers (or one undefined pointer and one pointer with a valid value) will return a meaningless Boolean value. *Don't do it.*

POINTER ASSIGNMENT

Pointers may be assigned to one another. Again, the two pointers must be the same type or the compiler will flag a type conflict error. The logic with pointer assignment is that when you assign one pointer to a second pointer, the second pointer then points to the identical dynamic variable that the first pointer was pointing to. This should make sense, since both pointers now contain the same physical memory address. Read this example carefully:

```
VAR
  APtr,BPtr : PDynaRec;

New(APtr);          { APtr^ is a dynamic record         }
New(BPtr);          { BPtr^ is another dynamic record }
BPtr := APtr;       { What used to be BPtr^ is lost!  }
```

Here, two pointers are each set at first to point to a different dynamic variable. Keep in mind that each call to **New** produces a separate and distinct dynamic variable on the heap.

Then, however, in the assignment statement **BPtr** is assigned the value of **APtr**. Both pointers now point to the same dynamic record, which is the record **APtr** pointed to originally. **APtr^** and **BPtr^** are now the identical record. Furthermore, the record that was originally created by the call **New(BPtr)** is now lost forever. *Once you "break" a pointer away from its referent, that variable is utterly inaccessible.*

GONE BUT NOT DEALLOCATED

This situation is worse, in fact, than it sounds. Even though the original **BPtr^** is inaccessible, *it still exists,* and occupies memory, memory that now cannot be used for anything else. Do *not* just cut a dynamic variable loose—unlike a kite or balloon that will fly away and cease being a problem, a "lost" dynamic variable will remain on the heap as long as the program that created it continues running. The memory it occupies is useless and cannot be recovered for other purposes. If you cut loose too many dynamic variables you could conceivably run out of heapspace and be unable to create any additional dynamic variables.

17.6 Disposing of Dynamic Variables

The way out is to clean house correctly when dynamic variables are no longer needed. Turbo Pascal contains a predefined procedure called **Dispose**, which is very much the opposite of **New**:

```
Dispose(APtr);
```

The **Dispose** procedure takes a pointer as its parameter. **Dispose** releases the memory occupied by **APtr^** (the dynamic variable pointed to by **APtr**) and causes the value of **APtr** to become undefined. Don't make the mistake of thinking that **Dispose** forces the value of its pointer parameter to **NIL**. The value becomes undefined, just as it was before you assigned a value to the pointer when the program began running.

The memory once occupied by **APtr^** goes back into a "pool" of free memory and becomes available for **New** to allocate to other dynamic variables.

One common misapprehension is that **Dispose** also makes the *pointer* passed to it go away. Not so—if **APtr** is a static variable, it remains behind, minus its referent, after a call to **Dispose**. You can then use **APtr** in another call to **New**, to give it a new dynamic variable as a referent. Dynamic referents come and go, but a static pointer remains as long as the program containing it is running.

17.7 Managing the Heap's Resources

When a program begins running, it reserves some quantity of RAM for dynamic variables. In the Turbo Pascal environment, the default condition is that all memory not allocated to code, static data, or stack will be allocated to the heap. This parceling out of memory can be modified by using the **$M** compiler command, as explained in Section 15.4. **$M** is also discussed in Section 19.10, in connection with the **Exec** procedure in Turbo Pascal's standard **DOS** unit.

MEMAVAIL AND MAXAVAIL

Knowing how much memory is actually available for the creation of dynamic variables can be critical. The Turbo Pascal runtime code keeps track of how much memory remains for the heap, and if you request more than is available, a runtime error will occur.

The key is not to create a dynamic variable that is larger than the available heap memory. Turbo Pascal provides two functions for measuring available memory: **MemAvail** and **MaxAvail**. They are predeclared and their definition looks like this:

```
FUNCTION MemAvail : LongInt;
FUNCTION MaxAvail : LongInt;
```

MemAvail returns a value that indicates the total amount of memory available for dynamic variables, in bytes. Note that this is different from the **MemAvail**

in Turbo Pascal 3.0, which returned the value in *paragraphs* to avoid overflowing a 16-bit integer. Long integers have put that problem into the past; now when you ask for the amount of free heapspace, there is nothing further to calculate; what **MemAvail** tells you is what you have.

MaxAvail returns a value that is the size of the largest single block of free memory in the heap; again, in bytes.

The difference between **MemAvail** and **MaxAvail** has to do with how the heap works. Dynamic variables are created with **New**, as described a little earlier in this chapter. When you're finished with a dynamic variable, you can erase it with **Dispose**. **Dispose** frees up the heap memory formerly occupied by the dynamic variable. The problem is that, unlike the stack, which holds data items in strict order and releases them in strict order, the heap holds dynamic variables anywhere it has room. Disposing of them at random tends to cut the heap up into small slices of free memory, each where a disposed-of dynamic variable used to exist.

This means that it is possible to have 16K of heapspace according to **MemAvail**, and *still* not be able to create a new dynamic variable. If there is no single free block of memory large enough to hold a dynamic variable of a given type, you cannot safely invoke **New** and create that variable. To do so will trigger this runtime error:

```
Error 203: Heap overflow
```

and terminate your program.

Thus the function of **MaxAvail** is to determine if it is possible to safely create any given dynamic variable:

```
IF MaxAvail < SizeOf(MyType)
   THEN Writeln('Not enough room!');
```

This example calculates the size that a dynamic variable will be, by invoking **SizeOf** on the *type* of the dynamic variable. If that size figure is greater than the value returned by **MaxAvail**, then no single block of memory exists that is large enough to hold another dynamic variable of that type.

What can you do if you find you have no spot large enough to create a new dynamic variable? Nothing automatic; there is no facility in Turbo Pascal that can shuffle the heap around, gathering free memory together into a single contiguous block. (This is sometimes called "garbage collection" and it is *very* hard to do.) About all you can do is start disposing of existing dynamic variables until a large-enough block opens up somewhere.

The real answer, of course, is to anticipate this problem and not keep large dynamic variables or structures (like linked lists; see Chapter 20) hanging around on the heap when they are not needed. Create them. Use them. Then *immediately* throw them away!

PART FOUR

Advanced
Turbo Pascal

Most people think of the word "advanced" as meaning "difficult to understand" or "hard to do." That's true in a lot of cases (mostly when the "difficult" material has been explained by twits) but there's an additional connotation: that of *specialization*. Advanced material is usually not as general in application as "the basics." Freshman-year English 101 can be A Survey of World Literature, but by the time you get to grad school, English 567 is likely to be something like Death and Dismemberment Themes in the Poetry of John Milton, In His Last Years When He Was Blind and Hallucinating About Giant Lobsters. As I said, that advanced stuff starts to get a little narrow.

What's true about English Lit is true about programming as well. Up until now in this book, most of what I've covered has been fundamental Pascal that works pretty much identically whether you're programming for DOS or for Windows. At this point things begin to diverge. Most of the material in the rest of this book will either not apply to Windows programming, or get you in various kinds of trouble if you attempt to apply it. Big parts of Chapter 24 will not apply to DPMI protected-mode programming as well. Protected mode is a very advanced topic that could fill a book all by itself. (I hope to write it someday. But first things first.)

Many of the tricks you're learning for real-mode DOS programming will have to be unlearned when you attack Windows or especially protected-mode programming. Why learn them at all, then? Well, why learn anything? Hey, if something is useful, it's worth knowing. DOS real-mode programming is a limited environment, and to write truly ambitious programs you need all the help you can get, including a very full bag of tricks. The processor and operating system don't give you a lot of help, and the amount of memory you have available to work in is strictly limited.

Yet there's a place for real-mode programming. Tens of millions of machines will never run either Windows or protected mode, because they don't have the raw speed or the advanced CPUs like the 286, 386, and 486. And plenty of applications and utilities don't really need the bulk of protected-mode programming.

Finally, to a lot of people, Windows is an acquired taste that they have no interest in acquiring. That's cool; I don't like beer and cheerfully deflect the flak with a shrug. I've lived 40 very rich years without beer, and people who genuinely don't want Windows' help generally get along very well without it, too. A good book remains to be written on Pascal for protected mode, but Tom Swan's excellent *Borland Pascal 7.0 Programming for Windows* (also in the Borland/Bantam series) can get you a whopping head start in the Windows world.

With the exception of the pointers material, the rest of this book will be of value mostly to the real-mode DOS people. Ignore it at your peril; you never know when you'll need to understand John Milton's lobster hallucinations—or the nature of real-mode memory.

Chapter 18

Type Conversion and Type Casting

STEPPING OVER THE RAILING WHEN YOU MUST

One roasty summer Saturday some years back (when I was still working for Borland in California), Mr. Byte and I were steaming over the Hill in the Magic Van to pick up some end mills in San Jose when the KWSS DJ caught my ear:

"… and up next is the great new single by Pizza Terra!"

Pizza Terra? What a *great* name for a rock band! We haven't seen names like that since the Strawberry Alarm Clock and the Peppermint Trolley Company, and I was duly impressed—if also wondering why I hadn't ever heard of Pizza Terra before.

Then he played the song. And moment by moment I found myself thinking, Boy, that sure sounds like Peter Cetera…

Peter Cetera … Pete Cetera … *Pizza Terra!*

I'd been type casted!

18.1 One Variable on Top of Another

Among the last parts of Pascal to resist my understanding was the subject of type casting, and in Pizza Terra I've found a wonderful metaphor to make it go down easier. What the DJ said was perfectly correct: Four spoken syllables that sounded like "pee-tzuh-tear-uh." Given your typical California DJ's level of enunciation, those four syllables could as easily be taken to mean "Pizza Terra" as "Pete Cetera."

And that's the whole point.

Type casting is the process of taking a variable of one type and treating it as a variable of another type. This sticks to the roofs of most mouths fed on Pascal and Modula-2, both of which are pretty hardnosed about type checking. Type

471

casting jumps the type checking safety railing, allowing you to get in two different kinds of trouble if you're not careful.

One kind of trouble is semantic nonsense. Both Turbo Pascal and Modula-2 allow a variable of type **Char** to be cast onto a variable of type **Boolean** through this notation:

```
MyChar := Char(MyBoolean);
```

This is completely legal. But what does it *mean*? Can a character be **True**? Is **False** an aspect of the letter 'Q'? It sounds like nonsense to me—which is a major reason we have type checking in civilized languages like Pascal.

The Pascal statement above implies that some sort of conversion process is going on, and that processor cycles are being spent somehow converting data from type **Boolean** to type **Char** before copying them to variable **MyChar**. Not so—the data is simply copied from **MyBoolean** to **MyChar** with nary a thought for data typing. It's like picking up a cylindrical crucible of molten aluminum and pouring the metal into a cubical mold. The *shape* of the aluminum changes, but the metal itself is still aluminum. It doesn't change to copper or zinc.

Underneath the level of Pascal, a **Boolean** variable is just a single byte of memory with some bit pattern in it. Like the syllables of speech, what a byte of memory means to us is pretty much what we decide it is to mean, according to some pre-agreed scheme. If a byte of memory with the value $01 is poured into a mold marked **Boolean**, we agree that it has the value **True**; if we pour the *same* byte into a mold marked **Char**, it comes up on the screen as a white smiley-face.

Think of type casting as another form of metal casting: pouring raw materials into a mold. The mold dictates the shape of the metal, but the underlying nature of the raw material is unchanged in the process. Cast the four syllables "pee-tzuh-tear-uh" into a mold marked "male vocalist" and you get Pete Cetera. Cast the same four syllables into a mold marked "imaginary Sixties rock band" and you get Pizza Terra.

18.2 Type Casting and Type Conflicts

It's easy enough to imagine a second kind of trouble connected with breaking the rules of type checking: What happens if you have more data in one type than in another? If you cast 6 bytes of data into 10 bytes of data, what do you have? Or, worse, if you cast 10 bytes of data into 6 bytes of data, does anything overflow? Do you overwrite unrelated variables that just happen to be adjacent in memory?

Casting between any two ordinal, pointer, or integer types is possible, even when the two types are not the same size. (When an array, string, record, or set type is involved in a type cast, the compiler insists that the two types be of the same size.) If the source type is smaller than the destination type, you end up with a partially-filled destination type. The generated code simply picks up bytes from the source type, starting with the lowest memory address, and drops bytes into the destination type until there are no more bytes to drop. Coping with the resulting semantic nonsense is left to you, but there's no danger of overwriting adjacent data.

When there's more source than destination, the code copies bytes from the source until the destination is full, then stops. This eliminates any danger of overwriting data adjacent in memory.

VALUE VERSUS VARIABLE TYPE CASTS

Turbo Pascal actually offers two different syntactic ways of coding up a type cast: value and variable type casts. The differences between the two are subtle and deserve a little discussion.

What most people think of as a type cast is called a *value type cast*:

```
MyLongInt := LongInt(MyBoolean);
```

What happens in a value type cast is that the compiler begins at the lowest-order memory location of the source value and begins dropping bytes into the destination value until either the source or destination value runs out of bytes.

In this particular case, the compiler takes the sole byte in **MyBoolean** and drops it into **MyLongInt**. One byte is all **MyBoolean** has, so it's a one-step operation.

It remains a one-step operation if you turn it around:

```
MyBoolean := Boolean(MyLongInt);
```

Only this time, the first byte taken from **MyLongInt** fills the destination **MyBoolean**, so the assignment stops, again after moving one byte.

Value type casts can best be thought of this way: You have a source, you have a destination, and you have a filter. The source is moved to the destination through the filter. The filter and the destination have the same type. The filter prevents any more bytes from coming through than the destination can hold. (See Figure 18.1.)

Now, a *variable type cast* is a lot less common. Many people aren't even aware that it exists. You can, however, operate this way:

```
Pointer(MyLongInt) := Addr(SomethingOrOther);
```

The filter metaphor fails here. What we're telling the compiler, in a sense, is to simply suspend strong typing and go ahead with the assignment as though source and destination were the same type. Hence the requirement with a variable type cast is that the source and the destination be the same *size*. (Not necessarily the same *type!*)

The compiler, moreover, checks and enforces this at compile time. If you try a variable type cast between two values of different sizes, you'll get a compiler error.

"STANDARD FUNCTION" TYPE CASTS

You may not think of them as such, but the Pascal standard defines a number of standard type casts that you use all the time—even if you've never heard the

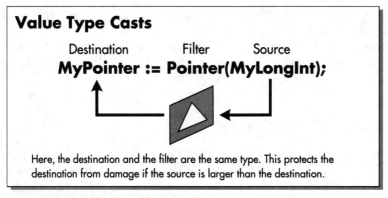

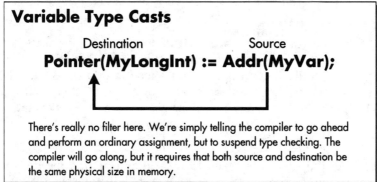

Figure 18.1 Value and Variable Type Casts

term "type cast" before. A type cast, remember, is a way of converting data from one type to another. Several standard functions do exactly that. This one, for example, ought to be familiar to you:

```
MyChar := Chr(MyInteger);
```

While nominally a function call to standard function **Chr**, what I've shown above is in fact a value type cast of a character onto an integer. The compiler simply picks up the lowest-order byte of **MyInteger** and drops it into **MyChar**. There's no procedure call, no "crunching." It's just an assignment statement made through a **Char**-shaped filter.

Or, consider this standard "function" call:

```
MyBoolean := Odd(MyInteger);
```

The same functional model applies here. The compiler simply takes the low-order byte of **MyInteger** and drops it into **MyBoolean**. Now, a Boolean value actually expresses nothing more than the state of the lowest-order bit of the single byte comprising the Boolean value. If that bit is a 0-bit, the Boolean value is considered **False**; and if that bit is a 1-bit, the Boolean value is considered **True**.

An odd integer *always* has its lowest-order bit set to 1. (Work out a couple on paper—or on your programmer's calculator—if this isn't immediately obvious to you.) So if you take the lowest-order byte of an odd integer and drop it into a Boolean value, the Boolean value becomes **True**. No processing is involved. We're simply interpreting the same single bit in two different ways.

Similarly, the **Ord** standard function is just a type cast of an integer onto a character.

18.3 Sign Extension and Numeric Casts

One hiccup in the casting process occurs when data from one numeric type is moved into another. The notion of simply moving bytes blindly from one variable to another no longer applies.

Turbo Pascal performs something called *sign extension* when data is moved between a signed numeric type into a larger signed numeric type; for example, from type **Integer** to type **LongInt**. The sign bit of the shorter type is moved into the sign bit of the larger type, even though the bytes from the shorter type do not entirely fill the larger type. The end result is that a negative integer value cast onto a long integer will result in a negative long integer value.

Most Turbo Pascal users take sign extension for granted, because numeric types are nearly always assignment-compatible, and explicit casting between numeric types never needs to be done. However, even if you explicitly cast an integer onto a long integer, sign extension will still happen.

Numeric types demonstrate one Pascal safety railing that *can't* be jumped: Turbo Pascal somewhat remarkably forbids a type cast of any real number type onto any integer type, just as it forbids assignment of any real number type to any integer type. Type **Real** cannot, in fact, be cast onto *any* other type. To get at the bytes inside type **Real**, you have to use union labor, as I'll explain below. (Modula-2, by contrast, allows byte-by-byte casting of real numbers onto any non-numeric type at all. Dr. Wirth evidently had second thoughts about this.)

18.4 Type Casting through Free Unions

One problem with type casting in Turbo Pascal is that it's not really part of the Pascal language, and other compilers in other environments may or may not implement it. For most of us that doesn't matter; I consider the differences in paradigms among environments (say, DOS, Mac, OS/2, and Unix) far more of a barrier to portability than any deviation from a high-level language's syntactic standard.

But the issue remains for those who care: There is really only one portable way to perform type casts in Pascal. This is the *free union variant record*, (or simply the *free union*) and it is about the most peculiar thing Niklaus Wirth decided to include in his definition of Pascal.

The best way to approach free unions is to start with their less libertarian relatives, discriminated unions. (We usually call discriminated unions *variant records*.) The familiar Pascal variant record looks like this:

```
ID =
 RECORD
  CASE Alien : Boolean OF
   True  : (HomeStarID : StarID);
   False : (EarthID : CountryID);
 END;
```

There are three fields defined here (**Alien, HomeStarID**, and **EarthID**) but only *two* exist at any one time. The Boolean field **Alien** is called the *tag field* and is *always* present in any instance of the record type. Which of the other two fields is considered present in the record depends on the value loaded into **Alien**. If **Alien** contains **True**, then the other field in the record is **HomeStarID**. If **Alien** contains **False**, then the other field is **EarthID**.

Beginners often ask, Well, who *enforces* that? Nobody; there's nothing to enforce. People who think "enforcement" are thinking backward. The tag field exists to tell users of the record what information was written into the record earlier so that those users can know how to interpret what they find. *The tag field is a flag, not a switch.* Changing the value of **Alien** has no effect on the data in the rest of the record. Given an instance of **ID** named **ScienceOfficer**, the tag field is used this way:

```
WITH ScienceOfficer DO
 IF Alien THEN
   SendHyperwaveTo(HomeStarID)
 ELSE
   SendTelegramTo(EarthID);
```

Changing the value in **Alien** in violation of the agreed-upon scheme (i.e., setting it to **False** for that guy Spock) will cause confusion, but only semantic confusion. The system won't crash.

If you're sharp it may occur to you that variant records are themselves a means of type casting, and you're right. Once you write a **HomeStarID** into an **ID** record, you can ignore the tag field and read the *identical* data right back as an **EarthID** type, essentially casting a **HomeStarID** type onto an **EarthID** type.

And if the only reason for the record is to cast one type onto another, who needs the tag field? In fact, dropping the tag field is how we turn a discriminated union into a free union:

```
ScreenAtom =
 RECORD
  CASE Boolean OF
   True : (Ch  : Char;
           Attr : Byte);
   False : (Atom : Word);
 END;
```

Like the Cheshire cat, the tag field has vanished, but its *type* remains. The need for the tag field as flag is gone, but we need something to enumerate the different variants; the lonely type specifier **Boolean** does that quite well by providing the **True** and **False CASE** labels. Any ordinal type (**Char, Integer, Word, Byte**, or enumerations) would do as well, and you don't have to account for every value in the type as long as you define at least two.

So what do we have here? A record of type **ScreenAtom** occupies 2 bytes of storage and that's all. The two variants may be considered two molds into which those 2 bytes of storage may be cast. One mold provides two byte-sized compartments called **Ch** and **Attr**. The other is a single 2-byte field called **Atom**. We can write a word-sized value to the **Atom** field and then pick out its two component bytes separately as **Ch** or **Attr**. The reverse, of course, is just as true: We can build an atom in two operations, first by storing a character in **Ch**, and then by storing its attribute in **Attr**. That done, we can read the finished atom out as **Atom**:

```
MyAtom.Ch   := 'A';
MyAtom.Attr := $07;
MEMW[$B800 : 0] := MyAtom.Atom;
```

A character on the PC's text screen is stored as 2 bytes side-by-side: the ASCII code for the character, and a byte specifying the attribute of the character, such as, its color for color screens, or things like underlining and reverse video for monochrome screens. **ScreenAtom** lets us look at these two bytes as a unit, or else as the two individual components, as we choose.

In the case of **ScreenAtom**, both of the two variants are of the same size, so everything's tidy. That's not a requirement; if the several variants vary in size, the record as a whole is as large as its largest variant. This prevents any danger to adjacent data.

18.5 The DOS Unit's Registers Union

The best example of a free union whose variants are *not* the same size is the **Registers** type exported by the Turbo Pascal **DOS** unit. The idea is to provide access to the 86-family CPU registers. Here 'tis:

```
TYPE
  Registers = RECORD
        CASE Integer OF
          0 : (AX,BX,CX,DX,BP,SI,DI,DS,ES,Flags : Word);
          1 : (AL,AH,BL,BH,CL,CH,DL,DH : Byte);
      END;
```

There are 10 accessible registers altogether: AX, BX, CX, DX, BP, SI, DI, DS, ES, and Flags. However, the first four are commonly treated in two ways: as 16-bit units whose names end in "X," or with each 16-bit unit seen as two 8-bit components ending in "H" (for High) and "L" (for Low). For example, AX is composed of AL and AH, BX of BL and BH, etc.

Both free unions provide easy access to the four general-purpose registers AX, BX, CX, and DX as both 16-bit units and pairs of 8-bit halves. Given an instance of type **Registers** named **Regs**, when you want to access all of AX, you specify **Regs.AX**. If you simply want to access the high half of AX without disturbing the low half (say for passing parameters to a DOS or BIOS service) you specify **Regs.AH**.

A diagram of the internals of the Turbo Pascal **Registers** type is shown in Figure 18.2. Each variant maps a different structure onto the same 20 bytes of memory. The 0 variant partitions those 20 bytes into 10 2-byte words. The 1 variant treats the first 8 bytes as single-byte quantities—and ignores the remaining 12 bytes.

In summary, what the **Registers** variants provide are two different interpretations of the same region of memory, safely and with zero overhead in processor cycles. Like Pizza Terra and Pete Cetera, it all depends on how you look at (or listen to) things.

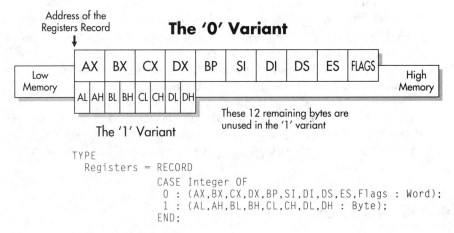

```
TYPE
    Registers = RECORD
                CASE Integer OF
                0 : (AX,BX,CX,DX,BP,SI,DI,DS,ES,Flags : Word);
                1 : (AL,AH,BL,BH,CL,CH,DL,DH : Byte);
                END;
```

Figure 18.2 The Registers Type

Chapter 19

DOS and the Borland DOS Unit

USING THE TOOLS THE OPERATING SYSTEM PROVIDES

The best 8086 software toolkit bargain going is DOS. For $90.00 or so you get a host of machine-code subprograms of remarkable power, that taken together do most of the dullest and most difficult routine work of a PC program: telling the time and date, spinning the disks, managing memory. All of this power is available through the standard Turbo Pascal unit, **DOS**. The most widely-used functions have their own high-level procedures and functions within the **DOS** unit that hide much of the arcana connected with loading and unloading machine registers and so on. To access DOS functions not graced with their own high-level subprograms, a generalized DOS-call primitive is provided from which *any* DOS call can be made with a little study and care.

Only some of the material in this section can genuinely be called *advanced*, particularly that connected with software interrupts and "naked" DOS calls. Take it slow and easy, and read everything with an eye for the details. If it doesn't become clear immediately, do come back to this section once you've worked up some confidence in general Pascal programming.

19.1 The Evolution of a Toolkit

Those of us who shrug at the thought of an application program that *requires* 640K (like Xerox's Ventura Publisher) might find the notion of an operating system living in less than 12K almost miraculous — until we ponder how very little such an operating system actually accomplished. The operating system, of course, was CP/M-80, the overwhelming favorite personal computer operating system before the appearance of the IBM PC. By 1993, CP/M-80 is virtually forgotten, but to forget it is to lose sight of why DOS has evolved the way it has.

DOS 1.X was simply a clone of CP/M-80 written in 8086 assembler rather than 8080/Z80 assember. The first 36 function calls (up to function $24, Set Random Record) are nearly identical to CP/M-80's function calls. Though tightly written, CP/M-80 cannot be accused of having been beautifully designed, and its function calls have a haphazard way of dealing with input values, return values, and error codes. Fortunately, the more fundamental DOS calls are hidden by the Turbo Pascal runtime code and the routines in the standard units, and you'll have very little need to call them directly through the **MSDOS** procedure. When you do, pay attention to the documentation and make no assumptions.

When it accessed files, CP/M-80 set up control blocks in memory called FCBs (File Control Blocks). In general terms, an application wrote necessary information into an FCB and then made the CP/M function call. PC DOS 1.X inherited this system for file I/O function calls, and all of the file I/O function calls in the first 36 DOS functions require the use of FCBs.

The break between PC DOS 1.X and DOS 2.0 was a fundamental one, far more fundamental than the break between 2.X and 3.X. For version 2, Microsoft rewrote DOS from scratch, modeling it on the Unix minicomputer operating system developed by AT&T. DOS 2 and 3 may be seen as stripped-down single-user, single-tasking Unix clones, containing most of the genuine Unix innovations without Unix's wretchedly slow performance.

Unix's most important contributions to DOS are subdirectories and their associated pathnames, allowing structure to be imposed on massive linear directories containing hundreds of separate files. The file I/O code within DOS 1.X was too set in its ways to be expanded to support pathnames and subdirectories, so Microsoft created a whole "second set" of file I/O function calls for DOS 2.X. These new calls provide all the functions of the original set and then some, and do it in a much cleaner fashion. DOS 2.X hid the FCBs within itself, making interface to files much simpler and more consistent. Rather than being associated with an FCB, a file, when opened, became associated with a "file handle;" a 16-bit code number associated with a file control table somewhere inside DOS.

Most of the fooling around connected with file I/O is, again, handled transparently by the Turbo Pascal runtime code and you needn't study the arcane details of working with file handles. What you need to understand is the reason why there are two DOS function calls for most file operations: The old ones do not understand pathnames or subdirectories; the new ones do. There are subtler reasons for using the newer set of file function calls, but for brevity's sake I'll ask you to take my word for it. Because Turbo Pascal has not run under DOS 1.X since V3.0, you have absolutely no reason *not* to use the newer function calls.

A certain number of new function calls have been added to every upgrade of DOS since 3.3, up to the now-current 6.0. These newer calls are arcane to the nines (seeming to point the way to yet more future enhancements rather than being immediately useful) and I will not be covering them here.

19.2 Real-Mode Software Interrupts

Most people think that DOS is the controlling hand within the PC, and while largely true, it doesn't credit the assistance of the ROM BIOS (Basic Input/Output System), which does much of the work for DOS. Many of the toolkit routines in this book rely on either DOS or ROM BIOS calls. In both instances, those calls are accomplished through software interrupts. In this short section I'll review the concept of a software interrupt and how the concept is made real in the 86-family of CPUs.

Traditionally, an *interrupt* is a tap on the CPU's shoulder, indicating that it must pay attention to something else *now*. Interrupt mechanisms have always been part of microprocessor systems. Until the development of the 8086 (and its slightly gimp-legged child, the 8088) all interrupts were *hardware* interrupts.

Hardware interrupts work this way: An electrical signal on one pin of the CPU chip causes the CPU logic to save the "state" of the currently-running program. This includes the program counter (which keeps track of where execution is at within a program), flags register, and the code segment register, CS. The CPU is then free to service the request from outside the chip to execute some bit of code unrelated to its ongoing task. Once the request for service is satisfied, the CPU restores the registers it had saved and picks up its ongoing task as though nothing had happened.

With the 86-family architecture, Intel presented the concept of the *software* interrupt. Software interrupts work exactly the same way as hardware interrupts do, except that the triggering request is a machine instruction (software) rather than an external electrical signal on a CPU pin (hardware).

There were a number of reasons for doing this. Since the only difference between hardware and software interrupts is the means by which the interrupt request is triggered, it is possible to test hardware interrupt service routines before the interrupting hardware is perfected, by using software interrupts to simulate the incomplete external hardware device.

A far more important use of software interrupts is in the devising of a system of standard entry points to system software. When any kind of interrupt happens, the CPU first saves essential registers, and then performs a "long jump" to the location of the interrupt service routine somewhere in memory.

The way the CPU locates this interrupt service routine is critical. The 256 8086 interrupts are numbered, from 0 to 255. When an interrupt happens, the CPU must receive the number of the requested interrupt. For hardware interrupts, this number comes from the interrupt priority controller chip outside the CPU. For software interrupts, the interrupt number is built into the interrupt instruction. For example, the 8086 instruction

```
INT 21H
```

will trigger software interrupt $21.

The first 1024 bytes of the 8086 memory map are reserved for *interrupt vectors*. "Vector" can be taken to mean "pointer," and pointers are exactly what occupy those 1024 bytes of memory. Each of the 256 different interrupts has its own 4-byte region of this 1024-byte memory block. (256 x 4 = 1024.) This 4-byte region contains a 32-bit pointer to the first instruction of the interrupt's service routine.

The first 4 bytes of 8086 memory contain the interrupt vector for interrupt 0. The next 4 bytes of memory contain the vector for interrupt 1, and so on up to 255. (See Figure 19.1.) Obviously, if the CPU knows the interrupt number, it can multiply that number by four and go immediately to the interrupt vector for any given interrupt. The first 2 bytes of the interrupt vector are the program counter value for the start of the service routine, and the second 2 bytes are the code segment value where that service routine exists. The CPU need only load the code segment value into the CS register and the program counter value into the program counter register, and it is off and running the interrupt service routine.

The important fact here is that the code that wishes to use a software interrupt service routine need not know where that routine is in memory. It only needs to know the interrupt *number*. Indeed, the actual location of the service routine can change over time, as the routine is altered or expanded. As long as the computer's boot or startup code stores the correct interrupt vectors into the lowermost 1024 bytes of memory, software interrupt service routines may be anywhere and still be used quickly and easily by application programs.

This is the spirit of the PC's ROM BIOS. The BIOS is a collection of software interrupt service routines stored in a ROM (Read-Only Memory) at the very top of the 8086's memory address space. The interrupt numbers are assigned according to the general function performed by the interrupt service routine. For example, interrupt 16 ($10) controls video services for the PC. Interrupt 22 ($16) controls access to the keyboard.

Not all software interrupts are reserved for the use of the ROM BIOS. DOS uses a few, and most of them are not used at all. The Microsoft Mouse driver makes use of a software interrupt. Quite a few peripheral driver programs, in fact, make use of software interrupts. The PC as we know it would have been impossible without them.

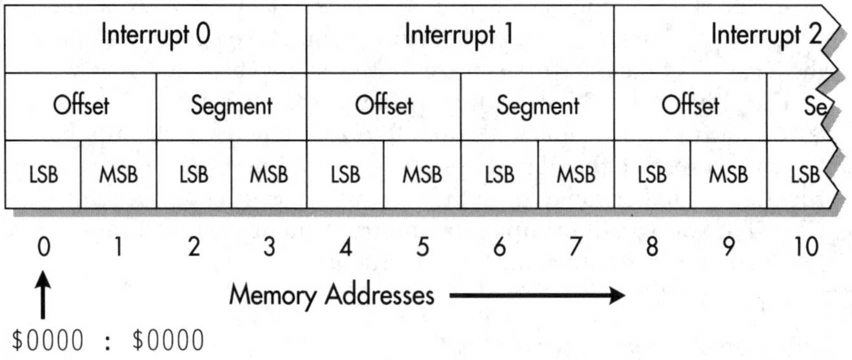

Figure 19.1 The Interrupt Vector Table

EXPLORING THE INTERRUPT VECTOR TABLE WITH GETINTVEC AND SETINTVEC

Exploring the interrupt vector jump table (the first 1024 bytes of 8086 memory where all the vectors are stored) can be done with DOS's DEBUG utility, but a fairly simple program can make the vectors easier to read and change. The **VECTORS.PAS** program is a utility called **Vectors** that can display and change interrupt vectors, and also display a hexdump of the first 256 bytes of memory pointed to by a vector. Changing an interrupt vector can be strong medicine, and shouldn't be done unless you know what you're doing. Altering the timer tick interrupt carelessly can freeze your machine solid in no more than 55 milliseconds' time. But if you intend to write programs that intercept interrupt vectors, **Vectors** can save a lot of aggravation during development.

One problem in reading simple hexdumps of the vector table is that the vectors' components are stored backward in memory from the way we generally write them. (See Figure 19.1.) The offsets are stored before the segments, and the least significant bytes of both segments and offsets are stored before the most significant bytes.

Vectors reformats the interrupt vector table for our eyes, and allows us to perform certain useful operations on the table. For example, it allows us to zero out all 32 bits of a vector, and also allows us to change the offset or segment portion of any vector to the value of our choice.

Vectors depends on two routines from Turbo Pascal's **DOS** unit, **GetIntVec** and **SetIntVec**:

```
PROCEDURE GetIntVec(IntNumber : Byte; VAR Vector : Pointer);
PROCEDURE SetINtVec(IntNumber : Byte; Vector : Pointer);
```

In both cases, **IntNumber** contains the number of the interrupt whose vector you wish to read or change, and **Vector** is a generic pointer containing the address read from or written to that vector. **GetIntVec** returns vector **IntNumber** in **Vector**; and **SetIntVec** places the address in pointer **Vector** in the vector table for interrupt **IntNumber**. These are "well-behaved" routines for reading and setting vectors from the interrupt vector table. We say "well-behaved" because the vector table is just an ordinary region of memory, accessible by way of the **MEM**, **MEMW**, and **MEML** statements, which I will not be covering in this particular book. These, however, are considered highly "ill-behaved" ways of manipulating interrupt vectors.

Why so?

Well, think about this: Suppose you're in the midst of altering a vector in the table, and have half of a new value written, when something somewhere in the system calls that interrupt. At the moment the CPU recognizes the interrupt, you may have a new segment in place but have not overwritten the old offset yet. The CPU sends execution charging off on this half-baked vector, which lands in the middle of a data buffer, starts executing data as code, and freezes the machine solid.

DOS has a pair of functions for reading and setting interrupt vectors that does it correctly by first *disabling* interrupts before reading or altering a vector. Only when the vector is completely read or completely changed will DOS re-enable interrupts. That way, your programs will not end up reading a half-correct vector, or (much worse) allowing the CPU to transfer control to a half-correct vector.

VECTORS' OTHER TRICK

The **Vectors** utility knows another trick—it can provide a look at what any vector is in fact pointing to. Any initialized interrupt vector points to an inter-rupt service routine of some sort. **Vectors** will on command hexdump the first 256 bytes of memory pointed to by any given interrupt vector. People who can read 8086 binary machine code in their heads can track the logic of simple service routines. The rest of us can look for service routine "signatures," typi-cally in the form of copyright notices embedded in the binary machine code. If you have the Logitech Mouse driver loaded, **Vectors** will show you the Logitech signature at an offset of 16 bytes into the driver, pointed to by interrupt 51 ($33).

Vectors tests every vector it displays and indicates whether the vector points to a binary $CF value. This is the machine-code equivalent of the **IRET** (Inter-rupt Return) instruction. Pointing an interrupt to an **IRET** instruction is a safety measure that prevents havoc in case an interrupt occurs for which the vector is uninitialized. If an unused vector is made to point to an **IRET**, the worst that can happen if that interrupt is triggered is nothing at all—the **IRET** sends execution back to the caller without taking any action.

In the best of all worlds, all unused interrupt vectors are initialized to point to an **IRET**. But as you'll see once you run **Vectors**, only a few vectors are so disarmed. Most point to segment zero, offset zero, which is in fact an interrupt vector itself, the vector for interrupt 0, the first entry in the jump table. If such an interrupt occurs, the CPU will attempt to execute the interrupt jump table as though it were code—which will almost certainly crash the machine hard.

Vectors is simple in operation. It cycles through the 256 interrupt vectors one at a time, displaying the current value of the current interrupt vector, and then pausing for a command. "Jumping" to another interrupt vector is done by entering its value as either a decimal number or a hexadecimal value preceded by a "$."

Changing a vector value is done with the E command. E prompts individu-ally for the segment and offset portion of the vector. If you don't wish to change one or both, simply press Enter and nothing will be altered. As with jumping to a new value, vector values can be entered in either decimal or hex.

D dumps the 256 bytes pointed to by the current vector. If the first byte of the block is an **IRET** instruction, **Vectors** will say so.

Z changes both the offset and segment portion of a vector to zero. This can be useful in cases where you are testing some software that modifies interrupt vectors—and may be modifying the wrong ones. Zeroing a vector allows you to come back after your test software has run, and tell at a glance if the zeroed vector or vectors have stayed zeroed.

Either Q or X will exit **Vectors**.

The procedure **WriteHex** figures prominently in **Vectors**, as the mechanism by which the interrupt vectors are displayed, and also the core of a hexdump routine, **DumpBlock**, that dumps 256 bytes of memory at the location pointed to by the current vector.

```
{----------------------------------------------------------------}
{                          VECTORS                               }
{                                                                }
{                  Interrupt vector utility                      }
{                                                                }
{                     by Jeff Duntemann                          }
{                     Turbo Pascal V7.0                          }
{                    Last update 4/12/93                         }
{                                                                }
{ This program allows you to inspect and change 8086 interrupt   }
{ vectors, and look at the first 256 bytes pointed to by any     }
{ vector.  This allows the spotting of interrupt service         }
{ routine "signatures" (typically the vendor's copyright         }
{ notice) and also indicates when a vector points to an IRET.    }
{                                                                }
{ Note that it can be VERY dangerous to arbitrarily change       }
{ values in interrupt vectors.  Many vectors are essential to    }
{ continuing system operating and should not be "messed with."   }
{                                                                }
{   From: BORLAND PASCAL FROM SQUARE ONE   by Jeff Duntemann     }
{----------------------------------------------------------------}


PROGRAM Vectors;

USES DOS;      { For GetIntVec and SetIntVec }

CONST
  Up = True;


TYPE
  String80     = String[80];
  Block        = ARRAY[0..255] OF Byte;
  PtrPieces    = ARRAY[0..3] OF Byte;


VAR
  I             : Integer;
  VectorNumber  : Integer;
  Vector        : Pointer;
  VSeg,VOfs     : Integer;
```

```
  NewVector      : Integer;
  MemBlock       : Block;
  ErrorPosition  : Integer;
  Quit           : Boolean;
  Command        : String80;
  CommandChar    : Char;

PROCEDURE StripWhite(VAR Target : OpenString);

CONST
  Whitespace  : SET OF Char = [#8,#10,#12,#13,' '];

BEGIN
  WHILE (Length(Target) > 0) AND (Target[1] IN Whitespace) DO
    Delete(Target,1,1)
END;


PROCEDURE WriteHex(BT : Byte);

CONST
  HexDigits : ARRAY[0..15] OF Char = '0123456789ABCDEF';

VAR
  BZ : Byte;

BEGIN
  BZ := BT AND $0F;
  BT := BT SHR 4;
  Write(HexDigits[BT],HexDigits[BZ])
END;


FUNCTION ForceCase(Up : BOOLEAN; Target : String) : String;

CONST
  Uppercase : SET OF Char = ['A'..'Z'];
  Lowercase : SET OF Char = ['a'..'z'];

VAR
  I : INTEGER;

BEGIN
  IF Up THEN FOR I := 1 TO Length(Target) DO
    IF Target[I] IN Lowercase THEN
      Target[I] := UpCase(Target[I])
```

```
      ELSE { NULL }
    ELSE FOR I := 1 TO Length(Target) DO
      IF Target[I] IN Uppercase THEN
         Target[I] := Chr(Ord(Target[I])+32);
    ForceCase := Target
END;



PROCEDURE ValHex(HexString : String;
                    VAR Value : LongInt;
                    VAR ErrCode : Integer);

VAR
  HexDigits  : String;
  Position   : Integer;
  PlaceValue : LongInt;
  TempValue  : LongInt;
  I          : Integer;

BEGIN
  ErrCode := 0; TempValue := 0; PlaceValue := 1;
  HexDigits := '0123456789ABCDEF';
  StripWhite(HexString);    { Get rid of leading whitespace }
  IF Pos('$',HexString) = 1 THEN Delete(Hexstring,1,1);
  HexString := ForceCase(Up,HexString);
  IF (Length(HexString) > 8) THEN ErrCode := 9
    ELSE IF (Length(HexString) < 1) THEN ErrCode := 1
    ELSE
      BEGIN
        FOR I := Length(HexString) DOWNTO 1 DO  { For each character }
          BEGIN
            { The position of the character in the string is its value: }
            Position := Pos(Copy(HexString,I,1),HexDigits) ;
            IF Position = 0 THEN    { If we find an invalid character... }
              BEGIN
                 ErrCode := I;      { ...set the error code... }
                 Exit               { ...and exit the procedure }
              END;
            { The next line calculates the value of the given digit }
            { and adds it to the cumulative value of the string: }
            TempValue := TempValue + ((Position-1) * PlaceValue);
            PlaceValue := PlaceValue * 16;  { Move to next place }
          END;
        Value := TempValue
      END
END;
```

```
     PROCEDURE DumpBlock(XBlock : Block);

VAR
  I,J,K : Integer;
  Ch    : Char;

BEGIN
  FOR I:=0 TO 15 DO          { Do a hexdump of 16 lines of 16 chars }
    BEGIN
      FOR J:=0 TO 15 DO      { Show hex values }
        BEGIN
          WriteHex(Ord(XBlock[(I*16)+J]));
          Write(' ')
        END;
      Write('   |');              { Bar to separate hex & ASCII }
      FOR J:=0 TO 15 DO           { Show printable chars or '.' }
        BEGIN
          Ch:=Chr(XBlock[(I*16)+J]);
          IF ((Ord(Ch)<127) AND (Ord(Ch)>31))
          THEN Write(Ch) ELSE Write('.')
        END;
      Writeln('|')
    END;
  FOR I:=0 TO 1 DO Writeln('')
END; { DumpBlock }


PROCEDURE  ShowHelp;

BEGIN
  Writeln;
  Writeln('Press Enter to advance to the next vector.');
  Writeln;
  Writeln
  ('To display a specific vector, enter the vector number (0-255)');
  Writeln
  ('in decimal or preceded by a "$" for hex, followed by Enter.');
  Writeln;
  Writeln('Valid commands are:');
  Writeln;
  Writeln
  ('D : Dump the first 256 bytes pointed to by the current vector');
  Writeln
  ('E : Enter a new value (decimal or hex) for the current vector');
  Writeln('H : Display this help message');
  Writeln('Q : Exit VECTORS ');
  Writeln('X : Exit VECTORS ');
```

```
        Writeln('Z : Zero segment and offset of the current vector');
        Writeln('? : Display this help message');
        Writeln;
        Writeln
        ('The indicator ">>IRET" means the vector points to an IRET
          instruction');
        Writeln;
        Writeln
        ('Change vectors with GREAT CAUTION.  You can lock up your system');
        Writeln('very easily by changing vectors carelessly!');
        Writeln;
   END;



PROCEDURE DisplayVector(VectorNumber : Integer);

VAR
   Bump : Integer;
   Chunks : PtrPieces;
   Vector : Pointer;
   Tester : ^Byte;

BEGIN
   GetIntVec(VectorNumber,Vector);{ Get the vector }
   Tester := Vector;                { Can't dereference untyped pointer }
   Chunks := PtrPieces(Vector);    { Cast Vector onto Chunks }
   Write(VectorNumber : 3,' $');
   WriteHex(VectorNumber);
   Write('  [');
   WriteHex(Chunks[3]);             { Write out the chunks as hex digits }
   WriteHex(Chunks[2]);
   Write(':');
   WriteHex(Chunks[1]);
   WriteHex(Chunks[0]);
   Write(']');
   IF Tester^ = $CF                 { If vector points to an IRET, say so }
      THEN Write(' >>IRET ')
      ELSE Write('        ');
   END;



PROCEDURE DumpTargetData(VectorNumber : Integer);

VAR
   Vector : Pointer;
   Tester : ^Block;
```

```
      BEGIN
        GetIntVec(VectorNumber,Vector);   { Get the vector }
        Tester := Vector;       { Cast the vector onto a pointer to a block }
        MemBlock := Tester^;    { Copy the target block into MemBlock }
        IF MemBlock[0] = $CF THEN { See if the first byte is an IRET }
          Writeln('Vector points to an IRET.');
        DumpBlock(MemBlock)         { and finally, hexdump the block. }
      END;


    PROCEDURE  ChangeVector(VectorNumber:  Integer);

    VAR
      Vector : Pointer;
      LongTemp,TempValue : LongInt;
      SegPart,OfsPart : Word;

    BEGIN
      GetIntVec(VectorNumber,Vector);      { Get current value of vector }
      LongTemp := LongInt(Vector);         { Cast Pointer onto LongInt }
      SegPart := LongTemp SHR 16; { Separate pointer segment from offset }
      OfsPart := LongTemp AND $0000FFFF;   { And keep until changed }
      Write('Enter segment ');
      Write('(RETURN retains current value): ');
      Readln(Command);
      StripWhite(Command);
      IF Length(Command) > 0 THEN
      { If something other than RETURN was entered }
        BEGIN
          Val(Command,TempValue,ErrorPosition);  { Evaluate as decimal }
          IF ErrorPosition = 0 THEN SegPart := TempValue
            ELSE   { If it's not a valid decimal value, evaluate as hex: }
              BEGIN
                ValHex(Command,TempValue,ErrorPosition);
                IF ErrorPosition = 0 THEN SegPart := TempValue
              END;
          Vector := Ptr(SegPart,OfsPart);
           { Reset the vector with any changes }
          SetIntVec(VectorNumber,Vector);
        END;
      DisplayVector(VectorNumber);
       { Show it to reflect changes to segment part }
      Writeln;
      Write('Enter offset  ');       { Now get an offset }
      Write('(RETURN retains current value): ');
      Readln(Command);
      StripWhite(Command);
```

```
      IF Length(Command) > 0 THEN
      { If something other than RETURN was entered }
        BEGIN
          Val(Command,TempValue,ErrorPosition);  { Evaluate as decimal }
          IF ErrorPosition = 0 THEN OfsPart := TempValue
            ELSE    { If it's not a valid decimal value, evaluate as hex: }
              BEGIN
                ValHex(Command,TempValue,ErrorPosition);
                IF ErrorPosition = 0 THEN OfsPart := TempValue
              END
        END;
      Vector := Ptr(SegPart,OfsPart);
      { Finally, reset vector with any change: }
       SetIntVec(VectorNumber,Vector);
  END;


  BEGIN
    Quit := False;
    VectorNumber := 0;
    Writeln('>>VECTORS<< V3.00 by Jeff Duntemann');
    Writeln('          From the book: BORLAND PASCAL FROM SQUARE ONE');
    Writeln('          Bantam Books, 1993');
    Writeln;
    ShowHelp;

  REPEAT
    DisplayVector(VectorNumber);    { Show the vector # & address }
    Readln(Command);                { Get a command from the user }
    IF Length(Command) > 0 THEN     { If something was typed:      }
      BEGIN
        { See if a number was typed; if one was, it becomes the
          current }
        { vector number.  If an error in converting the string to a  }
        { number occurs, Vectors then parses the string as a command. }
         Val(Command,NewVector,ErrorPosition);
         IF ErrorPosition = 0 THEN VectorNumber := NewVector
           ELSE
             BEGIN
               StripWhite(Command);        { Remove leading whitespace }
               Command := ForceCase(Up,Command); { Force to upper case }
               CommandChar := Command[1]; { Isolate first char.    }
               CASE CommandChar OF
                   'Q','X' : Quit := True;   { Exit VECTORS }
                   'D'     : DumpTargetData(VectorNumber); { Dump data }
                   'E'     : ChangeVector(VectorNumber);
                             { Enter new value }
```

```
            'H'     : ShowHelp;
            'Z'     : BEGIN              { Zero the vector }
                        Vector := NIL;   { NIL is 32 zero bits }
                        SetIntVec(VectorNumber,Vector);
                        DisplayVector(VectorNumber);
                        Writeln('zeroed.');
                        VectorNumber := (VectorNumber + 1) MOD 256
                      END;
            '?'     : ShowHelp;
          END {CASE}
        END
      END
    { The following line increments the vector number, }
    { rolling over to 0 if the number would have exceeded 255: }
    ELSE VectorNumber := (VectorNumber + 1) MOD 256
  UNTIL Quit;
END.
```

19.3 Registers and Register Structures

In broad strokes, the previous section described the nature and use of software interrupts. Your Turbo Pascal programs can make use of software interrupts quite easily. Understanding how requires some discussion of 8086 machine registers.

A register is nothing more than a storage location inside the CPU chip itself. The 8086 has quite a few of them. Nearly all of them are 16 bits, or 2 bytes, wide. Some of the registers have specific duties to perform in the 8086's execution of its programs. Many are simply convenient places to tuck things away for a moment. How the registers contribute to the 8086 instruction set is too large a topic to cover here in detail. What's important now is to understand how machine registers are used in connection with calling software interrupt service routines from Turbo Pascal.

Most software interrupt service routines like those in the PC's ROM BIOS require input values, and return output values when processing is finished. These values are passed back and forth between a Turbo Pascal program and the interrupt service routine in machine registers.

Turbo Pascal's **DOS** unit contains the **Intr** procedure, whose job is to invoke software interrupts. **Intr** requires an interrupt number and a special data structure containing word and byte fields corresponding to most of the 8086's registers:

```
Intr(IntNumber: Word; Regs : Registers);
```

The **Registers** type is defined in the interface part of the **DOS** unit. It is a free-union variant record (see Section 18.4) that maps byte fields corresponding to the general-purpose register halves over registers AX, BX, CX, and DX:

```
Registers =
  RECORD
```

```
CASE Integer OF
  0 : (AX,BX,CX,DX,BP,SI,DI,DS,ES,Flags : Word);
  1 : (AL,AH,BL,BH,CL,CH,DL,DH : Byte);
END;
```

Each of the fields of **Registers'** "0" variant (that is, the fields defined on the line following "0:") is named after an 8086 machine register. When **Intr** is called by your program, it copies the 10 values from these 10 fields into each field's corresponding 8086 register. Then it invokes the software interrupt you requested. When the interrupt service routine returns control to **Intr**, **Intr** copies each of the 10 8086 registers into its corresponding field in **Registers**. The interrupt service routine may or may not have changed any of the 10 machine registers, but if any *were* changed, the changed values will be available in **Registers** for your program to use.

At first glance, this seems straightforward enough. One persistant problem is that many of the 8086's registers are treated by interrupt service routines not as single 16-bit quantities, but as independent 8-bit quantities. In particular, registers AX, BX, CX, and DX are often treated as pairs of 8-bit registers. Within AX are AH and AL (Think, "A High" and "A Low"), within BX are BH and BL, and so on for CX and DX. You are often called upon to place separate values in the two halves of a given register.

For example, consider the BIOS VIDEO routine that positions the cursor to a particular location on the CRT screen. Before you call software interrupt 16 (the ROM BIOS video services interrupt) you have to place the desired row/column position in register DX. The row number goes in DH, and the column number in DL. **Registers** considers DX, defined as a **Word**. How do you put two different values into the two halves of a **Word**?

This is what the second variant line is for. Its eight fields are bytes, not words. This means that it takes two byte fields to equal the size of one word field—an important characteristic. (Turn back to Figure 18.2 in the last chapter if this isn't clear to you. Figure 18.2 is a memory diagram of how the different variants of type **Registers** are mapped into memory when Turbo Pascal allocates space for a **Registers** variable.)

Both variants begin at the same point in memory, which is the address of the record as a whole. The "0" variant is 10 words long, and encompasses everything contained in the record. The "1" variant, by contrast, is only 8 bytes—four words—long. It too begins at the beginning of the record, but its fields only extend 4 bytes in, corresponding in memory to the AX, BX, CX, and DX registers of the "0" variant. For example, fields AL and AH of the "1" variant are located at the same memory location as field AX of the "0" variant. This means that whatever exists in that memory location will be copied into the AX register when **Intr** is executed, whether it was written to memory as part of the AX field of the "0" variant, or as part of either the AH or AL fields of the "1" variant.

As I said in the last chapter, the **Registers** record type is just a way of casting two **Byte** types onto one **Word** type. Notice that there are no half-registers mapped onto BP, SI, DI, DS, ES, or Flags. In most cases these registers are not treated by halves. If you need to access half of one of these other registers independently of its other half, you will need to resort to either logical operators (AND or OR) or create a special record type of your own to facilitate the type cast:

```
TYPE
  Halfer =
    RECORD
      LoHalf,HiHalf : Byte
    END;
```

With type **Halfer** defined, you can type cast byte quantities into the correct portion of any word variable:

```
VAR
  Regs : Registers;

  Halfer(Regs.SI).LoHalf := $FF;  { Load the low half of BP }
  Halfer(Regs.SI).HiHalf := $1A;  { Load the high half of BP }
```

These statements use type casting to treat a **Word** value (**Regs.SI**) as a record of type **Halfer**, and assign values to one of **Halfer**'s fields. This notation is *not* standard Pascal, and is a Turbo Pascal enhancement to standard Pascal called "variable type casting." See Section 18.2 for more on this particular Turbo Pascal trick.

INTR IN ACTION

The best way to show you how to use the **Intr** procedure is with a simple toolkit routine that depends on it. Read the definition of **FlushKey** over carefully:

```
{->>>>FlushKey<<<<-------------------------------------------------}
{                                                                   }
{ Filename: FLUSHKEY.SRC - Last modified 2/13/93                     }
{                                                                   }
{ This routine uses ROM BIOS services to flush waiting              }
{ characters from the keyboard buffer. This should be done          }
{ immediately before user prompts which must NOT be answerable }
{ via type-ahead:  Go-aheads for file erasures, things like         }
{ that.                                                             }
{                                                                   }
{    From: BORLAND PASCAL FROM SQUARE ONE  by Jeff Duntemann    }
{-------------------------------------------------------------------}


PROCEDURE FlushKey;

VAR
  Regs : Registers;  { USES DOS unit! }

BEGIN
  Regs.AH := $01;               { AH=1: Check for keystroke }
```

```
    Intr($16,Regs);                { Interrupt $16: Keyboard services}
    IF (Regs.Flags AND $0040) = 0 THEN   { If chars in buffer }
      REPEAT
        Regs.AH := 0;              { Char is ready; go read it... }
        Intr($16,Regs);            { ...using AH = 0: Read Char }
        Regs.AH := $01;            { Check for another keystroke... }
        Intr($16,Regs);            { ...using AH = 1 }
      UNTIL (Regs.Flags AND $0040) <> 0;
  END;
```

FlushKey flushes the keyboard typeahead buffer. In other words, if any characters are waiting to be read in the typeahead buffer, **FlushKey** reads them and throws them away. Why is this useful? There are times when you do *not* want to allow a user to answer a question by typing ahead, presumably before the question's prompt appears on the screen. If you are asking a user whether or not he wants to delete the old version of his master data file, you would prefer that he read the question and think about it for a moment, rather than insert an answer in the typeahead queue and wait for the machine to catch up with his responses. He might slip and type the wrong character, or forget that the question comes up.

Therefore, immediately before prompting the user for responses which may have drastic consequences, call **FlushKey** to empty the typeahead buffer.

FlushKey uses the keyboard services interrupt of ROM BIOS, interrupt 22 (16 hex, or $16 in the listing). The very first line of the body of **FlushKey** loads a value of 1 into the high byte of register AX:

```
    Regs.AH := $01;
```

This notation selects the **AH** field of variant record **Regs** and loads $01 into it. Recall that **AH** indicates a byte-sized field.

Now, consider line 33:

```
    IF (Registers.Flags.Word AND $0040) = 0 THEN
```

This time, we're testing for one bit (the Zero bit) out of the **Flags** register. **Flags** is here treated as a 16-bit word quantity. **Flags** is not traditionally broken into halves, as AX, BX, CX, and DX so often are. While we could separately access the two halves of **Flags** for bit-testing purposes, I recommend against it for clarity's sake. There is no speed advantage to testing a single bit within an 8-bit byte over testing for that same bit within a 16-bit integer. (There may in fact be a speed disadvantage, since nearly all members of the 86 family of CPUs access data in word form faster than in byte form!)

A short program to demonstrate **FlushKey** is given below. The idea in **FlushTest** is to perform some time-consuming activity (in this case, incrementing a variable to 1000 and printing it all the while) and then query the keyboard to see if this counting should be done again. **FlushKey** is there to clear the keyboard buffer before asking the question. If **FlushKey** were not invoked, the user could type characters into the typeahead buffer and answer the question before it was asked. (Comment out **FlushKey**'s invocation at line 25 and try it!)

Flushkey guarantees that the user will read and question and (with any luck) think it over before responding.

```
{----------------------------------------------------------------}
{                          FlushTest                             }
{                                                                }
{         Keyboard buffer flush demonstration program            }
{                                                                }
{                       by Jeff Duntemann                        }
{                       Turbo Pascal V7.0                        }
{                       Last update 2/13/93                      }
{                                                                }
{   From: BORLAND PASCAL FROM SQUARE ONE  by Jeff Duntemann      }
{----------------------------------------------------------------}

PROGRAM FlushTest;

USES Crt,DOS;

VAR I,J : Integer;
    Ch  : Char;

{$I FLUSHKEY.SRC}

PROCEDURE Counter;

BEGIN
  FOR I := 1 TO 10000 DO  { Cut this to 1000 or 5000 for slow machines!}
    BEGIN
      GotoXY(1,WhereY); ClrEol;
      J := J + 1;
      Write(J)
    END;
  Writeln
END;

BEGIN
  REPEAT
    Counter;
    FlushKey;
    Write('End program now? (Y/N): ');
    Readln(Ch);
  UNTIL Ch IN ['Y','y']
END.
```

19.4 BIOS and BIOS Services

FlushKey provides a good introduction to the concept of ROM BIOS services. As I explained earlier, each broad function of BIOS (video, keyboard, printer, serial port) has its own software interrupt. However, within most BIOS functions are two or more separately invocable services that are called using the same software interrupt. Within the video function (software interrupt 16), for example, are services to position the cursor, write a character to the screen, scroll a rectangular window up or down, change text and graphics modes, write pixels to a graphics screen, read characters from a text screen, and quite a few more.

The BIOS video function is selected by invoking software interrupt 16. Invoking an individual video service is done by placing a service code in the high half of the AX register, AH. This is a custom in the use of the PC's ROM BIOS services: To select a service within a function, place the service code in AH.

FlushKey does this several times, initially at line 21. Service 1 for the BIOS keyboard function checks for the availability of a character in the typeahead buffer. **FlushKey** first checks to see if there is at least one character in the buffer by examining the Zero bit in the Flags register. Service 1 communicates its result to the calling logic by setting or clearing the Zero bit. If the Zero bit comes back cleared (i.e., set to 0), a character is in the buffer. If the Zero bit comes back set (i.e., set to 1), no character is waiting in the typeahead buffer.

Notice that if the first check for waiting characters comes back positive, **FlushKey** enters a **REPEAT/UNTIL** loop. The loop is entered only if a character is known to be in the buffer, so keyboard service 0 is called immediately. Service 0 returns the first waiting character in the typeahead buffer. If no character is waiting to be read, service 0 will sit and wait for a character to be typed. This is the reason we must check for the presence of a character before attempting to read one with service 0. Trying to read a character when none has been typed will give the appearance of a hung system until some key is pressed.

The loop reads a character and then checks for the presence of yet another character. If no further characters are detected via keyboard service 1, the buffer is empty and **FlushKey** has done its job. If more characters are detected, the read-and-check-for-more loop is repeated until the buffer comes up empty. This state is indicated by a set Zero flag. Note that nothing is done with the characters read; **FlushKey** simply reads them and throws them away to get them out of the buffer. You could expand **FlushKey** to return a string variable containing any characters found in the typeahead buffer if it was important not to ignore an important keypress, such as an "escape" code or other "hot key."

POLLING THE KEYBOARD WITH GETKEY

With only a little more complication, we can get from the BIOS virtually all it has to offer in terms of keyboard support. There are only three services available under the BIOS keyboard function, interrupt 22. **FlushKey** uses 0 and 1. Service 2 returns the current state of the PC's various shift-type keys.

There are four shift-type keys on the PC keyboard, and four lock-type keys. Shift-type keys create a condition only when pressed; when released, that condition goes away. The four shift-type keys are Control (Ctrl), Alt, Left Shift, and Right Shift. In terms of uppercase and lowercase characters, Left Shift and Right Shift are identical, but at the BIOS level they are two separate keys that may be tested for independently.

The lock-type keys are Insert (Ins), Caps Lock, Num Lock, and Scroll Lock. These keys control keyboard "toggles"—flags that can be switched between two states but which remain in a given state until switched to the opposite state, much like a toggle switch controlling a light fixture. Flip it once, and the light goes on and stays on until you flip it again to turn it off. This analogy is especially apt for some non-IBM keyboards, which have little LED lamps built into the lock-type keys so that you can always tell which state the key is in at a glance. With the IBM keyboard you have to remember, or take a chance by pressing a key and seeing what happens.

Keyboard interrupt service 2 returns an 8-bit byte in AL containing eight flag bits. The meaning behind each bit is shown below in Table 19.1.

The state of the shift-type keys (bits 0–4) is returned for the moment the interrupt call is made. There is *no* buffering of shift keys.

Below is **GetKey**, a keyboard sampling routine that will tell you everything the BIOS is capable of telling you about the PC keyboard. **GetKey** is a "polling" routine. It doesn't wait for a character or a string to be typed at the keyboard. At the moment you call **GetKey**, it jumps out and takes a look at the keyboard and the typeahead buffer. If a character is waiting in the typeahead buffer, **GetKey** will grab it and bring it back, setting its function return value to **True**. If no character is ready, **GetKey**'s function return value will come back as **False**. In *either* case, **GetKey** returns the current state of the shift-type keys and the lock-type keys in a byte named **Shifts**.

Table 19.1 Keyboard Service 2 Flags

Bit #	Meaning	Type
0	1 = Left Shift depressed	Shift
1	1 = Right Shift depressed	Shift
2	1 = Ctrl depressed	Shift
3	1 = Alt depressed	Shift
4	1 = Scroll Lock active	Lock
5	1 = Num Lock active	Lock
6	1 = Caps Lock active	Lock
7	1 = Insert active	Lock

```
{->>>>GetKey<<<<-----------------------------------------------}
{                                                               }
{ Filename: GETKEY.SRC - Last modified 2/13/93                  }
{                                                               }
{ This routine uses ROM BIOS services to test for the presence }
{ of a character waiting in the keyboard buffer and, if one is  }
{ waiting, return it. The function itself returns a TRUE        }
{ if a character has been read. The character is returned in    }
{ Ch. If the key pressed was a "special" (non-ASCII) key, the   }
{ Boolean variable Extended will be set to TRUE and the scan    }
{ code of the special key will be returned in Scan. In          }
{ addition, GETKEY returns shift status each time it is called  }
{ regardless of whether or not a character was read. Shift      }
{ status is returned as eight flag bits in byte Shifts,         }
{ according to the bitmap below:                                }
{                                                               }
{            BITS                                               }
{    7 6 5 4 3 2 1 0                                            }
{    1 . . . . . . . INSERT      (1=Active)                     }
{    . 1 . . . . . . CAPS LOCK   (1=Active)                     }
{    . . 1 . . . . . NUM LOCK    (1=Active)                     }
{    . . . 1 . . . . SCROLL LOCK (1=Active)                     }
{    . . . . 1 . . . ALT         (1=Depressed)                 }
{    . . . . . 1 . . CTRL        (1=Depressed)                 }
{    . . . . . . 1 . LEFT SHIFT  (1=Depressed)                 }
{    . . . . . . . 1 RIGHT SHIFT (1=Depressed)                 }
{                                                               }
{ Test for individual bits using masks and the AND operator:    }
{                                                               }
{   IF (Shifts AND $0A) = $0A THEN CtrlAndAltArePressed;        }
{                                                               }
{   From: BORLAND PASCAL FROM SQUARE ONE  by Jeff Duntemann     }
{---------------------------------------------------------------}


FUNCTION GetKey(VAR Ch       : Char;
                VAR Extended : Boolean;
                VAR Scan     : Byte;
                Var Shifts   : Byte) : Boolean;

VAR Regs  : Registers;
    Ready : Boolean;

BEGIN
  Extended := False; Scan := 0;
  Regs.AH := $01;      { AH=1: Check for keystroke }
  Intr($16,Regs);        { Interrupt $16: Keyboard services}
  Ready := (Regs.Flags AND $40) = 0;
```

```
  IF Ready THEN
    BEGIN
      Regs.AH := 0;          { Char is ready; go read it... }
      Intr($16,Regs);        { ...using AH = 0: Read Char }
      Ch := Chr(Regs.AL);    { The char is returned in AL }
      Scan := Regs.AH;       { ...and scan code in AH.    }
      IF Ch = Chr(0) THEN Extended := True ELSE Extended := False;
    END;
  Regs.AH := $02;            { AH=2: Get shift/alt/ctrl status }
  Intr($16,Regs);
  Shifts := Regs.AL;
  GetKey := Ready
END;
```

There is an additional complication to the notion of "returning a character" from the PC keyboard. There are keys that do not represent characters—the function keys and arrow keys are prime examples. Your programs may need to use those keys. How to get them?

The BIOS divides keystrokes into "ASCII" and "extended" keys. ASCII keys are keys which stand for an ASCII letter, numeral, or symbol having a numeric code of 0–127. If an ASCII key is pressed, **GetKey** returns the ASCII character in its character parameter **Ch**. The extended keys are the function keys, arrow keys, PgUp, PgDn, Home, End, and various combinations of those keys and Ctrl, Alt, and Shift. Each extended key has a code from 0–255. This code is returned for extended keys in **GetKey**'s **Scan** parameter. If an extended code is being returned, **GetKey** will also return a Boolean value of **True** in its **Extended** parameter.

All the various features of **GetKey** are exercised in the short demo program **KeyTest** given below. **KeyTest** samples the keyboard and displays the last character or extended key pressed, along with the current state of the shift keys and the lock keys. The ASCII character or scan code of the last key pressed will be shown in the middle of the screen. The current state of the shift keys is shown by upward- or downward-pointing arrows. If a particular lock key is active, the "sunburst" character symbol (character 15) will be displayed next to that key's label. It's interesting to note that of all the shift keys or lock keys, only Insert returns an extended code.

```
{-------------------------------------------------------------------}
{                          KeyTest                                  }
{                                                                   }
{         Full keyboard access demonstration program               }
{                                                                   }
{                      by Jeff Duntemann                            }
{                      Turbo Pascal V7.0                            }
{                      Last update 2/13/93                          }
{                                                                   }
{    From: BORLAND PASCAL FROM SQUARE ONE   by Jeff Duntemann      }
{-------------------------------------------------------------------}
```

```
PROGRAM KeyTest;

USES Crt,DOS;

VAR Ch : Char;
    Extended : Boolean;
    Scan,Shifts : Byte;
    Ready : Boolean;

{$I FLUSHKEY.SRC }
{$I GETKEY.SRC }
{$I CURSOFF.SRC }

BEGIN
  Ch := ' ';
  Ready := False;
  ClrScr;
  CursorOff;  { Get the cursor out of the way; we don't need it. }
  GotoXY(20,1); Write('< COMPLETE TURBO PASCAL Keyboard Read Demo >');
  GotoXY(30,2); Write('(Press ESC to exit...)');

  { First we set up the labels for the shift keys: }
  GotoXY(12,17); Write('Ctrl: ');
  GotoXY(5,18);  Write('Left Shift: ');
  GotoXY(48,18); Write('Right Shift: ');
  GotoXY(13,19); Write('Alt: ');

  { Here we set up the labels for the toggle keys: }
  GotoXY(50,19); Write('Caps Lock: ');
  GotoXY(64,19); Write('Insert: ');
  GotoXY(52,13); Write('Num Lock: ');
  GotoXY(64,13); Write('Scroll Lock: ');

  GotoXY(31,7); Write('<Last key pressed: >');

  FlushKey; { Empty any waiting keystrokes from the typeahead buffer }
  REPEAT
     Ready := GetKey(Ch,Extended,Scan,Shifts);
     GotoXY(29,8);
     IF Ready THEN  { If a character key has been pressed... }
       IF Extended THEN Write('Extended; Scan code = ',Scan)
         ELSE Write('            ',Ch,'            ');
     GotoXY(17,18); IF (Shifts AND $02) <> 0 THEN   { Left Shift }
        Write(Chr(31)) ELSE Write(Chr(30));
     GotoXY(62,18); IF (Shifts AND $01) <> 0 THEN   { Right Shift }
        Write(Chr(31)) ELSE Write(Chr(30));
     GotoXY(18,17); IF (Shifts AND $04) <> 0 THEN   { Ctrl }
```

```
              Write(Chr(31)) ELSE Write(Chr(30));
        GotoXY(18,19); IF (Shifts AND $08) <> 0 THEN   { Alt }
              Write(Chr(31)) ELSE Write(Chr(30));

        GotoXY(61,19); IF (Shifts AND $40) <> 0 THEN   { Caps Lock }
           Write(Chr(15)) ELSE Write(' ');
        GotoXY(72,19); IF (Shifts AND $80) <> 0 THEN   { Insert }
           Write(Chr(15)) ELSE Write(' ');
        GotoXY(62,13); IF (Shifts AND $20) <> 0 THEN   { Num Lock }
           Write(Chr(15)) ELSE Write(' ');
        GotoXY(77,13); IF (Shifts AND $10) <> 0 THEN   { Scroll Lock }
           Write(Chr(15)) ELSE Write(' ');

    UNTIL Ch = Chr(27);        { Until you press ESC... }
    TextMode(3);               { ...then restore cursor and quit. }
  END.
```

19.5 Making DOS Calls

Like most everything else in an 8086 environment, DOS is called through a software interrupt. We could, in fact, call DOS using Turbo Pascal's **Intr** software interrupt routine, by setting up values in a register structure and calling interrupt $21.

However, Turbo Pascal provides a somewhat more readable DOS call facility:

```
MSDOS(Regs);
```

where **Regs** is a record variable of the **Registers** type we examined in the previous section. Interrupt $21 does not have to be specified, as it is always the same for DOS calls and the interrupt calling code is built into the implementation of **MSDOS**.

The various functions performed by DOS each has a number. To invoke a function, this number must be loaded into register AH. Most individual DOS services require that additional parameters be loaded into various other registers before making the actual DOS call. We'll be providing numerous examples of **MSDOS** in use a little later.

DOS ERROR MESSAGES AND THE DOSERROR VARIABLE

Things go wrong. When a DOS function cannot complete successfully, DOS takes its best guess at what the problem is and returns an appropriate code in register AX. I say "best guess" because unusual situations have been known to knock DOS for a loop and return completely inappropriate error codes. You must therefore interpret DOS error codes carefully, and make provisions for situations when the returned error codes don't bear any relation at all to the problem at hand.

Beginning with DOS 2.0, a set of 19 error code values was defined and used in a standard fashion across all the new DOS function calls first included in DOS 2.0. This set begins with function call $2F, Set DTA Address. Function calls with numbers lower than $2F probably *don't* return error codes from this set. By and large, the routines in unit **DOS** use the newer DOS function calls. If you use function calls with numbers prior to $2F, double-check the DOS documentation to be sure you understand the errors such a call may return.

Table 19.2 summarizes the standard DOS error codes.

In summary: To make a DOS call, have defined a register variable of type **Registers** as described above, load the DOS service number into AH, load any other required parameters into the proper registers, and pass the structure to Turbo Pascal's **MSDOS** procedure:

```
Regs.AH := $36;   { "Get free disk space" service }
Regs.DL := $01;   { Request A: (drive 1) }

MSDOS(Registers);     { Make the DOS call }
```

Table 19.2 Standard DOS Error Codes

Code	Meaning
$00	No error; function call completed correctly
$01	Invalid function number
$02	File not found
$03	Path not found
$04	No handle available; all are in use
$05	Access denied
$06	Invalid handle
$07	Memory control blocks destroyed
$08	Insufficient memory
$09	Invalid memory block address
$0A	Invalid DOS environment
$0B	Invalid format
$0C	Invalid access code
$0D	Invalid data
$0E	*Not used by DOS!*
$0F	Invalid drive specification
$10	Attempt to remove current directory
$11	Not same device
$12	No more files to be found

If an error occurs, the error code will be returned in AX. Turbo Pascal's **DOS** unit contains a variable, **DOSError**, into which this error code is moved after a call to a DOS function that can return an error code.

Microsoft's documentation of DOS services is not always the best, especially if you're just learning your way around the PC at the system level. I don't have room to go over every single DOS service (there are about 85 in all) in this book. Experiment, but keep in mind that this is strong stuff—if you misunderstand the purpose of a parameter or put it in the wrong register, you could very easily blow your DOS session away and force a warm or cold reboot. Be careful—read it twice—and keep your cool!

DISK SIZE AND DISK FREE SPACE

DOS function call $36 does double duty, in that it returns both the free space on a disk and the total possible space on a disk. The Turbo Pascal **DOS** unit contains two functions that use this function call to provide the same service at a higher level: **DiskFree** and **DiskSize**.

DiskSize returns the total number of bytes that may be stored on a specified disk:

```
FUNCTION DiskSize(Drive : Byte) : LongInt;
```

Parameter **Drive** is used to specify which drive in the system is to be sampled. A disk must be present in the drive for this function to work correctly, as the disk will be accessed. In a somewhat contrary fashion, **Drive** does *not* contain the letter specifier for a disk drive, but a number indicating the drive, where 1 stands for drive A:, 2 stands for drive B:, and so on. To determine the size of the default drive, pass a 0 in **Drive**.

If the number passed in **Drive** does not correspond to a valid disk drive (for example, passing a 4 on a system with only drives A:, B:, and C:) **DiskSize** returns a -1.

DiskFree returns the number of free bytes available on a specified disk:

```
FUNCTION DiskFree(Drive : Byte) : LongInt;
```

The **Drive** parameter works in exactly the same way as it works in function **DiskSize**: Pass 1 to return the free bytes on drive A:, 2 for drive B:, and so on. A -1 value returned from the function indicates that the drive specified in **Drive** is invalid.

19.6 Times, Dates, Stamps, and Files

"You can ask me for anything you like, except time," said Napoleon Bonaparte. Your PC won't provide you with an empire, but time—well, time is easy. (The day of the week is another matter, but we'll get to that.) Setting and reading the time and date from the PC's real-time clock are relatively simple matters given the machinery in the **DOS** unit. Using the clock's time values to measure duration (the distance in time from one point to another) is fairly simple and can be quite useful. This section will cover the details of dealing with time on the PC, with a little help from Turbo Pascal.

HOW THE PC KEEPS TIME

Understanding *how* the PC keeps time is best begun by knowing *where* it "keeps" time. At $0040 : $006C is a 4-byte storage area that keeps a count of clock "ticks." These ticks occur roughly 18.2 times per second. Four bytes of zeroes at this location indicates midnight, and the count increases by 18.2 for every second past midnight. When DOS sets the clock to a particular time of day, it works backward from the requested time to the number of ticks that should have occurred by that time each day, and forces that number into the count storage location. When DOS needs to read the current time of day, it reads the 4 bytes from that storage location and converts the number of ticks to hours, minutes, and seconds. (The date is kept elsewhere, as I'll describe shortly.)

Now 18.2 ticks per second is a peculiar number, but it can be understood in the context of the ancient misty origins of the PC's hardware. As Figure 19.2 indicates, the original IBM PC's timing mechanism provided several different frequencies for several different purposes, all from the same master reference frequency. On the PC motherboard is an 8284 clock controller chip with a crystal-controlled reference oscillator that produces a 14.31818 Mhz square wave signal. This frequency was chosen as a convenience to the Color Graphics Adapter, which requires a 3.579545 Mhz input to correctly create what is called the "color burst" signal. The color burst signal helps format color information onto the composite video output produced in the CGA. As some quick work with your calculator will show, 3.579545 is 14.31818 divided by 4. (Those unfamiliar with computer hardware should understand that dividing a frequency by a factor of 2 or 3 or some power of 2 or 3 is easily done with a couple of standard flip-flop circuits.)

Another familiar number will appear if you divide 14.31818 by 3: 4.7727, which in Mhz is the CPU clock speed of the IBM PC. Dividing 14.31818 Mhz by 12 yields 1.19318 Mhz. This frequency is used as an input to a three-channel counter/timer chip called the 8253. (8254 on the PC/AT.) The 8253 is a busy creature, controlling as it does the timer tick interrupt, dynamic RAM refresh, and speaker output, all at once. Channel 0 is the one that controls the timer tick, which is of the most immediate interest.

Channel 0 of the 8253 divides the incoming signal (in this case 1.19318 Mhz) by up to 16 bits, or 65,536. Run that through your calculator and you'll see that it yields 18.206482. (This is why we say that the PC clock ticks at "roughly" 18.2 timer ticks per second. The precise figure is given by the ratio 1,193,180 / 65,536.) 18.2 is the fewest output pulses per second obtainable from the 8253, given an input frequency of 1.19318 Mhz.

So the output of channel 0 of the 8253 is a series of pulses coming at roughly 18.2 per second. Each time a pulse is output by the 8253, the 8259 interrupt

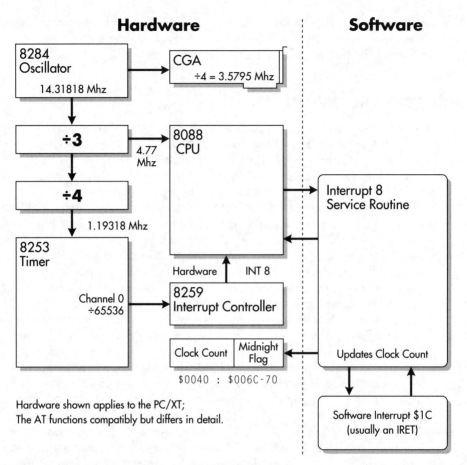

Figure 19.2 The PC/XT Clock/Timer Mechanism

controller chip generates a hardware interrupt. The interrupt service routine for this interrupt (interrupt 8) is in the PC ROM BIOS. This interrupt service routine increments the clock reference count at $0040 : $006C.

With each tick, the INT 8 service routine tests the reference count for a particular value: 1,573,040 (in hex, $1800B0). This is the number of timer ticks occurring in 24 hours. (18.206482 times 86400, the number of seconds in a 24-hour day.) When it detects this value, the count "rolls over" to zero, on the assumption that midnight has just occurred. It also writes a 1 into another location in memory at $0040 : $0070, immediately above the clock reference count. This is the "midnight flag" that indicates that midnight has occurred since the last time the clock was set.

The INT 8 service routine also generates a software interrupt $1C with each clock tick. This interrupt ordinarily does nothing, and the interrupt vector associated with it initially points to an **IRET** instruction, which does nothing but bounce control back to INT 8 like a ping-pong ball. However, it is possible to install a service routine for INT $1C that will execute some task 18.2 times per second. By making this task a process scheduler, some minimal multitasking support is possible. Of course, as anyone who has ever tried to run Unix on a 4.77 Mhz IBM PC should be aware, you can't expect much in terms of performance. The interrupt can be very useful in certain limited applications, like print spoolers. "Background" tunes can also be played by using interrupt $1C to feed new timer values to 8253 channel 2, which controls the speaker. (Consider that application a "tone spooler" if you will.)

Another note: Some people have leapt to the conclusion that 65,536 clock ticks occur in an hour, which is close but not true, since the true figure is 65,543 clocks and change.

The machinery I've described was what IBM built into its original PC back in 1981. Since then, PCs have gotten many times faster, but for compatibility's sake nearly all of them have a separate clock oscillator on them running at 14.31818 Mhz—even if their "real" clock (that is, the one controlling the CPU) is running at 33 or 50 Mhz.

Obviously, the clock count is only maintained while the PC is powered up and working properly. During periods when the power is off, the correct time must be maintained elsewhere. This elsewhere is a battery-maintained clock and CMOS RAM storage chip. A small lithium battery keeps an oscillator and a clock chip alive, and when the PC is powered up, BIOS reads the battery-powered clock and loads its value into the clock reference count at 0040:006C. Some early PCs lack built-in clocks and rely on many strange devices to keep time in hardware. The end result, however, is the same for all of them: The reference count resides at 0040:006C.

READING AND SETTING THE TIME THROUGH DOS

Turbo Pascal's **DOS** unit provides several functions connected with the PC's time and date: **GetDate**, **SetDate**, **GetTime**, and **SetTime**. Internally, these amount to very little more than "wrappers" around four DOS function calls made through the **MSDOS** procedure. They exist to hide the details of loading and unloading values between the register structure and more tractable parameters, but you should be aware of what is going on beneath the surface.

GetTime returns the time as currently maintained in the PC by using DOS Function 44 ($2C). It is declared this way:

```
PROCEDURE GetTime(VAR Hour,Minute,Second,Sec100 : Word);
```

Its information ultimately comes from the clock reference count at 0040:006C, but DOS converts the raw count of ticks since midnight into the familiar hours, minutes, seconds, and a slightly ersatz hundredths of seconds figure.

The hundredths figure is questionable because the PC's clock doesn't really resolve to a single hundredth of a second. Since there are only 18.2 clock ticks per second, the duration of a single tick is about 0.055 seconds (the reciprocal of 18.2). What DOS does is interpolate a given tick to its closest decimal equivalent within a second. This figure can be useful as long as you understand that there is that inescapable roundoff to the closest near-twentieth of a second.

Retrieving the time through DOS is trivial, then—as long as all we need is time in the form of four numbers. In everyday programming, time values are useful in a number of forms. A time-fetch routine can start with DOS's basic numeric time values and calculate these additional forms.

One common use of time is simply to display it, in a convenient format, for a human reader. The format I like is the one most familiar to PC users—the DOS DIR time format, which is a colon-separated 12-hour format with a single-letter AM/PM indicator: **12:17p**. Creating a string containing such a time format can be done with a little use of Turbo's **Str** built-in procedure and some concatenation.

There is one more form in which time can be expressed that you may find useful: a "time stamp" that expresses the time in 16 bits so that one such stamp may be compared with another to see which is later in time. This is a little tricky, as it isn't quite possible to express all four time units (hours, minutes, seconds, and hundredths of seconds) in one 16-bit time stamp. The matter of time stamps is important in dealing with DOS files, and I will devote considerable time to it later in this section.

In my own programming, I have combined these three different expressions of time into a single Pascal record:

```
TimeRec =
  RECORD
    TimeComp    : Word;  { DOS time stamp format }
    TimeString : String80;
    Hours,Minutes,Seconds,Hundredths : Integer
  END;
```

Filling such a record with the current time is done in two steps. The first step is simply to use Turbo Pascal's **GetTime** function to fill in the hours, minutes, seconds, and hundredths of seconds:

```
VAR
   TimeNow : TimeRec;

WITH TimeNow DO GetTime(Hours,Minutes,Seconds,Hundredths);
```

GetTime itself only makes the DOS call and loads the **TimeRec** integer fields. A separate routine, **CalcTime,** is used to calculate the string version of the time value and the time stamp value. I broke this out as a separate procedure so that time values originating elsewhere than the system clock can be put into the same format as system time values.

```
{->>>>CalcTime<<<<-------------------------------------------------}
{                                                                  }
{ Filename: CALCTIME.SRC - Last Modified 2/13/93                   }
{                                                                  }
{ This routine "fills out" a TimeRec passed to it with only        }
{ the DOS time values (hours, minutes, seconds, hundredths)        }
{ valid. It generates the TimeComp and TimeString fields.          }
{                                                                  }
```

```
{       TimeRec = RECORD                                              }
{                   TimeComp    : Word;       (DTA time stamp)        }
{                   TimeString : String80;                            }
{                   Hours,Minutes,Seconds,Hundredths : Integer        }
{               END;                                                  }
{                                                                     }
{ which, of course, also requires definition of type String80.       }
{                                                                     }
{   From: BORLAND PASCAL FROM SQUARE ONE   by Jeff Duntemann          }
{---------------------------------------------------------------------}


PROCEDURE CalcTime(VAR ThisTime : TimeRec);

TYPE
  String5 = String[5];

VAR
  Temp1,Temp2 : String5;
  AMPM        : Char;
  I           : Integer;

BEGIN
  WITH ThisTime DO
    BEGIN
      I := Hours;
      IF Hours = 0 THEN I := 12;    { "0" hours = 12am }
      IF Hours > 12 THEN I := Hours - 12;
      IF Hours > 11 THEN AMPM := 'p' ELSE AMPM := 'a';
      Str(I:2,Temp1); Str(Minutes,Temp2);
      IF Length(Temp2) < 2 THEN Temp2 := '0' + Temp2;
      TimeString := Temp1 + ':' + Temp2 + AMPM;
      TimeComp :=
        (Hours SHL 11) OR (Minutes SHL 5) OR (Seconds SHR 1)
    END
END;
```

Note that while the integer value **Hours** is left in 24-hour format, the string representation of the time converts its hours figure to a 12-hour format with the 'a' and 'p' to indicate AM or PM. **CalcTime** creates the time stamp by shifting the hours, minutes, and seconds numbers into their proper orientation and then ORing them into what amounts to a bitmap, as I'll explain in detail shortly.

Setting the time is easily done with the **SetTime** procedure in the **DOS** unit:

```
PROCEDURE SetTime(Hour,Minute,Second,Sec100 : Word);
```

Keep in mind that while **GetTime** and **SetTime** are included in the **DOS** unit, you will have to predefine **TimeRec** somewhere. On the listings diskette for this book I have provided a file called **TIMEREC.DEF**, containing the required definitions:

```
TimeRec = RECORD
            TimeComp    : Word;          { DOS time stamp format }
            TimeString  : String80;
            PM          : Boolean;
            Hours,Minutes,Seconds,Hundredths : Integer
          END;
```

READING AND SETTING THE DATE THROUGH DOS

There's a little-understood but critical difference between the way the PC handles the time and the date. Actually, the difference is that the PC *doesn't* handle the date at all in the same sense that it keeps time. Time on the PC is very nearly a hardware function. The hardware timer generates time-of-day interrupts (INT 8), which are serviced by a routine in ROM, which updates the clock reference count at $0040:$006C. The only information relevant to date-keeping is a single flag at $0040:$0070. This is the "midnight" flag, and it is set by the time-of-day interrupt service routine to a value of 1 when the clock reference count rolls over to zero at midnight.

That's it. The date, if it is to be kept at all, must be kept either by the operating system or by the application software. DOS maintains the current date, but it keeps the date value in a peculiar place: inside COMMAND.COM, the DOS command processor program. This location can be found by some DEBUG snooping, but it's different for each version of DOS and like any "undocumented" DOS location could disappear entirely or reappear in a completely incompatible form without any warning. So while you can muck around with the clock reference count and derive your own time values from it by going directly to memory at $0040:$006C, the *only* way to set or read the date is to do it DOS's way, through DOS function calls 42 ($2A) and 43 ($2B).

DOS uses the midnight flag to determine when to increment its date value. If DOS goes out to read the clock reference count through ROM BIOS service $1A and discovers that the midnight flag has been set, it increments its date value within COMMAND.COM. It certainly does this at boot time, but for a PC that is left on continuously, it is unclear when DOS actually goes out and looks at the clock reference count.

There is an excellent reason not to use ROM BIOS service $1A to read the clock reference count in your own programs: *any* reading of the count through this service (by you or by DOS) clears the midnight flag to zero. If your program uses BIOS service $1A before DOS gets around to updating its date value (again, on a PC that stays on all the time), your date will fall one day behind. For this reason, consider BIOS service $1A DOS's private creature—if you must read the clock reference count itself, go directly to memory with **MEMW** at $0040:$006C. (It's far from clear to me why you'd ever need to do this, however.)

When you read the date from DOS through DOS service $2A, it provides the year, month, day, and day-of-the-week, all as integer quantities. The mechanism is a procedure called **GetDate** in the **DOS** unit:

```
PROCEDURE GetDate(VAR Year,Month,Day,DayOfWeek : Word);
```

As with the time, I created a record type to hold DOS's date values, two string representations of the date, and a "date stamp" word (described a little later) that follows the DOS date stamp format used in its directory entries:

```
TYPE
  DateRec =
    RECORD
      DateComp        : Word;
      LongDateString  : String80;
      DateString      : String80;
      Year,Month,Day  : Integer;
      DayOfWeek       : Integer
    END;
```

As with my **TimeRec** record, filling a **DateRec** with information from DOS is a two-step process: First, **GetDate** fills the integer fields of a **DateRec** with the correct values:

```
VAR
  Today : DateRec;

WITH Today DO GetDate(Year,Month,Day,DayOfWeek);
```

A separate routine, **CalcDate**, calculates the date stamp and the two string representations of the date:

```
{->>>>CalcDate<<<<---------------------------------------------}
{                                                              }
{ Filename: CALCDATE.SRC - Last Modified 2/13/93               }
{                                                              }
{ This routine fills in the DateString, LongDateString, and    }
{ DateComp fields of the DateRec record passed to it. It       }
{ requires that the Year, Month, and Day fields be valid on    }
{ entry. It also requires prior definition of types DateRec    }
{ and String80. DateString is formatted this way:              }
{                                                              }
{     Wednesday, July 17, 1986                                 }
{                                                              }
{ DateRec is declared this way:                                }
{                                                              }
{     DateRec = RECORD                                         }
{                 DateComp        : Word;                      }
{                 LongDateString : String80;                   }
{                 DateString     : String80;                   }
{                 Year,Month,Day : Integer;                    }
{                 DayOfWeek      : Integer                     }
{               END;                                           }
{                                                              }
```

```
{ DayOfWeek is a code from 0-6, with 0 = Sunday.                 }
{ DateComp is a cardinal generated by the formula:              }
{                                                                }
{      DateComp = (Year-1980)*512 + (Month*32) + Day            }
{                                                                }
{ It is used for comparing two dates to determine which is      }
{ earlier, and is the same format used in the date stamp in     }
{ DOS directory entries.                                        }
{                                                                }
{ NOTE: This routine calls another routine from this book,      }
{ CalcDayOfWeek.                                                }
{                                                                }
{   From: BORLAND PASCAL FROM SQUARE ONE by Jeff Duntemann      }
{----------------------------------------------------------------}


PROCEDURE CalcDate(VAR ThisDate : DateRec);

TYPE
   String9 = String[9];

CONST
   MonthTags : ARRAY [1..12] of String9 =
       ('January','February','March','April','May','June','July',
        'August','September','October','November','December');
   DayTags   : ARRAY [0..6] OF String9 =
       ('Sunday','Monday','Tuesday','Wednesday',
        'Thursday','Friday','Saturday');

VAR
   Temp1 : String80;

BEGIN
   WITH ThisDate DO
     BEGIN
       DayOfWeek := CalcDayOfWeek(Year,Month,Day);
       Str(Month,DateString);
       Str(Day,Temp1);
       DateString := DateString + '/' + Temp1;
       LongDateString := DayTags[DayOfWeek] + ', ';
       LongDateString := LongDateString +
         MonthTags[Month] + ' ' + Temp1 + ', ';
       Str(Year,Temp1);
       LongDateString := LongDateString + Temp1;
       DateString := DateString + '/' + Copy(Temp1,3,2);
       DateComp := (Year - 1980) * 512 + (Month * 32) + Day
     END
END;
```

The two string representations cover the two most common expressions of a date in human-readable form: A "short" form with slashes: **6/29/93**; and a long form spelling it all out: **Friday, January 2, 1993**. Subsets of the long form can easily be extracted (for example, without the day-of-the-week or simply the month and the day) by using the Turbo Pascal built-in string function **Copy**.

CalcDate calls another routine, **CalcDayOfWeek**, to calculate the 0–6 day of the week figure. I'll go into this in detail a little later in this section.

TIME AND DATE STAMPS

A more intriguing use of time is in the comparison of two time values to see which is the older of the two. Using the four different integer values in a comparison would involve a lot of **IF/THEN** testing, since if the hours are equal, then the minutes have to be tested, and if the minutes are also equal, then the seconds have to be tested, and so on. It would be handy if there were a way to combine the elements of a time value into a single number that could be used in a single compare operation to tell if one value is older than another. A number like this is often called a *time stamp*.

The obvious way is simply to express a time as the number of hundredths of a second in all the hours, minutes, and seconds of a day. In a 24-hour day this works out to 8,640,000. This would fit nicely in a 32-bit long integer—but having a time stamp that fits in 16 bits would be faster to manipulate and more compact.

We can drop the hundredths—they're a little too ersatz for my tastes anyway. This cuts the figure to 86,400—agonizingly close to 65,536 but still too high to express in 16 bits.

Compromises must then be made. By dividing the maximum number of seconds in the time stamp by two—to 30 instead of 60—the number of bits required to express the seconds in a minute drops from six to five. Granting this slight reduction in the time stamp's precision, we can now express the number of hours in a day in 5 bits (0–23); the number of minutes in an hour in 6 bits (0–59); and the number of "seconds" in 5 bits (0–29). 5+6+5 = 16. (See Figure 19.3.)

Losing hundredths and every other second means that if two time stamps are within a second of one another, they will be identical. This might not be the time stamp method of choice in a system making rapid laboratory measurements in real-time, but for expressing the creation time of a file (which usually takes more than one second to create, write, and close anyway) it works out quite well.

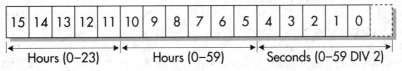

TimeStamp := (Hours SHL 11) OR (Minutes SHL 5) OR (Seconds SHR 1);

Figure 19.3 DOS Time Stamp Format

A 16-bit date stamp can be constructed by shifting the years figure 9 bits to the left (actually by multiplying it by 512, which is the same thing); adding that to the months figure shifted left by 7 bits (i.e. multiplying the months figure by 64), and then adding in the days value unchanged. Because the "19" portion of the year value is not incorporated into the date stamp, there are plenty of bits to go around.

I can't take credit for the 16-bit time stamp and date stamp formats described here. They are used by DOS to stamp its own files. And although I described them separately for clarity's sake, DOS actually stores a file's time and the date stamp side-by-side so that they can be used together to determine which of two files was updated most recently. Turbo Pascal 4.0 and later have a 32-bit long integer type, which can hold DOS's time and date stamps quite handily. Two such combined stamps stored in long integers can be compared with a single relational operator, rather than having to first compare the date stamps and then the time stamps.

Turbo Pascal's support for DOS file time and date stamps consists of four procedures, all in the **DOS** unit: **GetFTime**, **SetFTime**, **PackTime**, and **UnpackTime**.

A file's time and date stamps are read together into a single long integer parameter by using the **GetFTime** procedure in the **DOS** unit:

```
PROCEDURE GetFTime(VAR F; Time : LongInt);
```

The untyped parameter **F** must be an *opened* file of any type: text, typed, or untyped. Its time and date stamps are read into long integer parameter **Time**, with the date stamp occupying the high-order 16 bits.

The long integer stamps retrieved from files can be compared directly:

```
VAR
   FileX, FileZ : Text;
   FileXStamp, FileZStamp : LongInt;

Assign(FileX,'FILEX.TXT');  Reset(FileX);
Assign(FileZ,'FILEZ.TXT');  Reset(FileZ);
GetFTime(FileX,FileXStamp);
GetFTime(FileZ,FileZStamp);
IF FileXStamp > FileZStamp THEN
   Writeln('FileX is older than FileZ.')
ELSE
   Writeln('FileZ is older than FileX.');
```

Of course, you may wish to treat the time and date portions of the stamp separately, and you will almost certainly want to separate out the stamp into integer quantities for year, month, day, hours, minutes, seconds, and so on. Turbo Pascal provides two translation routines for combining the separate time and date values into a long integer stamp, and separating them out again. The **PackTime** procedure creates a long integer stamp from separate time and date values:

```
PROCEDURE PackTime(VAR DTData : DateTime; VAR Stamp : LongInt);
```

The **DateTime** type is a record defined in the interface section of the **DOS** unit:

```
DateTime =
  RECORD
    Year,Month,Day,Hour,Min,Sec : Word
  END;
```

PackTime takes values from a **DateTime** record and combines them into long integer parameter **Stamp**.

Going the other way involves procedure **UnpackTime**:

```
PROCEDURE UnpackTime(Stamp : LongInt; VAR DTData : DateTime);
```

The parameters are the same as those used with **PackTime**. Here, however, the input parameter is the long integer **Stamp** and the output is returned in **DTData**.

Just as the time and date stamps of a file may be returned to your Turbo Pascal program by **GetFTime**, there is a **DOS** unit function to set the stamps to some specified value:

```
PROCEDURE SetFTime(VAR F; Time : LongInt);
```

This procedure is very much the reverse of **GetFTime**, in that the parameters are the same types and have the same meaning. Only the direction the data is moving changes.

A "TOUCH" UTILITY

One good example of several of these time and date routines in use lies in a "touch" utility. On the surface, **Toucher** is very simple: It opens a file specified on the command line, reads the current time and date, and then sets the time and date stamps of the opened file to the current time and date read from the system clock. If, for example, you used **Toucher** on a file that was last modified sometime last May, any further DIR listings of that file would seem to indicate that it had been modified the moment **Toucher** "touched" it.

We define a **DateTime** record (the definition is in the **DOS** unit) named **Now**, and then use the two procedures **GetDate** and **GetTime** to fill in the time and date values for right now, i.e., when **Toucher** executes. The time and date stamp values are then "packed" into a single long integer value using the **PackTime** procedure. Finally, **SetFTime** applies the combined long integer stamp to the file itself. Close the file, and **Toucher** has done its work.

Now—why all this fuss? Of what possible use is a utility that simply tells a lie about the last time a file was modified? Well, a lie is what it is, but a lie with a purpose. As I will be describing later in this book, Turbo Pascal since version 4.0 has contained a Make facility that helps you handle the complexity of a large project with many interdependent source and object files. The Make logic within the compiler chooses to compile or not compile a given file depending on whether any files on which it is dependent were modified *after* the file in question. In other words, if module **A** USES module **B**, and module **B** was modified more recently than module **A**, then the compiler will choose to compile both modules; otherwise, it will only recompile module **A**.

But suppose you would like to compile both? (Perhaps you accidently erased the .TPU file for module **B** . . .) Apart from manually invoking the compiler separately, bypassing the Make logic altogether, you can artificially force module **B**'s source file to look as if it was modified more recently than module **A**, causing Make to invoke the compiler first for module **B** and then for module **A**. The way, of course, is to "touch" module B with **Toucher**.

Or suppose you just restored module **B** from a backup disk, and now you want to recompile both **A** and **B**. **B**'s newly restored file will have an older date than **A**, so if you want both files to recompile, you need to update **B**'s date by using **Toucher** on it.

If it seems peculiar, bear with me for now. Once you begin to use Turbo Pascal's Make facility, **Toucher**'s purpose will become a great deal clearer.

```
{------------------------------------------------------------------}
{                            TOUCHER                               }
{                                                                  }
{          'Touch' utility for DOS unit demonstration              }
{                                                                  }
{                          by Jeff Duntemann                       }
{                          Turbo Pascal V7.0                       }
{                          Last update 2/13/93                     }
{                                                                  }
{    From BORLAND PASCAL FROM SQUARE ONE   by Jeff Duntemann       }
{------------------------------------------------------------------}

PROGRAM Toucher;

USES DOS;

VAR
   I        : Integer;
   Stamp    : LongInt;
   Now      : DateTime;
   Target   : File;
   Sec100   : Word;
   DayOfWeek   : Word;

BEGIN
   IF ParamCount < 1 THEN
     BEGIN
        Writeln('>>TOUCHER  V2.00 by Jeff Duntemann');
        Writeln('          From the book BORLAND PASCAL FROM SQUARE ONE');
        Writeln;
        Writeln('  Calling Syntax:');
```

```
            Writeln('  TOUCHER <filename>');
            Writeln;
            Writeln('  TOUCHER is a "touch" utility that replaces ');
            Writeln('  the time/date stamp of a file with the current');
            Writeln('  date and time. This can be used to force a remake');
            Writeln('  on a project depending on that file.');
        END
    ELSE
        BEGIN
            Assign(Target,ParamStr(1));
            {$I-} Reset(Target); {$I+}
            I := IOResult;
            IF I <> 0 THEN
                BEGIN
                    Writeln('>>Error!  Named file cannot be opened...');
                END
            ELSE
                BEGIN
            WITH Now DO GetTime(Hour,Min,Sec,Sec100);
            WITH Now DO GetDate(Year,Month,Day,DayOfWeek);
            PackTime(Now,Stamp);
            SetFTime(Target,Stamp);
            Close(Target);
            END
        END
    END
END.
```

CALCULATING THE DAY-OF-THE-WEEK

DOS contains a (slightly flawed) algorithm for calculating the day-of-the-week given the date, so that when you read the date through **DOS** unit procedure **GetDate** (which uses DOS function $2A), you get a day-of-the-week indicator along free. Sunday is represented as a 0, and Saturday as a 6. Under the assumption that I would at some point need to fill a **DateRec** that did not come from DOS function $2A, I needed a means to calculate the day-of-the-week from the date.

DOS has a built-in way of doing this, but it has a fundamental flaw: It does not understand dates prior to January 1, 1980. There are other difficulties with it as well, having to do with leap years, but that's minor compared to a "year zero" only 13 years past.

The answer is an algorithm devised by a chap named Zeller in 1887, which I translated to Pascal directly from his paper—which my educated colleague Hugh Kenner was kind enough to translate from the original German. Explaining how it works would take most of a chapter all its own—so for now, simply assume that it does work, and works better than the algorithm built into DOS itself.

In using **CalcDayOfWeek**, make sure you pass the entire year; that is, 1993, rather than 93. The calculation will work on the value 93, but it will give you the day of the week for the year *93*—that is, back in biblical times.

```
{-  >>>>CalcDayOfWeek<<<<-------------------------------------}
{                                                             }
{ Filename: DAYOWEEK.SRC - Last modified 2/14/93              }
{                                                             }
{ This routine uses Zeller's Congruence to derive the day of  }
{ the week given the full date as year, month, and day. The   }
{ day of the week is returned as an integer where 0 = Sunday, }
{ 1 = Monday, etc.                                            }
{                                                             }
{ Day is a value from 1-31. Month is a value from 1-12.       }
{ Year *must* be passed as the full year; i.e., 1993, not 93. }
{ This allows us to determine weekday for dates well ahead and }
{ well back on the calendar.                                  }
{                                                             }
{    From: BORLAND PASCAL FROM SQUARE ONE by Jeff Duntemann   }
{-------------------------------------------------------------}

FUNCTION CalcDayOfWeek(Year,Month,Day : Integer) : Integer;

VAR
   Century,Holder : Integer;

{ This function implements true modulus, rather than    }
{ the remainder function as implemented in Pascal's MOD. }

FUNCTION Modulus(X,Y : Integer) : Integer;

VAR
  R : Real;

BEGIN
  R := X/Y;
  IF R < 0 THEN
    Modulus := X-(Y*Trunc(R-1))
  ELSE
    Modulus := X-(Y*Trunc(R));
END;


BEGIN
  { First test for error conditions on input values: }
```

```
  IF (Year < 0) OR
     (Month < 1) OR (Month > 12) OR
     (Day < 1)  OR (Day > 31) THEN
     CalcDayOfWeek := -1 { Return -1 to indicate an error }
  ELSE
     { Do the Zeller's Congruence calculation as Zeller himself }
     { described it in "Acta Mathematica" #7, Stockholm, 1887. }
     BEGIN
        { First we separate out the year and the century figures: }
        Century := Year DIV 100;
        Year  := Year MOD 100;
        { Next we adjust the month such that March remains month #3, }
        { but that January and February are months #13 and #14,    }
        { *but of the previous year*: }
        IF Month < 3 THEN
          BEGIN
            Inc(Month,12);
            IF Year > 0 THEN Dec(Year,1)   { The year before 2000 is }
              ELSE                 { 1999, not 20-1...   }
                BEGIN
                  Year := 99;
                  Dec(Century);
                END
          END;

     { Here's Zeller's seminal black magic: }
     Holder := Day;           { Start with the day of month }
     Holder := Holder + (((Month+1) * 26) DIV 10); { Calc the increment }
     Holder := Holder + Year;       { Add in the year }
     Holder := Holder + (Year DIV 4);   { Correct for leap years }
     Holder := Holder + (Century DIV 4);  { Correct for century years }
     Holder := Holder - Century - Century; { DON'T KNOW WHY HE DID THIS! }

     Holder := Modulus(Holder,7);      { Take Holder modulus 7 }

     { Here we "wrap" Saturday around to be the last day: }
     IF Holder = 0 THEN Holder := 7;

     { Zeller kept the Sunday = 1 origin; computer weenies prefer to }
     { start everything with 0, so here's a 20th century kludge:    }
     Dec(Holder);

     CalcDayOfWeek := Holder; { Return the end product! }
  END;
END;
```

19.7 Understanding DOS Disk Directories

There are two ways to look at disk files: the logical and the physical. The physical file is a collection of magnetic disturbances arranged on a floppy disk. The logical file is a sequence of sectors stored on a disk, where a sector is a "slice" of a disk file comprising some number of bytes of data. The physical location of any individual sector on the disk itself is of no concern in the logical view of the file. The physical file has no name; it is only a collection of sectors scattered buckshot-style across the face of the disk.

DOS intermediates between the two views of a file. It is possible to go around DOS and take charge of the physical reality of the file's naked sectors, but there's plenty of danger in that and very little profit, unless you intend to play copy protection games, which will earn you no points with anyone these days.

So I won't be going into the physical view of a file here, nor explain the FAT—which is the ultimate arbiter between physical and logical—nor most of the other DOS internals that could fill a book on their own. At the logical level, the most important entities aside from the disk files themselves are disk directories. By and large, this section concerns disk directories, how DOS formats them, and how the information contained there can be used.

ROOT DIRECTORIES AND SUBDIRECTORIES

A directory is like a phone book; there is one entry in a directory on a disk for every file on that disk, and this entry contains information essential for opening and using that file. There are two types of directories available under DOS. Every disk volume (which is a mass storage entity responding to a drive specifier like A:, B:, C:, etc.) has one and only one root directory. The root directory is of a fixed size, although the size of root directories varies depending on the type of disk you're dealing with.

Subdirectories may exist within the root directories, or within other subdirectories. They are tools for organizing groups of disk files into logical structures, revealing those of interest while hiding those that are not needed for the time being. They also serve to keep unused directory space from hogging precious disk space—like dynamic variables in Pascal, subdirectories can be created as needed in unlimited numbers (since they can be nested) and erased when no longer required.

A subdirectory is in fact a special type of file. Until DOS 3.0, in fact, subdirectories could be read and processed by the same function calls used to process ordinary data files. As part of DOS's ongoing evolution toward a protected-mode multitasking operating system, this and other shortcuts have been removed. DOS provides adequate tools for dealing with subdirectories at the Turbo Pascal program level. For disk diagnostic routines and other very low-level utilities, stronger measures (such as tracing through the labyrinth of the FAT) are required.

DIRECTORY ENTRIES VERSUS DTA

Echoing the logical/physical dichotomy of the disk file, there are two faces to a directory entry. One is the entry as it is actually stored on the disk, and the other is the way DOS shows us that entry when we search for it and find it. There are two reasons for this split personality: 1) The "real" directory entry contains information—specifically, the starting FAT cluster—that DOS would prefer to keep to itself. 2) There is information that is useful for repeated directory searches that is created and deleted after the searches are completed, and does not need to be stored away on disk.

The directory entry as stored on disk is not of any serious concern except for the writing of low-level disk utilities like the Norton Utilities. For everyday work with files the second manifestation of the directory entry—the entry as it is shown to us in a place called the Disk Transfer Area—is the one I will be describing and using here.

As you might expect, there are DOS function calls that go out to the directory and search for entries that match a particular filespec. These calls are embodied in a pair of procedures in Turbo Pascal's **DOS** unit (**FindFirst** and **Findnext**) that read and inspect disk directories. These two procedures allow for a program to go out and see what is actually on the disk before attempting to open something, or to make lists of file names for the program to manipulate in some way. I'll be describing them in detail a little later in this chapter.

FindFirst and **FindNext** place information about files in a table called the *Disk Transfer Area*, or DTA. The DTA table is the closest DOS will let us get to a directory entry without goosing it beneath the belt. The DTA's organization is best explained and used by setting it up as a Pascal record:

```
SearchRec =
  RECORD
    Fill : ARRAY[1..21] OF Byte;
    Attr : Byte;
    Time : LongInt;
    Size : LongInt;
    Name : String[12]
  END;
```

This record type is defined in the **DOS** unit, and may be used to declare variables of this type for use in programs incorporating the **FindFirst** and **FindNext** procedures.

The first 21 bytes are reserved, and DOS *means* that—don't think that in this case "reserved" means "unused." DOS uses those 21 bytes to hold information over from one type of DOS call to the next; if you try tucking something away in there, your file searches won't work.

Time should be familiar from the previous section. It is the combined time and date stamp DOS keeps for every file in its directory entry, and may be used in a numeric comparison to determine which of two files was modified more recently.

Size is the size of the file as it exists on disk, in bytes.

Name is the name of the file. This includes the dot *if* there are more than 8 characters in the name. The file name is an "ASCIIZ" string. This means that it is a string of characters without a length byte, plus a "null" character—ASCII character 0—appended to the end to indicate that it does in fact end somewhere.

Attr is the DOS file attribute byte. File attributes are "colors" a file may take on under certain special conditions so that it may be treated in special ways. Six of the eight bits in the attribute byte are significant, and they are outlined in Figure 19.4. Bits are considered "active" if set to 1.

Bit 0, if set to 1, marks a file as "read-only," meaning it cannot be deleted or modified via normal DOS operations. To delete or change the file you must first use a particular DOS call (CHMOD) to zero out the read-only bit, or use a DOS utility called ATTRIB from the command line to lower the read-only flag.

Bit 1 marks a file as "hidden," which means the file exists but cannot be seen or modified by most DOS operations. Some DOS calls will detect hidden files (those function calls used by **FindFirst** and **FindNext**, notably), but in most cases you need to make a CHMOD call to "unhide" them (or use ATTRIB from the command line) before you can do much with them. Out of sight, out of mind, I guess—and that old devil ERASE *.* won't touch hidden files.

Bit 2 marks a file as a "system" file, but has no real significance that I can identify. Peter Norton says it is a holdover from CP/M-80, but that's unclear to me. Ignore it.

Bit 3, if set, marks the file as the current "volume label," an 11-character name that can be given to any disk volume. Volume labels are little used, in part because of a DOS weirdness that prevents you from altering a volume label once one is created. More on this a little later.

Bit 4 marks a file as a subdirectory. Subdirectories are, in fact, files—and in DOS 2.X they could even be read as files using ordinary DOS calls. DOS 3.X will not allow subdirectories to be opened and read like files, but this attribute bit still allows you to identify such files as subdirectories, as we'll see in designing the **Locate** program shortly.

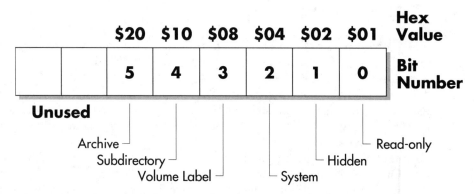

Figure 19.4 The DOS File Attribute Bits

Bit 5 is the archive bit, and is set to one every time a file is changed somehow. The idea is that a backup utility can inspect a directory and only back up files with the archive bit set. Then, once a file is archived, the utility can set its archive bit back to zero, so that it will be ignored by the next archiving operation. Once the file is again modified, its archive bit will be set back to one, making it fair game for the backup utility. Unless you use a backup utility, this bit will be set to one on virtually all files all the time.

INSPECTING AND CHANGING A FILE'S ATTRIBUTE BYTE

The attribute byte says a lot about a file, and it is important enough so that Turbo Pascal's **DOS** unit contains two procedures for reading and setting the attribute byte. Reading the attribute byte from a file's disk directory entry is done with **GetFAttr**:

```
PROCEDURE GetFAttr(VAR F; VAR Attr : Word);
```

Here, **F** is an untyped **VAR** parameter that may take any any type of file variable, once the file variable has been assigned some physical file name and opened. (Untyped **VAR** parameters are a variety of type cast, and I won't be explaining them in detail in this book.) When invoked, **GetFAttr** returns the attribute byte as the low-order byte of **Word** variable **Attr**. It is unclear why **Attr** is a **Word** and not a **Byte**.

Changing the attribute byte of a file is done with **SetFAttr**:

```
PROCEDURE SetFAttr(VAR F; Attr : Word);
```

Again, **F** can take any assigned and opened file variable, and **Attr** contains the desired attribute information in its low 8 bits.

After using either **SetFAttr** or **GetFAttr**, you should check the **DOSError** variable (defined in the **DOS** unit) to make sure that the operation went through successfully. This is especially important since nothing prevents you from passing *anything* in variable **F**: integers, records, sets, characters, whatever. Obviously, only a file variable will do, but it is up to you to make sure a file variable is what is actually passed in **F**.

TELLING DOS ABOUT THE DTA

When a program begins running, DOS sets up a default DTA at offset $80 into the file. This is the same address at which the "command-line tail" is placed, which is why you must pick up and save the command-line parameters *before* you begin searching for or opening and reading any files. While it is certainly possible to use the DTA at offset $80, I feel it is a better idea to declare a **SearchRec** as a variable, and then instruct DOS to use that variable as its DTA.

A DOS call, **$1A**, exists for this purpose. You can use it to set up a **SearchRec** as the current DTA:

```
VAR
  CurrentDTA : SearchRec;
  Regs      : Registers;

. . . . .

WITH Regs DO
  BEGIN
    AH := $1A;
    DS := Seg(CurrentDTA);
    DX := Ofs(CurrentDTA);
  END;
MSDOS(Regs);
```

The idea here is to place the address of the first byte of the new DTA in DS (the segment portion) and DX (the offset portion). As with all DOS calls, the number of the function goes in register AH.

You might get a little nervous about placing a new value in DS, when DS holds the segment address for Turbo Pascal's data segment, but in fact the current value of DS is saved and restored by the code generated for the **MSDOS** procedure by Turbo Pascal.

After this code is executed, any time DOS requires the use of a DTA, it will use the one mapped out at the address passed in DS : DX; in this case, record variable **CurrentDTA**. This particular **SearchRec** was declared as a variable, but you can also pass DOS the addresses of **SearchRec**s passed as parameters or declared as record constants.

A BETTER RECORD FORMAT FOR DIRECTORY INFORMATION

The DTA format embodied in **SearchRec** is what DOS gives us, but it's not necessarily the best that can be done. The combined time and date stamp is very compact, but not very useful except for determining the older of two files. To be used at all it must be processed by the **UnpackTime** procedure in the **DOS** unit, and even then the values are strictly numeric, when what is often needed is a nicely-formatted string equivalent of the date and time.

To make directory information from the DTA more accessible to Turbo Pascal programs, I have defined a different record type providing better Pascal representation of DTA information, and pointers for use in linked lists:

```
DIRRec =
  RECORD
    FileName  : String15;
    Attrib    : Byte;
    FileSize  : LongInt;
    TimeStamp : TimeRec;
    DateStamp : DateRec;
    Prior     : DIRPtr;
    Next      : DIRPtr;
  END;
```

(This record definition is included in the listings diskette for this book under the name **DIRREC.DEF.**) The reserved DOS work area in the DTA has been omitted. The file name field is now a Pascal string with a length byte. The time and date stamps have been replaced with the time and date records described in Section 19.6. A separate time and date stamp are present in these records, but have been expanded to individual values for hours, minutes, and seconds; months, day, and year, and English-reading string representations of time and date.

The two pointer fields allow doubly linked lists of these records to be constructed on the heap. I'll be describing this process in considerable detail in Section 20.3.

Converting between the DTA format and the **DIRRec** format is accomplished by a single routine, **DTAToDIR**. The routine is not especially subtle.

```
{->>>>DTAtoDIR<<<<-----------------------------------------------}
{                                                                }
{ FILENAME DTATODIR.SRC - Last modified 2/14/93                  }
{                                                                }
{ This procedure converts data as returned by DOS FIND          }
{ calls $4E & $4F in the Disk Transfer Area (DTA) to a more      }
{ tractable form as defined by my own record type DIRRec.       }
{ This involves converting the time from a word timestamp to    }
{ a TimeRec, and the date from a word datestamp to a DateRec.   }
{                                                                }
{ DTAToDIR requires the prior definition of types DIRRec,       }
{ DIRPtr, and DTAPtr; and procedures CalcTime and CalcDate.     }
{ Note that CalcDate calls CalcDayOfWeek as well.               }
{                                                                }
{   From: BORLAND PASCAL FROM SQUARE ONE by Jeff Duntemann      }
{----------------------------------------------------------------}


PROCEDURE DTAtoDIR(VAR OutRec : DIRRec);

VAR
    DTData     : DateTime;  { This type imported from DOS unit }
    I          : Integer;
    InRec      : SearchRec; { Also imported from the DOS unit }
    RegPack    : Registers; { Also imported from the DOS unit }
    CurrentDTA : DTAPtr;

BEGIN
    RegPack.AX := $2F00; { Find current location of DTA }
    MSDOS(RegPack);
    WITH RegPack DO CurrentDTA := Ptr(ES,BX);
    InRec := CurrentDTA^;
    UnpackTime(InRec.Time,DTData);
    WITH OutRec DO         { Now extract and reformat data }
      BEGIN
        FileName := InRec.Name; { Extract the file name }
```

```
          Attrib := InRec.Attr; { Extract the attribute field }
          WITH TimeStamp DO     { Expand integer time stamp }
            BEGIN
              TimeComp := InRec.Time SHR 16;
              Hours := DTData.Hour;
              Minutes := DTData.Min;
              Seconds := DTData.Sec;
              Hundredths := 0;
            END;
          CalcTime(TimeStamp);  { Fill in the other time fields }
          WITH DateStamp DO     { Expand integer date stamp }
            BEGIN
              DateComp := InRec.Time AND $0000FFFF;
              Day := DTData.Day;
              Month := DTData.Month;
              Year := DTData.Year;
            END;
          CalcDate(DateStamp);  { Fill in the other date fields }
          FileSize := InRec.Size;
          Next := NIL;            { Initialize the "next" pointer }
          Prior := NIL;           { Ditto the "prior" pointer }
        END
    END; { DTAtoDIR }
```

One point of interest is that you don't explicitly pass **DTAToDIR** a **SearchRec** to act as input. **DTAToDIR** gets its input in a somewhat unusual fashion, by querying DOS (by way of DOS function call **$2F**) to find out where the current DTA is, and assigns the address returned from DOS in ES : BX to a pointer. The DTA information is then accessed through that pointer.

It didn't have to be done that way, but I looked upon it as some guarantee that only the most current DTA would get converted (as encouragement to get information out of it and be done with the DTA format) and also as a demonstration of a DOS function call I might not otherwise be able to demonstrate. If you intend to keep **SearchRec**s around and need to convert them regardless of whether or not they are set as the current DOS DTA, it's trivial to pass a **SearchRec** as a value parameter.

DTAToDIR uses the **CalcDate** and **CalcTime** procedures from Section 19.6 to fill in the time and date stamp records in the **DIRRec** returned to the calling logic.

FROM DIRECTORY TO STRING

Because directory information needs to be displayed to the user in a great many applications, it would be handy to have a further conversion between information as stored in a **DIRRec** record and a string easily displayable via **Write** or **Writeln**. Such a conversion function is provided by the string function **DIRToString**.

```
{->>>>DIRToString<<<<---------------------------------------}
{                                                            }
{ Filename : DIRSTRIN.SRC - Last Modified 2/14/93            }
{                                                            }
{ This routine returns a String value containing all the     }
{ significant information from a directory record, formatted }
{ in a fashion similar to that used by the DOS DIR command   }
{ when it displays a file and its information. A typical      }
{ string returned by DIRToString would look like this:       }
{                                                            }
{    DIRSTRIN.BAK 1697 01/07/87   3:04p                      }
{                                                            }
{ Type DIRRec must be predefined.                            }
{                                                            }
{  From: BORLAND PASCAL FROM SQUARE ONE by Jeff Duntemann    }
{------------------------------------------------------------}

FUNCTION DIRToString(InputDIR : DIRRec) : STRING;

CONST
  Blanker = '                       ';

VAR
  Temp,WorkString : String80;
  DotPos : Integer;

BEGIN
  WITH InputDIR DO
    BEGIN
      Temp := '                    ';
      {If the entry has the directory attribute, format differently: }
      IF (Attrib AND $10) <> 0 THEN  { Bit 4 is the directory attribute }
        BEGIN
          Insert
          (FileName,Temp,1); { No extensions on subdirectory names }
          Insert
          ('<DIR>',Temp,14)   { Tell the world it's a subdirectory }
        END
      ELSE
        {This compound statement separates the file from its extension }
        { and converts the file size to a string. Note that we did not }
        { insert a file size figure into Temp for subdirectory entries. }
        BEGIN
          DotPos := Pos('.',FileName);
          IF DotPos > 0 THEN { File name has an extension }
            WorkString := Copy(FileName,1,DotPos-1) +
              Copy(Blanker,1,9-DotPos) + '.' +
```

```
                    Copy(FileName,DotPos+1,Length(FileName)-DotPos)
            ELSE
                WorkString := FileName + Copy
                (Blanker,1,8-Length(FileName)) + '.';
                Insert(WorkString,Temp,1);
                Str(FileSize:7,WorkString);
                Insert(WorkString,Temp,15)
            END;
        WITH DateStamp DO
          BEGIN
            { This is what it takes to assemble three separate integer}
            { figures for month, day, and year into a string equivalent.}
            IF Month < 10 THEN Insert('0',DateString,1);
            IF Day < 10 THEN Insert('0',DateString,4);
            Insert(DateString,Temp,24);
          END;
        Insert(TimeStamp.TimeString,Temp,34);
        { Finally, insert the time }
      END;
    Delete(Temp,42,Length(Temp)-42);
    DIRToString := Temp
END;
```

There's nothing especially subtle about **DIRToString**; it fills a string with information plucked from the **DIRRec** passed in parameter **InputDIR**. For a typical directory entry of a DOS file, the string returned by **DIRToString** looks like this:

```
DIRSTRIN.BAK    2623 01/13/87   7:53p
```

This string value returned by **DIRToString** is exactly 39 characters long, meaning that two such strings can be displayed side-by-side on an 80-column screen, with two spaces between them in the middle.

DIRToString will play a key role in two utility programs described later in this book: **Locate** and **Spacer**.

SEARCH AND SEARCH AGAIN

On the surface of it, you'd think that the simplest method possible for searching for a given file would simply be to attempt to open it—but that ignores the possibility of using "ambiguous" file names, that is, file names containing "wild card" characters that can match one file or many files. These file names are valid at the keyboard, and they are valid from within a program as well. For example, making use of ambiguous file names would allow your program to identify every file on a disk with an extension of .PAS—by using the ambiguous file name "*.PAS"—and work only with those files.

There are two kinds of wildcard characters: ? and *. The question mark character replaces one character in a file name, and no more; in other words, MODE?ERR.MSG would apply equally to MODE1ERR.MSG, MODE2ERR.MSG,

MODE3ERR.MSG, and so on. The asterisk means "I match anything from here to the end." The "end" here is either the dot character, for the main portion of the file name, or the end of the file name proper, for the file name extension. In other words, MODE*.MSG would match all of the three file names mentioned earlier in this paragraph, and the familiar *.* matches anything at all.

DOS's mechanism for dealing with one file specification matching many files involves two separate DOS function calls: FIND FIRST ($4E) and FIND NEXT ($4F). It works like this: You assemble a "file spec" for the file or files you wish to locate. A file spec is the string containing a full file specifier including the drive unit and path name. For example, while "LOCATE.PAS" is a file name, its full file spec might be something like "D:\TURBO\HACKS\LOCATE.PAS." You pass this file spec to FIND FIRST, and it will locate the first file matching that file spec if one exists, or return an error message if there is no match at all. If at least one is found, you then can call FIND NEXT repeatedly, and FIND NEXT will keep returning matching directory entries in the DTA until no more files match the file spec. Then an appropriate error code is returned in AX.

At first glance, it seems odd that two DOS function calls would be required to do this. A single FIND call could both begin the search and keep searching until it found all directory entries matching the file spec passed to it. DOS's two-call system is actually very efficient, since FIND FIRST does all the setting up of the file spec, and arranges some special information in the DTA to make the search possible. After that setup has been done once, it need not be done again; if the DTA is not disturbed, FIND NEXT need only continue the search, and not bother setting up all the search machinery for each additional search on the same file spec.

THE FINDFIRST AND FINDNEXT PROCEDURES

Turbo Pascal hides much of the messiness of using the FIND FIRST and FIND NEXT DOS function calls by embedding them within two procedures in the **DOS** unit: **FindFirst** and **FindNext**.

Setting up the DTA (in the form of a **SearchRec**) and performing the first search for a matching file is done by **FindFirst**:

```
PROCEDURE FindFirst(Spec : String; Attr : Word; VAR F : SearchRec);
```

The full file spec including the path is passed in **Spec**. **Spec** may be ambiguous; in other words, it may contain wildcard characters. If no directory information is included, the current directory is searched. **Attr** contains the attribute bits that are to apply to the search. There is some trickiness involved here, as I'll explain in connection with searching for volume labels and subdirectories a little later. Finally, **F** is the DTA to be used for the search.

You can tell if a **FindFirst** call has been successful in locating a matching file by checking the **DOSError** variable declared in the **DOS** unit. A 0 returned in **DOSError** indicates that the search was successful, and that the DTA contains the first matching file located. (Remember that that may not be the *only* file to match the file spec, since the file spec may contain wildcard characters.) Any other value indicates some sort of error. Errors to watch for are:

2 ($02) File not found

3 ($03) Path not found

18 ($12) No more files to be found

Error 2 occurs when you pass a subdirectory name as part of **Spec** and DOS can't find that subdirectory. Other errors may occur under special circumstances, but these three are the most common. A successful search will leave **DOSError** set to 0 and present you with a **SearchRec** filled with information about the found file.

LOOKING FOR THE NEXT ONE

Now as we said, finding a file through **FindFirst** is the last word *only* if the file spec passed in **Spec** was unambiguous; in other words, it contains no wild card characters. If you're searching for a group of files (perhaps all of those ending in .PAS), you need to process the information returned by **FindFirst** and continue the search. Continuing is done with **FindNext**:

```
PROCEDURE FindNext(VAR F : SearchRec);
```

Here, **SearchRec** is the *same* **SearchRec** you passed to **FindFirst** during the first part of the search. Keep in mind that you cannot call **FindNext** without first having called **FindFirst**. Furthermore, the call to **FindFirst** must have been successful; you must have received a 0 in **DOSError**.

I must emphasize that you cannot change search specs in the middle of the search by tinkering with **SearchRec** parameter **F**. For example, you can't decide to change the file attribute during repeated calls to **FindNext** by changing the **Attr** field in **F**. Once you begin a search with **FindFirst**, the only way to change the search conditions is to execute **FindFirst** again with the new spec and attribute byte. At that point, of course, it becomes a whole new search.

FindNext can be called repeatedly after the initial call to **FindFirst**, and the process can continue until error 2 or error 18 comes back in **DOSError**. At this point it's fruitless to go on, since DOS has failed to find any further matching files.

19.8 Creating and Reading Volume Labels

Reading volume labels provides an interesting first exercise in the use of **FindFirst**. Before we get into that, some discussion of volume labels and their role in PC DOS must come first.

Volume labels are a tip of the DOS hat to mainframe operating systems, which have long provided for the application of a unique machine-readable label to a storage volume, be it removable disk pack, fixed disk pack, or magnetic tape. Anyone can stick an adhesive label on a diskette, of course, but volume labels allow both the human user and the application program to "read" the label on the diskette. That way, if the program directs the user to "Insert the

ACCOUNTS diskette in drive A:" the program can immediately determine if the right diskette made it into the drive without having to poll the names of the files on the disk to make sure.

PC DOS first supported volume labels with V2.0, but the support in DOS 2.X is limited and crude. My recommendation is that you do *not* try to build volume label support into your applications unless they can be guaranteed to run only under DOS 3.X or higher.

For that reason, this particular section makes the same assumption, that the **CreateLabel** and **GetLabel** routines will only be run under DOS 3.X. I have not tested them under DOS 2.X and cannot guarantee that they will work under all circumstances for DOS 2.X.

THE NATURE OF A VOLUME LABEL

A volume label is physically nothing more than an empty file (that is, a file with zero bytes in it) with the volume label attribute bit set to 1. (See Figure 19.4.) All directory entry fields aside from creation time and date, file name, and attribute byte are zeroed out. DOS will only set attribute bit 3 (the Volume Label bit) on a file created in the root directory. By going beneath the level of DOS it is possible to set the Volume Label bit on a file in a subdirectory, of course, but how DOS would deal with such a file I couldn't say.

It's also possible to set the Volume Label bit on multiple files in the root directory, but only the one having the first directory entry physically will be treated as the real DOS volume label.

Reading and creating volume labels is easy. Changing or deleting them is *not*. Once a directory entry has had its Volume Label bit raised to one, none of the familiar DOS function calls will touch it, and only FIND FIRST will be able to detect its presence, and then only if it's the *first* directory entry with the bit set. Whether this is a bug due to Microsoft's forgetfulness or a feature supporting media security is unclear; that depends on how much you love Microsoft or how paranoid you are. I lean toward the former view; it seems silly to restrict the modification of volume labels so severely when *creating* them is so simple.

So once again, care must be counseled. Before you create a volume label for a disk volume, make triple sure the label you're creating is the label you want. The only safe recourse to an undesired label is to reformat the disk and recreate the label in the process.

There have been, of course, published methods of deleting and changing volume labels by locating the directory sectors on the disk and physically altering the sectors to change the directory entry tagged as the volume label. This operates beneath the level at which DOS wants you to work, and there's more than just "sticking to the rules" at stake here. The number of disk storage devices has grown explosively in the last few years, and some of them (the Bernoulli Box comes to mind) are significantly different from either floppy disks or traditional hard disks. I have not yet seen any truly reliable way of determining where the directory physically begins on the disk for any arbitrary disk type, and when you're talking about writing to sectors involving the disk directory or

FAT, *you do not want to get it wrong.* If your application tries to alter the volume label on a customer's 1.2GB odd-format hard disk drive and scrambles it in the process, you will at the very least lose the customer and possibly hear from his lawyers as well, since the likelihood of a disk device being fully backed up at all times varies inversely with its capacity.

For this reason, the two volume label routines presented here either read or create a volume label, but do not alter or delete volume labels that already exist. My hunch is that future releases of DOS will correct this oversight, since history has shown that volume label support has grown better as DOS has evolved. Furthermore, when you move to operating systems like OS/2 that support multitasking and multiple users, the OS must by need get very, very hardnosed about keeping applications from snooping critical system resources (like the FAT and disk directories) from under the table. The ability is not there now— but I don't think you'll have to wait very long for it.

READING A VOLUME LABEL

Since a DOS volume label is the first file in the root directory of a volume with bit 3 of the attribute byte set, the FIND FIRST DOS function call (as embodied in procedure **FindFirst**) is an intuitive means of reading a volume label. It is, in fact, the *only* means short of directly reading the directory sectors on the disk. The function **GetLabel** uses **FindFirst** to return the DOS volume label in the **SearchRec** record **F**.

```
{->>>>GetLabel<<<<-------------------------------------------------}
{                                                                  }
{ Filename : GETLABEL.SRC - Last Modified 2/15/93                  }
{                                                                  }
{ This function returns a string value that is the volume          }
{ label of the drive passed in DriveSpec. No check is made         }
{ as to the validity of the character in DriveSpec; if there       }
{ is no corresponding drive the system may hang or return an       }
{ error depending on the specifics. If no volume label exists      }
{ for the specified volume, a null string (zero length) will       }
{ be returned and parameter LabelFound will be set to FALSE.       }
{                                                                  }
{   From: BORLAND PASCAL FROM SQUARE ONE by Jeff Duntemann         }
{-----------------------------------------------------------------}


FUNCTION GetLabel(DriveSpec : String; { Include the colon! }
                  VAR LabelFound : Boolean) : String;

TYPE
  String80 = String[80];
```

```
VAR
  I          : Integer;
  SearchSpec : String80;
  Temp       : String80;
  Regs       : Registers;
  ASCIIZ     : ARRAY[1..81] OF Char;
  DTA        : SearchRec;

BEGIN
  SearchSpec := DriveSpec + '\*.*' + Chr(0);
  FindFirst(SearchSpec,$08,DTA);

  Temp := ''; { So we can return null string if no label found }
  IF (DOSError = 2) OR (DOSError = 18) THEN   { Label not found }
    LabelFound := False
  ELSE
    BEGIN
      LabelFound := True;
      Temp := DTA.Name;
      { If a dot exists in the DTA file name, get rid of it: }
      IF Pos('.',Temp) > 0 THEN Delete(Temp,Pos('.',Temp),1);
    END;
  GetLabel := Temp;       { Assign function return value }
END;
```

FindFirst requires a search spec, which is the full pathname of the file to be searched for, including the drive specifier. In this case, the file name we want to locate is the familiar "*.*" meaning any file name at all—since we don't know what the volume label is, we need to use a completely ambiguous file name. In other applications, we might want to find a file with a particular name, perhaps to see if it exists on the specified volume. In that case, the file name would be part of the search spec, rather than "*.*".

The search spec is constructed in a string variable by concatenating the drive specifier and the pathname "*.*", meaning any file name *in the root directory.* (Remember that the drive specifier here *must* include the colon after the letter indicating which drive you wish to read.) In other applications, the search spec could include a path down through several levels of subdirectories to a specific file or "*.*" within a specific subdirectory. Here, we stick with the root, because a volume label can only exist in the root directory.

The $08 value passed to **FindFirst** is a byte with only the volume label attribute bit (bit 3) set. This is how we direct **FindFirst** to locate a volume label directory entry and nothing else.

This exclusive treatment of the volume label attribute bit is a special case. The other attribute bits are treated very differently by FIND FIRST, as I will explain a little later when we start using **FindFirst** to look for ordinary files.

When DOS returns after **FindFirst** is invoked, two situations are possible: Either an error message comes back in **DosError**, or the DTA has been filled with a directory entry containing the DOS volume label on the specified volume.

DOS documentation states that the error message will be either 2 (File not found) or 18 (No more files to be found), but in practice I have never seen anything but error 18 returned under DOS 5.0. **GetLabel** itself does not return an error code to the calling logic; if the volume label was not found, **VAR** parameter **LabelFound** will return a value of **FALSE**.

One peculiarity about volume labels is that, although they are actually file names, DOS displays them without splitting them into the traditional file name/ file extension duo, divided by a period character. So when you retrieve a volume label from a DTA, you need to remove the period character *if* the volume label is longer than eight characters. In other words, the volume label "CALIBAN" will be found in the DTA as "CALIBAN" but the longer volume label WIDDERSHINS will be found as "WIDDERSH.INS." One string **Delete** statement does the job.

CREATING A VOLUME LABEL

If a disk volume does not already have a label, you can create one with a single DOS function call. DOS function call $3C (CREATE) is used to create a file anywhere on a disk, given its full file spec including path. Function $3C does not actually write any information into the file. It simply creates a directory entry and fills out the time and date stamps, name, and attribute byte. The resulting file has zero length, and occupies no space on the disk other than the space taken by the directory entry. Furthermore, if the attribute byte passed to function $3C contains bit 3 set to one, the created file will become the volume's volume label. (That is, of course, assuming that the volume in question doesn't already have a label.)

```
{->>>>CreateLabel<<<<--------------------------------------------}
{                                                                }
{ Filename : CREATLBL.SRC - Last Modified 2/15/93                }
{                                                                }
{ This procedure creates a new volume label on the unlabeled     }
{ DOS volume passed in DriveSpec. No check is made               }
{ as to the validity of the character in DriveSpec; if there     }
{ is no corresponding drive the system may hang or return an     }
{ error depending on the specifics. If a volume label already    }
{ exists on the specified volume, CreatedLabel will return       }
{ FALSE with an ErrorReturn value of 0. This is not really an    }
{ error condition, but DOS makes no provision for altering a     }
{ volume label that already exists, so at best we go home with   }
{ our tail between our legs. If some sort of true error          }
{ occurs, the DOS error code will be returned in ErrorReturn,    }
{ and CreatedLabel will be set to FALSE. If CreatedLabel         }
{ comes back TRUE, the label was in fact created.                }
{                                                                }
{ Function GetLabel(presented in this book) must be predefined.}
```

```
{                                                              }
{    From: BORLAND PASCAL FROM SQUARE ONE by Jeff Duntemann    }
{--------------------------------------------------------------}

PROCEDURE CreateLabel(DriveSpec        : String; { Include colon! }
                      NewLabel         : String;
                      VAR CreatedLabel : Boolean;
                      VAR ErrorReturn  : Word;
                      ShowError        : Boolean);

TYPE
   ErrorCode = 0..18;  { DOS function call error codes }
   String80 = String[80];

VAR
   I            : Integer;
   SearchSpec   : String80;
   FileSpec     : String80;
   CurrentLabel : String80;
   Regs         : Registers;
   ASCIIZ       : ARRAY[1..81] OF Char;
   DTA          : SearchRec;
   Error        : ErrorCode;
   FoundLabel   : Boolean;

BEGIN
   CurrentLabel := GetLabel(DriveSpec,FoundLabel);
     IF NOT FoundLabel THEN { No label exists yet }
       BEGIN
         FileSpec := DriveSpec + '\' + NewLabel + Chr(0);
           Move(FileSpec[1],ASCIIZ,Sizeof(FileSpec));

         WITH Regs DO
           BEGIN
             AH := $3C;     { $3C = Create File }
             DS := Seg(ASCIIZ); { Put address of ASCIIZ }
             DX := Ofs(ASCIIZ); { in DS : DX }
             CL := $08;     { Set Volume Label attribute }
           END;
         MSDOS(Regs);            { Make CHMOD DOS call }

         { If the Carry Flag is found to be set, it's an error: }
         IF (Regs.Flags AND $0001) = 1 THEN
           BEGIN
             CreatedLabel := False; { No luck }
             ErrorReturn := Regs.AX; { Return error code as parameter }
             Error := ErrorReturn; { Make an ordinal of the error code }
```

```
                IF ShowError THEN
                  CASE Error OF
                    2 : Writeln('Label file not found.');
                    3 : Writeln('Bad path error - possible disk failure.');
                    5 : Writeln
                    ('Access to label denied - Disk write protected?');
                    ELSE Writeln
                    ('Unexpected DOS error ',Error,' on label write.')
                  END; { CASE }
            END
          ELSE CreatedLabel := True   { No error - created the label }
        END
    ELSE  { Label already exists; can't re-create it... }
      BEGIN
        CreatedLabel := False;
        ErrorReturn := 0;
      END
  END;
```

DOS function call $3C is used to create a volume label in the procedure **CreateLabel**. To determine if a label already exists on the requested volume, **CreateLabel** calls **GetLabel**. If a label already exists, the Boolean variable **CreatedLabel** is returned to the calling logic set to **FALSE**. If no label is found, **CreateLabel** sets up function call $3C with $08 in CL—again, $08 is the numeric value of the attribute byte with bit 3, the volume label bit, set to 1.

CreateLabel gives you the option of returning an error code without any visible display of an error message, or actually displaying an error message on the console for the user.

Ordinarily, you wouldn't need to use DOS function $3C to create a file, since you can create a zero-length file simply by using **Assign** to assign a file variable to a pathname, and **Rewrite** to write the directory entry to the disk. **Assign** and **Rewrite** do not, however, give you access to the attribute byte, which is why function $3C must be used to create a volume label.

19.9 Searching for Groups of Files

FindFirst will locate the first file matching a given file spec. DOS has a streamlined method to take it from there: Once **FindFirst** has set up the necessary criteria, the FIND NEXT function call (as embodied in the **FindNext** procedure in the **DOS** unit) will repeatedly search the specified path until no more files are found that match the file spec specified to **FindFirst**.

After calling the **FindNext** procedure, when control returns to your Turbo Pascal program, either a found directory entry will be in **FindNext**'s **SearchRec** parameter (which is simply a DTA mapped upon a Pascal record) or an error code will be in **DOSError** indicating that no more files are to be found on that path.

The example program I've written to illustrate the use of **FindFirst** and **FindNext** is a truly useful one, now that 120 MB hard disks are common and 600 MB hard disks are not out of reach of many of us. If it hasn't already, a situation like this will soon arise: Somewhere on your hard disk you suspect there is a public domain utility program called FASTVID.COM—or was it FASTV.COM? Or FASTVID.EXE? Or were you imagining it all along? With 5,000 files scattered across 75 nested subdirectories, it could take quite a bit of searching to locate the mystery utility.

Or you could let the computer do what it does best and find it for you. This is the purpose of the program **Locate** that I will be describing shortly. **Locate** searches any directory and all its child subdirectories for files that match a given file specification, including wildcards. (If no directory is given, **Locate** will search the entire disk.)

Locate is a more difficult program than most to understand because it operates recursively. Some people just have a hard time dealing with recursion, and if you're one of those, **Locate** will have that uncomfortable feeling of black magic about it.

RECURSIVE TREE SEARCH

You may have heard the term "tree-structured directories" in reference to DOS V2.X subdirectory structures, particularly when there are several layers of nested subdirectories involved. The "tree" metaphor stems from the fact that one "root" directory can have any number of "branch" directories, each of which can itself have more "branch" directories, and so on. The directory structure "spreads out" from one single root directory into a structure reminiscent of a tree.

Figure 19.5 is a slightly-simplified diagram of a system of nested subdirectories. The top directory is the root, with each vertical partition representing one directory entry. Directory entries are either files or subdirectories. Each subdirectory entry in a directory points to its own subdirectory proper, and subdirectories may be nested in this fashion as deeply as desired.

The single-dot and double-dot symbols should be familiar from DIR listings of subdirectories. The single dot represents the current directory, and the double dot the parent directory. Why directory entries are required for the current and parent directories is complex and has to do with the way DOS keeps track of disk storage. In a sense, a tree-structured directory is a doubly-linked list of directories, but if that makes no sense to you, forget it; it is not germane to the current discussion. Note that the root directory has entries for neither parent directory (obviously) nor for itself; this is one way in which the root directory is special and distinct from subdirectories.

Searching a tree structure like this recursively can best be explained by following the search path on a diagram. Refer to Figure 19.6. For the sake of discussion, imagine a Pascal procedure named **SearchDirectory**. You pass it a directory specifier and a file name, and it searches that directory and any of its child directories for anything matching that file name, printing out the name and full path of any file it finds.

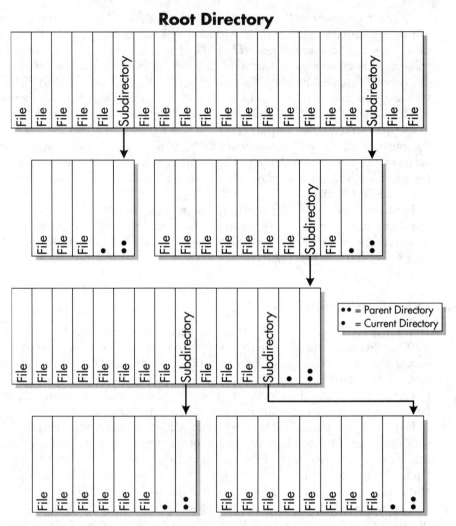

Figure 19.5 Tree-structured Directories

The search begins at the root directory. **SearchDirectory** is called, given the root directory specifier (the solo backslash "\") as the directory to search. Directory entries are examined one by one, to see if the file names match the search spec. This prosaic process continues until **SearchDirectory** encounters a subdirectory entry; let's call it subdirectory **TURBO**. **TURBO** needs to be searched too. This is where recursion happens.

SearchDirectory calls itself. What happens here is that the current "state" of **SearchDirectory** is pushed on the stack, and an entirely new copy of **SearchDirectory**'s local variables and parameters is created. This is called an *instantiation* of **SearchDirectory**. The new "copy" of **SearchDirectory** is passed the root directory specifier "\" *plus* the name of the new subdirectory, **TURBO**. It then begins searching directory **TURBO** for file matches.

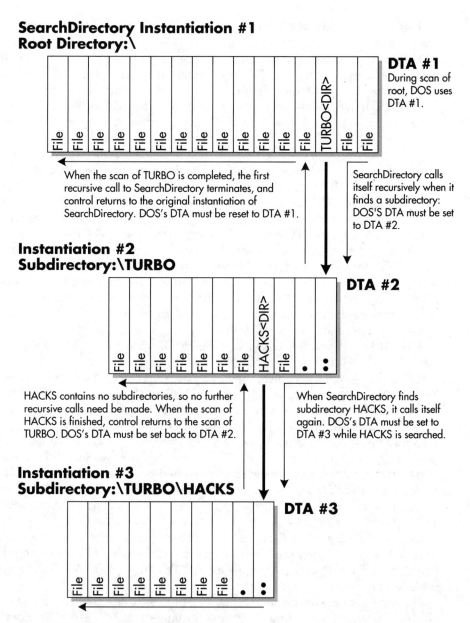

Figure 19.6 Recursive Directory Search

As it did with the root directory, **SearchDirectory** examines the directory entries in **\TURBO** one by one for matches. It displays any it finds. Along the way it discovers another subdirectory, a child directory to **\TURBO** called **HACKS**. **HACKS** needs to be searched, just as any other directory does. So **SearchDirectory** calls itself once again.

This time, the parent directory specifier **\TURBO** is prefixed to **HACKS** (with a backslash separator) making the new directory specifier **\TURBO\HACKS**. A third instantiation of **SearchDirectory** is created after the second has been safely pushed onto the stack. Yet again, directory entries are examined one by one for file matches, keeping an eye out for more subdirectories.

HACKS, however, has no subdirectories. When the scan of **HACKS** is completed, the third instantiation of **SearchDirectory** terminates. As with any Pascal subprogram that finishes execution, it returns control to the calling logic. In this case, the calling logic was the second instantiation of **SearchDirectory**. The second instantiation is popped from the stack and begins running again, checking directory entries in **\TURBO** for file matches as though nothing had interrupted it.

Subdirectory **\TURBO**, as it happens, has no more subdirectories. If it had, they would have been searched in exactly the same way **HACKS** was searched, via another recursive call to **SearchDirectory**. So the rest of **\TURBO** is searched for matching files. Eventually the search is completed. The second instantiation of **SearchDirectory** terminates, and returns control to the first instantiation, the one searching the root directory. The first instantiation of **SearchDirectory** is popped off the stack, and the search of the root directory continues. Once the scan of the root is completed, the original instantiation of **SearchDirectory** terminates, having searched the entire disk for files matching the given file spec.

From 10 steps back, this is all that happens. Beneath the surface, however, is an additional detail that has to be tended to: the current DTA.

The actual search mechanism used by **SearchDirectory** is DOS's FIND FIRST & FIND NEXT function calls (through the **DOS** unit's **FindFirst** and **FindNext** procedures), which require the use of the DOS DTA through a Pascal record called a **SearchRec**. FIND NEXT only works over a single directory, and each directory being searched needs its own exclusive use of a DTA. From a Pascal perspective this is no problem—Pascal creates a new **SearchRec** called **CurrentDTA** on the stack for each new instantiation of **SearchDirectory**. However—*DOS doesn't "know" that it must switch to the new instantiation's SearchRec.* DOS, in a sense, isn't in on the recursion process, which is handled entirely by the Turbo Pascal runtime code.

So—each time a call to **FindFirst** or **FindNext** is made, DOS must be "told" which DTA to use. You don't have to worry about that part of the problem, since **FindFirst** and **FindNext** each contain a call to DOS function $1A, which sets the address of the current DTA.

It's enough to make your head spin. The process is best followed along on a diagram; again, trace through the three instantiations of **SearchDirectory** in Figure 19.6. Each directory needs its own DTA for the search process, and the three DTA's are numbered from one to three. DTA #1 is used during the search of the root directory. When the first recursive call to **SearchDirectory** is made, an explicit call to DOS function $1A is made within **FindFirst**, changing the current DTA (that is, the one DOS will use) to DTA #2. DTA #2 remains the current DTA as long as the second instantiation of **SearchDirectory** has control. But when the third instantiation is created to search the third directory

\TURBO\HACKS, the current DTA must be changed yet again, to DTA #3. DTA #3 remains the current DTA as long as subdirectory \TURBO\HACKS is being searched.

\TURBO\HACKS is the bottom of the tree; from that point we start going home, and the whole process of changing DTA's as we wove our way downward through the directory tree must be undone as we move back upward again. The first change happens as we leave the third instantiation behind. DTA #3 was in force during the search of \TURBO\HACKS; now we are returning to the search of \TURBO, and we need to go back to DTA #2. (DTA #2 was waiting on the stack, safe and sound, still containing setup information from the **FindFirst** call that began the search of \TURBO.) When the search of \TURBO is finished, DTA #2's job is done. Control returns to the first instantiation of **SearchDirectory** to finish out the search of the root directory, and the current DTA must be changed again from DTA #2 to DTA #1, again on the stack, waiting to go back to work and finish the **FindNext** sequence that inspects directory entries one by one.

Each time we need to change *back* from the DTA used during a recursive call to **SearchDirectory**, a call must be made to DOS function $1A. Again, this is done safely within **FindNext**; but if you were working with raw DOS calls through Turbo Pascal's **MSDOS** procedure, you would have to call function $1A yourself, as did the earlier version of **Locate** originally published in my 1987 book *Turbo Pascal Solutions.*

PROGRAM LOCATE

With all of that convolution safely beneath your belt, take a long, close look at the actual code for program **Locate**. The entirety of **Locate** the program is only a frame for procedure **SearchDirectory**, which does the only real work in **Locate**. The search process was built into a procedure so that it could call itself; programs in Pascal cannot call themselves recursively.

```
{ ------------------------------------------------------------------ }
{                            LOCATE                                  }
{                                                                    }
{             Disk file tree-search search utility                  }
{                                                                    }
{                       by Jeff Duntemann                           }
{                       Turbo Pascal V7.0                           }
{                       Last update 2/10/93                         }
{                                                                    }
{ This utility searches a tree of directories (from the root        }
{ or from any child directory of the root) for a given file         }
{ spec, either unique or ambiguous. It provides a good              }
{ example of the use of the DOS 2.X/3.X FIND FIRST/NEXT             }
{ function calls. See the main program block for instructions       }
{ on its use.                                                       }
```

```
{                                                                    }
{    From: BORLAND PASCAL FROM SQUARE ONE   by Jeff Duntemann     }
{----------------------------------------------------------------}

PROGRAM Locate;

USES DOS;

TYPE
   String80 = String[80];
   String15 = String[15];

{ These include files are type definitions of structures used }
{ in this program, presented in Chapter 19 of the book: }

{$I TIMEREC.DEF}    { Described in Section 19.6 }
{$I DATEREC.DEF}    { Described in Section 19.6 }
{$I DIRREC.DEF}     { Described in Section 19.7 }


   DTAPtr  = ^SearchRec;


VAR
   I,J              : Integer;
   SearchSpec       : String80;
   InitialDirectory : String80;
   Searchbuffer     : SearchRec;

{ The include files are all subprograms presented elsewhere    }
{ in Chapter 19 of the book: }

{$I  DAYOWEEK.SRC}
{$I  CALCDATE.SRC}
{$I  CALCTIME.SRC}
{$I  DIRSTRIN.SRC}
{$I  DTATODIR.SRC}


{->>>>SearchDirectory<<<<--------------------------------------}
{                                                             }
{ This is the real meat of program LOCATE. The machinery       }
{ for using FIND FIRST and FIND NEXT are placed in a procedure }
{ so that it may be recursively called. Recursion is used      }
{ because it is the most elegant way to search a tree, which   }
{ is really all we're doing here. All the messiness (and it    }
{ IS messy!) exists to cater to DOS's peculiarities.           }
{                                                             }
```

```
{ For example, note that each recursive instantiation of      }
{ SearchDirectory needs its own DTA. No problem-one is         }
{ created on the stack each time SearchDirectory is called.    }
{ BUT-DOS is not a party to the recursion, so the DTA address  }
{ must be set both before AND after the recursive call, so     }
{ that once control comes BACK to an instance of               }
{ SearchDirectory that has been left via recursion, DOS can    }
{ "come back" to the temporarily dormant DTA, which may still  }
{ contain information necessary to execute a FIND NEXT call.   }
{                                                              }
{ Much of the rest of the fooling around involves formatting   }
{ the search strings correctly for passing to the next         }
{ instantiation of SearchDirectory.                            }
{                                                              }
{ It's not documented, but I have found that DOS returns error }
{ code 3 (Bad Path) on a file FIND when the path includes a    }
{ nonexistent directory name. Error code 2, on the other       }
{ hand, while documented, never seems to come up at all.       }
{--------------------------------------------------------------}


PROCEDURE SearchDirectory(Directory,SearchSpec : String);

VAR
  NextDirectory : String;
  TempDirectory : String;
  CurrentDTA    : SearchRec;
  CurrentDIR    : DIRRec;
  Regs          : Registers;



{>>>>DisplayData<<<<}
{ Displays file data and full path for the passed file }

PROCEDURE DisplayData(Directory : String; CurrentDIR : DIRRec);

VAR
  Temp : String;

BEGIN
  Temp := DIRToString(CurrentDIR);
  Delete(Temp,1,13);
  Write(Temp,Directory);
  IF Directory <> '\' THEN Write('\');
  Writeln(CurrentDIR.FileName);
END;
```

```
BEGIN
  { First we look for any subdirectories. If any are found, }
  { we make a recursive call and search 'em too: }

  { Suppress unnecessary backslashes if we're searching the root: }
  IF Directory = '\' THEN
    TempDirectory := Directory + '*.*'
  ELSE
    TempDirectory := Directory + '\*.*';

  { Now make the FIND FIRST call for directories: }

  FindFirst(TempDirectory,$10,CurrentDTA);


  { Here's the tricky stuff. If we get an indication that there is  }
  { at least one more subdirectory within the current directory,    }
  { (indicated by lack of error codes 2 or 18) we must search it    }
  { by making a recursive call to SearchDirectory. We continue      }
  { recursing and returning from the searched subdirectories until  }
  { we get a code indicating none are left. }
  WHILE (DOSError <> 2) AND (DOSError <> 18) DO
    BEGIN
      IF  ((CurrentDTA.Attr AND $10) = $10)    { If it's a directory }
      AND (CurrentDTA.Name[1] <> '.') THEN   { and not '.' or '..' }
        BEGIN
          { Add a slash separating sections of the path if we're not }
          { currently searching the root: }
          IF Directory <> '\' THEN NextDirectory := Directory + '\'
            ELSE NextDirectory := Directory;

          { This begins with the current directory name, and copies }
          { the name of the found directory from the current DTA to }
          { the end of the current directory string. Then the new   }
          { path is passed to the next recursive instantiation of   }
          { SearchDirectory. }
          NextDirectory := NextDirectory + CurrentDTA.Name;

          { Here's where we call "ourselves." }
          SearchDirectory(NextDirectory,SearchSpec);

        END;
      FindNext(CurrentDTA);  { Now we look for more... }
    END;

  { Now we can search for files, once we've run out of directories.  }
  { This is conceptually simpler, as recursion is not involved.      }
```

```
{ We combine the path and the file spec into one string, and make  }
{ the FIND FIRST call: }

{ Suppress unnecessary slashes for root search: }
IF Directory <> '\' THEN
   TempDirectory := Directory + '\' + SearchSpec
ELSE TempDirectory := Directory + SearchSpec;

{ Now, make the FIND FIRST call: }
 FindFirst(TempDirectory,AnyFile,CurrentDTA);

IF DOSError = 3 THEN        { Bad path error }
   Writeln('Path not found; check spelling.')

{ If we found something in the current directory matching the filespec.}
{ format it nicely into a single string and display it: }
ELSE IF (DOSError = 2) OR (DOSError = 18) THEN
   { Null; Directory is empty }
ELSE
   BEGIN
      DTAtoDIR(CurrentDIR);      { Convert first find to DIR format.. }
      DisplayData(Directory,CurrentDIR);      { Show it pretty-like }

      IF DOSError <> 18 THEN { More files are out there... }
        REPEAT
          FindNext(CurrentDTA);
          IF DOSError <> 18 THEN  { More entries exist }
            BEGIN
               DTAtoDIR(CurrentDIR);
               { Convert further finds to DIR format }
               DisplayData(Directory,CurrentDIR)    { and display 'em }
            END
        UNTIL (DOSError = 18) OR (DOSError = 2)  { Ain't no more! }
   END
END;


BEGIN
   IF ParamCount = 0 THEN
     BEGIN
        Writeln('>>LOCATE<<  V3.00  By Jeff Duntemann');
        Writeln
        ('          From the book, BORLAND PASCAL FROM SQUARE ONE');
        Writeln('          Bantam Books, 1993');
        Writeln;
        Writeln('This program searches for all files matching a given ');
```

```
            Writeln
            ('filespec on the current disk device, in any subdirectory.');
            Writeln('Now that 32MB disks are getting cheap, we can pile up');
            Writeln
            ('great heaps of files and easily forget where we put things.');
            Writeln
            ('Given only the filespec, LOCATE prints out the FULL PATH');
            Writeln('of any file matching that filespec.');
            Writeln;
            Writeln('CALLING SYNTAX:');
            Writeln;
            Writeln('LOCATE <filespec>');
            Writeln;
            Writeln
            ('For example, to find out where your screen capture files');
            Writeln('(ending in .CAP) are, you would enter:');
            Writeln;
            Writeln('LOCATE *.CAP');
            Writeln;
            Writeln
            ('and LOCATE will show the pathname of any file ending in .CAP.');
          END
        ELSE
          BEGIN
            Writeln;
            SearchSpec := ParamStr(1);
            { A "naked" filespec searches the entire volume: }
            IF Pos('\',SearchSpec) = 0 THEN
                SearchDirectory('\',SearchSpec)
            ELSE
              BEGIN
                { This rigamarole separates the filespec from the path: }
                I := Length(SearchSpec);
                WHILE SearchSpec[I] <> '\' DO I := Pred(I);
                InitialDirectory := Copy(SearchSpec,1,I-1);
                Delete(SearchSpec,1,I);
                SearchDirectory(InitialDirectory,SearchSpec);
              END;
          END
      END
  END.
```

The operation of **Locate** differs in small ways from the recursive search process described in connection with Figure 19.6. A single **FindFirst/FindNext** operation cannot, in fact, inspect directories for both subdirectory and file entries. To find all subdirectories we have to use a search spec of *.*, due to the way DOS handles attribute bits during file searches (more on this below); to find a specific file or group of files, we need a search spec naming that file or group. Obviously, this means we must search first for directories and then, once all of a directory's child directories have been searched, inspect the files.

So **SearchDirectory** searches for subdirectories first. To make the **FindFirst** call in its search for directories, **SearchDirectory** must assemble a search spec. For directories, this is nothing more than the current path passed to **SearchDirectory** in parameter **Directory** plus the totally ambiguous file specifier "*.*". Note the $10 value passed as the attribute parameter to **FindFirst**. This is an attribute byte with the subdirectory flag set to 1. The idea is that we are searching for any directory entry that has this bit set to 1.

We did something like this in searching for volume labels, by using **FindFirst** with the attribute byte set to $08, which is the value of the byte with the volume label flag set to 1. Unfortunately, DOS is inconsistent here. Executing **FindFirst** with the attribute byte set to $08 (i.e., with the volume label bit set) finds *only* the first directory entry with this bit set. Executing **FindFirst** with bit 4 (the subdirectory bit) set to 1 will find a subdirectory entry, but it will also find any ordinary file as well. A search for directory entries with the volume label bit set is *exclusive* in that it finds *only* volume label entries. A search for subdirectory entries is *inclusive* because it finds ordinary file entries *and* subdirectory entries.

This means we have to test any directory entry returned from a FIND FIRST or FIND NEXT in our search for subdirectories to make sure the returned entry is not just an ordinary file. This is done by masking out the subdirectory bit in the attribute byte and testing it:

```
IF (CurrentDTA.Attr AND $10) = $10
```

The Boolean expression here will return true only if the directory entry in **CurrentDTA** is a subdirectory entry.

Yet (as life is wont) there is another catch. All subdirectories (but *not* the root directory) contain two additional directory entries that are not really subdirectories. You've seen these on DOS DIR displays: "." (current directory) and ".." (parent directory). Both of these directory entries have bit 4 set to 1, so our search will find them. They are not part of **SearchDirectory**'s search strategy, however. We are already searching the current directory, so making a recursive call to search "." is meaningless. And due to the way **SearchDirectory** operates, we have already searched the parent directory by the time we are searching any child directory, so searching ".." is redundant.

This is why we must also discriminate against "." and ".." in testing for subdirectory entries. So if the following Boolean expression turns up a value of **TRUE**, we know we have a subdirectory in hand:

```
IF ((CurrentDTA.Attr AND $10) = $10
AND (CurrentDTA.FileName[1] <> '.') THEN
```

This test is made within a **WHILE** loop that inherits the initialized DTA from **FindFirst** and makes calls to **FindNext** continuously until an error message indicates no more files are to be found.

Once we know we have a subdirectory entry in the DTA, we have to search it. The only tricky thing about making the recursive call is passing the correct directory path to the next instantiation of **SearchDirectory**. A string variable, **NextDirectory**, is provided to hold the string carrying the directory path to be searched by the recursive call. **NextDirectory** is loaded with the path of the directory currently being searched, in a variable called **Directory**. Generating the new path involves appending the name of the subdirectory to the end of the directory path we are currently searching. A backslash needs to be added as a separator *unless* we're still searching the root directory, whose path *is* a backslash:

```
IF Directory <> '\' THEN NextDirectory := Directory + '\'
   ELSE NextDirectory := Directory;
```

Then, after a backslash acting as a separator, the name of the "found" directory (in **CurrentDTA**) needs to be appended to **NextDirectory**:

```
NextDirectory := NextDirectory + CurrentDTA.Name;
```

Once the new path has been created in string variable **NextDirectory**, we're ready to make the recursive call. The search spec in **SearchSpec** (that is, the file name or ambiguous file name we're searching for) is unchanged, and the directory path in **NextDirectory** reflects the name of the subdirectory we found in executing **FindFirst** and **FindNext**.

If **SearchDirectory** did not have to be called recursively (in other words, if all we had were "flat" directories as in DOS 1.X), none of this complication would be necessary; we could simply set the DTA address when the program began running and then forget about it.

But we can't. While being searched, each directory demands exclusive use of a DTA. Each time **SearchDirectory** is instantiated, a local variable called **CurrentDTA** is allocated on the stack. **CurrentDTA** is meant to function as the DOS DTA for as long as its instantiation of **SearchDirectory** has control. When an instantiation of **SearchDirectory** takes control and calls **FindFirst**, **FindFirst** sets the address of the DOS DTA to its own copy of **CurrentDTA**. When the current instantiation of **SearchDirectory** terminates and returns control to the prior instantiation of **SearchDirectory**, *that* instantiation must *again* set the address of the DOS DTA to its own copy of **CurrentDTA**. This is done within the **FindNext** call, which always sets the DOS DTA address to its own **SearchRec** parameter when it is invoked.

The first scan of a directory takes action only on subdirectories; files are ignored. Once a given scan determines that no further subdirectories exist within the current directory, a second scan is begun, this time a search for the file or files specified in string variable **SearchSpec**.

As with the search for directories, the current directory string must be combined with the search spec to produce the full path name of the file or files to be searched for. In setting up **FindFirst** to look for subdirectories, we used a search spec of "*.*". This won't do here—**SearchSpec** contains the very specific file name we're trying to match.

The attribute byte is set to $00 for this search—in other words, no attribute bits are set. An attribute of $00 causes **FindFirst** to return *only* ordinary files. It will not locate directories, hidden files, system files, or volume labels. This means that any file turned up as a match is indeed a match, and no further testing (as was necessary in looking for subdirectories) of the found files needs to be done.

If **DOSError** returns error code 2 or 18, then the directory is empty and that particular instantiation of **SearchDirectory** has done its job. It terminates, either ending the **Locate** program completely or passing control back upward to a prior instantiation of **SearchDirectory** to continue the search.

More likely, a file will be turned up. Its information is translated and moved from **CurrentDTA** to a more compliant form embodied by the **DIRRec** record variable **CurrentDIR**. This translation is accomplished by the **DTAToDIR** procedure described a little earlier in this chapter. The information in **CurrentDIR** is then displayed along with the full pathname of the found file by rearranging the information generated by the **DIRToString** procedure also described earlier.

Once any information turned up by **FindFirst** is displayed, control enters a **REPEAT** loop that calls **FindNext** repeatedly, displaying any matching files it finds, until DOS error 2 or 18 turns up in **DOSError**. Either error indicates that no more matching files remain in the current directory. At that point, **SearchDirectory** terminates, either ending **Locate** or passing control back to the prior instantiation of **SearchDirectory**.

That is about all there is to **Locate**. A typical session looks like this:

```
D:\>LOCATE  *.BAK

    1101   11/06/91    7:26p    \TEXT\HEADER.BAK
   11503   01/14/93   11:15a    \TURBO\LOCATE.BAK
    2623   01/13/93    7:53p    \TURBO\DIRSTRIN.BAK
    6055   01/14/93    9:33a    \TURBO\SPACER.BAK
    8595   01/14/93    9:31a    \TURBO\GETDIR.BAK
    2701   01/13/93   11:18a    \TURBO\DTATODIR.BAK
     215   02/12/93    1:12p    \CONFIG.BAK
```

It's interesting to note that the only file found in the root directory (CONFIG.BAK) turns up *last* in the display, even though DOS DIR lists it *before* both subdirectories \TURBO and \TEXT. Given your understanding of the workings of **Locate**, can you explain why this happens?

If you can, you are more than capable of writing and using recursive procedures like **SearchDirectory** and utilities that turn on their own particular brand of black magic.

19.10 Spawning Child Processes with Exec

DOS contains machinery to do something truly remarkable: "suspend" the currently running program and "spawn" a new program above the old program in memory. The new program behaves just as it would if you had executed it from the DOS prompt, *except* that it has less memory to work with. (The program that spawned it is lurking beneath it, sleeping but still taking up room.)

The running copy of the program that does the spawning is called the parent process, and the spawned program is called the child process. We call them processes because they might well be the same program, loaded from the same copy stored on disk. The Turbo Pascal IDE has this ability, and you might try executing a second copy of Turbo Pascal from the Files I DOS Shell menu item.

There is a DOS call, EXEC, which actually accomplishes the loading and executing of child processes. Setting up registers in preparation for a call to EXEC is far from trivial, however, and it is best to think of the **Exec** procedure in the **DOS** unit as a proven black box.

The declaration for **Exec** is disarmingly simple for something so powerful:

```
PROCEDURE Exec(Path,CmdLine : String);
```

To use **Exec**, you pass the full path and file name of the program to be executed in **Path**, and any command line you wish to pass the program in **CmdLine**. Any program that may be executed from the DOS prompt may be executed from **Exec**, and any legal command line may be passed in **CmdLine**:

```
Exec('C:\UTILS\LOCATE.EXE','*.PAS');
```

This invocation of **Exec** runs the **Locate** program described in the previous section, and passes it the command line '*.PAS'. This is equivalent to the following DOS command line:

```
C:\>UTILS\LOCATE *.PAS
```

Too easy? Did I hear you say that there must be a catch? There is indeed, and it involves that nastiest of all DOS bugaboos: memory management. The problem comes down to this: For a program to use **Exec** to spawn a child process, there must be enough free memory above the parent process to contain the child process. This includes the child process's data, stack, and heap.

So—how much free memory ordinarily exists above a loaded and running Turbo Pascal program? *None.*

Unless you specifically set up memory to allow it, spawning child processes will not work.

You have the power to allocate differing amounts of memory to your programs' stack and heap. The default values (i.e., those that are in force until you change them) give 16K of memory to the stack, and *all the rest of memory* to the heap. Obviously, if all remaining memory goes to the heap of the parent process, there will be no space left for spawning children.

ALLOCATING MEMORY FOR CHILD PROCESSES WITH $M

To work with **Exec**, then, you must rearrange memory. There are two ways to do this: one is from the menu in the Turbo Pascal IDE. The other way is through the **$M** compiler command, embedded in a comment at the beginning of your program source code file for both parent and child processes.

The correct way to do it is to use the **$M** command, since memory allocation is generally something you perform on a program-by-program basis. A memory setup for a parent process would not be the same as one for a program that does not use **Exec**.

An **$M** command looks like this:

```
{$M 16384,0,655360}
```

The three parameters (from left to right) specify stack size, minimum heap size, and maximum heap size. This particular **$M** command is the default memory allocation for a Turbo Pascal 7.0 program. In other words, if you do not add a specific **$M** command of your own to a program, the values shown above are the ones that are in force.

The stack size figure is quite simply the amount of memory devoted to the stack segment. If you write a program with a great deal of recursion (which uses the stack to hold recursive instantiations of subprograms), you may need to increase this figure.

The minimum heap and maximum heap values will take some explanation. The amount of memory available when you execute a program is not always the same. A transient program is always the highest thing running in memory. Beneath it are DOS, DOS's device drivers, and TSR programs like Sidekick, WindowDOS, READY! and so on. These things all take up memory, and your own program, running up at the top of the heap, gets what is left over. If you need more memory, you can remove resident programs from memory and perhaps do without special-purpose DOS device drivers, but even then you have DOS, different versions of which are different sizes.

This forces DOS to be careful what it allows you to run from the command line. Baked into the beginning of any .EXE file is information that tells DOS how much room a program requires to run. Before DOS will load an .EXE file from disk and run it, it checks to see how much room the program requires, and compares that against the amount of free memory it currently has. If the program to be run needs more memory than DOS has, DOS will refuse to run it, and you'll see this error message:

```
Program too big to fit in memory
```

The minimum heap size value from the **$M** command figures into this process. The code size (which is fixed for any given sequence of program statements), stack size, and minimum heap size are what Turbo Pascal adds up to determine how much memory a program *must* have to run. This is *not* reflected in the size of the .EXE file Turbo Pascal writes to disk! The .EXE file contains only code and typed constants. No space is reserved inside a .EXE file for stack or heap.

How large you should make the minimum heap figure depends on how much heap space your program *must* have to be able to perform its work at all. If a program doesn't use the heap at all, set *both* heap figures to 0:

```
{$M 16384,0,0}
```

There's no point in specifying a maximum heap size if the minimum heap size is zero. If your program builds data structures on the heap, you'll need to make some calculations and decide on a minimum figure, remembering that if Turbo Pascal doesn't allocate any memory for the heap when compiling your program, using the heap in a program running in a system with little free memory may prevent your program from running.

It will not necessarily crash your system, but if you've loaded up a lot of TSRs and your Turbo Pascal program nearly fills the remainder of memory, trying to allocate heap space may cause your program to abort prematurely for lack of memory. Furthermore, if your program is small and there is lots of free memory in your system, your program may run correctly even if it doesn't allocate any room for the heap. Ensuring that your programs will run under all circumstances requires keeping track of what resources they need and allocating them with **$M**.

The maximum heap figure is the amount of memory that the Turbo Pascal runtime watchdogs will allow the heap to take, if memory is available. This "permission" will be reflected in the returned values from the **MemAvail** function. If you set the maximum heap value to 655360 (essentially, all of memory) then your heap will be allowed to take all free memory DOS has available, right up to the top. You can't actually *get* 655,360 bytes for the heap (both DOS and your program's code take up some portion of that space!), but whatever is free will be available to your heap. In short, the minimum heap size figure is the amount of heap your program *needs* to run, while the maximum heap size figure is how much heap space you'd like your program to have.

Of course, if you request all available memory for your heap, DOS will grant whatever is left and then insist that no more is available for child processes. This is why, to execute a child process with **Exec**, you must set the maximum heap size figure down far enough so that there will be enough room to run the child process. The best way to do this is to make the minimum and maximum heap size allocations the same:

```
{$M 16384,32768,32768}
```

This **$M** command allocates 16K to the stack and 32K to the heap. The program will be given 32K for the heap and no more, but if it runs at all it will have *at least* 32K of heap.

THE TWO KINDS OF EXEC ERRORS

It may not always be possible to execute a child process, even if you have carefully kept heap size to a minimum. There may simply not be enough room once DOS and the TSRs have taken their share. There is no convenient way you can test for sufficient memory before you try to execute a child process. On the other hand, you can simply make the attempt, and if insufficient memory is available, DOS will return an error message and nothing ugly will happen. The error message is returned in the predefined variable **DOSError**. Typically you will see Error 8, Insufficient Memory. If some other error occurs, something else (and probably something serious) is wrong with your program or with DOS's memory allocation system.

If there is enough memory and DOS executes the child process, there is the possibility that the child process will get in trouble somehow. If your child process aborts with some sort of DOS error, the error code will be returned in another predefined variable, **DOSExitCode**. If your parent program depends on something the child process does, you must check **DOSExitCode** after the child process returns control to the parent. It is your only indication that things went well. As with most error codes, a 0 indicates success, and anything else indicates an error of some kind. The error codes are the same ones returned by runtime errors through DOS ERRORLEVEL.

EXECUTING DOS COMMANDS THROUGH COMMAND.COM

One of the most interesting programs to run as a child process is COMMAND.COM, the doorway to DOS itself. COMMAND.COM has some secret hooks into DOS, certainly, but by and large it is only a command parser that contains some very limited command code of its own. DIR, ERASE, and COPY are its most commonly-used built-in commands, and you can execute them from within a program by spawning COMMAND.COM as a child process.

It isn't enough just to execute COMMAND.COM. You need to pass it the name of the command you wish to execute, and that is done through the command-line string passed along with the name of the program to be executed. For example, to execute a DIR command from within a Turbo Pascal program, you would use this syntax:

```
Exec('C:\COMMAND.COM','/C DIR *.PAS');
```

Note that you must pass the full path to COMMAND.COM if it is not in the current directory. The "/C" is a special directive indicating to COMMAND.COM that a built-in command is present on the same command line.

Keep in mind that you *only* have to execute COMMAND.COM to invoke a built-in command; that is, a command that is not itself a separate program like FORMAT.COM or CHKDSK.COM.

"SHELLING OUT" TO DOS

Ducking out of your program to the DOS prompt temporarily is one of the most powerful uses of **Exec**. To pull this trick, all you need to do is execute **COMMAND.COM** by itself without a command line:

```
Exec(C:\COMMAND.COM,'');
```

That's all there is to it . . . sort of. You will see the COMMAND.COM sign-on message, and then the DOS prompt will appear:

```
Microsoft(R) MS-DOS(R) Version 5.00
        (C) Copyright Microsoft Corp 1981-1991

C:\>
```

You can then do anything you could do at the DOS prompt under ordinary circumstances, within the possible limitation of having a smaller available memory pool to draw on. When you wish to return to the parent program, simply type EXIT at the command prompt. At that point the copy of COMMAND.COM that had been running as a child process will terminate, and you will return to your parent program.

One thing to remember is that nothing "magical" is done to preserve the screen as it exists at the moment you "shell out" to DOS. If you disrupt the screen while working from the DOS prompt, the screen will remain disrupted when you return to the parent program. Neither will the parent program's cursor position be retained. To bring back the parent program's screen as it was when you left it, you must save that screen somewhere along with the cursor position, and restore them when you return.

The obvious place to store a screen pattern is on the heap, where space is relatively plentiful. Moving information to and from the heap can be done very quickly with the **Move** statement (which I won't be covering in detail in this book) for the sizes we're talking about, between 4000 and 8000 bytes.

The procedure **SaveScreen** moves the current screen pattern onto the heap, and the procedure **RestoreScreen** moves it back from the heap into display memory. Keeping a screen intact across a DOS command session becomes no more difficult than this:

```
SaveScreen(ScreenPointer);
Exec('C:\COMMAND.COM','');
RestoreScreen(ScreenPointer);
```

Here, **ScreenPointer** is a generic pointer, and the routines are interesting because they utterly hide the details of how and where the saved screen is stored.

```
{->>>>SaveScreen<<<<-----------------------------------------------}
{                                                                  }
{ Filename : SAVESCRN.SRC - Last Modified 2/14/93                  }
{                                                                  }
{ This routine saves the current display buffer out to the        }
{ heap, regardless of how large the current display format is.    }
{ The routine queries the BIOS to determine how many lines are    }
{ currently on the screen, and saves only as much data to the     }
{ heap as necessary.                                              }
{                                                                  }
{ Use the companion routine, RestoreScreen, to bring a screen     }
{ back from the heap.                                              }
{                                                                  }
{ Note that this routine calls several of the video query         }
{ routines described earlier in the book.                         }
{                                                                  }
{   From: BORLAND PASCAL FROM SQUARE ONE  by Jeff Duntemann       }
{------------------------------------------------------------------}

PROCEDURE SaveScreen(VAR StashPtr : Pointer);

TYPE
```

```
    VidPtr   = ^VidSaver;
    VidSaver = RECORD
                  Base,Size : Word;
                  BufStart  : Byte
               END;


VAR
  VidBuffer : Pointer;
  Adapter   : AdapterType;
  StashBuf  : VidSaver;
  VidVector : VidPtr;


BEGIN
  Adapter := QueryAdapterType;
  WITH StashBuf DO
    BEGIN
      CASE Adapter OF
        MDA,EGAMono,VGAMono,MCGAMono : Base := $B000;
        ELSE Base := $B800;
      END;  { CASE }
      CASE DeterminePoints OF
        8  : CASE Adapter OF
               CGA               : Size := 4000;  { 25-line screen }
               EGAMono,EGAColor : Size := 6880;  { 43-line screen }
               ELSE              Size := 8000;  { 50-line screen }
             END; { CASE }
       14 : CASE Adapter OF
               EGAMono,EGAColor : Size := 4000;  { 25-line screen }
               ELSE              Size := 4320;  { 27-line screen }
             END; { CASE }
       16 : Size := 4000;
      END; { CASE }
      VidBuffer := Ptr(Base,0);
    END;

GetMem(StashPtr,StashBuf.Size+4); { Allocate heap for whole shebang }
{ Here we move *ONLY* the VidSaver record (5 bytes) to the heap: }
Move(StashBuf,StashPtr^,Sizeof(StashBuf));
{ This casts StashPtr, a generic pointer, to a pointer to a VidSaver:}
VidVector := StashPtr;
{ Now we move the video buffer itself to the heap. The video data is }
{ written starting at the BufStart byte in the VidSaver record, and  }
{ goes on for Size bytes to fit the whole buffer. Messy but hey, this }
{ is PC land! }
Move(VidBuffer^,VidVector^.BufStart,StashBuf.Size);
END;
```

```
{->>>>RestoreScreen<<<<-----------------------------------------}
{                                                                }
{ Filename : RSTRSCRN.SRC - Last Modified 2/14/93                }
{                                                                }
{ This routine accepts a pointer generated by the SaveScreen     }
{ routine and brings back the saved display buffer from the      }
{ heap and loads it into the refresh buffer of the display       }
{ card.                                                          }
{                                                                }
{   From: BORLAND PASCAL FROM SQUARE ONE   by Jeff Duntemann     }
{----------------------------------------------------------------}


PROCEDURE RestoreScreen(StashPtr : Pointer);

TYPE
   VidPtr   = ^VidSaver;
   VidSaver = RECORD
                 Base,Size : Word;
                 BufStart  : Byte
              END;

VAR
   VidVector : VidPtr;
   VidBuffer : Pointer;
   DataSize  : Word;

BEGIN
   VidVector := StashPtr;  { Cast generic pointer onto VidSaver pointer }
   DataSize  := VidVector^.Size;
   { Create a pointer to the base of the video buffer: }
   VidBuffer := Ptr(VidVector^.Base,0);
   { Move the buffer portion of the data on the heap to the video buffer:}
    Move(VidVector^.BufStart,VidBuffer^,VidVector^.Size);
   FreeMem(StashPtr,DataSize + 4);
END;
```

Most of the trickiness of the system lies in **SaveScreen**, and that stems from the fact that a screen may be 25, 27, 43, or 50 lines in size. The routine determines the size of the screen by using the **DeterminePoints** function described in Section 12.4. The size of the screen is determined by the size of the font currently in use. Another more familiar complication is that video display buffers in the PC family may exist in one of two places: at segment $B000 (for monochrome modes) or $B800 (for color modes). This is determined by using the **QueryAdapterType** function, also presented in Section 12.4.

Once the size and location of the current screen has been determined, the rest is a suite of tricks with pointers. A generic pointer must be passed to **SaveScreen**, and this pointer is used to reference a block of storage on the heap allocated with **GetMem**. **GetMem** allocates enough space on the heap to hold the screen itself plus 4 additional bytes. These 4 bytes provide room for two **Word** variables indicating the size of the screen and the segment base of the video buffer.

The data is moved to the heap in two operations. The first moves only the segment base value and the screen size, in the form of a record type called **VidSaver**. There is a "dummy" field in **VidSaver**, called **BufStart**, that exists only to provide a starting point for the second move operation. This second move operation moves the video buffer data from the video buffer to the heap address at which **BufStart** exists.

The **RestoreScreen** routine is considerably simpler. It receives the pointer to the stored screen on the heap, and casts that pointer onto **VidVector**, a pointer to the **VidSaver** type. This allows **RestoreScreen** to easily bring the video buffer segment and screen size values from the heap by dereferencing the **VidVector** pointer. With the screen size and buffer segment in hand, moving the screen data itself from the heap to the display buffer is nothing more than another call to Turbo Pascal's **Move** procedure.

The only caution in shelling out to DOS between calls to **SaveScreen** and **RestoreScreen** is this: Don't change the size of the screen while you're out working with DOS. **RestoreScreen** assumes when it goes to work that the size of the screen is what it was when **SaveScreen** moved the screen image onto the heap. If the screen size is different, you won't see what you were seeing when you ducked out to COMMAND.COM.

The short demo program **ShellOut** shows **SaveScreen** and **RestoreScreen** in use. A simple screen is constructed, then saved out to the heap just before executing COMMAND.COM. Once COMMAND.COM returns, **RestoreScreen** brings the screen back in from the heap, correcting any disruption that occurred during the interactive session with COMMAND.COM.

```
{---------------------------------------------------------------------}
{                              ShellOut                               }
{                                                                     }
{    "Shell to DOS" with screen save demonstration program           }
{                                                                     }
{                          by Jeff Duntemann                          }
{                          Turbo Pascal V7.0                          }
{                          Last update 2/14/93                        }
{                                                                     }
{    From: BORLAND PASCAL FROM SQUARE ONE  by Jeff Duntemann          }
{---------------------------------------------------------------------}

PROGRAM ShellOut;

{$M 16384,16384,16384}   { Reserve some heap to save the screen }

USES DOS,CRT,BoxStuff;
```

```
TYPE
   AdapterType = (None,MDA,CGA,EGAMono,EGAColor,VGAMono,
                  VGAColor,MCGAMono,MCGAColor);

VAR
   Stash : Pointer;

{$I WRITEAT.SRC}      { Described in Section 12.3 }
{$I QUERYDSP.SRC}     { Described in Section 12.4 }
{$I FONTSIZE.SRC}     { Described in Section 12.4 }
{$I SAVESCRN.SRC}     { Described in Section 19.10 }
{$I RSTRSCRN.SRC}     { Described in Section 19.10 }

BEGIN
   ClrScr;
   MakeBox(1,1,80,24,PCLineChars);
   WriteAt(-1,3,True,False,'** Relatively Dumb Parent Program **');
   GotoXY(10,10); Write('Press Enter to shell to DOS: '); Readln;
   SaveScreen(Stash);
   Exec('C:\COMMAND.COM','');
   RestoreScreen(Stash);
   GotoXY(10,13); Write('Press Enter to terminate program: '); Readln;
END.
```

19.11 Reading the DOS Environment

One of the little strangenesses of PC DOS V2 and later is an item called the "DOS environment block" (usually referred to as "the environment"). DOS reserves a region of memory somewhere, in a location that doesn't change, as a "bulletin board" reserved for the posting of string-data notices. These notices are for applications programs that load, run for awhile under DOS, and then terminate. They have the ability to peek at the bulletin board and see what notices have been posted.

The notices can be anything at all, but are typically useful things about the DOS configuration of the system: Where COMMAND.COM is stored, what the current DOS search path is for program execution, and so on. Additionally, the user has the ability to place notices in the DOS environment by using DOS's SET command. By entering a command like

```
SET SYMLIB=D:\M2LIB\SYM
```

it's possible to post the string "SYMLIB=D:\M2LIB\SYM" on the DOS environment's bulletin board. Then, when a utility program needs to know where the Modula 2 symbol files are kept, it can peek at the environment and get the path attached to the identifier "SYMLIB."

Early implementations of DOS limited the size of the environment block to about 160 bytes, which was grossly inadequate. Since DOS 3.2 the environment block has been enlargeable with DOS's SHELL command, and most people give it about 1000 bytes or so, which allows it to become truly useful.

THE NATURE AND LOCATION OF THE DOS ENVIRONMENT

The environment is an area of reserved memory within DOS in which strings may be written. The strings stored in the environment are ASCIIZ strings, meaning that they are arrays of characters terminated with a binary 0. (In Pascal, Chr(0).) The end of significant information in the environment is signaled by the presence of another binary 0 after the binary 0 signalling the end of the last string in the environment. If the environment *begins* with a binary 0, nothing has been stored into it.

The location of the DOS environment is stored at the beginning of the code segment of your Pascal program, in a 256-byte area called the "Program Segment Prefix," of PSP. At offset $2C into the PSP is a 2-byte segment address, which is the segment of the first byte of the DOS environment. (The offset of the first byte of the environment is always assumed to be 0.) So finding the environment is only as difficult as saying:

```
EnvSegment := MEMW[CSEG : $2C];
```

where **EnvSegment** is an integer.

You don't have to worry about where the environment is in memory, however—Turbo Pascal locates it without assistance.

COUNTING ENVIRONMENT STRINGS

If you're interested in reading everything the environment contains, it's helpful to know how many strings have been stored there. Turbo Pascal 5.0 and later give you the **EnvCount** built-in function that returns the number of individual strings existing in the environment. **EnvCount** is declared this way:

```
FUNCTION EnvCount : Integer;
```

FETCHING ENVIRONMENT STRINGS BY INDEX

Once you know how many strings are lurking in the environment, retrieving them is done with the **EnvStr** function, which is present in Turbo Pascal versions 5.0 and later. **EnvStr** is passed the index of a string in the environment. The first string is string number 1, the second string number 2, and so on up to the number of strings reported by **EnvCount** as explained above. **EnvStr** is declared this way:

```
FUNCTION EnvStr(Index : Integer) : String;
```

A one-statement program can display the full contents of the DOS environment to your screen, using **EnvCount** and **EnvStr**:

```
PROGRAM ShowEnvironment;

USES DOS;

VAR
  I : Integer;

BEGIN
  IF EnvCount > 0 THEN
    FOR I := 1 TO EnvCount DO
      Writeln(EnvStr(I))
END.
```

READING A NAMED ENVIRONMENT STRING

If you know the name of an environment string (that is, the portion of a string on the left side of the '= ' sign), Turbo Pascal provides a way of reading the portion of the string on the right side of the '=' sign, using its **GetEnv** function. **GetEnv** is declared this way:

```
FUNCTION GetEnv(EnvironmentVariable : String) : String;
```

The use of **GetEnv** is best explained by example. The following short program prompts for an environment variable name (such as PATH, or COMSPEC) and searches the environment for a string of that name. If the string is found, the program displays its value:

```
PROGRAM ShowEnvironmentVariable;

USES DOS;

VAR
  Name,Value : String;

BEGIN
  Write('Enter the name of an environment variable: ');
  Readln(Name);
  Value := GetEnv(Name);
  IF Length(Value) = 0 THEN
    Writeln('That variable is not in the environment.')
  ELSE
    Writeln('The value of ',Name,' is ',Value,'.');
END.
```

For example, you might see the following session:

```
Enter the name of an environment variable: PATH

The value of PATH is C:\DOS;D:\UTILS;D:\WP42;C:\TURBO5
```

If **GetEnv** cannot find the named string, it returns a zero-length string.

Chapter **20**

Dynamic Data Structures

SINGLY- AND DOUBLY-LINKED LISTS ON THE HEAP

The whole point of having dynamic variables is to be able to create and destroy them as needed, without having to predeclare them at compile time. For single variables, this hardly seems worth the bother. Dynamic variables really come into their own when you begin building entire structures of variables out in heapspace—structures whose size and shape may not be known at compile time, and which may change drastically from execution to execution of the program, depending on whatever job it's called upon to do.

The subject of data structures is a tricky one, with a lot of wrinkles and corners where dust collects. It encompasses structures like circular buffers, linked lists, doubly-linked lists, trees, and sparse matrices. I don't have the room in this introductory book to go deeply into dynamic data structures; that subject can itself do justice to an entire book. What I can do here is introduce you to the ideas of dynamic data structures on the heap, and cement the principles in your mind by demonstrating, in detail, the two most-used dynamic structures: singly- and doubly-linked lists.

20.1 Linked List Fundamentals

We no longer have a phone next to our bed.

I used to get a lot of weird phone calls during the night, from well-meaning hacker-fans who assumed that, like them, I stayed up until all hours of the night beating on code. Not so—I hit the rack at 10:30 every night without fail, and that's one way I've managed to keep my youthful outlook, even if my hair has taken a walk in the meantime.

Like dreams, midnight help-calls tend to get forgotten. There was indeed one morning when, over coffee, Carol reminded me that I had been trying to explain something to somebody who had called on the far side of 2:00 ayem. "You got pretty agitated," she said. "It was weird. You were talking about lists of kites."

561

"Kites?" I was dipping cornflakes in my coffee and feeding them to Mr. Byte. "I haven't built a kite in 15 years."

"No. You were in metaphor mode. And *loud*. You were yelling, 'Look, lists aren't that hard to understand. Think of a guy flying a kite! Now think of a guy sitting on his kite, flying another kite! And a third guy sitting on the second guy's kite, flying another kite!'"

"Must have been big kites."

"Don't change the subject. Next time you take a call in the middle of the night, I'm going to pull that phone out by the roots."

I'm glad she brought it up; for the life of me, I don't remember that little session. But the notion of a bunch of kites connected together as a metaphor for linked lists makes a certain amount of sense. (It even works in real life. You can in fact fly a kite, then tie the kite string to the string of another kite and fly that kite, and so on. I took a half dozen dime-store kites one summer day and linked them together in the air. It was, to borrow a fine old Sixties term, psychedelic.)

Why so? Because a linked list is just a bunch of data blocks on the heap, connected by pointers. You can imagine them as kites if you like. But if you just take it step-by-step, you won't have any trouble understanding the concept at all.

DRAW IT OUT!

Linked lists are tailor-made for drawing out in diagram form. In fact, that's about the only way most people ever get them down straight, and I powerfully recommend that you spend some time studying the diagrams in this chapter. Furthermore, if you ever get in a tight spot in trying to understand some dynamic structure, dig out your old Ticonderoga #2, put a point on it, and *draw* the silly thing. If you find the notion embarrassing, close your door while you do it—and remind yourself that I do the same thing when structures get tangled in my mind.

Figure 20.1 summarizes the different symbols I'll be using to represent pointers and the records that make up singly- and doubly-linked lists discussed in this section.

RECORDS WITH POINTERS INSIDE THEM

When we first looked at dynamic variables, back in Chapter 17, we saw that a dynamic variable is tethered to its program's static data area by a pointer variable. Dynamic variables have no names, so the only way to use them is to work from the pointer variable, which *does* have a name.

But consider a record type that includes, as one of its fields, a pointer variable to another record like itself:

```
TYPE
  NAPPtr = ^NAPRec;
```

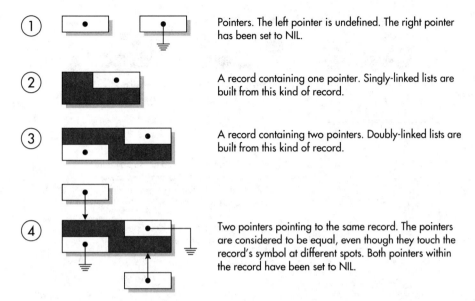

① Pointers. The left pointer is undefined. The right pointer has been set to NIL.

② A record containing one pointer. Singly-linked lists are built from this kind of record.

③ A record containing two pointers. Doubly-linked lists are built from this kind of record.

④ Two pointers pointing to the same record. The pointers are considered to be equal, even though they touch the record's symbol at different spots. Both pointers within the record have been set to NIL.

Figure 20.1 Typographical Conventions for Linked Lists

```
NAPRec = RECORD
           Name    : String;
           Address : String;
           City    : String;
           State   : String;
           Zip     : String;
           Next    : NADPtr
         END;
```

One of these records, once created out in heapspace and tethered to the static data area, could be made to point to another such record out in heapspace, and it to another, and so on. (Just like kites tied together by their strings. Get it?) We could have an entire long string of records, each one pointing to the next, with the whole tied to our program by just a single pointer variable.

Such a collection of dynamic records linked by pointers is called a *linked list*. (See Figure 20.2.) The very last record in the list contains a pointer whose value is **NIL**—again, remember that **NIL** only means a pointer that points to nothing. The **NIL** pointer signals the end of the linked list.

TRAVERSING A LINKED LIST

As with any dynamic variable, the list has no name. Its tether to reality is a pointer variable with a name. But neither the records themselves nor the pointers that link them have names. The pointer that tethers the list to the static data area is often called the *root*.

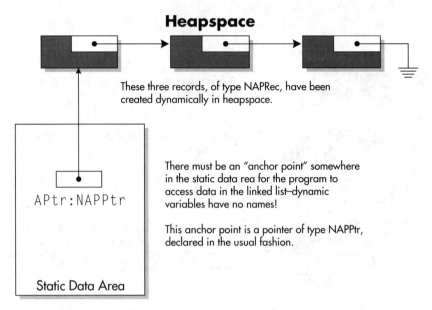

Heapspace

These three records, of type NAPRec, have been created dynamically in heapspace.

APtr:NAPPtr

There must be an "anchor point" somewhere in the static data rea for the program to access data in the linked list–dynamic variables have no names!

This anchor point is a pointer of type NAPPtr, declared in the usual fashion.

Static Data Area

Figure 20.2 A Linked List

How do we access the records in a linked list? The first record, pretty obviously, is **Root^**, since the pointer variable **Root** points to it. But how about the record pointed to by the pointer buried inside **Root^**? You can in fact say **Root^.Next^**, which can be read (most awkwardly) as "the record pointed to by the **Next** pointer contained in the record pointed to by **Root**." Obviously, it gets still worse for the third record in the list, **Root^.Next^.Next^**. Subject to certain limits of the compiler, you can go on this way for many levels: **Root^.Next^. Next^.Next^.Next^.Next^** and so on.

But that won't work. Why? *It assumes that we know how many records are in the linked list at compile time.* And, recall that the reason to use dynamic variables is to create structures whose size and shape may *not* be known at compile time. If you know how many records are there at compile time, you might as well just put them into an array.

No—the way to deal with dynamic structures is to be dynamic. We must move along the linked list, looking at one record at a time, until we detect the end of the list. This process is called *traversing* a linked list.

Traversing a list requires a little extra machinery. Specifically, we need a new pointer to help us, in addition to the root pointer. Look over the following code, which displays data from records of a linked list pointed to by **Root**:

```
Current := Root;              { Current and Root both point to list }

WHILE Current <> NIL DO
  BEGIN
    ShowRecord(Current^);     { Displays data in record Current^ }
```

```
    Current := Current^.Next { Points Current to next record }
  END;
```

Assigning one pointer to another, you'll recall, means that both pointers now point to the same item. **Current** and **Root** both point to the first record in the list. **Root** is the list's anchor into reality; we must *not* change it without good reason.

But we can make **Current** "travel" along the list by assigning to it the value of the **Next** field in the record it currently points to. Eventually **Current** is pointing to the last record in the list. The **Next** field inside that last record has a value of **NIL**. When **Current** is assigned **Current^.Next**, then **Current** takes on the value **NIL**. The **WHILE** loop tests for the **NIL** value, and when it finds **NIL**, it is satisfied and the loop terminates.

BUILDING LINKED LISTS

We covered traversing a linked list before explaining how a linked list is built, because traversing the list is often a part of the process of building the list. How the list is built depends upon your needs.

Linked lists are either *ordered* or not. An ordered list is built so that when you traverse the list, you will encounter the items in the list in some sort of order according to the data carried in the items. If, as you traverse a list, you find that all the items are in alphabetical order by one of the item's data fields, then that is an ordered list.

Building a list that is not ordered is simplicity itself. Given **GetRec**, a procedure that supplies filled records (of type **NAPRec** as given above) this code will construct a linked list:

```
VAR
   WorkRec      : NAPRec;
   Root,Holder  : NAPPtr;

Root := NIL;
Holder := Root;
FOR I := 1 TO 10 DO
  BEGIN
    GetRec(WorkRec);          { Fill the (static) work record  }
    New(Root);                { Create empty dynamic record    }
    WorkRec.Next := Holder;   { Copy root pointer into WorkRec }
    Root^ := WorkRec;         { Copy work record into Root^    }
    Holder := Root            { Point Holder to list root again }
  END;
```

The critical point here is that new records are inserted at the *beginning* of the list rather than at the end. The very first record loaded into the list becomes the *tail* of the list, pushed farther and farther from the root by each new record returned by **GetRec**.

A short list may not have to be ordered, because even a beginning-to-end sequential search on a short list (less than 100–200 items) is so fast that ordering it is not worth the small amount of time saved in searches.

But there are other reasons to order a list: We may want to *use* the data in some order in addition to simply searching it for matching data. For example, searching for names in an unordered list may be acceptably fast, but you wouldn't want to print out the names (say, for an address book) in random order.

Building an ordered list involves some traversing. Briefly, to add an item to an ordered list you must traverse the list until you find the place in the list where the new item must be inserted to keep the list in order. Once you find the proper spot, you insert the item. The following procedure builds an ordered list of records by adding a record in proper order to a list pointed to by **Root**:

```
PROCEDURE Builder(VAR Root : NAPPtr; WorkRec : NAPRec);

VAR
   Current,Last : NAPPtr;

BEGIN
   IF Root = NIL THEN        { List is empty! }
     BEGIN
       New(Root);
       WorkRec.Next := NIL;
       Root^ := WorkRec
     END
   ELSE                      { List already contains some records }
     BEGIN
       Current := Root;
       REPEAT                { Traverse list to find correct spot }
         Last := Current;
         Current := Current^.Next
       UNTIL (Current = NIL) OR (Current^.Name > WorkRec.Name)
                             { Found spot-now insert new record  }
       IF Root^.Name > WorkRec.Name THEN   { Record becomes new }
         BEGIN                             { first item on list }
           New(Root);                { Create new record for Root }
           WorkRec.Next := Last;     { Copy root pointer to Next  }
           Root^ := WorkRec          { Copy WorkRec to new record }
         END
       ELSE                              { Record belongs in  }
         BEGIN                           { mid-list somewhere }
           New(Last^.Next);        { Create new record for Last}
           WorkRec.Next := Current; { Point new rec to Current  }
           Last^.Next := WorkRec;   { Copy WorkRec to new record}
         END
     END
END;
```

In the code shown above, there are three possibilities that must be dealt with separately:

1. The list is empty. **Root** is equal to **NIL**. The record passed to **Builder** becomes the first record in the list. No traversing is necessary at all.

2. Testing the first record in the list (**Root^**) shows that the record to be inserted must be inserted *before* **Root^**. The new record must then become **Root^**, and its **Next** field must be made to point to the old **Root^**.

3. Traversing the list shows that the record must be inserted somewhere within the list or at its end. The record must be inserted between two existing records, or between the last record and **NIL**.

It is to cater to possibility #3 that the pointer **Last** was created. (See Figure 20.3.) **Last**, as its name implies, points to the last record pointed to by **Current**. **Last** is always one record behind **Current**, once **Current** moves off "home base." Having **Last** right behind **Current** makes it easy to insert a record into the list. With **Current** safely pointing to the rest of the list, the list is broken at **Last^.Next** and a new dynamic record is created for **Last^.Next** to point to:

```
New(Last^.Next);
```

Now to "heal" the break in the list: **WorkRec**'s **Next** field is pointed to **Current^**. **WorkRec** is now part of the second fragment of the list. Finally, **WorkRec**

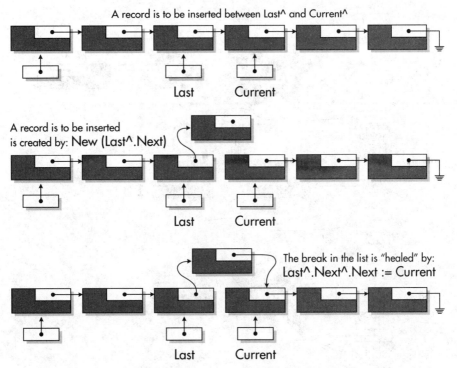

Figure 20.3 Inserting a Record into a Linked List

is assigned to **Last^.Next**. The list is whole once again, with **WorkRec** inserted between **Last^** and **Current^**.

DISPOSING OF A LINKED LIST

We have emphasized that you don't throw away a linked list by cutting the list free of its root pointer. The space in memory is still occupied, albeit by unreachable and now useless records. A linked list must be disposed of in an orderly manner. In some respects, getting rid of a linked list is the mirror image of the method used to create it. Since the order of the records doesn't matter when you're disposing of them, the same method is used to dispose of both ordered and non-ordered lists. (See Figure 20.4.)

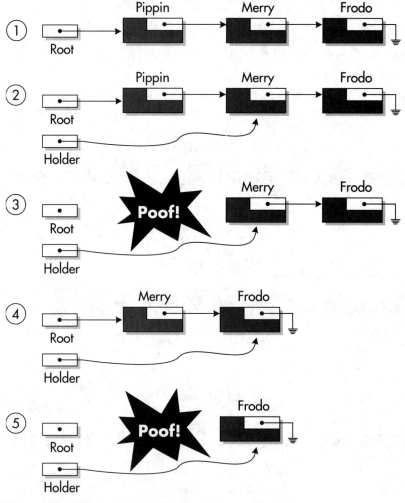

Figure 20.4 Disposing of a Linked List

Pointer **Root** anchors the list to be disposed of. A second pointer, **Holder**, is also needed. With **Root** pointing to the first record in the list, **Holder** is made to point to the second record. Now **Holder** is anchoring the list from one record further on than **Root**. **Root^** can thus be safely disposed of.

Root is then pointed to **Holder^**. With **Root** now also at the new beginning of the list, **Holder** may be moved up to the second record in the list, allowing **Root^** to be disposed of. The loop continues until no more records remain:

```
PROCEDURE ListDispose(VAR Root : NAPPtr);

VAR
  Holder : NAPPtr;

BEGIN
  IF Root <> NIL THEN        { Can't dispose if no list!   }
    REPEAT
      Holder := Root^.Next;  { Grab the next record...     }
      Dispose(Root);         { ...dispose of the first...  }
      Root := Holder         { and make the next the first }
    UNTIL Root = NIL END;
```

One slightly silly image to apply here is to think of pulling in a string of sausages hand-over-hand from a second-story balcony. You grasp the next one in line while you cut the first one free. Then you reach forward to what is now the next one, repeating the process until all of the sausages are safe in their pot.

20.2 A Simple List Manager Program

To reinforce all the various ways of manipulating linked lists, I'll present a simple list manager program in this section. **ListMan** is the skeleton of a "personal address book" to contain names, addresses, and (if you add another field to the **NAPRec** record type) phone numbers. **ListMan** is more than just a demonstration of linked list handling—it is your chance to show your stuff by building on it.

ListMan creates and adds records to ordered lists, saves them to disk, loads them from disk, and disposes of them gracefully when they are no longer needed. After each change to the size of the list, the number of records that may be added is displayed at the top of the screen.

The **AddRecords** procedure in **ListMan** is an expansion of the **Builder** procedure given above. **AddRecords** performs an additional service: It looks for duplicate names. There may be two distinct John Browns in your Christmas card list, but you may also have accidentally typed his name in twice. **AddRecords** shows you both duplicate records on the screen at once, and allows you to throw away the most recently entered one if it is in fact a duplicate.

CheckSpace shows how **MemAvail** is used. **MaxAvail** is not used because records are not deleted at random. Lists are deleted all at once, so no heapspace fragmentation will occur. If you were to expand **ListMan** to allow the deletion of records from the list at random (a good idea—what if you don't get a Christmas card from John Brown this year?), you will have to begin using **MaxAvail**.

Another function lacking in **ListMan** is search-and-edit. In other words, if John Brown moves, you will need to search the list for his name and change the address data stored in his record. The code to do this could be cribbed from **AddRecords**, which already searches the list for duplicates of the record to be inserted. You might, in fact, "break out" the search-for-duplicate code into a separate procedure that may be called by both **AddRecords** and your hypothetical search-and-edit procedure. In the same way, you could use the **GetString** procedure presented in Chapter 10 to write a more general data entry/edit procedure replacing the sequence of **Readln**s in **AddRecords**. Both **AddRecords** and your search-and-edit procedure could call the new data entry/edit procedure.

This is much of the magic of Pascal: the building of "toolkit" routines that may be called by two or more procedures within a program. In this way, the richness of function of a program may be increased tremendously without turning the program into something of Godzillan size.

```
{ --------------------------------------------------------------- }
{                                                                 }
{                           ListMan                               }
{                                                                 }
{     Mailing list manager demo using dynamic (heap) storage      }
{                                                                 }
{                       by Jeff Duntemann                         }
{                       Turbo Pascal V7.0                         }
{                     Last update 11/24/92                        }
{                                                                 }
{    From: BORLAND PASCAL FROM SQUARE ONE   by Jeff Duntemann     }
{ --------------------------------------------------------------- }


PROGRAM ListMan;

USES Crt;

TYPE
   String30 = String[30];        { Using derived string types }
   String6  = String[6];         { makes type NAPRec smaller }
   String3  = String[3];

   NAPPtr = ^NAPRec;
   NAPRec = RECORD
               Name    : String30;
               Address : String30;
               City    : String30;
               State   : String3;
               Zip     : String6;
               Next    : NAPPtr       { Points to next NAPRec }
```

```
        END;                          { in a linked list }

    NAPFile = FILE OF NAPRec;



VAR
  Ch      : Char;
  Root    : NAPPtr;
  Quit    : Boolean;



{$I YES.SRC }      { Contains function Yes, from Chapter 11 }


PROCEDURE ClearLines(First,Last : Integer);

VAR
  I : Integer;

BEGIN
  FOR I := First TO Last DO
    BEGIN
      GotoXY(1,I);
      ClrEOL
    END
END;




PROCEDURE ShowRecord(WorkRec : NAPRec);

VAR
  I : Integer;

BEGIN
  ClearLines(17,22);  { Clear away anything in that spot before }
  GotoXY(1,17);
  WITH WorkRec DO
    BEGIN
      Writeln('>>Name:      ',Name);
      Writeln('>>Address:   ',Address);
      Writeln('>>City:      ',City);
      Writeln('>>State:     ',State);
      Writeln('>>Zip:       ',Zip)
    END
END;
```

```pascal
PROCEDURE CheckSpace;

VAR
  Space      : LongInt;
  RealRoom   : Real;
  RecordRoom : Real;

BEGIN
  Space := MemAvail;
  RecordRoom := Space / SizeOf(NAPRec);
  ClearLines(2,3);
  Writeln
  ('>>There is now room for ',RecordRoom:6:0,' records in your list.');
END;



PROCEDURE ListDispose(VAR Root : NAPPtr);

VAR
  Holder : NAPPtr;

BEGIN
  GotoXY(27,10); Write('>>Are you SURE? (Y/N): ');
  IF YES THEN
    IF Root <> Nil THEN
      REPEAT
        Holder := Root^.Next;   { First grab the next record...        }
        Dispose(Root);          { ...then dispose of the first one... }
        Root := Holder          { ...then make the next one the first }
      UNTIL Root = Nil;
  ClearLines(10,10);
  CheckSpace
END;



PROCEDURE AddRecords(VAR Root : NAPPtr);

VAR
  I       : Integer;
  Abandon : Boolean;
  WorkRec : NAPRec;
  Last    : NAPPtr;
  Current : NAPPtr;

BEGIN
  GotoXY(27,7); Write('<<Adding Records>>');
  REPEAT                { Until user answers 'N' to "MORE?" question... }
```

```
      ClearLines(24,24);
      FillChar(WorkRec,SizeOf(WorkRec),CHR(0));   { Zero the record }
      ClearLines(9,15);
      GotoXY(1,9);
      WITH WorkRec DO              { Fill the record with good data }
        BEGIN
          Write('>>Name:      '); Readln(Name);
          Write('>>Address:   '); Readln(Address);
          Write('>>City:      '); Readln(City);
          Write('>>State:     '); Readln(State);
          Write('>>Zip:       '); Readln(Zip)
        END;
      Abandon := False;
                                { Here we traverse list to spot duplicates: }


      IF Root = Nil THEN        { If list is empty point Root to record }
        BEGIN
          New(Root);
          WorkRec.Next := Nil;  { Make sure list is terminated by Nil }
          Root^ := WorkRec;
        END
      ELSE                      { ...if there's something in list already }
        BEGIN
          Current := Root;        { Start traverse at Root of list }
          REPEAT
            IF Current^.Name = WorkRec.Name THEN { If duplicate found }
              BEGIN
                ShowRecord(Current^);
                GotoXY(1,15);
                Write
      ('>>The record below duplicates the above entry''s Name.  Toss entry?
      (Y/N): ');
                IF Yes THEN Abandon := True ELSE Abandon := False;
                ClearLines(15,22)
              END;
            Last := Current;
            Current := Current^.Next
          UNTIL (Current = Nil) OR Abandon
                            OR (Current^.Name > WorkRec.Name);

          IF NOT Abandon THEN     { Add WorkRec to the linked list  }
            IF Root^.Name > WorkRec.Name THEN { New Root item!      }
              BEGIN
                New(Root);               { Create a new dynamic NAPRec }
                WorkRec.Next := Last;   { Point new record at old Root }
                Root^ := WorkRec       { Point new Root at WorkRec    }
              END
```

```
                ELSE
                  BEGIN
                    NEW(Last^.Next);           { Create a new dynamic NAPRec, }
                    WorkRec.Next := Current;{ Points its Next to Current    }
                    Last^.Next^ := WorkRec; { and assign WorkRec to it      }
                    CheckSpace              { Display remaining heapspace   }
                  END;
            END;
        GotoXY(1,24); Write('>>Add another record to the list? (Y/N): ');
      UNTIL NOT Yes;
    END;


    PROCEDURE LoadList(VAR Root : NAPPtr);

    VAR
      WorkName : String30;
      WorkFile : NAPFile;
      Current  : NAPPtr;
      I        : Integer;
      OK       : Boolean;

    BEGIN
      Quit := False;
      REPEAT
        ClearLines(10,10);
        Write('>>Enter the Name of the file you wish to load: ');
        Readln(WorkName);
        IF Length(WorkName) = 0 THEN    { Hit (CR) only to abort LOAD }
          BEGIN
            ClearLines(10,12);
            Quit := True
          END
        ELSE
          BEGIN
            Assign(WorkFile,WorkName);
            {$I-} Reset(WorkFile); {$I+}
            IF IOResult <> 0 THEN          { 0 = OK; 255 = File Not Found }
              BEGIN
                GotoXY(1,12);
                Write
                ('>>That file does not exist.  Please enter another.');
                OK := False
              END
            ELSE OK := True                { OK means File Is open }
          END
```

```
        UNTIL OK OR Quit;
   IF NOT Quit THEN
      BEGIN
         ClearLines(10,12);
         Current := Root;
         IF Root = Nil THEN                    { If list is currently empty }
            BEGIN
               NEW(Root);                       { Load first record to Root^ }
               Read(WorkFile,Root^);
               Current := Root
            END                       { If list is not empty, find the end: }
         ELSE WHILE Current^.Next <> Nil DO Current := Current^.Next;
         IF Root^.Next <> Nil THEN
         { If file contains more than 1 record }
         REPEAT
            NEW(Current^.Next);               { Read and add records to list }
            Current := Current^.Next;         { until a record's Next field  }
            Read(WorkFile,Current^)           { comes up Nil    }
         UNTIL Current^.Next = Nil;
         CheckSpace;
         Close(WorkFile)
      END
END;


PROCEDURE ViewList(Root : NAPPtr);

VAR
   I        : Integer;
  WorkFile  : NAPFile;
  Current   : NAPPtr;

BEGIN
   IF Root = Nil THEN                    { Nothing is now in the list }
      BEGIN
         GotoXY(27,18);
         Writeln('<<Your list is empty!>>');
         GotoXY(26,20);
         Write('>>Press (CR) to continue: ');
         Readln
      END
   ELSE
      BEGIN
         GotoXY(31,7); Write('<<Viewing Records>>');
         Current := Root;
         WHILE Current <> Nil DO { Traverse and display until Nil found }
```

```
            BEGIN
              ShowRecord(Current^);
              GotoXY(1,23);
              Write('>>Press (CR) to view Next record in the list: ');
              Readln;
              Current := Current^.Next
            END;
          ClearLines(19,22)
      END
  END;


PROCEDURE SaveList(Root : NAPPtr);

VAR
  WorkName : String30;
  WorkFile : NAPFile;
  Current  : NAPPtr;
  I        : Integer;

BEGIN
  GotoXY(1,10);
  Write('>>Enter the filename for saving out your list: ');
  Readln(WorkName);
  Assign(WorkFile,WorkName);    { Open the file for write access }
  Rewrite(WorkFile);
  Current := Root;
  WHILE Current <> Nil DO      { Traverse and write }
    BEGIN
      Write(WorkFile,Current^);
      Current := Current^.Next
    END;
  Close(WorkFile)
END;



BEGIN         { MAIN }
  ClrScr;
  GotoXY(28,1); Write('<<Linked List Maker>>');
  CheckSpace;
  GotoXY(17,8);   Write('----------------------');
  Root := Nil; Quit := False;
  REPEAT
    ClearLines(5,7);
    ClearLines(9,24);
    GotoXY(1,5);
```

```
      Write
      ('>>[L]oad, [A]dd record, [V]iew, [S]ave, [C]lear list, or [Q]uit: ');
      Readln(Ch);                    { Get a command }
      CASE Ch OF
        'A','a' : AddRecords(Root);   { Parse the command & perform it }
        'C','c' : ListDispose(Root);
        'L','l' : LoadList(Root);
        'S','s' : SaveList(Root);
        'V','v' : ViewList(Root);
        'Q','q' : Quit := True;
      END; { CASE }
    UNTIL Quit
END.
```

20.3 Doubly-Linked Lists

Singly-linked lists (like those we spoke of in the last section) are a necessary first step in understanding dynamic data structures and how they go together. But as lists go, they're underpowered and not especially useful, in that they're a little like crystal radios: Everyone who cares about radios should build one to get an important appreciation for radio fundamentals. But I wouldn't willingly attempt to listen all the way through "Prairie Home Companion" on a crystal set.

Our radios—and our linked lists—should be a little more advanced than that.

ADDING A SECOND LINK

Singly-linked lists are held together by that ever-present **Next** pointer in their component records. The fundamental problem with singly-linked lists is that pointers are inescapably one-way devices. A pointer can point from one record to another, but you *cannot* look "back" along a pointer to see from where you've come. Needless to say, you can only traverse a singly-linked list in one direction. "Backing up" during the traversal of a singly-linked list requires the use of secondary pointers that "follow" the main traversing pointer one or two nodes behind.

It can be easier than that.

First of all, let's consider a dynamic record as part of a singly-linked list of string values:

```
TYPE
   String80 = STRING[80];
   PStringListNode = ^TStringListNode;
   TStringListNode = RECORD
                        StringData : String80;
                        Next       : PStringListNode;
                      END;
```

This is precisely the same kind of record we worked with in the last chapter when we created a simple name-and-address list manager using singly-linked lists. Making the record a suitable node for use in a doubly-linked list simply requires the addition of a second pointer:

```
TYPE
   TStringListNode = RECORD
                      Prior      : PStringListNode;
                      StringData : String80;
                      Next       : PStringListNode;
                    END;
```

The sense of both pointers' uses should be apparent from their names: The **Next** pointer points to the next node in the list, and the **Prior** pointer points to the node *before* it in the list.

Most of the same concepts we learned in working with singly-linked lists apply here. There's simply a second pointer to be handled.

20.4 Non-Ordered Doubly-Linked Lists

The very simplest kind of doubly-linked list is one in which the nodes are added in the order that they "come in." In other words, you don't attempt to place the nodes in alphabetical or any other kind of order. You simply get a piece of information, allocate a new node for it, and add that new node to the head of the list. The list grows from the root, with the first node allocated moving farther and farther away from the root with each new node allocated, like a kite being let out on the end of a string.

We can design such a list-builder very easily, and it can even perform a useful job for us. Suppose we want to build a doubly-linked list of the command-line parameters entered when a Turbo Pascal program is invoked at the DOS command line. Turbo Pascal has the **ParamCount** and **ParamStr** built-in procedures for this (see Section 10.4), but having the parameters in a linked list allows you to pass those parameters *as a list* to generalized procedures that operate on arbitrary lists of strings.

Having a doubly-linked list of the parameters would allow us to traverse the list forward or backward, processing the parameters in either order. For example, if you had this DOS command line:

```
C:\>MYPROG Fee Fie Foe Fum
```

you could process the parameters in the order "Fee, Fie, Foe, Fum" or "Fum, Foe, Fie, Fee."

The algorithm for building a non-ordered singly-linked list is best shown graphically. Figure 20.5 takes it step-by-step. Look closely at the figure and follow along with it through the following discussion. The full code for the creation of the list is in the PARAMTST.PAS program shown on pages 583–85.

BUILDING THE LIST

The singly-linked lists we worked with in the last chapter were tethered to reality through a single pointer called **Root**. Here we have to have *two* root pointers in the static data area: one to start with in traversing the list in ascending order, and another to start when traversing the list in descending order. These two root pointers are called **Ascending** and **Descending**.

The list is built from the "bottom" and grows "downward" from the bottom, by adding new nodes to the end of the existing list. This is why the **Descending** pointer acts as the working root pointer while we're building the list—we're building it from the end, and **Descending**, by definition, points to the end of the list. Note well that the first node allocated is considered the "start" node or the "head" of the list, whereas the last node allocated is considered the "end" node or the "tail" of the list.

We also need a temporary "holding" pointer called **Holder**.

The list is actually constructed in a loop. In our particular example, we use a **FOR..NEXT** loop, because we know (courtesy of **ParamCount**) exactly how many parameters need to be inserted in the list. For other applications, you may not know how many items have to be inserted into the list, so you might have to use a **WHILE** or **REPEAT** loop. The exact form of the loop doesn't matter, as long as you know when to start—and stop—the loop.

Before starting through the loop for the first time, set **Holder** to **NIL**. *This is important!* We'll use the value of **Holder** to determine when we're allocating the very first node in the list, which has to be handled a little differently from nodes allocated later.

So start the list-builder loop here: Allocate the first node in the list and load its string data: (See Figure 20.5a.)

```
New(Descending);
Descending^.StringData := ParamStr(I);
```

We've now got a record on the end of the **Descending** pointer with some data in it. That done, we need to get all the pointers pointed correctly. The first job there is to set both **Next** and **Prior** pointers of the newly-allocated record to their correct referents:

```
Descending^.Prior := Holder;
Descending^.Next  := NIL;
```

The job of **Next** and **Prior**, of course, is to point to other records in the list. The **Next** pointer at the end of the list has nothing to point to, and it signals that condition by pointing to **NIL**. Similarly, the **Prior** pointer at the *start* of the list has nothing to point to (that is, nothing is "prior" to it in the list) and it signals that condition by pointing to **NIL** as well.

When we allocate the first node on the list, that node is both the beginning and the end of the list, so both **Next** and **Prior** should point to **NIL**. **Next** is pointed to **NIL** explicitly, as is the **Next** pointer of each new record we add to the list. **Prior**, however, is assigned the value of **Holder**, a temporary pointer.

Why? **Holder**'s job throughout the creation of the list is to point to the end node of the list. It "holds" the existing list while we allocate a new node to append at the end of the list. On the first pass through the loop, there is no list on the heap, so **Holder** points to **NIL**. On later passes, **Holder** points to the end

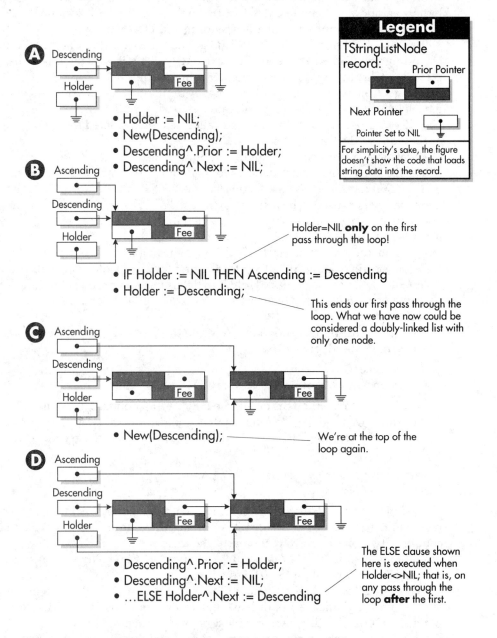

Legend

TStringListNode record:

Prior Pointer

Next Pointer

Pointer Set to NIL

For simplicity's sake, the figure doesn't show the code that loads string data into the record.

A Descending

Holder

- Holder := NIL;
- New(Descending);
- Descending^.Prior := Holder;
- Descending^.Next := NIL;

B Ascending

Descending

Holder

Holder=NIL **only** on the first pass through the loop!

- IF Holder := NIL THEN Ascending := Descending
- Holder := Descending;

This ends our first pass through the loop. What we have now could be considered a doubly-linked list with only one node.

C Ascending

Descending

Holder

- New(Descending);

We're at the top of the loop again.

D Ascending

Descending

Holder

- Descending^.Prior := Holder;
- Descending^.Next := NIL;
- ...ELSE Holder^.Next := Descending

The ELSE clause shown here is executed when Holder<>NIL; that is, on any pass through the loop **after** the first.

Figure 20.5 Building a Non-Ordered Doubly-Linked List

of the list, and that's where we want **Prior** of the new node to point. The "old" end of the list is now immediately prior to the "new" end of the list. That's why we assign **Holder** to **Prior**.

At this point, we come to the only conditional statement in the loop. The sole point of the test is to determine if this is the first node to be allocated:

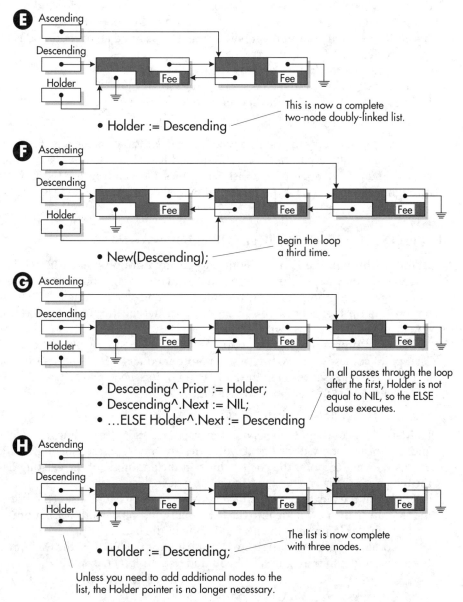

E Ascending

Descending

Holder

This is now a complete two-node doubly-linked list.

• Holder := Descending

F Ascending

Descending

Holder

Begin the loop a third time.

• New(Descending);

G Ascending

Descending

Holder

In all passes through the loop after the first, Holder is not equal to NIL, so the ELSE clause executes.

• Descending^.Prior := Holder;
• Descending^.Next := NIL;
• ...ELSE Holder^.Next := Descending

H Ascending

Descending

Holder

The list is now complete with three nodes.

• Holder := Descending;

Unless you need to add additional nodes to the list, the Holder pointer is no longer necessary.

Figure 20.5 Building a Non-Ordered Doubly-Linked List (Continued)

```
IF Holder = NIL Then Ascending := Descending
ELSE Holder^.Next := Descending;
```

We can tell if we're making our first pass through the loop because *only* on the first pass through the loop will **Holder** be equal to **NIL**. On all subsequent passes, **Holder** points to the end of the list we're building on the heap.

On the first pass through the loop, we point the **Ascending** pointer at the first node allocated. That's **Ascending**'s job: to point to that start node. And once we point it to the start node on the first pass through the loop, that's all the action **Ascending** sees. It continues to point to that start node as we add nodes onto the opposite end of the list.

We'll discuss the **ELSE** clause a little later.

The final step in our first pass through the loop (Figure 20.5b) is to update the **Holder** pointer to point to the new end node in the list:

```
Holder := Descending;
```

All the other pointers are pointing where they should, so the new record is now fully and officially a part of the doubly-linked list. Hence **Holder** is updated to hold the new end node on the list. This frees **Descending** for the next pass through the loop, when we use **Descending** to allocate another node for the loop.

THE SECOND PASS THROUGH THE LOOP

One pass through the loop is enough to create a doubly-linked list with one node, which may happen from time to time. (In our case, it may happen often—a great many programs take only a single command-line parameter.) There's no reason to stop there, however. In Figure 20.5, we go through it three times, however, and create a list with three nodes.

The second pass through the loop goes just like the first pass, up to a point. That point comes when we test to see if **Holder** equals **NIL**. On the second and all subsequent passes through the loop, **Holder** does *not* equal **NIL**, so the **ELSE** clause of the **IF** statement executes, in Figure 20.5d:

```
ELSE Holder^.Next := Descending;
```

Holder's job is to point to the end of the existing list. We're adding a new node, and that new node will be "next" after the end node on the existing list. This means we have to point the **Next** pointer in the end node of the existing list to the new node. This is what the **ELSE** clause does.

Updating the **Next** pointer in the end node of the existing list is the last step in integrating the new node into the list. Finally, just as we did the first time, we update **Holder** to point to the *new* end node in the list.

All additional passes through the loop are identical. Follow all the way through the steps shown in the figure until you understand it *thoroughly*.

TRAVERSING A DOUBLY-LINKED LIST

Traversing a doubly-linked list is really the same as traversing a singly-linked list. The difference is that you can choose which direction to go. (You also have the ability to back up if you need to.) If you start with the **Ascending** pointer, you will traverse the nodes in the list in the order that they were inserted into the list. On the other hand, if you begin traversing from the **Descending** pointer, you will traverse the list in the order *reverse* to that in which the nodes were added to the list. This code snippet traverses the list in order, beginning with the first node that was added to the list:

```
Runner := Ascending;
WHILE Runner <> NIL Do
  BEGIN
    Writeln(Runner^.StringData);
    Runner := Runner^.Next;
  END;
```

And this code snippet traverses the list in reverse order. Note the differences:

```
Runner := Descending;
WHILE Runner <> NIL Do
  BEGIN
    Writeln(Runner^.StringData);
    Runner := Runner^.Prior;
  END;
```

In the first case, you start with the **Ascending** pointer and use the **Next** pointers within the nodes; in the second, you start with the **Descending** pointer and use the **Prior** pointers within the nodes. Apart from that, the algorithm is precisely the same.

Once it all starts to make sense to you, run the PARAMTST.PAS program below and enter various command-line parameters. Watch the display after you press Enter. The parameters will be displayed first in forward order, and then in reverse order.

```
{----------------------------------------------------------------}
{                         ParamTest                              }
{                                                                }
{ Doubly-linked list demo: Creates list of command-line parms    }
{                                                                }
{                     by Jeff Duntemann                          }
{                     Turbo Pascal V7.0                          }
{                     Last update 11/24/92                       }
{                                                                }
{    From: BORLAND PASCAL FROM SQUARE ONE  by Jeff Duntemann      }
{----------------------------------------------------------------}
```

```
PROGRAM ParamTest;

TYPE
   String80 = STRING[80];
   PStringListNode = ^TStringListNode;
   TStringListNode = RECORD
                        Prior     : PStringListNode;
                        StringData : String80;
                        Next      : PStringListNode
                     END;


VAR
   I : Integer;
   Ascending,Descending,Runner,Holder : PStringListNode;


BEGIN
   Holder := NIL;  { Holder is NIL until the *second* node is created! }
   FOR I := 1 TO ParamCount DO
     BEGIN
       New(Descending);                      { Allocate a new node     }
       Descending^.StringData := ParamStr(I);{ Put data in the node    }
       Descending^.Prior := Holder;          { Point node's Prior ptr }
       Descending^.Next  := NIL;      { Next of new node is always NIL }

       { Special case: For first node, both Ascending }
       { & Descending point to the very same record:  }
       IF Holder = NIL Then Ascending := Descending
       { And for all *except* the first node, Next    }
       { is pointed to the newly allocated node:       }
         ELSE Holder^.Next := Descending;

       { Now move Holder "back" to point to the newly allocated node: }
       Holder := Descending;
     END;

   { Here we display the command-line parameters in forward order: }
   Runner := Ascending;
   WHILE Runner <> NIL Do
     BEGIN
        Writeln(Runner^.StringData);
        Runner := Runner^.Next;
     END;

   { Now we display the command-line parameters in reverse order: }
   Runner := Descending;
   WHILE Runner <> NIL Do
```

```
    BEGIN
      Writeln(Runner^.StringData);
      Runner := Runner^.Prior;
    END;


  Readln;
END.
```

20.5 A Practical Command-Line List Generator

The code shown above can come in handy if you ever need to process command-line parameters in linked list form. Why would you need to, if Turbo Pascal provides **ParamStr** and **ParamCount**? Most often you won't—but you may at some point discover you've written a text-processing routine of some sort that accepts a pointer to a linked list of strings as its input. To pass the command-line parameters to such a routine, you'll need them in the form of a list.

The unit shown below does a good job and doesn't take much code. The list of command-line parameters is built when the unit's initialization section runs, before the first statement of the main program ever executes. All you need to do is place the unit's name in your **USES** statement, and by the time your main program begins running, the command-line parameters are all ready to roll in a predefined doubly-linked list.

```
{----------------------------------------------------------------}
{                        ParamLst                                }
{                                                                }
{ Practical unit that creates linked-list of DOS command-line    }
{ parameters before program startup.                             }
{                                                                }
{                     by Jeff Duntemann                          }
{                     Turbo Pascal V7.0                          }
{                     Last update 11/24/92                       }
{                                                                }
{    From: BORLAND PASCAL FROM SQUARE ONE  by Jeff Duntemann     }
{----------------------------------------------------------------}

UNIT ParamLst;

INTERFACE

TYPE
   String80 = STRING[80];
   PStringListNode = ^TStringListNode;
   TStringListNode = RECORD
                     Prior      : PStringListNode;
                     StringData : String80;
```

```
                        Next        : PStringListNode
                    END;

    VAR
       Ascending,Descending : PStringListNode;

    IMPLEMENTATION

    VAR
       I : Integer;
       Runner,Holder : PStringListNode;

    { Everything is done in the initialization section: }

    BEGIN
       Holder := NIL; { Holder is NIL until the *second* node is created! }
       FOR I := 1 TO ParamCount DO
         BEGIN
           New(Descending);                      { Allocate a new node   }
           Descending^.StringData := ParamStr(I); { Put data in the node  }
           Descending^.Next  := Holder;          { Point node's Next ptr }
           Descending^.Prior := NIL;    { Prior of new node is always NIL }

           { Special case: For first node, both Ascending }
           { & Descending point to the very same record:  }
           IF Holder = NIL Then Ascending := Descending
           { And for all *except* the first node, Prior   }
           { is pointed to the newly allocated node:      }
             ELSE Holder^.Prior := Descending;

           { Now move Holder "back" to point to the newly allocated node: }
           Holder := Descending;
         END;
    END.
```

20.6 Ordered Doubly-Linked Lists

In the previous discussion of singly-linked lists, the process of building a list was very simple because the list was not an "ordered" list—its nodes were placed in the list as they were created without any regard for how the data in one node related to the data in any of the others. Essentially, building a non-ordered list is no more complex than inserting each node at the head of the list, rather like letting out the string of a kite.

Building an ordered list involves more overhead. For *each* insertion, the list must be traversed in order to find the correct place in the list for the inserted node. When the proper point is found, the new node is inserted at that point.

Three possible scenarios can arise in locating the proper spot for a new node: The new node can fall at the ascending end of the list, at the descending end of the list, or somewhere in the middle. The code for handling each situation is a little different.

The code for list insertion follows, and it takes into account all three scenarios. Assume that the list is to be ordered on a record field called **KeyField**. Also assume while you read the code below that the node to be inserted has been created through a pointer called **Holder**, and that **Holder^** has already been filled with data. Read the code below carefully—I'll be discussing it in detail over the next several pages.

```
Current := Ascending;
REPEAT
  IF Current^.KeyField > Holder^.KeyField THEN
     PositionFound := True ELSE PositionFound := False;
  IF NOT PositionFound THEN Current := Current^.Next
UNTIL PositionFound OR (Current = NIL);
IF PositionFound THEN { Record falls at beginning or middle }
  BEGIN
    IF Current = Ascending THEN    { Insert at the beginning }
      BEGIN
        Holder^.Next := Root;
        Current^.Prior := Holder;
        Ascending := Holder;
        Ascending^.Prior := NIL
      END
    ELSE       { Insert in the middle, right before Current^ }
      BEGIN
        Holder^.Next := Current;
        Holder^.Prior := Current^.Prior;
        Current^.Prior^.Next := Holder;
        Current^.Prior := Holder
      END
  END
ELSE                       { Record falls at the end }
  BEGIN
    Descending^.Next := Holder;
    Descending^.Next^.Prior := Descending;
    Descending := Descending^.Next;
    Descending^.Next := NIL
  END;
```

TRAVERSING TO FIND THE INSERTION POINT

The **REPEAT** statement accomplishes the traversal of the linked list. At each node in the list, the data in **Holder^** is compared to the data in **Current^**. If

Current^ is not found to be greater than **Holder^**, then the pointer **Current** is bumped to point to the next record in the list. Boolean flag **PositionFound** simply marks when the code decides that it knows where the record should go.

This traversal could apply to a singly-linked list as well as a doubly-linked list, since it is only testing in one direction. The **Prior** field of the nodes in the list has no function during traversal.

Inserting nodes into the list at any point must be done with some care. The order in which the pointers are modified is important. Changing the order could "break" the list; while doubly-linked lists are easier to mend than singly-linked lists (since there are two independent threads holding the list together), there's no sense in doing more than you have to in managing the list.

INSERTING AT THE BEGINNING OF THE LIST

Inserting a node at the beginning of the list first involves pointing **Holder^** at **Ascending^**—this places the inserted node at the head of the list. The **Prior** pointer in the node that used to be the first node in the list must be pointed "back" at the new head of the list. (Its previous value was **NIL**.) **Ascending** must now be moved so that it points to the new head of the list. This is done by assigning it **Holder**'s value. Finally, the **Prior** field of the new head record is set to **NIL**, because it now points to nothing—there is no record prior to the record at the head of the list.

APPENDING TO THE END OF THE LIST

Appending a record to the opposite end of the list is the mirror image of that process. The tail end record's **Next** pointer is pointed to the new record. The **Prior** pointer of the new end node is pointed back at the old end node. **Descending** is moved to point to the new end of the list. Finally, the **Next** field of the new end node is set to **NIL**, since there is no "next" node beyond it. (Don't just read this paragraph—relate it to the code back on page 587!)

INSERTING A NODE INTO THE MIDDLE OF THE LIST

Inserting a node into the middle of a doubly-linked list is summarized by Figure 20.6. Bullet 1 shows the situation before the insertion: A new node pointed to by **Holder** is ready for insertion. The next step, shown by bullet 2, involves pointing the **Prior** and **Next** pointers in the new node to their appropriate new target nodes in the list.

Now, at this point it might seem that the new node has somehow become attached to the list, but not so—if something happened to **Holder**, the new node would be completely inaccessible, because although it points to two other nodes in the list, nothing points to *it*. Remember that pointers are strictly a one-

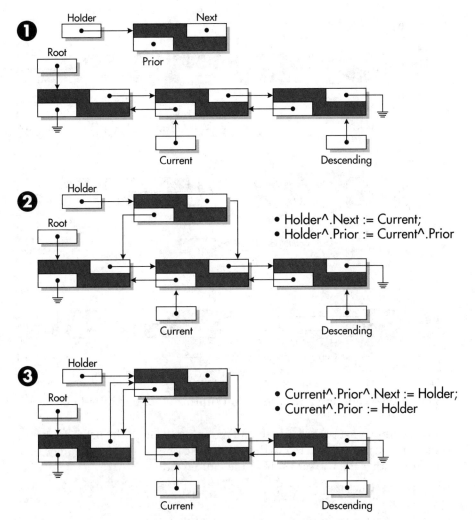

Figure 20.6 Inserting a Record into a Doubly-Linked List

way street. The referent of a pointer cannot look "back along the pointer" to identify who is pointing to it.

Bullet 3 completes the process, by repointing the two nodes (between which the new node falls) back to the new node. All in all, four nodes must be altered in order to insert the new node.

DELETING A NODE FROM A DOUBLY-LINKED LIST

The process of deleting a node from the middle of a list is considerably simpler, as shown in Figure 20.7. Two pointers are required, because deleting an entire

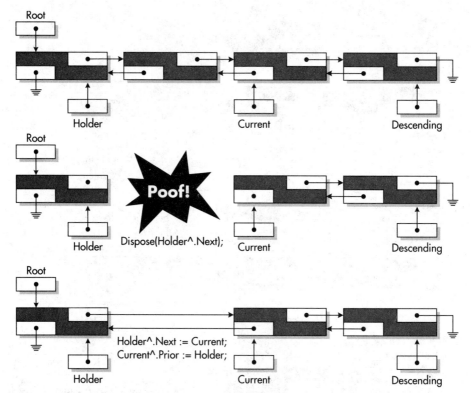

Figure 20.7 Deleting a Record from Within a Doubly-Linked List

node within a list breaks *both* threads running through the list. The space occupied by the node is deleted with the **Dispose** procedure, and it can be disposed of from either the **Current** side or the **Holder** side:

```
Dispose(Current^.Prior);
Dispose(Holder^.Next);
```

After that, "healing" the break simply involves pointing the two nodes alongside the break to one another:

```
Holder^.Next  := Current;
Current^.Prior := Holder;
```

20.7 Creating a List of Directory Entries

The addition of late binding and polymorphism to the Turbo Pascal language spec has some interesting consequences for the creation of linked lists. In fact, Turbo Pascal 5.5 introduced a standard list object that works polymorphically and can contain *any* kind of object—not just one single type, as we've been assuming thus far. However, before you can understand that sort of mystical magical list management, you had better have a solid grasp on the way it was done up until the age of objects. In the meantime, let's build a very useful tool around an ordered doubly-linked list.

Procedure **GetDirectory** returns two pointers to a doubly-linked list of directory entries matching a given filespec. The two pointers are again called **Ascending** and **Descending**.

The full search spec, including the path and disk specifier, is passed to **GetDirectory** in parameter **FileSpec**. As with any use of DOS's FIND FIRST/FIND NEXT function call sequence (see Chapter 19), the search spec must be assembled into an ASCIIZ string, and the string's address loaded into registers DS and DX. The attribute byte is also set, but by choice we're intending to read every kind of file except for the volume label: hidden files, system files, subdirectories, and of course ordinary DOS data files. Taken together, the hidden file bit, the system file bit, and the subdirectory bit, represent a binary value of $16, which is passed to DOS in register CL.

If DOS error messages 2 or 18 are returned by FIND FIRST, the directory is empty, and both **Ascending** and **Descending** are returned with a value of **NIL**. Otherwise, a new **DIRRec** record is created as the root of the new list, and filled with information returned by DOS in the DTA. Repeated calls by FIND NEXT will read the remainder of the directory, until an error message indicates that there are no further entries to be read. As each directory entry is read, **GetDirectory** adds the entry to the doubly-linked list it is building.

GetDirectory offers two different ways to build the list: in the order the directory entries physically appear on the disk, or in sorted order by file name or last-modified time and date. The caller's preference is passed to **GetDirectory** in Boolean parameter **Sorted**. If sorted order is selected (**Sorted** set to **True**), there is the further choice of sorting the list on either the name of the file or subdirectory (**SortOnName = True**), or on the time and date of last modification (**SortOnName = False**).

Determining which of two string records is greater than another in alphanumeric sort order is simple: They can be compared via Pascal's Boolean operators. Determining which of two time/date combinations is the earlier is a little trickier, even with the time and date present as single-word quantities in variables **TimeComp** and **DateComp**. If the "left" date is greater than the "right" date, then the time does not have to be taken into account, but if the dates are equal then the time stamps must also be compared. To aid the readability of the procedure, this process was set off in a short function called **LaterThan**, which accepts pointers to **DIRRecs** and returns a Boolean value of **TRUE** if the left entry is greater than the right entry as passed in the parameter line.

The logic of adding a record to the list is very close to the code example given on page 587, with some additional conditional logic to allow ordering the list on either the name or the time/date fields. Read the code example on page 587, and compare it to the actual code for **GetDirectory**.

```
{-------------------------------------------------------------------}
{                          DirStuff                                 }
{                                                                   }
{ Practical unit that creates linked-list of DOS directory          }
{ entries, including expanded time and date string formats.         }
{                                                                   }
{                     by Jeff Duntemann                             }
{                     Borland Pascal V7.0                           }
{                     Last update 11/24/92                          }
{                                                                   }
{   From: BORLAND PASCAL FROM SQUARE ONE   by Jeff Duntemann        }
{-------------------------------------------------------------------}

UNIT DirStuff;

INTERFACE

USES DOS;

TYPE
   String15 = STRING[15];
   String80 = STRING[80];

   DateRec = RECORD
                DateComp         : Word;
                LongDateString   : String80;
                DateString       : String80;
                Year,Month,Day   : Integer;
                DayOfWeek        : Integer
             END;

   TimeRec = RECORD
                TimeComp   : Word;           { DOS time stamp format }
                TimeString : String80;
                PM         : Boolean;
                Hours,Minutes,Seconds,Hundredths : Integer
             END;

   DIRPtr = ^DIRRec;
   DIRRec = RECORD
                FileName  : String15;
                Attrib    : Byte;
                FileSize  : LongInt;
                TimeStamp : TimeRec;
                DateStamp : DateRec;
                Prior     : DIRPtr;
                Next      : DIRPtr;
             END;
```

```
PROCEDURE CalcDate(VAR ThisDate : DateRec);

FUNCTION  CalcDayOfWeek(Year,Month,Day : Integer) : Integer;

PROCEDURE CalcTime(VAR ThisTime : TimeRec);

FUNCTION  DIRToString(InputDIR : DIRRec) : String;

PROCEDURE DTAtoDIR(VAR OutRec : DIRRec);

PROCEDURE GetDirectory(Filespec    : String80;
                       Sorted      : Boolean;
                       SortOnName  : Boolean;
                       VAR Ascending  : DIRPtr;
                       VAR Descending : DIRPtr);


IMPLEMENTATION

{ This routine is here simply to give a mathematically-correct MOD  }
{ routine to the Zeller's congruence algorithm in CalcDayOfWeek.    }

FUNCTION Modulus(X,Y : Integer) : Integer;

VAR
  R : Real;

BEGIN
  R := X/Y;
  IF R < 0 THEN
    Modulus := X-(Y*Trunc(R-1))
  ELSE
    Modulus := X-(Y*Trunc(R));
END;


{->>>>CalcDayOfWeek<<<<----------------------------------------------}
{                                                                    }
{ Last Modified 11/24/92                                             }
{                                                                    }
{ This routine returns an integer value indicating the day of        }
{ the the week, given the year, the month, and the day.  The         }
{ algorithm is Zeller's Congruence, for which I thank Hugh           }
{ Kenner of the University of Georgia, who graciously                }
{ translated the gist of Zeller's original 1887 paper for me!        }
{                                                                    }
{   From: BORLAND PASCAL FROM SQUARE ONE  by Jeff Duntemann          }
{--------------------------------------------------------------------}
```

```
FUNCTION CalcDayOfWeek(Year,Month,Day : Integer) : Integer;

VAR
  Century,Holder : Integer;

BEGIN
  { First test for error conditions on input values: }
  IF (Year < 0)  OR
     (Month < 1) OR (Month > 12) OR
     (Day < 1)   OR (Day > 31) THEN
     CalcDayOfWeek := -1  { Return -1 to indicate an error }
  ELSE
    { Do the Zeller's Congruence calculation as Zeller himself }
    { described it in "Acta Mathematica" #7, Stockholm, 1887.  }
    BEGIN
      { First we separate out the year and the century figures: }
      Century := Year DIV 100;
      Year    := Year MOD 100;
      { Next we adjust the month such that March remains month #3, }
      {  but that January and February are months #13 and #14,     }
      {  *but of the previous year*: }
      IF Month < 3 THEN
        BEGIN
          Inc(Month,12);
          IF Year > 0 THEN Dec(Year,1)      { The year before 2000 is }
            ELSE                            { 1999, not 20-1...       }
              BEGIN
                Year := 99;
                Dec(Century);
              END
        END;

      { Here's Zeller's seminal black magic: }
      Holder := Day;                     { Start with the day of month }
      Holder := Holder + (((Month+1) * 26) DIV 10); { Calc increment }
      Holder := Holder + Year;                       { Add in the year }
      Holder := Holder + (Year DIV 4);     { Correct for leap years  }
      Holder := Holder + (Century DIV 4); { Correct for century years }
      Holder := Holder - Century - Century;

      Holder := Modulus(Holder,7);             { Take Holder modulus 7 }

      { Here we "wrap" Saturday around to be the last day: }
      IF Holder  = 0 THEN Holder := 7;

      { Zeller kept the Sunday = 1 origin; computer weenies prefer to }
      { start everything with 0, so here's a 20th century kludge:     }
```

```
        Dec(Holder);

        CalcDayOfWeek := Holder;  { Return the end product! }
      END;
  END;
END;


{->>>>CalcDate<<<<---------------------------------------------}
{                                                             }
{ Filename: CALCDATE.SRC - Last Modified 7/11/88              }
{                                                             }
{ This routine fills in the DateString, LongDateString, and   }
{ DateComp fields of the DateRec record passed to it.  It     }
{ requires that the Year, Month, and Day fields be valid on   }
{ entry.  It also requires prior definition of types DateRec  }
{ and String80.  DateString is formatted this way:            }
{                                                             }
{    7/17/86                                                  }
{                                                             }
{ LongDateString is formatted this way:                       }
{                                                             }
{    Wednesday, July 17, 1986                                 }
{                                                             }
{ DayOfWeek is a code from 0-6, with 0 = Sunday.              }
{ DateComp is a cardinal generated by the formula:            }
{                                                             }
{    DateComp = (Year-1980)*512 + (Month*32) + Day            }
{                                                             }
{ It is used for comparing two dates to determine which is    }
{ earlier, and is the same format used in the date stamp in   }
{ DOS directory entries.                                      }
{                                                             }
{   From: BORLAND PASCAL FROM SQUARE ONE  by Jeff Duntemann   }
{-------------------------------------------------------------}

PROCEDURE CalcDate(VAR ThisDate : DateRec);

TYPE
  String9 = String[9];

CONST
  MonthTags : ARRAY [1..12] of String9 =
      ('January','February','March','April','May','June','July',
       'August','September','October','November','December');
  DayTags   : ARRAY [0..6] OF String9 =
      ('Sunday','Monday','Tuesday','Wednesday',
       'Thursday','Friday','Saturday');
```

```
VAR
  Temp1 : String80;

BEGIN
  WITH ThisDate DO
    BEGIN
      DayOfWeek := CalcDayOfWeek(Year,Month,Day);
      Str(Month,DateString);
      Str(Day,Temp1);
      DateString := DateString + '/' + Temp1;
      LongDateString := DayTags[DayOfWeek] + ', ';
      LongDateString := LongDateString +
        MonthTags[Month] + ' ' + Temp1 + ', ';
      Str(Year,Temp1);
      LongDateString := LongDateString + Temp1;
      DateString := DateString + '/' + Copy(Temp1,3,2);
      DateComp := (Year - 1980) * 512 + (Month * 32) + Day
    END
END;



{->>>>CalcTime<<<<---------------------------------------------}
{                                                               }
{ Last Modified 11/24/92                                        }
{                                                               }
{ This routine "fills out" a TimeRec passed to it with only     }
{ the DOS time values (hours, minutes, seconds, hundredths)     }
{ valid.  It generates the TimeComp and TimeString fields.      }
{ which, of course, also require definition of type String80.   }
{                                                               }
{   From: BORLAND PASCAL FROM SQUARE ONE   by Jeff Duntemann    }
{---------------------------------------------------------------}

PROCEDURE CalcTime(VAR ThisTime : TimeRec);

TYPE
  String5 = String[5];

VAR
  Temp1,Temp2 : String5;
  AMPM        : Char;
  I           : Integer;

BEGIN
  WITH ThisTime DO
    BEGIN
      I := Hours;
```

```
        IF Hours = 0 THEN I := 12;   { "0" hours = 12am }
        IF Hours > 12 THEN I := Hours - 12;
        IF Hours > 11 THEN AMPM := 'p' ELSE AMPM := 'a';
        Str(I:2,Temp1); Str(Minutes,Temp2);
        IF Length(Temp2) < 2 THEN Temp2 := '0' + Temp2;
        TimeString := Temp1 + ':' + Temp2 + AMPM;
        TimeComp :=
          (Hours SHL 11) OR (Minutes SHL 5) OR (Seconds SHR 1)
      END
END;



{->>>>DIRToString<<<<----------------------------------------------}
{                                                                  }
{ Last Modified 11/24/92                                           }
{                                                                  }
{ This routine returns a String value containing all the          }
{ significant information from a directory record, formatted       }
{ in a fashion similar to that used by the DOS DIR command        }
{ when it displays a file and its information.  A typical          }
{ string returned by DIRToString would look like this:            }
{                                                                  }
{       DIRSTRIN.BAK 1697  01/07/87   3:04p                        }
{                                                                  }
{ Type DIRRec must be predefined.                                 }
{                                                                  }
{   From: BORLAND PASCAL FROM SQUARE ONE   by Jeff Duntemann      }
{------------------------------------------------------------------}


FUNCTION DIRToString(InputDIR : DIRRec) : String;

CONST
  Blanker = '                                   ';

VAR
  Temp,WorkString : String80;
  DotPos : Integer;

BEGIN
  WITH InputDIR DO
    BEGIN
      Temp := '                                 ';
        {If the entry has the directory attribute, format differently: }
        IF (Attrib AND $10) <> 0 THEN { Bit 4 is the directory attribute }
          BEGIN
            Insert(FileName,Temp,1);{ No extensions on subdirectory names }
            Insert('<DIR>',Temp,14) { Tell the world it's a subdirectory }
```

```
                END
              ELSE
                {This compound statement separates the file from its extension  }
                { and converts the file size to a string.  Note that we did not }
                { insert a file size figure into Temp for subdirectory entries. }
                BEGIN
                  DotPos := Pos('.',FileName);
                  IF DotPos > 0 THEN  { File name has an extension }
                    WorkString := Copy(FileName,1,DotPos-1) +
                      Copy(Blanker,1,9-DotPos) + '.' +
                        Copy(FileName,DotPos+1,Length(FileName)-DotPos)
                  ELSE
                    WorkString := FileName +
                                    Copy(Blanker,1,8-Length(FileName)) + '.';
                  Insert(WorkString,Temp,1);
                  Str(FileSize:7,WorkString);
                  Insert(WorkString,Temp,15)
                END;
            WITH DateStamp DO
              BEGIN
                { This is what it takes to assemble three separate integer  }
                { figures for month, day, and year into a string equivalent.}
                IF Month < 10 THEN Insert('0',DateString,1);
                IF Day < 10 THEN Insert('0',DateString,4);
                Insert(DateString,Temp,24);
              END;
            Insert(TimeStamp.TimeString,Temp,34); { Finally, insert the time }
          END;
        Delete(Temp,42,Length(Temp)-42);
        DIRToString := Temp
      END;


{->>>>DTAtoDIR<<<<---------------------------------------------------}
{                                                                    }
{ Last modified 11/8/87                                              }
{                                                                    }
{ This procedure converts data as returned by DOS FIND               }
{ calls $4E & $4F in the Disk Transfer Area (DTA) to a more          }
{ tractable form as defined by my own record type DIRRec.            }
{ This involves converting the time from a word timestamp to         }
{ a TimeRec, and the date from a word datestamp to a DateRec.        }
{                                                                    }
{ DTAToDIR requires the prior definition of types DIRRec,            }
{ and DIRPtr, and procedures CalcTime and CalcDate.                  }
{                                                                    }
```

```pascal
{   From: BORLAND PASCAL FROM SQUARE ONE  by Jeff Duntemann     }
{--------------------------------------------------------------}


PROCEDURE DTAtoDIR(VAR OutRec : DIRRec);

TYPE
  DTAPtr      = ^SearchRec;

VAR
  DTData      : DateTime;    { This type imported from DOS unit }
  I           : Integer;
  InRec       : SearchRec;   { Also imported from the DOS unit  }
  RegPack     : Registers;   { Also imported from the DOS unit  }
  CurrentDTA  : DTAPtr;

BEGIN
  RegPack.AX := $2F00; { Find current location of DTA }
  MSDOS(RegPack);
  WITH RegPack DO CurrentDTA := Ptr(ES,BX);
  InRec := CurrentDTA^;
  UnpackTime(InRec.Time,DTData);
  WITH OutRec DO                 { Now extract and reformat data }
    BEGIN
      FileName := InRec.Name; { Extract the file name }
      Attrib := InRec.Attr;   { Extract the attribute field }
      WITH TimeStamp DO       { Expand integer time stamp }
        BEGIN
          TimeComp := InRec.Time SHR 16;
          Hours := DTData.Hour;
          Minutes := DTData.Min;
          Seconds := DTData.Sec;
          Hundredths := 0;
        END;
      CalcTime(TimeStamp);    { Fill in the other time fields }
      WITH DateStamp DO       { Expand integer date stamp }
        BEGIN
          DateComp := InRec.Time AND $0000FFFF;
          Day := DTData.Day;
          Month := DTData.Month;
          Year  := DTData.Year;
        END;
      CalcDate(DateStamp);    { Fill in the other date fields }
      FileSize := InRec.Size;
      Next := NIL;                { Initialize the "next" pointer }
      Prior := NIL;              { Ditto the "prior" pointer }
    END
END; { DTAtoDIR }
```

```
{->>>>GetDirectory<<<<-------------------------------------------}
{                                                                 }
{ Filename: GETDIR.SRC - Last modified 7/2/88                     }
{                                                                 }
{ This routine returns a pointer to a linked list of type         }
{ DIRRec, which must have been previously defined this way,       }
{ along with pointer type DIRPtr to point to it:                  }
{                                                                 }
{ DIRPtr = ^DIRRec;                                               }
{ DIRRec = RECORD                                                 }
{               FileName  : String15;                             }
{               Attrib    : Byte;                                 }
{               FileSize  : LongInt;                              }
{               TimeStamp : TimeRec;                              }
{               DateStamp : DateRec;                              }
{               Prior     : DIRPtr;                               }
{               Next      : DIRPtr;                               }
{          END;                                                   }
{                                                                 }
{ The linked list will contain a record for every file in the     }
{ current directory.  Since the linked list is out in heap,       }
{ your directory data takes up NO space in your data segment.     }
{ If there are no files in the current directory, the pointer     }
{ returned is equal to NIL.                                       }
{                                                                 }
{ The types TimeRec and DateRec must be defined prior to using    }
{ GetDirectory.  String80 & DTAToDIR must be defined as well.     }
{                                                                 }
{   From: BORLAND PASCAL FROM SQUARE ONE   by Jeff Duntemann      }
{-----------------------------------------------------------------}


PROCEDURE GetDirectory(Filespec    : String80;
                       Sorted      : Boolean;
                       SortOnName  : Boolean;
                       VAR Ascending  : DIRPtr;
                       VAR Descending : DIRPtr);

TYPE
   String9 = String[9];

VAR
   I          : Integer;
   FindError  : Integer;
   Regs       : Registers;
   OurDTA     : SearchRec;
   Root       : DIRPtr;
```

```
      Current    : DIRPtr;
      Last       : DIRPtr;
      Holder     : DIRPtr;
      PositionFound : Boolean;



FUNCTION LaterThan(LeftEntry,RightEntry : DirPtr) : Boolean;

BEGIN
   IF LeftEntry^.DateStamp.DateComp > RightEntry^.DateStamp.DateComp
THEN
      LaterThan := True
   ELSE
      IF (LeftEntry^.DateStamp.DateComp = RightEntry^.DateStamp.DateComp)
         AND
         (LeftEntry^.TimeStamp.TimeComp > RightEntry^.TimeStamp.TimeComp)
      THEN LaterThan := True
      ELSE LaterThan := False
END;



PROCEDURE AppendToEnd(VAR Holder,Descending : DIRPtr);

BEGIN
   Descending^.Next := Holder;    { Add record to end of list }
   Descending^.Next^.Prior := Descending; { Set reverse pointer }
   Descending := Descending^.Next;   { Bump Current to next record }
END;



BEGIN  { GetDir }
   FindFirst(FileSpec,$16,OurDTA);      { Make FIND FIRST DOS call... }
   FindError := DOSError;
   IF FindError = 2 THEN  { No files found to match FileSpec }
      BEGIN
         Ascending := NIL;    { Both linked list pointers are NIL }
         Descending := NIL
      END
   ELSE                  { There was at least one file found, so... }
      BEGIN
         New(Root);            { Create a record for the first find }
         DTAtoDIR(Root^);      { Convert first find to DIR format }
         Current := Root;      { The current record is now the root }
         Descending := Root;   { And also the last record in the list! }
         IF FindError <> 18 THEN
```

```
REPEAT
  FindNext(OurDTA);          { Make FIND NEXT DOS call }
  FindError := DOSError;
  IF FindError <> 18 THEN { More entries exist }
    BEGIN
      New(Holder);  { Create a record with temporary pointer }
      DTAtoDIR(Holder^); { Convert additional finds to DIR format }
      { Sorted and unsorted lists are constructed differently. }
      { If we're building a sorted list we have to scan it for }
      { each entry to find the proper place in the list.  For  }
      { unsorted lists we just hang the latest found entry on   }
      { the end of the list and bump Current to the Next. }
      IF Sorted THEN
        BEGIN
          Current := Root;{ Traverse list to find insert spot: }
          REPEAT
            IF SortOnName THEN    { To sort list on file name }
              IF Current^.FileName > Holder^.FileName THEN
                PositionFound := True ELSE PositionFound := False
            ELSE                      { To sort list by time/date }
              IF LaterThan(Current,Holder) THEN
                PositionFound := True ELSE PositionFound := False;
            IF NOT PositionFound THEN
              Current := Current^.Next;  { Bump to next item }
          UNTIL (Current = NIL) OR PositionFound;
          { When PositionFound becomes True, the record needs }
          { to be inserted in the list BEFORE Current^- }
          { This needs to be done differently if Current^ is }
          { at the head of the list. (i.e., Current = Root)}
          IF PositionFound THEN  { Insert at beginning... }
            BEGIN            { ...or in the middle somewhere }
              { NOTE:  DO NOT change the order of the }
              { pointer assignments in the following }
              { IF/THEN/ELSE statement!! }
              IF Current = Root THEN  { Insert at beginning }
                BEGIN
                  Holder^.Next := Root;
                  Current^.Prior := Holder;
                  Root := Holder;
                END
              ELSE    { Insert in the middle: }
                BEGIN
                  Holder^.Next  := Current;
                  Holder^.Prior := Current^.Prior;
                  Current^.Prior^.Next := Holder;
```

```
                              Current^.Prior := Holder
                    END
                END
              ELSE
              { The new record belongs at the end of the list }
                AppendToEnd(Holder,Descending)
            END
          ELSE
          { If no sort, we add the record to the end of the list: }
            AppendToEnd(Holder,Descending)
        END
      UNTIL FindError = 18;
    Ascending := Root
  END
END;  {GetDirectory}


END.  {DirStuff}
```

A FILE SIZE TALLY UTILITY

As a practical example of **GetDirectory** in use, let me present **Spacer,** a utility that does something that DOS DIR did not do until version 5: present a tally of the sizes of the displayed files. (Did it have to take 10 years?) Many times I've had to clear out a couple of megabytes from a 70-megabyte hard disk (which always seems to stay stuck at 62 megabytes full, no matter what I do!) and I have had to become a good eyeball estimator of the space I'll save if I just do an ERASE *.BAK or something along those lines. **Spacer** eliminates the guesswork. To find out the space taken up in the current directory by backup files (or any other kind of files you specify) type:

```
C:\> SPACER *.BAK

LOCATE   .BAK     11503   01/14/93    11:15a
DIRSTRIN.BAK      2623    01/13/93     7:53p
SPACER   .BAK     6055    01/14/93     9:33a
GETDIR   .BAK     8595    01/14/93     9:31a
DTEST    .BAK     5328    01/15/93     5:54p
DISPDIR .BAK       443    01/15/93     5:59p
DTATODIR.BAK      2701    01/13/93    11:18a

Total space occupied by these files is     37248 bytes.
```

Spacer works by generating a doubly-linked list of the requested files, using **GetDirectory**. It then displays the list, keeping a running total of the sizes of the files as it displays them. When the display has been completed, **Spacer** adds an additional line giving the total number of bytes of disk space occupied by the files whose names have just been displayed.

At first glance, you might wonder why a linked list needs to be built at all. Why couldn't you just add a little code to keep a running tally of files displayed from **Locate**? Well, of course, you could—but when you display 'em as you find 'em, you lose the ability to display them sorted by name or by last-modified time and date. You can only display them in the order that the directory entries physically appear on the disk. To display them in some order *other* than their physical order on the disk, you need a linked list, and to offer the choice of displaying them either in ascending or descending order by your chosen sort field, you need a *doubly*-linked list.

```
{------------------------------------------------------------------}
{                             Spacer                               }
{                                                                  }
{              Directory lister with file size tally               }
{                                                                  }
{                        by Jeff Duntemann                         }
{                        BORLAND PASCAL 7.00                        }
{                        Last update 11/24/92                      }
{                                                                  }
{    From: BORLAND PASCAL FROM SQUARE ONE  by Jeff Duntemann       }
{------------------------------------------------------------------}

PROGRAM Spacer;

USES DOS,              { Standard Borland unit }
     DirStuff;         { My collection of directory machinery }

CONST
  SortByName = True;
  SortByDate = False;

TYPE
  String80 = String[80];
  String15 = String[15];
  DTAPtr   = ^SearchRec;

VAR
  Parms      : Byte;
  SpaceTaken : Real;
  RunUp      : DIRPtr;
  RunDown    : DIRPtr;
  Current    : DIRPtr;
  FileSpec   : String80;
  WorkString : String80;
  Sorted     : Boolean;
  SortSpec   : Boolean;
```

```pascal
  Ascending  : Boolean;
  I          : Integer;

BEGIN
  Sorted := False;                { Set default values }
  SortSpec := SortByName;
  Ascending := True;
  Parms := ORD(ParamCount);   { Convert parm count to ordinal value }
  CASE Parms OF
    0 :
    BEGIN
      Writeln('>>SPACER<<  V3.00  By Jeff Duntemann');
      Writeln
      ('                  From the book, BORLAND PASCAL FROM SQUARE ONE');
      Writeln;
      Writeln
      ('This program displays ALL files matching a given filespec.');
      Writeln('Hidden and system files are not immune.');
      Writeln
      ('Additionally, it will add up the cumulative file sizes of');
      Writeln
      ('the files matching the filespec, so you can tell how much');
      Writeln
      ('space files in a given subdirectory subtend, or how much');
      Writeln('space you have invested in .PAS files, and so on.');
      Writeln;
      Writeln('CALLING SYNTAX:');
      Writeln;
      Writeln('SPACER <filespec> N|D A|D');
      Writeln;
      Writeln
      ('where <filespec> is a legal DOS filespec, including wildcards.');
      Writeln('The second parameter is either N or D:');
      Writeln('N indicates sort by file name;');
      Writeln('D indicates sort by time and date stamp.');
      Writeln
      ('If not given, entries are displayed in physical order.');
      Writeln;
      Writeln('The third parameter is either A or D:');
      Writeln('A indicates ascending order of display;');
      Writeln('D indicates descending order of display.');
      Writeln('If not given, sort is ascending.');
      Writeln;
      Writeln('For example:');
      Writeln;
      Writeln('SPACER *.PAS N');
```

```
      Writeln('  will display all files with the .PAS extension,');
      Writeln('  in ascending sorted order by file name.  Or,');
      Writeln;
      Writeln('SPACER *.PAS D D');
      Writeln('  will display all files with the .PAS extension,');
      Writeln('  in descending order by last-modification date.');
      Halt;
    END;
  1 : FileSpec := ParamStr(1);
  2 : BEGIN
        Sorted := True;
        FileSpec := ParamStr(1);
        WorkString := ParamStr(2);
        CASE UpCase(WorkString[1]) OF
          'D' : SortSpec := SortByDate;
          'N' : SortSpec := SortByName;
          ELSE Sorted := False
        END
      END;
  3 : BEGIN
        Sorted := True;
        FileSpec := ParamStr(1);
        WorkString := ParamStr(2);
        CASE UpCase(WorkString[1]) OF
          'D' : SortSpec := SortByDate;
          'N' : SortSpec := SortByName;
          ELSE Sorted := False
        END;
        IF Sorted THEN
          BEGIN
            WorkString := ParamStr(3);
            CASE UpCase(WorkString[1]) OF
              'A' : Ascending := True;
              'D' : Ascending := False;
              ELSE Ascending := True
            END
          END
      END;
END; { CASE }
{ Now we actually go out and build a linked list of directory entries, }
{ based on the parms we have parsed out of the command line: }
 GetDirectory(FileSpec,Sorted,SortSpec,RunUp,RunDown);
IF Ascending THEN Current := RunUp
  ELSE Current := RunDown;
IF Current = NIL THEN Writeln('No files found.')
  ELSE
```

```
        BEGIN
          SpaceTaken := 0.0;
          IF Ascending THEN
            WHILE Current <> NIL DO
              BEGIN
                Writeln(DirToString(Current^));
                SpaceTaken := SpaceTaken + Current^.FileSize;
                Current := Current^.Next
              END
          ELSE
            WHILE Current <> NIL DO
              BEGIN
                Writeln(DirToString(Current^));
                SpaceTaken := SpaceTaken + Current^.FileSize;
                Current := Current^.Prior
              END;
          Writeln;
          Writeln
          ('Total space occupied by these files is ',
            SpaceTaken:9:0,' bytes.');
        END
    END.
```

One trick to keep in mind in using **Spacer** is that it sends its output to the DOS standard output device, allowing output redirection. You can take **Spacer**'s files list and send it to a disk file instead of to the screen:

```
C:\>SPACER *.PAS > PASFILES.DIR
```

This command creates a text file named **PASFILES.DIR** and writes the exact same text output to the file that you would ordinarily see on the screen.

DISPOSING OF A LIST OF DIRECTORY ENTRIES

The lists of directory entries created by **GetDirectory** exist on the heap, and take up heapspace. For utilities like **Spacer** this is not especially important, since the utility creates the linked list, displays it, and then returns to DOS. For more complicated applications that need to reuse heapspace, some method of disposing of the directory lists is required.

Such a routine, by this time, should almost seem trivial. Singly- and doubly-linked lists can be disposed of in nearly identical fashion, since only one thread is required to tether the list while the rootmost entry is disposed of. Procedure **DisposeOfDirectory** will do the job quickly and safely.

```
{->>>>DisposeOfDirectory<<<<-------------------------------------}
{                                                                }
{ Filename : DISPDIR.SRC - Last Modified 11/26/92                }
{                                                                }
```

```
{ This routine disposes of lists of DIRRec records as built by }
{ GetDirectory.  Type DIRRec and DIRPtr must be defined prior  }
{ to its inclusion.                                            }
{                                                              }
{    From: BORLAND PASCAL FROM SQUARE ONE by Jeff Duntemann    }
{--------------------------------------------------------------}

PROCEDURE DisposeOfDirectory(RootPointer : DIRPtr);

VAR
  Holder : DIRPtr;

BEGIN
  IF RootPointer <> NIL THEN     { Can't dispose if no list! }
  REPEAT
    Holder := RootPointer^.Next; { Grab the next record. }
    Dispose(RootPointer);        { Dispose of the first... }
    RootPointer := Holder        { ...and make the next the first... }
  UNTIL RootPointer = NIL        { ...until the list is all gone. }
END;
```

Chapter 21

Project Management

WORKING SMART WITH MAKE AND BUILD

I have said in many places that a computer language is a tool for managing complexity. Hiding the details of a process behind a procedure or function name allow you to think of that process as an integral whole without being distracted by internal details that implement the process. By choosing what details to hide and what details to reveal at what level in a program design, you can read that program at any level without being overwhelmed by details belonging to the next level up or down.

There is a second kind of complexity in computer programming, and that is the logistical complexity of implementing a very large software project that cannot be compiled as a single monolithic source code file. As soon as you must divide a program into parts, the number of individual files to be tended to explodes, since for every part of the program there will be a source code file, an object code file, a .BAK backup file, and (optionally) a .TPM file.

Keeping track of these files is what Turbo Pascal's project management features were created to do.

21.1 Integral Make and Build

Splitting off portions of a program into separately-compiled units is best done along functional lines. For example, a massive accounting program might have four major functions: accounts payable, accounts receivable, payroll, and budget. Putting each of the four major functions in a unit makes for a small, easily-understood main program and manageable modules for the four functions. Another advantage to breaking down the program this way is that the four major functional units may be specified as overlays (see Section 13.5) to reduce the memory requirements of the program as a whole.

Another reason for separate compilation is to move libraries of generally-useful procedures and functions into their own units, where they may be accessed in a compiled state and not recompiled each and every time the program as a whole is compiled, but only when one of the routines is itself actually changed.

THE BUILD FEATURE

The accounting program example is shown in Figure 21.1. Six utility libraries named **A, B, C, D, E,** and **F** are variously shared by the four functional units, **Payable, Receivable, Payroll,** and **Budget**. The arrows indicate visually which units use what other units. These relationships between units are called *dependencies*.

By the way the Turbo Pascal compiler works, the **USE**-er cannot be compiled until after the **USE**-ee is compiled. This implies a definite order in which the various units must be compiled if you choose to compile them all at one time. This order is reflected in Figure 21.1 by the units' position relative to the top of the figure. Unit **C** is the first to be compiled because unit **A** depends on unit **C**, and unit **Payable** depends on unit **A**. When compiling, the compiler threads its way down through this *dependency chain* until it reaches bottom, and then it

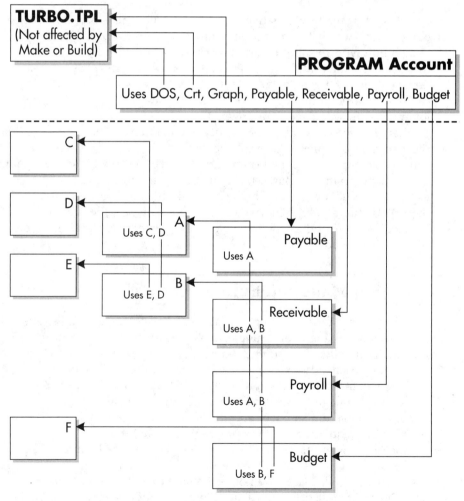

Figure 21.1 Compile Order in a Build Operation

climbs back out, compiling as it goes. Only after all the units are compiled is main program **Account** compiled.

This operation, of compiling all compilands (a *compiland* is any compilable source file, either unit or main program) contained in the program is called a *build*. You can initiate a build operation by selecting the **B**uild item on the Compile menu.

A build will look for the source code for any unit used by the program and attempt to compile it. You can perform a build on a program even if you don't have the source code for all the units; the BGI and Turbo Vision are good examples, along with any units in TURBO.TPL. Even if you have the source code for units residing in TURBO.TPL, you can't "re-build" TURBO.TPL just by recompiling the source for TURBO.TPL units. For source code changes to TURBO.TPL units to take effect, you must extract the unit from TURBO.TPL first, and then do the build.

THE MAKE FEATURE

A build is very much what Turbo Pascal 3.0 did every time you pressed "C": It compiled every line of source code in the entire program, regardless of what parts of the program had been changed since the last compile. Compiling every-thing every time is wasteful and unnecessary, and can be avoided by using Turbo Pascal's *integral Make* feature.

A *make* is a selective build. The Turbo Pascal compiler inspects the files in the dependency chain, and recompiles only those parts of the program that need compiling.

What does the compiler check? Primarily DOS *time stamps*; that is, the fields in every file's directory entry that indicate when the file was last modified. If a compiland's source code file was modifed more recently than its object code file (that is, its unit file), that means that you've made changes to the source code file since the last time the file was compiled. The object code file does not reflect those changes, and therefore must be recompiled.

If, on the other hand, the object code file is *newer* than the source code file, it means no changes have been made to the source code file since the last time it was compiled, and the object code file is therefore up-to-date and in no need of recompilation. Be careful when you restore unit source code files from backups. The compiler won't notice that the source code has changed if the "last-modified" date on the source code file is older than the compiled .TPU. If you restore source code from a backup copy, "touch" each source file with a touch utility (I present one in Section 19.6) or simply perform a build instead of a make, so that all available unit source code files will be recompiled.

The compiler makes this check individually on every unit file down the dependency chain from the primary file. It recompiles any file whose .TPU file is older than its source file. Note that in *any* make operation, the primary file is *always* compiled, whether or not its object code file is up-to-date.

Making sure every object code file is up-to-date with respect to its source code file is necessary, but it isn't enough. The second check the compiler makes as it moves along the dependency chain is that the interface part of any unit is older than the object code file of anything that uses it. This is much more subtle and will take some additional explanation.

Figure 21.2 will help. We have two units along a time line, with the dots on the time line marking the points at which each file was last modified. "Later" is to the right. Both units are up-to-date individually, in that FOO.TPU is later than FOO.PAS, and BAR.TPU is later than BAR.PAS. *However*, unit **Foo** uses unit **Bar**. Changes may have been made to BAR.PAS after the last time that FOO.PAS was compiled. These changes could invalidate the interface between the two units.

For example, unit **Bar** could contain a procedure **Crunchit**, originally defined this way:

```
PROCEDURE Crunchit(InVal,OutVal : Integer);
```

Unit **Foo** would have been compiled to use procedure **Crunchit** as defined above. Then, BAR.PAS could have been modified after **Foo** was last compiled, to add an additional parameter:

```
PROCEDURE Crunchit(InVal,OutVal,ErrVal : Integer);
```

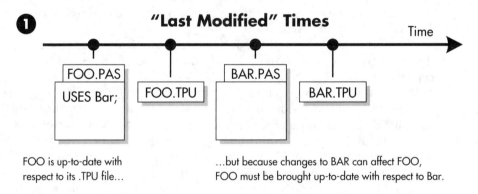

FOO is up-to-date with respect to its .TPU file...

...but because changes to BAR can affect FOO, FOO must be brought up-to-date with respect to Bar.

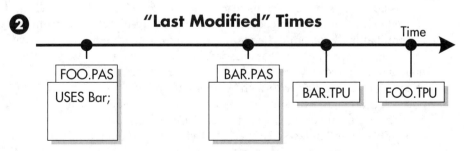

After a MAKE operation, only FOO is recompiled, to take into account any changes made to BAR since FOO's last compilation.

Figure 21.2 Inter-Unit Dependencies and Make

Now, the interface to procedure **Crunchit** is no longer what **Foo** expects it to be. To be sure that all changes to **Bar** are "known" to unit **Foo**, FOO.PAS must be recompiled so that **FOO.TPU** is newer than **BAR.TPU**.

If Turbo Pascal's Make feature detects the situation at bullet 1 of Figure 21.2, it will recompile FOO.PAS so that FOO.TPU is newer than BAR.TPU, as is the case at bullet 2. This way, all changes made to BAR.PAS will be recognized and synchronized with FOO.PAS.

Make does this all the way down the dependency chain. It makes sure that any unit using another unit is "newer" than the unit it uses. Returning to Figure 21.1 for a moment, a make operation would ensure that PAYABLE.TPU was newer than A.TPU, and that A.TPU was newer than both C.TPU and D.TPU. Furthermore, PAYROLL.TPU must be newer than A.TPU, B.TPU, C.TPU, D.TPU, and E.TPU, because all of those units are farther down the dependency chain than PAYROLL.TPU.

What this means is that changing the interface part of C.TPU would cause the Make feature to trigger compilation of every unit shown in the figure except for F.TPU, because F.TPU in no way depends on C.TPU.

Now, why do I specify the interface part, specifically? A unit communicates with other units and the main program only through its interface part. Anything defined in the implementation part of a unit is private to that unit and invisible to the "outside world." So changing the implementation part of a unit does not affect the way that unit links up with the other units and the main program. This isn't to say that changing a unit's implementation part has no effect on a program's operation; it only means that the smart linker will not be affected by changes in any unit's implementation part.

The Make feature performs a third and final check on every file in the dependency chain. If a unit file loads a .OBJ assembly language file through the $L directive, or if it loads an include file with the $I directive, the make operation ensures that the unit is recompiled if either the include files or the .OBJ files are newer than the unit's TPU file. This guarantees that any changes made to the .OBJ files or the include files are recognized by and reflected in the unit's .TPU file.

The nicest thing about the integral Make feature is that it's entirely automatic. You don't have to tell it what to do. Make knows how to inspect time stamps and compare them to find out which is newer. Make also knows which files depend on which other files, and knowing all that, it can compile whatever needs to be compiled to ensure that the program as a whole is up-to-date without compiling anything unnecessarily.

21.2 Conditional Compilation

Turbo Pascal since V4.0 has supported *conditional compilation*. By using conditional compilation directives, you can tell the compiler to compile certain portions of a source code file and ignore others, based on *conditional symbols* that you define.

An example is the best way to approach conditional compilation. I have a relatively simple ASCII text file lister utility called **JList2**. It prints a file neatly under page headers listing the file name, size, and last modified date and time. I designed **Jlist2** for use with laser printers, and it makes use of the "line printer" fonts many of the latest crop of laser printers support.

Now, the problem with using any printer-specific feature (and this is by no means limited to laser printers) is that you have to build printer-specific code or data into the lister program. Most printers respond to escape sequences (that is, series of characters initiated by the ESC character, $27) to change fonts, line spacing, and so on. As you might expect, each printer responds to a different set of escape sequences to do the same thing. There are simply no standards.

Ordinarily, you'd either have to have a separate source code file for each printer you want to support, or else juggle sets of incompatible escape sequences inside the program. There's another option that I've found attractive, and that is to use Turbo Pascal's conditional compilation to use a single source code file to generate several printer-specific versions of the resulting .EXE file.

Consider this: The HP Laserjet II laser printer is reset to its default state using the escape sequence ESC E. The Canon LBP-8 A1 laser printer is reset using the escape sequence ESC c. Supporting both printers can be done easily by using conditional compilation:

```
{ This version compiles if "HPLJII" is defined }
{$IFDEF HPLJII}
PROCEDURE  ResetPrinter;

BEGIN
   Write(LST,Chr(27)+'E');
END;

{$ENDIF}

{ This version compiles if "CANONA1" is defined }
{$IFDEF CANONA1}
PROCEDURE  ResetPrinter;

BEGIN
   Writeln(LST,Chr(27)+'c')
END;

{$ENDIF}
```

Here are two different versions of the same procedure. Obviously, both can't be compiled at once, or you would receive an error for duplicate identifiers on **ResetPrinter**. However, you can direct Turbo Pascal to compile only one of the two by defining only one of the two conditional symbols **HPLJII** and **CANONA1**. If the symbol **HPLJII** is defined, the first of the two procedures (everything between {**$IFDEF HPLJII**} and {**$ENDIF**}) will be compiled, and the second will be ignored. If **CANONA1** is defined, the second procedure (everything between {**$IFDEF CANONA1**} and {**$ENDIF**}) will be compiled and the first will be ignored.

One very important warning here: The IDE's MAKE feature is totally oblivious to the state of conditional symbols. In other words, you cannot force a make operation simply by passing a new conditional symbol state to the compiler. MAKE looks only at the time stamp of source code and object code files. It has no involvement whatsoever with the machinery of conditional compilation. Obviously, if you add the line **{$DEFINE HPLJII}** to a source code file and save it to disk, you will force a make operation, because the source code file has been changed. However, changing one of the symbol definitions in the Conditional defines part of the Options I Compiler dialog box will *not* force a make operation!

CONDITIONAL SYMBOLS

Now, what *is* a "conditional symbol," and how are such symbols defined? A conditional symbol is just that: a name that provides information to the compiler regarding conditional compilation. It is *not* a part of the program, bears no resemblance at all to Pascal identifiers, and takes no room in your data segment. Defining conditional symbols has no effect whatsoever on the efficiency of generated object code. If you name the symbol to the compiler, the compiler considers it defined. Otherwise, the symbol is unknown to the compiler and considered undefined. *The sole job of a conditional symbol is to be either defined or undefined.* It is very much like a Boolean variable intended for the compiler's use alone. *You cannot reference a conditional symbol in code.* A Pascal **IF** statement, for example, has no power to test whether a conditional symbol is defined or undefined.

When working within the IDE, you can define symbols from the Conditional defines item in the Options I Compiler dialog box. (This is why you sometimes hear the term "conditional define" as a noun meaning "conditional symbol." "Conditional symbol" is the term used in the Borland Pascal documentation. I think "conditional define" sounds verbish and funny and don't use it.) All you need do is enter the symbol's name in the dialog box that appears. More than one symbol can be defined by separating the symbols with semicolons. However, leave no intervening spaces between symbols.

When using Turbo Pascal's command-line compiler and working from the command line, use the /D directive to define conditional symbols:

```
C:\TURBO>TPC JLIST2 /DCANONA1
```

If you later wanted to compile the same source code file to support the HP Laserjet II, you would invoke TPC this way:

```
C:\TURBO>TPC JLIST2 /DHPLJII
```

Again, leave no space between the /D directive and the symbol name. The /D directive can take multiple symbols, separated by semicolons, or you can pass multiple /D directives to TPC with one symbol defined per directive. The choice is yours.

There are a number of predefined conditional symbols that are available whether or not you define them, as summarized in Table 21.1.

Table 21.1. Predefined symbols

Symbol	When defined
VER40	Always defined if running V4.0
VER50	Always defined if running V5.0
VER55	Always defined if running V5.5
VER60	Always defined if running V6.0
VER70	Always defined if running either Borland or Turbo Pascal V7.0
VER10	Always defined if Turbo Pascal for Windows 1.0 and Windows are running
VER15	Always defined if Turbo Pascal for Windows 1.5 and Windows are running
MSDOS	Always defined when the compiler is targeted for real-mode DOS
WINDOWS	Always defined when the compiler is targeted for Microsoft Windows
DPMI	Always defined when the compiler is targeted for DPMI (protected mode) DOS
CPU86	Always defined for Intel '86 processors
CPU87	Useful in V4.0 only, and there it was defined when a math coprocessor chip was detected at runtime. Since V5.0, emulation has made the distinction unnecessary, and the symbol is *always* defined, as a backward compatibility feature only.

The version symbols allow you to test which version of the compiler is in command. This can be useful if you're distributing source code to people who may be using earlier versions of Turbo Pascal. Each version of the compiler automatically defines its "own" version symbol; the others will always be undefined. For example, Borland and Turbo Pascal 7.0 define VER70 and leave the others undefined.

Three symbols are defined depending on how you set the compiler to generate code. If the compiler is targeted for DOS (that is, if you set the compiler to compile code for real-mode DOS) the **MSDOS** symbol will be defined. Note that only Borland Pascal allows you to target something other than real-mode DOS (by using the Compile | Target dialog box), so **MSDOS** will be the only targeting symbol ever defined in Turbo Pascal. The **WINDOWS** symbol will be defined if you target Windows applications using Compile | Target, and **DPMI** will be defined if you target DOS protected mode.

DOS is the only operating system supported by Borland Pascal products for the time being, but if a future version of Pascal appears for OS/2 or Unix, a symbol like **OS2** or **UNIX** would probably be defined in each version to indicate to the compiler which operating system is hosting the compile. This feature might allow you to cross-compile the same source code file for different operating systems.

Similarly, the **CPU86** symbol is always defined for Intel 86-family CPUs, and currently this is the only version available. One could imagine a **CPU68** for Motorola CPUs, or perhaps a **CPUALPHA** symbol for the DEC Alpha CPU, if Borland ever made the product available for those CPUs.

CONDITIONAL COMPILATION BASED ON SYMBOLS

As mentioned above, a conditional symbol is either defined or undefined. There is a separate test for a symbol's being defined and for its being undefined. The **$IFDEF <symbol>** directive causes the code which follows it to be compiled if **<symbol>** is defined, down to the **$IFDEF**'s matching **$ENDIF** directive. The **$IFNDEF <symbol>** directive, by contrast, causes compilation of the code that follows it if **<symbol>** is *not* defined.

For example, suppose you want to build diagnostic display routines into a program for use during testing stages only. During the test, the statements need to be added to a program; later on they must be removed. You could, for example, display the value of a variable this way:

```
{$IFDEF TESTMODE}
Writeln(LST,'<Diagnostic:> MedianAge =',MedianAge);
{$ENDIF}
```

If you compile with **TESTMODE** defined, this statement will be inserted into the executable program file. Later on, compile without defining **TESTMODE** and the statement will no longer be compiled.

For either/or situations there is an intermediate **$ELSE** directive that separates two alternate segments of source code, one to be compiled if the other is not. For example, if you want to use slightly different code for positioning the cursor with a mouse than with the keypad, you might do something like this:

```
{$IFDEF MOUSE}

IF ButtonPressed THEN
  BEGIN
    GetMouseXY(X,Y);
    GotoXY(X,Y)
  END;

{$ELSE}

IF InChar IN CursorKeySet THEN
  BEGIN
    DeltaXY(InChar,X,Y);
    GotoXY(X,Y)
  END;

{$ENDIF}
```

Here, you either use the mouse or you don't, and each case has its own particular means of processing cursor position information.

In the example at the beginning of this section, I used a separate **$IFDEF** directive for each of two different printers, rather than the **$ELSE** directive. The reason was that I might want to add support for a third or a fourth printer eventually, and with **$IFDEF/$ELSE** you can only choose one of *two* different alternatives. If I wanted to choose one of several different printer reset strings I could set it up this way:

```
{$IFDEF CANONA1}
    ResetString := Chr(27)+'c';
{$ENDIF}
{$IFDEF HPLJII}
    ResetString := Chr(27)+'E';
{$ENDIF}
{$IFDEF LJ400}
    ResetString := Chr(27)+'@';
{$ENDIF}
{$IFDEF PTIGER}
    ResetString := Chr(27)+'*R';
{$ENDIF}
```

If you wanted, you could add additional conditional clauses later on to support additional printers. One caution here is that *you* are responsible for ensuring that only *one* of the various printer symbols is defined at a time. In the earlier example, the compiler would stop on a duplicate identifier error. However, if in this example more than one symbol is defined, the compiler will compile the statement corresponding to each defined printer, and only the *last* of them will be the one that actually carries its value into the rest of the program. *No error will be generated.*

DEFINING AND UNDEFINING SYMBOLS WITHIN THE SOURCE CODE FILE

You have the option of defining and undefining symbols within your source code itself using the **$DEFINE** and **$UNDEF** directives. The following directive:

```
{$DEFINE TESTMODE}
```

is completely equivalent to defining symbol **TESTMODE** from the command line using TPC, or from the **Options | Compiler** menu item within the IDE.

Similarly, you can undefine a symbol this way:

```
{$UNDEF TESTMODE}
```

If **TESTMODE** is not already defined, the **$UNDEF** directive does nothing.

CONDITIONAL COMPILATION BASED ON COMPILER TOGGLES

Turbo Pascal's conditional compilation feature also has the ability to test the state of switch-type compiler options, and will either compile or ignore blocks of code depending on the state of a particular option. The **$IFOPT <option>** directive does this. **$IFOPT** is the function equivalent of **$IFDEF** except that it tests a compiler option rather than a symbol.

The best example involves floating-point support under Turbo Pascal 4.0, which did *not* have the math coprocessor emulation feature introduced with V5.0. If you wanted to write a V4.0 program that compiled to "twin" .EXES for running on machines with and without math coprocessors, you needed to use conditional compilation.

The problem centers around the incompatible types **Real** and **Double**. **Real** is the 6-byte software-only real, which under V4.0 is the only floating-point type available on machines without an Intel math coprocessor. **Double** is the double-precision hardware real number type, which required a math coprocessor in order to be used in a V4.0 program. The **$N+** option enables the use of hardware reals, and the **$N-** option disables the use of hardware reals.

In defining groups of numeric variables to be used in floating-point calculations, you can use conditional compilation based on the state of the **$N** option to determine whether to define the variables as type **Real** or type **Double**:

```
VAR
{$IFOPT N+}
  R,S,Perimeter,Area : Double;
{$ELSE}
  R,S,Perimeter,Area : Real;
{$ENDIF}
```

$IFOPT can also test the state of the $B, $D, $F, $I, $L, $N, $R, $S, $T, or $V options.

CONDITIONAL COMPILATION CAUTIONS

One problem with the example just shown, however, is that the size of your data items changes on you. Type **Double** is eight bytes in size, whereas type **Real** is six bytes in size. If you compile a program to use type **Real** and then write values of type **Real** out to a binary file, you will not be able to read that file back in with a separate .EXE version of the program that had been compiled to use type **Double**.

When you use conditional compilation in this way, you actually end up with two different programs with two different feature sets. The .EXE using **Double** will have greater numeric precision than the .EXE using **Real**—so the two copies might not produce exactly the same results for a given set of real-number data. The programs might react differently on a numeric overflow condition. The two .EXEs will certainly be of different physical sizes.

As I mentioned earlier, the IDE MAKE facility is indifferent to changes in defined and undefined conditional symbols, and doesn't help you much when you're trying to maintain two different versions of the same program. Worse, conditional compilation makes your source code somewhat schizophrenic and difficult to read.

As useful as some of my friends hold conditional compilation to be, I myself have used it only rarely and have a hard time endorsing it. Cross-platform development has become extremely complicated with the advent of GUI platforms like Windows and OS/2, and if you want to work in multiple worlds from one set of source code, you're far better off using a portability library designed for the purpose.

In general, use conditional compilation sparingly, and try to find another solution to any perceived need for it before you haul out the $IFs.

Chapter 22

The Borland Graphics Interface (BGI)

CREATING THE LIGHT FANTASTIC, PIXEL BY PIXEL

There are as many ways to display graphics images as there are to constructing tribal lays (as Mr. Kipling might have said), and each and every one of them is important to someone, somewhere. It would be useful and lovely to support every one of those diverse graphics boards from a high-level language, but up until now the problem of writing fast drivers for many different boards has kept Turbo Pascal graphics limited to IBM's Color Graphics Adapter and its clones.

Those days are past. Starting with Turbo Pascal 4.0, Borland's Pascal products have included a device-independent graphics system called the Borland Graphics Interface (BGI). In its first release, the BGI supported all IBM graphics adapters including the CGA, EGA, VGA, MCGA, and PC3270 graphics adapters. The initial release also supported the popular Hercules Graphics Adapter and the ATT 400-line graphics board found in ATT machines. Version 5.0 added support for IBM's 8514 graphics adapter and 256-color VGA mode. Version 7.0 added support for VESA-standard video modes, as well as graphics in protected mode.

22.1 Understanding Graphics, Borland-Style

The schism between text and graphics displays is now well understood: In a text display, a coarse grid (typically 25 × 80 but possibly larger) contains patterns of *characters*. These include the familiar letters, digits, and punctuation marks, but may also include the many special characters supported by the IBM PC: foreign language and mathematical characters, box-drawing characters, halftones, and bargraph elements. The key here is that characters are indivisible atoms from which screen displays are built. The characters themselves appear on the screen as patterns of tiny dots, but the individual dots *within* a character may not be changed or otherwise controlled.

A graphics display, by contrast, is a much finer grid of individual illuminated dots called *pixels*. Here, the pixels are the indivisible atoms from which other figures are constructed. These other figures may be anything at all, but in a typical graphics software system there are procedures for drawing lines, rectangles, circles, arcs, and polygons, and more complex figures are constructed from those simpler elements. Text characters may be built from pixels, but with the greater control over individual dots, a broader selection of character styles is possible. Collections of stylistically-similar character figures are called *fonts*. Furthermore, because of the complete pixel-by-pixel control over character size and position, a graphics font may be *proportionally spaced*; for example, characters take up only the horizontal space they need. An "i" is narrower than a "w," and so on.

Any piece of hardware that controls the display of pixels on a CRT screen or display panel of some kind is called a graphics *device*. The number of the pixels in the grid determines a graphics device's *resolution*. The Hercules Graphics Adapter, for example, displays a grid of pixels 720 wide by 348 high. We say that its resolution is 720×348. The Hercules device displays only two *colors*. On a green screen these might by called "green and black," since a pixel on a Hercules screen is either illuminated or not illuminated. On the other hand, some people run the Hercules device with an amber or white screen, so it makes more sense to call the Hercules a *monochrome* device, and think of its two colors as "on" and "off."

With devices that work with color monitors, pixels may be one of several colors in a group called a *palette*. The original and now almost-extinct IBM Color Graphics Adapter (CGA) supports two different palettes: One contains the colors red, green, and yellow; the other contains the colors cyan, magenta, and white. IBM's now-fading Enhanced Graphics Adapter (EGA) is a more complex device that supports a palette of 16 different colors. The now-standard Video Graphics Array (VGA) is more complex still, with the ability to display 256 different graphics colors.

A single graphics device may be capable of displaying different resolutions and different color palettes, depending on how it is initialized by a program. Each different resolution and color palette combination is called a graphics *mode*. IBM's CGA, for example, has two modes: One has a resolution of 320×200 and a palette of four colors, while the other has a resolution of 640×200 and a palette of only two colors.

Most display devices these days are capable of operating in both text mode and graphics mode, by turns. The default is nearly always text mode, with graphics mode looked upon as something a little more special. This is why we say we get "into" and "out of" graphics mode; text mode is the mode in which most work is generally done. The Turbo Pascal IDE works only in text mode, but may produce .EXE program files that work in text mode, in graphics mode, or switch from one to the other as their work requires. Borland Pascal and Turbo

Pascal for Windows do work in graphics mode, but only graphics mode as managed by Windows itself. That is, you can use the graphics resolution and palette that Windows was installed for, and no other. (I won't be covering Windows programming in this book, as it is a seriously advanced topic that is best approached once you've had some experience working with Turbo Pascal for DOS.)

THE LIMITS OF "DEVICE INDEPENDENCE"

Supporting more than one graphics device has been possible all along with the help of some third-party graphics software libraries. The special trick performed by the BGI is that it detects *at runtime* what graphics device is installed in the host machine, and loads an appropriate driver at that time. In other words, the very same .EXE file you create can (with a little care) run identical graphics on many different graphics devices *without recompiling*. This is why the BGI is called a *device-independent* graphics system. The device drivers are separate DOS files with a .BGI extension. Your program must know where the drivers will be stored at compile time, but it need not know directly which driver will be used.

The BGI is not *quite* device independent in that the resolution of the individual graphics devices must be taken into account by the programmer. In other words, some graphics devices (like IBM's CGA) have only a 200-pixel vertical resolution, while devices like the EGA have a 350-pixel, and the VGA a 480-pixel (or higher) vertical resolution. Your program can query the BGI to determine what resolution the currently-loaded driver can handle, and it must adjust its drawing calculations accordingly. For example, if you want to draw a line around the entire screen, your program must be prepared to draw vertical lines for the sides 200 pixels high for the CGA and 350 pixels high for the EGA. There are completely device-independent graphics systems that write all graphics to a virtual screen using *world coordinates* that are scaled to fit whatever resolution the designated output device can offer. The BGI does not go quite that far.

22.2 Getting into and out of Graphics Mode

Getting into graphics mode requires knowing what graphics device is installed in the computer executing a Turbo Pascal program. You have the option of specifying which graphics device explicitly, or of letting the BGI determine what device is installed. There is also the issue of a graphics mode: If you specify a specific graphics device, you must also specify a graphics mode that is valid for the installed graphics device. If you let the BGI determine what device is installed in the system, the BGI will also select a mode. Your software can query this mode, and change to another mode if the mode selected by the BGI is not the one you wish to use for the given graphics device.

LETTING THE BGI DETECT THE GRAPHICS DISPLAY DEVICE

The easiest way to get into graphics mode is to let the BGI go out and take a look at the hardware to see what sort of display board you have installed, and then automatically initialize the highest-resolution mode valid for that board. Directing the BGI to detect the installed graphics device is done with the **DetectGraph** procedure:

```
PROCEDURE DetectGraph(VAR GraphDriver : Integer;
                      VAR GraphMode   : Integer);
```

To work correctly, **DetectGraph** must be passed the value 0 in the **GraphDriver** parameter. The best way to do this is to use the constant **Detect**, which is predefined in the **Graph** unit with a value of 0:

```
GraphDriver := Detect;
DetectGraph(GraphDriver,GraphMode);
```

Keep in mind that while constant **Detect** is predefined, the variables **GraphDriver** and **GraphMode** I used here are *not*, and they or some other two integer variables must be defined in your program for passing to **DetectGraph**.

DetectGraph returns the driver code for the installed display board in **GraphDriver**, and the highest-resolution mode valid for that board in **GraphMode**. These codes are given in Tables 22.1 and 22.2.

The procedure that actually initializes the BGI is **InitGraph**:

```
PROCEDURE InitGraph(VAR GraphDriver : Integer;
                    VAR GraphMode   : Integer;
                    DriverPath      : STRING);
```

The variable passed to **InitGraph** as the **GraphDriver** parameter must contain a value from 0–10. The **Graph** unit contains a set of named constants for these

Table 22.1 BGI Graphics Device Constants

Constant	Value	Meaning
Detect	0	Tells the BGI to attempt device detection
CGA	1	IBM Color Graphics Adapter (or clone)
MCGA	2	IBM Multi Color Graphics Array
EGA	3	IBM EGA (or clone) with 256K RAM
EGA64	4	IBM EGA with 64K RAM
EGAMono	5	IBM 256K EGA connected to monochrome screen
IBM8514	6	IBM 8514 graphics card (version 5.0 only)
HercMono	7	Hercules Graphics Adapter
ATT400	8	AT & T 400-line display adapter
VGA	9	IBM Virtual Graphics Array (or clone)
PC3270	10	IBM 3270 PC display adapter

values to help you in remembering which is which and what each means, as shown in Table 22.1. Other graphics devices may have been added to the driver collection by the time you read this book—this, after all, is what device-independent graphics was designed to make possible. Check the README file on your Turbo Pascal distribution disk to see if there have been any late additions.

The variable passed to **InitGraph** as the **GraphMode** parameter specifies the graphics mode to use, and must contain a value *only* if you specify a driver in **GraphDriver**. In most cases, you will simply carry over a value from a previous call to **DetectGraph**, which detected the installed graphics device. If you pass **Detect** in **GraphDriver**, the graphics mode will be chosen for you and *returned* in the variable passed as **GraphMode**. If you specify a specific driver in **GraphDriver** and a specific graphics mode in **GraphMode** without a previous call to **DetectGraph**, the mode specified in **GraphMode** must be legal for the driver specified in **GraphDriver**. As with the driver-specifier values, the **Graph** unit contains predefined constants for each legal mode for each supported driver. The constants and their values are summarized in Table 22.2.

The modes **EGA64Lo** and **EGA64Hi** operate with early IBM-built EGA boards that had only 64K of graphics memory installed. Note that the IBM 8514 driver is not present in Turbo Pascal 4.0. Neither the IBM8514 nor the ATT400 board can be autodetected by the BGI. The ATT board will be seen as a CGA, and the 8514A will be detected as a VGA. To use the 8514 driver, you must explicitly specify the 8514 driver by passing the value of the predefined constant **IBM8514** to **InitGraph** in the **GraphDriver** parameter. Similarly, to use the ATT400 driver, you must pass the value of the predefined constant **ATT400** to **InitGraph** in **GraphDriver**. In both cases, you must choose a graphics mode valid for the board in question and pass the code for that graphics mode explicitly in **GraphMode** when calling **InitGraph**. As I'll explain below, you cannot simply pass the constants—you must assign the constants to variables and then pass those variables in **InitGraph**'s parameters.

The **DriverPath** parameter contains either a null string, indicating that the BGI should expect to find its device drivers in the current directory, or else the full pathname of the directory where the drivers are stored.

Something important to keep in mind: **InitGraph**'s parameters **GraphDriver** and **GraphMode** are **VAR** parameters. The **Graph** unit contains all these handy predefined constants summarized in the last two tables, but *you can't pass the constants in GraphDriver or GraphMode*. **VAR** parameters cannot be constants. You must first assign one of the constants to an integer variable and pass the variable in **GraphDriver** or **GraphMode** instead:

```
VAR
   CurrentDriver, CurrentMode : Integer;

CurrentDriver := MCGA;
CurrentMode   := MCGAC2;

InitGraph(CurrentDriver,CurrentMode,'C:\TURBO\BGI');
```

Table 22.2 GraphMode Constants Supported by the BGI

Constant	Value		Meaning	
CGAC0	0	320×200	Light Green/Light Red/Yellow	1 page
CGAC1	1	320×200	Light Cyan/Light Magenta/White	1 page
CGAC2	2	320×200	Green/Red/Brown	1 page
CGAC3	3	320×200	Cyan/Magenta/Light Gray	1 page
CGAHi	4	640×200	2 color	1 page
MCGAC0	0	320×200	Light Green/Light Red/Yellow	1 page
MCGAC1	1	320×200	Light Cyan/Light Magenta/White	1 page
MCGAC2	2	320×200	Green/Red/Brown	1 page
MCGAC3	3	320×200	Cyan/Magenta/Light Gray	1 page
MCGAMed	4	640×200	2 color	1 page
MCGAHi	5	640×480	2 color	1 page
EGALo	0	640×200	16 color	4 pages
EGAHi	1	640×350	16 color	2 pages
EGA64Lo	0	640×200	16 color	1 page
EGA64Hi	1	640×350	4 color	1 page
EGAMonoHi	3	640×350	2 color	
			64K on card:	1 page
			256K on card:	2 pages
HercMonoHi	0	720×348	2 color	2 pages
ATT400C0	0	320×200	Light Green/Light Red/Yellow	1 page
ATT400C1	1	320×200	Light Cyan/Light Magenta/White	1 page
ATT400C2	2	320×200	Green/Red/Brown	1 page
ATT400C3	3	320×200	Cyan/Magenta/Light Gray	1 page
ATT400Med	4	640×200	2 color	1 page
ATT400Hi	5	640×400	2 color	1 page
VGALo	0	640×200	16 color	4 pages
VGAMed	1	640×350	16 color	2 pages
VGAHi	2	640×480	16 color	1 page
PC3270Hi	0	720×350	2 color	1 page
IBM8514Lo	0	640×480	256 colors	1 page
IBM8514Hi	1	1024×768	256 colors	1 page

BGI INITIALIZATION ERRORS

The BGI will do its best to initialize itself and the graphics system when you invoke **InitGraph**. Your programs need to be able to deal with the possibility that something will go wrong. Possible problems include these:

- You try to detect a graphics device and no graphics device is installed in the system.
- The BGI cannot find its drivers.
- The driver that was loaded was found to be faulty somehow.
- There was not enough memory to load the driver.

The error codes supplied by the BGI are always negative integers. The codes are returned in two places: in the **GraphDriver** parameter, and by an integer function called **GraphResult**. By testing the **GraphDriver** parameter immediately after a call to **InitGraph** to see if it is negative, you can tell an error code from a valid driver number, which will always be positive. The error codes are the same in both cases, and are summarized in Table 22.3. The most commonly encountered error is -3, which occurs when the BGI cannot find the requested driver. Recall that the pathname of the driver must be passed in the string parameter **DriverPath**. If **DriverPath** is passed a null string, the BGI will assume that the drivers are in the current directory.

Note in the example invocation of **InitGraph** given on page 624, that the driver pathname is "hard-coded" into the **InitGraph** procedure call. In general, that's not a good thing to do. *You* may always have your drivers stored on drive C: in a subdirectory called BGI, but someone else who may want to run your programs may not.

The preferred method is to assume that the drivers are in the current directory and *try* to load them; if on checking the value returned in **GraphDriver** or **GraphResult** you find an error, bring up a prompt for the user asking him to enter the pathname for the graphics drivers. Once the user enters a pathname, you should re-attempt BGI initialization with a second call to **InitGraph**.

Table 22.3 BGI Initialization Error Codes

Error	Meaning
-1	No graphics device is detected in the system
-3	The BGI cannot find the driver file
-4	The driver that was loaded is invalid
-5	There is insufficient memory to load the required driver

I'm not entirely comfortable with that scheme, as it assumes that the user knows where the BGI drivers are; in reality, the user may not even know what a BGI driver *is*. An interesting project in Turbo Pascal would be to take the general algorithm from the **Locate** utility given in Section 19.9 and build a search routine that will search the current disk drive for files with a .BGI extension, pausing to attempt BGI initialization anywhere it finds one. This would be an ideal application for the directory search "engine" described in Chapter 23.

RETURNING TO TEXT MODE

If your program operates in graphics mode, it can't simply return to DOS when it finishes its work. DOS functions strangely in graphics mode at times; you may get a solid block cursor, but you may get no cursor at all, or you may get a graphics board that simply goes nuts. *Always go back to text mode before returning control to DOS.*

Furthermore, the place to do it is in your program's exit procedure. Why? In case of a runtime error of some sort, the exit procedure will *always* be executed before control returns to DOS. If you simply code the return to text mode at the normal exit point from the program, a runtime error will leave the user in graphics mode when it aborts your program and returns to DOS.

The procedure that does the job is this:

```
PROCEDURE CloseGraph;
```

It takes no parameters. When invoked, **CloseGraph** returns to the text mode that was in force when **InitGraph** was executed to enter graphics mode. The dynamic memory that was occupied by the loaded graphics driver is returned to the heap.

The method for invoking **CloseGraph** from within an exit procedure is shown in the **Scribble** program given in Section 22.9.

MOVING BETWEEN TEXT AND GRAPHICS MODES

The procedures **InitGraph** and **CloseGraph** are the beginning and ending of graphics activity. In between, you may wish to bounce back and forth between text and graphics modes for various reasons. You needn't initialize the BGI from scratch every time you wish to enter graphics mode. Once the BGI has been successfully initialized via **InitGraph**, you can reenter graphics mode quickly using the **SetGraphMode** procedure:

```
PROCEDURE SetGraphMode(Mode : Integer);
```

The **Mode** parameter must contain a graphics mode code that is valid for the current graphics device. Trying to set an invalid mode will trigger an error code of −10 that will be returned in the **GraphResult** function. The legal modes for the supported graphics devices are given in Table 22.2.

SetGraphMode clears the graphics screen, and when called from within graphics mode may be used as a graphics equivalent of the **ClrScr** routine used for clearing the text screen.

SetGraphMode is also necessary for changing the graphics mode from the mode the BGI sets when it detects a graphics device in the system. If the detected device supports more than one graphics mode, the BGI will enter the mode providing the highest resolution possible. If for some reason you wish to use a lower-resolution mode with that device, you will have to use the **SetGraphMode** procedure to change to that mode.

Returning to text mode without shutting down the BGI is done with another procedure:

```
PROCEDURE RestoreCRTMode;
```

No parameters are necessary; **RestoreCRTMode** returns to the text mode that was in force when **InitGraph** was first called to initialize the BGI. If the text mode was changed during some previous foray into text mode through **RestoreCRTMode**, the original text mode will be reasserted.

Using **SetGraphMode** and **RestoreCRTMode** you can alternate between text and graphics modes as many times as you need to. The BGI remains initialized and the current driver remains loaded in memory until **CloseGraph** shuts it down and returns memory occupied by the driver to the heap's free list.

QUERYING THE CURRENT GRAPHICS MODE

The BGI includes a function that will return the current graphics mode:

```
FUNCTION GetGraphmode : Integer;
```

The value returned is one of the mode values summarized in Table 22.2.

OBTAINING NAMES OF GRAPHICS DRIVERS AND MODES

Obtaining the graphics driver name is done through a simple string function:

```
FUNCTION GetDriverName : String;
```

Obviously, you can't call **GetDriverName** until you successfully complete a call to **InitGraph**. The string name returned is one of the constant identifiers summarized in Table 22.1.

Querying the name of a graphics mode is done through another string function:

```
FUNCTION GetModeName(ModeNum : Word) : String;
```

Here, the number of the mode (from Table 22.2) is passed as a word value, and the string name (from that same table) is returned as the string function result.

Obtaining the maximum mode number for the currently loaded graphics driver is done through the **GetMaxMode** function:

```
FUNCTION GetMaxMode : Word;
```

The result is the highest ordinal mode number supported by that driver, obtained by querying the driver directly.

What are these three functions for? Borland allows third-party vendors to provide graphics drivers for the BGI, drivers for which neither the BGI nor Borland's documentation may have any knowlegde. By and large, within a given driver the highest-numbered mode provides the highest resolution and by implication the best quality graphics. Once a driver is loaded, **GetmaxMode** allows you to specify a graphics mode without either specifying an invalid mode or a mode that does not yield the best quality graphics.

22.3 Coordinates, Viewports, and Basic Drawing Tools

The pixels on a graphics screen are specified by two numbers: An X value indicating their distance from the left margin of the screen, and a Y value indicating their distance from the top of the screen. The two numbers are given as a pair of coordinates, with the X coordinate given first. For example, 17,141 indicates an X value of 17 and a Y value of 141. The upper left corner of the screen is the *origin*, and it is always numbered 0,0.

Because the BGI operates with many different kinds of graphics devices, the largest legal values for X and Y cannot be hard-coded into the BGI or into your programs. Your programs can call two functions that return the largest legal values for X and Y:

```
FUNCTION GetMaxX : Word;
FUNCTION GetMaxY : Word;
```

GetMaxX returns the X coordinate of the leftmost edge of the display screen. **GetMaxY** contains the Y coordinate of the bottommost edge of the display screen. Keep in mind that these boundary numbers are *not* equal to the resolution of the screen, but rather to the resolution reduced by one, since the origin begins at zero. In other words, for a screen with a resolution of 320 × 200, **GetMaxX** will return 319, and **GetMaxY** will return 199. (See Figure 22.1.)

Since they are ordinary Pascal functions, you can use them within expressions to "generalize" your drawing routines to take varying screen sizes into account. For example, this statenent will draw a line around the outermost boundary of the screen, regardless of the screen's resolution:

```
Rectangle(0,0,GetMaxX,GetMaxY);
```

ABSOLUTE COORDINATES

Specifying the coordinates of a pixel on the screen as a specific X and Y value is known as using *absolute coordinates*. In other words, identifying a pixel as 17,244 is a use of absolute coordinates.

Some of the drawing procedures in the BGI use absolute coordinates. The best example is the routine that simply plots a single pixel at absolute coordinate X,Y:

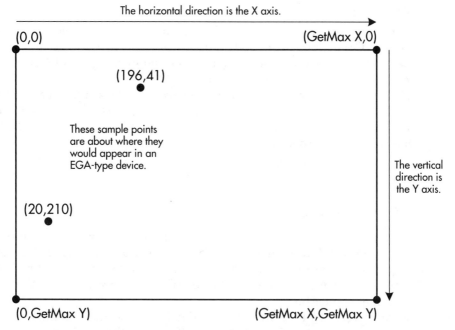

Figure 22.1 The Graphics Screen Coordinate System

```
PROCEDURE PutPixel(X,Y : Integer; PixelColor : Word);
```

Here, the absolute coordinates of the position at which you want to plot a pixel are passed as **X** and **Y**. The **PixelColor** parameter is a number specifying the color of the plotted pixel. What values are legal or meaningful here depend heavily on what sort of graphics device you are using. Handling issues of color and line style is described in Section 22.4.

The BGI also includes a routine that plots a straight line between two points, where the points are specified as two pairs of absolute coordinates:

```
PROCEDURE Line(X1,Y1,X2,Y2 : Integer);
```

Here, the two integers **X1** and **Y1** comprise one set of absolute coordinates, and the integers **X2** and **Y2** comprise the other set. The two locations may be anywhere on the screen; for example, the point defined by the first set of coordinates does not need to be above or to the left of that defined by the second set of coordinates.

Line draws its line in the current color and line style, which are set with the **SetColor** and **SetLineStyle** procedures, which will be discussed in detail in Section 22.4.

Two sets of coordinates are sufficient to specify a line, but they are also sufficient to specify a rectangle whose sides are parallel to the sides of the display screen. All you need to do is specify the upper left hand corner of the rectangle, and the lower right-hand corner of the rectangle, and it's done. The BGI uses this procedure to do the work:

```
PROCEDURE Rectangle(X1,Y1,X2,Y2 : Integer);
```

As with **Line**, the color and style are those currently in force, which may be set with the **SetColor** and **SetLineStyle** procedures, as described in Section 22.4.

The relationship between the output of **Line** and **Rectangle** for the same two sets of absolute coordinates is shown in Figure 22.2.

In Figure 22.2, the upper left corner of the rectangle was given in **X1** and **Y1**, but that is not a requirement. The very same rectangle as shown in the figure could have been drawn by reversing the two pairs of coordinates, and specifying the lower right corner first:

```
Rectangle(400,280,80,180);
```

THE CURRENT POINTER (CP)

Absolute coordinates are easy to understand, but in a lot of drawing applications they are more work than they need to be. There are some shorthand techniques offered by the BGI using a more flexible system called *relative coordinates*, and a very handy (if invisible) helper called the *current pointer*. We'll look at the current pointer first.

The current pointer (usually abbreviated to CP), is the graphics-mode analog to the familiar text cursor. One important difference is that the CP is not visible, as the text cursor is. The CP is actually a pair of coordinates that the BGI keeps within itself as a means of remembering the location of the last pixel drawn to the screen with certain BGI procedures.

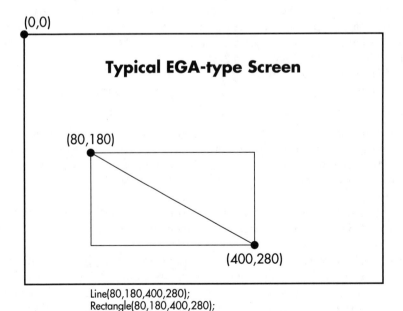

```
Line(80,180,400,280);
Rectangle(80,180,400,280);
```

Figure 22.2 Drawing with Absolute Coordinates

When you first initialize the BGI with a call to **InitGraph**, the CP is at 0,0. It represents a starting point for a slightly different method of drawing lines, using a BGI procedure called **LineTo**:

```
PROCEDURE LineTo(X,Y : Integer);
```

Note that **LineTo** only gives you *one* set of coordinates—and to draw a line you need two ends. The other end is provided by the CP. **LineTo** draws a straight line between the CP, wherever it currently happens to be, and the pixel represented by **X,Y**. After the line is drawn, the CP is moved to the other end of the drawn line; in other words, to **X,Y**.

If the CP isn't exactly where you want it to be when you want to draw a line using **LineTo**, you can easily move it with another BGI procedure:

```
PROCEDURE MoveTo(X,Y : Integer);
```

MoveTo does nothing more than move the CP to **X,Y**. Some people find it helpful to think of **MoveTo** as **LineTo** with some mystical "pen" lifted from the screen so that the line is not actually drawn, but I think it is plainer to imagine the CP as an invisible marker that you pick up and carry to a new screen location with **MoveTo**.

The BGI allows you to query the absolute coordinates of the current position of CP. Two functions are provided for this:

```
FUNCTION GetX : Integer;
FUNCTION GetY : Integer;
```

GetX returns the X coordinate of the CP, and **GetY** returns the Y coordinate of CP. These two functions return a value that is "viewport relative," that is, they return the position of CP *relative to the origin of the current viewport*. We'll come back to what that means later in this section when we discuss viewports. Unless you set the current viewport to some subset of the screen, the current viewport is always the entire screen. So in your early explorations of the BGI you needn't worry about the consequences of being viewport-relative.

RELATIVE COORDINATES

The true power of the current pointer is realized only in conjunction with a different system of specifying locations on the screen, known as *relative coordinates*. Absolute coordinates, to review, may be used to draw a line by naming the ends of the line as specific locations on the screen:

```
Line(0,0,100,280);
```

Relative coordinates do not deal in specific screen locations given as X,Y coordinate pairs. Relative coordinates instead specify a *distance* from some point on the screen, usually CP. Relative coordinates are almost always given as pairs, where the first value in the pair is the distance along the X axis in pixels, and the second value is the distance along the Y axis.

In other words, if you assume your starting point is CP, a relative coordinate pair 5,10 specifies a point 5 pixels to the right of CP and 10 pixels below CP.

These distances in X and Y can be negative as well as positive. A negative X value indicates a position to the *left* of CP, and a negative Y value indicates a position *above* CP. Figure 22.3 shows the difference between absolute and relative coordinates for several points on the graphics screen.

The BGI includes a procedure to move a CP to a new position relative to its current position:

```
PROCEDURE MoveRel(DX,DY : Integer);
```

The parameters **DX** and **DY** (named after "delta X" and "delta Y" meaning "change in X" and "change in Y") are the relative coordinates to which CP is moved. For example, if those relative coordinates were 10,–12, the CP would be moved 10 pixels to the right of its current position and 12 pixels above its current position. Keep in mind that a positive distance in X is to the right, while a negative distance in X is to the left; and a positive distance in Y is downward while a negative distance in Y is upward.

The most common use of relative coordinates is probably the drawing of lines from CP to a second position given as relative to CP. The BGI contains a procedure to do this:

```
PROCEDURE LineRel(DX,DY : Integer);
```

DX and **DY** are, again, relative coordinates. CP is one endpoint of the line to be drawn, and the other endpoint is given relative to CP.

As an example, see Figure 22.3. The first statement:

```
MoveRel(235,-100);
```

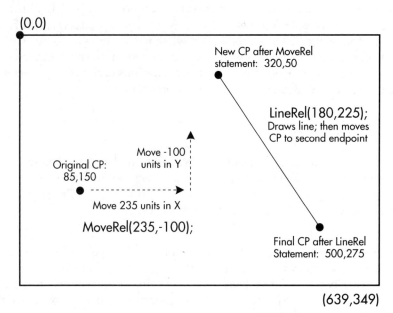

Figure 22.3 Drawing with Relative Coordinates

moves the CP from its current position at 85,150 to a new position at 85,150 added to the relative coordinates 235,–100, yielding a new absolute position for the CP at 320,50. The second statement:

```
LineRel(180,225);
```

draws a line from CP to the point 180 pixels to the right of CP and 225 pixels below CP. After the line is drawn, **LineRel** moves CP to the second endpoint of the line, at 500,275.

LineRel and **MoveRel** can be used to draw irregular figures specified by a set of points. The sets of points may be stored in an array, and the figure may be drawn by a simple procedure to which the array is passed.

Such a routine, **DrawMarker**, is given below. It draws small figures that are called *polymarkers* in the traditional graphics industry. Polymarkers are small figures used to visibly mark a location on a screen in a distinctive fashion. (The "poly" comes from the fact that the figures are composed of several straight lines and are therefore considered polygons.) The typed constants defined above the procedure itself contain the pairs of relative coordinates used to draw the markers. Three markers are given: a lozenge (i.e., a diamond standing on one point), a cross, and a square.

The first relative coordinate pair in each typed constant is considered a move coordinate by **DrawMarker**, and represents a move *away* from the CP before beginning to draw the marker. If a marker actually begins drawing at the CP (as **Cross** does) this first coordinate pair is 0,0.

After the first move is made, a **WHILE** loop continues drawing lines until a 0,0 relative coordinate is encountered, indicating that the figure is complete.

```
{->>>>DrawMarker<<<<------------------------------------------------}
{                                                                   }
{ Filename : DRAWMARK.SRC - Last Modified 2/19/93                   }
{                                                                   }
{ This routine uses relative line draws to draw "polymarkers"       }
{ at the current pointer (CP).  The patterns to be drawn are        }
{ arrays of "deltas", each delta being a "change in X" and          }
{ "change in Y" integer pair.  The first pair is a MOVE not a       }
{ line draw, to allow the marker to be drawn entirely away          }
{ from the CP.                                                      }
{                                                                   }
{ This routine may only be used in graphics mode.                   }
{                                                                   }
{    From: BORLAND PASCAL FROM SQUARE ONE   by Jeff Duntemann       }
{------------------------------------------------------------------}

TYPE
   PointArray = ARRAY[0..9,0..1] OF Integer;

CONST
   Lozenge : PointArray =
```

```
        ((0,-3),(-3,3),(3,3),(3,-3),(-3,-3),(0,0),(0,0),(0,0),(0,0),(0,0));
     Cross    : PointArray =
        ((0,0),(0,-3),(0,6),(0,-3),(3,0),(-6,0),(0,0),(0,0),(0,0),(0,0));
     Square   : PointArray =
        ((-2,-2),(0,4),(4,0),(0,-4),(-4,0),(0,0),(0,0),(0,0),(0,0),(0,0));

  PROCEDURE DrawMarker(Marker : PointArray);

  VAR
     I : Integer;

  BEGIN
     MoveRel(Marker[0,0],Marker[0,1]);   { First pair is relative move }
     I := 1;     { Start drawing with coordinate pair 1, not 0! }
     WHILE NOT ((Marker[I,0] = 0) AND (Marker[I,1] = 0)) DO
        BEGIN
           LineRel(Marker[I,0],Marker[I,1]);
           Inc(I)
        END
  END;
```

Once drawn, a marker can be erased by setting the current color to the background color and drawing the marker again in the background color.

The markers I've defined here are tiny things, but there is no reason **DrawMark** could not draw any larger figure bounded by eight lines or fewer. Just define the figure in terms of nine points and create a **PointArray** containing the point coordinates relative to the starting point.

VIEWPORTS AND VIEWPORT-RELATIVE DRAWING

The BGI supports *viewports*, which are rectangular windows within your graphics screen. BGI viewports do two things: They *clip*; that is, if you put a viewport in force and draw to the viewport, any graphics that extend beyond the boundaries of the viewport will not be drawn. We say that those "loose ends" are clipped. Also, BGI viewports *translate*. The upper left corner of the viewport becomes position 0,0, and both relative and absolute coordinates are calculated from the upper left corner of the viewport rather than the upper left corner of the entire screen.

Also, you can clear a viewport without disturbing graphics existing outside the boundaries of the viewport.

You should note that viewports do not *scale*; that is, a viewport is not a miniature screen to which all graphics are drawn reduced in size in proportion. A square measuring 50 pixels on a side when drawn on the default viewport (the entire screen) will still be 50 pixels on a side when drawn within a smaller viewport.

When **InitGraph** is executed, the current viewport defaults to the entire screen. The BGI includes a procedure that defines a smaller viewport:

```
  PROCEDURE SetViewPort(X1,Y1,X2,Y2 : Integer; Clip : Boolean);
```

The first four parameters contain two sets of coordinates; as with the **Rectangle** procedure, they specify the upper left corner and the lower right corner of the new viewport. The **Clip** parameter is a Boolean value indicating whether or not graphics should be clipped to the new viewport. If **Clip** is passed a value of **True**, then lines or other figures specified as extending beyond the viewport will not be fully drawn. Only those portions of the graphics figures falling within the viewport will be drawn. On the other hand, a value of **False** passed in **Clip** will force all graphics to be drawn regardless of where it falls on the screen.

Keep in mind that, of necessity, the edges of the physical screen are clipping boundaries.

Once a viewport is set, the upper left corner of that viewport becomes the new 0,0 position for graphics. All graphics commands executed will calculate their coordinates relative to that corner. Figure 22.4 shows a simple example. The exact same sequence of graphics statements is executed twice: once with the current viewport set to the entire screen, and again with the viewport set to a rectangle in the lower right portion of the screen.

```
Rectangle(0,0,GetMaxX,GetMaxY); { Draw a line around the screen }
Circle(50,50,25);               { Draw a thingie }
Line(50,50,100,50);
Line(50,50,50,200);
Line(50,50,100,100);
Rectangle(50,165,100,200);

SetViewPort(320,175,600,300,True);  { Create a viewport }

Rectangle(0,0,GetMaxX,GetMaxY); { Draw a line around the viewport }
Circle(50,50,25);               { Draw the thingie again }
Line(50,50,100,50);
Line(50,50,50,200);
Line(50,50,100,100);
Rectangle(50,165,100,200);
```

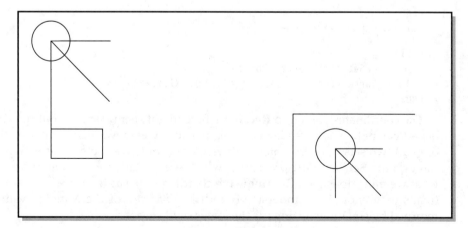

Figure 22.4 Graphics Clipping with Viewports

Notice that everything is drawn with absolute coordinates, which are the same in both cases, but that the coordinates are *translated* by the viewport to become *viewport-relative*. The graphics figure is drawn the same size in both cases, but its position changes when drawn within the viewport. Also, when drawn within the viewport, the graphics figure loses its bottom half (a square and part of the vertical line) to clipping.

There's one other interesting thing about Figure 22.4: The line supposedly drawn around the viewport is only drawn on two sides of the viewport. The bottom and the right side of the line are clipped. This points up an error in logic in the graphics statement

```
Rectangle(0,0,GetMaxX,GetMaxY);
```

when drawn within the viewport. *GetMaxX and GetMaxY are not viewport-relative*. They are one of the few features of the BGI that have no truck whatsoever with viewports. **GetMaxX** and **GetMaxY** return the coordinates of the lower right-hand corner of the physical screen, no matter what the current viewport happens to be.

Is there any way to query the BGI for the coordinates of the current viewport? Yes indeed:

```
PROCEDURE GetViewSettings(VAR PortSpec : ViewPortType);
```

When invoked, **GetViewSettings** returns a record value of type **ViewPortType**, which is predefined in the **Graph** unit:

```
ViewPortType = RECORD
                 X1,Y1,X2,Y2 : Word;
                 Clip : Boolean
               END;
```

The proper way to draw a line around the periphery of the current viewport would be this:

```
PROCEDURE  OutlineCurrentPort;

VAR
  CurrentPort : ViewPortType;

BEGIN
  GetViewSettings(CurrentPort);
  WITH CurrentPort DO Rectangle(0,0,X2-X1,Y2-Y1);
END;
```

The coordinates passed to **Rectangle** here might seem peculiar. But remember—**Rectangle** is *always* viewport-relative, and **GetViewSettings** returns the original two sets of coordinates that were used to define the current viewport through the **SetViewPort** procedure, which were relative to the *full screen*. So what we must do is pass **Rectangle** the coordinates 0,0 as the upper left corner (that's easy enough to understand) and the *difference* of the X and Y values returned by **GetViewSettings** as the lower right corner.

That is something to remember: *The coordinates passed to **SetViewPort** are always relative to the full screen.* If they were not, how else would you reset the viewport to anything larger than the current viewport?

Setting the current viewport back to the full screen, in fact, is done this way:

```
SetViewPort(0,0,GetMaxX,GetMaxY);
```

The interior of a viewport can be erased to the background color in one easy operation, using yet another BGI built-in procedure:

```
PROCEDURE ClearViewPort;
```

This will, of course, erase the line drawn around the periphery of the viewport with the **OutlineCurrentPort** procedure shown above, since the outline is *within* the viewport and is considered part of the viewport.

THE HEARTBREAK OF RECTANGULAR PIXELS

Little things do count, and little errors can add up to disastrous problems. One of the worst errors committed by IBM in creating the PC architecture lay in creating numerous graphics adapters that displayed rectangular pixels. In fact, all PC-compatible graphics adapters in common use, except for the 8514 and the "480" modes in the VGA and MCGA, display rectangular pixels.

It isn't just a small matter of a few percent. High-resolution mode on the CGA produces pixels that are more than *twice* as high as they are wide.

Hey, what's the problem? Pixels are too small to see their shape, anyway, right?

Yes, but—put a lot of them in a row on the screen and the discrepancy adds up. For example, execute the following statement in BGI graphics mode:

```
Rectangle(0,0,100,100);
```

This draws a square from the upper left corner of the screen at 0,0 to a point at 100,100. The figure is therefore 100 pixels on a side. It should be a square, right? It is not. (Not unless you're using a 640 × 480 pixel mode on a VGA or MCGA, that is.) How severely rectangular it is depends on what graphics board you're actually using, and in what mode.

The first and most serious problem with rectangular pixels is that calculations based on geometric principles have to be adjusted to operate correctly in the ill-behaved Cartesian grid represented by your screen. You may think you're drawing a square, but it comes out a rectangle. The proportions of your graphics and diagrams may be misleading, stretched significantly in the vertical and compressed in the horizontal.

The second, compounding problem is that the deviation from squareness varies all over the map, depending on the mode and the graphics device. CGA high resolution has a ratio of horizontal to vertical measure of 5/12; CGA medium resolution is better but still off at 5/6. This ratio of horizontal (X axis) measure to vertical (Y axis) measure is called *aspect ratio*. You'll have to deal with it if you expect your graphics to display in a similar fashion across all BGI-supported modes and devices.

Fortunately, the BGI provides a function that returns the aspect ratio at any given time:

```
PROCEDURE GetAspectRatio(VAR XAspect,YAspect : Word);
```

The two parameters return numbers whose ratio reflects the ratio between the width and the height of the screen pixels in the current graphics device and mode. These numbers are calculated internally to the BGI and are used by the BGI to make sure that the figures produced by **Circle**, **Arc**, and **PieSlice** (see Section 22.5) are always displayed as round, regardless of the current graphics device or mode.

The numbers are large positive integers, with the **YAsp** figure typically returned as 10000, and the **XAsp** figure some other number in proportion to the screen's current aspect ratio. The EGA's 640×350 graphics mode, for example, will return a **YAsp** = 10000 and an **XAsp** = 7750. The ratio of 7750/10000, or 0.775, accurately reflects the rectangular distortion of that mode.

To use the aspect ratio to draw a true square in any supported mode, you must take aspect ratio into account. The following procedure does all that is necessary:

```
{->>>>Square<<<<---------------------------------------------}
{                                                            }
{ Filename : SQUARE.SRC - Last Modified 2/20/93              }
{                                                            }
{ This routine draws a square at X,Y that is symmetrical     }
{ independent of the current graphics device and mode. The   }
{ Side parameter contains the measure in pixel of a side, and}
{ the MeasureXAxis is a Boolean that indicates whether the   }
{ figure passed in Side is measured along the X Axis or the Y}
{ axis. MeasureXAxis=True assumes that Side measures along   }
{ X axis, and False assumes that Side measures along the Y   }
{ axis.                                                      }
{                                                            }
{ The system must be in BGI graphics mode.                   }
{                                                            }
{   From: BORLAND PASCAL FROM SQUARE ONE by Jeff Duntemann   }
{------------------------------------------------------------}

PROCEDURE Square(X,Y,Side : Word; MeasureXAxis : Boolean);

VAR
  XA,YA : Word;
  XL,YL : Word;

BEGIN
  XL := Side; YL := Side;
  GetAspectRatio(XA,YA);
```

```
   IF MeasureXAxis THEN YL := Round((XA/YA)*Side)
      ELSE XL := Round((YA/XA)*Side);
   Rectangle(X,Y,X+XL,Y+YL);
END;
```

Here, we pass procedure **Square** the **X,Y** coordinates of the upper left corner of the square to be drawn, plus the length in pixels of one side. Now, we also need to specify along which axis this measure is to apply, since 100 pixels along the X axis is not as long as 100 pixels along the Y axis. This is the purpose of the **MeasureXAxis** parameter. If set to **True**, **MeasureXAxis** specifies that **Side** is to be measured along the X axis, and the Y length of a side in pixels is to be adjusted according to the aspect ratio. Similarly, if **MeasureXAxis** is set to **False**, then **Side** is assumed to be measured along the Y axis, and the X length in pixels is adjusted according to the aspect ratio. This means you may well get two very different-sized squares for two different Boolean values passed in **MeasureXAxis**, particularly if (as in CGA high-resolution mode) there is a drastic difference in proportion between the two axes.

Certain things cannot be adjusted by the aspect ratio; specifically, bitmapped things like fill patterns and bit images will look different depending on the device and mode, and there is nothing either you or the BGI can do about it.

FINE-TUNING THE ASPECT RATIO

The BGI corrects for rectangular pixels when drawing certain figures, most importantly circles using the **Circle** procedure. Each graphics adapter has a design aspect ratio (for example, 5/6 for the CGA in medium-resolution mode) and this is the ratio that the BGI assumes when performing its corrections. The *physical* aspect ratio (that is, the ratio you would get by actually laying a steel rule against the glass of your screen and measuring vertical against horizontal) depends somewhat on the nature of the display. Some lap-held machines have CGA-compatible displays with true square pixels. Or (more commonly) CRT monitors may be misadjusted in the vertical, causing a small but noticeable deviation from the design aspect ratio.

The BGI allows you to override its correct factor, which is the aspect ratio obtained by the **GetAspectRatio** function. The procedure that does this is **SetAspectRatio**:

```
PROCEDURE SetAspectRatio(XAspect,YAspect : Word);
```

This works a lot like **GetAspectRatio** in reverse: We provide values for **XAspect** and **YAspect** and the BGI uses them to calculate its new aspect ratio correction factor, which will be returned in subsequent calls to **GetAspectRatio**.

The two figures can be anything at all, but I recommend holding **XAspect** at 10000 and altering **YAspect** as necessary. In the case of a lap-held liquid crystal CGA-compatible display with square pixels, you would set **YAspect** to 10000 as well. Or, if your monitor is simply adjusted a little off, you may need a calibration routine that displays a square on the screen and allows you to "squeeze" it with the cursor keys until it looks right, each time changing the aspect ratio slightly. A program to explore aspect ratios in this fashion is given below. Using it, you can adjust the ratio until a square is precisely a square as measured on the faceplate of your CRT. Then you can use the display aspect ratio values as parameters to **SetAspectRatio** in the future to get the ratio just right.

Also, if you would like to build aspect-ratio adjustment into your own graphics programs, you can simply lift the **AdjustAspectRatio** procedure from the program and build it into your own.

```
{-------------------------------------------------------------}
{                       AspectRatio                           }
{                                                             }
{      Aspect ratio adjustment demonstration program          }
{                                                             }
{                    by Jeff Duntemann                        }
{                    Turbo Pascal V7.0                        }
{                    Last update 2/23/93                      }
{                                                             }
{   From: BORLAND PASCAL FROM SQUARE ONE by Jeff Duntemann    }
{-------------------------------------------------------------}


PROGRAM AspectRatio;

USES Crt,Graph;

VAR
   I,Color     : Integer;
   Palette     : PaletteType;
   GraphDriver : Integer;
   GraphMode   : Integer;
   ErrorCode   : Integer;



{$I SQUARE.SRC}    { Described in Section 22.3 }



PROCEDURE AdjustAspectRatio;

VAR Side       : Integer;
    W          : Word;
    Ch         : Char;
    Quit       : Boolean;
    Delta      : Integer;
    Color      : Word;
    Filler     : FillSettingsType;
    TheLine        : String;
    XAspect,YAspect : Word;
```

```
PROCEDURE  ShowRatio;

VAR
  Temp : String;

BEGIN
  SetFillStyle(0,0);  Bar(0,0,GetMaxX,20);
  WITH Filler DO SetFillStyle(Pattern,Color);
  GetAspectRatio(XAspect,YAspect);
  TheLine := 'Current ratio: ';
  Str(XAspect:6,Temp);
  TheLine := TheLine + Temp + '/';
  Str(YAspect:6,Temp);
  TheLine := TheLine + Temp + ' Up/down arrows to adjust; Q quits...';
  OutTextXY(10,10,TheLine)
END;


BEGIN
  Quit := False; Side := 180;
  Color := GetColor; GetFillSettings(Filler);
  GetAspectRatio(XAspect,YAspect);
  Delta := YAspect DIV 100;
  Square((GetMaxX DIV 2)-(Side DIV 2),
         (GetMaxY DIV 2)-(Side DIV 2),Side,True);

  ShowRatio;
  REPEAT
    Ch := ReadKey;
    IF Ch <> #0 THEN
      IF Ch in ['Q','q'] THEN Quit := True ELSE Quit := False
    ELSE
      BEGIN
        Ch := ReadKey;
        CASE Ord(Ch) OF
          $48 : BEGIN
                  SetColor(0);
                  Square((GetMaxX DIV 2)-(Side DIV 2),
                         (GetMaxY DIV 2)-(Side DIV 2),Side,True);
                  {Kluge fix:} W := YAspect+Delta;
                  SetAspectRatio(XAspect,W);
                  SetColor(Color);
                  Square((GetMaxX DIV 2)-(Side DIV 2),
                         (GetMaxY DIV 2)-(Side DIV 2),Side,True);
                  ShowRatio;
                END;
          $50 : BEGIN
```

```
                    SetColor(0);
                    Square((GetMaxX DIV 2)-(Side DIV 2),
                            (GetMaxY DIV 2)-(Side DIV 2),Side,True);
                    {Kluge fix:} W := YAspect-Delta;
                    SetAspectRatio(XAspect,W);
                    SetColor(Color);
                    Square((GetMaxX DIV 2)-(Side DIV 2),
                            (GetMaxY DIV 2)-(Side DIV 2),Side,True);
                    ShowRatio;
                END;
          END; { CASE }
        END
      UNTIL Quit
    END;


  BEGIN
    GraphDriver := Detect; { Let the BGI determine what board we're using }
    DetectGraph(GraphDriver,GraphMode);
    InitGraph(GraphDriver,GraphMode,'');
    ErrorCode := GraphResult;
    IF ErrorCode <> 0 THEN
      BEGIN
          Writeln('>>Halted on graphics error: ',GraphErrorMsg(ErrorCode));
        Halt(2)
      END;

    AdjustAspectRatio;

    CloseGraph;
  END.
```

22.4 Colors, Palettes, Fills, and Floods

There are quite a number of routines in the **Graph** unit for setting and querying the use of color in programs that use the BGI. If you're using a monochrome display like the Hercules board, most of them will be unnecessary and you can use the default values. But if you wish to make effective use of color, you should spend a little time understanding the way the BGI throws colors to your screen.

FOREGROUND AND BACKGROUND

In its most commonly-encountered form, graphics consists of illuminated pixels on a dark (generally black) background. This is actually a special case of the more general truth: All pixels that are not specifically set to some *foreground color* remain set to some *background color*. Metaphorically, the background may be seen as a sheet of paper on which foreground graphics can be drawn in several colors. There can be many foreground colors (up to 16 in the current release of the BGI, for those graphics devices that support 16 colors), but only *one* background color.

The background color can be changed, and when it is changed, all pixels that belong to the background change to the new color at once.

Colors are specified to the BGI as numbers, but there are 16 predefined constants that help you in remembering which color goes with which number. These are summarized in Table 22.4. Note that not all of these colors are available in every graphics device. The CGA, for example, only supports four colors at once in its **CGAC0** through **CGAC3** modes, and the Hercules board supports none of them at all except for **Black** and **White**.

Setting the background color is done with a single BGI procedure:

```
PROCEDURE SetBkColor(Color : Word);
```

You may specify the **Color** parameter as a variable, a literal, or as one of the constants from the table above. All pixels belonging to the background change to the new color instantly. Furthermore, the background color does not respect viewport boundaries. When you set the background color, you set it for the entire visible screen, *even if a smaller viewport is currently in force*.

Querying the background color is done with a simple BGI function:

```
FUNCTION GetBkColor : Word;
```

The returned value ranges from 0–15, depending on what the current graphics device and mode allow.

The drawing routines we have discussed already (**Line**, **LineRel**, and **Rectangle**) draw in the *current drawing color*. This is a color selected from one of the valid colors for the current graphics device, and the drawing routines set pixels to that color as a foreground color. The current drawing color is set with another BGI procedure:

```
PROCEDURE SetColor(Color : Word);
```

Table 22.4 BGI Predefined Color Constants

Constant	Value	Constant	Value
Black	0	DarkGray	8
Blue	1	LightBlue	9
Green	2	LightGreen	10
Cyan	3	LightCyan	11
Red	4	LightRed	12
Magenta	5	LightMagenta	13
Brown	6	Yellow	14
LightGray	7	White	15

As with **SetBkColor**, the parameter **Color** may be passed a variable, a numeric literal, or one of the color constants from the table given above.

Querying the current drawing color is done with a BGI function:

```
FUNCTION GetColor : Word;
```

The value returned will range from 0–15, depending on what the current graphics device and mode allow.

The way to erase a figure already drawn in one color is to draw it again, after having temporarily set the current drawing color to the background color:

```
VAR
  SavedColor : Word;

  SavedColor := GetColor; { Record the current drawing color }
  Rectangle(0,0,100,100); { Draw a rectangle in the current color }
  SetColor(GetBkColor);    { Set drawing color to background color }
  Rectangle(0,0,100,100); { Draw the rectangle again, erasing it }
  SetColor(SavedColor);    { Re-assert the previous drawing color }
```

The number of colors supported by the current driver and mode may be queried with the following function:

```
FUNCTION GetMaxColor : Word;
```

GetMaxColor will return 16 for EGA 640 × 350 mode, and 256 for the VGA 320 × 200 256 color mode. The value returned is the largest value that can be passed to the **SetColor** procedure.

QUERYING THE COLOR OF A PIXEL

It may be useful to determine the color of any given pixel on the screen. The BGI provides a function for this purpose:

```
FUNCTION GetPixel(X,Y : Word) : Word;
```

The parameters **X** and **Y** are viewport-relative coordinates of the desired pixel. The result value may range from 0–15, depending on what the current graphics device and mode allow.

PALETTES

The BGI provides an additional level of versatility in setting display colors, in the form of *palettes*. A palette is, in effect, a translation table for color values. A color value used in drawing by the BGI may be set to any physical color supported by the graphics device with the palette as an intermediary. For example, you can define the BGI's color 3 (ordinarily blue) to be drawn as red by redefining color 3 in the current palette.

Because the palette includes the background color as color 0, you can also change the background color by redefining the palette.

Table 22.5 will help make the matter clearer. The left half of the table contains the default palette, in this case for a graphics device like the EGA, VGA, and MCGA, all of which support 16 simultaneous colors. (The CGA, by contrast, only supports four.) Notice that each color is "passed through" the table as itself. In other words, color 0 is drawn as color 0; color 1 is drawn as color 1, and so on.

In the right half of the table, the palette has been redefined randomly, so that every color is redefined as some other color. In other words, once the new palette is put into effect, color 0 will be drawn as color 14; color 1 will be drawn as color 4, and so on. All colors do not have to be changed; you may redefine only one, or redefine all but one, or any combination. In the redefined table, BGI color 11 was left defined as physical color 11, Light Cyan.

Physically, the palette is a table kept somewhere in memory by the BGI. When you alter the current palette, you change values in this table. There are two BGI routines that perform this palette redefinition. One of them redefines one color at a time, and the other allows you to redefine all of them at once. Redefining a single color is done with this procedure:

```
PROCEDURE SetPalette(DrawColor : Word; PhysicalColor : ShortInt);
```

The meaning of the two parameters is something you should keep in mind: **DrawColor** is the value you would use in setting a current drawing color through

Table 22.5 Default and Custom Palettes

Default Palette BGI Color	Drawn as	*Redefined Palette* BGI Color	Drawn as
0	0 (Black)	0	14 (Yellow)
1	1 (Blue)	1	4 (Red)
2	2 (Green)	2	10 (LightGreen)
3	3 (Cyan)	3	1 (Blue)
4	4 (Red)	4	9 (LightBlue)
5	5 (Magenta)	5	6 (Brown)
6	6 (Brown)	6	12 (LightRed)
7	7 (LightGray)	7	15 (White)
8	8 (DarkGray)	8	13 (LightMagenta)
9	9 (LightBlue)	9	0 (Black)
10	10 (LightGreen)	10	3 (Cyan)
11	11 (LightCyan)	11	11 (LightCyan)
12	12 (LightRed)	12	7 (LightGray)
13	13 (LightMagenta)	13	8 (DarkGray)
14	14 (Yellow)	14	5 (Magenta)
15	15 (White)	15	2 (Green)

the **SetColor** procedure. **PhysicalColor** is the actual color in which that current drawing color would appear on the screen.

For example, if you wished color 4 (which defaults to red) to specify light blue on the screen, you would execute this statement:

```
SetPalette(4,LightBlue);
```

Setting a value for all colors in the palette may be done with a different procedure:

```
PROCEDURE SetAllPalette(VAR Palette);
```

As you can tell from the presence of an untyped **VAR** parameter here, the BGI is hedging its bets about the actual physical representation of its internal palette translation table. By refusing to build a specific structure into the BGI procedure definition, Borland has the ability to rearrange the table to some degree in a future release without changing the definition of the **SetAllPalette** procedure.

For the time being, the structure of the palette table is a record as shown below:

```
CONST
  MaxColors = 15;

TYPE
  PaletteType = RECORD
                  TableSize : Byte;
                  Colors    : ARRAY[0..MaxColors] OF ShortInt
                END;
```

The constant **MaxColors** is predefined in the **Graph** unit, and for the current release is limited to 16 colors. Version 5.0 supports more simultaneous colors and a larger palette, particularly under the 256-color modes present in the IBM VGA, 8514, and MCGA graphics devices.

The **TableSize** field in the **PaletteType** record specifies the number of bytes occupied by the translation table. For the time being, that will be equivalent to **MaxColors** plus one, since **MaxColors** counts from 0.

To use **SetAllPalette**, define a variable of type **PaletteType** and assign your translation values to the various fields as needed. Then invoke **SetAllPalette** with your **PaletteType** variable as the parameter. You may assign a value of –1 to any of the elements of the **Colors** array (this is the reason the values are of type **ShortInt**, which is a signed, 1-byte integer) and the –1 value indicates that the previous value in the BGI's table for that color is not to be changed.

Something to keep in mind is that color 0 in the palette table specifies the background color. Unless you wish the background color to be something other than black, don't redefine color 0.

Another thing to remember is that changing the palette affects all graphics information *currently* on the screen, as well as graphics figures drawn *after* the palette is changed. When you change any color in the palette, any graphics drawn in that color anywhere on the screen changes *instantly*.

SetAllPalette allows you to change the palette temporarily and then restore the original palette. To do this requires a little help from another BGI procedure:

```
PROCEDURE GetPalette(VAR CurrentPalette : PaletteType);
```

You can use **GetPalette** to return the current palette translation table in the parameter **CurrentPalette**, which is a record of the **PaletteType** type defined above. With the current palette saved in a holding variable of type **PaletteType**, you can change the palette to your special, temporary palette, do what work needs to be done, and then change the palette back to the saved palette:

```
VAR
    PaletteStash : PaletteType;

    GetPalette(PaletteStash);
    SetAllPalette(NewPalette);
    DrawSomething;
    SetAllPalette(PaletteStash);
```

As an example of how palettes work, I offer the following short program. It draws a large number of lines in random positions in random foreground colors. Then it alters the palette randomly, and each line drawn in a given color *instantly* changes to the new color. The lines are not being redrawn; the information on the screen is simply being reinterpreted within the new color translation scheme.

I call the program **PsychedelicFiberglass**, which might seem odd at first— but once you compile and run the program, you will see immediately how appropriate a name it is. Especially if (like me) you came of age in the Sixties.

```
{---------------------------------------------------------------}
{                      PsychedelicFiberglas                     }
{                                                               }
{                      by Jeff Duntemann                        }
{                      Turbo Pascal V7.0                        }
{                      Last update 2/19/93                      }
{                                                               }
{ This program demonstrates palette-switching through the BGI.  }
{ Children of the Sixties will understand the name.             }
{                                                               }
{     From BORLAND PASCAL FROM SQUARE ONE by Jeff Duntemann     }
{---------------------------------------------------------------}

PROGRAM PsychedelicFiberglas;

USES Crt,Graph;

VAR
    I,Color       : Integer;
    Palette       : PaletteType;
    GraphDriver   : Integer;
    GraphMode     : Integer;
    ErrorCode     : Integer;
```

```
BEGIN
  GraphDriver := Detect; { Let the BGI determine what board we're using }
   DetectGraph(GraphDriver,GraphMode);
   InitGraph(GraphDriver,GraphMode,'');
  ErrorCode := GraphResult;
  IF ErrorCode <> 0 THEN
    BEGIN
       Writeln('>>Halted on graphics error: ',GraphErrorMsg(ErrorCode));
      Halt(2)
    END;

  Randomize;

  GetPalette(Palette);
  FOR Color := 0 TO 10000 DO { Draw 10,000 lines in random colors }
    BEGIN
       SetColor(Random(Palette.Size));
       Line(Random(GetMaxX),Random(GetMaxY),
           Random(GetMaxX),Random(GetMaxY));
    END;

  REPEAT
    REPEAT I := Random(Palette.Size) UNTIL I <> 0;
    SetPalette(I,Random(Palette.Size));
  UNTIL KeyPressed;       { Cycle palettes until the user presses a key }

  CloseGraph; { Return to the text mode in force when we began }

END.
```

256-COLOR PALETTE ENHANCEMENTS

Turbo Pascal V5.0 expanded the maximum-sized palette to 256 colors, and added the IBM 8514A display device. This made palette management more complex than it was under the original V4.0 BGI. New routines were added to the BGI to deal with 256-color palette complexities.

The palette color lookup table varies in size depending on which graphics driver is loaded. A new function provides the preferred means of determining how many colors are in a particular driver's palette:

```
FUNCTION GetPaletteSize : Word;
```

The return value tells you how many colors are in the current driver's palette. This system replaces the 4.0 method, in which the **GetMaxColor** was the means used to query palette size.

The 8514 and VGA in 256 color mode presents a special problem for palette management, because they have a palette of 256 colors that may be chosen from among a group of 2^{18}, or 256,144. This massive number consists of three 6-bit values, one for Red, one for Green, and one for Blue. The 256-color palette comes filled with the standard default colors, the first 16 of which match the 16 standard colors used with the EGA and VGA high resolution modes. If you wish to experiment with some of those other 256,000-odd colors, you'll need to set them with the following procedure:

```
PROCEDURE SetRGBPalette(ColorNum,RedVal,GreenVal,BlueVal : Word);
```

Here, **ColorNum** specifies a number from 0–255 which is the entry in the 256-color palette you wish to specify, and the three remaining parameters provide the color values to be summed up as that entry in the table. Think of it as a means to specify a single 18-bit color number by breaking it down into component colors, each of which in turn are 6-bit intensity values for the red, green, and blue electron guns in an RGB analog monitor.

LINE STYLES

We tend to think of lines as mundane, from-here-to-there strokes of a single, uninterrupted color. In a simpler graphics system (such as that found in Turbo Pascal V3.0) this was the case. The BGI, however, allows you to add a little life to your lines, in two ways: thickness and "style," that is, lines that are drawn in a pattern of dots or dashes or combinations of both.

True, there are only two choices for line width: thin (one pixel wide) and thick (three pixels wide). But the combination of two-line thicknesses plus an almost unlimited variety of line styles (assuming you roll your own) provides a lot of latitude in laying down the line.

Line styles affect the patterns drawn by all of the following BGI draw routines: **Line**, **LineRel**, **Rectangle**, and **DrawPoly**. The procedures that draw curved lines (**Circle**, **Arc**, and **Ellipse**) are not affected, nor are the procedures that draw the stroke fonts.

Ordinarily, lines are drawn in the narrow width, without any specific line style. To change either line thickness or style (or both) you must use this BGI procedure:

```
PROCEDURE SetLineStyle(LineStyle : Word;
                       BitPattern : Word;
                       Thickness : Word);
```

There are a number of predefined constants to make your invocations of **SetLineStyle** more meaningful to the casual reader (including yourself, six months after the fact . . .). Table 22.6 summarizes the constants and what they mean.

All three of **SetLineStyle**'s parameters are type **Word**. The **LineStyle** parameter specifies either one of the BGI's four built-in line styles, or else a programmer-defined line style specified by the bit pattern in the second parameter, **BitPattern**. When using one of the four built-in line styles (**SolidLn**, **DottedLn**, **CenterLn**, or **DashedLn**) the **BitPattern** parameter should be passed a 0. The third parameter,

Table 22.6 BGI Line Style Constants

Constant	Value	Parameter	Comments
SolidLn	0	LineStyle	Solid line
DottedLn	1	LineStyle	Fairly coarse dotted line
CenterLn	2	LineStyle	Long dash/short dash pattern
DashedLn	3	LineStyle	Dashed line
UserBitLn	4	LineStyle	Causes BGI to use BitPattern
NormWidth	1	Thickness	1-pixel-wide lines
ThickWidth	3	Thickness	3-pixel-wide lines

Thickness, specifies one of the two BGI-supported line thicknesses. The only two legal values are 1 (**NormWidth**) or 3 (**ThickWidth**). Any other value passed in **Thickness** will be ignored, and lines will be drawn according to the last legal value passed in **Thickness**, or else the default (**NormWidth**) if **SetLineStyle** has not yet been called.

The best way to illustrate what **SetLineStyle** can do is by showing you an actual screen containing various types of lines drawn by the BGI. Figure 22.5 is such a screen. The **SetLineStyle** invocations that specified each of the 12 lines displayed in Figure 22.5 are given below, in the same order that the lines appear on the screen:

```
SetLineStyle(SolidLn,0,NormWidth);   { This is the default! }
SetLineStyle(DottedLn,0,NormWidth);
SetLineStyle(CenterLn,0,NormWidth);
SetLineStyle(DashedLn,0,NormWidth);

SetLineStyle(SolidLn,0,ThickWidth);
SetLineStyle(DottedLn,0,ThickWidth);
SetLineStyle(CenterLn,0,ThickWidth);
SetLineStyle(DashedLn,0,ThickWidth);

SetLineStyle(UserBitLn,$F99F,NormWidth);
SetLineStyle(UserBitLn,$AAAA,NormWidth);
SetLineStyle(UserBitLn,$C0C0,NormWidth);
SetLineStyle(UserBitLn,$E667,NormWidth);
```

The first **SetLineStyle** invocation given above is the default condition for line styles, and the values shown will be in force until you change them with a different set of values passed in **SetLineStyle**.

Custom line styles are represented by 16 bits, where a 1 bit will be drawn to the screen in the foreground color, and a 0 bit will be left in the background color. Designing custom bit patterns for your own line styles is as much a matter of trial-and-error as it is planning. Sketch out the line pattern you want to draw

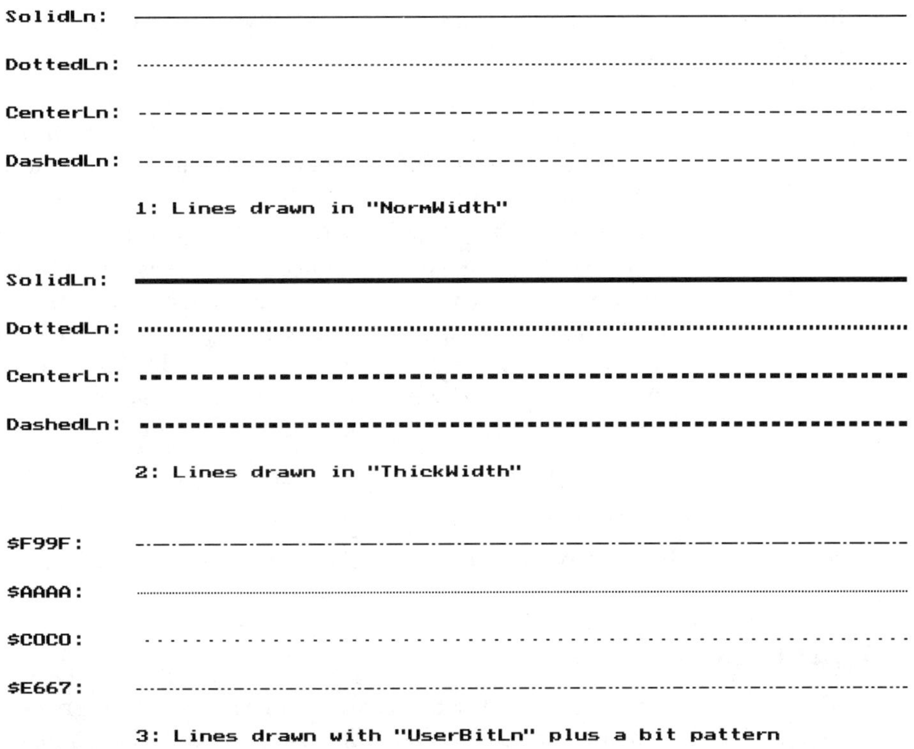

SolidLn: ————————————————————————————————

DottedLn: ···

CenterLn: — — — — — — — — — — — — — — — — — — —

DashedLn: — — — — — — — — — — — — — — — — — —

        1: Lines drawn in "NormWidth"

SolidLn: ████████████████████████████████████

DottedLn: ▪▪▪▪▪▪▪▪▪▪▪▪▪▪▪▪▪▪▪▪▪▪▪▪▪▪▪▪▪▪▪▪▪▪▪▪▪▪▪

CenterLn: ■ ■ ■ ■ ■ ■ ■ ■ ■ ■ ■ ■ ■ ■ ■ ■ ■ ■

DashedLn: ■■■ ■■■ ■■■ ■■■ ■■■ ■■■ ■■■ ■■■ ■■■ ■■■

        2: Lines drawn in "ThickWidth"

$F99F: — · — · — · — · — · — · — · — · — · — ·

$AAAA: ··

$C0C0: ·

$E667: — · · — · · — · · — · · — · · — · · — · ·

        3: Lines drawn with "UserBitLn" plus a bit pattern

Figure 22.5 Lines and Line Styles

on graph paper, blackening in the bits for the foreground color portions of the pattern. Then derive the binary bit pattern by translating the blackened blocks into 1-bits, and the empty blocks into 0-bits. Then display a line using your new line style, and if it isn't quite right, tweak it and try again. Remember always that the pattern "wraps" after 16 bits, and that bit 15 is right next to bit 0—there is no dead space left between them.

One final caution on line styles: The "gaps" in a styled line do not assert themselves when drawn over foreground color information. In other words, a styled line when drawn over a solid line or a filled bar of the same color will appear as solid. The gaps in the line are *allowed to remain* in the background color, but they are not *forced* to the background color! If the styled line is the same color as the foreground color of the graphics underneath it, the underlying graphics will show through, and the gaps will appear to vanish.

SETTING THE WRITE MODE FOR LINE DRAWING

Turbo Pascal 5.0 added a "write mode" feature to BGI line drawing. A *write mode* is the logical operation invoked when each pixel comprising the line being drawn is written to the screen. There are currently two write modes, present as named constants in the **BGI** unit:

CopyPut   with a value of 0. Here, pixels comprising the line are written directly to the screen, overwriting any pixels underneath the line on the screen. This is the only mode in which lines are written under Turbo Pascal 4.0.

XORPut   with a value of 1. When this write mode is in force, the pixels comprising the line are combined with pixels underneath the line on the screen, using the XOR logical operator. One interesting and useful property of the XOR logical operator is that a line written to the screen using write mode **XORPut** can be erased by simply writing the same line to the same place on the screen, again with write mode **XORPut** in force.

Setting the write mode is done with a new 5.0-specific procedure:

```
PROCEDURE SetWriteMode(WriteMode : Integer);
```

Here, **WriteMode** may have a value of 0 or 1. The default write mode is **CopyPut**.

FILL PATTERNS

What line styles are to lines, fill patterns are to areas. Actually, there are two ways of filling areas on the screen. One, fill styles, we will discuss here. The other, flood filling, will be discussed in the following section.

The BGI includes a number of relatively ordinary fill patterns, but it also gives you the option of defining your own. With a little cleverness you can fill an area with a pattern that looks like bricks, or shingles, or staring eyeballs.

Filling an area requires that we specify a fill style and a fill color. There are two different procedures to do this: **SetFillStyle** selects one of the predefined fill patterns; and **SetFillPattern** sets the current fill pattern to a custom pattern defined in an array of 8 bytes. In either case, the style is the pattern that fills the specified area, and the color is the color in which the pattern is drawn.

To choose one of the predefined patterns and an associated color, use **SetFillStyle**:

```
PROCEDURE SetFillStyle(Pattern : Word; Color : Word);
```

The **Color** parameter takes the number of a color that is legal for the current graphics device and mode. Currently, it cannot be larger than 15 for any supported graphics device.

In the **Pattern** parameter you pass one of several legal codes corresponding to predefined BGI fill patterns. As with most of the numerous codes valid for BGI operations, the **Graph** unit contains a number of predefined constants to make remembering the fill pattern codes easier:

Table 22.7 BGI Fill Pattern Constants

Constant	Value	Meaning
EmptyFill	0	Fills with background color
SolidFill	1	Fills with solid foreground color
LineFill	2	Horizontal line fill
LtSlashFill	3	Light forward slant line fill
SlashFill	4	Heavy forward slant line fill
BkSlashFill	5	Heavy backward slant line fill
LtBkSlashFill	6	Light backward slant line fill
HatchFill	7	Light crosshatch fill
XHatchFill	8	Heavy crosshatch fill
InterleaveFill	9	Interleaved line fill
WideDotFill	10	Wide-spaced dot fill
CloseDotFill	11	Narrow-spaced dot fill
UserFill	12	User-defined fill pattern

The best way to describe these patterns is simply to show them to you. Figure 22.6 is an actual screen dump of all 12 predefined fill patterns supplied with the BGI. The default fill pattern (that is, the fill pattern that is in force until you explicitly set another one with **SetFillStyle** or **SetFillPattern)** is a solid fill with white foreground pixels.

The fill pattern that you select using **SetFillPattern** is the pattern that the BGI will use when you draw filled graphics figures using the **Bar**, **Bar3D**, **FillPoly**, and **PieSlice** procedures.

I wrote a simple program that displays the 12 standard BGI fill patterns shown in Figure 22.6. It's an interesting demonstration of how to write a program that operates in a resolution-independent manner. Note that the regions displayed with the **Bar3D** routine are not positioned at any absolute X,Y location on the screen. That is, I didn't "hard-code" region coordinates into the program. Instead, I derived several initial values from the maximum width and height of the screen via **GetMaxX** and **GetMaxY**. These include the width and height of the regions, and the size in pixels of the space between them. All the calculations that position the regions on the screen are derived from those basic calculations.

It isn't absolutely resolution-independent, but you'll find that the ShowFill program displays the 12 regions in pretty much the same way on any BGI-supported graphics device.

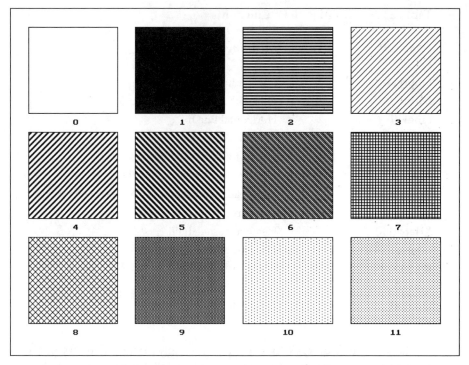

Figure 22.6 The Predefined BGI Fill Patterns; Captured from SHOWFILL.PAS

```
{--------------------------------------------------------------------}
{                           ShowFill                                 }
{                                                                    }
{ Demo program that displays all 12 of the standard fill styles }
{ included with the BGI in a resolution-independent way.            }
{                                                                    }
{                    by Jeff Duntemann                               }
{                    Turbo Pascal V7.0                               }
{                    Last update 2/20/93                             }
{                                                                    }
{    From: TURBO PASCAL FROM SQUARE ONE  by Jeff Duntemann          }
{--------------------------------------------------------------------}
PROGRAM ShowFill;

USES Graph;

TYPE
  String5 = STRING[5];

VAR
```

```
        GraphDriver : Integer;
        GraphMode   : Integer;
        ErrorCode   : Integer;
        I,J,K       : Integer;
        BoxWidth    : Integer;
        BoxHeight   : Integer;
        Offset      : Integer;
        ThisStyle   : Integer;
        StyleNumString : String[5];
        StartX,StartY : Integer;

    BEGIN
      GraphDriver := Detect;  { Let the BGI detect the board we're using }
      DetectGraph(GraphDriver,GraphMode);
      InitGraph(GraphDriver,GraphMode,'');
      ErrorCode := GraphResult;
      IF ErrorCode <> 0 THEN
        BEGIN
          Writeln('>>Halted on graphics error:',
                   GraphErrorMsg(ErrorCode));
          Halt(2)
        END;

      Rectangle(0,0,GetMaxX,GetMaxY);  { Draw frame around full screen }

      { Derive region-positioning values in a resolution-independent way: }
      Offset := GetMaxX DIV 24;
      BoxWidth  := GetMaxX DIV 5;
      BoxHeight := GetMaxY DIV 4;

      { This sets the text box position for display of the pattern number: }
      SetTextJustify(CenterText,CenterText);

      FOR I := 0 TO 3 DO     { Loop from left to right }
        FOR J := 0 TO 2 DO   { Loop from top to bottom }
          BEGIN
            ThisStyle := (J*4)+I; { Derive a single number value for style }
            Str(ThisStyle:2,StyleNumString); { Convert that value to string }
            SetFillStyle(ThisStyle,White); { Set the style for drawing    }
            { Derive upper left corner values for the next region: }
            StartX := Offset + (Offset+BoxWidth)*I;
            StartY := Offset + (Offset+BoxHeight)*J;
            { We use Bar3D with Depth=0 to draw region with a border:}
              Bar3D(StartX,StartY,
                  StartX+BoxWidth,StartY+BoxHeight,0,TopOn);
            { Draw the number of each fill pattern beneath its display: }
```

```
        OutTextXY(StartX+(BoxWidth DIV 2),
                   StartY+BoxHeight+(Offset DIV 2),
                   StyleNumString);
      END;

   Readln;        { Wait for the user to press Enter }
   CloseGraph;    { Shut down the BGI and return to text mode }
END.
```

DEFINING YOUR OWN FILL PATTERNS

The BGI provides 12 predefined fill patterns, but you aren't stuck with only those 12. Another BGI procedure allows you to define a custom fill pattern of your own and make it the current fill pattern:

```
PROCEDURE SetFillPattern(Pattern : FillPatternType; Color : Word);
```

The **FillPatternType** is defined in unit **Graph** and is nothing more than an array of 8 bytes:

```
TYPE
   FillPatternType : ARRAY[1..8] OF Byte;
```

Think of the 8 bytes in **FillPatternType** as a bitmap that is endlessly replicated throughout the area being filled. A 1-bit in any of the eight bytes becomes an illuminated pixel within the pattern. A 0-bit does not "erase" what is underneath it; rather, you should think of 0-bit portions of the fill pattern as being transparent and will allow any graphics beneath them to "shine through."

Designing a fill pattern, as with line styles, is best begun on square-ruled graph paper. Lay out an 8×8 pixel square area, and darken in the pixels that you wish to be illuminated in your pattern. Translate the pattern of darkened and white blocks into binary bytes, where the darkened squares are 1-bits and the white squares 0-bits. The top row of the design square becomes element 1 of a **FillPatternType** array, the second row of the design square becomes element 2 of the array, and so on. It takes some practice, because you tend to forget that the edges of the pattern join up with themselves. The block you lay out may bear little resemblance to the final pattern it produces in a filled region.

Figure 22.7 shows three such design squares and their translations into binary bytes, along with filled rectangles suggestive of how such patterns appear on an actual screen. Note especially the non-intuitive connection between the design square for the "squiggles" pattern and the pattern itself. It took some considerable trial-and-error to get "squiggles" right, because the wrap from top edge to bottom edge is crucial to the "squiggleness" of the pattern. "Blocks," by contrast, is a self-contained little pattern, its screen appearance obvious from the design square.

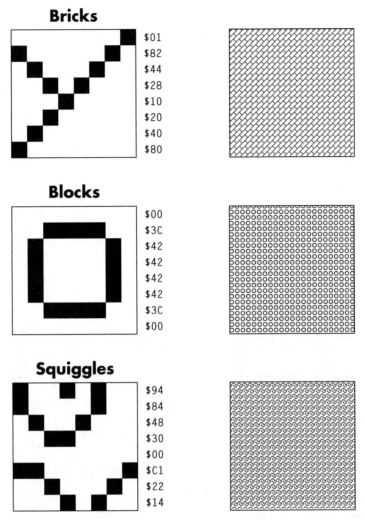

Figure 22.7 Pattern Design

I generally store my custom fill patterns as array constants, which is a compact and easily-readable way to represent them. The short program given below, PATTERNS.PAS, demonstrates how to store such patterns as array constants, assert them via **SetFillPattern**, and then use them to fill rectangles with the **Bar** procedure. **Patterns** simply draws six rectangles and fills them with six custom fill patterns in white. It is reasonably device-independent and should run on most any BGI-supported graphics device.

```
{------------------------------------------------------------------}
{                          Patterns                                }
{                                                                  }
{          Graphics pattern demonstration program                 }
{                                                                  }
{                               by Jeff Duntemann                  }
{                               Turbo Pascal V7.0                  }
{                               Last update 2/20/93                }
{                                                                  }
{     From: BORLAND PASCAL FROM SQUARE ONE   by Jeff Duntemann    }
{------------------------------------------------------------------}


PROGRAM Patterns;

USES Graph;

CONST
  Halftone1 : FillPatternType =
                ($CC,$33,$CC,$33,$CC,$33,$CC,$33);
  Halftone2 : FillPatternType =
                ($AA,$55,$AA,$55,$AA,$55,$AA,$55);
  Squiggles : FillPatternType =
                ($94,$84,$48,$30,$00,$c1,$22,$14);
  Vertical  : FillPatternType =
                ($CC,$CC,$CC,$CC,$CC,$CC,$CC,$CC);
  Bricks    : FillPatternType =
                ($01,$82,$44,$28,$10,$20,$40,$80);
  Blocks    : FillPatternType =
                ($00,$3C,$42,$42,$42,$42,$3C,$00);


VAR
  GraphDriver : Integer;
  GraphMode   : Integer;
  ErrorCode   : Integer;


BEGIN
  GraphDriver := Detect;   { Let the BGI detect the board we're using }
  DetectGraph(GraphDriver,GraphMode);
  InitGraph(GraphDriver,GraphMode,'');
  ErrorCode := GraphResult;
  IF ErrorCode <> 0 THEN
    BEGIN
      Writeln('>>Halted on graphics error: ',GraphErrorMsg(ErrorCode));
      Halt(2)
    END;
```

```
   SetFillPattern(Halftone1,White);
   Bar(0,0,99,100);
   Rectangle(0,0,99,100);

   SetFillPattern(Halftone2,White);
   Bar(110,0,209,100);
   Rectangle(110,0,209,100);

   SetFillPattern(Squiggles,White);
   Bar(220,0,319,100);
   Rectangle(220,0,319,100);

   SetFillPattern(Vertical,White);
   Bar(0,105,99,199);
   Rectangle(0,105,99,199);

   SetFillPattern(Bricks,White);
   Bar(110,105,209,199);
   Rectangle(110,105,209,199);

   SetFillPattern(Blocks,White);
   Bar(220,105,319,199);
   Rectangle(220,105,319,199);

   Readln;
   CloseGraph;
END.
```

QUERYING FILL PATTERNS AND COLORS

As with nearly all graphics attributes supported by the BGI, the fill patterns and colors may be queried by your programs. The routine that does this is:

```
PROCEDURE GetFillSettings(VAR FillData : FillSettingsType);
```

The settings are returned in a record of type **FillSettingsType**, which is predefined within the **Graph** unit:

```
TYPE
   FillSettingsType = RECORD
                         Pattern : Word;
                         Color   : Word
                      END;
```

If you're sharp you'll notice a weakness here—there is only one 2-byte word in which to report the fill pattern. What **GetFillSettings** reports is only the number of the predefined fill pattern that is currently in force. These numbers are given in Table 22.7. If a custom fill pattern is in force, **Pattern** will contain the code 12. The **Color** field will contain the color value passed to the BGI in **SetFillStyle** or **SetFillPattern**.

FLOOD FILLING

Regular, predictable figures such as rectangles, polygons, and pie-slices can be filled using a technique called *scan conversion* which is fast but limited to that sort of figure whose boundaries are mathematically predictable. Filling a region with irregular or unpredictable boundaries requires another sort of fill technique, called *flood filling*. In simplest terms, when the BGI does a flood fill, it picks a point on the screen at which to begin, and then propagates the pattern away from that point, stopping only when it reaches a boundary of a specified color. The procedure to do it is this:

```
PROCEDURE FloodFill(StartX,StartY : Integer; BoundaryColor : Word);
```

The parameters **StartX** and **StartY** specify a point in the viewport called a *seed*, which is where the flood operation begins. Flooding is limited by the boundaries of the current clipping viewport, the borders of the physical screen, or a region of foreground color specified by **BoundaryColor**.

The pattern used by **FloodFill** is the current fill pattern, set by either **SetFillStyle** or **SetFillPattern**, as described above. You will notice that flood filling is considerably slower than filling by scan conversion. There is a lot more testing to do; the BGI must literally test every graphics byte in the display buffer before it fills it, to be sure it doesn't try to fill over or beyond a proper color boundary.

One caution in using **FloodFill** is to be sure the region you intend to fill is truly closed. In other words, the boundary of foreground color specified by **BoundaryColor** must be complete and unbroken, all the way around. Even a one-pixel gap will let the fill pattern or color "leak out" and spread to fill the entire remaining empty area of the screen or viewport.

In general, use **Bar**, **Bar3D**, **FillPoly**, or **PieSlice** to generate filled areas whenever possible. Not only are they faster methods to fill space with color or a pattern, they appear to be more in line with Borland's future plans for the evolution of the BGI. Particularly, if Borland ever intends to make the BGI a true "world coordinate" graphics system, then flood filling becomes extremely difficult and may be eliminated altogether. The rift began with Turbo Pascal 5.0, since the 8514 driver added with that release does *not* support flood filling.

22.5 Polygons, Bars, Arcs, Circles, and Ellipses

We've discussed the basic BGI routines for drawing lines and rectangles, and used the **Bar** routine in the previous section to demonstrate the BGI's fill patterns. In this section we'll talk about the other BGI routines that actually draw figures on your screen.

DRAWING GENERIC POLYGONS

In computer graphics terms, a *polygon* is any figure composed only of straight lines. We're used to thinking of polygons as *closed* figures, that is, where one endpoint comes around and meets the other endpoint, forming an enclosed region. In fact, a wandering line composed of some number of line segments is just as genuinely a polygon, though it is variously called an *open polygon* or a *hull*. The easiest way to define such a figure (given that nothing requires it to be a *regular* polygon) is by defining a set of coordinate points acting as its vertices, and drawing lines from vertex to vertex until the figure is complete. This is the way the BGI operates, through this procedure:

```
PROCEDURE DrawPoly(PointCount : Word; VAR PointSet);
```

Here, **PointCount** specifies the number of vertices the polygon will have. One quirk here is that the beginning and ending vertex are considered separate points and must have separate coordinates, even if they are at an identical position on the screen. This is necessary, again, because in an open polygon the two end vertices *are* separate and distinct points. Obviously, the number of vertices will vary from call to call, so passing the coordinates of the vertices is a bit of a problem. The problem is solved by making the **PointSet** parameter untyped, so that any data type at all can be passed through it.

Actually, for **DrawPoly** to work correctly, what the BGI expects in **PointSet** is an array of a record type called **PointType**. The definition of **PointType** is in unit **Graph**:

```
TYPE
    PointType = RECORD
                    X,Y : Integer
                END;
```

You can create arrays of **PointType** as array constants, or build the arrays on the heap, or simply make them global and fill them with assignment statements. Something important to keep in mind: *The vertices of a polygon are specified as absolute and not relative coordinates.* This is a shame, in some ways, because to relocate a polygon to another position on the screen you must recalculate and change *all* values in *every* **PointType** record that specifies a vertex. For a complicated polygon this could take a significant amount of time, but for now it can't be helped.

Below is an array constant that contains the vertex definitions for a tolerable (if not entirely regular) pentagon:

```
Pentagon  : ARRAY[0..5] OF PointType =
              ((X : 100; Y :  10),
               (X : 200; Y :  80),
               (X : 155; Y : 160),
               (X :  45; Y : 160),
               (X :   0; Y :  80),
               (X : 100; Y :  10));
```

To define a polygon with more or fewer vertices, simply extend or reduce the number of elements in the array specification at the top, and fill in or trim the definition accordingly. Drawing the pentagon would be done this way:

```
DrawPoly(6,Pentagon);
```

Remember that the **PointCount** parameter takes the number of vertices in **PointSet**, *not* the high index of the array. Also remember that for closed polygons the number of vertices is one more than we might, from common sense, expect, since two of the vertices are the same and lie "atop" one another on the screen. The polygon is drawn in the current line style and color, as set by **SetLineStyle**.

The BGI has machinery for drawing filled polygons in a very similar fashion, using a separate procedure:

```
PROCEDURE FillPoly(PointCount : Word; VAR PointSet);
```

In terms of its parameters and its calling syntax and conventions, **DrawPoly** and **FillPoly** are absolutely identical. Their only difference is what they draw on the screen. Both draw the outline of the polygon in the current line style and color, but **FillPoly** also fills the polygon with the current fill pattern. As with **DrawPoly**, the perimeter of the filled polygon is drawn in the current line style and color, as set by **SetLineStyle**.

Ahh, but you may think of the catch: What about open polygons? Common sense tells us that you can't fill an open polygon (which may be no more than a jagged line) and common sense is correct. If you pass an open polygon to **FillPoly**, the BGI will draw the shortest line between the two end vertices and *then* fill it. No error will be generated. In a sense, the BGI guarantees that **FillPoly** will always work with a closed polygon by closing any open polygon that happens to be passed to **FillPoly**.

The short program below defines two polygons, one open, and one closed. The closed polygon is the pentagon defined above, and the open polygon is a crooked line with some passing resemblance to the Big Dipper. POLYGON.PAS demonstrates how polygons are defined in typed constants, and shows how the BGI closes an open polygon before it fills the open polygon with **FillPoly**.

The program also demonstrates one easy method for moving a polygon: Using a **FOR** loop to step through either the X or Y coordinates and adding or subtracting the same value to all coordinates. POLYGON.PAS only moves them in the Y direction, but there is no reason you could not use a single FOR statement to shift a polygon in both the X and Y dimensions at the same time.

```
{------------------------------------------------------------------}
{                          Polygons                                }
{                                                                  }
{        Polygon draw/polygon fill demonstration program           }
{                                                                  }
{                        by Jeff Duntemann                          }
{                        Turbo Pascal V7.0                          }
{                        Last update 2/20/93                        }
{                                                                  }
{    From: BORLAND PASCAL FROM SQUARE ONE   by Jeff Duntemann       }
{------------------------------------------------------------------}
PROGRAM Polygons;
```

```
USES Graph;

CONST
  Squiggles : FillPatternType =
              ($94,$84,$48,$30,$00,$c1,$22,$14);

  Pentagon  : ARRAY[0..5] OF PointType =
              ((X : 100; Y :  10),
               (X : 200; Y :  80),
               (X : 155; Y : 160),
               (X :  45; Y : 160),
               (X :   0; Y :  80),
               (X : 100; Y :  10));

  BigDipper : ARRAY[0..5] OF PointType =
              ((X : 350; Y :  20),
               (X : 420; Y :  35),
               (X : 475; Y : 100),
               (X : 450; Y : 160),
               (X : 530; Y : 195),
               (X : 600; Y : 150));

VAR
  I           : Integer;
  GraphDriver : Integer;
  GraphMode   : Integer;
  ErrorCode   : Integer;

BEGIN
  GraphDriver := Detect; { Let the BGI determine what board we're using }
   DetectGraph(GraphDriver,GraphMode);
   InitGraph(GraphDriver,GraphMode,'');
  ErrorCode := GraphResult;
  IF ErrorCode <> 0 THEN
    BEGIN
      Writeln('>>Halted on graphics error: ',GraphErrorMsg(ErrorCode));
      Halt(2)
    END;

  SetFillPattern(Squiggles,White);

  DrawPoly(6,Pentagon);
  FOR I := 0 TO 5 DO     { Translate the pentagon down 160 pixels }
    Pentagon[I].Y := Pentagon[I].Y + 160;
  FillPoly(6,Pentagon);

  DrawPoly(6,BigDipper);
```

```
FOR I := 0 TO 5 DO      { Translate the Big Dipper down 140 pixels }
   BigDipper[I].Y := BigDipper[I].Y + 140;
 FillPoly(6,BigDipper);

 Readln;
 CloseGraph;
END.
```

Figure 22.8 is a screen shot of the patterns produced by POLYGON.PAS. Note the way that the Big Dipper figure was filled by the BGI, as two separate closed figures formed when the two endpoints of the figure were connected by the shortest line between them.

DRAWING RECTANGLES AND BARS

We've already used the BGI's **Rectangle** procedure informally. It draws an outline rectangle in the current line style and color:

```
PROCEDURE Rectangle(X1,Y1,X2,Y2 : Integer);
```

where **X1,Y1** specify the upper left corner of the rectangle, and **X2,Y2** specify the lower left corner of the rectangle. **Rectangle** is viewport-relative.

Drawing a filled rectangle is done with the **Bar** procedure:

```
PROCEDURE Bar(X1,Y1,X2,Y2 : Integer);
```

Bar is basically identicial to **Rectangle**, except that the interior of the rectangle is filled with the current fill color or pattern, as set by **SetFillStyle** or **SetFillPattern**. The perimeter of the bar is *not* drawn—only the interior portion is generated in the fill color or pattern, and the pattern goes out to the edges. If you want a line

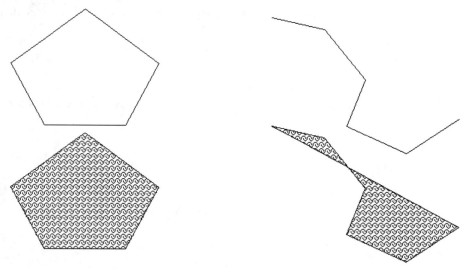

Figure 22.8 Open and Closed Polygons

perimeter around your bars, you must draw them separately, with the **Rect-angle** statement, *after* the bar is drawn. (There's another trick you can use: Draw a 3-D bar with the **Bar3D** routine, and specify a depth of 0.) If you draw the perimeter first with **Rectangle** and *then* try to fill the rectangle with the **Bar** statement, you'll discover that your perimeter disappears under the fill color or pattern. Like **Rectangle**, **Bar** is viewport-relative.

Far more interesting than either **Rectangle** or **Bar** is **Bar3D**:

```
PROCEDURE Bar3D(X1,Y1,X2,Y2 : Integer;
                Depth       : Word;
                Top         : Boolean);
```

The idea is to facilitate the generation of 3-D bar graphs, which are very popular with the desktop-presentation set. The first four parameters operate identically to those of **Rectangle** and **Bar**, and set the upper left corner and lower right corner of the front-facing rectangle of the 3-D bar to be drawn. The **Depth** parameter specifies the depth of the 3-D bar in pixels. The **Top** parameter speci-fies whether the top portion of the bar's 3-D extension is to be drawn. This becomes important if you want to stack bars of different colors or fill patterns, as is often done in bar graphs to indicate different meanings for portions of the same numeric figure.

Unlike **Bar**, an outline *is* drawn around the filled portion of the bar. This outline is drawn in the current line color and style. You can use this feature to your advantage in drawing "flat" bars by specifying a **Depth** parameter of 0. When **Depth=0**, a single-line border appears around the bar. This is the easiest way to draw a patterned bar with a border in the BGI.

The best way to appreciate **Bar3D** is to see it operate. Figure 22.9 shows the BGI's rectangle family. Note the two stacked bars filled with different patterns. The bottom bar was drawn with **Top** set to **False**, so that the top of the bar was not drawn. The top bar was drawn with **Top** set to **True**, so that a top was drawn, properly finishing it off as the top of the entire bar.

The four figures shown in Figure 22.9 were drawn on an EGA screen with the statement sequence below. The two patterns, **Squiggles** and **Bricks**, were de-fined in the **Patterns** program given in the previous section.

```
SetFillPattern(Squiggles,White);   { Set a fill pattern }
Rectangle(50,50,150,420);          { Draw an outline rectangle }
Bar(200,50,300,420);               { Draw a filled bar }
Bar3D(350,50,450,420,10,True);     { Draw a filled 3-D bar }
Bar3D(500,50,600,148,10,True);     { Draw top portion of a 2-part bar }
SetFillPattern(Bricks,White);      { Change fill pattern }
Bar3D(500,148,600,420,10,False);   { Draw bottom part of a 2-part bar }
```

DRAWING ELLIPSES AND ELLIPTICAL ARCS

Drawing curved figures of any kind is always harder than creating things out of straight lines. The BGI does a tolerable job of certain kinds of curved figures,

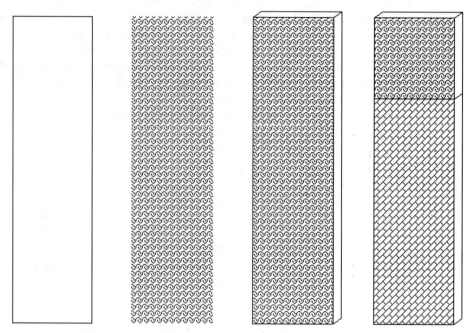

Figure 22.9 Rectangular Figures

although it has no general procedure for drawing curved lines. Specifically, the BGI draws ellipses, circles (which are special cases of the more general ellipse), portions of ellipses or circles called arcs, and filled segments of circles called *pie slices* from their only real use in generating the ever-popular pie chart.

The most general routine for drawing curved figures with the BGI draws ellipses and elliptical arcs:

```
PROCEDURE Ellipse(X,Y : Integer; StartAngle,EndAngle : Word;
                  XRadius,YRadius : Word);
```

The **X** and **Y** parameters specify a "center" point for the ellipse or arc. If you know geometry this might seem odd, since ellipses actually have two centers. In the context of the BGI, however, the center of a drawn ellipse is the midpoint of the major axis. This major axis is always either horizontal or vertical; it is not possible to draw an ellipse on an oblique axis. (See Figure 22.10.)

Specifying the shape of an ellipse must be done by passing **Ellipse** two separate radius figures. **XRadius** specifies the distance in pixels from the center of the ellipse to the edge of the ellipse along the X (horizontal) axis. **YRadius** specifies the distance from the center of the ellipse to its edge along the Y (vertical) axis. Bullet 1 in Figure 22.10 shows a complete ellipse with its relation to the center point at **X,Y** and the two radius figures, **XRadius** and **YRadius**.

The ellipse will be drawn in the current drawing color; however, ellipses do not use styled lines and will be drawn only in a single-pixel solid line.

There is no generalized curve-drawing routine in the BGI for drawing spline curves. (That is, generalized curved figures with no required regular formula to

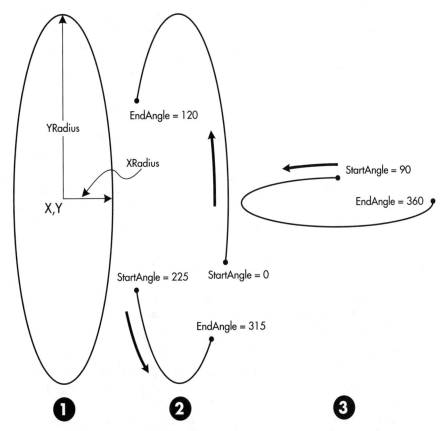

Ellipse(X, Y, StartAngle, EndAngle, XRadius, YRadius);

Figure 22.10 The Structure of Ellipses and Arcs

them.) However, the **Ellipse** procedure is versatile enough to draw elliptical arcs, which (with some cleverness and patience) may be pieced together to form continuous curves.

An elliptical arc is nothing more than a portion of the perimeter of an ellipse. Bullet 2 in Figure 22.10 shows two such portions of the same ellipse shown in Bullet 1. By varying the axes of the ellipse and the portion of the ellipse "lifted" out as a curve, most simple curved segments can be produced.

Specifying the portions of an ellipse drawn as elliptical arcs is done with angular measurement. The ellipse is divided into 360 degrees, with the 0 point at 3 o'clock. The degree measurement increases in a counterclockwise direction, all the way around the ellipse until the 360 degree point, which is the same as the 0 point. 90 degrees is at 12 o'clock, 180 degrees at 9 o'clock, 270 degrees at 6 o'clock, and so on. The upper curve at Bullet 2 in Figure 22.10 starts at 0 degrees and continues to 120 degrees. The curve may start anywhere along the perimeter of the ellipse; the bottom curve at Bullet 2 begins at 225 degrees and continues to 315 degrees.

As with complete ellipses, elliptical arcs are drawn only in a solid, single-pixel width line. Line styles and thicknesses do not operate at all within the **Ellipse** procedure. Portions of a drawn ellipse extending beyond the bounds of the current clipping viewport or beyond the physical screen are clipped and not displayed.

DRAWING FILLED ELLIPSES

Creating filled ellipses is done with the following procedure:

```
PROCEDURE FillEllipse(X,Y : Integer; XRadius,YRadius : Word);
```

Functionally, **FillEllipse** is identical to **Ellipse** minus **Ellipse**'s ability to draw elliptical arcs. (Filling an arc is meaningless, so the **StartAngle** and **EndAngle** parameters are not present.) The ellipse, when drawn, is filled with the current fill pattern using scan conversion.

DRAWING CIRCLES AND CIRCULAR ARCS

In geometry, a circle is actually a special case of an ellipse. The same is true to some extent in the BGI. Circles are needed often enough to warrant their having a procedure all to themselves:

```
PROCEDURE Circle(X,Y : Integer; Radius : Word);
```

Circles are simpler creatures than ellipses. The **X,Y** parameters specify the coordinates of the circle's center point, and **Radius** specifies the radius of the circle in pixels. The circle is drawn using the current drawing color, but, as with **Ellipse**, line styles do not operate on circles.

The BGI supplies a separate routine for drawing circular arcs:

```
PROCEDURE Arc(X,Y : Integer; StartAngle,EndAngle,Radius : Word);
```

A circular arc is simply a segment of a circle. The **X,Y** parameters, again, specify the center point of the circle of which the arc is a segment. **Radius** is the radius of the arc. **StartAngle** and **EndAngle** operate precisely as they do in **Ellipse**: They indicate the angular portion of the circle which the arc represents. The 0 point is at 3 o'clock, and so on, just as for **Ellipse**.

Why are there separate routines for drawing circles and arcs? Over the years, computer scientists have developed tricky methods for drawing circles very quickly that depend on the circle's radial symmetry. Only *one eighth* of the circle is actually calculated; the remaining seven sections are plotted as "reflections" of the single calculated segment. In drawing an arc, the code does not know up front what angular portion of the arc will be drawn. It must be ready to calculate and draw all portions of the arc, and for a sizeable arc this could take much longer than for a circle of equal radius. In short, the BGI draws circles about as quickly as it is possible to draw them; arcs, being a messier problem to solve, are drawn with their own procedure.

As with circles and ellipses, circular arcs are drawn in the current drawing color but without adhering to the current line style.

The BGI allows programs to query the coordinates of the last arc drawn using the **Arc** procedure:

```
PROCEDURE GetArcCoords(VAR ArcCoords : ArcCoordsType);
```

The procedure returns a record type that is predefined within the **Graph** unit:

```
TYPE
   ArcCoordsType = RECORD
                     X,Y : Integer;
                     XStart,YStart : Word;
                     Xend,YEnd : Word
                   END;
```

The **X,Y** fields are the coordinates of the center point of the last arc drawn. **XStart,YStart** are the coordinates of the starting point of the arc, and **XEnd,YEnd** are the coordinates of the last point drawn. All coordinates are relative to the current viewport.

Why is this useful? Remember that when you specify an arc, you don't specify the coordinates for the starting and ending points. You specify *angles*. The BGI then calculates what pixels on the screen these angles represent. If you want to merge a straight line seamlessly with the end of an arc, you need to know the exact X,Y coordinates of the end in question.

A good example of how this feature might be used lies in the drawing of "rounded rectangles." Most people feel that rectangles with rounded corners are slightly more aesthetically pleasing than rectangles that come to sharp points at all four corners. Drawing four 90° arcs as the corners of a rectangle and then connecting the endpoints of the arcs with straight lines will produce a rounded rectangle. The following procedure generalizes the idea:

```
{->>>>RoundedRectangle<<<<------------------------------------------}
{                                                                   }
{ Filename : ROUNDRCT.SRC - Last Modified 2/20/93                   }
{                                                                   }
{ This routine draws a rectangle at X,Y; Width pixels wide and }
{ Height pixels high; with rounded corners of radius R.             }
{                                                                   }
{ The Graph unit must be USED for this procedure to compile.   }
{                                                                   }
{   From: BORLAND PASCAL FROM SQUARE ONE  by Jeff Duntemann   }
{-------------------------------------------------------------------}

PROCEDURE RoundedRectangle(X,Y,Width,Height,R : Word);

VAR
   ULData,LLData,LRData,URData : ArcCoordsType;

BEGIN
  { First we draw each corner arc and save its coordinates: }
  Arc(X+R,Y+R,90,180,R);
```

```
        GetArcCoords(ULData);
        Arc(X+R,Y+Height-R,180,270,R);
        GetArcCoords(LLData);
        Arc(X+Width-R,Y+Height-R,270,360,R);
        GetArcCoords(LRData);
        Arc(X+Width-R,Y+R,0,90,R);
        GetArcCoords(URData);
        { Next we draw the four connecting lines: }
        Line(ULData.XEnd,ULData.YEnd,LLData.XStart,LLData.YStart);
        Line(LLData.XEnd,LLData.YEnd,LRData.XStart,LRData.YStart);
        Line(LRData.XEnd,LRData.YEnd,URData.XStart,URData.YStart);
        Line(URData.XEnd,URData.YEnd,ULData.XStart,ULData.YStart);
    END;
```

A separate record of type **ArcCoordsType** is defined for each of the four corners. After each corner is drawn, its coordinates are immediately queried and stored in the appropriate record. Only when all four corners have been drawn are the straight lines drawn to connect the rounded corners. Can you explain why?

It is possible to put nonsense values for R (a radius larger than the rectangle is wide, for example) but aside from bizarre graphics on the screen, no harm will come of it. Keep in mind that if you have a line style in force, the straight lines in the drawn figure will use the line style whereas the rounded corners will not.

PIE SLICES

The BGI includes a routine that will draw a filled circle, or a "filled arc" more commonly called a *pie slice*:

```
    PROCEDURE PieSlice(X,Y : Integer; StartAngle,EndAngle,Radius : Word);
```

The parameter list here is identical to that of the **Arc** procedure, both in declaration and operation. An arc is drawn just as it would be using the **Arc** procedure, using the current drawing color. Next, its endpoints are joined to the arc's center point at **X,Y** by two straight lines. These lines will be drawn in the current drawing color *and current line style*. Finally, the region enclosed by the arc and the two radius lines is filled using the BGI's scan converter and the current fill color or pattern.

This provides a means of drawing a filled circle—assuming it is filled by the current drawing color:

```
    PieSlice(100,100,0,360,40);
```

This statement will draw a circle filled with the current drawing color. Notice that the start angle is 0 and the end angle is 360—indicating a complete circle. The problem with drawing filled circles arises if they are to be filled with a pattern or some color *other* than the current drawing color. The radius lines running between the center point and the end points of the arc will still be drawn, even if the arc specified is a complete circle. What you have is a line from the center of the circle to the 3 o'clock position, as shown in the uppermost of the two filled circles in Figure 22.11.

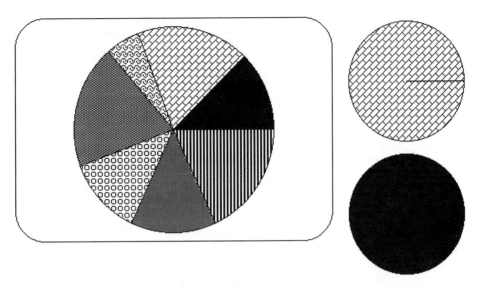

Figure 22.11 Pie Slices in Various Uses

The way around this is to use the **SetColor** procedure to set the current drawing color to the same color as the fill color you specify with **SetFillStyle**. This will yield the bottom circle of the pair in Figure 22.11.

The only important use of **PieSlice** lies in generating segments of filled circles for inclusion in pie chart graphs. Figure 22.11 shows such a chart, with seven separate pie slices sharing a common center point, each filled with a different fill pattern. The box around the pie chart was drawn with the **RoundedRectangle** procedure presented earlier.

The program below, PIEMAN.PAS, generated the graphics shown in Figure 22.11.

```
{-------------------------------------------------------------}
{                           PieMan                            }
{                                                             }
{             PieSlice demonstration program                  }
{                                                             }
{                            by Jeff Duntemann               }
{                            Turbo Pascal V7.0               }
{                            Last update 2/20/93             }
{                                                             }
{   From: BORLAND PASCAL FROM SQUARE ONE   by Jeff Duntemann }
{-------------------------------------------------------------}


PROGRAM PieMan;

USES Graph;

CONST        { Fill Patterns for pie chart: }
  Halftone1 : FillPatternType =
```

```
                              ($CC,$33,$CC,$33,$CC,$33,$CC,$33);
     Halftone2 : FillPatternType =
                   ($AA,$55,$AA,$55,$AA,$55,$AA,$55);
     Squiggles : FillPatternType =
                   ($94,$84,$48,$30,$00,$c1,$22,$14);
     Vertical  : FillPatternType =
                   ($CC,$CC,$CC,$CC,$CC,$CC,$CC,$CC);
     Bricks    : FillPatternType =
                   ($01,$82,$44,$28,$10,$20,$40,$80);
     Blocks    : FillPatternType =
                   ($00,$3C,$42,$42,$42,$42,$3C,$00);


VAR
  GraphDriver : Integer;
  GraphMode   : Integer;
  ErrorCode   : Integer;


{$I ROUNDRCT.SRC}   { RoundedRectangle }


BEGIN
  GraphDriver := Detect; { Let the BGI determine what board we're using }
  DetectGraph(GraphDriver,GraphMode);
  InitGraph(GraphDriver,GraphMode,'');
  ErrorCode := GraphResult;
  IF ErrorCode <> 0 THEN
    BEGIN
      Writeln('>>Halted on graphics error: ',GraphErrorMsg(ErrorCode));
      Halt(2)
    END;


  RoundedRectangle(30,30,380,260,35);   { Draw the pie graph frame }


  PieSlice(220,160,0,45,120);                { Draw the pie chart segments }
  SetFillPattern(Bricks,White);
  PieSlice(220,160,45,110,120);
  SetFillPattern(Squiggles,White);
  PieSlice(220,160,110,130,120);
  SetFillPattern(Halftone1,White);
  PieSlice(220,160,130,200,120);
  SetFillPattern(Blocks,White);
  PieSlice(220,160,200,245,120);
  SetFillPattern(Halftone2,White);
  PieSlice(220,160,245,295,120);
  SetFillPattern(Vertical,White);
  PieSlice(220,160,295,360,120);


  SetFillStyle(SolidFill,White); { Set White as fill color }
```

```
    PieSlice(500,260,0,360,70);      { Draw a color-filled circle }
    SetFillPattern(Bricks,White);    { Set a fill pattern }
    PieSlice(500,105,0,360,70);      { Draw a pattern-filled circle }

    ReadIn;
    CloseGraph;
END.
```

DRAWING ELLIPTICAL SECTORS

The BGI extends the concept of a circular pie slice to an elliptical pie slice, more formally called a *sector*. A sector is a portion of an elliptical arc with the end-points of the arc joined to the center of the ellipse. It is, in essence, a pie slice with an X radius and a Y radius:

```
PROCEDURE Sector(X,Y : Integer;
                 StartAngle,EndAngle,
                 XRadius,YRadius : Word);
```

As with **PieSlice**, **Sector** fills the region enclosed by the arc with the current fill color and style.

22.6 Bit Fonts and Stroke Fonts

The word "font" is a relatively recent addition to the IBM PC vocabulary, since until fairly recently there was only one font available—the one embedded in ROM on the display board. The EGA graphics board had the ability to load several text fonts, but no software really took advantage of the power. With the appearance of faster machines and more sophisticated graphics software, fonts become an essential part of graphics programming. The BGI's font support is considerable, and in this section we'll examine it in detail.

BIT FONTS

A *bit font* is a font defined as a pattern of individual pixels—each one repre-sented by one bit in a table somewhere in memory. All text-mode fonts are bit fonts, generally burned into Programmable Read Only Memory chips (PROMs) on the graphics board. The BGI provides a bit font for use in graphics modes. The character patterns in the BGI's bit font are limited to a character cell 8 pixels high and 8 pixels wide. The bit font is thus called an "8 × 8" font.

An 8 × 8 font may seem small, but it can be made larger by representing each pixel in the character patterns by four pixels arranged in squares. Enlarging it therefore means doubling its size at each level of enlargement, which is not a great deal of control. Furthermore, as the font gets larger it starts looking "blockier"; and therefore becoming uglier and harder to read.

Bit fonts have the advantage that they can be displayed on the screen very rapidly, since displaying a bit font character is only a matter of moving 8 bytes from one location in memory (the character pattern table) to another (the video display buffer).

STROKE FONTS

Another kind of font is the *stroke font*, so called because its characters are defined as sequences of straight lines or *strokes*, as of the stroke of a pen. Stroke fonts can be made very elaborate, almost calligraphic and ornamental, and very pleasing compared to the blockier bit fonts. Since they are composed of straight lines, stroke fonts are easily scaled up or down in size in very fine increments, simply by making each line comprising each character a little bit longer or a little bit shorter, with everything in proportion. These stylistic and scaling features come at the cost of speed, since every character requires several (or perhaps 15 or 20) line-draw operations. Also, because the lines on a typical PC graphics device are relatively coarse, stroke font characters can only be made so small before they blur into unintelligible blobs. In use they tend to be much larger on the screen than bit font characters, more suitable for titles and banners on presentation slides than for dense text.

SETTING FONT TYPE, SIZE, AND DIRECTION

A BGI font has three characteristics: font type—that is, which font from the BGI's repertoire; font size on the screen; and the direction the text is to read—from left to right in a horizontal direction, or from bottom to top in a vertical direction. Fonts are drawn in the current drawing color, but even though stroke fonts are drawn with straight lines, they are *not* affected by the current line style. In other words, you can draw stroke fonts only in continuous rather than dashed or dotted lines.

Setting font parameters is done with a single procedure:

```
PROCEDURE SetTextStyle(Font,Direction,CharSize : Word);
```

"Normal" size for a bit font is 1, and for a stroke font is 4. Stroke fonts will display with a **CharSize** value from 1–3, but they will rarely be readable and are almost never attractive. The largest value accepted for any font is 10. Passing a value larger than 10 in **CharSize** will not trigger any sort of error; however, the BGI will treat the oversize value as though it were the value 10, and the characters will be drawn no larger than they would if 10 were passed in **CharSize** instead.

For the other two parameters, a number of constants have been defined to make dealing with raw numeric codes a little easier. Table 22.8 summarizes the font constants as defined in the BGI.

The **Direction** parameter indicates which way the text will be displayed on the screen. With **Direction** set to 0, text will be displayed normally, from left to

Table 22.8 BGI Font Constants

Constant	Value	Parameter	Meaning
DefaultFont	0	Font	The BGI's default 8×8 bit font
TriplexFont	1	Font	"Three line" serif stroke font
SmallFont	2	Font	Highly reduceable stroke font
SansSerifFont	3	Font	"Two-line" font without serifs
GothicFont	4	Font	"Ye Olde English" ornamental font
HorizDir	0	Direction	Left to right, horizontally
VertDir	1	Direction	Bottom to top, vertically

right in a horizontal direction. When **Direction** is set to 1, text will be displayed vertically, starting from the bottom and going toward the top of the screen.

The available BGI fonts are easier to display than describe. I've shown a sampling of all fonts in Figure 22.12. Font 2, **SmallFont**, is an attempt to define a stroke font that is readable and tolerably attractive in small sizes. Unlike most of the other fonts, it loses something with a gain in size. It begins to look slightly bizarre when enlarged, because it is comprised of relatively few strokes, and individual characters come to resemble something off the cover of a heavy metal rock album. It is the only stroke font that can hold its own at the same size as the default font 0. Keep in mind, though, that it takes longer to display text with **SmallFont** than with **DefaultFont**, even when they are scaled to approximately the same size.

GothicFont is highly ornamental and difficult to read at any size. Its deliberately antique nature clashes severely with the high-tech look of a graphics application on a color screen. The two best fonts for use at fairly large sizes are **TriplexFont** and **SansSerifFont**, which differ almost entirely in that one has serifs and the other doesn't. A "serif" in font jargon is one of those little swellings at the extremities of certain characters, for example, at the bottom of the uppercase "T" and lowercase "p." Fonts without serifs (called "sans serif" fonts; "sans" is French for "without") look simpler and more modern and may be slightly easier to read than fonts with serifs, but apart from that serifs matter only in questions of aesthetics.

THE "OTHER" BGI STROKE FONTS

They're not mentioned in the V7.0 documentation, but there are several additional BGI stroke fonts packaged with V7.0 that may be used in almost the same way as the four standard fonts shown in Figure 22.12. The main difference is that these additional fonts do *not* have a predefined constant exported by the **Graph** unit. You use them in the same way, but you must pass a numeric value to **SetTextStyle** rather than a predefined constant. I've summarized them in Table 22.9.

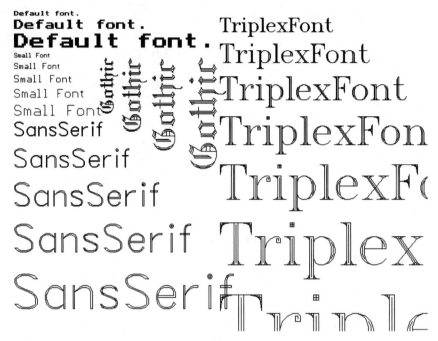

Figure 22.12 The BGI Standard Fonts

Note that although I've suggested a constant to represent each of these fonts to be consistent with the constants representing the four standard BGI stroke fonts, these constants have to be defined by you in your code before you can use them. You have the option of simply passing the stated font value to **SetTextStyle**, but the constants make things much easier to understand when reading your code.

Aside from not having predefined constants, these additional fonts are used just like the standard fonts. As with the standard fonts, make sure the .CHR files are where your program can find them! For sample output from the additional fonts, see the screen shot in Figure 22.13.

Table 22.9 Undocumented BGI Stroke Fonts

Font Name	*Style Value*	*Font File*	*Suggested Constant*
Script	5	SCRI.CHR	ScriptFont
Simplex	6	SIMP.CHR	SimplexFont
Triplex Script	7	TSCR.CHR	TriplexScriptFont
Complex	8	LCOM.CHR	ComplexFont
European	9	EURO.CHR	EuroFont
Bold	10	BOLD.CHR	BoldFont

Figure 22.13 The Undocumented BGI Fonts

FONT INITIALIZATION ERRORS

When you execute **SetTextStyle**, the BGI must load and prepare a font file for use. This means that it is at the mercy of your disk system. If the font file is not found on the disk, or if the drive is not ready for access, errors will be generated. You should check **GraphResult** after calling **SetTextStyle** to see if all went well. The possible errors are summarized in Table 22.10.

The Default font (font 0) is the only font that does *not* need to be loaded from a disk file. Its character patterns are part of the BGI and are always kept in memory. All other fonts are separate files with a .CHR extension. You should

Table 22.10 Font Initialization Error Codes

Error	Meaning
-8	Font file not found
-9	Not enough memory to load the font selected
-12	Graphics I/O error
-13	Invalid font file
-14	Invalid font number

keep in mind that alternating rapidly between stroke fonts will cause delays as the fonts are loaded and reloaded repeatedly from disk.

DISPLAYING TEXT ON THE SCREEN

Two routines are provided for actually displaying graphics text on your screen:

```
PROCEDURE OutText(TextString : String);
PROCEDURE OutTextXY(X,Y : Integer; TextString : String);
```

They differ only in how the position of the text on the screen is determined. **OutText** places the text at the current pointer (CP), while **OutTextXY** places the text at the coordinates passed in **X,Y**.

As you might have begun to think, in looking at Figure 22.13, there's a little more to it than that. A text string executed with a variable-sized font occupies a varying amount of space on the screen. Where is the positioning point? And where does an **OutText** operation leave the CP?

You have to learn to think of displaying text under the BGI as a process of generating a rectangular box full of graphics and then positioning it somewhere on the screen. I call this the *text box*, even though the "box" is invisible and only the text is ever actually displayed. The positioning point when text is displayed through **OutTextXY** is, as you might expect, the upper left corner of the rectangular box occupied by the graphics text. **OutTextXY** does *not* update the CP.

The interaction of CP with **OutText** and the text box is a little more complex. CP is the positioning point, but the relationship of the text box to CP depends on two parameters set with yet another BGI routine:

```
PROCEDURE SetTextJustify(H,V : Word);
```

Both **H** and **V** accept values ranging from 0–2. As with most numeric codes used in the BGI, the **Graph** unit includes several named constants to make them easier to remember, as shown in Table 22.11. **H** defaults to 0 and **V** defaults to 1. Therefore, unless you change the defaults with a call to **SetTextJustify**, **OutText** positions the text box at the upper left corner of CP.

Table 22.11 BGI Text Justification Constants

Constant	Value	Parameter	Meaning
LeftText	0	H	CP at left edge of text box
CenterText	1	H or V	CP centered in text box
RightText	2	H	CP at right edge of text box
BottomText	0	V	CP at bottom of text box
TopText	2	V	CP at top of text box

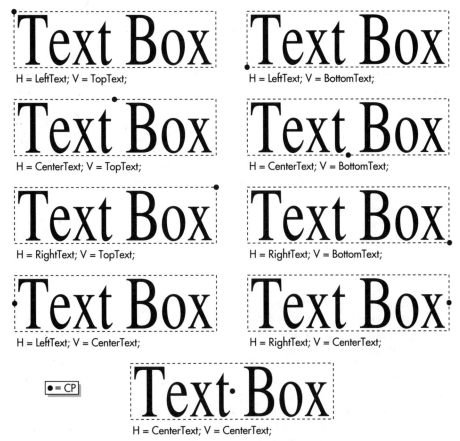

H = LeftText; V = TopText;

H = LeftText; V = BottomText;

H = CenterText; V = TopText;

H = CenterText; V = BottomText;

H = RightText; V = TopText;

H = RightText; V = BottomText;

H = LeftText; V = CenterText;

H = RightText; V = CenterText;

● = CP

H = CenterText; V = CenterText;

Figure 22.14 The Relation of CP to the Text Box

As with many matters of computer graphics, the situation is easier to show than to explain. Figure 22.14 shows the relationship of the CP and the text box for various combination of **H** and **V**. The question that follows is where CP goes after a call to **OutText**. Again, it depends on the combination of factors set by **SetTextStyle** and **SetTextJustify**.

First of all, when you set **Direction** to **VertDir** and write text in a vertical direction, the CP is *never* altered by **OutText**. When writing in a horizontal direction (**Direction** set to **HorizDir**), the CP is moved *only* when **H** is set to **LeftText**. **V** may be set to any of its legal values, but as long as **H** is set to **LeftText**, the CP will be moved to the *right* edge of the text box at whatever orientation specified by **V**. In other words, if **V** is set to **CenterText**, then CP will be moved from the left edge of the text box to the center of the right edge of the text box.

The program FONTS.PAS is given below as an example of how text is written to the screen in various fonts and various sizes, using the **OutTextXY** procedure. This program was used to generate the image shown in Figure 22.12.

```
{-----------------------------------------------------------------}
{                            FONTS                                }
{                                                                 }
{ Demonstration unit that displays the four "standard" BGI        }
{ fonts, both horizontally and vertically drawn.                  }
{                                                                 }
{                      by Jeff Duntemann                          }
{                      Turbo Pascal V7.0                          }
{                      Last update 2/20/93                        }
{                                                                 }
{    From: BORLAND PASCAL FROM SQUARE ONE  by Jeff Duntemann      }
{-----------------------------------------------------------------}

PROGRAM Fonts;

USES Graph;

VAR
  I,J,K : Integer;
  GraphDriver : Integer;
  GraphMode   : Integer;
  ErrorCode   : Integer;
  TestString  : STRING;

BEGIN
  GraphDriver := Detect;  { Let the BGI detect the board we're using }
  DetectGraph(GraphDriver,GraphMode);
  InitGraph(GraphDriver,GraphMode,'');
  ErrorCode := GraphResult;
  IF ErrorCode <> 0 THEN
    BEGIN
      Writeln('>>Halted on graphics error: ',GraphErrorMsg(ErrorCode));
      Halt(2)
    END;

  { Demonstrate the default font: }
  J := 0;
  FOR I := 1 TO 3 DO
    BEGIN
      SetTextStyle(DefaultFont,HorizDir,I);
      OutTextXY(0,J,'Default font.');
      J := J+5+TextHeight('DefaultFont');
    END;


  { Demonstrate the small font: }
  J := 60; TestString := 'Small Font';
```

```
FOR I := 4 TO 8 DO
  BEGIN
    SetTextStyle(SmallFont,HorizDir,I);
    OutTextXY(0,J,'Small Font');
    J := J+5+TextHeight(TestString);
  END;

{ Demonstrate the Triplex font: }
J := 0; TestString := 'TriplexFont';
FOR I := 4 TO 10 DO
  BEGIN
    SetTextStyle(TriplexFont,HorizDir,I);
    OutTextXY(320,J,TestString);
    J := J+5+TextHeight(TestString);
  END;

{ Demonstrate the Sans Serif font: }
J := 155; TestString := 'SansSerif';
FOR I := 4 TO 10 DO
  BEGIN
    SetTextStyle(SansSerifFont,HorizDir,I);
    OutTextXY(0,J,TestString);
    J := J+5+TextHeight(TestString);
  END;

{ Now give poor weird Gothic a chance: }
J := 123; TestString := 'Gothic';
FOR I := 4 TO 7 DO
  BEGIN
    SetTextStyle(GothicFont,VertDir,I);
    OutTextXY(J,70,TestString);
    J := J+TextHeight(TestString);
  END;

Readln;
CloseGraph;
END.
```

THE SIZE OF THE TEXT BOX

Sometimes, deciding where to position text on the screen depends heavily on how large the text box is. The BGI provides two routines for returning the size of the text box, given a string of text:

```
FUNCTION TextWidth(TextString : String)  : Word;
FUNCTION TextHeight(TextString : String) : Word;
```

Both routines take the text style into account when making their calculations. In other words, the values you pass to the BGI through the procedure **SetTextStyle** are used to calculate the dimensions of the text box.

The value returned by **TextWidth** is always the X-dimension of the text box, even when the text is being displayed in a vertical direction. Similarly, the value returned by **TextHeight** is always the Y-dimension of the text box.

One other procedure can affect the size of the text box by altering the vertical-to-horizontal proportions of stroke characters:

```
PROCEDURE SetUserCharSize(MultX,DivX,MultY,DivY : Word);
```

The idea here is to compress or expand stroke font characters in one dimension without affecting the other dimension. You can make stroke characters shorter and fatter, or taller and thinner, by passing the correct values in the four parameters.

The parameters **MultX** and **DivX** act as a pair to specify a multiplier for the X-dimension, to change the width of stroke characters without changing their height. Think of the calculation this way:

$$\text{New Character Width} = \frac{\text{MultX}}{\text{DivX}} * \text{Standard Character Width}$$

Similarly, the parameters **MultY** and **DivY** act together to specify a multiplier for the Y= dimension. They operate this way:

$$\text{New Character Height} = \frac{\text{MultY}}{\text{DivY}} * \text{Standard Character Height}$$

For example, if you want to make the text twice as wide without altering the height, specify a value of 2 for **MultX** and 1 for **DivX**. Or, to make the text half as high without affecting its width, specify a value of 1 for **MultY** and 2 for **DivY**.

The default for all four parameters is 1. This is the normal proportion of width to height set for the stroke fonts. To return to the default, simply make this call:

```
SetUserCharSize(1,1,1,1);
```

Under Turbo Pascal 4.0, you must call **SetTextStyle** immediately after a call to **SetUserCharSize** to make the new character size multipliers take effect. Since V5.0 this is no longer the case: A call to **SetUserCharSize** takes effect immediately.

CLIPPING CAUTIONS

Something you must keep in mind: Stroke fonts are clipped at the screen boundaries and at viewport boundaries. *Bit fonts are never clipped.* If you attempt to write a string to the display using a bit font, and part of the string extends beyond the boundaries of the screen or current viewport, *none* of that string will be displayed. The **OutText** or **OutTextXY** procedure will simply have no effect.

This is an excellent reason to use the **TextHeight** and **TextWidth** functions to keep an eye on the size of your text when using a bit font. One little corner over the edge, and nothing gets displayed at all.

QUERYING BGI TEXT SETTINGS

Your programs can query the BGI for the current state of the various text settings by calling this procedure:

```
PROCEDURE GetTextSettings(VAR TextInfo : TextSettingsType);
```

The type returned in the **VAR** parameter **TextInfo** is a record defined within the **Graph** unit:

```
TYPE
  TextSettingsType =
    RECORD
    Font      : Word;  { Font code 0-4 }
    Direction : Word;  { 0 = horizontal; 1 = vertical }
    CharSize  : Word;  { 1-10 }
    Horiz     : Word;  { 0=left; 1=center; 2=right }
    Vert      : Word   { 0 = bottom; 1 = top }
    END;
```

The fields return either the default values or the values that were set with **SetTextStyle** and **SetTextJustify**.

GENERATING BGI ERROR MESSAGE STRINGS

The BGI very conveniently includes a function that returns a descriptive string for each error message:

```
FUNCTION GraphErrorMsg(ErrorCode : Integer) : String;
```

This makes it unnecessary to hard-code such strings into your own programs, assuming you consider the BGI's error messages adequate. Essentially, after a graphics operation that affects **GraphResult**, you can pass the value returned by **GraphResult** to **GraphErrorMsg** and then display the string in an error message window in the size, font, and screen location of your choosing. This is certainly better than having the BGI simply burst in with an error message of its own anywhere it chooses.

Using **GraphErrorMsg** is simple:

```
SetTextStyle(TriplexFont,HorizDir,6);
OpResult := GraphResult;
IF OpResult <> 0 THEN
  OutTextXY(MsgX,MsgY,'>>Error! '+ GraphErrorMsg(OpResult));
```

Don't try to pass **GraphResult** to **GraphErrorMsg** directly! **GraphResult** is reset to 0 after each call, much as the **IOResult** file I/O error function is. If you call it twice in a row, the second call will always return a 0, regardless of what error code it returned on the first call. Call it once, immediately after a graphics operation, and assign the value it returns to an integer variable. Then make all tests on that variable, and use the variable to pass the error value to **GraphErrorMsg**.

22.7 Bitmaps and Bitblts

So far in our discussion of the BGI, everything has been concerned with putting graphics information up on the screen. Nothing interacts with graphics information *after* it appears on the display with the exception of two procedures that manipulate *bitmaps*.

All the graphics devices supported by the BGI contain their own video memory, and they encode pixel information in that memory by relating bits in memory to pixels on the screen. We say that bit information in video memory *maps* somehow to pixels displayed on the screen. In most cases, a 1-bit indicates foreground color on the screen, whereas a 0-bit indicates background color. The EGA and VGA consist of several separate but congruent *bit planes*, each representing one of the primary colors. A 1-bit in the red bit plane means that the pixel corresponding to that position in the bit plane will contain red information. If the corresponding bit in the green bit plane also contains a 1, the pixel will contain both red and green information, and the color of the pixel will be brown.

You needn't understand this to make use of bitmaps, but some understanding of the background technology often helps. In short, a bitmap is a collection of bits in memory that represent some rectangular pattern of graphics on the screen. Functionally, you can think of a bitmap as a rectangular subset of the screen.

The BGI gives you the ability to "lift" a rectangular section of the graphics screen (we'll call those sections bitmaps from now on) from the display and store it in a variable, and then "drop" the same bitmap back onto the display, perhaps at a different position. Lifting the bitmap from the display is done with this procedure:

```
PROCEDURE GetImage(X1,Y1,X2,Y2 : Integer; VAR BitMap);
```

Here, we pass the procedure two coordinate pairs that define a rectangular region of the screen, just as we pass to **Rectangle** or **Bar**. The **BitMap** parameter is untyped, and is therefore nothing but an address of a location in memory. When called, **GetImage** will read the bit information representing the rectangular region defined by the coordinates, and store that information in memory starting at the address passed in **BitMap**.

This means that the actual parameter passed in **BitMap** had better be big enough to contain the graphics information, because no checks will be done — the BGI starts laying down bit information at the first byte of **BitMap** and continues until it's done. If your actual parameter is smaller than the information from the screen, adjacent storage may be overwritten, with unpredictable (but predictably bad) results.

The organization of the bitmap in memory is simple: The first word of the bitmap gives the width of the rectangular region stored as the bitmap, in pixels, counting from 1 and not 0. The second word is the height of the region in pixels, again counting from 1 and not 0.

The easiest way to lift a bitmap safely is to allocate storage for the bitmap on the heap. The **GetMem** procedure allows you to reserve a region of the heap memory of a specified size and return a pointer to it. All that remains is finding out how much memory a given section of screen will occupy. The BGI has a function that will tell you:

```
FUNCTION ImageSize(X1,Y1,X2,Y2) : Word;
```

If you pass the coordinates that define a rectangular region of the screen to **ImageSize**, the function will return the number of bytes of storage that the region will occupy when "lifted" by **GetImage**. Putting it all together, storing a region of the screen on the heap is done this way:

```
VAR
   ImageChunk : Pointer;

GetMem(ImageChunk,ImageSize(0,0,100,50));
GetImage(0,0,100,50,ImageChunk^);
```

Laying down the bitmap elsewhere on the screen is done with another BGI routine:

```
PROCEDURE PutImage(X,Y : Integer; VAR BitMap; BitBlt : Word);
```

Here, the **X,Y** coordinates indicate the upper left corner of where the bitmap is to be positioned on the screen. **BitMap**, again, is the untyped parameter containing the stored bitmap. And third, something new under the BGI sun: the parameter **BitBlt** (pronounced *bit blit*), which is a code specifying how the stored bitmap is to be logically combined with the information over which it will be written.

The word *bitblt* comes from the mnemonic for an ancient machine-code instruction in a primordial DEC minicomputer meaning "bit block transfer." Understanding the notion of bitblt will be easier if you understand bit manipulation in general, which is admittedly a somewhat advanced topic. **BitBlt's** legal values and their meanings are summarized in Table 22.12, along with the predefined constants from the **Graph** unit.

You might think of **PutImage** as a *two-dimensional* bitwise logical operator. You have a two-dimensional plane of bits stored on the heap (it was put there by **GetImage**) and another two-dimensional plane of bits in graphics screen memory. **PutImage** combines the two, according to the logical operator passed in the **BitBlt** parameter. Here are the ways it can work:

Table 22.12 Legal Values for the BitBlt Parameter

Constant	Value	Meaning
NormalPut	0	**BitMap** bits replace screen bits (V4.0 only)
CopyPut	0	Identical to **NormalPut** (V5.0 and later)
XORPut	1	**BitMap** bits XOR with screen bits
ORPut	2	**BitMap** bits OR with screen bits
ANDPut	3	**BitMap** bits AND with screen bits
NOTPut	4	Negated **BitMap** bits replace screen bits

CopyPut (originally named **NormalPut** in Turbo Pascal 4.0) is a simple "bit move" operator. Each bit from the source plane replaces its corresponding bit in the screen plane. This replicates both foreground and background information on the screen. In essence, you have dropped the "lifted" bitmap *whole* onto its new position in the screen, completely replacing whatever was there before. This is probably the commonest mode for **PutImage**.

XORPut uses the logical exclusive OR operator. Each bit from the source plane is XORed with its corresponding bit in the screen plane. XOR is a slightly magical creature in its effects. If you XOR a bit plane over itself on the screen, all bits in the bitmap will be set to zero. In effect, you can erase a bitmap by first lifting it from the screen with **GetImage** and then using **PutImage** with **XORPut** to lay it back down over itself. This is useful in animation; you can move a graphics object around the screen by XORing it at one position, XORing it over itself to erase it, and then XORing it back down again at a new position.

ORPut uses the logical OR operator. Each bit in the source plane is ORed with its corresponding bit in the screen plane. In effect, foreground information is transferred from **BitMap** to the screen, *but background information is not*. This is the way you would combine two images that overlap into a single larger image.

ANDPut uses the logical AND operator. Each bit in the source plane is ANDed with its corresponding bit in the screen plane. What happens here is that foreground bits will be transferred from **BitMap** to the screen *only* if their corresponding screen bits are *also* foreground bits. There isn't much use for this sort of bit-combination, but it's available if you ever need it.

NOTPut uses the NOT operator, which inverts the bits in **BitMap** before moving them to the screen in the same way that **CopyPut** does. In other words, each 1 bit from the source plane is inverted to a 0 bit and then replaces its corresponding bit in the screen plane; and each 0 bit from the source plane is inverted to a 1 bit, and then replaces its corresponding bit in the screen plane. Again, this is not tremendously useful, but **NOTPut** may be used to "flash" a window by lifting the window into memory with **GetImage**, dropping it back over itself with **PutImage** and **NOTPut**, and then putting it back down again with **PutImage** and **CopyPut**.

One very important use of **GetImage** and **PutImage** lies in menuing and windowing systems. "Popping up" a menu over a graphics background demands that the background be saved somewhere first so that it can be restored later once you put the popped-up menu away. This is easily done by using **GetImage** to "lift" the background area onto the heap, then drawing the menu where the saved area had been. To restore the background area overwritten by the menu, you use **PutImage** to "drop" the saved area back down over the menu, covering it completely and making the screen look as it did before the menu popped into view.

I use this technique a great deal in the **PullDown** unit described in Section 22.9 in this chapter. For ambitious examples of **GetImage** and **PutImage** in use, I refer you to that section.

CLIPPING CAUTIONS

Clipping works a little oddly with respect to bitmaps. As with bit font output, if the entire bitmap cannot be laid down on the visible screen, it will not be laid down at all. There is one exception: The lower edge of the visible screen will clip a bitmap being laid down by **PutImage**. Viewports (in contrast to the full visible screen) cannot clip bitmaps at all.

22.8 Graphics Paging

A few of the BGI's supported graphics devices contain enough video memory to allow more than one distinct graphics screen. With more than one screen, "building" a complicated image can be done invisibly by directing graphics output to the screen that is not currently displayed. Then, at the appropriate time, the invisible screen can be made the visible screen, and the image will appear all at once.

One problem with this feature is that not all graphics devices support it, although many do. Currently, the only BGI-supported devices that include multiple graphics pages are the EGA, VGA, and Hercules. This means that to use paging in applications that may run on many different graphics devices, you must test for the presence of a multipage device before attempting to use paging.

Two procedures control the BGI's graphics paging feature:

```
PROCEDURE SetActivePage(Page : Word);
PROCEDURE SetVisualPage(Page : Word);
```

SetActivePage controls which graphics page graphics output is written to. **SetVisualPage** controls which graphics page is currently visible:

```
SetVisualPage(1);        { Separate the visible from active pages }
SetActivePage(0);
DrawComplicatedThingie; { Draw a complex image in the invisible page }
SetVisualPage(0);        { Now make it appear like magic! }
```

Values passed in **Page** must be legal for the current graphics device and mode. Table 22.13 sums up the various multipage devices and modes currently supported by the BGI, in terms of the values and constants used by **InitGraph** to select those modes.

If you pass an invalid page number to either of the paging control procedures, the operation will be ignored, but no error will be generated.

In general, the scattered nature of the PC video adapter universe makes it unadvisable to build an application that depends utterly on built-in hardware video paging. If you want to do this sort of thing, you're probably better off building a paging system of your own that uses the heap for the alternate page and then "flashes" the alternate page into video memory when it is fully drawn.

22.9　A Graphics Pull-Down Menuing System

There are two ways to design graphics support into an application. The low road is to write the application in text mode and enter graphics mode *only* when graphics-oriented work needs to be done. This is the design strategy of Borland's Quattro Pro spreadsheet. The spreadsheet work is done entirely in text mode, with the business graphics feature accessible at the touch of a function key. The high road is simply to design the whole application in graphics, whether the

Table 22.13 Multipage Devices and Modes

Constant	Value	Meaning		
EGALo	0	640×200	2 color	4 pages
EGAHi	1	640×350	16 color	2 pages
EGAMonoHi	3	640×350	2 clr;	
			64K:	1 page;
			256K:	4 pages
HercMonoHi	0	720×348	2 color	2 pages
VGALo	0	640×200	16 color	4 pages
VGAMed	1	640×350	16 color	2 pages

immediate work being done is graphics-oriented or not. Most people who do this today work with Microsoft Windows as the graphics environment, rather than a far more simple toolkit like the BGI.

Windows fully solves the ugly problem that the BGI only partially solves: It is a truly device-independent graphics system, and graphics applications written to the Windows Application Programming Interface (API) look essentially the same whether you're running on a 640 × 480 pixel resolution VGA, or (as I do) on a 768 × 1024 super VGA (SVGA).

If you're a devoted graphics fan, Windows is definitely the way of the future. Virtually no PCs are being sold today that contain a processor less powerful than the 80386 SX. The 80286 is now a quaint oddity (I see no ads anywhere for new 286 machines except in the "leftovers" mail-order discount catalogs), and the 8088 is virtually forgotten. This leaves a vast number of older machines still in use, however, and if you have something with a 286 or older CPU, you simply can't run Windows effectively.

The BGI is CPU-independent, which is its primary advantage for the graphics programmer. Furthermore, the BGI is *enormously* easier to understand and work with than Windows, which is a skull-cracker of the highest order. Sooner or later, if you're going to stay in the programming game, you're going to have to learn to deal with graphics under Windows. In the meantime, the BGI will do you quite nicely, and is an excellent education in the basic principles of graphics.

MICE, MENUS, AND BOUNCING BARS

Over the past few years, environments like Microsoft Windows have cemented certain ideas in the public mind about what an all-graphics application should look like. Most familiar is the notion of a *pull-down menuing user interface*. An always-present white bar across the top of the screen contains several key words, each of which represents a menu. These menus can be "pulled down" from the bar by depressing a mouse button while the mouse pointer points at or near the desired menu key word. When a menu is pulled down, a white "bounce bar" can be moved up or down a list of commands or other options by moving the mouse, highlighting whatever the bar covers in white. When the bar covers the desired option, the mouse button is released, and the option is considered selected.

If a menu is pulled down by mistake, or if the menu does not contain what the user wants to select, the mouse pointer is simply moved away from the menu, which then vanishes without further effect. It's an easily-explorable, non-threatening system of program control. An example of a pull-down menu system in use is shown in Figure 22.15.

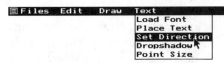

Figure 22.15 A Pull-Down Menu

THE MENU AS DATA STRUCTURE

Designing such a menuing system takes a certain amount of thought. It should be general enough so that it can be table-driven. In other words, the names of the menus, their positions on the bar, the number of items in each menu, and the identifying code returned for each item should be part of some sort of data structure, rather than constants or literals hard-coded into the menuing routines themselves.

Such a data structure can be encapsulated in the data types shown below:

```
String15  = STRING[15];    { To keep the size of things down! }

ItemRec   = RECORD
               Item       : String15;
               ItemCode   : Byte;
               ItemActive : Boolean
            END;

MenuRec   = RECORD
               XStart,XEnd : Word;
               Title       : String15;
               MenuSize    : Word;
               Imageptr    : Pointer;
               Active      : Boolean;
               Choices     : Byte;
               ItemList    : ARRAY[0..18] OF ItemRec
            END;

MenuDesc  = ARRAY[0..12] OF MenuRec;
```

Within this system, an *item* is one of the choices in a menu, and a *menu* is a collection of items represented by an outlined box beneath the menu bar. Items are defined as variables of type **ItemRec**. Each item has a string that describes it on the screen (**Item**) and a numeric code that uniquely defines it (**ItemCode**). No other item within a given menu system may have that same numeric code. When a given item is selected by the user, the menuing procedure returns that item's code to the calling logic.

The last item in the **ItemRec** definition is a Boolean flag that indicates whether or not the item is *active*; that is, whether the item will appear on the screen and be selectable at any given time. For example, in a text-editing program, you might wish to disable any menu items involving editing of text until such time as the user selects and opens a file to edit. After the file is opened, editing again makes sense and the items should become available for selection. The menuing unit **PullDown** that I will describe shortly includes procedures to activate and deactivate items at random at any time.

Items grouped together into a menu are part of a larger data structure embodying one menu of the several in the system as a whole. This structure is a record type called **MenuRec**. Like each item, the menu as a whole has a title, given by the field **Title**. This word or phrase is what appears in the white menu bar at the top of the screen. The user points to the title and depresses the left mouse button to pull down that menu. There is a region of the bar within which any left button click will pull down a menu. The left and right bounds of this region are given by the fields **XStart** and **XEnd**. The **Title** string is displayed within these bounds.

Like items, menus may be active or inactive during the execution of a program. The Boolean flag **Active** specifies whether the menu will be available for pulling down. The field **Choices** contains the number of items in the menu. An array called **ItemList** contains the items themselves, expressed as **ItemRec** records. Each menu may contain up to 19 items. The other fields in **MenuRec** we'll return to a little later, as they involve practical considerations of displaying the menu boxes quickly.

Finally, the collection of menus that are available across the menu bar is described by an array of **MenuRec** called **MenuDesc**. Up to 13 menus are possible in this system as I've implemented it. The maximum menu count across the bar (13) and the maximum number of items within a single menu (19) were compromises chosen to keep the total maximum number of items in the system under 255.

All of the procedures that display and manipulate the menus are passed a variable of type **MenuDesc**. Now, **MenuDesc** is monstrous as data structures go (4,810 bytes in 832 fields) and if you define an ordinary variable of type **MenuDesc** you will somehow have to fill all 832 fields with their appropriate data. The practical alternative is to define **MenuDesc** structures as typed constants, which puts the burden of filling the structure with its data on the compiler, where it belongs. I have defined a single **MenuDesc** structure called **DemoMenu**, which is included on the listings diskette. It can be used as a "boilerplate" menu structure; modify it to create your own menus rather than typing in the entire monstrosity from scratch.

The alternative to using typed constants is to write the **MenuDesc** to disk as a binary file, and then read it back from disk into ordinary variables of type **MenuDesc**. This is less convenient than using typed constants, since it demands an editor of some sort that edits the binary data.

```
{->>>>DemoMenu<<<<--------------------------------------------}
{                                                              }
{ Filename : DEMOMENU.DEF - Last Modified 2/28/93             }
{                                                              }
{ This may be the largest structured constant you'll ever see. }
{ It defines a menu used by the PULLDOWN.PAS menu unit, which  }
{ implements a pulldown menuing system using the BGI.  You can }
{ copy this file to a new file and modify it to suit your      }
{ own applications.                                            }
{                                                              }
{ The MenuDesc type is defined in unit PullDown.              }
{                                                              }
{    From: BORLAND PASCAL FROM SQUARE ONE  by Jeff Duntemann  }
{--------------------------------------------------------------}
```

```
CONST
  DemoMenu : MenuDesc =
              ((XStart    : 18; XEnd : 58;
                Title     : 'Files';
                MenuSize  : 11;
                Imageptr  : NIL;
                Active    : True;
                Choices   : 5; ItemList  :
                ((Item : 'Retrieve'; ItemCode : 21; ItemActive : True),
                 (Item : 'Save';     ItemCode : 22; ItemActive : True),
                 (Item : 'Delete';   ItemCode : 23; ItemActive : True),
                 (Item : 'Rename';   ItemCode : 24; ItemActive : True),
                 (Item : 'Quit';     ItemCode : 25; ItemActive : True),
                 (Item : ''; ItemCode : 0; ItemActive : False),
                 (Item : ''; ItemCode : 0; ItemActive : False),
                 (Item : ''; ItemCode : 0; ItemActive : False),
                 (Item : ''; ItemCode : 0; ItemActive : False),
                 (Item : ''; ItemCode : 0; ItemActive : False),
                 (Item : ''; ItemCode : 0; ItemActive : False),
                 (Item : ''; ItemCode : 0; ItemActive : False),
                 (Item : ''; ItemCode : 0; ItemActive : False),
                 (Item : ''; ItemCode : 0; ItemActive : False),
                 (Item : ''; ItemCode : 0; ItemActive : False),
                 (Item : ''; ItemCode : 0; ItemActive : False),
                 (Item : ''; ItemCode : 0; ItemActive : False))),
               (XStart    : 74; XEnd     : 114;
                Title     : 'Edit';
                MenuSize  : 11;
                Imageptr  : NIL;
                Active    : True;
                Choices   : 9; ItemList  :
                ((Item : 'Grab';      ItemCode : 31; ItemActive : True),
                 (Item : 'Pull';      ItemCode : 32; ItemActive : True),
                 (Item : 'Erase';     ItemCode : 33; ItemActive : False),
                 (Item : 'Join';      ItemCode : 34; ItemActive : False),
                 (Item : 'Swap';      ItemCode : 35; ItemActive : False),
                 (Item : 'Invert';    ItemCode : 36; ItemActive : True),
                 (Item : 'Recolor';   ItemCode : 37; ItemActive : True),
                 (Item : 'Split';     ItemCode : 38; ItemActive : True),
                 (Item : 'Duplicate'; ItemCode : 39; ItemActive : True),
                 (Item : ''; ItemCode : 0; ItemActive : False),
                 (Item : ''; ItemCode : 0; ItemActive : False),
                 (Item : ''; ItemCode : 0; ItemActive : False),
                 (Item : ''; ItemCode : 0; ItemActive : False),
                 (Item : ''; ItemCode : 0; ItemActive : False),
```

```
      (Item : ''; ItemCode : 0; ItemActive : False),
      (Item : ''; ItemCode : 0; ItemActive : False),
      (Item : ''; ItemCode : 0; ItemActive : False),
      (Item : ''; ItemCode : 0; ItemActive : False),
      (Item : ''; ItemCode : 0; ItemActive : False))),
 (XStart    : 129; XEnd     : 175;
  Title     : 'Draw';
  MenuSize  : 11;
  Imageptr  : NIL;
  Active    : True;
  Choices   : 4; ItemList   :
  ((Item : 'Freehand';  ItemCode : 41; ItemActive : True),
   (Item : 'Polyline';  ItemCode : 42; ItemActive : True),
   (Item : 'Spray';     ItemCode : 43; ItemActive : True),
   (Item : 'Dragstamp'; ItemCode : 44; ItemActive : True),
   (Item : ''; ItemCode : 0; ItemActive : False),
   (Item : ''; ItemCode : 0; ItemActive : False),
   (Item : ''; ItemCode : 0; ItemActive : False),
   (Item : ''; ItemCode : 0; ItemActive : False),
   (Item : ''; ItemCode : 0; ItemActive : False),
   (Item : ''; ItemCode : 0; ItemActive : False),
   (Item : ''; ItemCode : 0; ItemActive : False),
   (Item : ''; ItemCode : 0; ItemActive : False),
   (Item : ''; ItemCode : 0; ItemActive : False),
   (Item : ''; ItemCode : 0; ItemActive : False),
   (Item : ''; ItemCode : 0; ItemActive : False),
   (Item : ''; ItemCode : 0; ItemActive : False),
   (Item : ''; ItemCode : 0; ItemActive : False),
   (Item : ''; ItemCode : 0; ItemActive : False),
   (Item : ''; ItemCode : 0; ItemActive : False))),
  (XStart    : 179; XEnd     : 215;
   Title     : 'Text';
   MenuSize  : 11;
   Imageptr  : NIL;
   Active    : True;
   Choices   : 5; ItemList   :
   ((Item : 'Load Font';ItemCode : 51; ItemActive : True),
    (Item : 'Place Text';ItemCode : 52; ItemActive : True),
    (Item :
      'Set Direction'; ItemCode : 53; ItemActive : True),
    (Item : 'Dropshadow';ItemCode : 54; ItemActive : True),
    (Item : 'Point Size';ItemCode : 55; ItemActive : True),
    (Item : ''; ItemCode : 0; ItemActive : False),
    (Item : ''; ItemCode : 0; ItemActive : False),
    (Item : ''; ItemCode : 0; ItemActive : False),
    (Item : ''; ItemCode : 0; ItemActive : False),
    (Item : ''; ItemCode : 0; ItemActive : False),
```

```
                    (Item : ''; ItemCode : 0; ItemActive : False),
                    (Item : ''; ItemCode : 0; ItemActive : False),
                    (Item : ''; ItemCode : 0; ItemActive : False),
                    (Item : ''; ItemCode : 0; ItemActive : False),
                    (Item : ''; ItemCode : 0; ItemActive : False),
                    (Item : ''; ItemCode : 0; ItemActive : False),
                    (Item : ''; ItemCode : 0; ItemActive : False),
                    (Item : ''; ItemCode : 0; ItemActive : False),
                    (Item : ''; ItemCode : 0; ItemActive : False))),
            (XStart    : 15; XEnd      : 55;
    Title      : '';
    MenuSize   : 0;
    Imageptr   : NIL;
    Active     : False;
    Choices    : 0; ItemList   :
    ((Item : ''; ItemCode : 0; ItemActive : False),
     (Item : ''; ItemCode : 0; ItemActive : False),
     (Item : ''; ItemCode : 0; ItemActive : False),
     (Item : ''; ItemCode : 0; ItemActive : False),
     (Item : ''; ItemCode : 0; ItemActive : False),
     (Item : ''; ItemCode : 0; ItemActive : False),
     (Item : ''; ItemCode : 0; ItemActive : False),
     (Item : ''; ItemCode : 0; ItemActive : False),
     (Item : ''; ItemCode : 0; ItemActive : False),
     (Item : ''; ItemCode : 0; ItemActive : False),
     (Item : ''; ItemCode : 0; ItemActive : False),
     (Item : ''; ItemCode : 0; ItemActive : False),
     (Item : ''; ItemCode : 0; ItemActive : False),
     (Item : ''; ItemCode : 0; ItemActive : False),
     (Item : ''; ItemCode : 0; ItemActive : False),
     (Item : ''; ItemCode : 0; ItemActive : False),
     (Item : ''; ItemCode : 0; ItemActive : False),
     (Item : ''; ItemCode : 0; ItemActive : False),
     (Item : ''; ItemCode : 0; ItemActive : False))),
            (XStart    : 15; XEnd      : 55;
    Title      : '';
    MenuSize   : 0;
    Imageptr   : NIL;
    Active     : False;
    Choices    : 0; ItemList   :
    ((Item : ''; ItemCode : 0; ItemActive : False),
     (Item : ''; ItemCode : 0; ItemActive : False),
     (Item : ''; ItemCode : 0; ItemActive : False),
     (Item : ''; ItemCode : 0; ItemActive : False),
     (Item : ''; ItemCode : 0; ItemActive : False),
     (Item : ''; ItemCode : 0; ItemActive : False),
     (Item : ''; ItemCode : 0; ItemActive : False),
```

```
            (Item : ''; ItemCode : 0; ItemActive : False),
            (Item : ''; ItemCode : 0; ItemActive : False),
            (Item : ''; ItemCode : 0; ItemActive : False),
            (Item : ''; ItemCode : 0; ItemActive : False),
            (Item : ''; ItemCode : 0; ItemActive : False),
            (Item : ''; ItemCode : 0; ItemActive : False),
            (Item : ''; ItemCode : 0; ItemActive : False),
            (Item : ''; ItemCode : 0; ItemActive : False),
            (Item : ''; ItemCode : 0; ItemActive : False),
            (Item : ''; ItemCode : 0; ItemActive : False),
            (Item : ''; ItemCode : 0; ItemActive : False),
            (Item : ''; ItemCode : 0; ItemActive : False))),
          (XStart    : 15; XEnd      : 55;
Title      : '';
MenuSize   : 0;
Imageptr   : NIL;
Active     : False;
Choices    : 0; ItemList  :
          ((Item : ''; ItemCode : 0; ItemActive : False),
           (Item : ''; ItemCode : 0; ItemActive : False),
           (Item : ''; ItemCode : 0; ItemActive : False),
           (Item : ''; ItemCode : 0; ItemActive : False),
           (Item : ''; ItemCode : 0; ItemActive : False),
           (Item : ''; ItemCode : 0; ItemActive : False),
           (Item : ''; ItemCode : 0; ItemActive : False),
           (Item : ''; ItemCode : 0; ItemActive : False),
           (Item : ''; ItemCode : 0; ItemActive : False),
           (Item : ''; ItemCode : 0; ItemActive : False),
           (Item : ''; ItemCode : 0; ItemActive : False),
           (Item : ''; ItemCode : 0; ItemActive : False),
           (Item : ''; ItemCode : 0; ItemActive : False),
           (Item : ''; ItemCode : 0; ItemActive : False),
           (Item : ''; ItemCode : 0; ItemActive : False),
           (Item : ''; ItemCode : 0; ItemActive : False),
           (Item : ''; ItemCode : 0; ItemActive : False),
           (Item : ''; ItemCode : 0; ItemActive : False),
           (Item : ''; ItemCode : 0; ItemActive : False))),
          (XStart    : 15; XEnd      : 55;
Title      : '';
MenuSize   : 0;
Imageptr   : NIL;
Active     : False;
Choices    : 0; ItemList  :
          ((Item : ''; ItemCode : 0; ItemActive : False),
           (Item : ''; ItemCode : 0; ItemActive : False),
           (Item : ''; ItemCode : 0; ItemActive : False),
           (Item : ''; ItemCode : 0; ItemActive : False),
```

```
                     (Item : ''; ItemCode : 0; ItemActive : False),
                     (Item : ''; ItemCode : 0; ItemActive : False),
                     (Item : ''; ItemCode : 0; ItemActive : False),
                     (Item : ''; ItemCode : 0; ItemActive : False),
                     (Item : ''; ItemCode : 0; ItemActive : False),
                     (Item : ''; ItemCode : 0; ItemActive : False),
                     (Item : ''; ItemCode : 0; ItemActive : False),
                     (Item : ''; ItemCode : 0; ItemActive : False),
                     (Item : ''; ItemCode : 0; ItemActive : False),
                     (Item : ''; ItemCode : 0; ItemActive : False),
                     (Item : ''; ItemCode : 0; ItemActive : False),
                     (Item : ''; ItemCode : 0; ItemActive : False),
                     (Item : ''; ItemCode : 0; ItemActive : False),
                     (Item : ''; ItemCode : 0; ItemActive : False),
                     (Item : ''; ItemCode : 0; ItemActive : False))),
             (XStart    : 15; XEnd      : 55;
              Title     : '';
              MenuSize  : 0;
              Imageptr  : NIL;
              Active    : False;
              Choices   : 0; ItemList  :
             ((Item : ''; ItemCode : 0; ItemActive : False),
              (Item : ''; ItemCode : 0; ItemActive : False),
              (Item : ''; ItemCode : 0; ItemActive : False),
              (Item : ''; ItemCode : 0; ItemActive : False),
              (Item : ''; ItemCode : 0; ItemActive : False),
              (Item : ''; ItemCode : 0; ItemActive : False),
              (Item : ''; ItemCode : 0; ItemActive : False),
              (Item : ''; ItemCode : 0; ItemActive : False),
              (Item : ''; ItemCode : 0; ItemActive : False),
              (Item : ''; ItemCode : 0; ItemActive : False),
              (Item : ''; ItemCode : 0; ItemActive : False),
              (Item : ''; ItemCode : 0; ItemActive : False),
              (Item : ''; ItemCode : 0; ItemActive : False),
              (Item : ''; ItemCode : 0; ItemActive : False),
              (Item : ''; ItemCode : 0; ItemActive : False),
              (Item : ''; ItemCode : 0; ItemActive : False),
              (Item : ''; ItemCode : 0; ItemActive : False),
              (Item : ''; ItemCode : 0; ItemActive : False),
              (Item : ''; ItemCode : 0; ItemActive : False))),
             (XStart    : 15; XEnd      : 55;
              Title     : '';
              MenuSize  : 0;
              Imageptr  : NIL;
              Active    : False;
              Choices   : 0; ItemList  :
             ((Item : ''; ItemCode : 0; ItemActive : False),
```

```
(Item : ''; ItemCode : 0; ItemActive : False),
(Item : ''; ItemCode : 0; ItemActive : False),
(Item : ''; ItemCode : 0; ItemActive : False),
(Item : ''; ItemCode : 0; ItemActive : False),
(Item : ''; ItemCode : 0; ItemActive : False),
(Item : ''; ItemCode : 0; ItemActive : False),
(Item : ''; ItemCode : 0; ItemActive : False),
(Item : ''; ItemCode : 0; ItemActive : False),
(Item : ''; ItemCode : 0; ItemActive : False),
(Item : ''; ItemCode : 0; ItemActive : False),
(Item : ''; ItemCode : 0; ItemActive : False),
(Item : ''; ItemCode : 0; ItemActive : False),
(Item : ''; ItemCode : 0; ItemActive : False),
(Item : ''; ItemCode : 0; ItemActive : False),
(Item : ''; ItemCode : 0; ItemActive : False),
(Item : ''; ItemCode : 0; ItemActive : False),
(Item : ''; ItemCode : 0; ItemActive : False),
(Item : ''; ItemCode : 0; ItemActive : False))),
(XStart    : 15; XEnd      : 55;
Title      : '';
MenuSize   : 0;
Imageptr   : NIL;
Active     : False;
Choices    : 0; ItemList   :
((Item : ''; ItemCode : 0; ItemActive : False),
 (Item : ''; ItemCode : 0; ItemActive : False),
 (Item : ''; ItemCode : 0; ItemActive : False),
 (Item : ''; ItemCode : 0; ItemActive : False),
 (Item : ''; ItemCode : 0; ItemActive : False),
 (Item : ''; ItemCode : 0; ItemActive : False),
 (Item : ''; ItemCode : 0; ItemActive : False),
 (Item : ''; ItemCode : 0; ItemActive : False),
 (Item : ''; ItemCode : 0; ItemActive : False),
 (Item : ''; ItemCode : 0; ItemActive : False),
 (Item : ''; ItemCode : 0; ItemActive : False),
 (Item : ''; ItemCode : 0; ItemActive : False),
 (Item : ''; ItemCode : 0; ItemActive : False),
 (Item : ''; ItemCode : 0; ItemActive : False),
 (Item : ''; ItemCode : 0; ItemActive : False),
 (Item : ''; ItemCode : 0; ItemActive : False),
 (Item : ''; ItemCode : 0; ItemActive : False),
 (Item : ''; ItemCode : 0; ItemActive : False),
 (Item : ''; ItemCode : 0; ItemActive : False))),
(XStart    : 15; XEnd      : 55;
Title      : '';
MenuSize   : 0;
Imageptr   : NIL;
```

```
Active    : False;
Choices   : 0; ItemList  :
((Item : ''; ItemCode : 0; ItemActive : False),
 (Item : ''; ItemCode : 0; ItemActive : False),
 (Item : ''; ItemCode : 0; ItemActive : False),
 (Item : ''; ItemCode : 0; ItemActive : False),
 (Item : ''; ItemCode : 0; ItemActive : False),
 (Item : ''; ItemCode : 0; ItemActive : False),
 (Item : ''; ItemCode : 0; ItemActive : False),
 (Item : ''; ItemCode : 0; ItemActive : False),
 (Item : ''; ItemCode : 0; ItemActive : False),
 (Item : ''; ItemCode : 0; ItemActive : False),
 (Item : ''; ItemCode : 0; ItemActive : False),
 (Item : ''; ItemCode : 0; ItemActive : False),
 (Item : ''; ItemCode : 0; ItemActive : False),
 (Item : ''; ItemCode : 0; ItemActive : False),
 (Item : ''; ItemCode : 0; ItemActive : False),
 (Item : ''; ItemCode : 0; ItemActive : False),
 (Item : ''; ItemCode : 0; ItemActive : False),
 (Item : ''; ItemCode : 0; ItemActive : False),
 (Item : ''; ItemCode : 0; ItemActive : False))),
(XStart   : 15; XEnd      : 55;
Title     : '';
MenuSize  : 0;
Imageptr  : NIL;
Active    : False;
Choices   : 0; ItemList  :
((Item : ''; ItemCode : 0; ItemActive : False),
 (Item : ''; ItemCode : 0; ItemActive : False),
 (Item : ''; ItemCode : 0; ItemActive : False),
 (Item : ''; ItemCode : 0; ItemActive : False),
 (Item : ''; ItemCode : 0; ItemActive : False),
 (Item : ''; ItemCode : 0; ItemActive : False),
 (Item : ''; ItemCode : 0; ItemActive : False),
 (Item : ''; ItemCode : 0; ItemActive : False),
 (Item : ''; ItemCode : 0; ItemActive : False),
 (Item : ''; ItemCode : 0; ItemActive : False),
 (Item : ''; ItemCode : 0; ItemActive : False),
 (Item : ''; ItemCode : 0; ItemActive : False),
 (Item : ''; ItemCode : 0; ItemActive : False),
 (Item : ''; ItemCode : 0; ItemActive : False),
 (Item : ''; ItemCode : 0; ItemActive : False),
 (Item : ''; ItemCode : 0; ItemActive : False),
 (Item : ''; ItemCode : 0; ItemActive : False),
 (Item : ''; ItemCode : 0; ItemActive : False),
 (Item : ''; ItemCode : 0; ItemActive : False))));
```

MAKING MENUS

All the data structures and subprograms it takes to use the menuing system are gathered together into a unit, **PullDown**. The heart of **PullDown** is the menuing routine itself, **Menu**. All the other functions and procedures in the unit support **Menu** somehow.

SetupMenu creates the menu bar across the top of the screen. This consists of drawing the white bar using the **Bar** procedure, then displaying the menu titles within their **XStart**, **XEnd** ranges across the bar. It also draws the small figure called the "amulet" at the far left corner of the menu bar. The purpose of the amulet is to give a point on the menu that selects something that is *not* a menu. What this might be is up to you. When the user clicks on the amulet, a Boolean flag named **Amulet** is returned to the calling logic, which can then do what it must. A click on the amulet might trigger termination of the application (similar to the function of the Close Box in Microsoft Windows) or the forcing of the application to a background task from the foreground in a multitasking environment.

The best way to understand how menus are created and displayed is to follow the Pascal code of **Menu** through an invocation. The menu bar across the top of the screen is 12 pixels high. Any click on the mouse buttons when the mouse pointer Y value is less than 13 pixels from the top of the screen means that the user has clicked on the menu bar. An application should give control to **Menu** whenever it detects such a click.

From the top, then: **Menu**'s first task is to save the current draw color in a temporary variable called **SaveColor**. **Menu** uses only white, for simplicity's sake, but the application may be drawing in some other color when **Menu** is called.

That done, **Menu** polls the mouse to find out where within the menu bar the pointer is. The first check is for a click on the amulet. If the click was on the amulet, the **Amulet** parameter is set to **True** and **Menu** terminates. If the amulet was not the target of the user's click, **Menu** begins scanning the 13 menus in the **CurrentMenu** parameter to find out if the pointer lies within the title range for any active menu. This is done by testing the pointer X position against the **XStart** and **XEnd** fields in each menu in turn, starting with the leftmost menu. The scan continues until it finds an active menu, or until it finds a "null" menu; that is, a menu whose title is an empty string. By convention, all defined menus are grouped toward the left. Totally unused and empty menus should not be left within a group of defined menus; keep them at the end of the **MenuDesc** array. A defined menu coming *after* a null menu will not be detected in this initial scan.

If the pointer was not within the title range of an active menu, **Menu** terminates. Otherwise, the menu box is pulled down so that the user can select one of the menu's items.

The dimensions of the menu box enclosing a menu's list of items is not kept anywhere within the **MenuDesc** data structure. The width and height of the box is calculated each time the menu is pulled down. This is not difficult and it can be done quickly. The list of items is scanned to find the longest item title string. The width of the menu box is then calculated based on the length of this longest string, with a little margin space on either side of the string for clarity. The height of the menu box is easily calculated, since the entire system assumes the BGI 8×8 font, making each item's height exactly 12 pixels (eight for the font and four for breathing room above and below the characters themselves). The upper left corner coordinates are placed in variables **M1X** and **M1Y** and the left right corner coordinates are placed in variables **M2X** and **M2Y**.

That done, we now know exactly what portion of the screen the menu box will cover when pulled down. The size in bytes that this region occupies is calculated using the **ImageSize** BGI function and saved in a **MenuRec** field named **MenuSize**.

We have to save whatever is underneath that part of the screen. This is done by allocating space on the heap for a bitmap (using the **MenuSize** figure), and then saving the screen area under the menu box to the heap as a bitmap, using the BGI procedure **GetImage**.

Once the area under the menu box is safely stored on the heap, we can start building the menu box itself. The first thing to go up is the bounce bar. It is drawn using the BGI **Bar** procedure, and immediately stored on the heap using **GetImage**. We will need it again, frequently, later on.

The fastest way to show a menu on the screen is to move a bitmap containing the menu box pattern from the heap directly to screen memory using **PutImage**. The menu box pattern has to first get onto the heap somehow before we can do that. The way **Menu** was designed, the *first* time a menu box is shown to the user, it is drawn right on the screen using the various BGI procedures. Once drawn, it is saved out to the heap, and every time after that is is "flashed" to the screen using **PutImage**, which is several times faster than drawing the menu box piecemeal.

How does **Menu** tell whether a given menu box has been drawn once before? In the **MenuRec** record is a pointer field called **ImagePtr**. A typed constant can only initialize a pointer field to **NIL**, and **NIL** is the value **ImagePtr** has until its menu box is drawn onto the screen. When the menu box pattern is moved to the heap, **ImagePtr** is made to point to the pattern on the heap using **GetMem**. After that, **ImagePtr** will no longer be equal to **NIL**. So when **Menu** sees a menu's **ImagePtr** pointer equal to **NIL**, it knows that the menu has not been shown before and must be drawn from scratch on the screen.

In connection with this, note that changing the active/inactive status of an item or menu alters the pattern of the menu box that contains that item. The procedures that change the active/inactive status of an item or menu (**ActivateItem**, **DeactivateItem**, **ActivateMenu**, and **DeactivateMenu**) force **ImagePtr** to NIL, which in turn forces **Menu** to draw that menu from scratch the next time the user pulls it down.

The menu box border is drawn with the BGI **Rectangle** procedure, and the item titles are drawn using **OutTextXY**. Note that the top item is drawn in black rather than white—remember that we have already drawn the bounce bar on the screen, and the top item in a menu is drawn on top of the bounce bar. After the first item is drawn, the draw color is returned to white using the BGI **SetColor** procedure. When the entire menu box pattern has been drawn, it is saved to the heap using **GetImage**.

At this point the menu box pattern exists on the heap, whether it was just drawn and stored there or stored there the last time the menu was pulled down. **PutImage** is thus used to bring the menu box pattern from the heap to the display.

With the menu down and on display, the next step is to bounce the bounce bar up and down the list of items following the motion of the mouse pointer. This is done with a **REPEAT..UNTIL** loop that repeatedly samples the mouse pointer using **PollMouse**. The loop keeps track of where the mouse pointer is in relation to the bounce bar, and when the mouse pointer moves up or down beyond the limits of the bounce bar, the bounce bar is "bounced" up or down to follow the mouse pointer. (Checks are, of course, made to ensure that the bounce bar is not bounced off the top or the bottom of the menu box.)

Bouncing the bar is done using the **XOROpt** parameter to **PutImage**. The bounce bar pattern is a plain white bar stored on the heap. The top item in the menu, if you recall, was written with black letters on the original white bounce bar. If the plain bounce bar image on the heap is XORed over the bounce bar and its black letters, the black letters will become white—and the white bounce bar will disappear.

Contrariwise, if the plain white bounce bar is XORed over white letters against black screen, the result will be a white bar with black letters. Using **PutImage** and **XOROpt**, the bounce bar is erased from its original position and written again either one position up or one position down. The upper and lower bounds of the bar are changed accordingly, as is a "pick" value that started out as 0 and indicates which of the menu items the bounce bar is currently highlighting.

As the user moves the mouse pointer up and down while holding the left mouse button depressed, the bounce bar follows, highlighting one menu item or another. All this time the loop code waits for one of the following things to happen:

1. The user presses the right mouse button. This indicates that the user has had a change of heart and no longer wishes to select a menu item. It's like pressing the Esc key; the idea is to put the menu away without selecting anything. The menu box is erased (we say, "put away") by writing the previously-saved portion of the screen back over it (this happens within the **RestoreUnderMenuBox** local procedure), and **Menu** returns a 0 code to the calling logic in the **ReturnCode** parameter.

2. The user moves the mouse pointer outside the bounds of the menu box. This is equivalent to pressing the right mouse button. The menu box is put away and a 0 code is returned by **Menu** to the calling logic.

3. The user *releases* the left mouse button while the bounce bar is highlighting an active item. This indicates selection of that item. The item's code is passed back to the calling logic in **ReturnCode**, and the menu is put away.

If the user releases the left button while the pointer is pointing to an inactive menu item, a 0 code will be returned. Note that the bounce bar does not highlight inactive menu items; they remain black and without a visible item title.

```
{------------------------------------------------------------------}
{                          PULLDOWN                                }
{                                                                  }
{                Graphics pull-down menuing system                 }
{                                                                  }
{                        by Jeff Duntemann                         }
{                        Turbo Pascal V7.0                         }
{                        Last update 2/28/93                       }
{                                                                  }
{    From: BORLAND PASCAL FROM SQUARE ONE   by Jeff Duntemann      }
{------------------------------------------------------------------}

UNIT PullDown;

INTERFACE

USES DOS,Graph,Crt,    { Standard Borland units }
     Mouse;            { Described in Chapter 13.3 }

TYPE
  String15  = String[15];

  ItemRec   = RECORD
                Item       : String15;  { Title of item }
                ItemCode   : Byte;      { Code number of item }
                ItemActive : Boolean    { True if item is active }
              END;

  MenuRec   = RECORD
                XStart,XEnd : Word;      { Pixel offset along menu bar
                Title       : String15; { Menu title }
                MenuSize    : Word;      { Size of menu image on heap }
                Imageptr    : Pointer;   { Points to menu image on heap }
                Active      : Boolean;   { True if menu is active }
                Choices     : Byte;      { Number of items in menu }
                ItemList    : ARRAY[0..18] OF ItemRec  { The items }
              END;

  MenuDesc  = ARRAY[0..12] OF MenuRec; { Up to 13 items along menu bar }


{->>>>ActivateMenu<<<<---------------------------------------------}
{                                                                  }
{ Filename : PULLDOWN.PAS - Last Modified 12/25/87                 }
{                                                                  }
{ This routine makes the menu specified by MenuNumber active.      }
```

```
{ regardless of whether it was active or inactive at        }
{ invocation.  ImagePtr is set to NIL so that the menu will be }
{ redrawn the next time it is pulled down.                  }
{                                                           }
{ Types MenuRec, ChoiceRec, MenuDesc and String15 must be   }
{   predefined.                                             }
{-----------------------------------------------------------}

PROCEDURE ActivateMenu(VAR CurrentMenu : MenuDesc;
                           MenuNumber    : Byte);


{->>>>DeactivateMenu<<<<------------------------------------}
{                                                           }
{ Filename : PULLDOWN.PAS - Last Modified 12/25/87          }
{                                                           }
{ This routine makes the menu specified by MenuNumber       }
{ inactive, regardless of whether it was active or inactive at }
{ invocation.  ImagePtr is set to NIL so that the menu will be }
{ redrawn the next time it is pulled down.                  }
{                                                           }
{ Types MenuRec, ChoiceRec, MenuDesc and String15 must be   }
{   predefined.                                             }
{-----------------------------------------------------------}

PROCEDURE DeactivateMenu(VAR CurrentMenu : MenuDesc;
                             MenuNumber    : Byte);


{->>>>ActivateItem<<<<--------------------------------------}
{                                                           }
{ Filename : PULLDOWN.PAS - Last Modified 12/25/87          }
{                                                           }
{ This routine sets the item whose code is given in Code to }
{ active, regardless of the state of the item at invocation. }
{ ImagePtr is set to NIL so that the menu will be redrawn   }
{ the next time it is pulled down.                          }
{                                                           }
{ Types MenuRec, ChoiceRec, MenuDesc and String15 must be   }
{   predefined.                                             }
{-----------------------------------------------------------}

PROCEDURE ActivateItem(VAR CurrentMenu : MenuDesc;
                           Code          : Byte);
```

```
{->>>>DeactivateItem<<<<----------------------------------------}
{                                                               }
{ Filename : PULLDOWN.PAS - Last Modified 12/25/87              }
{                                                               }
{ This routine sets the item whose code is given in Code to     }
{ inactive, regardless of the state of the item at invocation.  }
{ ImagePtr is set to NIL so that the menu will be redrawn       }
{ the next time it is pulled down.                              }
{                                                               }
{ Types MenuRec, ChoiceRec, MenuDesc and String15 must be       }
{   predefined.                                                 }
{---------------------------------------------------------------}


PROCEDURE DeactivateItem(VAR CurrentMenu : MenuDesc;
                             Code         : Byte);




{->>>>InvalidMenu<<<<-------------------------------------------}
{                                                               }
{ Filename : PULLDOWN.PAS - Last Modified 12/25/87              }
{                                                               }
{ This function checks for duplicate item codes within the      }
{ menu array passed in CurrentMenu.  The menuing system always  }
{ assumes that every menu item has a unique code.  Run this     }
{ function on any menu array you intend to use and abort if a   }
{ duplicate code is detected.                                   }
{                                                               }
{ Types MenuRec, ChoiceRec, MenuDesc and String15 must be       }
{   predefined.                                                 }
{---------------------------------------------------------------}


FUNCTION InvalidMenu(CurrentMenu : MenuDesc;
                     VAR BadCode : Byte) : Boolean;




{->>>>SetupMenu<<<<---------------------------------------------}
{                                                               }
{ Filename : PULLDOWN.PAS - Last Modified 12/25/87              }
{                                                               }
{ This routine does the initial display of the menu bar, menu   }
{ titles, and the menu bar amulet.                              }
{                                                               }
{ Types MenuRec, ChoiceRec, MenuDesc and String15 must be       }
{   predefined.                                                 }
{---------------------------------------------------------------}
```

```
PROCEDURE SetupMenu(CurrentMenu : MenuDesc);
```

```
{->>>>Menu<<<<----------------------------------------------------}
{                                                                  }
{ Filename : PULLDOWN.PAS - Last Modified 12/25/87                 }
{                                                                  }
{ This is the main menuing routine.  It requires that both         }
{ InvalidMenu and SetupMenu be run before it.  It directly         }
{ samples the mouse pointer position and decides which menu        }
{ within the menu bar has been selected.  It then allows the       }
{ user to bounce the menu bar up and down within the menu          }
{ until an item is chosen or the right button is pressed or        }
{ the pointer is moved out of the pulled-down menu.  The code      }
{ of the chosen item is returned in ReturnCode.  If no item is     }
{ chosen, ReturnCode returns a 0.  The returned code is            }
{ within the range 0-255.                                          }
{                                                                  }
{ Menu is responsible for drawing pull-down menus and storing      }
{ them on the heap so that once drawn a menu does not need to      }
{ be drawn again until it is changed somehow, typically by         }
{ deactivating or reactivating an item.                            }
{                                                                  }
{ Types MenuRec, ChoiceRec, MenuDesc and String15 must be         }
{   predefined.                                                    }
{------------------------------------------------------------------}

PROCEDURE Menu(CurrentMenu    : MenuDesc;
               VAR ReturnCode : Word;
               VAR Amulet     : Boolean);




IMPLEMENTATION


PROCEDURE ChangeItemStatus(VAR CurrentMenu : MenuDesc;
                           Code            : Byte;
                           ToActive        : Boolean);

VAR
   I          : Byte;
   MenuNumber : Byte;
   ItemFound  : Boolean;
```

```
BEGIN
  MenuNumber := 0; ItemFound := False;
  REPEAT
    WITH CurrentMenu[MenuNumber] DO
      BEGIN
        I := 0;
        REPEAT      { Here we scan menu items to find the right one }
          IF ItemList[I].ItemCode = Code THEN  { We found it ! }
            BEGIN
              ItemList[I].ItemActive := ToActive;  { Mark item }
              ItemFound := True;
              { Since we've changed the data in a menu, we must     }
              { remove any menu image from the heap, and force      }
              { the code to redraw it the next time it's pulled down: }
              IF ImagePtr <> NIL THEN  { If an image is on the heap }
                BEGIN
                  FreeMem(ImagePtr,MenuSize);  { Deallocate heap image }
                  ImagePtr := NIL            { Make pointer NIL again }
                END;
            END
          ELSE
            Inc(I)
        UNTIL ItemFound OR (I > Choices)
      END;
    Inc(MenuNumber)
  UNTIL ItemFound OR (MenuNumber > 12);
END;



{----------------------------------------------------------------------}
{   IMPLEMENTATION Definitions above this bar are PRIVATE to the unit. }
{----------------------------------------------------------------------}


PROCEDURE ActivateMenu(VAR CurrentMenu : MenuDesc;
                           MenuNumber   : Byte);

BEGIN
  WITH CurrentMenu[MenuNumber] DO
    BEGIN
      ImagePtr := NIL;
      Active   := True
    END
END;


PROCEDURE DeactivateMenu(VAR CurrentMenu : MenuDesc;
                             MenuNumber   : Byte);
```

```
BEGIN
  WITH CurrentMenu[MenuNumber] DO
    BEGIN
      ImagePtr := NIL;
      Active   := False
    END
END;




PROCEDURE ActivateItem(VAR CurrentMenu : MenuDesc;
                           Code         : Byte);

BEGIN
  ChangeItemStatus(CurrentMenu,Code,True)
END;




PROCEDURE DeactivateItem(VAR CurrentMenu : MenuDesc;
                             Code         : Byte);

BEGIN
  ChangeItemStatus(CurrentMenu,Code,False)
END;




FUNCTION InvalidMenu(CurrentMenu : MenuDesc;
                     VAR BadCode : Byte) : Boolean;

VAR
  I,J            : Word;
  CmdSet         : SET OF Byte;
  DuplicateFound : Boolean;

BEGIN
  DuplicateFound := False;
  CmdSet := [];  { Start out with the empty set }
  FOR I := 0 TO 12 DO      { Check each menu }
    WITH CurrentMenu[I] DO
      BEGIN
        J := 0; { Reset item counter to 0 for each new menu }
        REPEAT  { Here we scan menu items to check each one }
          IF ItemList[J].ItemCode > 0 THEN
            IF ItemList[J].ItemCode IN CmdSet THEN
```

```
                         BEGIN
                            DuplicateFound := True;                { Flag duplicate }
                            BadCode := ItemList[J].ItemCode { Return dupe in BADCODE }
                         END
                       ELSE
                         BEGIN
                            { Add item's command code to the set: }
                            CmdSet := CmdSet + [ItemList[J].ItemCode];
                            Inc(J)
                         END
                    ELSE Inc(J)
                  UNTIL (J > Choices) OR DuplicateFound
            END;
     InvalidMenu := DuplicateFound
END;




PROCEDURE SetupMenu(CurrentMenu : MenuDesc);

VAR
   I,DrawX,DrawY : Word;

BEGIN
   { Show bar and amulet: }
    SetFillStyle(SolidFill,White); Bar(0,0,GetMaxX,11);
    SetColor(0); Rectangle(2,1,12,9);
    FOR I := 3 TO 8 DO IF Odd(I) THEN Line(4,I,10,I);

    { Display menu titles in bar: }
    DrawX := CurrentMenu[0].XStart; DrawY := 2; I := 0;
    REPEAT
       OutTextXY(DrawX,DrawY,CurrentMenu[I].Title);
      Inc(I);
       DrawX := CurrentMenu[I].XStart;
    UNTIL (Length(CurrentMenu[I].Title) = 0) OR (I > 13);
END;




PROCEDURE Menu(CurrentMenu    : MenuDesc;
                  VAR ReturnCode : Word;
                  VAR Amulet     : Boolean);

VAR
   PointerX,PointerY : Word;        { Current position of mouse pointer }
   Left,Center,Right : Boolean;      { Current state of mouse buttons }
   I,J               : Integer;
```

```
    MenuWidth            : Integer;       { Width in pixels of target menu }
    M1X,M1Y,M2X,M2Y      : Integer;       { Coordinates of menu box }
    FoundMenu            : Boolean;
    SaveColor            : Integer;       { Holds caller's draw color }
    UnderMenu            : Pointer;       { Points to saved screen area }
    BounceBar            : Pointer;       { Points to bounce bar pattern }
    Pick                 : Word;          { Number of item under bounce bar }
    UpperBound,
      LowerBound         : Integer;       { Current Y-limits of bounce bar }


PROCEDURE  RestoreUnderMenuBox;

BEGIN
  PointerOff;
  PutImage(M1X,M1Y,UnderMenu^,NormalPut);
  PointerOn
END;



BEGIN
  Amulet := False;
  SaveColor := GetColor; SetColor(White);
  PollMouse(PointerX,PointerY,Left,Right,Center);
  { Check to see if the amulet is under mouse pointer: }
  IF (PointerX > 1) AND (PointerX < 13) AND
     (PointerY > 0) AND (PointerY < 10)
  THEN
    BEGIN
      Amulet := True;   { We've clicked on the amulet }
      SetColor(SaveColor);
      Exit               { THIS IS AN EXIT TO MENU! }
    END;
  { Now we find out which menu to pull down: }
  I := -1;
  REPEAT
    I := I + 1;
    IF (PointerX >= CurrentMenu[I].XStart) AND  { If pointer is in }
       (PointerX <= CurrentMenu[I].XEnd)   AND  { menu's range }
       CurrentMenu[I].Active                    { and menu is active }
    THEN FoundMenu := True ELSE FoundMenu := False;
  UNTIL FoundMenu OR                            { We hit an active menu }
        (Length(CurrentMenu[I].Title) = 0) OR   { We hit a null menu }
        (I > 13);                               { Only 13 menus max! }
  IF FoundMenu THEN  { Pull it down and pick! }
    BEGIN
      PointerOff;
```

```
WITH CurrentMenu[I] DO{ We're only working with current menu now }
BEGIN
    { Calc coordinates of the found menu box: }
    MenuWidth := 0;        { First we have to calc menu width : }
    FOR J := 0 TO Choices-1 DO   { Find longest item string }
      IF Length(ItemList[J].Item) > MenuWidth
        THEN MenuWidth := Length(ItemList[J].Item);
    MenuWidth := MenuWidth * 8; { We're using the 8 X 8 font }
    M1X := XStart; M1Y := 11;
    M2X := XStart+MenuWidth+6;
    M2Y := (Choices+1) * 12;
    MenuSize := ImageSize(M1X,M1Y,M2X,M2Y);

    { We must save the screen area beneath the menu box: }
    GetMem(UnderMenu,MenuSize);              { Allocate space on heap }
    GetImage(M1X,M1Y,M2X,M2Y,UnderMenu^);{ Save area out to heap   }

    { First we clear the menu box: }
    SetFillStyle(SolidFill,Black);
    Bar(M1X,M1Y,M2X,M2Y);

    { Here we create the bounce bar pattern on the heap: }
    SetFillStyle(SolidFill,White);
    GetMem(BounceBar,ImageSize(M1X+1,M1Y+1,M2X-1,M1Y+12));
    Bar(M1X+1,M1Y+1,M2X-1,M1Y+12);
    GetImage(M1X+1,M1Y+1,M2X-1,M1Y+12,BounceBar^);

    { If menu has not yet been shown for the first time, or if }
    { the active/inactive status of any menu item has changed since }
    { we last pulled it down, the image pointer is NIL and we must }
    { draw it and then store it on the heap.  Any time AFTER the }
    { first time it comes in from the heap FAST.                }
    IF ImagePtr = NIL THEN     { We must draw the menu }
      BEGIN
        Rectangle(M1X,M1Y,M2X,M2Y);  { Draw the menu box }
        { The first item must be drawn in black on the
          white bar: }
        SetColor(Black);
        IF ItemList[0].ItemActive THEN
          OutTextXY(XStart+3,14,ItemList[0].Item);
        SetColor(White);
        { Items after the first are drawn in white on black: }
        FOR J := 1 TO Choices-1 DO IF ItemList[J].ItemActive THEN
          OutTextXY(XStart+3,14+(J*12),ItemList[J].Item);
        { Now we allocate heap space and move image to heap }
        GetMem(ImagePtr,MenuSize);
        GetImage(M1X,M1Y,M2X,M2Y,ImagePtr^);
      END;
```

```
{ Bring the menu box image in from the heap: }
PutImage(M1X,M1Y,ImagePtr^,NormalPut);
PointerOn;  { We need the pointer on to bounce the bar }

{ Now we enter the "bounce loop" that moves the bounce bar  }
{  up and down the menu box, attached to the mouse pointer: }
UpperBound := 12; LowerBound := 24; Pick := 0;
REPEAT
   PollMouse(PointerX,PointerY,Left,Center,Right);
   { If the pointer leaves the menu box, it's an "escape" }
   {   identical in effect to pressing the right button:   }
   IF (PointerX < M1X) OR (PointerX > M2X) OR
      (PointerY > M2Y) THEN Right := True
   ELSE
     BEGIN
     IF PointerY < UpperBound THEN
       { We bounce the bar UPWARD: }
       IF PointerY > 12 THEN
         { If we're not above the top line }
         BEGIN
           PointerOff;
           { Erase bar at current position if item is active: }
           IF ItemList[Pick].ItemActive THEN
             PutImage(M1X+1,UpperBound,BounceBar^,XORPut);
           { Decrement bounds and pick number: }
           UpperBound := UpperBound - 12;
           LowerBound := LowerBound - 12;
           Pick := Pick - 1;
           { Show bar at new position if item is active: }
           IF ItemList[Pick].ItemActive THEN
             PutImage(M1X+1,UpperBound,BounceBar^,XORPut);
           PointerOn;
         END;
     IF PointerY > LowerBound THEN
       BEGIN
         PointerOff;
         { Erase bar at current position if item is active: }
         IF ItemList[Pick].ItemActive THEN
           PutImage(M1X+1,UpperBound,BounceBar^,XORPut);
         { Increment bounds and pick number: }
         UpperBound := UpperBound + 12;
         LowerBound := LowerBound + 12;
         Pick := Pick + 1;
         { Show bar at new position if item is active: }
         IF ItemList[Pick].ItemActive THEN
           PutImage(M1X+1,UpperBound,BounceBar^,XORPut);
         PointerOn;
```

```
                        END;
                     END;
                  UNTIL (NOT Left) OR Right;
                  RestoreUnderMenuBox;
                  { Now we set up the function return code.  The right button  }
                  { always indicates "escape;" i.e., 0; Take No Action.        }
                  { Picking an inactive menu item also returns a 0.  An active }
                  { item returns its item code as the function result. }
                  IF Right THEN ReturnCode := 0
                     ELSE IF ItemList[Pick].ItemActive THEN
                              ReturnCode := ItemList[Pick].ItemCode
                           ELSE ReturnCode := 0
               END;   { WITH statement }
            PointerOn;
         END;
      SetColor(SaveColor);    { Restore caller's drawing color }
   END;

   { No initialization section...}

   END.
```

A GRAPHICS SCRATCHPAD APPLICATION

To illustrate the **PullDown** unit, I have written a very simple graphics scratchpad application called **Scribble**. Between **PullDown** and **Scribble**, you have examples of the majority of the routines built into Turbo Pascal's **Graph** unit.

Scribble doesn't actually do very much aside from allow you to create freehand sketches on the screen. The majority of the menu items in the **DemoMenu** structure are dummies. All of the command structure is in place for you to expand **Scribble**, however, just by adding new case handlers to the central **CASE..OF** statement. It does show you how to initialize the BGI and enter graphics mode, check for BGI errors, and exit graphics mode courteously without abandoning the user in some anomalous state with a scrambled screen and no cursor.

An important point of interest is that the "cleanup" work of turning off the mouse driver and reentering text mode are done from the main program's exit procedure. This ensures that, in the event of a runtime error of some sort, the system will return to text mode no matter where in the program the runtime error occurred. This is tested by deliberately staging a divide-by-zero error when the RENAME option in the FILES menu is selected. If **CloseGraph** had not been present in the exit procedure when that error is triggered, **Scribble** would return to DOS while remaining in text mode, leaving the user up the proverbial creek without a cursor.

```
{----------------------------------------------------------------}
{                          SCRIBBLE                              }
{                                                                }
{      Simple freehand graphics sketchpad program               }
{                                                                }
{                     by Jeff Duntemann                          }
{                     Turbo Pascal V7.0                          }
{                     Last update 2/28/93                        }
{                                                                }
{    From: BORLAND PASCAL FROM SQUARE ONE  by Jeff Duntemann     }
{----------------------------------------------------------------}

PROGRAM Scribble;

USES DOS,Crt,Graph, { Standard Borland units }
     Mouse,          { Described in Section 13.3 }
     PullDown;       { Described in Section 22.9 }

{$I DEMOMENU.DEF }   { This is a LARGE include file containing a }
                     { sample menu array of type MenuDesc }

VAR
  GraphDriver : Integer;
  GraphMode   : Integer;
  ErrorCode   : Integer;
  I           : Integer;
  R           : Real;
  M1,M2,M3,M4 : Word;
  ReturnCode  : Word;
  XText,YText : String;
  Mule        : String;
  PointerX,
    PointerY  : Word;
  Left,Center,
    Right     : Boolean;
  Amulet      : Boolean; { True if amulet was clicked on within Menu }
  Quit        : Boolean;
  DuplicateCode : Byte;
  ExitSave    : Pointer;

VAR
  SavedColor : Word;
  Palette : PaletteType;
  Color   : Word;


{$F+} PROCEDURE ReturnToTextMode; {$F-}
```

```
BEGIN
  PointerOff;              { Turn off the mouse pointer }
  CloseGraph;              { Go back to text mode }
  ExitProc := ExitSave
END;


BEGIN
  ExitSave := ExitProc;         { This ensures that we will ALWAYS      }
  ExitProc := @ReturnToTextMode;{ re-enter text mode on return to DOS! }

  ClrScr;
  { Check the menu structure to be sure all codes are unique: }
  IF InvalidMenu(DemoMenu,DuplicateCode) THEN
    BEGIN
      Writeln('>>Halted for invalid menu: Duplicate code ',
              DuplicateCode);
      Halt(1)
    END;

  GraphDriver := Detect; { Let the BGI detect the board we're using }
  DetectGraph(GraphDriver,GraphMode);
  InitGraph(GraphDriver,GraphMode,'');
  IF GraphResult <> 0 THEN
    BEGIN
      Writeln('>>Halted on graphics error: ',GraphErrorMsg(GraphResult));
      Halt(2)
    END;

  SetupMenu(DemoMenu);
  PointerOn;

  SetColor(Yellow); Quit := False;
  REPEAT
    PollMouse(PointerX,PointerY,Left,Center,Right);
    IF Left THEN
      BEGIN
        IF PointerY < 12 THEN { We're in the menu bar; call Menu: }
          BEGIN
            Menu(DemoMenu,ReturnCode,Amulet);
            { Update graphics CP to reflect motion while in Menu: }
            PollMouse(PointerX,PointerY,Left,Center,Right);
            MoveTo(PointerX,PointerY);

            { The CASE statement parses menu items and takes action }
            IF ReturnCode <> 0 THEN
```

```
              CASE ReturnCode OF
                25 : Quit := True;
              { Here is where you parse out other codes returned from }
              { procedure Menu.  Put a CASE selector for each valid   }
              { code, and then implement some action for each CASE     }
              { selector. }
                END;  { CASE }
          END
        ELSE
          IF (GetX <> PointerX) OR (GetY <> PointerY) THEN
            BEGIN   { If we're not in the menu bar, then we sketch: }
            PointerOff;
            LineTo(PointerX,PointerY);
            PointerOn
          END
      END
    ELSE MoveTo(PointerX,PointerY)
  UNTIL KeyPressed OR Quit;

  { Note that CloseGraph is executed from the MAIN exit procedure! }
END.
```

Chapter 23

Procedural Types

USING PROGRAM CODE AS
THOUGH IT WERE DATA

My former colleague Dan Beale of *PC Tech Journal* posed an interesting (if slightly rhetorical) question to me once as I struggled to make a tight left turn out of a Burger King parking lot during rush hour in South Baltimore:

"What *is* data, anyway?"

I guess Dan found danger intellectually stimulating. I put the question aside until it was clear that we would survive, and it has haunted me a little ever since.

You and I might say that data is the stuff in the **VAR** section of a program, and while that's true enough for us, keep in mind that Dan is a LISP hacker. In LISP, anything can be either code or data as you like. It's not that the line between code and data in LISP is thinly drawn; the line is not drawn at all so much as imagined. Whether a run of memory locations is code or data to LISP depends powerfully on how you care to think about it.

Turbo Pascal has kept us from thinking such thoughts, both in dangerous situations and while sitting at home in the bathtub—until now. Starting with Turbo Pascal 5.0, the Pascal notions of code and data moved decidedly LISPward, by allowing procedures or functions to become data types and be passed as parameters.

This may strike you as not especially useful, or perhaps even dangerous— but it's really no more dangerous than eating at Burger King, and lots more useful than other peculiar things like variant records that we've long since come to terms with. Let's take a closer look.

23.1 Procedures As Types

If data can be thought of as a cupful of information in memory, then a data type is a mold to cast the information in. A type gives shape and form to data, just as a mold turns molten iron into boxcar wheels, or molten ice into rocket-shaped popsicles. The binary pattern 01000001 when cast in a character mold (type

Char) is the letter 'A'. The same pattern cast in a numeric mold (type **Byte**) is the number 65.

The notion of data types as frames or molds comes into its own when we speak of Pascal records. Here, we glue together several partitions in a particular order, and the whole assemblage is given a name as a data type:

```
TYPE
  DemoRec =
    RECORD
      Name   : String60;
      Age    : Byte;
      Sex    : Boolean;
      Weight : Integer
    END;
```

Notice and remember that there is no actual *data* in this type definition at all. There is only a specification for a container that can later be filled with data — a mold, if you will. We're not speaking of any actual record, but only of the *shape* of a record that could be created at some time in the future.

Now, consider what we do when we define the header of a procedure in the interface portion of a Turbo Pascal unit:

```
PROCEDURE DisplayFileData(DTA : SearchRec; Path : STRING);
```

What we've specified here is the name of a procedure, along with the names, types, and order of two parameters. (Ignore what the procedure is supposed to do for the time being.) Compare the definition above with the definition below:

```
PROCEDURE DeleteFile(ItsDTA : SearchRec; ItsPath : STRING);
```

Both this and the previous header define procedures. Both procedures have two parameters: the first is of type **SearchRec** (which is defined in Turbo Pascal's **DOS** unit) and the second is a default-length string. From a Pascal standpoint (assuming you ignore the bodies of the two procedures) these two procedure definitions are identical.

Just as with Pascal records, a procedure definition can be thought of as a series of data items of a particular type, defined in a particular order. This implies that we could specify a frame for procedures, just as we have record type definitions as frames for Pascal records. In fact, we can.

Study the following type definition, which is legal under V5.0 and later:

```
TYPE
  ActionProc = PROCEDURE(FileDTA : SearchRec; FilePath : STRING);
```

What we've done here is distilled the essence of both of the procedure headers shown earlier, and defined a type that applies to both procedures. The fact that type **ActionProc** specifies a procedure (as opposed to a function) is shown by the reserved word **PROCEDURE**; and the types of the two parameters are shown, as is their order. Also, the **ActionProc** definition specifies that neither parameter is a **VAR** parameter simply by the lack of the **VAR** reserved word.

Those who probe such things should realize that type **ActionProc** also defines the complete structure of the stack frame for calling any procedure of this type. Except . . . depending on where a procedure is defined, the stack frame is created for near calls or far calls. "Far" calls incorporate full 32-bit addresses, while "near" calls incorporate only the 16-bit offset of a procedure into the current code segment. A near procedure can therefore be called only from within its own code segment. Procedures defined in the interface section of a unit are always far procedures. Procedures defined in the implementation section of a unit are near procedures, as are procedures defined within the main program.

This means that a procedural type definition fails in providing one important piece of information: whether the procedure is a near or far procedure. Getting this wrong would guarantee that your program runs off into the bushes, so the compiler demands that all procedures that will be considered to be of a procedural type *must* be far procedures, no matter where they're defined. This is best guaranteed by bracketing headers of typed procedures with {$F+} and {$F-} compiler directives:

```
{$F+}
PROCEDURE DisplayFileData(DTA : SearchRec; Path : String);
{$F-}
```

Bracketing procedures defined in the interface section of a unit isn't necessary, since all procedures defined in the **INTERFACE** section of a unit are considered far procedures.

Failing to specify a procedure as a far procedure when it would otherwise be a near procedure will generate compile-time error 143: Invalid procedure or function reference.

One other restriction on procedural types is that procedures used as procedural variables or parameters must be declared at the global scoping level.

23.2 Procedures As Variables

The existence of procedural types implies procedural variables. Given type **ActionProc** above, we can define variables that are instances of type **ActionProc**:

```
VAR
   DoThis : ActionProc;
```

What can be done with a procedure variable of type **ActionProc**? Not much. You can assign the name of a type-compatible procedure to it:

```
DoThis := DisplayFileData;
```

And, as you might imagine, you can execute the procedure assigned to the procedural variable by naming the variable in the source code. Keep in mind that when you intend to execute a procedural variable, you need to provide actual parameters, just as though you were executing the procedure through its defined name:

```
DoThis := DisplayFileData;
DoThis(CurrentDTA,CurrentPath);   { Executes DisplayFileData }
```

You can use the **SizeOf** function on a procedural variable, but the answer will invariably be 4, regardless of how many parameters the procedural type has. In physical reality, a procedural variable is nothing but a 32-bit address; that is, the address of the procedure currently assigned to the variable. Assuming that **DisplayData** has been assigned to **DoThis**, the same address contained in the procedural variable **DoThis** will be returned by the notation **@DisplayData** or **Addr(DisplayData)**.

Built-in functions **Seg** and **Ofs** can also be used with procedural variables, and return the code segment and code segment offset address, respectively, for the named procedural variable.

Procedural variables cannot take part in any kind of comparison, either with other procedural variables of the same type or with compatible procedures. Attempting to do so will generate error **143: Invalid procedure or function reference**. This brings up the question of how you can tell whether a procedural variable has been assigned some value. You can't test a procedural variable against NIL, as you can with pointers, because procedural variables can't take part in comparison statements. Fortunately, Borland has added a new function to version 7 of both Borland and Turbo Pascal that allows you to determine if a procedural variable has been assigned a value.

The function is **Assigned**. It returns the Boolean value **True** if the procedural variable has been assigned some value, and **False** if the variable has had no value assigned to it and is therefore undefined.

You can use it this way:

```
IF Assigned(DoThis) THEN
    DoThis(CurrentDTA,CurrentPath)
ELSE Writeln('Error!  Action procedure is undefined!');
```

You *can* define a file of some procedural type, and write procedural variables of that type to that file. What gets written to disk is the 4-byte address of the procedure assigned to the variable. Parameters are *not* written to the file.

23.3 Procedures As Parameters

So far, none of this has come across as especially useful. Procedural types and variables really come into their own only when used in connection with procedural parameters.

In the Pascal subculture, it's easy enough to think of a procedure as a little machine, the quintessential "black box." Its parameters are the data we feed into the machine, and also the processed data we get back. This metaphor, however, has always been limited to feeding *information* to the procedure. Procedural parameters now let us feed the procedure part of its instructions as well.

The aim here is to make a procedure that is more general than is possible under standard Pascal. Think of it this way: A certain procedure makes chairs. We pass the procedure the dimensions of the chair, and the raw materials (oak, cherry, walnut, whatever) and the procedure returns a finished chair.

Now suppose we change the chair-making procedure so that we can also pass a set of instructions that tells the procedure what to make. If we need a chair, we pass the dimensions and materials for the chair, along with the way the chair is made. Or, if we need a table instead, we pass the dimensions and the materials and instructions for making tables. The procedure is no longer a chair-making procedure but a furniture-making procedure, and it is *enormously* more powerful.

This can, and should, change the way we think about and design our procedures. Two apparently unrelated tasks can have a large number of common elements. In the metaphor of the furniture-making procedure, the making of tables and the making of chairs have many common elements: planing the wood, drilling holes and routing joints, gluing joints, sanding and finishing surfaces, and so forth.

Or consider several simple disk utilities: One creates a linked list of all the files in a directory. Another copies all files whose archive attribute bit is cleared to some backup device. A third counts the number of bytes occupied by all the files in a directory of some given file spec. These might seem to be relatively distinct, but they have one strong common element: all three need to scan a disk directory for files matching some file spec and attribute combination.

So in designing procedures to perform the three tasks mentioned above, we start by building an underlying procedure that does the actual scanning of a disk directory. To this underlying procedure we pass a procedural parameter that specifies the task-specific portion of the code for each desired task. The underlying procedure becomes a file-search "engine" that does one thing and one thing only: It accepts a file spec and attribute byte, and it searches a directory for files matching the spec and attribute. Each time it finds a matching file, it passes that file to a procedural parameter that does something to or with that file. In this it is an extension of the directory search program LOCATE.PAS that we investigated back in Chapter 19.

23.4 A Directory-Search Unit

We can take the file search engine and make it a unit, and pass whatever actions we want the search engine to perform as procedural parameters. I've implemented such a unit in SCANNER.PAS, shown below. As you can see, there's not a great deal to it. The **Scan** procedure scans a directory named in **DirPath** for files matching the file specification **FileSpec** and the attribute value **Attribute**. Each time **Scan** finds a matching file, it calls the procedure passed in procedural parameter **Action**.

If **DirPath** contains a null string, **Scan** queries DOS for the name of the current directory and uses that string instead. If the name of the directory does not end in a backslash, **Scan** appends a backslash to it before concatenating the path and the file spec.

Once the pathname is set up, the remainder of **Scan** simply uses the **FindFirst** and **FindNext** procedures from the **DOS** unit. (I explained the use of these procedures in detail back in Chapter 19.) Each time **FindFirst** or **FindNext** returns a 0 error code, it means a matching file was located, and information about that file has been stored in the DOS disk transfer area (DTA). **FindFirst** and **FindNext** set the DOS DTA address to a parameter of type **SearchRec**, a record type predefined in the standard **DOS** unit. Its definition is shown below:

```
SearchRec = RECORD
              Fill: ARRAY[1..21] OF Byte;
              Attr: Byte;
              Time: Longint;
              Size: Longint;
              Name: String[12];
            END;
```

Note that while **SearchRec** contains the file's name, it does *not* contain the file's path.

Each time a matching file is found, **Scan** calls a procedure named **Action**. Or at least **Action** *looks* like a procedure—but in fact, **Action** is a procedural parameter of type **ScanProc**. **Action** takes two parameters: the DTA of the found file, and the found file's path. Taken together, these two data items tell us everything about a file that DOS is capable of telling us before we actually open the file and begin reading its contents.

That's all **Scan** does: It scans a directory for files matching a set of criteria. Each time such a file is found, it hands control to a procedural parameter to do something specific with the found file. One thing—and one thing well done.

```
{--------------------------------------------------------------}
{                         Scanner                              }
{                                                              }
{ Practical unit that demonstrates procedural types and        }
{ parameters, by implementing a directory scanner to which     }
{ "action" routines are passed as parameters.                  }
{                                                              }
{                    by Jeff Duntemann                         }
{                    Turbo Pascal V7.0                         }
{                    Last update 3/1/93                        }
{                                                              }
{   From: BORLAND PASCAL FROM SQUARE ONE  by Jeff Duntemann    }
{--------------------------------------------------------------}
```

```
{$F+}
UNIT Scanner;

INTERFACE

USES DOS;

TYPE
  ScanProc = PROCEDURE(DTA : SearchRec; Path : String);


PROCEDURE Scan(FileSpec  : String;
               DirPath   : String;
               Attribute : Byte;
               Action    : ScanProc);


IMPLEMENTATION

PROCEDURE Scan(FileSpec  : String;
               DirPath   : String;
               Attribute : Byte;
               Action    : ScanProc);

VAR
  ScanDTA : SearchRec;    { Defined in DOS unit }

BEGIN
  IF DirPath = '' THEN GetDir(0,DirPath);
  IF DirPath[Length(DirPath)] <> '\' THEN DirPath := DirPath+'\';
  FileSpec := DirPath+FileSpec;
  FindFirst(FileSpec,Attribute,ScanDTA);      { Look for directories }
  IF DOSError <> 2 THEN
    BEGIN
      Action(ScanDTA,DirPath);
      REPEAT
        FindNext(ScanDTA);
        IF DOSError = 0 THEN Action(ScanDTA,DirPath);
      UNTIL DOSError <> 0
    END
END;


{ No initialization section }
END.
```

ENGINE ACTIONS

I've coded up a very simple application that uses unit **Scanner.** The program is called **Spacer,** shown below, but in your listings diskette it will be called SCANTEST.PAS. There's another program SPACER.PAS described in this book (in Chapter 20) and while the programs are similar in their function, they need separate names. This is a good point to reiterate that the name you give a program in the **PROGRAM** statement doesn't have to match the file name under which the program is stored on disk. You don't, in fact, have to give a program a name at all! The **PROGRAM** statement is optional in Borland's Pascal products, and you can leave it out if you prefer. (I think leaving it out makes Pascal programs look more than a little peculiar.) If you choose to behead your program files, make sure you leave off the reserved word **PROGRAM** as well as the name; you must either have them both, or have neither.

```
{-----------------------------------------------------------------}
{                          ScanTest                               }
{                                                                 }
{ Demonstration of the use of procedural parameters in a          }
{ simple directory scanning utility that "does something" when    }
{ each file matching a file spec is found during the scan.        }
{                                                                 }
{                      by Jeff Duntemann                          }
{                      Turbo Pascal V7.0                          }
{                      Last update 3/1/93                         }
{                                                                 }
{    From: BORLAND PASCAL FROM SQUARE ONE  by Jeff Duntemann      }
{                                                                 }
{ This file is called SCANTEST.PAS because there is another       }
{ SPACER.PAS in this book.  This does what SPACER.PAS does,       }
{ more or less, but uses procedural procs to get it all done.     }
{-----------------------------------------------------------------}

PROGRAM Spacer; { File is SCANTEST.PAS! }

USES DOS,      { Standard Borland unit }
     Scanner;  { Procedural proc demo unit from Chapter 23 }

VAR
  Total : LongInt;

{ DO NOT FAIL to make procedures passed as procs FAR calls! }

{$F+} PROCEDURE ShowEm(DTA : SearchRec; Path : String); {$F-}

BEGIN
```

```
    Writeln(DTA.Name:13,DTA.Size:10);
    Total := Total + DTA.Size;
END;


BEGIN
  IF ParamCount < 1 THEN
    Writeln('Enter "SCANTEST" plus a file spec; i.e., "SCANTEST
*.PAS"')
  ELSE
    BEGIN
      Total := 0;
      Scan(ParamStr(1),'',0,ShowEm); { ShowEm is a procedural parameter }
      Writeln('Listed files occupy ',Total,' bytes.')
    END
END.
```

The **Spacer** program does what its namesake in Chapter 20 does: display all files in the current directory matching a given file spec, and then provide a figure giving the total size in bytes of all files listed. DOS didn't even do this most obvious task until V5.0, and it's a good, simple illustration of how to pass a procedure as a parameter.

Spacer contains a short procedure called **ShowEm** that adheres to the spec for procedural type **ActionProc**, defined in unit **Scanner**. It is a procedure (rather than a function) and it has two parameters: one a **SearchRec**, and the other one a **STRING**, in that order. That means we can pass **ShowEm** as a parameter to **Scan**, so that **ShowEm** will be executed each time **Scan** makes a "hit" on the file spec and attribute value.

Note that nothing explicitly declares procedure **ShowEm** to be of type **ActionProc**. **ShowEm** as defined simply fits the mold—and if by some chance it didn't, the compiler would call foul when we tried to pass **ShowEm** as a parameter to **Scan**.

Spacer does what it does simply by having **Scan** execute **ShowEm** each time a file is found. **ShowEm** adds the size of the found file to long integer variable **Total**, producing a running total of the bytes occupied by the found files. After **Scan** finishes its scan of the specified directory (indicating that no more files are to be found) **Spacer** prints out the final value of **Total**. Voila! A useful disk utility in 25 lines!

Spacer is a pretty trivial example of the use of procedural parameters. I've created a more sophisticated descendent of **Spacer** in program **DirSort**, shown below. Program **DirSort** builds on **Spacer** by producing a sorted directory listing. It does this by creating a linked list of DTA records and inserting each DTA into the list such that the list remains in sort order. **DirSort** provides some flexibility by allowing us to specify the sort order as being alphabetical by file name, or by time stamp, with the oldest files displayed first.

```
{------------------------------------------------------------}
{                        DirSort                             }
{                                                            }
{ Sorted directory demo program, demonstrating the use of    }
{ procedural parameters.                                     }
{                                                            }
{                   by Jeff Duntemann                        }
{                   Turbo Pascal V7.0                        }
{                   Last update 3/2/93                       }
{                                                            }
{    From: BORLAND PASCAL FROM SQUARE ONE  by Jeff Duntemann }
{------------------------------------------------------------}

PROGRAM DirSort;

USES DOS,       { Standard Borland unit }
     Scanner;   { From Chapter 23 }

CONST
  ByName = False;
  ByDate = NOT ByName;

TYPE
  NodePtr = ^DTANode;
  DTANode = RECORD
              DTA    : SearchRec;
              Prior  : NodePtr;
              Next   : NodePtr;
            END;

  TestFunc = FUNCTION(LeftRec,RightRec : DTANode) : Boolean;

VAR
  Current,Root,Descending : NodePtr;
  TakeAction              : ScanProc;
  FindSpec                : String;
  Total                   : LongInt;


{ This routine returns TRUE if the file name in the left parameter }
{ is greater than the file name in the right parameter.            }

{$F+} FUNCTION TestName(LeftRec,RightRec : DTANode) : Boolean; {$F-}

BEGIN
  IF LeftRec.DTA.Name > RightRec.DTA.Name THEN TestName := True
    ELSE TestName := False
END;
```

```
{ This routine returns TRUE if the time/date stamp in the left     }
{ parameter is later than the time/date stamp in the right parm.   }

{$F+} FUNCTION TestTime(LeftRec,RightRec : DTANode) : Boolean; {$F-}

BEGIN
  IF LeftRec.DTA.Time > RightRec.DTA.Time THEN TestTime := True
    ELSE TestTime := False
END;




{ This procedure inserts a new record into a linked list with the root }
{ passed in ListRoot.  Note the proc parm IsGreater, which returns True }
{ if the first of two records is to be considered greater than the second. }
{ *How* the judgement is made is up to the individual procedure passed in  }
{ the parameter IsGreater.                                          }

PROCEDURE
    InsertNode(VAR ListRoot  : NodePtr; { Root pointer of sorted list }
                   NewDTA     : SearchRec; { The DTA to be inserted }
                   IsGreater : TestFunc); { Tells which node is greater }

VAR
  Current,NewNode : NodePtr;
  PositionFound     : Boolean;

BEGIN
  { First we create a node on the heap for the found DTA: }
  New(NewNode);
  NewNode^.DTA := NewDTA;

  { Next we traverse the linked list to find an insertion position: }
  Current := ListRoot;
  PositionFound := False;
  IF Current <> NIL THEN
    REPEAT
      IF IsGreater(Current^,NewNode^) THEN PositionFound := True
        ELSE Current := Current^.Next
    UNTIL PositionFound OR (Current = NIL);
  { Finally, we insert the new node into the list: }
  { It goes either at the beginning or middle }
  IF PositionFound OR (Current = NIL) THEN
    BEGIN
      IF Current = ListRoot THEN { Insert it at the beginning of the list }
        BEGIN
          NewNode^.Next := ListRoot;
          Current^.Prior := NewNode;
```

```
                    Root := NewNode;
                    Root^.Prior := NIL
                  END
                ELSE    { Insert it in the middle, right before Current^ }
                  BEGIN
                    NewNode^.Next := Current;
                    NewNode^.Prior := Current^.Prior;
                    Current^.Prior^.Next := NewNode;
                    Current^.Prior := NewNode
                  END
              END
          ELSE        { The new node goes at the end of the list }
            BEGIN
              Descending^.Next := NewNode;
              Descending^.Next^.Prior := Descending;
              Descending := Descending^.Next;
              Descending^.Next := NIL
            END
        END;


{$F+} PROCEDURE InsertByName(CurrentDTA : SearchRec; Path : String);
{$F-}

BEGIN
   InsertNode(Root,CurrentDTA,TestName);
  Total := Total + CurrentDTA.Size;
END;


{$F+} PROCEDURE InsertByTime(CurrentDTA : SearchRec; Path : String);
{$F-}

BEGIN
   InsertNode(Root,CurrentDTA,TestTime);
  Total := Total + CurrentDTA.Size;
END;


BEGIN
  CASE Ord(ParamCount) OF
   0 : BEGIN
         Writeln('DIRSORT    V2.00 by Jeff Duntemann');
         Writeln;
         Writeln
         ('This utility produces a sorted directory listing.  The');
         Writeln('default sort field is the file name, in ascending');
```

```
           Writeln('alphabetical order.');
           Writeln;
           Writeln('Calling syntax:');
           Writeln('  DIRSORT <filespec> [/D|d]');
           Writeln
           ('Where <filespec> is any legal DOS file spec inc. path;');
           Writeln
           ('and an optional specifier "/D" indicates sort by DOS');
           Writeln('time stamp instead of file name.');
           Halt(1);   { THIS IS AN EXIT FROM DIRSORT }
       END;
   1 : BEGIN
           FindSpec := ParamStr(1);
           TakeAction := InsertByName;
       END;
   2..255 : BEGIN
           FindSpec := ParamStr(1);
           IF (ParamStr(2) = '/D') OR (ParamStr(2) = '/d') THEN
             TakeAction := InsertByTime ELSE
             TakeAction := InsertByName
       END
   END; { CASE }


   Total := 0; Root := NIL; Descending := NIL;
   Scan(FindSpec,'',0,TakeAction);         { Build the linked list }
   Current := Root;
   WHILE Current <> NIL DO                  { Now traverse & display it: }
     BEGIN
         Writeln(Current^.DTA.Name:14,Current^.DTA.Size:10);
         Current := Current^.Next
     END;
   Writeln('Listed files occupy ',Total,' bytes.');
END.
```

Far more than **Spacer, DirSort** demonstrates the power of thinking of code as data. Two different procedural types come into play within **DirSort**. The first is type **ActionProc**, the same type defined in unit **Scanner** and used in **Spacer**. **DirSort** contains two procedures of type **ActionProc**: **InsertByName** and **InsertByTime**. Both call a larger procedure, **InsertNode**, which actually inserts DTA records into the linked list.

At the start of **DirSort**, either **InsertByName** or **InsertByTime** is assigned to procedural variable **TakeAction**, depending on the command-line parameters passed to **DirSort**. **TakeAction** is then passed as a procedural parameter to search engine procedure **Scan**. If we pass **InsertByName** to **Scan**, the linked list will be created with the nodes in alphabetical order by name. If we pass **InsertByTime** to **Scan**, the linked list will be created with the nodes in order by DOS time stamp, oldest files first. We could have passed a Boolean flag indicating which action to take. But if the only purpose of the flag would be to specify an action, why not eliminate the middleman and pass the *action itself* as data? This is, in fact, what we're doing by selecting one of the two procedures **InsertByName** and **InsertByTime** and passing it as a parameter to **InsertNode**.

23.5 Procedural Functions

As their names imply, **InsertByName** and **InsertByTime** differ in the way they insert the DTA record into the linked list. Both call **InsertNode**, but each passes **InsertNode** a slightly different set of parameters. Note in the definition of **InsertNode** that it has a parameter named **IsGreater**. **IsGreater** is another procedural parameter, this time a *function* parameter. The procedural type for procedural parameter **IsGreater** is defined in the type-definition part of **DirSort**:

```
TYPE
   TestFunc = FUNCTION(LeftRec,RightRec : DTANode) : Boolean;
```

DirSort contains two functions of type **TestFunc**: **TestName** and **TestTime**. Both take two records of type **DTANode** and return a Boolean value indicating which of the two records is considered "greater." **TestName** tests the name fields of the two DTA nodes, and returns **True** if the left parameter is greater than the right parameter on the ASCII sort sequence. **TestTime**, on the other hand, compares the DOS time stamps of the two DTA nodes, and returns **True** if the left parameter is later in time than the right parameter.

Looking back to the difference between **InsertByName** and **InsertByTime**, you can see that the difference involves nothing more than which one of **TestName** and **TestTime** is passed to **InsertNode** as a parameter: **InsertByName** passes **TestName** to **InsertNode**, and **InsertByTime** passes **TestTime** to **InsertNode**.

Is the difference between code and data beginning to fuzz up a little bit for you?

Whether you realize it immediately or not, **DirSort** is the core of a DOS "sweep" utility that gathers files into a linked list and then allows the user to perform various tasks with the files in the list. Typically, a sweep utility allows the user to continually scroll through the files in the list, marking one or more files in the list to be deleted, printed, or moved to a backup device. Such a utility can be simplified by treating the various actions as procedures defined to be of a procedural type, and then passing that procedure to a list-processing procedure that actually invokes it upon the list of marked files.

Chapter 24

Pointers and Real-Mode Memory

SEEING AND USING THE CONNECTION BETWEEN POINTERS AND ADDRESSES

Well, there's tricks and then there's *tricks*. Everything we've talked about so far has been relatively aboveboard, nonsneaky standard Pascal, just like what you'd learn in school. This chapter, on the other hand, focuses on all the devious, nonstandard Turbo Pascal-ish pointer lore that makes life interesting and some truly fabulous programming possible.

Lord knows why you'd ever want to, but should you at some point need to learn the C language, you had better have a thorough understanding of low-level pointer theory. Consider this chapter a *necessary* segue into C or C++. On the other hand, the easiest and perhaps sanest way to write a C program is to pay somebody else to write it—and if you can do that, hey, you might as well stick with familiar territory.

(There is, by the way, *nothing* that can be done in C or C++ that cannot also be done in Pascal—except, perhaps, routinely take three times as long to get anything significant finished!)

24.1 The Nature of PC Memory

As I said early in Chapter 17, a pointer is a full 80x86 32-bit *address*—but that's about all I said in regard to its nature. Understanding what pointers look like under the sheets requires understanding the nature of 80x86 addresses—which further implies that you understand the nature of the PC's segmented memory system. Let's take a closer look at it.

The 80x86 processors can contain and use up to a megabyte of directly-addressable *real mode* memory. The more advanced processors in the family (the 286 and later) can address larger (sometimes *much* larger) amounts of *extended*

733

memory when operating in *protected mode*. Turbo Pascal does not operate in protected mode, so without the most violently underhanded gymnastics, extended memory is forbidden to Turbo Pascal users. Borland Pascal 7.0 finally opened up the world of protected mode programming, and while protected mode work isn't difficult, it's a subject all its own. And, as you can tell (having followed along with me for 734 pages) this book has to stop somewhere, and soon. I'm afraid protected mode will have to await another book.

THE ANATOMY OF A MEGABYTE

A megabyte of memory is actually not 1,000,000 bytes of memory, but 1,048,576 bytes. It doesn't come out even in our base 10 because computers insist on base 2. 1,048,576 bytes expressed in base 2 is 100000000000000000000b bytes. That's 2^{20}, a fact that we'll return to shortly. The number 100000000000000000000b is so bulky that it's better to express it in the compatible (and much more compact) base 16, which we call hexadecimal. 2^{20} is equivalent to 16^5, and may be written in hexadecimal as 100000H.

The address of a byte in any block of memory is just the number of that byte *starting from zero*. This means that the last, or highest address in a memory block containing one megabyte is 100000H minus one, or 0FFFFFH.

The addresses in a megabyte of memory, then, run from 00000H to 0FFFFFH. In binary notation, that is equivalent to the range of 00000000000000000000b to 11111111111111111111b. That's a lot of bits—20, as I mentioned earlier. When the processor is operating in real mode, there are 20 pins on the CPU chip that "talk" to the rows of memory chips comprising the PC memory system. Those 20 bits of address are connected to those 20 CPU pins to allow the CPU to select locations in memory.

16-BIT BLINDERS

The 80×86 processors in real mode "see" a full megabyte. That is, the CPU chips can pass a full 20-bit address to the memory system external to the CPU. From that perspective, it seems pretty simple and straightforward. However . . . the bulk of all the trouble you're likely ever to have understanding the 80×86 CPUs stems from this fact: That whereas those CPUs can see a full megabyte of memory, they are constrained to look at that full megabyte through 16-bit blinders.

You may call this peculiar. (If you ever do any amount of low-level programming, as with an assembler, you'll probably call it much worse.) But to get the most out of your Pascal programming you had better understand it, and understand it thoroughly.

The blinders metaphor is closer to literal than you might think. Look at Figure 24.1. The long rectangle represents the megabyte of memory that the 8088 can address. The CPU is off to the right. In the middle is a piece of metaphorical cardboard with a slot cut in it. The slot is 1 byte wide and 65,536 bytes long. The CPU can slide that piece of cardboard up and down the full length of its memory system. However, *at any one time*, it can only access 65,536 bytes.

The CPU's view of memory *is* peculiar. It is constrained to look at memory in chunks, where no chunk is larger than 65,536 bytes in length.

64K is an important number, just as 1MB is. (We call 65,536 "64K" for the same reason that we call 1,048,576 "1MB"—it's just shorthand for what is actually a binary—not decimal—number that "comes out even.")

65,536 in binary is 1000000000000000b; that is, 1 followed by 16 zeroes. In hex it's 10000H. The important characteristic of 64K is that the number can be expressed in 16 bits. 16 bits, being a multiple of one byte, carries with it some of the magic quality of the byte as data atom in our computer universe. 65,536 is an important number because it is the maximum size of a segment—a limitation you will encounter more and more as you hone your skills in Turbo Pascal.

THE NATURE OF SEGMENTS

In real mode 86 × 86 tech-speak, a *segment* is a region of memory that begins on a paragraph boundary and extends for some number of bytes less than or equal to 64K (65,536). A *paragraph* is a measure of memory equal to 16 bytes. The term paragraph is almost never used, *except* in connection with the places where segments may begin.

Any memory address evenly divisible by 16 is called a *paragraph boundary*. The first paragraph boundary is address 0. The second is address 10H; the third address 20H, and so on. Any paragraph boundary may be considered the start of a segment.

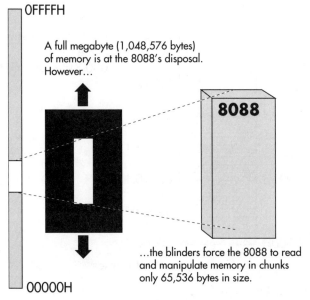

OFFFFH

A full megabyte (1,048,576 bytes) of memory is at the 8088's disposal. However…

8088

…the blinders force the 8088 to read and manipulate memory in chunks only 65,536 bytes in size.

00000H

Figure 24.1 Seeing a megabyte through 64K blinders

This *doesn't* mean that a segment actually starts every 16 bytes up and down throughout that megabyte of memory. A segment is like a shelf in one of those modern adjustable bookcases. On the back face of the bookcase are a great many little slots spaced one half inch apart. A shelf bracket can be inserted into any of the little slots. However, there aren't hundreds of shelves, but only four or five. Most of the slots are empty. They exist so that a much smaller number of shelves may be adjusted up and down the height of the bookcase as needed.

In a very similar manner, paragraph boundaries are little slots at which a segment may be begun. A Turbo Pascal program might make use of only four or five segments, but each of those segments may begin at nearly any of the 65,536 paragraph boundaries existing in the 8088's megabyte of memory.

There's that number again: 65,536; our beloved 64K. There are 64K different paragraph boundaries where a segment may begin. Each paragraph boundary has a number. As always, the numbers begin from 0, and go to 64K minus one; in decimal 65,535, or in hex 0FFFFH. Because a segment may begin at any paragraph boundary, the number of the paragraph boundary at which a segment begins is called the *segment address* of that particular segment. We rarely, in fact, speak of paragraphs or paragraph boundaries at all. When you see the term "segment address," keep in mind that each segment address is 16 bytes (one paragraph) farther along in memory than the one before it. See Figure 24.2.

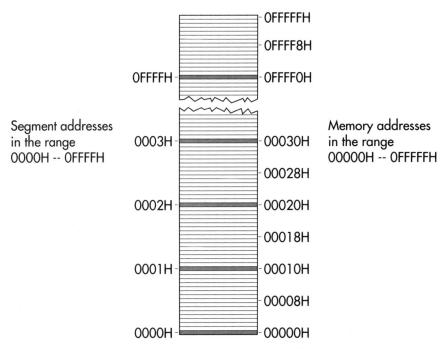

Segment addresses in the range 0000H -- 0FFFFH

Memory addresses in the range 00000H -- 0FFFFFH

Figure 24.2 Memory addresses versus segment addresses

In short, segments may begin at any segment address. There are 65,536 segment addresses evenly distributed across the full megabyte of real mode 80x86 memory, 16 bytes apart. A segment address is more a permission than a compulsion; for all the 64K possible segment addresses, only five or six are ever actually used to begin segments at any one time. Remember to think of segment addresses as slots where segments may be placed.

So much for segment addresses; now, what of segments themselves? A segment may be up to 64K bytes in size, but it doesn't *have* to be. A segment may be only one byte long, or 256 bytes long, or 21,378 bytes long, or any length at all short of 64K bytes.

A HORIZON, NOT A PLACE

You define a segment primarily by stating where it begins. What, then, defines how *long* a segment is? Nothing, really—and we get into some tricky semantics here. A segment is more a *horizon* than a *place*. Once you define where a segment begins, that segment can encompass any location in memory between that starting place and the horizon—which is 65,536 bytes down the line.

I think of segments this way: *A segment is the location in memory at which the CPU's 64K blinders are positioned.* In looking at memory through the blinders, you can see bytes starting at the segment address, and going on until the blinders cut you off, 64K bytes down the way. The CPU can "look" at one of these segments, and read and write memory or execute code from one, but to switch from one segment to another the CPU must perform some swapping around of values in registers—essentially moving the blinders from one location to another.

Each unit in Turbo Pascal gets its own code segment. In addition, there is one data segment for the application as a whole, and one stack segment. I won't go into a great deal of detail here about how segments are used at an assembly-language level. It's enough that you understand what they are—because the notion of pointers depends utterly on them and the addresses that they specify.

STORING 20-BIT ADDRESSES IN 16-BIT REGISTERS

Those of you who understand something of 32-bit CPU internals (that is, the internals of the 386 and 486 CPU families) need to keep in mind that real mode is the *only* mode present in the older 16-bit 8086 and 8088 CPUs. Real mode continues to exist as a "compatibility mode" with the older CPU, and its functioning is 16-bit in nature, even though some of the registers in the newer CPUs are 32 bits in size. The way things are laid out, in the newer CPUs only the first 16 bits of the 32-bit registers are actually used in real mode.

Registers do many jobs, but one of their more important jobs is holding addresses of important locations in memory. Expressing a megabyte (that is, expressing the quantity 1,048,576) requires a total of 20 bits.

Now, how do you put a 20-bit memory address in a 16-bit register?
Easy. You don't.

You put a 20-bit address in *two* 16-bit registers.

What happens is this: From the CPU's perspective, all locations within the 80×86's megabyte of memory have not one address but *two*. Every byte in memory is assumed to reside in some segment. A byte's complete address, then, consists of the address of its segment, along with the distance of the byte from the start of that segment. The address of the segment is (as we said before) the byte's *segment address*. The byte's distance from the start of the segment is the byte's *offset address*. Both addresses must be specified to completely describe any single byte's location within the full megabyte of real mode memory.

When written, the segment address comes first, followed by the offset address. The two are separated with a colon. Segment:offset addresses are generally written in hexadecimal, with the additional convention that when you write out both items at once with their colon, you needn't prefix the two values with Pascal's "$" symbol indicating a hexadecimal quantity.

I've drawn Figure 24.3 to help make this a little clearer. A byte of data we'll call **MyByte** exists in memory at the location marked. Its address is given as 0001:001D. This means that **MyByte** falls within segment 0001H, and is located 001DH bytes from the start of that segment.

The universe is perverse, however, and clever eyes will perceive that **MyByte** can have two other perfectly legal addresses: 0:002D; and 0002:000D. How so? Keep in mind that a segment may start every 16 bytes throughout the full megabyte of real memory. A segment, once begun, embraces all bytes from its origin to 65,535 bytes further up in memory. There's nothing wrong with seg-

MyByte could have any of
the three possible addresses:

0000H : 02DH
0001H : 01DH
0002H : 00DH

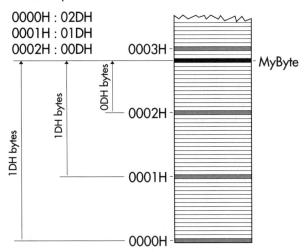

Figure 24.3 Segments and offsets

ments overlapping, and in Figure 24.3 we have three overlapping segments. **MyByte** is **$2D** bytes into the first segment, which begins at segment address 0000H. **MyByte** is **$1D** bytes into the second segment, which begins at segment address $0001. It's not that **MyByte** is in two or three places at once. It's only in one place, but that one place may be described in any of three ways.

It's a little like Chicago's street number system. Howard Street is 76 blocks from Chicago's "origin," Madison Street. Howard Street is, however, only four blocks from Touhy Avenue. You can describe Howard Street's location relative to either Madison Street or Touhy Avenue, depending on what you want to do.

An arbitrary byte somewhere in the middle of the 80x86's megabyte of memory may fall within literally tens of thousands of different segments. Which segment the byte is *actually* in is strictly a matter of convention.

This problem appears in real life to confront programmers of the IBM PC. The PC keeps its time and date information in a series of memory bytes that starts at address 0040:006C. There is also a series of memory bytes containing PC timer information located at 0000:046C. You guessed it—we're talking about exactly the same starting byte. Different writers speaking of that same byte may give its address in either of those two ways, and they'll all be completely correct.

The way, then, to express a 20-bit address in two 16-bit quantities is to put the segment address into one 16-bit quantity, and the offset address into another 16-bit quantity. The two registers taken together identify one byte among all 1,048,576 bytes in a megabyte.

24.2 Untyped Pointers and Pointer Type Casts

And that, in a nutshell, is what a pointer actually is: an address expressed as a 16-bit segment and a 16-bit offset, laid side-by-side in memory as a single 32-bit type. There is *nothing* in the low-level representation of a pointer that specifies what type a pointer points to. When allocated in memory, all pointers are essentially alike. The compiler does type-checking on typed pointers based on information it saves in its symbol table at compile time.

BUILDING POINTER VALUES WITH PTR

You can give a pointer a value by assigning it the value of another valid pointer. You can give a pointer the value of **NIL** (which means the pointer points to nothing) by assigning it the predefined constant **NIL**. You can give a pointer a value by using it in a call to **New** (as we saw in Chapter 17) or in a call to **GetMem** (as we'll see in the next section). You can read a value into a pointer from data stored in a file.

And there is one additional way to put a value into a pointer: by "building" a pointer value through a call to the predefined procedure **Ptr**. **Ptr** takes two 16-bit values as its parameters and returns as its function result a 32-bit pointer.

One 16-bit parameter is a segment address, and the other 16-bit parameter is an offset address.

Given a segment address of **$B800**, and an offset address of 0 (for example, the start of the video refresh buffer), **Ptr** may be used to return a pointer to the start of the buffer this way:

```
BufferStartPtr := Ptr($B800,0);
```

Here, **BufferStartPtr** may be any pointer type at all. It may even be (as I'll explain in the next section) an "untyped" pointer. Any pointer variable of any type may be assigned a value from the **Ptr** function.

In fact, most of the time you'll use **Ptr** will be as a means of putting a value into an untyped pointer. Let's investigate untyped pointers a little further.

UNTYPED POINTERS

Turbo Pascal is unique among Pascal compilers in giving you the ability to break nearly any rule if you really, *really* need to. (This is in sharp contrast to C, which comes close to having no rules at all.) Most of the time, you must define a pointer type as pointing to some other type. This is a rule well worth breaking on occasion, however, and the way to do it is with the predefined type **Pointer**, Turbo Pascal's untyped or "generic" pointer.

The untyped pointer differs from the standard pointer in that it doesn't have a base type; it isn't defined as a pointer to some type or another, but simply as a variable of type **Pointer**:

```
VideoBuffer : Pointer;
```

Here, **VideoBuffer** is a pointer, but it cannot be directly dereferenced, since it has no base type. In other words, you cannot use this syntax:

```
Char1 := VideoBuffer^;        { Will not compile! }
```

This statement is not only illegal (generating Error 26: Type conflict) but also logically meaningless. If **VideoBuffer** has no base type, what sort of thing is **VideoBuffer^**?

What *can* be done (and we're getting a little ahead of ourselves here) is type cast the generic pointer's referent when assigning the referent to some variable:

```
Char1 := Char(VideoBuffer^);  { Will compile }
```

This becomes meaningful, in that the compiler can take the first byte it finds at the location pointed to by **VideoBuffer** and consider that byte a value of type **Char**. Of course, you have to make sure that the byte you're casting onto a character variable makes sense as a character. This is less of a problem with type **Char** (which can legally contain any 8-bit value) than with another type like **Boolean** that can have only two specific values, 1 and 0. If you cast a value of 17 onto a **Boolean**, what do you have? Truth and More? No. Confusion, mostly.

Generic pointers are part of Turbo Pascal's suite of low-level system hooks, and are actually a way of dressing up a raw machine address in a suit of clothes that Pascal will tolerate. Type **Pointer** is assignment-compatible with any other pointer type, including other generic pointers.

The uses for generic pointers generally involve situations where the *size* of the referent is not known at compile time, or may change even at run time. Video buffers are a good example of this: The EGA display board has a 4,000-byte video buffer when operating in 25 × 80 mode, but a 6,880-byte buffer when operating in 43 × 80 mode. If the user is allowed to switch modes while a program is operating, a pointer to a video buffer must be capable of dealing with two different sizes of buffers; the sanest way to do that is not to entrust the pointer with any knowledge of the buffer's size at all.

NORMALIZED POINTERS

If you examine the actual values of a number of pointers returned by **New**, an interesting trend shows up: The offset portion of the pointer is either zero or a very small number. The short program below will provide you with 50 pointer values to look at. It allocates 50 items on the heap, returning pointers to an array of 50 pointers allocated as static data. Once the items are allocated on the heap, the program prints the values of each of the 50 pointers to your printer in segment:offset form.

The program is also an interesting example of a type cast in action: A record is defined containing two word fields, and the pointers being examined are type cast onto the record. This allows the pointer to be treated by **Writeln** as a pair of word values, which **Writeln** knows how to handle. If you had tried to feed an actual pointer to **Writeln**, the compiler would have issued

```
Error 64: Cannot read or write variables of this type
```

as you have probably discovered in your earlier work.

The program, as shown below, allocates 50 copies of an 80-byte string on the heap. Run the program as is, and then change the array type in line 14 to **^Integer** or **^STRING**, or perhaps a pointer to some synthetic type you've defined and can import or paste into the program.

```
PROGRAM PtrDump;

USES Printer;

TYPE
  PtrSplitter =
    RECORD
      PtrOffset,PtrSegment : Word
    END;
  String80 = STRING[80];

VAR
  I : Integer;
  PtrArray : ARRAY[1..50] OF ^String80;
BEGIN
```

```
              Write('Allocating 50 pointers');
              FOR I := 1 TO 50 DO
                BEGIN
                  New(PtrArray[I]);
                  Write('.');
                END;
              Writeln('done.');
              Write('Now writing the pointer values to hardcopy...');
              FOR I := 1 TO 50 DO
                BEGIN
                  Writeln(Lst,PtrSplitter(PtrArray[I]).PtrSegment,
                              ':',
                          PtrSplitter(PtrArray[I]).PtrOffset);
                  Dispose(PtrArray[I]);
                END;
              Write(Lst,Chr(12));  { Form feed to printer }
              Writeln('Done!');
            END.
```

When you run the program as shown, with the array pointing to 80-byte strings, the output will look something like this:

```
26068:0
26073:8
26079:0
26084:8
26090:0
26095:8
```

and so on. The first figure is the pointer's segment component, and the second figure is the pointer's offset component. If you run it for an array of **^Integer**, you'll see something like this:

```
26068:0
26068:8
26069:0
26069:8
26070:0
26070:8
```

The actual segment values will differ on your own machine, because of variations in the size of DOS, device drivers, and other things in low memory. What's important to note is that no matter what you allocate on the heap, Turbo Pascal will *always* return a pointer with an offset value less than 15.

What Turbo Pascal returns from a call to **New** is a *normalized pointer,* meaning a pointer whose offset is less than 16 bytes. This conflicts with many people's idea of a "segment." Turbo Pascal does *not* stake out 64K regions of heap memory with a single segment value and then relentlessly take bites from that big segment (by using increasingly large offset values) until the segment is all gone. Instead, each pointer's segment value is as close as the heap manager code can bring it to the actual physical location of the allocated dynamic variable in memory.

HEAP GRANULARITY

If you play around a little bit with **PtrDump** and examine the spacing between adjacent allocated memory blocks, you'll find that even for data types as small as one byte (**Char**, **Boolean**, etc.) the heap manager will still allocate 8 bytes. So in practice, you'll never see an offset value other than 8 or 0. The offset will be 8 for data types smaller than 8 bytes, and 0 for data types from 9–16 bytes in size. In allocating larger blocks, the offset value depends on whether or not the size of the data item being allocated is an even multiple of 8 bytes.

For example, if you allocate a string defined as **STRING[79]**, the actual string's physical size is 80 bytes (don't forget the hidden length byte), which is an even multiple of 8—and all offset values will be zero. A string defined as **STRING[80]** is actually 81 bytes in size, so there will be some "leftovers" and you'll see some offsets of 8.

What's going on here is that the heap manager has a *granularity* of 8 bytes—meaning that it allocates no slice of the heap smaller than 8 bytes, regardless of how small the dynamic variable being allocated is. Furthermore, for larger dynamic variables, the heap is only allocated in 8-byte chunks. A 1-byte variable is allocated 8 bytes. A 9-byte variable is allocated 16 bytes—as is a 10-byte variable or anything up to 16 bytes. An 81-byte variable (like the common **STRING[80]**) is allocated 88 bytes. To determine the number of bytes of heap space to allocate to a given data type, the heap manager looks at the physical size of the type (the value you'd see returned by the **SizeOf** function) and then rounds *up* to the nearest multiple of 8 bytes.

On the surface, this may seem wasteful. Why waste 7 bytes on the heap just to allocate a **Char**? But then again, why allocate individual **Char** values on the heap at all? Characters are so small that you might as well create arrays for them to live in. Most of the time, you'll be allocating some sort of record on the heap, and records are almost always 8 bytes or larger in size.

You can take knowledge of heap granularity into account when designing a program, and arrange things so that records to be allocated on the heap are some even multiple of 8 bytes in physical size. That way, no heap space is wasted on every allocation.

POINTER COMPARISON PROBLEMS

Turbo Pascal's normalization of pointers ordinarily doesn't matter much, and won't matter at all if the only pointers you ever use are the pointers handed back to you by the heap manager. When you get in trouble is when you "build" your own pointers using **Ptr** or other mechanisms, and then try to compare those pointers for equality to the heap manager's normalized pointers.

When you compare two pointers, Turbo Pascal's internal code does *not* work out a full 20-bit address from the segment and offset portions of the pointers being compared. It simply does a bit-by-bit 32-bit compare on the two pointers. If both the segment values are not bit-for-bit identical, *and* if both the offset values are not bit-for-bit identical, the two pointers will not be considered equal, *even if they actually point to the very same physical location in memory.*

Take a look at the little program shown below. It builds two pointers to the same location in memory. One is a normalized pointer and the other is not. It compares the two and finds them unequal.

```
PROGRAM IDByte;

VAR
  Normal,AbNormal : ^Byte;

BEGIN
  Normal    := Ptr($FFFF,$E);
  AbNormal := Ptr($F000,$FFFE);
  Writeln(Normal^,'  ',AbNormal^);
  IF Normal = Abnormal THEN
    Writeln('Turbo Pascal considers these pointers equal.')
  ELSE
    Writeln('Turbo Pascal considers these pointers unequal.');
  Readln;
END.
```

The location in question is the "Equipment ID byte" found near the top of memory in most PC-compatible machines. The clone people have used some odd numbers in that location from time to time, but most people have simply adopted IBM's original codes, shown in Table 24.1.

Table 24.1 Equipment ID Codes at F000:FFFE

Model ID Byte Hex/Decimal	Indicated machine
FF /255	PC
FE /254	XT and Portable PC
FD /253	PCjr
FC /252	AT, XT/286, PS/2 mod 50/60
FB /251	Later XTs
FA /250	PS/2 mod 30
F9 /249	IBM PC Convertible
F8 /248	PS/2 mod 80

Sadly, because of the somewhat chaotic situation in the clone BIOS business, these codes can't be relied upon to tell you anything useful unless you already know you're running on a true IBM-built PC.

COMPARING POINTERS FOR CONGRUENCE

Two pointers are *congruent* when they point to the *same* physical memory location, regardless of how the physical address is apportioned between segment and offset. The two pointers demonstrated in the **IDByte** program shown above are not equal, but they *are* congruent.

Two pointers are said to be congruent if they both cook down to the same 20-bit physical address. Testing for congruence is simple: You only have to convert both pointers to 20-bit physical addresses and then compare them.

The only Turbo Pascal data type big enough to hold a 20-bit address is **LongInt**. The algorithm for the conversion from a segmented address to a 20-bit address is this:

Shift the segment portion of the pointer left by four bits;

Then add to this value the offset portion of the pointer.

That's all it takes, and it's pretty simple. That is what, in fact, the 80×86 processors do when they need to take a segmented real-mode address and access memory with it: Convert it first to a 20-bit address and then send that address out to the 20 memory addressing lines of the CPU chip.

In Turbo Pascal terms, the conversion looks like this:

```
TYPE
  PtrSplitter =
    RECORD
      PtrOffset,PtrSegment : Word
    END;
  String80 = STRING[80];

Full20BitAddress :=
  LongInt(PtrSplitter(Ptr1).PtrSegment) SHL 4 +
          PtrSplitter(Ptr1).PtrOffset;
```

The variable **Full20BitAddress** is a **LongInt**. Look very carefully at the use of the *double* type cast—at first glance, it's a very strange breed of dog. (Hey, *all* breeds of *cats* are strange.)

The inner type cast casts the pointer (which, remember, contains a segmented address) onto a **PtrSplitter** record that allows separate access to the segment and offset portions of the pointer. It's just a way of laying a different template over the same region of memory occupied by the pointer. Or in another sense, you're telling the compiler to bend the rules a little, and treat the pointer as though it were two **Word** types side by side. This way, you can access one half of the pointer without disturbing (or bringing along) the other half.

The type cast allows you to take the segment portion of the pointer and shift it left by 4 bits. The outer type cast treats the result of the shift operation as a **LongInt**. This is necessary because shifting a 16-bit quantity like **Word** to the left by 4 bits makes it too big (now, 20 bits) to fit in a **Word** anymore. So the intermediate value in the expression is now a **LongInt**. Adding the offset portion of the pointer to the **LongInt** value containing the shifted offset is easy— and that's all you need to do.

The function given below tests the two pointers passed as parameters for congruence. It performs the conversion described above on both pointers, and then compares the two 20-bit addresses stored as **Longint** values for equality. If the two 20-bit addresses are the same, the two pointers point to the same location in real-mode memory. Otherwise, the two pointers point to different locations.

```
FUNCTION AreCongruent(Ptr1,Ptr2 : Pointer) : Boolean;

TYPE
  PtrSplitter =
    RECORD
      PtrOffset,PtrSegment : Word
    END;
  String80 = STRING[80];

BEGIN
  IF LongInt(PtrSplitter(Ptr1).PtrSegment) SHL 4 +
            PtrSplitter(Ptr1).PtrOffset
      =
     LongInt(PtrSplitter(Ptr2).PtrSegment) SHL 4 +
            PtrSplitter(Ptr2).PtrOffset
  THEN AreCongruent := True
  ELSE AreCongruent := False;
END;
```

You can test the **AreCongruent** function by using a simple extension of the **IDByte** program presented earlier. The **Congruent** program given below tests the two pointers to the equipment ID byte for equality, and then tests them for congruence. You might change one or both of the pointers to different values and run the program again to see how the comparisons go. Try to create several congruent pointers with distinct segment and offset values. It's good practice, and will sensitize you to the possibilities that turn up when dealing with pointers at the bit-pattern level.

```
PROGRAM Congruent;

VAR
  Normal,AbNormal : ^Byte;

FUNCTION AreCongruent(Ptr1,Ptr2 : Pointer) : Boolean;

TYPE
  PtrSplitter =
    RECORD
```

```
          PtrOffset,PtrSegment : Word
      END;
    String80 = STRING[80];

BEGIN
    IF LongInt(PtrSplitter(Ptr1).PtrSegment) SHL 4 +
              PtrSplitter(Ptr1).PtrOffset

        =

        LongInt(PtrSplitter(Ptr2).PtrSegment) SHL 4 +
              PtrSplitter(Ptr2).PtrOffset
    THEN AreCongruent := True
    ELSE AreCongruent := False;
END;


BEGIN
    Normal   := Ptr($FFFF,$E);
    AbNormal := Ptr($F000,$FFFE);

    Writeln('Below are the referents of two pointers:');
    Writeln(Normal^,'   ',AbNormal^);

    { Test the pointers for ordinary equality: }
    IF Normal = Abnormal THEN
      Writeln('Turbo Pascal considers these pointers equal...')
    ELSE
      Writeln('Turbo Pascal considers these pointers unequal...');

    { Now test the pointers for congruence: }
    IF AreCongruent(Normal,AbNormal) THEN
      Writeln('...but they actually point to the same location.')
    ELSE
      Writeln('...and they do in fact point to different locations.');
END.
```

NORMALIZING POINTERS

There may come a situation where you have a pointer that is *not* normalized, and need to get it into normalized form. Normalizing a pointer is straightforward—it's basically reversing the process of creating a 20-bit address from a segmented pointer.

The algorithm:

- Convert the "non-normal" pointer to a 20-bit address;
- Mask out and save the low-order 4 bits of the address;
- Shift the full 20-bit address to the *right* by 4 bits. Store the result in the segment portion of the normalized pointer;
- Store the low-order 4 bits of the address in the offset portion of the normalized pointer.

This algorithm satisfies the requirement that a normalized pointer have an offset portion that is never higher than 15. The highest value expressible by 4 bits (which is all the bits that are stored in the offset portion) is 15.

The function shown below takes any pointer as its parameter and returns the pointer in normalized form, using the above algorithm.

```
FUNCTION Normalizer(InPtr : Pointer) : Pointer;

VAR
   Address20Bit : LongInt;
   OutPtr       : Pointer;

TYPE
   PtrSplitter =
     RECORD
       PtrOffset,PtrSegment : Word
     END;
   String80 = STRING[80];

BEGIN
   Address20Bit := LongInt(PtrSplitter(InPtr).PtrSegment) SHL 4 +
                           PtrSplitter(InPtr).PtrOffset;
   PtrSplitter(OutPtr).PtrSegment := Address20Bit SHR 4;
   PtrSplitter(OutPtr).PtrOffset  := Address20Bit AND $0000000F;
   Normalizer := OutPtr;
END;
```

24.3 Pointer and Linked List Constants

Pointer typed constants have been with us for some time, but prior to version 6.0, the only value a pointer constant could be initially assigned was **NIL**:

```
CONST
   IntPtr : ^Integer = Nil;
```

POINTER CONSTANTS CREATED USING PTR

Beginning with V6.0, pointer constants may be values other than **NIL**. You can construct a pointer constant by using the **Ptr** function:

```
MonoOrigin  : Pointer = Ptr($B000,0);
ColorOrigin : Pointer = Ptr($B800,0);
```

Pointer constant definitions like these can be built into other typed constants as well. A good example would be the two addresses for PC text video refresh buffers:

```
TYPE
   VidTypes = (Mono,Color);
```

```
CONST
  VidOrigins : ARRAY[VidTypes] OF Pointer =
                 (Ptr($B000,0), Ptr($B800,0));
```

Here, I've defined an array constant that has as its two elements the two pointer constants I defined just above. By using the enumerated type **VidTypes** as indices, you can choose one of the two origin pointers with an easy-to-read syntax:

```
MyOrigin := VidOrigins[Mono];
```

Actually, that syntax isn't especially useful, because you want your program to detect which origin to use automatically. I've defined a function that queries BIOS for the type of video in use, and returns a value of type **VidTypes**:

```
FUNCTION VidType : VidTypes;

VAR
  Regs : Registers;

BEGIN
  Intr($11,Regs);  { Call Equipment Configuration Information }
  IF (Regs.AX AND $0030) = $0030 THEN
    VidType := Mono
  ELSE
    VidType := Color;
END;
```

By using this function, you can choose the proper origin pointer automatically:

```
MyOrigin := VidOrigins[VidType];
```

POINTER CONSTANTS DEFINED WITH ADDR

Pointer constants may also be given address values through the use of the address-of operators **@** or **Addr**:

```
TYPE
  StringPtr = ^STRING;

CONST
  Message  : String[20] = 'Time is running out!';
  PMessage : StringPtr = Addr(Message);
```

This might not seem immediately useful, but what it does in fact allow you to do is create *linked list constants* that are instantly available without your having to explicitly build the constant list with **New**.

LINKED LIST CONSTANTS

The notion of a linked list constant is a little weird, but they have a very definite use: to define a set of default values in cases where you have values stored in a linked list. The ability to create record constants has existed for some time in Turbo Pascal, and is used for the same general purpose. Linked lists allow you to take fields that belong together and run them out into a linked list rather than group them together in a record.

But why store related data fields in a linked list when you can logically group them together in a record? Minimizing memory use would be one reason. You may find yourself dealing with complicated data groups that vary enormously in the size of the significant data.

Here's a possible scenario: Suppose you're creating a system to track significant medical history information for individuals. You want to be able to summarize any unusual medical conditions existing back to the great-grandparent level. Each person has two parents, four grandparents, and eight great-grandparents, and you might wish to allocate the individual and each of his or her ancestors a 255-character string field to describe medical anomalies. That's 15 strings requiring 3,840 bytes of storage—if you store them in a record. Keep in mind that **STRING** types stored in a record occupy 256 bytes of storage, even if they're totally empty.

Now, most people are pretty healthy, so an average person would have at most two or three ancestors with any significant medical problems. Most of the descriptor strings would then simply be blank, and every blank string would waste 256 bytes of storage. Start creating records for a few hundred people and the wasted space adds up fast.

Instead, create a linked list for each individual, with the medical history strings as the important portions of the nodes in the list. The node would look like this:

```
TYPE
  RelationID   =
  (Self,
   Father,Mother,
    PGFather,PGMother,MGFather,MGMother,
    PPGGFather,PPGGMother,PMGGFather,PMGGMother,
      MPGGFather,MPGGMother,MMGGFather,MMGGMother);

  PHistoryNode = ^THistoryNode;
  THistoryNode =
    RECORD
      IDCode    : Word;
      Relation  : RelationID;
      Next      : PHistoryNode;
      History   : STRING;
    END;
```

A default "record" (which is in fact a linked list) could be laid out as a linked list constant:

```
CONST
  NodeMMGGMother : THistoryNode =
  (IDCode : 0; Relation : MMGGMother; Next : NIL; History : '');
```

```
NodeMMGGFather : THistoryNode =
(IDCode : 0; Relation : MMGGFather;
 Next : @NodeMMGGMother; History : '');
NodeMPGGMother : THistoryNode =
(IDCode : 0; Relation : MPGGMother;
 Next : @NodeMMGGFather; History : '');
NodeMPGGFather : THistoryNode =
(IDCode : 0; Relation : MPGGFather;
 Next : @NodeMPGGMother; History : '');
NodePMGGMother : THistoryNode =
(IDCode : 0; Relation : PMGGMother;
 Next : @NodeMPGGFather; History : '');
NodePMGGFather : THistoryNode =
(IDCode : 0; Relation : PMGGFather;
 Next : @NodePMGGMother; History : '');
NodePPGGMother : THistoryNode =
(IDCode : 0; Relation : PPGGMother;
 Next : @NodePMGGFather; History : '');
NodePPGGFather : THistoryNode =
(IDCode : 0; Relation : PPGGFather;
 Next : @NodePPGGMother; History : '');
NodeMGMother : THistoryNode =
(IDCode : 0; Relation : MGMother;
 Next : @NodePPGGFather; History : '');
NodeMGFather : THistoryNode =
(IDCode : 0; Relation : MGFather;
 Next : @NodeMGMother;   History : '');
NodePGMother : THistoryNode =
(IDCode : 0; Relation : PGMother;
 Next : @NodeMGFather;   History : '');
NodePGFather : THistoryNode =
(IDCode : 0; Relation : PGFather;
 Next : @NodePGMother;   History : '');
NodeMother   : THistoryNode =
(IDCode : 0; Relation : Mother;
 Next : @NodePGFather;   History : '');
NodeFather   : THistoryNode =
(IDCode : 0; Relation : Father;
 Next : @NodeMother;     History : '');
NodeSelf     : THistoryNode =
(IDCode : 0; Relation : Self;
 Next : @NodeFather;     History : '');

DefaultRoot : PHistoryNode = Addr(NodeSelf);
```

This is a complete linked list of 15 nodes, along with its "root" pointer, **DefaultRoot**. There's one very important wrinkle to notice here: The linked list constant is declared "backwards" from what we might consider intuitive. The root pointer is declared *after* the list itself, and the nodes are present in reverse order. Traversing the list might generally *begin* with the **NodeSelf** node, but that node must be declared last.

The problem is that Turbo Pascal, being a one-pass compiler, has to "know" each identifier before referencing that identifier. It's building a symbol table as it goes, remember. The **NodeSelf** node references the **NodeFather** node—but if you declared **NodeSelf** first, the compiler would not yet have encountered **NodeFather** and would not have **NodeFather** in its symbol table.

Think of it this way: When you set the table for Thanksgiving dinner, you grab the good china plates off the top of the stack to lay them out on the table. That is, you *use* the plates in order from the top of the stack down.

Your mother, on the other hand, is washing the plates (which have gotten dusty since last Christmas) and she's building the stack from the bottom *up*. That's the only way she *can* build the stack, since she can't hang a plate in the air and then hang another plate beneath it. She needs a foundation plate to place each plate on, and the last plate you end up placing on the table is in fact the first plate she washed.

Apart from that, the rest of the linked list constant's definition should seem straightforward. There may be better ways to solve this particular problem (a record containing 15 pointers might be less hassle), but the core theory is valid, and when someday you discover that you need a linked list constant for something you ought to know that the option is available.

24.4 GetMem

When you create a dynamic variable with **New**, you don't have to tell Turbo Pascal how much memory to allocate on the heap for that variable. Apart from generic pointers, a pointer is always a pointer to *something*, and that something (a data type) has a size that is fixed at compile time and never changes. So Turbo Pascal can tell from the type to which the pointer points how much memory will be needed for the dynamic variable.

Dynamic variables and **New** and **Dispose** are all part of Standard Pascal. They allow you to create variables on the heap without specifying how many or in what order they are created. Turbo Pascal lets you take it one step further: You can allocate blocks of memory on the heap for data whose size is *not* known at compile time.

Just as Turbo Pascal extends Standard Pascal pointer concept with generic pointers, it provides "generic" versions of **New** and **Dispose**. These are **GetMem** and **FreeMem**. **GetMem** is the generic counterpart of **New**. It allocates a block of memory on the heap of a size that you the programmer specify:

```
PROCEDURE GetMem(VAR AnyPtr : <any pointer type>; Size : Word);
```

The pointer variable passed as the first parameter may be any type of pointer at all, including a generic pointer. Furthermore, if the pointer is a typed pointer, the size of the type to which it points need not be the same as the value passed in **Size**. (It isn't an especially good idea to use typed pointers with **GetMem** if you can avoid it, however. Turbo Pascal's generated code always assumes that the referent of a typed pointer is the size of that pointer's target type.)

On return from a call to **GetMem**, **AnyPtr** will point to a block of memory on the heap consisting of **Size** bytes. As with **New**, if Turbo Pascal's heap manager can't find a single block of heap memory large enough to satisfy the request, a runtime error will be generated. This situation can be improved somewhat by installing a custom heap error handler. (See Section 24.6.)

24.5 FreeMem

Just as **GetMem** is the generic counterpart of **New**, **FreeMem** is the generic counterpart of **Dispose**:

```
PROCEDURE FreeMem(VAR AnyPtr : <any pointer type>; Size : Word);
```

FreeMem deallocates the memory allocated to the referent of **AnyPtr** and forces the value of **AnyPtr** to be undefined. (*Not* **NIL**!) It is crucial that the value passed in **Size** is *precisely* the same value that had previously been allocated to the referent of **AnyPtr**. If not, you will corrupt the heap and unexpected (but certainly unwanted) things may begin to happen. The burden is on you to make sure that this does not happen; there is *nothing* in Turbo Pascal to protect the heap from careless use of **FreeMem**.

GetMem and **FreeMem** are most often used to create buffers on the heap whose size is not known at compile time. The best example of this involves the saving of portions of a graphics screen on the heap, using the **GetImage** procedure from the **Graph** unit. (**Graph** is discussed in detail in Chapter 22.) Saving a small portion of the screen requires a certain amount of heap memory, and saving a larger portion requires more. Using **GetMem** allows you to allocate only as much heapspace as you need to save a piece of the graphics screen, no more, no less. The **Move** procedure (which I won't be covering in detail in this book) is another way to move data into and out of a buffer allocated with **GetMem**.

Good examples of **GetMem** and **FreeMem** in use may be found in the **Scribble** program and the **PullDown** unit it uses. These are described in Chapter 22.

24.6 The Heap Error Function

Ordinarily, if you request allocation of a block of memory on the heap through a call to **New** or **GetMem** and there is not enough memory in any single block to satisfy the request, a fatal runtime error occurs and your program aborts to DOS or to the Turbo Pascal IDE. This can always be avoided by using **MaxAvail** before each attempted allocation. Turbo Pascal allows slightly more sophisticated handling of such an error by installing a custom heap error function that takes control in the event of a heap overflow.

Why bother? In a sense, it allows you to give **New** or **GetMem** a "second chance" in case they fail at allocating a memory block. Once you have installed a heap error handler, the handler will get control whenever a heap memory allocation attempt fails. The heap error handler is passed the size of the block that was requested. You can then have the handler attempt to free up enough memory on the heap to satisfy the request. If the heap error handler is successful, **New** or **GetMem** can then be called again, automatically, to retry the heap allocation.

How the heap memory is to be freed up is your decision, and will probably be application-dependent. You might devise a simple "garbage collector" routine that packs all existing dynamic variables onto the heap, squeezing out wasted "holes" in heap memory. This is genuinely difficult stuff, since your garbage collector must have the ability to change the value of any pointer that points into the heap. You can't just move a block of heap memory—some pointer somewhere may be pointing to it, and if someone dereferences that pointer, they'll be in for a possibly nasty surprise.

A generalized garbage collector is something best not attempted. The easiest alternative would be to ask the user what data might simply be thrown away, and then disposing of that specific data. If you are designing an application that makes heavy use of the heap, you might keep this possibility in mind.

The heap error handler must be declared this way:

```
FUNCTION <name> (Size : Word) : Integer; FAR;
```

The actual name of the function is up to you; it could be **HeapErrorHandler**, **TrashMan**, or whatever you like. But it must have one **Word** parameter, it must return a value of type **Integer**, and it must be followed by the **FAR** reserved word so that it will be invocable via an 80x86 FAR call.

You install the heap error handler by assigning its address to a predefined generic pointer variable called **HeapErr**:

```
HeapErr := @TrashMan;
```

When a heap overflow error occurs, Turbo Pascal's runtime code transfers control to the address stored in **HeapErr**, assuming a **Word** parameter on the stack. This parameter will contain the size in bytes of the memory block that was requested during the failed allocation attempt. The heap error handler's mission (should it decide to accept it) is to free up that much space on the heap.

It should try, and one would hope that it would succeed. There's no guarantee of that, of course, so provision is made to pass a value *back* to the Turbo Pascal runtime code that indicates whether the second chance was successful or not. The value is in fact the function return value, and before terminating the heap error handler should assign one of three values to its return value:

0—Failed; issue a runtime error and halt. This is the default, and will occur on every heap error unless you install a replacement heap error handler.

1—Failed; assign **Nil** to the pointer passed with the failed allocation attempt. The **Nil** pointer will indicate that the allocation attempt failed, and no runtime error will be issued.

2—Successful; the amount of memory passed to the error handler in the parameter **Size** was freed by the error handler. This return value signals to the Turbo Pascal runtime code that the **New** or **GetMem** heap allocation should be attempted again.

THE END-RUN!

Taken together, type casting, generic pointers, the @ function, **GetMem**, **FreeMem**, and the **Ptr** function provide a nearly-complete end-run around Standard Pascal's strong typing straightjacket. Turbo Pascal is now the functional equivalent of the C language, with all the power—and danger—that that implies. There is a whole second level of things you can do with pointers that has less to do with the heap than with manipulating the system at a low level. This involves reading values from DOS and BIOS work areas, working directly with video bitmaps, and so on. You should be fairly comfortable with the standard features of Turbo Pascal and at least passingly comfortable with machine internals before attempting things of this sort.

But once you *do* understand them, nothing will stand in your way. Go for it!

Chapter 25

Onward to Objects!

A QUICK LOOK AT THE NEXT LEVEL OF PROGRAM STRUCTURE

Say something is an alien often enough, and it'll start growing fangs on you. Sometimes I think we've been doing that with the whole subject of object-oriented programming, and now the newcomers to Pascal are thoroughly afraid of the dark.

This is dumb. Those of us who explain programming have been entranced by the novelty of objects, and thus we've focused on how different object-oriented programming is from that ordinary type of programming we've all been doing for years. And in emphasizing the differences we've neglected the similarities to the extent that objects have become another sort of arcana in a field with arcana shoved into every crevice.

I think it might well be time to turn this trend around.

There's a lot to be learned about objects, so much so that I can't treat it all in one book. And this one short chapter won't make you an expert, but I write it with the sincere hope that it will allow you to explore the subject on your own, and get you far enough so that you can either master it yourself or hold out until I can get another book in print.

The naked truth is that objects bear plenty of similarities to things you've been using all along in Pascal: records, units, and most especially the notion of *structure*. For at the bottom of it all, object-oriented programming is simply another level of structure that you can impose upon a program in the cause of making it easier to understand and maintain. Like anything else in programming, it can be done well or badly—and the choice, as always, is yours.

25.1 Objects As Packages

The best way to start explaining objects is to belay all this yammer about paradigms and programming models and state a simple fact: An object is a box to put code and data in. It is, to be sure, a special sort of box with certain interesting and nonobvious properties, but we'll get to those in time. For now, it's a box. Furthermore, objects bear a striking resemblance to something else you should be familiar with by now: units. Let's begin by drawing on our previous experience with units.

UNITS AS PHYSICAL CONTAINERS

When you create a unit, you're creating a physical container (a .TPU file) for holding code and data that belong together for some reason. The data can be any kind of data: variables, constants, or typed constants. The code can be procedures, or functions, or any mix of both. A unit has no real structure except that some items belonging to the unit may be hidden, and others may be visible to other programs. That's still significant, and units are a marvelous mechanism for controlling the interface between groups of code and data and the outside world.

In the interface section of a unit you have the procedure and function headers that define how those procedures and functions are seen and used by the outside world. Later on in the unit, you have the actual bodies of those procedures and functions in the implementation section of the unit. Data items may exist in either the interface or implementation section. Data defined in the interface section is for the use of the outside world; data defined in the implementation section is for the private use of the unit alone. Finally, at the end of a unit you may optionally create an initialization section, which executes before the program that uses the unit, and allows the unit to set itself up before allowing other code to use it. This setting up might consist of assigning values to exported variables, generating memory-based tables, and other housekeeping that has to be done somewhere, and somewhen, ideally before anyone in the outside world gets a chance to use the unit.

One subtle fact rarely called out is that a unit's structure is a *physical* structure. By physical I mean that it truly is reflected in the actual bytes of data stored on disk as a .TPU file. Inside the physical file is a table of identifiers that the unit *exports*; that is, makes available to code that wishes to use the unit. If an identifier isn't in that table, that identifier can't be accessed from outside the unit. The difference between an identifier in the interface section of a unit and in the implementation section of a unit is thus a physical one: whether or not that identifier exists in the unit's table of exported identifiers.

Keep this in mind; it's important.

OBJECTS AS LOGICAL CONTAINERS

There are some amazing similarities between units and objects that I rarely hear anyone comment on. An object is a grouping-together of code and data. Inside an object may be variables (though not constants), procedures, and functions. Furthermore, there is a line that may be drawn inside an object between what is available for use by the outside world, and what is for the private use of the object alone.

Finally, an object may optionally have a mechanism called a *constructor*, which sets up the values in the object's variables. The constructor works very much like the initialization section of a unit, and exists for precisely the same reasons.

(Let me pause here and pacify the object-extremists, who are probably sharpening their axes about now and imagining my head on a block. Yes, there is a lot more to objects than this. But we have to start somewhere, and I think it's wiser to begin on familiar soil than to immediately parachute far behind enemy lines.)

The first and most significant difference between objects and units is that a unit (as I said earlier) is a physical structure, whereas an object is a *logical* structure.

Now, what can I mean by this?

A unit's identity is to a large degree tied up in its physical separateness from other code in programs or other units. You cannot, for example, store two units within a single .TPU file. A unit does have a name and thus a logical identity, but without a physical .TPU file to live in, a unit simply cannot exist.

An object, on the other hand, is entirely a logical structure. To have a separate physical identity, an object must be stored inside a unit; you cannot compile an object to some sort of physical "object" file. One or many objects may be stored in a single .TPU file or inside of a program. Units have two names: the name you provide in the **UNIT** statement, and the name you give to the source code file on disk. (It is true that these two names must be the same for any single unit. Still, it's true that *both names must exist*.) Objects are known by their "inside" names only—those are the only names they have.

This is about as far as I need to go in a purely conceptual sense. Let's get a look at how objects are defined, so that we can take the comparison between units and objects further.

25.2 Objects As Logical Structures

When most people begin explaining objects, they invariably say something like, "Objects are a lot like records." This is a little like saying a lamp is just like a refrigerator because they both contain light bulbs. Superficial appearances don't do justice here. Objects are a much more cosmic concept than records, so don't tie yourself too tightly to that very superficial resemblance.

But on the surface of it, an object definition looks a little like a record definition. Here's a simple object that draws on some of the code we've already worked with in this book:

```
TYPE
  String20 = STRING[20];
  String50 = STRING[50];

  Date =
    OBJECT
      Year,Month,Day : Word;
      DayOfWeek      : Word;
      DateStamp      : Word;
```

```
          AsString          : String20;
          AsLongString      : String50;
          PROCEDURE PutToday;
          PROCEDURE PutNewYMD(NewYear, NewMonth, NewDay : Word);
          PROCEDURE CalcStampFromDate;
          PROCEDURE CalcDateFromStamp;
          PROCEDURE CalcDateStringForms;
       END;
```

True enough, the **OBJECT..END** syntax is reminiscent of **RECORD..END**. But records can't contain procedure definitions as shown here. It's true that records may contain procedural variables, as I explained in Chapter 23. But a record may *not* contain the definition of the procedural variable, which is essentially what we have in terms of procedure headers defined within objects.

What does this object definition mean? First and foremost, it defines a logical association between a group of variables and a group of procedures. These variables are (as with records) generally called *fields*, and the procedures are generally called *methods*. A record also defines a logical association among its fields, but one that isn't taken very far. Furthermore, the association among the fields of a record is a physical one as well as a logical one. All fields of a record are arranged side by side in memory once a record variable is declared.

With an object, the fields are indeed allocated side by side in memory. But what of the methods? *There is nothing physically in an object that represents its methods.* You can't do a memory dump of an object and see anything like a pointer or a procedural variable. There's just nothing there. The object defines a relationship between fields and methods that is strictly logical. No physical association exists.

METHOD IMPLEMENTATION

So where are the methods? They must be fully implemented (that is, the procedure bodies must be present) somewhere else in the same module. You cannot, for example, define an object in a program and then implement its methods in a unit. If the object definition is present in a unit, the method implementations must exist in that same unit. If the object definition is present in a program file, the methods must be implemented in the same program file.

The actual form of a method implementation is very much the same as an ordinary procedure or function implementation. The only twist is that when you implement a method belonging to an object definition, you must place the name of the object type before the name of the method, separated by a dot. Here's the full implementation of one of the methods of the **Date** object:

```
PROCEDURE Date.PutToday;

BEGIN
  GetDate(Year,Month,Day,DayOfWeek);   { From Borland's DOS unit }
  CalcStampFromDate;     { Method; Calculates 16-bit "date stamp" }
```

```
    CalcDateStringForms; { Method: Calculates string forms of date }
  END;
```

The purpose of this method is to read the current date from the PC system clock and place it in the various fields of the **Date** object. Note the <object>.<method> syntax of the method name, which nails down the logical association between the object type (here, **Date**) and one of its methods (**PutToday**). The method simply fetches the date through the **DOS** unit's **GetDate** routine, and then messages the values returned by **GetDate**, using other methods belonging to the **Date** object.

The full implementation of all of the **Date** object's methods is given in the short test program given below. Read it over carefully, looking for similarities and differences between objects and units.

```
{----------------------------------------------------------------}
{                          DateTest                              }
{                                                                }
{ Demonstration of a simple "date" object encapsulating date     }
{ data and date manipulation code into a single entity.          }
{                                                                }
{                       by Jeff Duntemann                        }
{                       Turbo Pascal V7.0                        }
{                       Last update 3/14/93                      }
{                                                                }
{    From: BORLAND PASCAL FROM SQUARE ONE  by Jeff Duntemann     }
{----------------------------------------------------------------}

PROGRAM DateTest;

USES Crt,DOS;

TYPE
  String9  = STRING[9];
  String20 = STRING[20];
  String50 = STRING[50];

  WhenUnion =              { This allows us to pull apart    }
    RECORD                 { the 32-bit DOS file time stamp }
      TimePart : Word;
      DatePart : Word;
    END;

  Date =
    OBJECT
      Year,Month,Day : Word;
      DayOfWeek      : Word;
      DateStamp      : Word;
      AsString       : String20;
```

```
        AsLongString   : String50;
        PROCEDURE PutToday;
        PROCEDURE PutNewYMD(NewYear, NewMonth, NewDay : Word);
        PROCEDURE PutNewDateStamp(NewDateStamp : Word);
        PROCEDURE CalcStampFromDate;
        PROCEDURE CalcDateFromStamp;
        PROCEDURE CalcDateStringForms;
      END;

CONST
  MonthTags : ARRAY [1..12] of String9 =
     ('January','February','March','April','May','June','July',
      'August','September','October','November','December');
  DayTags   : ARRAY [0..6] OF String9 =
     ('Sunday','Monday','Tuesday','Wednesday',
      'Thursday','Friday','Saturday');

{$I DAYOWEEK.SRC }   { Calculates day of the week; see Section 19.6 }


PROCEDURE  Date.PutToday;

BEGIN
  GetDate(Year,Month,Day,DayOfWeek);  { From Borland's DOS unit }
  CalcStampFromDate;   { Method: Calculates 16-bit "date stamp" }
  CalcDateStringForms; { Method: Calcs string representations of date }
END;


PROCEDURE Date.PutNewYMD(NewYear, NewMonth, NewDay : Word);

BEGIN
  Year := NewYear; Month := NewMonth; Day := NewDay;
  DayOfWeek := CalcDayOfWeek(Year,Month,Day);
  CalcStampFromDate;
  CalcDateStringForms;
END;


PROCEDURE Date.PutNewDateStamp(NewDateStamp : Word);

BEGIN
  DateStamp := NewDateStamp;
  CalcDateFromStamp;
END;
```

```
PROCEDURE  Date.CalcStampFromDate;

BEGIN
  DateStamp := ((Year - 1980) SHL 9) OR (Month SHL 5) OR Day;
END;


PROCEDURE  Date.CalcDateFromStamp;

BEGIN
  Year := (DateStamp SHR 9) + 1980;
  Month := (DateStamp SHR 5) AND $000F;
  Day := DateStamp AND $001F;
  DayOfWeek := CalcDayOfWeek(Year,Month,Day);
  CalcDateStringForms;
END;


PROCEDURE  Date.CalcDateStringForms;

VAR
  Temp1 : String9;

BEGIN
  { Calculate the "short" date string: }
  Str(Month,AsString);
  IF Month < 10 THEN AsString := '0' + AsString;
  Str(Day,Temp1);
  IF Day < 10 THEN Temp1 := '0' + Temp1;
  AsString := AsString + '/' + Temp1;
  Str(Year,Temp1);
  AsString := AsString + '/' + Temp1;
  { Calculate the "long" date string: }
  AsLongString := DayTags[DayOfWeek] + ', ';
  Str(Day,Temp1);
  AsLongString := AsLongString +
    MonthTags[Month] + ' ' + Temp1 + ', ';
  Str(Year,Temp1);
  AsLongString := AsLongString + Temp1;
END;


VAR
  Today     : Date;  { These are two Date objects }
  FileDate  : Date;
```

```
  TestFile      : TEXT;
  DOSTimeStamp  : LongInt;
  DTRec         : DateTime;

BEGIN
  { Load a Date object with today's date from the system clock: }
  Today.PutToday;
  Writeln('Today is ',Today.AsLongString,'.');

  { Load a Date object with the last-changed date of a DOS file: }
  Assign(TestFile,'DAYOWEEK.SRC');
  Reset(TestFile);
  GetFTime(TestFile,DOSTimeStamp);
  { This type casts the time stamp as a free-union variant record,   }
  { allowing us to "pull out" the date part of the 32-bit time stamp:}
   FileDate.PutNewDateStamp(WhenUnion(DOSTimeStamp).DatePart);
  Writeln
  ('The opened file''s "last-changed" date is ',FileDate.AsLongString);
END.
```

What we have here is in fact a new type of data, one that incorporates both traditional data (various expressions of a date) and code to manipulate it. The **Date** object expresses a calendar date in various forms, and packs along machinery to convert those date values from one form to another. Data conversion is almost always a messy business—so who should "know" better how to convert data from one form to another than the data itself? The conversion process is closely tied to the data being converted, and objects provide an orderly, structured way of associating data with a process closely tied to that data. The **CalcDateFromWord** procedure "belongs" to the object, as do the various year, month, and date fields that it acts upon. You're not working with a tin can full of loose tools anymore. You're working with data that packs its own tools along wherever it goes.

As with procedural types, the more you work with objects, the more you come to think of the code and the data comprising an object as inseparable aspects of the same entity.

25.3 Encapsulation and Access

The **Date** object I've just presented is about as simple as an object can be and still be tolerably useful. It's a good example of the most fundamental of the three characteristic aspects of object-oriented programming: *encapsulation.* Encapsulation is this binding together of data with the code that manipulates it. The other two aspects of object-oriented programming are considerably subtler, and I won't be covering them in exhaustive detail in this book. One is inheritance, through which you can modify an object by creating a derivative type that seamlessly melds the original object with your alterations. The third is polymorphism, which is the truly spooky one: It's a feature through which a family of distinct but related objects may all be addressed by a common command set— with each object reacting in an appropriate way to each command, and without the caller of the command having to know what exact object type will be receiving the command.

If that seems mystical or pointless to you, set it aside for now. It all comes with time, practice, and study.

For now, we're going to speak further about encapsulation.

OBJECTS IN USE

The main program body of the DATETEST.PAS program shown earlier demonstrates the basics of object use. You must declare a variable of an object type:

```
VAR
    Today     : Date;   { These are two Date objects }
    FileDate  : Date;
```

For all their special features and subtleties, objects are still types, and with types one creates variables, object-oriented or not. The declaration above gives us two "empty" date objects.

This is also a good place to point out a new and perhaps disorienting convention in the Turbo Pascal world: placing a **VAR** section immediately before the beginning of the main program block, after all the procedure and function bodies. Global objects are usually declared here, and while it feels funny for awhile, it's perfectly legal and makes a certain sense. (Look to DATETEST.PAS for an example if you haven't seen what I mean. Borland does it a lot in their example code.)

Placing a date value into a date object can be done through any of three methods written for that purpose. Here are some typical invocations of those three methods:

```
Today.PutToday;

FileDate.PutNewDateStamp(WhenUnion(TimeStamp).DatePart);

FileDate.PutNewYMD(1993,3,10);
```

Notice that you must always name the object that you're working on, either through "dotting" as shown above (the most common notation) or by using the same **WITH** syntax you use with record types:

```
WITH Today DO PutNewYMD(1993,3,10);
```

Once a legitimate date has been stored in the **Date** object, you can access the data fields of the object to express that date in whatever way you need. The individual year, month, day, and day-of-the-week figures are all available, as are a short and long string representation of the date. You simply use the object's fields as you would the fields of a record:

```
Writeln(Today.AsLongString);
```

(Perhaps objects aren't all that different from records after all. I guess it depends on what you want to do with them.)

One thing you *can't* do with objects is create files with an object type as the file's base type. In other words, things like this are illegal and won't compile:

```
TYPE
    DateFileType = FILE OF Date;   { Won't compile!}
```

The reason this was done is complex and has to do with polymorphism and something called *late binding* that makes object types somewhat slippery at runtime. A separate mechanism for object-oriented file I/O exists and is called *stream I/O;* however, using streams is an advanced and rather difficult business and I won't be covering it in this book.

THE GOAL OF ENCAPSULATION

Some people find the word "encapsulation" a little misleading in a Turbo Pascal context. It seems to promise more than it delivers. People who have been exposed to Smalltalk (as I was, having worked at Xerox when Smalltalk was developed) certainly think so. In Smalltalk, an object's fields simply cannot be referenced outside of the object and its suite of methods. They are definitely "encapsulated" within the very opaque capsule that is the object itself.

The idea in Smalltalk is to control access to an object's fields, for very good reasons. Consider our date object. You can just reach in with an assignment statement and modify any of the various representations of the date that the object supposedly represents. Now, suppose you modify one representation . . . and leave the others alone? This would be the situation, say, if the date held in **Today** were 3/11/93, and you assigned the string "2/14/92" to the **AsString** field. The object would not even agree among its own fields what date it was holding, which could have some very weird consequences in a piece of software designed to use the **Date** object—and to assume that *all* the field representations would represent the same date.

As it stands right now, the **Date** object relies on you the programmer maintaining the object's internal consistency. You have to discipline yourself to treat the fields as read-only and change the date by calling one of the three "put" methods. Each of the "put" methods takes care of *all* of the fields, thus keeping the object internally consistent.

This is the goal of encapsulation: to control access to the internal *state* of the object; that is, the values contained in all of its fields at any given time.

CONTROLLING ACCESS THROUGH PRIVACY

Date is as simple as I could make it and still make it useful. It can certainly be improved by using some of the mechanisms by which Turbo Pascal enforces encapsulation.

Most of these mechanisms are bound up in the notion of *privacy*. You can declare both fields and methods as private, using the **PRIVATE** standard directive. In an object type definition, anything above the **PRIVATE** directive may be accessed normally from any module that has access to the object type definition. Anything below the **PRIVATE** directive, however, can only be referenced from *within the module where the object type is defined*.

In other words, if we were to define a **DateObj** unit to contain the **Date** object, we could prevent code outside the **DateObj** unit from referencing fields or methods by using the **PRIVATE** directive. This might be our first cut:

```
Date =
  OBJECT
    PROCEDURE PutZero;
    PROCEDURE PutToday;
    PROCEDURE PutNewYMD(NewYear, NewMonth, NewDay : Word);
    PROCEDURE PutNewDateStamp(NewDateWord : Word);
  PRIVATE
    Year,Month,Day : Word;
    DayOfWeek      : Word;
    DateStamp      : Word;
    AsString       : String20;
    AsLongString   : String50;
    PROCEDURE CalcStampFromDate;
    PROCEDURE CalcDateFromStamp;
    PROCEDURE CalcDateStringForms;
  END;
```

There are now two parts to the object definition: a public part and a private part. I've moved the three "put" methods into the public part, and all the rest of the object has been declared private by virtue of falling after the **PRIVATE** directive.

Quick: What's wrong with this picture?

Easy: There's no way to *read* the date from the **Date** object anymore! You can set the date three different ways, but from outside the **DateObj** unit you can't look at any of the data fields or even know that they exist. This means we need to provide a few more methods. Here's a further improved **Date** object type:

```
Date =
  OBJECT
    FUNCTION  GetYear    : Word;
    FUNCTION  GetMonth   : Word;
    FUNCTION  GetDay     : Word;
    FUNCTION  GetDayOfWeek       : Word;
    FUNCTION  GetDateStamp       : Word;
    FUNCTION  GetDateString      : String20;
    FUNCTION  GetLongDateString  : String50;
    PROCEDURE PutZero;
    PROCEDURE PutToday;
    PROCEDURE PutNewYMD(NewYear, NewMonth, NewDay : Word);
```

```
    PROCEDURE PutNewDateStamp(NewDateWord : Word);
  PRIVATE
    Year,Month,Day  : Word;
    DayOfWeek       : Word;
    DateStamp       : Word;
    AsString        : String20;
    AsLongString    : String50;
    PROCEDURE CalcStampFromDate;
    PROCEDURE CalcDateFromStamp;
    PROCEDURE CalcDateStringForms;
  END;
```

Now we've got seven new function methods to return any of the object's fields, all in a "read-only" fashion that forbids altering the fields from outside the **DateObj** unit. As you might imagine, coding these additional methods is simplicity itself. Here's one as an example:

```
FUNCTION Date.GetYear : Word;

BEGIN
  GetYear := Year;
END;
```

The others work pretty much the same way. Notice that three of the methods are private as well as the fields. The "calc" methods are only useful to the object itself, so there's no sense in allowing people outside the object's immediate neighborhood to call them. They are, in a way, procedures local to the object itself, created in order to avoid duplication of code in the other methods.

I should reiterate at this point that the **PRIVATE** directive works in conjunction with Pascal's modular architecture. **PRIVATE** makes things private outside of the current module. If you define an object within a unit, anything inside that same unit can access the private fields or methods. If you define an object within a program, anything within that program can access the private fields or methods. If we went back and dropped the **PRIVATE** directive into the **Date** object definition in the DATETEST.PAS program on page 761, nothing would happen. The program is all one single module, so none of the privacy would actually be enforced.

This is why I recommend exiling your objects out to units; in fact, divide your objects into object families, and give each family a separate unit. This way, each family of objects will have the power to keep its own set of family secrets. I've implemented the **DateObj** unit mentioned above, and here it is, private fields and all. Read it carefully, until you understand thoroughly how it works.

```
{----------------------------------------------------------------}
{                          DateObj                               }
{                                                                }
{ A simple "date" object encapsulating date data and date        }
{ manipulation code into a single entity.                        }
{                                                                }
```

```
{                    by Jeff Duntemann                         }
{                    Turbo Pascal V7.0                         }
{                    Last update 3/15/93                       }
{                                                              }
{   From: BORLAND PASCAL FROM SQUARE ONE  by Jeff Duntemann    }
{--------------------------------------------------------------}

UNIT DateObj;

INTERFACE

USES Crt,DOS;

TYPE
  String9  = STRING[9];
  String20 = STRING[20];
  String50 = STRING[50];

  Date =
    OBJECT
      FUNCTION   GetYear     : Word;
      FUNCTION   GetMonth    : Word;
      FUNCTION   GetDay      : Word;
      FUNCTION   GetDayOfWeek        : Word;
      FUNCTION   GetDateStamp        : Word;
      FUNCTION   GetDateString       : String20;
      FUNCTION   GetLongDateString : String50;
      PROCEDURE PutZero;
      PROCEDURE PutToday;
      PROCEDURE PutNewYMD(NewYear, NewMonth, NewDay : Word);
      PROCEDURE PutNewDateStamp(NewDateStamp : Word);
    PRIVATE
      Year,Month,Day : Word;
      DayOfWeek      : Word;
      DateStamp      : Word;
      AsString       : String20;
      AsLongString   : String50;
      PROCEDURE CalcStampFromDate;
      PROCEDURE CalcDateFromStamp;
      PROCEDURE CalcDateStringForms;
    END;

IMPLEMENTATION

CONST
  MonthTags : ARRAY [1..12] of String9 =
      ('January','February','March','April','May','June','July',
       'August','September','October','November','December');
```

```
DayTags    : ARRAY [0..6] OF String9 =
   ('Sunday','Monday','Tuesday','Wednesday',
    'Thursday','Friday','Saturday');


{$I DAYOWEEK.SRC }  { Calculates day of the week; see Section 19.6 }


FUNCTION Date.GetYear : Word;

BEGIN
  GetYear := Year;
END;


FUNCTION Date.GetMonth : Word;

BEGIN
  GetMonth := Month;
END;


FUNCTION Date.GetDay : Word;

BEGIN
  GetDay := Day;
END;


FUNCTION Date.GetDayOfWeek : Word;

BEGIN
  GetDayOfWeek := DayOfWeek;
END;


FUNCTION Date.GetDateStamp : Word;

BEGIN
  GetDateStamp := DateStamp;
END;


FUNCTION Date.GetDateString : String20;

BEGIN
  GetDateString := AsString;
END;
```

```
FUNCTION Date.GetLongDateString : String50;

BEGIN
  GetLongDateString := AsLongString;
END;


PROCEDURE Date.PutZero;

BEGIN
  DateStamp := 0;
  Year := 0; Month := 0; Day := 0; DayOfWeek := 0;
  AsString := '';
  AsLongString := '';
END;


PROCEDURE Date.PutToday;

BEGIN
  GetDate(Year,Month,Day,DayOfWeek);   { From Borland's DOS unit }
  CalcStampFromDate;    { Method; Calculates 16-bit "date stamp" }
  CalcDateStringForms; { Method; Calcs string representations of date }
END;


PROCEDURE Date.PutNewYMD(NewYear, NewMonth, NewDay : Word);

BEGIN
  Year := NewYear; Month := NewMonth; Day := NewDay;
  DayOfWeek := CalcDayOfWeek(Year,Month,Day);
  CalcStampFromDate;
  CalcDateStringForms;
END;


PROCEDURE Date.PutNewDateStamp(NewDateStamp : Word);

BEGIN
  DateStamp := NewDateStamp;
  CalcDateFromStamp;
END;


PROCEDURE Date.CalcStampFromDate;

BEGIN
```

```
        DateStamp := ((Year - 1980) SHL 9) OR (Month SHL 5) OR Day;
    END;



    PROCEDURE  Date.CalcDateFromStamp;

    BEGIN
      Year := (DateStamp SHR 9) + 1980;
      Month := (DateStamp SHR 5) AND $000F;
      Day := DateStamp AND $001F;
      DayOfWeek := CalcDayOfWeek(Year,Month,Day);
      CalcDateStringForms;
    END;



    PROCEDURE  Date.CalcDateStringForms;

    VAR
      Temp1 : String9;

    BEGIN
      { Calculate the "short" date string: }
      Str(Month,AsString);
      IF Month < 10 THEN AsString := '0' + AsString;
      Str(Day,Temp1);
      IF Day < 10 THEN Temp1 := '0' + Temp1;
      AsString := AsString + '/' + Temp1;
      Str(Year,Temp1);
      AsString := AsString + '/' + Temp1;
      { Calculate the "long" date string: }
      AsLongString := DayTags[DayOfWeek] + ', ';
      Str(Day,Temp1);
      AsLongString := AsLongString +
        MonthTags[Month] + ' ' + Temp1 + ', ';
      Str(Year,Temp1);
      AsLongString := AsLongString + Temp1;
    END;

  END.
```

One thing to note is that the **DateStamp** field of **Date** is useful for comparing two dates to see which is prior on the time line:

```
IF Today.GetDateStamp > Tomorrow.GetDateStamp THEN
    Writeln('Something isn't quite right here...');
```

(Note that we're not referencing the **DateStamp** field directly here, but are instead using the function method that returns the *value* of **DateStamp** through a one-way door.) Using the "date stamp" value in comparisons prevents you from having to first compare the year, and if they're the same then compare the month, and if they're again the same compare the day, and so on.

25.4 Introduction to Inheritance

Encapsulation is the foundation of object-oriented programming, and you should understand it thoroughly before you try to work with OOP's more advanced concepts. But at this point you're ready to take on the notion of *inheritance*.

Inheritance is a mechanism allowing you to extend an object type without rewriting it. In a nutshell, you write a type by specifying that you will start with an existing type and build on it. The moment you name your new type, it *already contains* everything its foundation type contains. The foundation type on which you build is called the *parent* or *ancestor* type. You don't even need the ancestor type's source code to do this extending—which is one of the magics of object-oriented programming.

EXTENSION BY INHERITANCE

Suppose having a **Date** object is all well and good, but you want a new object that can pin down a given *time* within the specified date. You've already written the date machinery for object type **Date**—and you'd like to reuse that machinery with as little fooling around as possible. The way to go is to extend **Date** by creating a child object type of **Date** that adds some time machinery to the date machinery that's already there.

Syntactically, creating a child object type is easy. You define a new object type with the parent type's name in parentheses after the reserved word **OBJECT**:

```
TYPE
  DateTime =
    OBJECT(Date)
      FUNCTION GetHours : Word;
      FUNCTION GetMinutes    : Word;
      FUNCTION GetSeconds    : Word;
      FUNCTION GetTimeString : String20;
      FUNCTION GetTimeStamp  : Word;
      FUNCTION GetWhenStamp  : LongInt;
      PROCEDURE PutZero;
      PROCEDURE PutNow;
      PROCEDURE PutNewHMS(NewHours,NewMinutes,NewSeconds : Word);
      PROCEDURE PutNewTimeStamp(NewTimeStamp : Word);
      PROCEDURE PutNewWhenStamp(NewWhenStamp : LongInt);
    PRIVATE
      TimeStamp : Word;
      Hours,Minutes,Seconds : Word; { Seconds is always even! }
      TimeAsString : String20;
```

```
        WhenStamp : LongInt;
        PROCEDURE CalcTimeFromStamp;
        PROCEDURE CalcStampFromTime;
        PROCEDURE CalcTimeStringForm;
    END;
```

This new object type, **DateTime**, *begins* with everything contained in the **Date** object you name as its parent. All the methods and fields contained in **Date** are already present in **DateTime** before you define a single new method or field for **DateTime**, and the methods inherited from **Date** may be called just as they would be called from a **Date** object.

It's important to remember this when you extend an object, as we've done here with **Date**. All the method definitions for **Date** are off somewhere else . . . and therefore prone to be forgotten about. But what you have here is an object that stores both a date and a time, along with several different representations that fall into three general groups:

1. The numeric values for hours, minutes, seconds, year, month, day, and day-of-the-week.

2. String-based expressions of time and date like 3/7/93 and 4:32PM.

3. Binary "stamps" that express the date and the time as single numeric quantities that may be compared for equality and sort order. There's a separate stamp for time and date, and then a single 32-bit combined stamp that contains *both* time and date information. All the stamps express time and date information in the form that DOS does, in order to make the DateTime object useful in manipulating DOS files. I discussed the DOS binary time/date stamp format in Section 19.6.

The 32-bit combined time/date stamp expresses a complete "when," (both date and time on a given date) so I call it a "when stamp" to call it something. That's the nomenclature you see in the object definition.

Here's the complete listing for the unit that defines the **DateTime** object:

```
{-----------------------------------------------------------------}
{                           DaTime                                }
{                                                                 }
{ Unit implementing a "when" stamp through inheritance, by        }
{ adding time-oriented features to the "date stamp" object        }
{ defined in the DateObj unit presented in Section 25.3.          }
{                                                                 }
{                     by Jeff Duntemann                           }
{                     Turbo Pascal V7.0                           }
{                     Last update 3/15/93                          }
{                                                                 }
{    From: BORLAND PASCAL FROM SQUARE ONE   by Jeff Duntemann     }
{-----------------------------------------------------------------}
```

```
UNIT DaTime;

INTERFACE

USES DOS,      { Standard Borland unit }
     DateObj; { From Section 25.3 }

TYPE
  DateTime =
    OBJECT(Date)
      FUNCTION GetHours : Word;
      FUNCTION GetMinutes    : Word;
      FUNCTION GetSeconds    : Word;
      FUNCTION GetTimeString : String20;
      FUNCTION GetTimeStamp  : Word;
      FUNCTION GetWhenStamp  : LongInt;
      PROCEDURE PutZero;
      PROCEDURE PutNow;
      PROCEDURE PutNewHMS(NewHours,NewMinutes,NewSeconds : Word);
      PROCEDURE PutNewTimeStamp(NewTimeStamp : Word);
      PROCEDURE PutNewWhenStamp(NewWhenStamp : LongInt);
    PRIVATE
      TimeStamp : Word;
      Hours,Minutes,Seconds : Word; { Seconds is always even! }
      TimeAsString : String20;
      WhenStamp : LongInt;
      PROCEDURE CalcTimeFromStamp;
      PROCEDURE CalcStampFromTime;
      PROCEDURE CalcTimeStringForm;
    END;

IMPLEMENTATION

TYPE
  WhenUnion =              { This allows us to pull apart    }
    RECORD                 { the 32-bit DOS file time stamp }
      TimePart : Word;
      DatePart : Word;
    END;



FUNCTION DateTime.GetHours : Word;

BEGIN
  GetHours := Hours;
END;
```

```
FUNCTION DateTime.GetMinutes : Word;

BEGIN
  GetMinutes := Minutes;
END;


FUNCTION DateTime.GetSeconds : Word;

BEGIN
  GetSeconds := Seconds;
END;


FUNCTION DateTime.GetTimeString : String20;

BEGIN
  GetTimeString := TimeAsString;
END;


FUNCTION DateTime.GetTimeStamp : Word;

BEGIN
  GetTimeStamp := TimeStamp;
END;


FUNCTION DateTime.GetWhenStamp : LongInt;

BEGIN
  GetWhenStamp := WhenStamp;
END;


PROCEDURE DateTime.PutZero;

BEGIN
  Date.PutZero;
  TimeStamp := 0; WhenStamp := 0;
  Hours := 0; Minutes := 0; Seconds := 0;
  TimeAsString := '';
END;


PROCEDURE DateTime.PutNow;
```

```
VAR
  Hundredths : Word;
  NewWhenStamp : LongInt;

BEGIN
  { The date is part of "now," so read & store the date too: }
  PutToday;  { Don't need to qualify with name of parent! }
  GetTime(Hours,Minutes,Seconds,Hundredths);  { Discard hundredths }
  CalcStampFromTime;
  WhenUnion(NewWhenStamp).TimePart := TimeStamp;
  WhenUnion(NewWhenStamp).DatePart := GetDateStamp;
  PutNewWhenStamp(NewWhenStamp);
  CalcTimeStringForm;
END;




PROCEDURE  DateTime.PutNewHMS(NewHours,NewMinutes,NewSeconds  :  Word);

BEGIN
  Hours := NewHours; Minutes := NewMinutes; Seconds := NewSeconds;
  { Seconds value MUST be even for time to fit into 16 bits! }
  IF Odd(Seconds) THEN Inc(Seconds);
  CalcStampFromTime;
  CalcTimeStringForm;
END;




PROCEDURE  DateTime.CalcTimeFromStamp;

BEGIN
  Hours := TimeStamp SHR 11;
  Minutes := (TimeStamp SHR 5) AND $003F;
  Seconds := (TimeStamp SHL 1) AND $001F;
END;




PROCEDURE  DateTime.CalcStampFromTime;

BEGIN
  TimeStamp := (Hours SHL 11) OR (Minutes SHL 5) OR (Seconds SHR 1);
END;




PROCEDURE  DateTime.PutNewTimeStamp(NewTimeStamp  :  Word);

BEGIN
  TimeStamp := NewTimeStamp;
```

```
      CalcTimeFromStamp;
      CalcTimeStringForm;
   END;



PROCEDURE DateTime.PutNewWhenStamp(NewWhenStamp : LongInt);

BEGIN
   WhenStamp := NewWhenStamp;
   PutNewDateStamp(WhenUnion(WhenStamp).DatePart);  { Parent's method! }
    PutNewTimeStamp(WhenUnion(WhenStamp).TimePart);
END;



PROCEDURE DateTime.CalcTimeStringForm;

VAR
   Temp1,Temp2 : String9;
   AMPM        : Char;
   I           : Integer;

BEGIN
   I := Hours;
   IF Hours = 0 THEN I := 12;    { "0" hours = 12am }
   IF Hours > 12 THEN I := Hours - 12;
   IF Hours > 11 THEN AMPM := 'p' ELSE AMPM := 'a';
    Str(I:2,Temp1); Str(Minutes,Temp2);
   IF Length(Temp2) < 2 THEN Temp2 := '0' + Temp2;
   TimeAsString := Temp1 + ':' + Temp2 + AMPM;
END;


END.
```

SCOPE AND INHERITANCE

When you extend an object by defining a child object, the child object has full access to all of its parent's public methods and fields without qualification. In other words, to call one of **Date**'s methods, **DateTime** simply names it. There's no need to specify **Date.PutToday**; **PutToday** is quite properly one of **DateTime**'s own methods. The same is true of fields; all of **Date**'s public fields are within the scope of all of **DateTime**'s methods.

It's another matter where private fields and methods are involved. If the parent and child objects are defined in separate units (as I've done here), their private items remain private, even from one another. *Private fields and methods are within scope for child objects only when the child objects are defined within the same unit as the parent.* That is, the separate data fields in **Date** are *not* accessible to

DateTime. DateTime.PutNow, for example, cannot assign new values to **Year,** **Month,** or **Day** fields defined in **Date.**

Because the date is part of "now," **PutNow** does in fact cause new values to be stored in **Year, Month,** and **Day** (as well as all of **Date**'s other fields), but it does so in an orderly manner: by calling **Date.PutToday.** The "today-ness" of **DateTime** is inherited from **Date**—so why not just let **Date**'s methods handle date manipulation? This is a key tenet of object-oriented programming: *Add only what you must. Inherit (and therefore reuse) everything you can.*

OVERRIDING METHODS

Date has a method called **PutZero** that zeroes out all of the fields in the **Date** object. It's useful to have a reliable, testable state to indicate that a **Date** object contains no date at all—being to date objects what **NIL** is to pointers. You call **PutZero** to put a **Date** object into that state.

DateTime has a **PutZero** method as well, and it does exactly the same thing: Zero out all the data fields of the **DateTime** object, for the same purpose.

Now, both **Date** and its child object **DateTime** have a **PutZero** method. When a child object has a method of the same name as a method in its parent object, we say that the child's method *overrides* the parent's method of the same name. You override a parent object's method to alter the behavior of the parent object somehow, rather than simply inheriting that behavior intact. In this case, we need to alter the **PutZero** method to zero out *both* the date and time information, rather than simply the date information as **Date.PutZero** does.

A child object contains its parent object, so as you might imagine there are potential conflicts when both objects have a method with the same name. Turbo Pascal resolves this conflict through the rules of scope: Even though both **Date** and **DateTime** have a **PutZero** method, within the scope of **DateTime,** the only visible **PutZero** method is **DateTime.PutZero. Date.PutZero** is out of scope, and can only be invoked by fully qualifying the method name: **Date.PutZero.**

Note from the DATIME.PAS listing that **DateTime.PutZero** calls **Date.PutZero** to zero out **Date**'s data fields:

```
PROCEDURE  DateTime.PutZero;

BEGIN
   Date.PutZero;   { Call parent's method that this one overrides }
   TimeStamp := 0; WhenStamp := 0;
   Hours := 0; Minutes := 0; Seconds := 0;
   TimeAsString := '';
END;
```

In order to call **Date**'s **PutZero** method, you need to specify whose method it is. The default **PutZero** (that is, the one that is normally in scope) is **DateTime**'s **PutZero.**

Keep in mind that the parent object never "knows" about its children. (You could design parent and child together and have parent methods call child methods, but this is bad practice and I do not recommend it!)

It might seem useful on occasion, but you cannot override data fields as you can methods. In other words, we could not define a field named **AsString** to **DateTime**. The compiler would consider it a duplicate identifier error. And this leads us to another problem.

THE DISADVANTAGES OF PRIVACY

For all that it can be a valuable feature, private methods and fields exact a price once you begin using inheritance to extend object types. As I said just above, child objects cannot access private fields or methods inside their ancestor types, *unless* the child objects are defined within the ancestor types' module.

This was not an issue in extending **Date** to produce **DateTime**. We extended **Date** in a very strict sense; that is, we did nothing at all to modify what **Date** was already doing. We didn't change anything in **Date**; we just added some time machinery to it. In the one or two cases when calling a method in **DateTime** had to affect one of the fields in **Date**, **DateTime** called one of **Date**'s public methods to handle the date manipulation. Overriding the **PutZero** method is a good example of this: **DateTime** called **Date**'s own **PutZero** to zero out **Date**'s private fields.

A problem comes up when a child object must not only extend the behavior of its parent, but also modify that behavior in some way that involves private fields or methods without some way to do it through public method calls. Here's an example of the problem, incorporating the **Date** object:

Suppose you want to modify the **Date** object to express the string forms of the date in European format, which is day/month/year rather than the familiar American month/day/year. In **Date**, the method that generates the string forms of the date expressed in the object is called **CalcDateStringForms**. By the conventions of object-oriented programming, all you'd have to do to create a European extension of **Date** is simply create a child type of **Date** called **EuroDate**, and override the **CalcDateStringForms** method with a new version that just puts the day first in the **AsString** field, rather than the month.

One catch—*CalcDateStringForms is a private method, and all the fields it acts upon are private fields*. You can create a method called **CalcDateStringForms** in a child type, but the new **CalcDateStringForms** method would not be able to access the **AsString** and **AsLongString** fields to re-express them in European format. You can't create a new **CalcDateStringForms** with access to the private string fields unless you create it within the same module (in most cases, unit) that defines the original **Date** type. Maybe you "own" that unit and can create child types within the unit—but maybe you don't. Whether or not the **AsString** and **AsLongString** fields should really be private at all could be the subject of a lively debate. The security partisans would argue yes, and the extensibility partisans would argue no. The only "right" answer is the one that best serves the cause of getting your job done.

The more you get into object-oriented programming, the more you'll run into Pyrrhic design questions of this sort. In general, if you expect someone (including yourself) to create child types of a given object type outside of the parent type's unit, use private fields with extreme care.

25.5 The Mysteries of Polymorphism

This is as far as I'm going to take you in terms of a detailed tour through object-oriented programming. One major concept remains, but it's too large to treat in this chapter. The concept is that of virtual methods, by which Turbo Pascal implements polymorphism.

Polymorphism is a suitably mysterious term for an idea that catches most traditional structured programmers quite by surprise. It comes from the Greek for "many shapes," and it opens up an entirely new way to express program logic in Pascal.

The basic idea in polymorphism is to create a family of related objects, typically starting with a fundamental parent object and deriving a sequence of child objects from that parent object. Each of these objects implements a method with the same name. The name of the method may be the same, but how the method actually does its work is custom-tailored to fit the object that defines the method.

At runtime, you can call that method—the one held in common by all the objects in that family—*without necessarily knowing which type of object will receive the method call.* It doesn't matter, because each method responds to the method call in a way appropriate to its nature.

At least, that's the $5.00 way of describing polymorphism. It'll go down easier with a 2-bit metaphor.

THE KILLER-FROST PROBLEM

Up and down County Highway 42 in rural central Ohio are any number of farms. There are corn farms, wheat farms, apple farms, and cherry farms. Specialization is definitely the watchword of the Nineties, so each farm tends to produce only one crop—but each is *very* efficient at producing that one crop.

County agent Hank tries to help out the farmers in his county any way he can. Mostly he tries to let them know what sorts of things are going on in the outside world that affect *all* farmers—and then hopes that each will respond in an appropriate way.

It's early September in central Ohio, and within a few weeks harvest time will begin. County agent Hank is watching CNN, and sees a report of a massive weather front rushing down from northern Canada, carrying subzero air in its wake. The front has already reached northern Wisconsin, and it'll reach Ohio in no more than two days. A killer frost caught Wisconsin unawares, and most of the Wisconsin pickle crop has been destroyed.

Hank goes to work. One by one he calls the farmers along Highway 42, and leaves a very simple message with each of them, in person or on their answering machines: "Killer frost tomorrow. *Harvest your crops now.*"

Notice that Hank doesn't call Tony the apple farmer and say, "Tony, killer frost tomorrow. Get your ladders out, call up your cousins, and get your apples off the trees right now!" Tony is an apple farmer, and has been all his life. He knows damned well how to harvest his apples. Hank doesn't have to tell him that. Tony picks up Hank's message off his answerbox and understands immediately: *Harvest your crops now.* Hank need say no more; Tony knows exactly what to do.

The same applies to Sam the cherry farmer, George the corn farmer, and Roger the lettuce farmer. Agent Hank delivers the same identical message to all of them, and then each of them goes off and does what he does best: harvests his crops as his crops need to be harvested.

APPROPRIATE ACTION

What Agent Hank did is issue a polymorphic method call to all the farmers in his county. All of his clients are farmers; they have that in common. But each farms something different, and each knows perfectly well how to do his own farming. Hank need only say, *Harvest your crops now,* and each farmer will respond in a fashion appropriate to his crop.

Let's leap back into the realm of computer reality again, and consider an example of polymorphism in action that has admittedly been cited a lot in the literature—but which remains one of the best possible examples.

Consider a CAD or drawing program. The drawing program allows you to create various kinds of graphical figures on the screen. Some of the basic figures include rectangles, circles, ellipses, lines, and disk-based bitmaps. Each has a different appearance, but each is nonetheless a graphical figure with some visible presence on the screen of the drawing program.

Each type of graphical figure can be represented by a separate object type. A **Circle** object type would have fields that appropriately define a circle: an X,Y for the circle's center, plus a radius and perhaps a line color or thickness. A **Square** object type would have an X,Y for the upper left corner of the square, and then the length of a side, and perhaps a line color or thickness. Each of the different kinds of figures would have a different set of data fields to describe it. But on the other hand, each kind of figure ultimately has to be displayed on the screen. So let's give each of the different figure types a method named **Draw**. It's a different process to draw each type of figure to the screen, so all of the **Draw** methods contain a different sequence of code statements to actually accomplish that drawing. But the *name* of the method—**Draw**—is the same in every case.

We're leaving the details of drawing to the objects themselves. All we need do to draw any of the objects is simply to execute their **Draw** method:

```
MyCircle.Draw;
MySquare.Draw;
MyLine.Draw;
```

Each object goes out and "draws itself" in a sense, by responding in an appropriate fashion to a common command issued identically to every object. Cool, huh? *But that's only the half of it.*

LATE BINDING

All of the graphics figure object types in this scenario are derived from the same fundamental object type, the "root" type of a family of objects that we call an *object hierarchy.* This fundamental type might be called **Figure**. The graphics figures have object type **Figure** in common, just as all of Agent Hank's farmers have the career "farmer" in common. It's generally what they do—but each does it in a distinctly different way. From parent type **Figure** you might derive **Square, Line,** and **Circle,** and then from **Circle** you might derive yet another object type called **Ellipse.** Every one of these object types implements a **Draw** method in an appropriate way.

Borland Pascal loosens the rules of type checking a little for pointers to object types. Here's something important to remember: *A pointer to a parent type can also legally point to any object type descended from that parent type.* In other words, if you define a pointer type named **PFigure** that points to type **Figure,** that same pointer type could legally point to type **Circle, Square, Line,** or **Ellipse,** and the compiler won't object one whit.

Keep all that in mind. Now, suppose you're designing a drawing program with a toolbar to select different geometrical figures to draw. When the user clicks on one of the buttons in the toolbar, a graphical figure is created on the heap, and a pointer named **CurrentFigure** is assigned to point to the new figure. **CurrentFigure** needs to be able to point to *any* kind of figure presented on the toolbar, so of course it must have the type **PFigure.**

When you drag the mouse cursor across the screen to the location where you want to "drop" the new graphic figure, you make a single method call indicating that "this is the place":

```
CurrentFigure^.Draw;
```

Regardless of what sort of figure is actually on the other end of pointer **CurrentFigure,** the correct **Draw** method is called. The user doesn't actually select a figure type from the toolbar until the program runs, so you can't "hard-code" a specific type into the code like this:

```
MySquare.Draw;
```

You don't *know* that the user is going to choose to draw a square. The user could just as soon choose to draw a circle or an ellipse. *Your program won't know until runtime what actual type the pointer CurrentFigure will be pointing to.*

In traditional Pascal programming, every function call is given the address of the function being called at compile time. This is called *binding,* because a call statement is "bound" to the called code by the compiler. In object-oriented programming, binding can be very cleverly delayed until the actual moment that a method is called. This clever process is called *late binding*, and it is the lynchpin of polymorphism.

Late binding allows you to create situations with tremendous richness of expression in your programs. You can build incredibly elaborate data structures out on the heap, and control them with a vanishingly small set of common commands. You can identify what is common about all your many different object types, and build that commonality into a set of common methods. (These common methods are defined specially with the reserved word **VIRTUAL**, and they are called *virtual methods*.) That done, you can carefully hide what is *different* about each separate object type within the object itself.

This is structured programming with a vengeance: Reveal what needs revealing, and hide what needs hiding. At one level in your program, you need only consider what your family of objects has in common. At a deeper level, when you're "inside" an individual object, you can focus on one single individual object type, and consider that object's characteristic traits. This is the pinnacle of Wirth's ideal of structured programming as the artful hiding of details.

It's a *very* serious rush, once the lights come on inside your head.

CONCLUSION

Getting Smooth,
Getting Fast

There's a peculiar belief mired in the conventional wisdom of our culture that education is something you have to go somewhere to get poured into your head through a funnel—usually for an extraordinary amount of money, and the more money it costs, the better an education you get. Hoo-boy, what a fine little fib that is—witness the happy hordes pouring out of academia today without even the ability to construct a coherent sentence.

Reality is a little different: You go to college and pay that extorted fortune for credentials alone; *education* comes solely from within. Furthermore, it can occur anywhere you happen to be. If you choose to educate yourself, no power on Earth can keep you from becoming an educated person.

I learned this from the old man who had this extraordinary ability to make a B on a report card look like a case of ringworm. His perspective on education was remarkable, and I'll close this book (as I opened it) with one of his "old sayings" that I never heard anywhere else: "If you learn English and math, *you already know everything else.* All you have to do is read the books and work the problems."

He was right, as usual, and by that guiding principle I have learned everything I know today. To learn about telescopes and astronomy, I read the books, then built a telescope and looked at the stars. To learn electronics, I read the books and then built radios that I used to talk to guys like myself in South America. To learn programming, I read the books and I wrote programs. Lots of programs. Big ones, little ones, serious ones and silly ones. It was wonderful good fun, and it worked.

It's your turn. You've read the book you need to get you started. Now it's your responsibility to work the problems. Don't settle, furthermore, for problems somebody else wrote down in a book. Look around you; your life will suggest a multitude of challenges. I wanted a pocket memo book that neatly displayed the phone numbers and addresses of my friends and associates that I kept in a database. I wrote the program to print out that memo book, and thereby learned a lot about the process of text formatting and printing. I wanted a program to conveniently access MCI Mail through my modem, so I wrote JiveTalk, and thereby learned a lot about serial communications and file transfer protocols.

I wanted a program to help me compare mortgage payments while shopping for a house. So I wrote Mortgage Vision, and thereby learned a great deal about a multitude of programming concepts, from amortization algorithms to collection classes to application frameworks. (You can now buy Mortgage Vision in every K-Mart in the country, by the way, and that effort brings me a reliable chunk of money every month. Education pays!)

Now, what work needs doing? Set yourself some tasks and see them through. Getting smooth is only a matter of practice, and the more you practice, the faster and smoother your programming skills will become. You'll certainly be reading more books as you go (with luck I'll have written some of them), but practice is what makes excellence out of competence.

So get to work. Read the books. Work the problems. Oh—and one more thing: Reach out and help someone who is struggling with the dragons you've already conquered. I never learned anything so well as that which I took the time to explain to others.

Good luck. Let me know how you do.

Appendix

The Extended ASCII Code and Symbol Set

Dec	Hex	Binary	Symbol	Dec	Hex	Binary	Symbol
0	00	00000000		19	13	00010011	‼
1	01	00000001	☺	20	14	00010100	¶
2	02	00000010	☻	21	15	00010101	§
3	03	00000011	♥	22	16	00010110	▬
4	04	00000100	♦	23	17	00010111	↕
5	05	00000101	♣	24	18	00011000	↑
6	06	00000110	♠	25	19	00011001	↓
7	07	00000111	·	26	1A	00011010	→
8	08	00001000	▪	27	1B	00011011	←
9	09	00001001	○	28	1C	00011100	∟
10	0A	00001010	◉	29	1D	00011101	↔
11	0B	00001011	♂	30	1E	00011110	▲
12	0C	00001100	♀	31	1F	00011111	▼
13	0D	00001101	♪	32	20	00100000	
14	0E	00001110	♫	33	21	00100001	!
15	0F	00001111	☼	34	22	00100010	"
16	10	00010000	►	35	23	00100011	#
17	11	00010001	◄	36	24	00100100	$
18	12	00010010	↕	37	25	00100101	%

Dec	Hex	Binary	Symbol	Dec	Hex	Binary	Symbol
38	26	00100110	&	74	4A	01001010	J
39	27	00100111	'	75	4B	01001011	K
40	28	00101000	(	76	4C	01001100	L
41	29	00101001	)	77	4D	01001101	M
42	2A	00101010	*	78	4E	01001110	N
43	2B	00101011	+	79	4F	01001111	O
44	2C	00101100	,	80	50	01010000	P
45	2D	00101101	-	81	51	01010001	Q
46	2E	00101110	.	82	52	01010010	R
47	2F	00101111	/	83	53	01010011	S
48	30	00110000	Ø	84	54	01010100	T
49	31	00110001	1	85	55	01010101	U
50	32	00110010	2	86	56	01010110	V
51	33	00110011	3	87	57	01010111	W
52	34	00110100	4	88	58	01011000	X
53	35	00110101	5	89	59	01011001	Y
54	36	00110110	6	90	5A	01011010	Z
55	37	00110111	7	91	5B	01011011	[
56	38	00111000	8	92	5C	01011100	\
57	39	00111001	9	93	5D	01011101	]
58	3A	00111010	:	94	5E	01011110	^
59	3B	00111011	;	95	5F	01011111	_
60	3C	00111100	<	96	60	01100000	`
61	3D	00111101	=	97	61	01100001	a
62	3E	00111110	>	98	62	01100010	b
63	3F	00111111	?	99	63	01100011	c
64	40	01000000	@	100	64	01100100	d
65	41	01000001	A	101	65	01100101	e
66	42	01000010	B	102	66	01100110	f
67	43	01000011	C	103	67	01100111	g
68	44	01000100	D	104	68	01101000	h
69	45	01000101	E	105	69	01101001	i
70	46	01000110	F	106	6A	01101010	j
71	47	01000111	G	107	6B	01101011	k
72	48	01001000	H	108	6C	01101100	l
73	49	01001001	I	109	6D	01101101	m

Dec	Hex	Binary	Symbol	Dec	Hex	Binary	Symbol
110	6E	01101110	n	146	92	10010010	Æ
111	6F	01101111	o	147	93	10010011	ô
112	70	01110000	p	148	94	10010100	ö
113	71	01110001	q	149	95	10010101	ò
114	72	01110010	r	150	96	10010110	û
115	73	01110011	s	151	97	10010111	ù
116	74	01110100	t	152	98	10011000	ÿ
117	75	01110101	u	153	99	10011001	Ö
118	76	01110110	v	154	9A	10011010	Ü
119	77	01110111	w	155	9B	10011011	¢
120	78	01111000	x	156	9C	10011100	£
121	79	01111001	y	157	9D	10011101	¥
122	7A	01111010	z	158	9E	10011110	₧
123	7B	01111011	{	159	9F	10011111	ƒ
124	7C	01111100	¦	160	A0	10100000	á
125	7D	01111101	}	161	A1	10100001	í
126	7E	01111110	~	162	A2	10100010	ó
127	7F	01111111	⌂	163	A3	10100011	ú
128	80	10000000	Ç	164	A4	10100100	ñ
129	81	10000001	ü	165	A5	10100101	Ñ
130	82	10000010	é	166	A6	10100110	ª
131	83	10000011	â	167	A7	10100111	º
132	84	10000100	ä	168	A8	10101000	¿
133	85	10000101	à	169	A9	10101001	⌐
134	86	10000110	å	170	AA	10101010	¬
135	87	10000111	ç	171	AB	10101011	½
136	88	10001000	ê	172	AC	10101100	¼
137	89	10001001	ë	173	AD	10101101	¡
138	8A	10001010	è	174	AE	10101110	«
139	8B	10001011	ï	175	AF	10101111	»
140	8C	10001100	î	176	B0	10110000	░
141	8D	10001101	ì	177	B1	10110001	▒
142	8E	10001110	Ä	178	B2	10110010	▓
143	8F	10001111	Å	179	B3	10110011	│
144	90	10010000	É	180	B4	10110100	┤
145	91	10010001	æ	181	B5	10110101	╡

Dec	Hex	Binary	Symbol	Dec	Hex	Binary	Symbol
182	B6	10110110	╢	219	DB	11011011	█
183	B7	10110111	╖	220	DC	11011100	▄
184	B8	10111000	╕	221	DD	11011101	▌
185	B9	10111001	╣	222	DE	11011110	▐
186	BA	10111010	║	223	DF	11011111	▀
187	BB	10111011	╗	224	E0	11100000	α
188	BC	10111100	╝	225	E1	11100001	β
189	BD	10111101	╜	226	E2	11100010	Γ
190	BE	10111110	╛	227	E3	11100011	π
191	BF	10111111	┐	228	E4	11100100	Σ
192	C0	11000000	└	229	E5	11100101	σ
193	C1	11000001	┴	230	E6	11100110	µ
194	C2	11000010	┬	231	E7	11100111	τ
195	C3	11000011	├	232	E8	11101000	φ
196	C4	11000100	─	233	E9	11101001	θ
197	C5	11000101	┼	234	EA	11101010	Ω
198	C6	11000110	╞	235	EB	11101011	δ
199	C7	11000111	╟	236	EC	11101100	∞
200	C8	11001000	╚	237	ED	11101101	ø
201	C9	11001001	╔	238	EE	11101110	ε
202	CA	11001010	╩	239	EF	11101111	∩
203	CB	11001011	╦	240	F0	11110000	≡
204	CC	11001100	╠	241	F1	11110001	±
205	CD	11001101	═	242	F2	11110010	≥
206	CE	11001110	╬	243	F3	11110011	≤
207	CF	11001111	╧	244	F4	11110100	⌠
208	D0	11010000	╨	245	F5	11110101	⌡
209	D1	11010001	╤	246	F6	11110110	÷
210	D2	11010010	╥	247	F7	11110111	≈
211	D3	11010011	╙	248	F8	11111000	°
212	D4	11010100	╘	249	F9	11111001	∙
213	D5	11010101	╒	250	FA	11111010	·
214	D6	11010110	╓	251	FB	11111011	√
215	D7	11010111	╫	252	FC	11111100	^{n}
216	D8	11011000	╪	253	FD	11111101	^{2}
217	D9	11011001	┘	254	FE	11111110	■
218	DA	11011010	┌	255	FF	11111111	

Bibliography

Duntemann, Jeff. *Assembly Language from Square One*. Chicago: Scott Foresmann and Co., 1990.

Duntemann, Jeff. *Assembly Language Step-by-Step*. New York: John Wiley and Sons, 1992.

Nelson, Ted. *Computer Lib/Dream Machines*. Redmond: Tempus Books, 1987.

Penrose, Roger. *The Emperor's New Mind*. New York: Oxford University Press, 1989.

Sturtz, Richard. *8087 Applications and Programming for the IBM and other PCs*. New York: Brady, 1983.

Index